D1454206

ADVANCES IN THE DEMPSTER-SHAFER THEORY OF EVIDENCE

EDITED BY

Ronald R. Yager
Machine Intelligence Institute
Iona College, New Rochelle, NY

Janusz Kacprzyk
Systems Research Institute
Polish Academy of Sciences, Warsaw

Mario Fedrizzi
Faculty of Economics and Commerce
University of Trento

John Wiley & Sons, Inc.
New York • Chichester • Brisbane • Toronto • Singapore

In recognition of the importance of preserving what has been written, it is a policy of John Wiley & Sons, Inc. to have books of enduring value published in the United States printed on acid-free paper, and we exert our best efforts to that end.

This publication is designed to provide accurate and authoritative information in regard to the subject matter covered. It is sold with the understanding that the publisher is not engaged in rendering legal, accounting, or other professional service. If legal advice or other expert assistance is required, the services of a competent professional person should be sought. FROM A DECLARATION OF PRINCIPLES JOINTLY ADOPTED BY A COMMITTEE OF THE AMERICAN BAR ASSOCIATION AND A COMMITTEE OF PUBLISHERS.

Copyright © 1994 by John Wiley & Sons, Inc.

All rights reserved. Published simultaneously in Canada.

Reproduction or translation of any part of this work beyond that permitted by section 107 or 108 of the 1976 United States Copyright Act without the permission of the copyright owner is unlawful. Requests for permission or further information should be addressed to the Permissions Department, John Wiley & Sons, Inc.

Library of Congress Cataloging-in-Publication Data

Advances in the Dempster-Shafer theory of evidence / edited by Ronald R. Yager, Janusz Kacprzyk, Mario Fedrizzi.

p. cm.

Includes bibliographical references and index.

ISBN 0-471-55248-8

1. Neural networks (computer science). 2. Fuzzy systems. 3. Artificial intelligence. I. Yager, Ronald R., 1941– II. Kacprzyk, Janusz, 1947– III, Fedrizzi, Mario, 1949– QA76.87.A.39 1993 006.3--dc20

92-26536
CIP

Printed in the United States of America
10 9 8 7 6 5 4 3 2 1

CONTRIBUTORS

James F. Baldwin, University of Bristol, Queens Building, Bristol BS8 1TR, ENGLAND

Alain Chateauneuf, CERMSEM – Université de Paris I, 90, rue de Tolbiac, 75634 Paris Cédex 13, FRANCE

Bassam A. Chokr, Vladik Ya. Kreinovich, University of Texas, Computer Science Department, El Paso, TX 79968, USA

Didier Dubois, Henri Prade, Institut de Recherche en Informatique de Toulouse (I.R.I.T) – C.N.R.S., Université Paul Sabatier, 118 route de Narbonne, 31062 Toulouse Cédex, FRANCE

Jerzy Grzymała-Busse, Computer Science Department, University of Kansas, Lawrence, KS 66045, USA

Hung T. Hguyen, Elbert A. Walker, Department of Mathematical Sciences, New Mexico State University, Las Cruces, NM 88003, USA

John G. Hughes, Michael F. McTear, Dept. of Information Systems, University of Ulster at Jordanstown, Co. Antrim, BT370QB, UK

Jean-Yves Jaffray, Laboratoire d'Informatique de la Decision, Université P. et M. Curie (Paris VI), 4, Pl. Jussieu, 75005 Paris, FRANCE

George J. Klir, Department of Systems Science, State University of New York, Binghamton, NY 13902-6000, USA

Jürg Kohlas, Paul-André Monney, Institute for Automation and Operations Research, University of Fribourg, CH-1700 Fribourg, SWITZERLAND

Vladik Ya. Kreinovich, Andrew Bernat, Walter Borrett, Yvonne Mariscal, Elsa Vila, University of Texas, Computer Science Department, El Paso, TX 79968, USA

Rudolf Kruse, Frank Klawonn, Department of Computer Science, Technical University of Braunschweig, W-3300 Braunschweig, GERMANY

Maria T. Lamata, Serafin Moral, Department of Computer Science, University of Granada, 18071 – Granada, SPAIN

Weiru Liu, Dept. of Artificial Intelligence, University of Edinburgh, 80 South Bridge, Edinburgh, EH1 1HN, UK

Zdzisław Pawlak, Institute of Computer Science, Warsaw University of Technology, Nowowiejska 15/19, 00-665 Warsaw, POLAND

Alessandro Saffiotti, IRIDIA, Université Libre de Bruxelles, 50 av. F. D. Roosevelt, CP 194/6, B-1050 Bruxelles, BELGIUM

Prakash P. Shenoy, School of Business, University of Kansas, Lawrence, KS 66045–2003, USA

Andrzej Skowron, Institute of Mathematics, University of Warsaw, Banacha 2, 02-097 Warsaw, POLAND

Philippe Smets, IRIDIA, University of Brussels, 50 av. F. D. Roosevelt, CP 194/6, B-1050 Brussels, BELGIUM

Marcus Spies, IBM Germany – Scientific Center, Institute for Knowledge-Based Systems, Wilckensstrasse la, W-6900 Heidelberg, GERMANY

Thomas M. Strat, Artificial Intelligence Center, SRI International, 333 Ravenswood Avenue, Menlo Park, CA 94025, USA

Thomas Whalen, Department of Decision Sciences, Georgia State University, Atlanta, GA 30303-3083, USA

Sławomir T. Wierzchoń, Institute of Computer Science, Polish Academy od Sciences, ul. Ordona 21, Warsaw, POLAND

S. K. M. Wong, Y. Y. Yao, P. Lingras, Department of Computer Science, University of Regina, Regina, Saskatchewan, CANADA S4S 0A2

Hong Xu, Robert Kennes, IRIDIA, Université de Bruxelles, 50 av. F. D. Roosevelt, CP 194/6, B-1050 Brussels, BELGIUM

Ronald R. Yager, Machine Intelligence Institute, Iona College, New Rochelle, NY 10801, USA

Lianwen Zhang, Department of Computer Science, University of British Columbia, Vancouver, BC, CANADA V6T 1Z2

CONTENTS

Foreword

It is with great pleasure that I welcome this collection of diverse and stimulating contributions to the Dempster-Shafer theory of belief functions. These contributions demonstrate the vigor and fruitfulness of current research on belief functions, and their publication as a unit can serve to make that research even more vigorous. During the past decade, research on belief functions has suffered from fragmentation; the researchers involved have been spread over so many different disciplines, meetings, and journals that they have often been unaware of each other's work. By bringing together so many of the leading workers in the field, the editors of this volume have begun to create a new research community.

Though belief-function ideas can be found in eigteenth-century literature on the probability of testimony, the modern theory has its origins in work by A. P. Dempster in the 1960s. Dempster was inspired by R. A. Fisher's "fiducial" method – a brilliant but unsatisfactory method for computing probabilities for statistical parameters from observations. Dempster's generalization of Fisher's method produced nonadditive probabilities, which combined by a general rule that I later called "Dempster's rule of combination."

I added to Dempster's theory in various ways in the 1970s, but in retrospect, my most influential contributions were simplifications rather than elaborations. My 1976 book, *A Mathematical Theory of Evidence*, began as an article on non-Bayesian weights of evidence. In order to explain why these weights of evidence were important, I first had to explain belief functions, which took up more pages than I had expected; what had started as an article evolved into a book. Since the general theory of belief functions was aside from my main point, I kept the exposition as simple as possible – I considered, for example, only finite frames of discernment. As it turned out, it was this simple exposition that caught people's imagination. To my dismay, I still find it difficult to interest people in weights of evidence.

Though Dempster's work predated mine by ten years and included all the basic ideas of belief functions, the theory is now usually called the "Dempster-Shafer theory." I am proud to be associated with Dempster in this appellation. I have always been inspired by the quality of his work, and his personal support has always been invaluable to me.

The name "Dempster-Shafer theory" was coined by J. A. Barnett in 1981, in an article that marked the entry of the belief functions into the literature on artificial intelligence. It is appropriate that the theory should have been given a new name at that time. Dempster had pointed out in his foreword to my 1976 book that I was breaking his theory free from the narrow confines of Fisher's statistical problem. But in retrospect, the autonomy that I was able to gain for the theory in the 1970s seems very limited. It was not until the adventurous can-do spirit of artificial intelligence took hold of belief functions that they were fully freed from the mindset of statistics, where numerical degress of belief had to be either frequencies or betting rates.

Today belief functions sit in the middle of an exciting discussion in artificial intelligence. They provide a bridge, in a sense, between fuzzy reasoning, which has been remarkably successful in applications, and probability, which has been less widely useful but still seems to have stronger normative claims. During the 1980s, I came to agree with Piero Bonissone's view that managing uncertainty in artificial intelligence means choosing, on a case-by-case basis, between different formalisms and different ways of using these formalisms. Since belief functions sit in the middle, better understanding of how and when to use belief functions will contribute significantly to our understanding of uncertainty management using other formalisms. Thus this volume has a significance beyond the Dempster-Shafer theory itself; it is an important contribution to our general understanding of probability and uncertainty.

September 1992 Glenn Shafer

About the editors

MARIO FEDRIZZI is an alumnus of the University of Padua. He holds an MA degree in Mathematics, and a Ph.D. in Financial Mathematics. Since 1976 his work has concentrated on dealing with imprecision, mainly by means of fuzzy sets and fuzzy logic, and possibility theory, in various problems or decision making, in particular group and consensus formation, and knowledge-based decision support systems. Dr. Fedrizzi is a full professor of financial mathematics, and the dean of the Faculty of Economics and Commerce, University of Trento, Italy. He is the author of a book, coeditor of at least five volumes, and author or coauthor of at least sixty papers.

JANUSZ KACPRZYK is an alumnus of Warsaw University of Technology. He holds an MS degree in automatic control and computer science, a Ph.D. degree in systems analysis, and a Doctorate of Science degree in computer science. Since 1973, Dr. Kacprzyk's work has concentrated on various issues related to dealing with uncertainty and imprecision, in particular by means of fuzzy sets and logic, and possibility theory, in decision making and control, decision support systems, and knowledge-based systems and artificial intelligence. Dr. Kacprzyk is a research associate at the Systems Research Institute, Polish Academy of Sciences in Warsaw, Poland. He is a coeditor of *Archives of Control Sciences*, and also serves on the editorial boards of many journals including the *International Journal of Intelligent Systems*. Dr. Kacprzyk is the author of three books, coeditor of at least ten edited volumes, and author or coauthor of more than a hundred papers.

RONALD R. YAGER is Director of the Machine Intelligence Institute and Professor of Information Systems at Iona College. He received his undergraduate degree from City College of New York and his Ph.D. from the Polytechnic Institute of Brooklyn. He has served at the National Science Foundation as program director in the Information Sciences Program, and was a visiting scholar at Hunter College of the City University of New York. Dr. Yager was a NASA/Stanford fellow and a research associate at the University of California, Berkeley. He has served as a lecturer at the NATO

Advanced Study Institute, and is a research fellow of the Knowledge Engineering Institute, Guangzhou University, China. He is on the scientific committee of the Fuzzy Logic Systems Institute, Iizuka, Japan and co-president of the International Conference on Information Processing and Management of Uncertainty in Paris. He is editor-in-chief of the *International Journal of Intelligent Systems*, and also serves on the editorial board of a number of other journals including the *Journal of Approximate Reasoning, Fuzzy Sets and Systems*, and the *International Journal of General Systems*. He has published over 200 articles and has edited ten books.

1

DEMPSTER-SHAFER THEORY OF EVIDENCE: GENERAL ISSUES

1 What is Dempster-Shafer's model?

Philippe SMETS

Abstract: Several mathematical models have been proposed for the modeling of someone's degrees of belief. The oldest is the Bayesian model that uses probability functions. The upper and lower probabilities (ULP) model, Dempster's model, the evidentiary value model (EVM), and the probability of model propositions somehow generalize the Bayesian approach. The transferable belief model (TBM) is based on other premises and uses belief functions. None of these models is the best: each has its own domain of application. We illustrate through examples the underlying hypotheses that lead to the selection of an adequate model for a given problem. We give indications on how to choose the appropriate model. The major discriminating criterion is: if there exists a probability measure with known values, use the Bayesian model; if there exists a probability measure but with some unknown values, use the ULP models; if the existence of a probability measure is not known, use the TBM. Dempster's model is essentially a special case of ULP model. The EVM and the probability of modal propositions (provability, necessity,...) corresponds to a special use of the Bayesian model.[1]

Keywords: belief functions, Dempster-Shafer theory, belief modeling, upper and lower probabilities, transferable belief model.

---

[1] The following text presents research results of the Belgian national incentive-program for fundamental research in artificial intelligence initiated by the Belgian State, Prime Minister's Office, Science Policy Programming. Scientific responsibility is assumed by its author. A preliminary and much shorter version appeared in Smets (1990 a, b, c).

1. INTRODUCTION

1.1. Modeling beliefs

I do not know what Dempster-Shafer's model is,[2] except that it uses the mathematical object called "belief function." Usually its aim is the *modeling of someone's degrees of belief.* But there are so many interpretations of Dempster-Shafer's theory in the literature that it seems useful to present the various contenders in order to clarify their respective meanings and domains of applicability.

Beliefs result from *uncertainty* and the interpretations we present correspond to different forms of uncertainty. The uncertainty encountered here concerns the one usually quantified by probability functions. We do not tackle the problem of vagueness and ambiguity studied in fuzzy sets theory and possibility theory. Here, the uncertainty sometimes results from a random process (the objective probability case), and sometimes only from the lack of information that induces some "belief" (instead of some "knowledge"). The domain of application of the various models we study here is the same as the one studied by the Bayesians, but in some cases, as with the transferable belief model, we propose solutions different from those defended by the Bayesians.

We will consider successively the classical probability model, the upper and lower probabilities (ULP) model, Dempster's model, the transferable belief model (TBM), the evidentiary value model (EVM), and the provability/necessity model. Each model corresponds to a different form of uncertainty or to the introduction of some particular extra assumptions.

None of these models receives the *qualification of "Dempster-Shafer"* and I do not think any model deserves it. This qualification has a historical origin (Gordon and Shortliffe, 1984) but is misleading. Some people qualify any model that uses belief functions as Dempster-Shafer. This might be acceptable provided they did not blindly accept the applicability of both Dempster's rule of conditioning and combination. Such uncritical – and in fact often inappropriate – use of these two rules explains most of the errors encountered in the so-called Dempster-Shafer literature (Pearl, 1990).

---

[2] By a model, we simply mean a mathematical representation (idealization) of some process, the subjective, personal beliefs here. It should not be confused with the concept of a model encountered in logic.

Both Dempster and Shafer introduced models but I do not think they would recognize them as "Dempster-Shafer" models. Dempster's seminal work was not oriented toward the modeling of someone's beliefs. Shafer's idea was to use the mathematics introduced by Dempster in order to model someone's belief (Shafer, 1976a). We share this idea, but consider that Shafer did not justify his model in his book, and later justifications were too much based on random sets, one-to-many mappings and upper and lower probabilities–all approaches open to criticism, as shown in this paper. So we introduced the concept of the transferable belief model (TBM) in order to justify the use of belief functions (including Dempster's rule of conditioning and Dempster's rule of combination) to model someone's belief (Smets, 1988). This papers focuses more on a presentation of the TBM and a criticism of most of the justifications provided in the literature. The TBM was in fact developed to meet these criticisms. Justifications of the use of belief functions is in Smets and Kennes (1990). Justification of Dempster's rule of conditioning is in Smets (1990a, 1991a), and Klawonn and Schwecke (1990).

The problem with Dempster's model lies in the fact that it sets out to assess "beliefs" on some space Y on which the existence of a *probability measure is acknowledged, but not precisely known* in that the probability is known for some of its subsets, but not for all of them. The updating of this "partially defined" probability measure on Y by conditionalization cannot always be performed, but the solution proposed in Dempster's model (the D-conditioning in section 5) has been criticized for violating the basic rules of probability theory (Levi, 1983).

In the TBM, such probability measure on Y is not claimed. If there is such a probability measure, the TBM is reduced to the classic probabilistic model. But the TBM can be described without assuming such a probability measure on Y. And if such a probability measure on Y is not assumed, the constraints of the probability theory – because of its irrelevance – can no longer be brought into play to criticize the updated beliefs derived on Y after applying Dempster's rule of conditioning.

This explains why we described the TBM as a *purified model*, "purified" inasmuch as a connection with probability concepts is not necessary. In the TBM, we use the available information but no more. We do not assume the existence of a probability measure on every space as do the Bayesians. We keep only those probabilities that are justified. The obvious interest of the TBM is that it can be applied even in contexts where every probalility concept is absent. And when probabilities are defined everywhere, the TBM is reduced to the Bayesian model.

We study a paradigm, the unreliable sensor. We apply each model to it and show what the underlying hypotheses are that justify the use of each model. For each model, we successively present a short summary of the underlying theory followed by an analysis of the paradigm. For a real problem, the user will have to select the appropriate model, and that selection should be governed by the explicit acknowledgment of the underlying hypothesis. So in each context, there will be only one satisfactory analysis. There is no satisfactory general method; each case requires its own. What that method might be depends on the underlying hypothesis.

1.2. The static and dynamic components

Any model for belief has at least two components: static, which describes our state of belief, and dynamic, which explains how to update our belief given new pieces of information. We insist on the fact that both components must be considered in order to compare these models. Unfortunately, too many publications are restricted to the static component and fail to detect the differences between these models. In fact, the originality of the models based on belief functions lies essentially in their dynamic component.

The difference between the various models we have studied can be described through the Möbius transform of the various measures of belief presented here. Let Ω be a finite set Ω with its powerset denoted by 2^Ω. Given a function F: $2^\Omega \rightarrow [0, 1]$, its *Möbius transform m*: $2^\Omega \rightarrow [0,1]$ is:

$$m(A) = \sum_{X \subseteq A} (-1)^{|A|-|X|} F(X)$$

and

$$F(A) = \sum_{X \subseteq A} m(X)$$

where $|X|$ is the number of elements in X. When F is a probability function P, $m(A)$ is null whenever $|A| \neq 1$ and $m(\omega) = P(\{\omega\})$, for each $\omega \in \Omega$. When F is a belief function bel (or a lower probability function P_* in Dempster's model), then[3] $m(A) \geqslant 0$ for all $A \subseteq \Omega$, $m(\emptyset) = 0$ and m is called a *basic belief assignment*, and m's values are called the *basic belief masses*.

2. THE BREAKABLE SENSOR

Suppose I am a new technician and must check the temperature of a process. To do this, I have a sensor that can check the temperature of the process – a temperature that can be only hot or cold. If the temperature is hot (TH), the sensor light is red (R) and if the temperature is cold (TC), the sensor light is blue (B). The sensor is made of a thermometer and a device that turns on the blue-red light according to the temperature reading. Unfortunately, the thermometer may well be broken.

The only known information is what is written on the box containing the sensor. "Warning: the thermometer included in this sensor may be broken. The probability that it is broken is 20%. When the thermometer is not broken, the sensor is a perfectly reliable detector of the temperature situation. When the thermometer is not broken, red light means the temperature is hot, blue light means the temperature is cold. When the thermometer is broken, the sensor answer is unrelated to the temperature."

I am a new technician and have never seen this sensor before. I know nothing about it except the warning written on the box. I use it and the blue light goes on. How do I assess the temperature status? What is my opinion (belief) that the temperature status is hot or cold?

Before constructing any quantified description of our personal belief with respect to the temperature status, one must build a frame of discernment Ω (also called the universe of discourse or state space) on which beliefs will be allocated and updated. Its structure is a finite Boolean algebra of propositions or of sets, which here is equivalent. $\Omega = S \times T \times \Theta$, the Cartesian product of spaces S, T, and Θ where:

- $S = \{\text{B, R}\}$, the sensor status, Blue or Red
- $T = \{\text{TH, TC}\}$, the temperature status, Hot or Cold
- $\Theta = \{\text{ThW, ThB}\}$, the thermometer status, Working or Broken

[3] We accept the closed world assumption (as in Shafer's work). Under closed world assumption $m(\emptyset) = 0$. Under open world assumption, $m(\emptyset)$ may be positive, and bel $(A) = \sum_{\emptyset \neq X \subseteq A} m(X)$, in which case bel $(\Omega) = 1 - m(\emptyset)$. For the difference between the open and closed world assumptions, see Smets (1988).

The eight elements of the space Ω are detailed in Table 1.1.

Table 1.1: The labels of the eight elements of Ω.

	B		R	
	TH	TC	TH	TC
ThW	*a*	*b*	*c*	*d*
ThB	*e*	*f*	*g*	*h*

3. THE PROBABILITY MODEL

3.1. The model

In probability theory, the static component consists of the assessment of a probability density p on the elements of Ω such that $p: \Omega \to [0, 1]$, $\sum_{\omega \in \Omega} p(\omega) = 1$.

Degrees of belief on subsets of Ω are quantified by a probability distribution $P: 2^{\Omega} \to [0, 1]$ such that for all $\omega \in \Omega$, $P(\{\omega\}) = p(\omega)$ and for all A, $B \subseteq \Omega$ with $A \cap B = \emptyset$, $P(A \cup B) = P(A) + P(B)$ and $P(A) = \sum_{\omega \in A} p(\omega)$.

The only dynamic component is the conditioning rule: when you learn that $B \subseteq \Omega$ is true (and if $P(B) \neq 0$), P is updated into the conditional probability distribution $P(.|B)$ defined on 2^{Ω} such that $P(A|B) = P(A \cap B)/P(B)$.

3.2. The probabilist analysis

A probabilist will build a probability distribution P on 2^{Ω}. The information on the box induces the constraints:

$$P(\text{ThW}) = P(\{a, b, c, d\}) = p(a) + p(b) + p(c) + p(d) = 0.8$$
$$P(\text{ThB}) = P(\{e, f, g, h\}) = p(e) + p(f) + p(g) + p(h) = 0.2$$

When the sensor is working (ThW), the sensor is red (R) when the temperature is hot (TH), and blue (B) otherwise (TC). So

$$p(a) = p(d) = 0$$

When the sensor is broken (ThB), the sensor status (B or R) is unrelated to the temperature status. It translates as $P(\mathrm{B}|\mathrm{ThB}, \mathrm{TH}) = P(\mathrm{B}/\mathrm{ThB}, \mathrm{TC})$, that is:

$$\frac{p(e)}{p(e)+p(g)} = \frac{p(f)}{p(f)+p(h)}$$

Let $x = P(\mathrm{B}|\mathrm{ThB}) = \dfrac{p(e)+p(f)}{p(e)+p(f)+p(g)+p(h)}$ denotes the probability that the sensor is blue when the thermometer is broken and $\pi = P(\mathrm{TC}) = p(b) + p(f) + p(h)$ denotes the a priori probability that the temperature is cold (before we perform our measurement). Finally the status of the thermometer (ThB or ThW) is unrelated to the temperature (TH or TC): $P(\mathrm{ThW}|\mathrm{TH}) = P(\mathrm{ThW})$, that is, $\dfrac{p(a)+p(c)}{p(a)+p(c)+p(e)+p(g)} = 0.8.$

Table 1.2: Probability distribution on $\Omega = S \times T \times \Theta$.

	B		R	
	TH	TC	TH	TC
ThW	0	$.8\pi$	$.8(1-\pi)$	0
ThB	$.2(1-\pi)x$	$.2\pi x$	$.2(1-\pi)(1-x)$	$.2\pi(1-x)$

Table 1.2 presents the probability distribution p on Ω. The set of constraints is not sufficient to define uniquely π and x. There are several ways to describe the missing information; those used simplify the discussion as π and x have natural connotations. We must compute

$$P(\mathrm{TC}|\mathrm{B}) = \frac{p(b)+p(f)}{p(a)+p(b)+p(e)+p(f)} = \frac{(.8+.2x)\pi}{.8\pi+.2x}$$

Even if we knew π, what value should be given to x, the probability that the sensor status is blue when the thermometer is broken? Nothing in the available evidence tells us what value to give to x. A probabilist facing such a problem can follow several approaches:

- He can try to collect data about x... If he could, then his results would be the same as those obtained with the various alternative models analyzed hereafter. The problem we study is the one where no further data can be collected about x.
- He can propose extraneous assumptions like:

- the principle of insufficient reason: when the thermometer is broken, the sensor can only be blue or red. Knowing nothing more, I postulate that both options have the same probability, hence $x = 0.5$
- a maximum entropy argument that leads to the same result
- a meta-probability that describes his belief about the possible values of x... but how can one justify where the mata-probability comes from? (Remember all the technician knows is the warning on the box containing the sensor.)

So to perform a strict probability analysis, you must introduce some extraneous assumption. The value of your results will only reflect the value of this assumption. The classical probability approach therefore fails in such states of ignorance. This failure explains why other models have been proposed.

4. UPPER AND LOWER PROBABILITIES MODEL

4.1. The model

The upper and lower probabilities model is identical to the probability model except that it acknowledges that some probabilities might be unknown. Let the set Π of all those probability distributions be compatible with the available information. Instead of building a meta-probability distribution on Π as strict Bayesians would recommend, one considers critical values – usually the extremes – of the various probabilities one is interested in. Various forms of partly known probability models can be described. Sometimes Π is uniquely defined through its so-called upper and lower probabilities functions P^* and P_* where

$$\text{for all } A \subseteq \Omega,\ P^*(A) = \sup_{P \in \Pi} P(A), P_*(A) = \inf_{P \in \Pi} P(A)$$

In other cases, Π is a convex set of probability distributions (Kyburg, 1987). Sometimes Π is just a set of probability distributions, as in the case where we have a double head or double tail coin, but we do not know which; hence $P(\text{Head})$ is either 0 or 1 and Π has only two elements. When Π contains only one element, the model is reduced to the classic probability model.

In the usual upper and lower probabilities model, the static part consists of defining the upper probability distribution P^* or the lower probability distribution P_*, both from 2^Ω to $[0,1]$. For each P in Π, one has:

$$\text{for all } A \subseteq \Omega,\ P_*(A) \leqslant P(A) \leqslant P^*(A)$$

By construction, $P^*(A) = 1 - P_*(A)$.

Conditioning on $B \subseteq \Omega$ is obtained by considering each probability distribution P in Π, and conditioning them on B. Let Π_B be the resulting set of conditional probability distributions:

$$\Pi_B = \{P_B : \text{for all } A \subseteq \Omega, P_B(A) = P(A|B) = \frac{P(A \cap B)}{P(B)}, P \in \Pi\}$$

The upper and lower conditional probabilities functions are the upper and lower limits of these conditional probabilities:

$$\text{for all } A \subseteq \Omega, \qquad \begin{aligned} P_*(A|B) &= \inf_{P_B \in \Pi_B} P_B(A) = \inf_{P \in \Pi} P(A|B) \\ P^*(A|B) &= \sup_{P_B \in \Pi_B} P_B(A) = \sup_{P \in \Pi} P(A|B) \end{aligned}$$

4.2. The upper and lower probabilities analysis

In the probability approach, the missing information is π and x.They are only known to be in $[0,1]^2$. To each pair (π, x) there corresponds an element P of Π. We will also consider the case where π is known, in which case the set of compatible probability distributions is Π' where each value of x in $[0,1]$ defines an element P of Π'. (The ′ notation will distinguish the two cases.) These constraints describe the static part of the model.

The dynamic part is applied once the blue light (B) is observed. Suppose first that π and x are both unknown. Conditioning on B results in:

$$\begin{aligned} P_*(\text{TC}|\text{B}) &= \inf_{P \in \Pi} \text{P}(\text{TC}|\text{B}) = \inf_{(\pi, x) \in [0,1] \times [0,1]} \text{P}(\text{TC}|\text{B}) = 0 \\ P^*(\text{TC}|\text{B}) &= \sup_{P \in \Pi} \text{P}(\text{TC}|\text{B}) = \sup_{(\pi, x) \in [0,1] \times [0,1]} \text{P}(\text{TC}|\text{B}) = 1 \end{aligned}$$

Should π be known, then:

$$\begin{aligned} P'_*(\text{TC}|\text{B}) &= \inf_{P \in \Pi'} \text{P}(\text{TC}|\text{B}) = \inf_{x \in [0,1]} \text{P}(\text{TC}|\text{B}) = \pi(.8\pi + 0.2) \\ P'^*(\text{TC}|\text{B}) &= \sup_{P \in \Pi'} \text{P}(\text{TC}|\text{B}) = \sup_{x \in [0,1]} \text{P}(\text{TC}|\text{B}) = 1 \end{aligned}$$

So if the technician is ignorant of π, he is left in a state of total ignorance even after observing B. If he knows π, he can compute informative limits and try to make a decision given this partial knowledge about $P(\text{TC}|\text{B})$, a problem still open to discussion.

5. DEMPSTER'S MODEL

5.1. The model

Dempster (1967) introduced a special form of upper and lower probabilities model. For the static part of the model, he considers a space X endowed with a probability measure P_X and a mapping M from space X to space 2^Y. Let $M(x)$ denote the image of x under M for $x \in X$. He defines upper and lower probabilities measures P^* and P_* on Y such that, for all $A \subseteq Y$:

$$P_*(A) = P_X(M_*(A))$$

and

$$P^*(A) = P_X(M^*(A))$$

where

$$M_*(A) = \{x : x \in X,\ M(x) \subseteq A,\ M(x) \neq \emptyset\}$$

and

$$M^*(A) = \{x : x \in X,\ M(x) \cap A \neq \emptyset\}$$

The functions P_* and P^* are a belief function and plausibility function respectively (see section 6).

The upper and lower probabilities nature of Dempster's solution can be shown. One has:

$$\text{for all A} \subseteq \text{Y}, \quad \inf P_Y(A) = \inf \sum_{x \in X} P_Y(A|x) \cdot P_X(x)$$

where inf is taken over all possible values of $P_Y(A|x)$. Index of the P functions indicate the domain of P. One has $P_Y(A|x) = 1$ if $M(x) \subseteq A$, and anything in $[0, 1]$ otherwise. The minimum is obtained by taking $P_Y(A|x) = 0$ whenever possible. Hence:

$$\inf P_Y(A) = \sum_{x : M(x) \subseteq A} P_X(x) = P_X(M_*(A)) = P_*(A)$$

The Möbius transform m of the lower probability distribution P_* is nonnegative: for each $X \in X, m(M(x)) = P_X(\{x\})$, and all other m on 2^Y are null.

For the dynamic part of the model, two types of conditioning can be considered:

$$P_*(A|B) = \inf P_Y(A|B) = \inf \frac{\sum_{x \in X} P_Y(A \cap B|x) \cdot P_X(x)}{\sum_{x \in X} P_Y(B|x) \cdot P_X(x)} =$$

$$= \frac{P_*(A \cap B)}{P_*(A \cap B) + P^*(\bar{A} \cap \mathrm{B})}$$

where inf is taken over all possible values of $P_Y(A|x)$. This conditioning, hereafter called the *G*-conditioning, corresponds to the solution described in the upper and lower probabilities model in section 4. It is not the one considered by Dempster.

Instead he considers that conditioning on $B \subseteq Y$ means that the mapping $M: X \to 2^Y$ has been transformed into mapping $M_B: X \to 2^Y$ with:

$$M_B(x) = M(x) \cap \mathrm{B}$$

It corresponds to the idea that the conditioning information indicates that the set of images of each $x \in X$ is $M(x) \cap B$. Dempster postulates also that the knowledge of the conditioning event B does not modify P_X, that is, $P_X(x|B) = P_X(x)$, a requirement open to criticism (see section 5.3). In that case,

$$P_*(A|B) = \inf \sum_{x \in X} P_{Y|B}(A|x) \cdot P_X(x)$$

$$P^*(A|B) = \sup \sum_{x \in X} P_{Y|B}(A|x) \cdot P_X(x)$$

where $P_{Y|B}(A|x) = 1$ if $M(x) \cap B \subseteq A$ and anything in $[0, 1]$ otherwise. Then

$$P_*(A|B) = \frac{P_*(A \cup \bar{B}) - P_*(\bar{B})}{1 - P_*(\bar{B})} \qquad P^*(A|B) = \frac{P^*(A \cap B)}{P^*(B)}$$

which is what we call the *D*-conditioning. Dempster's model is defined as the one endowed with the *D*-conditioning rule.

Apart from the *D*-conditioning, Dempster also defines the so-called Dempster's rule of combination, a rule to combine the beliefs induced by two distinct pieces of information. It does not have an immediate counterpart in probability theory. It is not necessary for our presentation, so we shall not insist on it (see Shafer, 1986; Smets, 1990a).

5.2. Dempster's analysis

The static part of Dempster's model is perfectly acceptable by any probabilist. The constraints induce the same solutions as described with the upper and lower probabilities analysis in section 4. The X and Y spaces correspond to the Θ and the Ω spaces, respectively. The mapping M is such that $M(\text{ThW}) = \{a, b, c, d\}$ and $M(\text{ThB}) = \{e, f, g, h\}$. Finally, the probabilities defined on Θ induce the basic belief masses m on 2^{Ω}.

$$m(\{b, c\}) = 0.8$$

and

$$m(\{e, f, g, h,\}) = 0.2$$

Suppose π is unknown. Once B is known to have occurred (i.e., $\{c, d, g, h\}$ is impossible) one adapts the mapping M into M_B, where $M_B(\text{ThW}) = \{a, b\}$ and $M_B(\text{ThB}) = \{e, f\}$. Then

$$P_*(\text{TC}|\text{B}) = P_*(b, d, f, h\}|\{a, b, e, f\}) =$$

$$= \frac{P_*(\{b, c, d, f, g, h\}) - P_*(\{c, d, g, h\})}{1 - P_*(\{c, d, g, h\})} = \frac{0.8 - 0}{1 - 0} = 0.8$$

and

$$P^*(\text{TC}|\text{B}) = \frac{P^*(b, f\})}{P^*(\{a, b, e, f\})} = \frac{1}{1} = 1$$

Suppose π is known. The X domain is now the space $\text{T} \times \Theta$ and the Y domain is still Ω. The induced basic belief masses m on 2^{Ω} are given in Table 1.3. Then

$$P'_*(\text{TC}|\text{B}) = \frac{P'_*(\{b, c, d, f, g, h\}) - P'_*(\{c, d, g, h\})}{1 - P'_*(\{c, d, g, h\})} =$$

$$= \frac{\pi}{0.8\,\pi + 0.2}$$

$$P'^*(\text{TC}|\text{B}) = \frac{P'^*(b, f\})}{P'^*(\{a, b, e, f\})} = \frac{\pi}{0.8\,\pi + 0.2}$$

The fact $P'^* = P'_*$ reflects the Bayesian nature of the solution. As shown in Shafer (1976a), once a belief is quantified by a probability distribution, all updating will result in a probability distribution.

Table 1.3: List of elements x of the space $T \times \Theta$, with their image under M and the value of the basic belief masses m induced by P_X.

elements x of $X = T \times \Theta$	$M(x)$	$m(M(x)) = P_X(\{x\})$
ThW ∩ TH	$\{c\}$	$0.8(1 - \pi)$
ThW ∩ TC	$\{b\}$	0.8π
ThB ∩ TH	$\{e, g\}$	$0.2(1 - \pi)$
ThB ∩ TC	$\{f, h\}$	0.2π

5.3. Remarks

The adaptation of the mapping is perfectly acceptable. Disagreement appears in the dynamic part when the D-conditioning is used (Levi, 1983; Good, 1982; Williams, 1982; Shafer, 1986). Why does one keep the same probability distribution on Θ once B has been learned? Bona fide probability analysis would require that P_Θ also be updated once B is known to have occurred. One should have

$$P(\text{ThB}|\text{B}) = \frac{P(\text{ThB})\,P(\text{B}|\text{ThB})}{P(\text{B})} = \frac{0.2x}{0.2x + 0.8\pi}$$

$$P(\text{ThW}|\text{B}) = \frac{0.8\pi}{0.2x + 0.8\pi}$$

To be allowed to use $P(\text{ThB}|\text{B}) = P(\text{ThB}) = 0.2$, one must have $x = \pi$, a constraint unjustified in the context and one that usually cannot be justified in more elaborate examples. Of course, to answer Levi's criticisms will take us straight back to the upper and lower probabilities model.

An important point in Dempster's model is that one recognizes the existence of a probability distribution P_Y on Y. The statement $P_*(A) \leqslant P_Y(A) \leqslant P^*(A)$ is meaningful as $P_Y(A)$ exists, even though its exact value is unknown. The so-called Dempster-Shafer model usually corresponds to this interpretation. It is not the case with the transferable belief model (section 6) where no concept of probability distribution on Y is assumed or required.

The important point in Dempster's model is that one starts with a probability measure P_X on X and assumes a probability measure P_Y on Y.

Levi's criticism of Dempster-Shafer's analysis is based on the assumption that there is a probability distribution P_Y on Y, in which case Dempster's rule of conditioning is questionable. But if you do not assume a probability distribution on Y, the criticism becomes unfounded. This explains why we try to describe the TBM without assuming a probability distribution on Y, even though there may exist one on X. We reject the Bayesian postulate that *on any space* there is *always* a probability measure that quantifies our degree of belief. Introduce probabilities on Y, and Levi's criticisms must be resolved, but how? Shafer's (1986) answer is hardly convincing.

6. THE TRANSFERABLE BELIEF MODEL

6.1. The model

The transferable belief model is a mathematical, idealized model that sets out to represent someone's beliefs. For such a representation, it uses belief function where $\text{bel}(A)$ is true.

The *transferable belief model* is based on a two-level model:

- a *credal level* where beliefs are entertained, combined, and updated
- a *pignistic level* where beliefs are used to take decisions (from *pignus*, a bet in Latin)

At the credal level, each piece of evidence leads to the allocation of parts of some initial finite amount of belief to subsets of the universe of discourse Ω, also called the frame of discernment. If all these parts were allocated only to the singletons of Ω, the resulting model would correspond to the Bayesian model. But, in general, parts may be allocated to subsets. They represent that part of our belief that supports some subset of the frame of discernment, but that does not support any more specific subsets because of lack of information.

Suppose a mass $m(A)$ (called a *basic belief mass*) supports a set A of Ω, and then you learn that subset X of Ω is impossible. The basic belief mass given initially to A now supports $A \cap \bar{X}$. So the basic belief mass $m(A)$ is transferred to $A \cap \bar{X}$, hence the name of the model. This corresponds to Dempster's rule of conditioning.

The *degree of belief* $\text{bel}(A)$ given to the set A of Ω is defined as the sum of all masses that support A,

$$\text{bel}(A) = \sum_{\emptyset \neq X \subseteq A} m(X)$$

The *degree of plausibility* function pl(A) quantifies the total amount of belief that might support A:

$$\text{pl}(A) = \text{bel}(\Omega) - \text{bel}(\bar{A}) = \sum_{X \cap A \neq \emptyset} m(X)$$

The transferable belief model claims that beliefs are quantified by *a single number* (bel). In that, it differs from Kyburg's (1987) models that consider that states of belief are described by sets of probability distributions, and therefore do not require that degrees of beliefs be single-valued.

The transferable belief model is not a particular case; nor is it a generalization of probability models or of any meta-model based on probability distributions. We never assume the existence of a probability distribution on Ω (on the contrary, it is assumed in Dempster's model). Nevertheless, one must be careful to avoid the treacherous pitfall. Inasmuch as the quantification of our belief on Ω is represented by a belief function, one can always build an "artificial" space Θ endowed with a probability measure and with a one-to-many mapping between Θ and Ω, just as in Dempster's model. But here this is just a mathematical property without any practical meaning. This probability measure on Θ does not correspond to a measure of some subjective belief on Θ. It is merely a mathematical construct.

The existence of an underlying probability measure reflecting some beliefs is irrelevant to our approach. We only postulate the existence of basic belief masses assigned to subsets A of Ω, each expressing the support given specifically to A and induced by the evidence, and that could be transfered to more specific subsets of Ω should new pieces of evidence become available (the conditioning process).

In any modeling of uncertainty, it is required that a method should be provided for making decisions. If the TBM is to be more than just an artificial idealized mathematical model of how beliefs could be represented and updated, one must describe – and justify – a tool for decision making. Our solution is detailed in Smets (1990b) and Smets and Kennes (1990). Suppose one must bet on the elements of Ω. One must build on Ω a probability distribution (the pignistic probability distribution Bet P) derived from the belief function that describes our credal state. For all elements $x \in \Omega$:

$$\text{Bet}P(x) = \sum_{x \in A \subseteq \Omega} m(A)/|A| = \sum_{A \subseteq \Omega} m(A)|\{x\} \cap A|/|A|$$

where $|A|$ is the number of elements of Ω in A.

6.2. The transferable belief model analysis

When π is unknown, the static part results in the basic belief masses $m(\{b,c\}) = 0.8$ and $m(\{e,f,g,h\}) = 0.2$. Conditioning on B implies the transfer of all basic belief masses within the set $\{a,b,e,f\}$. The updated basic belief masses m_B are $m_B(\{b\}) = 0.8$ and $m_B(e, f\}) = 0.2$. So $\text{bel}(\text{TC}|B) = \text{bel}_B(\{b,f\}) = 0.8$, and $\text{pl}(\text{TC}|B) = \text{pl}_B(\{b,f\}) = 1$.

When π is known, the static part results in the basic belief masses m' with

$$m'(\{b\}) = 0.8\,\pi \quad m'(\{c\}) = 0.8\,(1-\pi) \quad m'(\{e,g\}) = 0.2\,(1-\pi)$$
$$m'(\{f,h\}) = 0.2\,\pi$$

Conditioning on B implies the transfer of all basic belief masses within the set $\{a, b, e, f\}$. The updated basic belief masses m'_B are

$$m'_B(\{b\}) = 0.8\,\pi \quad m'_B(\{e\}) = 0.2\,(1-\pi) \quad m'_B(\{f\}) = 0.2\,\pi$$

So

$$\text{bel}'(\text{TC}|B) = \text{bel}'_B(\{b,f\}) = \frac{\pi}{0.8\,\pi + 0.2}$$

and

$$\text{pl}'(\text{TC}|B) = \text{pl}'_B(\{b,f\}) = \frac{\pi}{0.8\,\pi + 0.2}$$

6.3. Remarks

These solutions are numerically the same as those obtained by Dempster's analysis. The difference does not reside in the numerical results, but in their interpretation. Nowhere have we postulated a probability distribution on Ω. But one might argue that the information used to build the initial basic belief masses is probability related. Though true, it is not necessarily so. To understand the exact nature of the origin of these masses and the relation with probability distribution, one must consider space Ω and the various algebra **R** one can build on Ω. If there exists an algebra $\mathbf{R}_0$ on which our belief happens to be quantified by a probability distribution P_0, whatever the origin of this probability distribution, then for all $A \in R_0$, $\text{bel}(A) = P_0(A)$. This is a requirement to be compared with Hacking's (1965) frequency principle:

$$\text{Belief}(A|\ \text{chance}(A) = p) = p$$

It here becomes:

> If there exists an algebra $R \subseteq 2^{\Omega}$ on which a probability distribution $P_0(A)$ is known for all $A \in R$, then $\text{bel}_R(A) = P_0(A)$

In case there are two algebras R_1 and R_2 on Ω on which our beliefs are quantified by probability distribution P_1 and P_2, and such that $R_1 \subseteq R_2$, then use P_2 to define your belief function bel on R_2. P_1 is neglected as it is less informative than P_2, and P_2 contains information included in P_1 (and even more in general). The case when neither of the two algebras is a subalgebra of the other is not studied here as not being fundamental to our discussion.

Suppose bel_0 is known on some algebra R_0 and belief must be expessed on 2^{Ω}. In the absence of any further information, build the vacuous extension bel of bel_0 on 2^{Ω}, with basic belief masses m such that:

$$m(A) = \begin{cases} m_0(A), & \text{for all } A \in R \\ 0, & \text{otherwise} \end{cases}$$

This is the extension used in our example when we wrote $m(\{b, c\}) = 0.8$ and $m(\{e, f, g, h\}) = 0.2$.

When no algebra can be founded on which a probability distribution could describe our beliefs, we can nevertheless assess basic belief masses using betting behaviors and varying betting frames as detailed in Smets and Kennes (1990).

7. THE EVIDENTIARY VALUE MODEL

Ekelöf (1982) intially proposed a theory of evidentiary value in the judicial context (see Gärdenfors et al.,1983 for a survey of the topic). The model is very close to Dempster-Shafer's model and the transferable belief model.

An evidentiary argument includes three components (Gärdenfors, 1983):

- an evidentiary theme that is to be proved
- evidentiary facts
- evidentiary mechanisms that state that an evidentiary fact is caused by an evidentiary theme

The authors suggest that the probability that the evidentiary mechanism has worked given the evidentiary facts is considered more important judicially than the probability of the evidentiary theme given the evidentiary facts.

This model fits in perfectly with the breakable sensor paradigm. The evidentiary value $EV(\mathrm{TC}|B)$ that the temperature is cold given the light is B is the probability that the fact B is caused by the theme TC, that is, the probability that the thermometer is working:

$$EV(\mathrm{TC}|\mathrm{B}) = P(\mathrm{ThW}) = 0.8$$

Identically, $EV(\mathrm{TH}|\mathrm{B}) = 0$ as a blue light B is not caused by a hot temperature. It can, of course, occur in such cases, but it would not result from a causal link.

Thus $EV(\mathrm{TC}|\mathrm{B}) = \mathrm{bel}(\mathrm{TC}|\mathrm{B})$ and $1 - EV(\mathrm{TH}/\mathrm{B}) = \mathrm{pl}(\mathrm{TC}|\mathrm{B})$. This equality has led some authors to consider that Dempster's model might find its justification in the evidentiary value model. But the problem with this approach is the same as with Dempster's model. Why do we keep $P(\mathrm{ThW}) = 0.8$ once B is learned, and why don't we use $P(\mathrm{ThW}|\mathrm{B})$ as the causal weight? Levi's criticisms apply here also.

Another problem appears once the prior probability π is known. What is then the probability that the fact B is caused by TC? In the context $\mathrm{ThW} \cap \mathrm{TC}$ (probability $0{,}8\pi$, see Table 1.3), B is caused by TC. But what about context $\mathrm{ThB} \cap \mathrm{TC}$ (with probability 0.2π): can we say that B is caused by TC? Hicks (1979, p. 13) requires four elements to assert that "TC causes B":

1. TC existed.
2. B existed.
3. The hypothetical situation in which TC did not exist, ceteris paribus, can be constructed.
4. If that situation had existed, B would not have occurred.

In context $\mathrm{ThW} \cap \mathrm{TC}$, the causality requirements are satisfied: TC and B existed, the hypothetical context is $\mathrm{ThW} \cap \mathrm{TH}$ (the ceteris paribus clause requires that the thermometer status is kept identical) and in that context, B cannot occur. Hence $P(\mathrm{ThW} \cap \mathrm{TC}) = 0.8\pi$ is part of the $EV(\mathrm{TC}|\mathrm{B})$.

In context $\mathrm{ThB} \cap \mathrm{TC}$, the causality requirements are not satisfied: TC and B existed, the hypothetical context is $\mathrm{ThB} \cap \mathrm{TH}$ and in that context, B can occur. So $P(\mathrm{ThB} \cap \mathrm{TC}) = 0.2\pi$ is not included in $EV(\mathrm{TC}|\mathrm{B})$.

When π is considered, Dempster's and the transferable belief solutions are different from the evidentiary value solution. Hence these models are different.

8. PROBABILITY OF MODEL PROPOSITIONS

Ruspini (1986) interprets Dempster-Shafer's model as a model to quantify not the probability that a proposition is true, but the probability that a proposition is necessary. Pearl (1988) interprets Dempster-Shafer's model as a model to quantify not the probability that a proposition is true, but the probability that a proposition is provable. Necessity and provability are very similar model concepts and can be represented by the modal operator $\Box$. So both interpretations of bel is that bel(A) is the probability of $\Box A$. These interpretations are similar to those in the evidentiary value model.

If $\text{bel}(A) = P(\Box A)$, then $\text{bel} = P\Box$. In that case it is easy to show that $P\Box$ is a capacity of order infinite (i.e., it satisfies all the inequalities that characterize a belief function). But difficulty appears in defining the concept of updating and justifying Dempster's rule of conditioning. What is $\text{bel}(A|B)$? Is it $P(\Box A|B)$, $P(\Box(A|B))$ or $P(\Box A|\Box B)$? The problem is still open. If one defines it as $P(\Box A|\Box B)$ (probably the most immediate proposal), one might expect that:[4]

$$\text{bel}(A|B) = P(\Box A|\Box B) = \frac{P(\Box \wedge \Box B)}{P(\Box B)} = \frac{P(\Box(A \wedge B))}{P(\Box B)} = \frac{\text{bel}(A \wedge B)}{\text{bel}(B)}$$

This conditioning rule is called the *geometrical rule of conditioning* (see Suppes and Zanotti, 1977; Shafer, 1976b; Smets, 1991a). It is encountered also in random sets theory (Hestir et al., 1991).

If one takes Nguyen's interpretation of $A|B$ as a conditional object (Goodman et al., 1991), one can obtain:

$$\text{bel}(A|B) = P(\Box(\text{A}|\text{B}) = \frac{P(\Box(A \wedge B)}{P(\Box B)} =$$

$$= \frac{\text{bel}(A \wedge B)}{1 + \text{bel}(A \wedge B) - \text{bel}(\neg B \vee A)}$$

But these two rules do not correspond to Dempster's rule of conditioning defended by Shafer and the TBM. Ruspini (1986) uses Dempster's rule of conditioning to define bel(A|B), but does not fully justify such a choice.

One could be tempted to claim that the TBM and other models based on belief functions are nothing but models for probability of modal propositions. This claim, though tempting, is not yet

[4] The context being propositional logic, we use the conjunction operator $\wedge$ instead of the set operator. In modal logic, $\Box A \wedge \Box B \equiv \Box(A \wedge B)$.

justified. To be acceptable, one will have to explain the origin of Dempster's rule of conditioning. In the TBM, it is an integral part of the model: it corresponds to the ability for each mass $m(A)$, $A \subseteq \Omega$, to move freely among the subsets of A if further information justifies it. In Dempster's model, it is deduced in the D-conditioning if one accepts the postulate that the knowledge of the conditioning event does not modify the probabilities (except for a possible rescaling) on the X space (see section 5.1).

9. THE COIN EXPERIMENT OR "DO WE NEED THE TBM?"

To explain the difference between the TBM, the Dempsterian, and the Bayesian analyses, we consider a classic example already analyzed in Shafer and Tversky (1985).

Suppose there are four men: Mr. Truth, Mr. False, Mr. Head, and Mr. Tail. They all look at the visible face of a coin you have put on the table (I did not say that you have tossed the coin before putting it on the table). I know that:

> Mr. Truth will say H when the face is Head, T when the face is Tail.
> Mr. False will say T when the face is Head, H when the face is Tail.
> Mr. Head will always say H.
> Mr. Tail will always say T.

One of the four men is selected by a random process. The selection is independent from the visible face of the coin. For each of the four men, the probability he will be selected is 0.25. I do not know who the randomly selected man is. I hear he says H. I wish to determine what my belief is that the face is Head.

Let Ω be the space $\{H, T\}$ and the collected information be denoted SH (for the selected person said H).

Both the TBM and the Dempsterian analysis of the scenario lead to a first conclusion that Mr. Tail was certainly not selected. The probabilities allocated to the other options therefore are proportionally rescaled into 0.33 (the closed world assumption is accepted for the TBM analysis). Then:

- the 0.33 allocated to Mr. Truth supports the fact that the H is true,

- the 0.33 allocated to Mr. False supports the fact that T is true, and
- the 0.33 allocated to Mr. Head supports nothing (hence Ω).

Hence bel($H|SH$) = 0.33, bel($T|SH$) = 0.33 and bel($H \cup T|SH$) = 1.

Levi's criticism is that the updating of the three probabilities is unjustified. For a Bayesian, the appropriate updated probabilities are the probabilities that Mr. Truth (False, Head, Tail) were indeed selected given that I know now that the selected person said H. Of course, the available data do not enable us to unambiguously define these probabilities, except for the one related to Mr. Tail, which is 0 by necessity. The missing information is the a priori probability that the face was H (or T).

Should you have tossed the coin, that probability would have been 0.5, and the Bayesian – as well as any other approach in fact – would have led to updating the initial 0.25 probabilities into:

$$P(\text{Mr. Truth}\,|\,SH) = P(\text{SH}\,|\,\text{Mr. Truth})\,P(\text{Mr. Truth})\,/\,P(SH) = \\ = 0.5 \times 0.25/0.5 = 0.25$$
$$P(\text{Mr. False}\,|\,SH) = P(\text{SH}\,|\,\text{Mr. False})\,P(\text{Mr. False})\,/\,P(SH) = \\ = 0.5 \times 0.25/0.5 = 0.25$$
$$P(\text{Mr. Head}\,|\,SH) = P(\text{SH}\,|\,\text{Mr. Head})\,P(\text{Mr. Head})\,/\,P(SH) = \\ = 1 \times 0.25/0.5 = 0.5$$
$$P(\text{Mr. Tail}\,|\,SH) = P(\text{SH}\,|\,\text{Mr. Tail})\,P(\text{Mr. Tail})\,/\,P(SH) = \\ = 0.0 \times 0.25/0.5 = 0.0$$

where the denominator 0.5 is the normalization factor such that the probabilities add to one as they should. Of course, one does not find the 0.33 of the previous analysis. It reflects the impact of the supplementary information about how the coin was dropped on the table.

But this is not the situation that prevails here. We ignore how the visible face of the coin was selected: no randomness, not even a probability measure were assumed on Ω.

For a Dempsterian analysis, one defines the spaces $\Omega = \{H, T\}$, $\Pi = \{$Mr. Truth, Mr. False, Mr. Head, Mr. Tail$\}$, $\Sigma = \{SH, \neg SH\}$ (the possible observations). The X and Y spaces and the M mappings of section 5.1 correspond here to the spaces Π, $\Pi \times \Omega \times \Sigma$ and the mapping defined by the four pieces of information on how each person answers once he has seen the face of the coin (e.g., M(Mr. Truth) = {(Mr. Truth, H, SH) ∪ (Mr. Truth, T, $\neg SH$)}, M(Mr. Head) = {Mr. Head, H, SH) ∪ (Mr. Head, T, SH)},...). Given the independence assumptions between the selection process on

Π and the value of Ω, the knowledge of a probability distribution on Ω would be sufficient to build the probability measure on $\Pi \times \Omega \times \Sigma$. One would then derive the probabilities on Ω once *SH* is learned, by a direct application of the probability calculus.

But such a probability on Ω is unknown, let alone the probability distribution on $\Pi \times \Omega \times \Sigma$. In a Dempsterian approach, one nevertheless somehow acknowledges that there exists some probability measure P on $\Pi \times \Omega \times \Sigma$, that one can speak of $P(A)$ for A in $\Pi \times \Omega \times \Sigma$. Of course, the value of $P(A)$ can only be claimed to be in some interval, the interval $[P_*(A), P^*(A)]$. Once *SH* is learned, according to the model, one should update the mapping (by deleting all elements with $\neg SH$ in the space $\Pi \times \Omega \times \Sigma$). But why was the probability measure on Π not updated as it should be in probability theory?

In the TBM, we do not postulate the existence of a probability measure on Ω, nor on $\Pi \times \Omega \times \Sigma$. We acknowledge an initial probability measure on Π. We build a belief function on $\Pi \times \Omega \times \Sigma$ by vacuously extending the initial information (according to the minimal commitment principle; see Smets, 1991a). The important point is that we never assumed a probability measure on $\Pi \times \Omega \times \Sigma$. Then we learn *SH*. The conditioning event is not "measurable" on Π, where "nonmeasurable on Π" means that the set of elements of $\Pi \times \Omega \times \Sigma$ that become impossible after we learn *SH* is not a cylindrical extension of a subset of Π on $\Pi \times \Omega \times \Sigma$ (i.e., is not a subset of $\Pi \times \Omega \times \Sigma$ that can be written as $\pi \times \Omega \times \Sigma$ where $\pi \subseteq \Pi$). In fact, the knowledge of *SH* leaves us ignorant as to what should become the probability on Π (except that we know that Mr. Tail was not selected). We can nevertheless update our belief on $\Pi \times \Omega \times \Sigma$ (by transfering the basic belief masses as would be given by Dempster's rule of conditioning), and derive the TBM results (which are, of course, numerically equal to those of the Dempsterian analysis).

A harsh critic could say: you had a probability on Π, and it induces your basic belief masses on $\Pi \times \Omega \times \Sigma$. Once you learn *SH*, you should have updated your probabilities on Π and used these to update your basic belief masses on $\Pi \times \Omega \times \Sigma$. This is only a rephrasing of Levi's criticisms. The problem is that the probability theory does not provide a method to update probabilities on nonmeasurable events. I know the probability on every subset of Π, and I could update these probabilities if I learn that some subset of Π is true by applying the conditioning operator $[P(A|B) = P(A \cap B)/P(B)$ for all $A, B \subseteq \Pi]$. But here I must condition on an event on $\Pi \times \Omega \times \Sigma$ that is nonmeasurable on Π. *SH* is not equivalent to a subset of Π. So probability theory does not put any constraints on how to update my probabilities on Π.

Now why do I later worry about distinguishing the TBM from the Dempsterian model? Because, in the last instance, one accepts a probability measure on $\Pi \times \Omega \times \Sigma$ (with some of its values unknown); hence, the probability measure on Π is the marginal of that "poorly known" probability measure on $\Pi \times \Omega \times \Sigma$. Once *SH* is known, the probability distribution on $\Pi \times \Omega \times \Sigma$ must be updated by the conditioning rule described in probability theory. And the update probability distribution on Π will be the marginal of the new conditional probability defined on $\Pi \times \Omega \times \Sigma$. *SH* is no longer a nonmeasurable event. It is measurable on $\Pi \times \Omega \times \Sigma$ and its impact on Π can be derived by the marginalization constraints. In fact, once a probability distribution on $\Pi \times \Omega \times \Sigma$ is introduced, it is back to an upper and lower probabilities scenario. But then Dempster's rule of conditioning (and combination) becomes irrelevant. Correct updating must be performed by the *G*-conditioning.

This argument has shown the danger of accepting a probability distribution on $\Pi \times \Omega \times \Sigma$. Reject it as in the TBM, and all problems related to Levi's criticisms are resolved because they no longer apply.

10. THE TBM VERSUS DEMPSTERIAN ULP

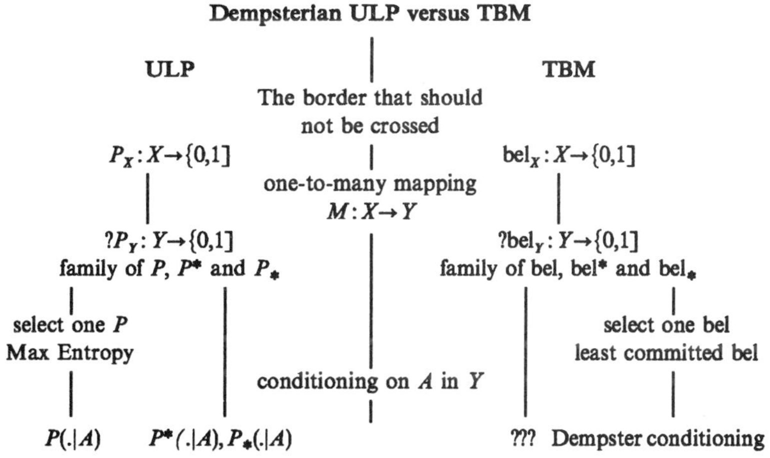

Figure 1.1: Comparing the Dempsterian ULP model and the TBM.

The next problem we wish to tackle is related to the misuses of Dempster's rule of conditioning (not speaking of the combination rule) in contexts where it should not be used. The error results from the erroneous assumption that Dempster's rule of conditioning is the *only* appropriate rule for updating all beliefs that happen to be quantified by belief functions, regardless of the context. Figure 1.1 summarizes the differences between the Dempsterian ULP model and the TBM.

10.1. Dempsterian ULP model context

Suppose a space X on which my belief is quantified by a probability distribution P_X. Updating of P_X on subsets B of X is performed by the probabilistic conditioning rule:

$$P_X(A|B) = \frac{P_X(A \cap B)}{P_X(B)}, \text{ for all } A, B \subseteq X$$

Suppose a one-to-many mapping M between space X and the power set 2^Y of a space Y. Suppose we postulate there is a probability distribution P_Y on Y. Can we build P_Y such that it satisfies the constraints due to the existence of the mapping M and the probability distribution P_X? Of course not; but we can define for every subset A of Y limits between which $P_Y(A)$ must be. Let these limits be $P_*(A)$ and $P^*(A)$ (see section 5.1.). These limits characterize a family of probability distributions Π on Y. Each element of Π is compatible with the mapping M and probability distribution P_X.

But suppose you would like to select the *best* representative of Π. You might want to select the element of Π that is the "least informative" on Y. The immediate translation of this requirement is: select the element of Π whose antropy is maximal. Let P^o be such an element of Π. You can then proceed with this probability distribution as if it was the *only* probability distribution induced by M and P_X on Y. So updating on $B \subseteq Y$ would be obtained by the classic conditioning rule of probability theory applied to P^o.

But you could also refuse to reduce Π to one of its elements and consider that all that is known is that P_Y is in Π. Then updating on $B \subseteq Y$ is obtained by considering each element of Π and conditioning it on B, and so deriving the set Π_B of all the conditional probability distributions on Y given B. This process is the very one that led to the G-conditioning in sections 4.1 and 5.1.

10.2. TBM context

A totally different scenario, but perfectly parallel in its form, can be constructed in the TBM context. Suppose a space X on which my belief is quantified by a belief function bel_X. Updating bel_X on subsets $A \subseteq X$ is obtained by Dempster's rule of conditioning.

Suppose then the same mapping M as above. On Y one can then define a family B of belief functions compatible with bel_X and M. One can define the upper and lower belief and plausibility functions bel^* and bel_*, pl^* and pl_* where, for instance, for all $A \subseteq Y$, $\text{bel}^*(A) = \max \text{bel}(A)$ and the max is taken on the elements of B. Mathematically, bel^* is a belief function, pl^* is the dual plausibility function (Dubois and Prade, 1986). The other two functions are neither belief nor plausibility functions.

As in the probabilistic approach one could select the *best* representative of B. In the TBM context, there is a principle, the *least commitment principle*, that allows the selection of the least informative belief function in B. For a pair of belief functions defined on a space Ω, one says that bel_1 is less committed than bel_2 if for all $A \subseteq \Omega$, $\text{bel}_1(A) \leqslant \text{bel}_2(A)$ (under closed world assumption only) or if for all $A \subseteq \Omega$, $\text{pl}_1(A) \geqslant \text{pl}_2(A)$ (under closed world assumption, both definitions are identical; under open world assumption, only the plausibility-based definition is valid [Smets, 1991b]). This principle expresses the idea that one should never commit more belief than is justified by the available information. It could, of course, be criticized, but it is surely much easier to defend than the maximum entropy principle. In the family B induced by bel_X and M, the least committed belief function is bel_*. This is the belief function that contains all and nothing but the information induced on Y by bel_X and M. So the normal attitude of the TBM analysis is to use this belief function and to proceed with it. Updating for some B in Y is realized by the application of Dempster's rule of conditioning.

One could try to simulate the ULP attitude, keep the family B of belief functions, condition each of them, and derive the set of compatible conditional belief functions on Y given B. This approach seems to have never been pursued, maybe because the approach based on selecting the least committed solution is convincing.

The parallelism between the two scenarios is quite obvious. Nevertheless an error is often encountered. It happens that the lower probability P_* induced by P_X and M on Y is a belief function. Discovering that property, users come to think that the appropriate rule for updating this lower probability is Dempster's rule of conditioning. It is totally unjustified (see Fagin and Halpern, 1990). The nature of the two scenarios is completely different: in one case one has a family of probability distributions on Y, in the other a family of belief functions on Y. The origin and nature of these sets must be recognized; the fact that P_* is a belief function does not entitle the user to cross the line between the two parallel scenarios and assimilate the lower probability to a belief function on which Dempster's rule of conditioning can be applied.

10.3. Final remarks on the difference

For every problem, the solutions obtained by the Dempsterian ULP analysis and the TBM analysis are numerically the same. So what is the difference between the two models? The difference lies essentially in the aim and nature of the two models.

In the TBM, the aim is to model degrees of belief. Any underlying concept of probability is irrelevant. One starts with the bbm allocated to subsets of Ω that cannot be allocated to more specific subsets because of a lack of information, but that will be transferred to more specific subsets of Ω in the light of new pieces of evidence. The dynamic nature of the model is part of its definition.

In the Dempsterian ULP model, the essential aim is not in modeling degrees of belief. The problem tackled is the evaluation of the boundaries between which lie some probabilities that are constrained by some underlying probabilities and a one-to-many mapping. The bbm are just incidental mathematical niceties and the conditioning rule is open to criticism like those of Levi.

Shafer's (1976a) initial contribution was to introduce the use of the Dempsterian ULP model to model degrees of belief, but his recent presentations are very much in line with the underlying probability measure and the one-to-many mapping. His modelization further acknowledges the presence of some probability measure on the frame of discernment and, as a result, it is open to Levi's criticisms.

11. CONCLUSIONS

Consider the mapping M between the X and 2^Y as presented in section 5.1. The major difference between the transferable belief and the probability approaches is, of course, in the way we create our beliefs on Y knowing the belief on X. The transferable belief model is based on what is available and nothing else whereas the probability analysis postulates the existence of a probability distribution on Y. Bayesians assume that whenever a probability distribution P_X is defined on X, then one can describe a probability distribution P_Y on Y where P_Y satisfies the constraints induced by P_x and the mapping M.

Reconsider the $x = P(B|ThB)$ parameter in the breakable sensor paradigm. Bayesians claim the existence of such a probability, that is, they claim that in context ThB, the B or R light data is governed by a random process, not by an arbitrary process as acknowledged in the transferable belief model analysis.

What is the *difference between a random and an arbitrary selection procedure?*

The *frequentists* suppose that an experience is repeated n times and a particular event X is observed r times. They claim there exists a limit for the ratio r/n when n tends to infinity (the limit being the probability of X). If the events are generated arbitrarily, the existence of such a limit is not claimed. We know *nothing* about an arbitrary process, whereas we know at least something about a random process: the existence of a limit.

In a classical frequentist analysis one knows the existence of a limit and its value; in an ULP analysis one knows the existence of a limit but not its value; in the transferable belief model one does not even know the existence of a limit (let alone its value).

The *Bayesian* can justify his probabilities through betting argument. The pignistic probabilites are such that Dutch books are avoided at the synchronic level. At the diachronic level, the argument is based on an assumption of temporal coherence that can be disposed of without falling into the Dutch Book trap (Smets and Kennes, 1990). The TBM and its related decision-making rules are so that there exists no a priori startegy that leads to a sure loss. In the TBM, contingent conditioning and updating are different concepts (Walley, 1991).

The requirement about the existence of a limit or of some coherent behaviour can be avoided in a logical approach like the one based on *Cox's axioms* (Cox, 1964), but at the cost of introducing the axiom: "the belief given to the complement of a proposition A is a function of the belief given to A." This postulate is not required in the transferable belief model (Smets et al., 1991).

All alternatives to the transferable belief model explicitly or implicitly accept the Bayesian assumption: the existence of probability distributions on all relevant spaces. The genuine difference between the transferable belief model and all its contenders lies in this assumption. Accept it and Levi's remarks are relevant. In the transferable belief model, one never postulates the existence of these probability distributions. One only recognizes that if a probability distribution can be defined on some algebra, it should induce coherence constraints on the way beliefs are allocated. But never infer that a probability distribution exists on those spaces on which we extend vacuously the belief function derived from the initial probability constraints.

At the credal level, nothing requires that beliefs be quantified by probability distributions, even though it may sometimes happen. All arguments in favor of representing degrees of belief by probability distributions and based on betting behavior or decisions theory are also satisfied in our model at the pignistic level.

Claiming the existence of a probability distribution on the space on which our beliefs are assessed is already a piece of information in itself. Should you accept it, then the upper and lower probabilities model should be applied.

We strongly reject the following interpretation where belief functions are used instead of upper and lower probabilities. Some authors consider that Dempster-Shafer's model (i.e., belief and plausibility functions) can be used to handle cases of ill-defined probabilities, cases where there exists a probability function on Ω but we only know that its values for each $A \subseteq \Omega$ ore contained between two limits. They claim that all that is known is a belief function bel (or eqivalently a plausibility function pl as $\mathrm{pl}(A) = 1 - \mathrm{bel}(\bar{A})$) such that:

$$\text{for all } A \subseteq \Omega, \quad \mathrm{bel}(A) \leqslant P(A) \leqslant \mathrm{pl}(A)$$

This might be the case; but then they should justify why the lower limits are quantified by a belief function, why the lower limits conform to the inequalities that characterize belief functions, why the Möbius transform of the lower limits are nonnegative. Furthermore, when conditioning is involved, how do they justify the use of the D-conditioning and not that of the G-conditioning? These questions have to be answered before using belief functions instead of lower probabilities functions as lower limits for the intervals and before using Dempster's rule of conditioning (and Dempster's rule of combination). All too often authors simply confuse the two theories. This explains why we felt justified in writing this paper. We hope we have succeeded in clarifying the matter.

Acknowledgments. The author wishes to thank Y.T. Hsia, R. Kennes, H.T. Nguyen, and A. Saffiotti for their help and contribution.

His thanks extend to all his friends who so often disagree with him, thereby forcing him to refine his arguments.

BIBLIOGRAPHY

Cox, R.T. (1946). Probability, frequency and reasonable expectation. *Amer. J. Phys.* 14:1–13.

Dempster, A.P. (1967). Upper and lower probabilities induced by a multi-valued mapping. *Annals of Math. Statistics* 38:325–39.

Dubois, D. and Prade, H. (1986). A set theoretical view of belief functions. *Int. J. Gen. Systems* 12:193–226.

Ekelöf, P.O. (1982). *Rättegång IV*. Fifth edition, Stockholm.

Fagin, R. and Halpern, J. (1990). A new approach to updating beliefs. *Sixth Conf. on Uncertainty in AI.*

Gärdenfors, P. (1983). Probabilistic reasoning and evidentiary value. In Gärdenfors P., Hansson, B., and Sahlin, N.E. (eds.), *Evidentiary value: Philosophical, judicial and psychological aspects of a theory*, pp. 44–57. Lund, Sweden: C.W.K. Gleerups.

Gärdenfors, P., Hansson, B., and Sahlin, N.E. (1983). *Evidentiary value: Philosophical, judicial and psychological aspects of a theory.* Lund, Sweden: C.W.K. Gleerups.

Good, I.J. (1982). Comments on Lindley's paradox, by G. Shafer. *J. Amer. Statist. Assoc.* 77:342–44.

Goodman, I.R., Nguyen, H.T., and Walker, E.A. (1991). *Conditional inference and logic for intelligent systems.* Amsterdam: Elsevier.

Gordon, J. and Shortliffe, E.H., (1984). The Dempster-Shafer theory of evidence. In Buchanan, B.G. and Shortliffe, E.H. (eds.), *Rule-based expert systems: The Mycin experiments of the Stanford Heuristic Programming Project*, pp. 272–92. Reading, MA: Addison-Wesley.

Hacking, I. (1965). *Logic of statistical inference.* Cambridge, UK: Cambridge University Press.

Hestir, K., Nguyen, H.T., and Rogers, G.S. (1991). A random set formalism for evidence reasoning. In Goodman, I.R., Gupta, M.M., Nguyen, H.T., and Rogers, G.S. (eds.), *Conditional logic in expert systems.* Amsterdam: Elsevier.

Hicks, J. (1979). *Causality in economics.* Oxford, UK: Basil Blackwell.

Klawonn, F. and Schwecke, E. (1990). On the axiomatic justification of Dempster's rule of combination. Submitted for publication.

Kyburg, H.E. Jr. (1987). Bayesian and non-Bayesian evidential updating. *Artificial Intelligence* 31:271–94.

Levi, I. (1983). Consonance, dissonance and evidentiary mechanisms. In Gärdenfors, P., Hansson, B., and Sahlin, N.E. (eds.), *Evidentiary value: Philosophical, judicial and psychological aspects of a theory.* pp. 27–43. Lund, Sweden: C.W.K. Gleerups.

Pearl, J. (1988). *Probabilistic reasoning in intelligent systems: Networks of plausible inference.* San Mateo, CA: Morgan Kaufmann.

Pearl, J. (1990). Reasoning with belief functions: An analysis of compatibility. *Intern. J. Approx. Reasoning* 4: 363–90.

Ruspini, E.H. (1986). The logical foundations of evidential reasoning. Technical note 408, SRI International, Menlo Park, CA.
Shafer, G. (1976a). *A mathematical theory of evidence*. Princeton, NJ: Princeton Univ. Press.
Shafer, G. (1976b). A theory of statistical evidence. In Harper and Hooker (eds.), *Foundations of probability theory, statistical inference, and statistical theories of science*. Dordrecht: Reidel.
Shafer, G. (1986). The combination of evidence. *Int. J. Intell. Systems* 1:155–80.
Shafer, G. and Tversky, A. (1985). Languages and designs for probability. *Cognitive Sci.* 9: 309–39.
Smets Ph. (1988). Belief functions. In Smets Ph., Mamdani, A., Dubois D., and Prade, H. (eds.), *Nonstandard logics for automated reasoning*, pp. 253–86. London: Academic Press.
Smets, Ph. (1990a). The combination of evidence in the transferable belief model. *IEEE-Pattern Analysis and Machine Intelligence* 12: 447–58.
Smets, Ph. (1990b). Constructing the pignistic probability function in a context of uncertainty. In Henrion, U., Shacter, R.D., Kanal, L.N., and Lemmer, J.F. (eds.), *Uncertainty in Artificial Intelligence* 5, pp. 29–40. Amsterdam: North-Holland.
Smets, Ph. (1990c). The transferable belief model and other interpretations of Dempster-Shafer's model. *Proc. Sixth Conf. on Uncertainty in AI*, Cambridge, MA.
Smets, Ph. (1991a). Axioms for belief functions. In preparation.
Smets, Ph. (1991b). Belief functions: The disjunctive rule of combination and the generalized Bayesian theorem. Submitted for publication.
Smets, Ph. and Kennes, R. (1990). The transferable belief model. Technical Report: TR-IRIDIA-90-14.
Smets Ph., Clarke, M.R.B., and Froidevaux, Ch. (1991). Uncertainty, conditional and nonmonotonicity: Positions and debate in nonstandard logics. Submitted for publication.
Suppes, P. and Zanotti, M. (1977). On using random relations to generate upper and lower probabilities. *Synthese* 36:427–40.
Walley, P. (1991). *Statistical reasoning with imprecise probabilities*. London: Chapman and Hall.
Williams, P.M. (1982). Discussion in G. Shafer, Belief functions and parametric models. *J. Roy. Statist. Soc.* B44: 322–52.

2 Measures of uncertainty in the Dempster-Shafer theory of evidence

George J. KLIR

Abstract: In the Dempster-Shafer theory, two types of uncertainty coexist: nonspecificity and discord. Well-justifiable measures of these two types of uncertainty are overviewed from both conceptual and mathematical points of view. A measure of total uncertainty, which is defined as the sum of nonspecificity and discord, is also discussed.

Keywords: uncertainty, information, nonspecificity, discord.

1. INTRODUCTION

The concept of *uncertainty* has lately been one of the most researched scientific concepts (Klir and Folger, 1988). In general, uncertainty in a problem situation emerges whenever information pertaining to the situation is deficient in some respect. It may be incomplete, imprecise, contradictory, vague, unreliable, fragmentary, or deficient in some other way. These various information deficiencies result in different types of uncertainty.

Uncertainty is also an important strategic resource. When an appropriate amount of uncertainty is allowed in dealing with a problem, the associated computational complexity may often be substantially reduced, while, at the same time, the credibility of the solution obtained is increased.

From the mid-seventeenth century (when the concept of numerical probability emerged) until the mid-twentieth century, uncertainty was conceived solely in terms of probability theory. This seemingly unique connection between uncertainty and probability theory, which was taken for granted for three centuries, has only lately been challenged. The challenge came from several mathematical theories that are either more general than or totally distinct from probability theory (Klir and Folger, 1988).

One way of generalizing classical probability theory is to allow the use of imprecise probabilities. The formalization of imprecise probabilities can be achieved in different ways (Kyburg, 1987; Walley, 1991), one of which is the Dempster-Shafer theory (Shafer, 1976). In this case, imprecise probabilities are captured by measures of two types, one of which is superadditive and the other subadditive, that replace the classical concept of the additive measure of probability theory. These measures, which are referred to as belief measures and plausibility measures, may be interpreted as lower and upper probabilities, respectively.

An important aspect of every mathematical theory that conceptualizes uncertainty of some kind is the capability to quantify the uncertainty involved. This requires that we can measure, in an adequately justified way, the amount of uncertainty involved in each possible characterization of uncertainty within the theory. Given a specific measurement unit, the value of uncertainty in each situation should be unique.

Assume that we can measure the amount of uncertainty involved in a problem-solving situation conceptualized in a particular mathematical theory. Assume further that the amount of uncertainty can be reduced by obtaining relevant information as a result of some action (finding a relevant new fact, designing a relevant experiment and observing the experimental outcome, receiving a requested message, discovering a relevant historical record). Then, the amount of information obtained by the action may be measured by the reduction of uncertainty that results from the action. In this sense, the amount of uncertainty (pertaining to a problem-solving situation) and the amount of information (obtained by a relevant action) are intimately connected. Furthermore, the amount of information contained in a mathematical description of a problem-solving situation may be measured by the difference between the maximum and actual amounts of uncertainty pertaining to the situation.

The nature of uncertainty (and the associated information) depends on the mathematical theory within which problem-solving situations are formalized. Each formalization of uncertainty in a problem-solving situation is a mathematical model of the situation. When we commit ourselves to a particular mathematical theory, our modeling becomes necessarily limited by the constraints of the theory. Clearly, a more general theory is capable of capturing uncertainties of some problem situations more faithfully than its less-general competitors.

A measure of probabilistic uncertainty was established by Shannon (1948). The issue of how to measure uncertainty in the various alternative theories, including the Dempster-Shafer theory, was investigated mostly in the 1980s (Klir and Folger, 1988). It became clear by these investigations that the Dempster-Shafer theory is capable of formalizing simultaneously two distinct types of uncertainty. This contrasts with probability theory, within which only one of these two types of uncertainty can be captured.

The purpose of this chapter is to overview results regarding the measurement of uncertainty in the Dempster-Shafer theory and in two special theories subsumed under it, probability theory and possibility theory.

2. TERMINOLOGY AND NOTATION

Let X denote in this chapter a universal set under consideration, assumed here to be finite for the sake of simplicity, and let $P(X)$ denote the power set of X. For our purpose, the Dempster-Shafer theory is formulated in terms of a function

$$m: P(X) \to [0,1]$$

such that

$$m(\emptyset) = 0 \text{ and } \sum_{A \subset X} m(A) = 1$$

This function is called a *basic probability assignment*; the value $m(A)$ represents the degree of evidential support that a specific element of X belongs to set A, but not to any particular subset of A. Every set $A \in P(X)$ for which $m(A) \neq 0$ is called a *focal element*. The pair (F,m), where F denotes the set of all focal elements of m, is called a *body of evidence*.

Associated with each basic assignment m is a pair of measures, a *belief measure*, Bel, and a *plausibility measure*, Pl, which are determined for all sets $A \in P(X)$ by the equations

$$\mathrm{Bel}(A) = \sum_{B \subset A} m(B) \tag{1}$$

$$\mathrm{Pl}(A) = \sum_{B \cap A \neq \emptyset} m(B) \tag{2}$$

These measures are connected by the equation

$$\mathrm{Pl}(A) = 1 - \mathrm{Bel}(A), \text{ for all } A \in P(\mathrm{X}), \tag{3}$$

where A denotes the complement of A. Furthermore,

$$\mathrm{Bel}(A) \leqslant \mathrm{Pl}(A), \text{ for all } A \in P(X). \tag{4}$$

A belief measure (or a plausibility measure) becomes a *probability measure*, Pr, when all focal elements are singletons. In this case, $\mathrm{Pr}(A) = \mathrm{Bel}(A) = \mathrm{Pl}(A)$, for all $A \in P(X)$, which follows immediately from (1) and (2), and we obtain the *additivity property* of probability measures. Any probability measure, Pr, on a finite set X can be uniquely determined by a *probability distribution function*

$$p\colon X \to [0,1]$$

via the formula

$$\mathrm{Pr}(A) = \sum_{x \in A} p(x) \tag{5}$$

From the standpoint of the Dempster-Shafer theory, function p is clearly equivalent to function m restricted to singletons.

When all focal elements are nested (ordered by set inclusion), we obtain special plausibility measures, which are called *possibility measures*, and the corresponding special belief measures, which are called *necessity measures*. A theory that deals with nested bodies of evidence in terms of these two measures is usually called a *possibility theory*. This theory is closely connected with the theory of fuzzy sets since α-cuts of every fuzzy set form also a family of nested subsets.

A possibility measure, Pos, is conveniently (and uniquely) determined by a *possibility distribution function*

$$r\colon X \to [0,1]$$

via the formula

$$\mathrm{Pos}(A) = \max_{x \in A} r(x) \tag{6}$$

for all $A \in P(X)$. The corresponding necessity measure, Nec, is then determined for all $A \in P(X)$ by a formula equivalent to (3),

$$\mathrm{Nec}(A) = 1 - \mathrm{Pos}(A) \tag{7}$$

It is useful to introduce the following special notation for possibility theory. Assume that $X = \{x_1, x_2, \ldots, x_n\}$ and let $A_1 \subset A_2 \subset \ldots \subset A_n$, where $A_1 = \{x_1, x_2, \ldots, x_i\}$, $i = 1,2,\ldots,n$, be a complete sequence of nested subsets that contains all focal elements of a possibility measure Pos. That is, if $m(A) \neq 0$, then $A \in \{A_1, A_2, \ldots, A_n\}$. *Let* $m_i = m(A_i)$ and $r_i = r(x_i)$ for all $i = 1,2,\ldots,$n. Then, the n-tuples $m = (m_1, m_2, \ldots, m_n)$ and $r = (r_1, r_2, \ldots, r_n)$ fully characterize the basic assignment and the possibility distribution, respectively, by which the possibility measure Pos is defined. The nested structure implies that $r_i \geqslant r_{i+1}$ for all $i = 1,2,\ldots,n$-1. Furthermore,

$$r_i = \sum_{k=i}^{n} m_k \tag{8}$$

$$m_i = r_i - r_{i+1} \tag{9}$$

for all $i = 1,2,\ldots,n$, where $r_{n+1} = 0$ by convention (Klir and Folger, 1988).

3. MEASURE OF NONSPECIFICITY

It follows from the nature of the Dempster-Shafer theory that it subsumes two distinct types of uncertainty. One of them is well characterized by the name *nonspecificity*. It is now well established that this type of uncertainty is properly measured by a function N defined by the formula

$$N(m) = \sum_{A \in F} m(A) \log_2 |A| \tag{10}$$

where $|A|$ denotes the cardinality of the focal element A and F signifies the set of all focal elements. This function, which was proven unique under appropriate requirements (Klir and Mariano, 1987; Ramer, 1987), measures nonspecificity of a body of evidence in units that are called *bits*: one bit of uncertainty expresses the total ignorance regarding the truth or falsity of one proposition. The range of the function is

$$0 \leqslant N(m) \leqslant \log_2|X|$$

$N(m) = 0$ when $m(\{x\}) = 1$ for some $x \in X$ (full certainty); $N(m) = \log_2|X|$ when $m(X) = 1$ (total ignorance).

Function N is connected with a simple measure of information (and uncertainty) that was proposed within the classical set theory by Hartley (1928). He showed that, given a finite set of *possible* alternatives, A, the amount of information (in bits), $I(A)$, needed to characterize one of the alternatives is given by the simple formula

$$I(A) = \log_2|A|$$

The uniqueness of this function was also proven, more rigorously, by Renyi (1970). Function N can clearly be viewed as a weighted average of the Hartley information for all focal elements.

When m characterizes a probability measure, (10) becomes

$$N(m) = \sum_{x \in X} m(\{x\}) \log_2 1$$

and, hence, $N(m) = 0$. That is, probability theory is devoid of nonspecificity. This raises an interesting question: what kind of uncertainty is captured by probability theory and measured by the Shannon entropy? I return to this question in the next section.

When m characterizes a possibility and necessity measures and we employ the notation introduced in Section 2, (10) can be rewritten as

$$N(m) = \sum_{i=l}^{n} m_i \log_2|A_i|$$

Since $|A_i| = i$ according to our notation, we obtain

$$N(m) = \sum_{i=l}^{n} m_i \log_2 i \tag{11}$$

Using (9) and recognizing that $\log_2 1 = 0$, we can also express possibilistic nonspecificity in terms of the possibility distribution r associated with m:

$$N(r) = \sum_{i=2}^{n} r_i \log_2 \frac{i}{i-1} \tag{12}$$

Although function N and the Shannon entropy measure totally different types of uncertainty, all relations among the various types of the Shannon entropy (simple, joint, conditional) have their exact counterparts expressed by function N. For example, let $N(X)$ (or

$N(Y)$), $N(X,Y)$, and $N(X|Y)$ (or $N(Y|X)$) denote the simple, joint, and conditional nonspecificities, respectively. Then (Klir and Folger, 1988):

$$N(X|Y) = N(X,Y) - N(Y)$$

$$N(Y|X) = N(X,Y) - N(X)$$

$$N(X,Y) \geqslant N(X) + N(Y)$$

$$N(X|Y) \leqslant N(X)$$

$$N(Y|X) \leqslant N(Y)$$

$$N(X) - N(Y) = N(X|Y) - N(Y|X)$$

$$N(Y) - \mathrm{N}(X) = N(Y|X) - N(X|Y)$$

We can also define information transmission for nonspecificity, $T_N(X,Y)$, in the same way in which it is defined for the Shannon entropy:

$$T_N(X,Y) = N(X) + N(Y) - N(X,Y)$$

Then, by simple algebraic manipulation, we also have

$$T_N(X,Y) = N(X) - N(X|Y)$$

$$T_N(X,Y) = N(Y) - N(Y|X)$$

4. MEASURE OF DISCORD

The second type of uncertainty captured by the Dempster-Shafer theory is clearly connected with the uncertainty type inherent in probability theory and measured by the Shanon entropy. The question of what the generalized counterpart of the Shannon entropy in the Dempster-Shafer theory should measure has been investigated since the early 1980s.

The Shannon entropy, H, which is applicable only to probability measures, assumes in the Dempster-Shafer theory the form

$$H(m) = \sum_{x \in X} m(\{x\}) \log_2 m(\{x\})$$

Since values $m(\{x\})$ are required to add to 1 for all $x \in X$, this formula can be rewritten as

$$H(m) = -\sum_{X \in X} m(\{x\}) \log_2[1 - \sum_{y \neq x} m(\{y\})] \tag{13}$$

Since $m(A) = 0$ for all sets that are not singletons, the term

$$\text{Con}(\{x\}) = \sum_{y \neq x} m(\{y\}) \tag{14}$$

in (13) represents the total evidential claim pertaining to focal elements that are different from the focal element $\{x\}$. That is, Con ($\{x\}$) expresses the sum of all evidential claims that fully conflict with the one focusing on $\{x\}$. Clearly, Con $(\{x\}) \in [0,1]$ for each $x \in X$. The function

$$-\log_2[1 - \text{Con}(\{x\})]$$

which is employed in (13), is monotonic increasing with Con ($\{x\}$) and extends its range from $[0,1]$ to $[0,\infty]$. The choice of the logarithmic function is a result of the axiomatic requirement that the joint uncertainty of several independent random variables be equal to the sum of their individual uncertainties (Aczel and Daroczy, 1975; Klir and Folger, 1988; Renyi, 1970).

It follows from these facts and from the form of (13) that the Shannon entropy is the mean (expected) value of the conflict among evidential claims within a given probabilistic body of evidence. Since $H(m) = 1$ for two focal elements with probabilities 0.5, it is clear that the Shannon entropy measures uncertainty in bits. Its range is $[0, \log_2|X|]$.

What is the generalized counterpart of the Shannon entropy in the Dempster-Shafer theory? Two candidates were proposed in the early 1980s:

$$E(m) = -\sum_{A \in F} \text{m(A)} \log_2 \text{Pl}(A) \tag{15}$$

$$C(m) = -\sum_{A \in F} m(A) \log_2 \text{Bel}(A) \tag{16}$$

Function E defined by (15), which is usually called a *measure of dissonance* (or *entropylike measure*) was proposed by Yager (1983). Function C given by (16), which is usually called a *measure of confusion*, was proposed by Höhle (1982). It is obvious that either of the functions collapses into the Shannon entropy when m defines a probability measure.

What do functions E and C acutally measure? From (2) and the general property of basic assignments (satisfied for every $A \in P(X)$),

$$\sum_{A \cap B = \emptyset} m(B) + \sum_{A \cap B \neq \emptyset} m(B) = 1$$

we obtain

$$E(m) = \sum_{A \in F} m(A) \log_2 [1 - \sum_{A \cap B = \emptyset} m(B)] \tag{17}$$

The term

$$K(A) = \sum_{A \cap B = \emptyset} m(B)$$

in (17) represents the total evidential claim pertaining to focal elements that are disjoint with the set A. That is, $K(A)$ expresses the sum of all evidential claims that fully conflict with the one focusing on the set A. Clearly, $K(A) \in [0,1]$. The function

$$-\log_2[1 - K(A)]$$

which is employed in (17), is monotonic increasing with $K(A)$ and extends its range from $[0,1]$ to $[0,\infty]$. The choice of the logarithmic function is motivated in the same way as in the classical case of the Shannon entropy.

It follows from these facts and the form of (17) that $E(m)$ is the mean (expected) value of the conflict among evidential claims within a given body of evidence (F,m); it measures the conflict in bits and its range is $[0, \log_2 |X|]$.

Function E is not fully satisfactory since we feel intuitively that $m(B)$ conflicts with $m(A)$ whenever $B \not\subset A$, not only when $B \cap A = \emptyset$. This broader view of conflict is expressed by the measure of confusion C given by (16). Let us demonstrate this fact.

From (1) and the general property of basic assignment (satisfied for every $A \in P(X)$),

$$\sum_{B \subset A} m(B) + \sum_{B \not\subset A} m(B) = 1$$

we get

$$C(m) = -\sum_{A \in F} m(A) \log_2 [1 - \sum_{B \not\subset A} m(B)] \tag{18}$$

The term

$$L(A) = \sum_{B \not\subset A} m(B)$$

in (18) expresses the sum of all evidential claims that conflict with the one focusing on the set A according to the broader view of conflict: $m(B)$ conflicts with $m(A)$ whenever $B \not\subset A$. The reasons for using the function

$$-\log_2[1 - L(A)]$$

instead of $L(A)$ in (18) are the same as already explained in the context of function E. The conclusion is that $C(m)$ is the mean (expected) value of the conflict, viewed in the broader sense, among evidential claims within a given body of evidence (F,m).

Function C is also not fully satisfactory as a measure of conflicting evidential claims within a body of evidence, but for a different reason than function E. Although it employs the broader, and more satisfactory, view of conflict, it does not properly scale each particular conflict of $m(B)$ with respect o $m(A)$ according to the degree of violation of the subsethood relation $B \subset A$. It is clear that the more this subsethood relation is violated the greater the conflict. As a result, function C has also some undersirable mathematical properties. For example, its maximum is greater than $\log_2|X|$.

To overcome the deficiencies of functions E and C as adequate measures of conflict in the Dempster-Shafer theory, it was recently proposed to replace them with the following function (Klir and Ramer, 1990):

$$D(m) = -\sum_{A \in F} m(A) \log_2 [1 - \sum_{B \in F} m(B) \frac{|B-A|}{|B|}] \tag{19}$$

Observe that the term $\text{Con}(A) = \sum_{B \in F} m(B) \frac{|B-A|}{|B|}$ in (19) expresses the sum of individual conflicts of evidential claims with respect to a particular set A, each of which is properly scaled by the degree to which the subsethood $B \subset A$ is violated. This conforms exactly to the intuitive idea of conflict that emerged from the critical reexamination of functions E and C. Let function Con, whose application to probability measures is given by (14), be called a *conflict*. Clearly, $\text{Con}(A) \in [0,1]$ and, furthermore,

$$K(A) \leqslant \text{Con}(A) \leqslant L(A) \tag{20}$$

The reason for using the function $-\log_2[1 - \text{Con}(A)]$ instead of Con in (19) is exactly the same as previously explained in the context of function E. This monotonic transformation extends the range of $\text{Con}(A)$ from $[0,1]$ to $[0,\infty]$.

Function D, which is called a *measure of discord*, is clearly a measure of the mean conflict (expressed by the logarithmic transformation of function Con) among evidential claims within each given body of evidence. It follows immediately from (20) that

$$E(m) \leqslant D(m) \leqslant C(m) \tag{21}$$

Observe that $|B-A| = |B| - |A \cap B|$ and, consequently, (19) can be rewritten as

$$D(m) = -\sum_{A \in F} m(A) \log_2 \sum_{B \in F} m(B) \frac{|A \cap B|}{|B|} \tag{22}$$

It is obvious that

$$\mathrm{Bel}(A) \leqslant \sum_{B \in F} m(B) \frac{|A \cap B|}{|B|} \leqslant \mathrm{Pl}(A) \tag{23}$$

Function D is applicable equally well to the fuzzified Dempster-Shafer theory provided that the cardinality $|A|$ of a fuzzy set A is defined by the formula

$$|A| = \sum_{x \in X} \mu_A(x)$$

where μ_A denotes the membership grade function of set A, and the set intersection is defined by the minimum operator.

It is easy to see that function D measures the conflict of evidential claims within each body of evidence in bits: $D(m) = 1$ is equivalent to a full conflict between the evidential claims regarding the truth or falsity of a single proposition. It has also been proven (Ramer and Klir, 1992) that the function is additive in the same sense as functions E and C (Dubois and Prade, 1987) and that its range is $[0, \log_2|X|]$. The minimum is obtained for all bodies of evidence with a single focal element; its maximum is obtained only when m defines the uniform probability distribution on X.

When we specialize to possibility theory and, hence, deal only with nested bodies of evidence, the measure of discord, D, is still applicable, while the measure of dissonance, E, is not. That is, nested bodies are consonant (in the sense of function E), but they are not, in general, totally conflict-free (in the sense of the more general function D). They are conflict-free only if they contain one focal element.

Hence, while probability theory is completely free of nonspecificity, possibility theory involves both nonspecificity and discord. It is known, however, that possibilistic bodies of evidence are almost discord-free (Geer and Klir, 1991). In particular, the maximum value of possibilistic discord is monotonic increasing with $n = |X|$ and converges to a constant, estimated as 0.892 for $n \to \infty$. This estimate, which is based on extrapolating numerical results calculated for $n \leqslant 21$, is safeguarded by an analytical result, according to which the maximum value of possibilistic discord cannot exceed the value $1/\log_e 2 \sim 1.443$ for any n. Hence, for large bodies of evidence, at least, discord is likely to be negligible when compared with nonspecificity. Neglecting discord, when justifiable, may substantially reduce computational complexity in dealing with large possibilistic bodies of evidence.

Using the notation introduced in Section 2, which is based upon the notion of a complete sequence of nested subsets that contains all focal elements, it is easy to derive the following possibilistic form of the measure of discord:

$$D(m) = -\sum_{i=1}^{n-1} m_i \log_2\left(\sum_{j=1}^{i} m_j + \sum_{j=i+1}^{n} m_j \frac{i}{j}\right) \tag{24}$$

Furthermore, using (9), we obtain

$$D(m) = -\sum_{i=1}^{n-1} (r_i - r_{i+1}) \log_2 [1 - i \sum_{j=i+1}^{n} \frac{r_j}{(j-1)j}] \tag{25}$$

5. MEASURE OF TOTAL UNCERTAINTY

In general, the two types of uncertainty, nonspecificity and discord, may coexist in a given body of evidence. It is thus reasonable to measure the total uncertainty, $T(m)$, in a given body of evidence (m,F) by adding the values of its nonspecificity and discord:

$$T(m) = N(m) + D(m) = \sum_{A \in F} m(A) \frac{|A|}{\sum_{B \in F} m(B) \frac{|A \cap B|}{|B|}} \tag{26}$$

Surprisingly, this function has also the same range, $[0, \log_2|X|]$, as each of its two components, N and D (Ramer, 1991). The minimum, $T(m) = 0$, is obtained whenever $m(\{x\}) = 1$ for some particular $x \in X$. The maximum, $T(m) = \log_2|X|$, is not unique. It is obtained not only for $m(X) = 1$ (which is the unique maximum of N) and for the uniform probability distribution on X (which is the unique maximum of D), but also for other bodies of evidence that seem to possess certain symmetries. For example, the maximum is obtained for the body of evidence defined on $X = \{1,2,3,4\}$ whose focal elements are $\{1,2\}$, $\{2,3\}$, $\{3,4\}$, $\{4,1\}$ and the values of the basic assignments are uniform (0.25 for each focal element).

Since both functions N and D are additive (Klir and Folger, 1988; Ramer and Klir, 1992), function T is also additive.

Function T is promising as a single measure of uncertainty in the Dempster-Shafer theory, but more work is needed to make a definite conclusion: we still need, for example, to investigate the various relations among the basic, joint, and conditional forms of T and, hopefully, to prove the uniqueness of T under some well-justifiable axiomatic requirements.

6. CONCLUSIONS

When a well-justified measure of probabilistic uncertainty and information was established, the Shannon entropy (Shannon, 1948), it was a significant event. It resulted in a new mathematical area, the classical information theory, which has been of major influence to almost all areas of science and engineering, and even to some areas of humanities and the arts (see, e.g., Attneave, 1959; Bell, 1953; Brillouin, 956; Gatlin, 1972; Guiasu, 1977; Klir, 1985; Moles, 1966; Theil, 1967; Webber, 1979). Two principles based upon the Shannon entropy, the principles of minimum and maximum entropy, have increasingly been recognized as fundamental principles of scientific methodology (Christensen, 1985, 1986; Jaynes, 1979; Kapur, 1983). The utility and success of these principles in statistical modeling, image processing, pattern recognition, and other areas is quite impressive.

Notwithstanding the success of classical information theory, it has some shortcomings. These are primarily the result of the probabilistic intolerance to nonspecificity or imprecision. It is reasonable to expect that a generalized and more powerful information theory will emerge as an outgrowth of the Dempster-Shafer theory. Although the development of such a theory will undoubtedly be a major undertaking, its feasibility is no longer questionable due to the well-justified measures of relevant types of uncertainty overviewed in this paper.

BIBLIOGRAPHY

Aczel, J., and Daroczy, Z. (1975). *On measures of information and their characterizations*. New York: Academic Press.

Attneave, F. (1959). *Applications of information theory to psychology*. New York: Henry Holt.

Bell, D.A. (1953). *Information theory and its engineering applications*. New York: Pitman.

Brillouin, L. (1956). *Science and information theory*. New York: Academic Press.

Christensen, R. (1985). Entropy minimax multivariate statistical modeling – I. Theory. *Intern. J. of General Systems* 11 (3): 231–77.

Christensen, R. (1986). Entropy minimax multivariate statistical modelling – II. Applications. *Intern. J. of General Systems* 12 (3): 227–305.

Dubois, D. and Prade, H. (1987). Properties of measures of information in evidence and possibility theories. *Fuzzy Sets and Systems* 24 (2): 161–82.

Gatlin, L.L. (1972). *Information theory and the living system*. New York: Columbia University Press.

Geer, J.F. and Klir, G.J. (1991). Discord in possibility theory. *Intern. J. of General Systems* 19 (2).

Guiasu, S. (1977). *Information theory with applications*. New York: McGraw-Hill.

Hartley, R.V.L. (1928). Transmission of information. *Bell System Technical Journal* 7: 535–63.

Höhle, U. (1982). Entropy with respect to plausibility measures. *Proc. Twelveth IEEE Symp. on Multiple-Valued Logic*, Paris, pp. 167–69.

Jaynes, E.T. (1979). Where do we stand on maximum entropy? In R.L. Levine and M. Tribus (eds.), *The maximum entropy formalism*, pp. 15–118. Cambridge, MA: MIT Press.

Kapur, J.N. (1983). Twenty-five years of maximum entropy principle. *J. Math. Phys. Sciences* 17 (2): 103–56.

Klir, G.J. (1985). *Architecture of systems problem solving*. New York: Plenum Press.

Klir, G.J. and Folger, T.A. (1988). *Fuzzy sets, uncertainty, and information*. Englewood Cliffs, NJ: Prentice-Hall.

Klir, G.J. and Mariano, M. (1987). On the uniqueness of possibilistic measure of uncertainty and information. *Fuzzy Sets and Systems* 24 (2): 197–219.

Klir, G.J. and Ramer, A. (1990). Uncertainty in the Dempster-shafer theory: A critical re-examination. *Intern. J. of General Systems* 18 (2): 155–66.

Kyburg, H.E. (1987). Bayesian and non-Bayesian evidential updating. *Artificial Intelligence* 31: 271–93.

Moles, A. (1966). *Information theory and esthetic perception*. Urbana, IL: University of Illinois Press.

Ramer, A. (1987). Uniqueness of information measure in the theory of evidence. *Fuzzy Sets and Systems* 24 (2): 183–96.

Ramer, A. (1991). Inequalities and nonprobabilistic information. *Proc. IFSA'91 Congress*, Brussels.

Ramer, A. and Klir, G.J. (1992). Measures of conflict and discord. *Information Sciences*. In press.

Renyi, A. (1970). *Probability theory*. Amsterdam: North-Holland. (Chapter 9, Introduction to Information Theory, pp. 540–616.)

Shafer, G. (1976). *A mathematical theory of evidence*. Princeton, NJ: Princeton University Press.

Shannon, C.E. (1948). The mathematical theory of communication. *Bell System Technical Journal* 27: 379–423, 623–56.

Theil, H. (1967). *Economics and information theory*. Amsterdam: North-Holland; and Chicago: Rand McNally.

Walley, P. (1991). *Statistical reasonning with imprecise probabilities*. London: Chapman and Hall.

Webber, M.J. (1979). *Information theory and urban spatial structure*. London: Croom Helm.

Yager, R. (1983). Entropy and specificity in a mathematical theory of evidence. *Intern. J. of General Systems* 9 (4): 249–60.

3 Representation, independence, and combination of evidence in the Dempster-Shafer theory

Lianwen ZHANG

Abstract: The Dempster-Shafer theory is an extension of the Bayesian theory. Technically, it allows us to propagate probabilities through logical links in addition to conditional links and it combines items of evidence by using Dempster's rule, a generalization of Bayes' rule. Practically, it allows us to derive beliefs for a question of interest from probabilities for a related question. The paper defends the representation adequacy of the belief function formalism, proposes a more concrete criterion for two items of evidence to be independent, and modifies Dempster's rule of combination to avoid counterintuitive examples.

Keywords: belief functions, Dempster's rule, representation adequacy, independence of evidence, moderate conditioning.

1. INTRODUCTION

Let us begin by giving the setup. There is a frame, that is, a finite set of possibilities, of which exactly one is true. One may know something and hence have beliefs about the truth. One may learn new things about the truth and consequently update his or her beliefs.

What formalism is appropriate for representing beliefs about the truth in a given frame? Beliefs lead to decisions. The Bayesian decision theory lays its foundation by figuring out a few principles that a rational decision maker should not violate, in the sense that any violation, once exposed, would be held to be ridiculous and the relevant decisions will be changed. Those principles are taken as axioms. There are several systems of axioms to choose from. All the axiom systems have the logical consequence that there exists a probability distribution and a utility function over the frame, and that the decision should be made by maximizing the subjective expected utility (see, for example, Savage [1954]; Lindley [1972]). The probability is presumably a representation of the decision maker's beliefs.

Consider the truth x in the frame X. Technically, the Bayesian theory begins with a prior probability P_0 over X, which represents one's prior beliefs about the truth. If it is later observed that the truth lies in a subset A of X, then our beliefs will be updated to the conditional probability $P_0(.|A)$. The degree of belief on a subset B, for instance, will change from $P_0(B)$ to $P_0(B|A)$, which is defined by

$$P_0(B|A) = \frac{P_0(B \cap A)}{P_0(A)} \tag{1}$$

Observations are usually made in frames different from but related to the frame of interest. To absorb the observation y_0 made in frame Y, the conditional probabilities $P_0(y_0|x)$ for all $x \in X$ have to be assessed. Bayes' rule, which follows from (1), is more commonly used for belief updating

$$P_0(x|y_0) = kP_0(x)\, P_0(y_0|x) \tag{2}$$

where k is the renormalization constant independent of x. As a function of x, $P_0(y_0|x)$ is called the likelihood of x given y_0. In words, Bayes' rule says that posterior is in direct proposition to the product of prior and likelihood.

In spite of the a priori arguments that establish, among other things, the existence of subjective probability, judgments have to be made in the practice of the Bayesian theory. We have to decide on a probability as best representing a group of evidence. This is done, according to the philosophy of constructive probability, by fitting evidence against a scale of canonical examples (Shafer, 1981).

The canonical examples are games where the outcomes are generated with known chances (Shafer, 1981). When one makes the judgment that $P(A) = p$, he is saying that his evidence provides support for A comparable to what would be provided by the knowledge that the truth is generated by a chance setup that produces a result in A exactly p of the time.

What if we are unable to directly compare our prior knowledge to canonical examples of games? What if we are unable to assess the conditional probabilities needed in (2)? The Dempster-Shafer theory is able to provide an answer for the first question when our prior knowledge can be represented by a probability over a frame that is related to the frame of interest through a compatibility relation. It also enables us to relax the demands by (2) for conditional probabilities to logical constraints (see section 2 for an example).

Issues about the Dempster-Shafer theory that have received a lot of discussion in recent years include: (1) What are belief functions? Are belief functions lower probabilities? (2) Is the belief function formalism adequate for representing knowledge? (3) Is Dempster's rule of combination valid? (4) What kind of independence is required for two items of evidence to be independent so that they can be combined by using Dempster's rule? (5) Is the belief function formalism computationally feasible?

The confusion of belief functions with lower probabilities has been disavowed by Shafer in several papers (See Shafer, 1981; 1987; 1990) and is becoming more and more widely known (Pearl, 1989; 1990 and Fagin and Halpern, 1990b). The question mark on the computational feasibility has been removed by works of, among others, Shafer and Shenoy (1988), Kong (1986), and Almond (1988). The conclusion is: if a problem is computationally feasible for a Bayesian solution, then it is also computationally feasible for a belief function solution.

The other three issues, however, are still alive for debate. Pearl (1989; 1990) argues against any belief function representation of individual conditional probabilities that do not constitute a complete probability model. Diaconis and Zabell (1982), Zadeh (1986), Pearl (1989), and Voorbaark (1991), among others, expressed their doubt on the validity of Dempster's rule of combination by analyzing examples, while other authors, like Dubois and Prade (1986b) and Smets (1988a), wrote in favor of the rule. The independence requirement for the use of Dempster's rule was also a topic of discussion in Walley (1987), Voorbaark (1991), Shafer (1981; 1990).

This paper will defend the representation adequacy of the belief function formalism, propose a concrete criterion for two items of evidence to be independent, and modify Dempster's rule to avoid drawing counterintuitive conclusions in the Three Prisoner Puzzle (Diaconis and Zabell, 1982).

The paper begins with a concise introduction to the Dempster-Shafer theory. An example illustrating and supporting the use of belief functions will be analyzed in terms of qualitative Bayesian networks (Pearl, 1988) and the idea of propagating probabilities through logical links will be emphasized.

2. THE DEMPSTER-SHAFER THEORY

Consider the following example. Betty tells me that a tree limb fell on my car. Based on experiences, my subjective probability for Betty being reliable is 0.8. The question is: How much should I believe that a *Tree* limb indeed fell *On my Car* (*TOC*)?

Either there is a tree limb on my car (*TOC*) or there is not ($\neg$ *TOC*). Let us denote the truth by x. Given that Betty is to testify, one can regard what she may testify (*BT*) as a causal result of the truth x and her being reliable *BR*. If Betty is being reliable and the truth is *TOC*, then she would testify so; if Betty is being reliable and the truth is not in $\neg$ *TOC*, then she would testify so as well; if Betty is not being reliable, then her testimony conveys no information about the truth. We therefore have a causal model of three variables x, *BR*, and *BT* as shown in Figure 3.1a.[1]

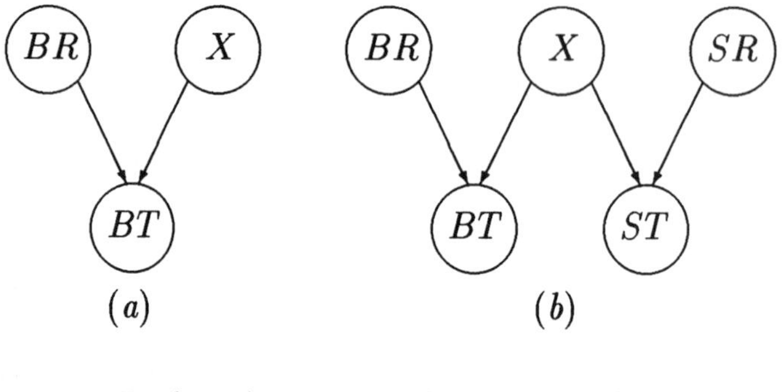

Figure 3.1: Testimonies as causal results of the truth and the reliabilities.

In the Bayesian language, the question becomes: What is the conditional probability $P(x = TOC \mid BT = TOC)$? It cannot be

[1] See Horsch and Poole (1990) for an interesting discussion on how to construct "causal" models for probabilistic reasoning.

answered because: (1) we do not have a prior on x, and (2) we do not have the conditional probability of BT given x and $\neg BR$ (Betty's not being reliable).[2] On the other hand, there do exist some logical constraints that relate probabilities on BR to x through the item of evidence $\{BT = TOC\}$. The Dempster-Shafer theory provides a way of making use of the probabilities on BR to answer the question about x.

The formal exposition of the Dempster-Shafer theory involves two frames, S and T, with a compatibility relation C in between. The compatibility relation is a subset of the Cartesian product $S \times T$, with the semantics that $(s, t) \in C$ if and only if s and t are compatible. We are interested in the truth in T, but a probability P is only available about the truth in S. This probability certainly tells us something about the truth in T through C. We summarize this information by a *belief function Bel* over T defined by

$$Bel(A) = P\{s \mid s \in S \text{ such that for all } t \text{ if } (s,t) \in C, \text{ then } t \in A\} \quad (3)$$

for any subset A of T. In the Bayesian theory, probabilities are used to capture intuitive degrees of belief. In the Dempster-Shafer theory, belief functions are used instead. Section 5.1 will discuss the characteristics of belief function (BF) – degrees of belief.

Continue our TOC example. Because of Betty's testimony, Betty's being reliable (BR) is compatible with TOC but not with $\neg TOC$, while Betty's not being reliable ($\neg BR$) is compatible with both TOC and $\neg TOC$. According to (3), my BF degree on TOC is 0.8, while my BF degree on $\neg TOC$ is zero. The zero does not mean that I am sure there is no limb on my car, as a zero probability would; it merely means that Betty's testimony gives me no reason to believe in $\neg TOC$.

2.1. Propagating probabilities through logical links

The Dempster-Shafer theory is an extension of the Bayesian theory not only because it solves new problems, but also because it introduces new techniques. One important technique it introduces, which has not received due emphasis in the belief function literature, is that of propagating probabilities through logical links. The reader

---

[2] Lower probabilities may be useful here. See Shafer (1981; 1990), Kyburg (1987), Fagin and Halpern (1990b) and many papers for the relationship between lower probabilities and belief functions. The author is not aware of any work on dealing with the forbidding complexity of the lower probability approach.

has already seen this in (3). For the sake of comparison, let us first see how the Bayesian theory propagates information through conditional links.

Suppose s and t are two variables and suppose we know the conditional probability $P(t|s)$. In the Bayesian theory:

1. A probability $P(s)$ on s can be propagated to t to get the probability $P(t) = \Sigma_s P(s) P(t|s)$.
2. A likelihood $l(t)$ on t can be propagated to s to get the likelihood $l(s) = \Sigma_t l(t) P(t|s)$.

What if the only information available between s and t is a logical constraint, a compatibility relation C? The Bayesian theory cannot do any nontrivial inference between s and t at all.[3] One important merit of the Dempster-Shafer theory is that it enables us to propagate probabilities through logical links. Actually, if evidence about s is represented by a probability $P(s)$, then its impacts on t are represented by the belief function induced from P by using (3), which can then be combined with information about t derived from other independent sources. The same thing can be done for s if there is a probability on t. Propagating probabilities through logical links is one of the important ideas underlying the Gister system (Lowrance, 1988), a system that supports the construction, modification, and analysis of evidential arguments.

2.2. Dempster's rule of combination

We are concerned with the truth t in frame T. We have a probability P_1 over frame S_1, which is related to T through compatibility relation C_1, giving rise to a belief function Bel_1; and we have a probability P_2 over frame S_2, which is related to T through relation C_2, giving rise to a belief function Bel_2. How should the two belief functions be combined?

According to *Dempster's rule of combination*, we proceed as follows. First form the Cartesian product $S_1 \times S_2$ of frames, the direct product $P_1 \times P_2$ of probabilities, and the join $C_1 \bowtie C_2$ of compatibility relations.[4] Some elements in $S_1 \times S_2$ may become impossibilities because of $C_1 \bowtie C_2$. Eliminate those impossibilities from

[3] One may cite lower probabilities here. See footnote 2.

[4] The join $C_1 \bowtie C_2$ is defined as follows. A triple $(s_1, s_2, t) \in C_1 \bowtie C_2$ if and only if $(s_1, t) \in C_1$ and $(s_2, t) \in C_2$. See Maier (1983).

$S_1 \times S_2$ to get S, condition $P_1 \times P_2$ on S to get P, and restrict $C_1 \bowtie C_2$ accordingly to get C. The result is the new frame S related to T by the compatibility relation C and the probability P over S. A belief function can thus be defined over T by using (3). This belief function, usually denoted by $Bel_1 \oplus Bel_2$, is called the *orthogonal sum* of Bel_1 and Bel_2 (Shafer, 1976).

To continue the *TOC* example, suppose that Sally comes along and testifies that nothing fell on my car. The frame of interest is $\{TOC, \neg TOC\}$. The frames where probabilities are available are $\{BR, \neg BR\}$ and $\{SR, \neg SR\}$. The Cartesian product of those two frames is $\{(BR, SR), (BR, \neg SR), (\neg BR, SR), (\neg BR, \neg SR)\}$. The combination (BR, SR) is an impossibility and has to be eliminated. If my subjective probability of Sally being reliable is also 0.8, then my combined BF degree of belief on *TOC* would be $\dfrac{0.8 \times 0.2}{0.8 \times 0.2 + 0.8 \times 0.2 + 0.2 \times 0.2} = 0.44$. So, Sally's contradicting testimony has weakend my belief on *TOC*.

There are some independence requirements on the items of evidence for the use of Dempster's rule. We will discuss those requirements in section 4. Counterintuitive examples can still be construed against Dempster's rule even when those independence requirements are satisfied. In section 5, we will modify Dempster's rule to avoid those counterintuitive examples.

2.3. Talking about belief functions with one frame

The standard way to introduce belief functions with only one frame T is to begin with a *basic probability assignment* (*bpa*) m, which is a probability over the power set $\mathbf{P}(T)$ of T. A belief function *Bel* can be defined by:

$$Bel(A) = \Sigma\{m(B) | B \subseteq A\} \tag{4}$$

A subset A is called a *focal element* if $m(A) > 0$.

To relate to the two frame setup, let us define a subset C_s of T for each $s \in S$ by $C_s = \{t | (s, t) \in C\}$, then a bpa m over T can be defined by:

$$m(B) = \Sigma\{P(C_s) | s \in S \text{ such that } C_s = B\} \tag{5}$$

The belief function induced by this bpa is exactly the same as the one directly given by (3).

Dempster's rule for combining two belief functions Bel_1 and Bel_2 can be defined by a relatively simple rule in terms of the corresponding bpa's m_1 and m_2. Let m be the bpa of $Bel_1 \oplus Bel_2$. Then we have

$$m(B) = \frac{\Sigma\{m_1(B_1)m_2(B_2) | B_1 \cap B_2 = B\}}{\Sigma\{m_1(B_1)m_2(B_2) | B_1 \cap B_2 \neq 0\}} \tag{6}$$

To condition a belief function on a subset A is to combine it with a belief function that establishes A with certainty, that is, with a belief function whose bpa m satisfies $m(A) = 1$ and $m(B) = 0$ for any other subset B.

3. REPRESENTING RELATIONAL INFORMATION

This section is concerned with the problem of representing relational knowledge by belief functions. The discussions will be carried out in terms of two related variables x and y. We will first point out the inappropriateness of the "conditional"[5] and then discuss what can be represented in the "joint setup."

Recall that belief functions, as well as probabilities, are to represent beliefs about the truth in a given frame. Because the variables x and y are related, assuming x to be a specific value will induce beliefs about y, the truth in the frame Y of y. Let us represent those beliefs by a belief function. When this belief function happens to be a probability, it is nothing but the conditional probability of y given x. Hence one may call this belief function the "conditional belief function" of y given x. Letting x run through all the possible values, we get a collection of "conditional belief functions." One can, of course, view this collection of "conditional belief functions" as a representation of the relationship between x and y. Unlike conditional probabilities, however, those "conditional belief functions" cannot, in Dempster-Shafer theory, be combined with others to arrive at a "joint belief function."

There have been several attempts to convert conditionals into joint belief functions. Smets (1978) proposed and embedding of conditional probabilities in belief functions, which was afterwards advocated by Shafer (1982). The embedding is based on the idea of translating a conditional probability statement, say $P(y = y_0 | x = x_0) = 0.5$, into

[5] Terms in quotes are to be understood in comparison to the corresponding terms in probability theory.

the material implication statement $P(\neg\{y = y_0\} \cup \{x = x_0\}) = 0.5$. This translation produces counterintuitive examples in inference chaining and contraposing, in reasoning by case and in dealing with specificity (Pearl, 1990). Also, the marginal of the embedding on y is not vacuous as it should be. Actually, the statement $P(A|B) = p$ cannot be converted into an equivalent statement of the form $P(f(A,B)) = q$, where f is some Boolean function of A and B (Goodman, 1987). Black and Laskey (1990) gave two other translations called consonant extension and dissonant extension, but neither seems well justified.

The "conditional setup" is thus not suitable, in the Dempster-Shafer theory, for representing information about the relationship between x and y. This leaves us with only one possible setup: the joint setup – the joint truth (x, y) in the joint frame $X \times Y$, where X and Y are frames of x and y respectively. Let us see a few examples of relational information that can be represented in this setup by belief functions.

A logical constraint C between X and Y is simply a subset of $X \times Y$, which spells out which combinations of the values of the two variables are logically possible and which are not. This can simply be represented by the belief function over $X \times Y$, which establishes C with certainty (section 2.3).

A belief function can be mathematically viewed as a random set (Nguyen, 1978). Randomized logical constraints can hence be naturally represented as belief functions.

Statistical models where variables are constrained by an equation except for an independent random error constitute a special kind of randomized logical constraints. Let us see an example.

The Kalman filter model (Dempster, 1990) is concerned with a sequence of states T_t progressing through times $t = 0, 1, 2, \ldots\ldots, n$, where T_t is typically a vector of unknowns describing the system at time t. The random evolution of the states is described by a system of state equations

$$T_{t+1} = G_{t+1}T_t + V_t \tag{7}$$

where the G_{t+1} are known matrices describing systematic linear behavior of the system, and the V_t are independent random disturbances with known distributions.

In the Kalman filter model, we have more than conditional probabilities. If there were only conditional probabilities, $P(T_{t+1}|T_t = value1)$ should tell us nothing about $P(T_{t+1}|T_t = value2)$. But here either one of those two conditional probabilities is actually determined by the other. We see no easy way to represent this extra information in the Bayesian formalism.

Probabilities are special random sets. So, joint probability over *x* and *y* can certainly be represented by belief functions (Shafer, 1976). A joint probability can be constructed from a group of conditional probabilities and some prior(s). In this sense, the Dempster-Shafer theory is able to accommodate groups of conditional probabilities that constitute complete probability models.

As pointed out earlier in this section and in Pearl (1989; 1990), however, the belief function formalism is unable to adequately represent individual conditional probabilities and probabilistic constraints, when they do not constitute a complete model. The question is, how useful are those individual conditional probabilities and probabilistic constraints if they do not constitute a complete model? When a lot parameters are missing, they are useless. In a general algorithm, we have only two choices: either to assign "reasonable" values to them or to carry them around through the whole computation. If we assign arbitrary "reasonable" values to them, the conclusions we reach will not make much sense. On the other hand, if we carry them through the whole computation, the complexity will be forbidding.

When only a few parameters are missing, we can either assign reasonable values to them (Pearl, 1989) or carry them around in the computation. Then we will be dealing with a complete probability model with unknown parameters and/or poorly supported numerical values. Therefore, the same thing can be done in the Dempster-Shafer theory.

In summary, the belief function formalism is most suitable for representing logical constraints and randomized logical constraints like statistical regression equations, which cannot be represented in the Bayesian theory formalism except for some special cases. A group of conditional probabilities and probabilistic constraints can also be represented by belief functions when it constitutes a complete probability model. When it does not constitute a complete probability model, the Dempster-Shafer theory can make as much, if not more, out of it than the Bayesian theory could.

4. THE INDEPENDENCE OF EVIDENCE

Dempster's rule should be used to combine belief functions that represent independent items of evidence. But when are items of evidence independent? How can we tell? This is probably the most frequent question asked about the Dempster-Shafer theory.

Let us discuss the question in terms of the independent witness metaphor. We are concerned with the truth x in the frame X, and we have a witness, say Betty, whose probability of being reliable is known. Betty's being reliable (BR) is related to the truth x in X because she testifies that the truth is in a subset A of X. As in section 2, we regard what Betty may testify (BT), given she is to testify, as a causal result of the truth x and her being reliable (Figure 3.1a).

Now, suppose Sally comes along and testifies that the truth is in another subset B of X. A similar causal model can be constructed for Sally and putting the two models together, we have a joint qualitative causal model of five variables (Figure 3.1b).

We propose to view Betty's testimony and Sally's testimony as two independent items of evidence if and only if the following two independencies, implicit in Figure 3.1b, are satisfied.

1. BR and SR are qualitatively independent[6] of each other.
2. Given x, BT is qualitatively independent of ST.

The need for condition (1) has been recognized by Shafer for quite some time (Shafer, 1981; 1985). Shafer (1990) wrote: "The independence required by Dempster's rule is simply probabilistic independence applied to the question for which we have probabilities rather than directly to the question of interest." Definition 5.1 of Voorbaark (1991) is nothing but another formal presentation of the condition.

To intuitively see why the condition is necessary, imagine that Betty and Sally are good friends and they intend to be reliable or unreliable at the same time on a given issue. Then condition 1 is violated and it is obviously wrong to combine the effects of Betty's testimony and those of Sally's testimony by using Dempster's rule.

Is condition 1 enough for the use of Dempster's rule? The answer is negative. The condition only requires that Betty's and Sally's reliabilities be independent a priori, when they are "viewed abstractly – i.e., before the interactions of the conclusions are taken into account" (Shafer, 1981, p. 49). It does not impose any constraints on the connections lying between the reliabilities and the truth x. Those connections may as well depend on each other. One way to ensure the independence between the connections is to require that Sally's testimony is conditional independent of Betty's testimony given the truth.

[6] See Pearl (1988, pp. 79–81) for the meaning of qualitative independence. The bottom line is the notion of independence is more basic than numerical probabilities. "People can easily and confidently detect dependencies even though they may not be able to provide precise numerical estimates of probabilities."

Shafer (1990) gave an interesting example that actually supports the need for condition (2). My neighbor Betty called me that she has heard my burglar alarm; I then called another neighbor Sally, who verified that my alarm sounded. Assume Betty's being reliable in general is independent of Sally's being reliable in general (before those reliabilities are tied to the problem). Then, condition (1) is satisfied. Is it appropriate to use Dempster's rule to combine those two items of evidence then? The answer would be negative if there might be some other noise similar to my burglar alarm. In this case, even given that my burglar alarm did not sound, Sally's testimony would still not be independent of Betty's: Betty's testimony would imply there was a similar sound, suggesting Sally's testimony would be the same (if she is more likely to be reliable than not).

So, conditions (1) and (2) are necessary for the use of Dempster's rule. Are they sufficient? In the next section, we will argue that there should also be some requirements on the items of evidence themselves in order for them to be combined by Dempster's rule (see section 6.3).

5. MODIFYING DEMPSTER'S RULE OF COMBINATION

Not only have the independencies required by Dempster's rule been questioned, but also the validity of the rule itself. Zadeh (1986), for instance, argues that the rule is valid only if there is a "conflict free parent relation behind evidence." Voorbaark (1991) claims that the rule favors focal elements with larger cardinalities. The most insightful criticism, though, was put forward by Diaconis and Zabell (1982) in terms of the Three Prisoner Puzzle. This section is an attempt to modify Dempster's rule to avoid this criticism.

5.1. The conservativeness of BF degrees of belief

In the Dempster-Shafer theory, intuitive degrees of belief are represented by the belief function (BF) degrees, instead of subjective probabilities. What are the characteristics of the BF degrees? How appropriate are they as representations of intuitive beliefs?

Well, belief function degrees are conservative. Recall the notation from section 3. Let s and t stand for the truths in S and T, respectively. Then, if s is s_0, t must be in C_{s_0}. Formula (3) can be rewritten as

$$Bel(A) = \Sigma\{P(s) \mid C_s \subset A\} \tag{8}$$

The $Bel(A)$ is conservative as a degree of belief about t because it consists of only those portions of P (on S) that render $t \in A$ a necessity. It is in this sense that Pearl (1989) calls BF degrees of belief degrees of necessity. In terms of betting, if P is the frequency of a game and we bet on A with rate $Bel(A)$, we will at least break even in the long run, with the possibility of a net win (Shafer, 1981).

In dual to Bel, there is another measure Pl called plausibility function which is given by

$$Pl(A) = \Sigma\{P(s) \mid C_s \cap A \neq 0\} \tag{9}$$

The $Pl(A)$ is radical as a degree of belief about t because it consists of all those portions of P (on S) that do not exclude $t \in A$ as an impossibility. In terms of betting, if P is the frequency of a game and we bet on A with rate $Pl(A)$, we will at most break even in the long run, with the possibility of a net loss (Shafer, 1981).

A probability mass of $P(s)$ is assigned to C_s. When we talk about belief on t being in a proper but nonempty subset A of C_s, $P(s)$ is always excluded from the conservative $Bel(A)$ and is always included in the radical $Pl(A)$. A moderate attitude would be to include only a portion of $P(s)$. A natural choice for that portion is $P(s)|A|/|C_s|$, where $|.|$ stands for cardinality. This leads to the *center probability* P_c of Bel, given by

$$P_c(A) = \sum_s \frac{|A \cap C_s|}{|C_s|} P(s) \tag{10}$$

Dubois and Prade (1986a) view P_c as a probability approximation to Bel, while Smets (1988a) derives (10) from a set of axioms presumably characterizing a generalization to the insufficient reason principle.

5.2. Conditioning

In this subsection, we will show how the conservativeness of the Bel and the radicalness of Dempster's rule combine to arrive at a counterintuitive conclusion in the Three Prisoner Puzzle (Gardner, 1961) and how a moderate approach toward conditioning can avoid it.

Three prisoners a, b, and c await their verdict, knowing that one of them will be declared guilty and the other two be released. Prisoner a asks the jailer, who knows the verdict, to pass a letter to either one of the other two prisoners – one of whom is going to be released; later the jailer tells prisoner a that he gave the letter to prisoner b. The problem is to assess prisoner a's chances of being the one declared guilty.

Let G_i stand for "prisoner i is declared guilty," where i can be a, b, or c; and let L_j stand for "the jailer gave the letter to prisoner j," where j can be b or c. The fact that prisoner b received the letter is represented by the belief function that establishes the subset $\{G_a, G_c\}$ with certainty.

There are two variables: the guilty prisoner and the letter recipient. Items of evidence are to be asessed on the Cartesian product of their frames. Due to the compatibility relation between the two frames, we actually need only consider a subset of the Cartesian product, namely: $\{(G_a, L_b), (G_a, L_c), (G_b, L_c), (G_c, L_b)\}$.

Suppose the judge is known to have had a hard time deciding the verdict and to have randomly selected the misfortunate from the three prisoners. Combining this with L_b by Dempster's rule results in equal degrees of 1/2 on both G_a and G_c. This is, according to the criticism, counterintuitive, because prisoner c, unlike a, could have been named by the jailer, and the fact that c is not named should render him more likely to be the one found guilty. To amplify this clash with intuition, imagine that a repeats the experiment with 1,000 independent jailers, and all name b as the letter recipient. Intuitively, this strange coincidence should trigger some question as to why c was never selected, suggesting that he is the one found guilty. But still, Dempster's rule will conclude equal degrees, 1/2, on both G_a and G_c.

Let Bel_A with bpa m_A be the result of conditioning a belief function Bel with bpa m on a subset A. Then

$$m_A(B) = k\Sigma\{m(C) | A \cap C = B\} \tag{11}$$

where k is the renormalization constant independent of B. We see that the probability mass $m(C)$ is included in $Bel_A(B)$ whenever the intersection of C and A is not empty and is a subset of B, regardless how much or how little of C lies within B. In this sense, we say Dempster's rule is "radical."

In the three prisoner example, the probability mass of 1/3 assigned to $\{(G_a, L_b), (G_a, L_c)\}$ gets included in the belief of $\{(G_a, L_b)\}$ after conditioning on $\{(G_a, L_b), (G_c, L_b)\}$, while the probability mass of 1/3 assigned to $\{(G_c, L_b)\}$ remains committed to $\{(G_c, L_b)\}$, rendering equal degrees of belief on $\{(G_a, L_b)\}$ and $\{(G_c, L_b)\}$.

A conservative approach would be to include $m(C)$ in the belief of B after conditioning on A only when $C \subseteq B$; that is, to set the bpa of B to be $k\Sigma\{m(C) | C \subseteq B\}$. This approach will not work either. In the three prisoner example, there are no focal elements that are subsets of $\{(G_a,$

$L_b)\}$. So the conservative approach would conclude a 0 degree of belief on G_a, which is anti-intuitive.

We therefore propose a moderate approach to conditioning. To distinguish, we use $Bel_{|A}$ and $m_{|A}$ instead of Bel_A and m_A, and define

$$m_{|A}(B) = k\Sigma\{\frac{|A \cap C|}{|C|} m(C) | A \cap C = B\} \tag{12}$$

where k is the renormalization constant independent of B.

In the three prisoner example, let L_b denote the set $\{(G_a, L_b), (G_c, L_b)\}$. If we condition the belief function on L_b by the moderate approach, we get

$$m_{|L_b}(\{(G_a, L_b)\}) = k\frac{|\{(G_a, L_b)\}|}{|\{(G_a, L_b), (G_a, L_c)\}|} m(\{(G_a, L_b), (G_a, L_c)\})$$
$$= k\frac{1}{2}\cdot\frac{1}{3} = \frac{k}{6}$$

and

$$m_{|L_b}(\{(G_c, L_b)\}) = k\frac{|\{(G_c, L_b)\}|}{|\{(G_c, L_b)\}|} m(\{(G_c, L_b)\}) = k\frac{1}{3}$$

Here, the normalization constant k is 2. So, we get a degree of belief 1/3 on $\{(G_a, L_b)\}$ and a degree of belief 2/3 on $\{(G_a, L_b)\}$. The clash with intuition disappears.

To end this subsection, let us point out that the center probability of $Bel_{|A}$ is same as $P_c(.|A)$, the result of conditioning the center probability P_c of Bel on A (Zhang, 1986a).

5.3. Combination

What kind of rule of combination would our moderate approach to conditioning lead to? Dempster's rule does not consider how focal elements intersect, from which originates the counterintuitive conclusion in the three prisoner example. A natural way to modify the rule is to take the intersections among focal elements into account.

Let Bel_1 and Bel_2 be two belief functions with bpa's m_1 and m_2. Let m be the bpa of the to-be-defined combination of the two belief functions. Our first assumption is

$$m(C) = k\Sigma\{r(A,B)m_1(A)m_2(B)|A \cap B = C\} \tag{13}$$

where k is the renormalization constant independent of C, m_1 and m_2, and $r(A,B)$ is a number independent of m_1 and m_2, presumably a measure of how A and B intersect.

If we want the combination rule to reduce to our moderate conditioning rule when one of the belief functions establishes a subset of the frame with certainty, and if we require the combination rule be commutative and associative, then (Zhang, 1986a) the only choice for $r(A, B)$ is

$$r(A,B) = \frac{|A \cap B|}{|A||B|} \tag{14}$$

We therefore have

$$m(C) = k\Sigma\{\frac{|C|}{|A||B|}m_1(A)m_2(B)|A \cap B = C\} \tag{15}$$

The corresponding belief function, denoted by Bel_1 © Bel_2, is called the *center combination* of Bel_1 and Bel_2.

If we use this new combination rule in our *TOC* example, the degree of belief on *TOC* would be 0.4, instead of 0.44.

Let us end this section with a few remarks about the center combination rule. First, Yen (1986) proposed a similar rule of combination in his attempt to extend the Dempster-Shafer theory by randomizing the compatibility relations. The reason for his new rule was that Dempster's rule "overweighs the prior probability."

Second, center combination of belief functions implies multiplication of center probabilities (Zhang, 1986a). Let P_1, P_2, and P be the center probabilities of Bel_1, Bel_2, and Bel_1 © Bel_2 respectively, then for any x in the frame

$$P(x) = k\,P_1(x)\,P_2(x) \tag{16}$$

Finally, the center combination rule reduces to Dempster's rule if $|A \cap B| = |A||B|$ for every pair of focal elements A and B of Bel_1 and Bel_2. This condition is satisfied when the two belief functions are over two different frames X_1 and X_2, the combination is performed over $X_1 \times X_2$, and the compatibility relation in between X_1 and X_2 does not rule out any elements in $X_1 \times X_2$ as impossibilities.

6. CONCLUSION

This paper has touched some basic issues of the Dempster-Shafer theory. Belief functions arise when there is a need, due to the lack of conditional links, to propagate probabilities thorugh logical links. It was argued that the belief function formalism is able to represent knowledge that is representable in the Bayesian theory and that is usable by general algorithms. A more concrete criterion was given for two items of evidence to be independent in terms of the independent witness metaphor. And a new rule of combination was proposed. Unlike Dempster's rule, this new rule does not produce counterintuitive results in the three prisoner example.

ACKNOWLEDGMENTS

This paper has benefited from comments on an earlier draft by M. Horsch, R. Qi, and Y. Zhang. The author wants to give his special thanks to D. Poole for informing him of several important relevant papers. Suggestions by the editors and an anonymous reviewer are also valuable. Research is supported by NSERC Grant OGP0044121.

BIBLIOGRAPHY

Almond, R. (1988). Fusion and propagation in graphical belief models. Research Report S-121, Deartment of Statistics, Harvard University.

Black, P. K. and Laskey, K. B. (1990). Hierarchical evidence and belief functions. In Shacter, R.D. et al. (eds.), *Uncertainty in artificial intelligence* 4, pp. 207–15. Amsterdam: North-Holland.

Dempster, A. P. (1967). Upper and lower probabilities induced by a multivalued mapping. *Annual of Mathematical Statistics* 38, 355–74.

Dempster, A. P. (1990). Construction and local computation of network of belief functions. In R. M. Oliver and J. Q. Smith (eds.), *Influence diagrams, belief nets, and decision analysis*, chap. 6. New York: Wiley.

Dempster, A. P. and Kong, A. (1988). Uncertain evidence and artificial analysis. *Journal of Statistical Planning and Inference* 20, 355–68.

Diaconis, P. and Zabell, S. L. (1982). Updating subjective probability. *Journal of the American Statistical Society* 77 (380): pp. 822–30.

Dubois, D. and Prade, H. (1986a). A set-theoretic view of belief functions. *International Journal of General Systems* 12, 193–226.

Dubois, D. and Prade, H. (1986b). On the unicity of Dempster rule of combination. *International Journal of Intelligent Systems* 1, 133–42.

Fagin, R. and Halpern, J. Y. (1990a). Updating beliefs vs. combining beliefs. *Proceedings of the Sixth Conference on Uncertainty in Artificial Intelligence*, Cambridge, MA, pp. 317–24.

Fagin, R. and Halpern, J. Y. (1990b). Two views of beliefs: Belief as generalized probability and belief as evidence. *Proceedings of the Eighth National Conference on Artificial Intelligence*, Boston, pp. 112–19.

Gardner, M. (1961). *Second Scientific American book of mathematical puzzles and diversions.* New York: Simon and Schuster.

Goodman, I. R. (1987). A measure free approach to conditioning. *Proceedings of the Third Workshop on Uncertainties in AI*, Seattle, pp. 270–77.

Horsch, M. and Poole, D. (1990). A dynamic approach to probabilistic inference. *Proceedings of the Sixth Conference on Uncertainty in Artificial Intelligence*, Cambridge, MA, pp. 155–61.

Kong, A. (1986). Multivariate belief functions and graphical models. Doctoral Dissertation Department of Statistics, Harvard University.

Kyburg, Jr., H. E. (1987). Bayesian and non-Bayesian evidential updating. *Artificial Intelligence* 31, 271–93.

Lemmer, J. F. (1986). Confidence factors, empiricism and the Dempster-Shafer theory of evidence. In L. N. Kanal and J. F. Lemmer (eds.), *Uncertainty in artificial intelligence*, pp. 117–25. Amsterdam: North-Holland.

Lindley, D. V. (1972). *Bayesian statistics: A review.* Philadelphia: SIAM.

Lowrance, J. D. (1988). Automating argument construction. *Journal of Statistical Planing and Inference* 20, 369–87.

Maier, D. (1983). *The theory of relational databases.* Rockville, MD: Computer Science Press.

Nguyen, H. T. (1978). On random sets and belief functions. *Journal of Mathematical Analysis and Applications* 65, 531–42.

Pearl, J. (1988). *Probabilistic reasoning in intelligent systems.* San Mateo, CA: Morgan Kaufmann.

Pearl, J. (1989). Bayesian and belief-functions formalisms for evidential reasoning: A conceptual analysis. Technical Report CSD-880054 R-106-S-II, Computer Science Department, University of California, Los Angeles.

Pearl, J. (1990). Which is more believable, the probably provable or the provably probable? *Proceedings of the Eighth Biennial Conference of the Canadian Society for Computational Studies of Intelligence*, University of Ottawa, pp. 1–7.

Savage, L. J. (1954). *The foundation of statistics.* New York: Wiley.

Shafer, G. (1976). A mathematical theory of evidence. Princeton, NJ: Princeton University Press.

Shafer, G. (1981). Constructive probability. *Synthese* 48: 1–60.

Shafer, G. (1982). Belief functions and parametric models (with discussions). *Journal of the Royal Statistical Society*, Series B 44, 322–52.

Shafer, G. (1985). Belief functions and possibility measures. In J. C. Bezdek (ed.), *The analysis of fuzzy information.* Boca Raton, FL: CRC Press.

Shafer, G. (1987). Probability judgement in artificial and expert systems. *Statistical Science* 2: 3–16.

Shafer, G. (1990). Perspective on the theory and practice of belief function. *International Journal of Approximate Reasoning* 4: 323–62.

Shafer, G. and Shenoy, P. P. (1988). Local computation in hypertrees. Working Paper 201, School of Business, University of Kansas.

Smets, P. (1978). Un model mathematico-statistique simulant le processus du diagnostic medical. Doctoral Dissertation at the Free University of Brussels, Presses Universitaires de Bruxelles.
Smets, P. (1988a). Belief functions versus probability functions. In B. Bouchon, L. Saitta, and R. R. Yager (eds.), *Uncertainty and intelligent systems*, pp. 17–24. Berlin: Springer-Verlag.
Smets, P. (1988b). Belief functions. In P. Smets, et al. (eds.), *Non-standard logics for automated reasoning*, pp. 253–86. London: Academic Press.
Voorbaark, F. (1991). On the justification of Dempster's rule of combination. *Artificial Intelligence* 48: 171–97.
Walley, P. (1987). Belief-function representations of statistical evidence. *Ann. Stat.* 10: 741–61.
Yen, J. (1986). A reasoning model based on an extended Dempster-Shafer theory. *Proceedings of AAAI-86*, Philadelphia, PA, pp. 125–31.
Yen, J. (1989). Can evidence be combined in the Dempster-Shafer theory? In L. N. Kanal, T. S. Levitt, and J. F. Lemmer (eds.), *Uncertainty in artificial intelligence 3*, pp. 63–72. Amsterdam: North-Holland.
Zadeh, L. A. (1986). A simple view of the Dempster-Shafer theory of evidence. *AI Magazine*, Summer, 85–90.
Zhang, L. (1986a). Weights of evidence and internal conflict for support functions. *Information Science* 38: 205–12.
Zhang, L. (1986b). Further investigations in theory of evidence and the theory of possibility. Unpublished Masters Thesis, Beijing Normal University, Beijing, China.

4 Focusing versus updating in belief function theory

Didier DUBOIS and Henri PRADE

Abstract: Dempster's rule of conditioning is carefully examined and compared to upper and lower conditional probabilities induced by a belief function. Although both notions are extensions of probabilistic conditioning they cannot serve the same purpose. The notion of focusing, as a change of reference class, is introduced and opposed to updating. Dempster's rule is good for updating, while the other form of conditioning expresses a focusing operation. The concept of focusing models the meaning of uncertain conditional statements in a more natural way than updating. The focusing view of conditioning seems to be a useful tool for the representation of rules in the treatment of nonmonotonic reasoning problems such as the well-known "penguin triangle" example.

Keywords: belief function, upper and lower probabilities, conditioning, updating.

1. INTRODUCTION

The theory of belief functions, as introduced by Shafer (1976b), is based on two basic components: a tool for representing belief, that is, a pair (*Bel*, *Pl*) of set-functions that quantify for any statement A to what extent available evidence implies A and is consistent with A, respectively; and a tool for combining evidence, also called the

Dempster rule of combination (Dempster, 1967). A particular case of Dempster's rule of combination is when a belief function must be combined with a sure fact S. Then, a form of conditioning is obtained that generalizes the probabilistic notion.

Dempster's rule of conditioning has been criticized because it is not in accordance with the view of the belief function *Bel* as a special kind of lower probability. Namely, if we condition each probability $P \geqslant Bel$ by event S, then the lower bound of the obtained conditional probabilities is not the result of the Dempster rule of conditioning on S (e.g., Kyburg, 1987; Pearl, 1990). The repeated answer to this type of criticism is that a belief function should not be regarded as a lower probability (Smets, 1988; Shafer, 1990) because the theory of evidence does not presuppose an unknown probability distribution whose values are bounded by the belief function.

However, recent results in upper and lower probabilities indicate than conditioning a family of probability distributions $P \geqslant Bel$ still leads to a belief function (Fagin and Halpern, 1990; Jaffray, 1990) and that moreover this belief function is also the lower bound of a family of belief functions (de Campos et al., 1990). These analyses suggest the existence of two types of conditioning in belief function theory. Rather than choosing between the two forms of conditioning, we suggest in this paper that both notions should be kept because they are not tailored for the same purpose. Dempster's rule of conditioning is a strong generalization of Bayes' conditioning well adapted to updating a belief function upon receiving a sure piece of information. In contrast, the other rule is a weaker, less informative generalization of Bayes' conditioning that corresponds to focusing on a subclass of a referential set. A result of this paper is a new expression of the focusing rule, in the spirit of Dempster's (1967) original view of the belief function as induced from a probability via a multivalued mapping. As a consequence the weak conditioning rule is like conditioning a probability on an ill-known event.

The second part of the paper is devoted to the representation of "if... then..." statements in belief function theory. It is argued that the focusing rule of conditioning offers a better model, especially when it comes to the treatment of cases involving generic knowledge tainted with exceptions. Dempster's rule of conditioning is compared with the focusing rule on classical examples in nonmonotonic reasoning. A by-product of the paper is that the usual assumption made in the literature of evidence theory regarding the independence of pieces of knowledge supplied by experts is generally untenable, and that a belief function representing the overall knowledge base cannot be derived by means of the Dempster rule of combination. On the contrary, following previous suggestions (Dubois and Prade, 1986), we advocate the idea that a set of default rules be modeled by means of a set of constraints on a global belief function, each constraint being obtained by means of the focusing rule of conditioning. Other discussions pertaining to belief function theory and its relevance to uncertain reasoning can be found in Dubois and Prade (1992), of which this paper is a companion.

2. UPDATING VERSUS FOCUSING

Consider these two situations (Dubois and Prade, 1992):

1. A die has been thrown 1,000,000 times, and $P(i)$ is the probability that facet i comes out of a throw. $P(i)$ is, of course, frequency-based. Consider the question: how often does i occur among odd facets? To do this we must compute $P(i \mid \text{odd})$ using Bayes' rule.
2. A die has been thrown by a player, but he has not seen the result yet. He has ideas about what are the most probable outcomes under the form of a probability distribution $P(i)$, $i = 1, n$ that expresses his subjective belief about the occurrence of each facet. Now before the official result is advertised a friend tells him that the result is an odd number. How does the player update his belief? Again by computing $P(i \mid \text{odd})$, the Bayesians say.

It should be clear to the reader that these situations are quite different. In the first situation $P(\text{even}) \neq 0$ because in the 1,000,000 throws some results have been even. Moreover, no updating takes place. We are always considering P as the probability distribution to be used. We are just changing the reference class and computing $P(i \mid \text{odd})$, which is the relative frequency of getting facet i among the occurrences of odd facets, that is, $P(i \mid \text{odd}) = P(i) / P(\text{odd})$ if i is odd, and 0 otherwise. In other words, we are *focusing* on the reference class "odd."

In the second situation, the player is computing a new probability distribution P' over the whole set $\{1, 2, 3, 4, 5, 6\}$ by forcing $P'(\text{even}) = 0$ due to the piece of evidence he received from his friend. P' has little to do with P except it is the result of *updating* P. Moreover, the prior P is not supposed to be necessarily derived from reading the results of the frequentist experiment. As a consequence, putting

$P'(i) = P(i \mid \text{odd})$ using Bayes'rule can be challenged. Other updating rules can be thought of, namely any rule that reassigns the mass $P(\text{even})$ to odd facets is a priori allowed. For instance, Lewis's (1976) rule of imaging is another updating rule that reassigns the mass of impossible outcomes to possible ones, based on proximity notions, namely $P(\bar{S})$ is allotted to the outcome in S, which is as close as possible to the complement $\bar{S}$ of S where S is the piece of evidence that leads us to assume $P'(S) = 1$. $P'(i) = P(i \mid \text{odd})$ can be justified in the framework of probability kinematics (e.g., Domotor, 1985) by means of a minimal change principle based on cross-entropy (Williams, 1980). Bayes' rule is also the only possible updating rule that does not change the degrees of probability in relative value:

$$\text{for all } A,B, \frac{P'(A \cap S)}{P'(B \cap S)} = \frac{P(A \cap S)}{P(B \cap S)} \text{ for } A,B \text{ such that } A \cap S \neq \emptyset,$$
$$B \cap S \neq \emptyset, \text{ and } P'(S) = 1$$

Bayes' conditioning rule in probability theory can thus correspond to two distinct operations here called focusing and updating. Focusing addresses the following problem: given a probability distribution that reflects a population, what is the probability distribution reflecting a subclass of this population? Updating is a belief change operation that expresses how to revise an a priori probability distribution describing some epistemic state into another probability distribution upon the arrival of a sure piece of information. For the sake of clarity, the result of focusing a measure of uncertainty g, defined on a set X, to a subset S of X will be denoted g_S. On the other hand, the result of updating g upon hearing that event S occurs will be denoted g_S^+. The difference between g_S and g_S^+ is that g_S is viewed as a consequence of g where g remains the reference uncertainty measure while g_S^+ is viewed as a new reference uncertainty measure g' when S is known to occur. In the latter case the prior $g(\bar{S}) \neq 0$ is acknowledged as being wrong, and changed into $g'(\bar{S}) = 0$ where $g' = g_S^+$. When Bayesian updating makes sense, focusing and updating take the same form since $g_S = g_S^+ = g(\cdot \mid S)$.

Now, assume the probability distribution P is only known to belong to a family $\mathbf{P}$ of probabilities. Then it can be seen that focusing and updating lead to different results. In the case of focusing on S, what is needed is to compute $P(\cdot \mid S)$ for the "true" distribution P on which only incomplete information is available. In other words, for all $A \subseteq X$, the possible values of $P(A \mid S)$ for all $P \in \mathbf{P}$ must be determined:

$$P_S^*(A) = \sup\{P(A|S), P\in\mathbf{P}\}; P_{S*}(A) = \inf\{P(A|S), P\in\mathbf{P}\} \quad (1)$$

This rule is used by Walley (1991) and all the people working with probability bounds. On the contrary, updating upon hearing that S has occurred corresponds to eliminating from $\mathbf{P}$ all probabilities P such that $P(\bar{S}) \neq 0$; that is, turn $\mathbf{P}$ into $\mathbf{P}^+{}_S = \{P\in\mathbf{P}, P(S) = 1\}$. The latter operation makes sense only if there exists a $P\in\mathbf{P}$, $P(S) = 1$, that is, $P^*(S) = \sup\{P(S), P\in\mathbf{P}\} = 1$. When $P^*(S) < 1$, a reasonable choice is to consider as the most plausible probabilities in $\mathbf{P}$ the set $\{P\in\mathbf{P}, P(S) = P^*(S)\}$ and to let $\mathbf{P}^+{}_S = \{P(\cdot\,|\,S), P\in\mathbf{P}, P(S) = P^*(S)\}$. This view is advocated by Moral and de Campos (1991) (see also Gilboa and Schmeidler [1991] who call it maximum likelihod updating). Moral and de Campos introduce a less drastic way of updating that takes into account all probabilities in $\mathbf{P}$ such that $P(S) > 0$, considering that the greater $P(s)$, the more plausible $P(\cdot\,|\,S)$ as a member of $\mathbf{P}^+{}_S$. If we let $\mathbf{P}_S = \{P(\cdot\,|\,S), P\in\mathbf{P}\}$ be the result of focusing $\mathbf{P}$ on S, it is clear that $\mathbf{P}^+{}_S \subset P_S$, that is, updating on the fact that S is true, is a much more drastic conditioning rule than focusing on S. Focusing and updating no longer coincide when applied to upper and lower probabilities, even when updating is based on Bayes' rule.

3. UPDATING AND FOCUSING WITH BELIEF FUNCTIONS

In this section, we shall consider belief functions à la Dempster (1967). Namely, let Ω be a population, and for all ω, let $x(\omega)\in X$ be the evaluation of ω according to some attribute (e.g., ω is a man and $x(\omega)$ is the amount of money in his bank account). We assume that the available information on the population is incomplete, that is, for all ω, $x(\omega)\in\Gamma(\omega)$ where $\Gamma(\omega)$ is a nonempty subset of X describing what is known about $x(\omega)$. For any $E\subseteq X$, let $m(E)$ be the proportion of the population for which $\Gamma(\omega) = E$. $m(E)$ is the probability that what is known about an individual in Ω is E exactly. Under this interpretation the quantities $Bel(A) = \sum_{E\subseteq A} m(E)$ and $Pl(A) = \sum_{E\cap A\neq\emptyset} m(E)$ are lower and upper bounds on the value of the probability that an individual ω in Ω is such that $x(\omega)\in A$, had the information describing the mapping x been complete.

Let us consider the focusing problem. Let $S\subseteq X$ be a subset of X, and we are asking the question: what is the proportion of the population Ω that belong to $A \subseteq X$(i.e., such that $x(\omega) \in A$) among those which belong to S? The answer may not be precise; indeed, all we know about ω is that $x(\omega) \in E$ and we must decide whether $x(\omega) \in S$ or not. Let $P_E(S)$ be the (actually unknown) proportion of those ω with $x(\omega) \in S$ among the ones for which all that is known is $\Gamma(\omega) = E$. There are three situations (de Campos et al., 1990):

- $E \subseteq S$ then $P_E(S) = 1$;
- $E \cap S = \emptyset$ then $P_E(S) = 0$;
- $E \cap S \neq \emptyset$ and $E \cap \bar{S} \neq \emptyset$ then $P_E(S)$ is unknown.

Assume $P_E(S)$ is known. The answer to the question of focusing *Bel* on S is then:

$$\text{for all } A \subseteq X,\ Bel_{S,P}(A) = \sum_{F \subseteq A} \frac{\sum_{E:E \cap S = F} m(E) \cdot P_E(S)}{\sum_E m(E) \cdot P_E(S)} \tag{2}$$

It is clearly a belief function that depends upon $P_E(S)$, for all $E \subseteq X$. Indeed each mass $m(E)$, such that $P_E(S) > 0$ is changed into $m_{S,P}(S,E) = m(E) \cdot P_E(S)$, which is the proportion of individuals that belong to S and are known at best to belong to E. This mass is allocated to $S \cap E$. The mass assignment of $Bel_{S,P}$ is simply defined as

$$\text{for all } E' \subseteq S,\ m_{S,P}(E') = \frac{\sum_{E:S \cap E = E'} \mathrm{m}(E) \cdot P_E(S)}{\sum_E m(E) \cdot P_E(S)} \tag{3}$$

assuming that we redistribute, to all E' such that $m_{S,P}(E') > 0$, all the mass $\sum_{E:P_E(S)=0} m(E)$ in a Bayesian way. When $P_E(\mathrm{S})$ is unknown for $E \cap S \neq \emptyset$, $E \cap \bar{S} \neq 0$, we can only compute a lower bound to $Bel_{S,P}$ as follows: $Bel_S(A) = \inf \{Bel_{S,P(S|.)}(A) \mid P_E(S) \in [0,1],\ E \cap S \neq \emptyset,\ E \cap \bar{S} \neq \emptyset\}$. As proved by de Campos et al. (1990), when $Pl(S) > 0$:

$$Bel_S(A) = \inf\left\{\frac{P(A) \cap \mathrm{S})}{P(S)} \mid P(A) \geqslant Bel(A), \text{ for all } A \subseteq S\right\} =$$

$$= \frac{Bel(A \cap S)}{Bel(A \cap S) + Pl(\bar{A} \cap S)} \tag{4}$$

and $Bel_S(A) = 0$ if $Bel(A \cap S) = Pl(\bar{A} \cap S) = 0$.

This conditioning rule, originally suggested by Dempster (1967), has been used by Ruspini (1986), Smets (1987), Walley (1991), and Fagin and Halpern (1990). The latter authors, as well as Jaffray (1990), proved that Bel_S is still a belief function. However, exhibiting its mass function is tedious. The form of (4) should not be surprising noticing that the conditional probability $P(A \mid S)$ can take the form

$$P(A \mid S) = \frac{1}{1 + \left(P(\bar{A}\cap S) / P(A\cap S)\right)}$$

and that the function $f(x,y) = \dfrac{1}{1 + x/y}$ is decreasing with x and increasing with y. Dually, the conditional plausibility function for focusing reads

$$Pl_S(A) = \frac{Pl(A\cap S)}{Pl(A\cap S) + Bel(\bar{A}\cap S)} \tag{5}$$

The focusing rule answers the following question: for some individual $\omega_0 \in \Omega$ we happen to know that $x(\omega_0) \in S$; what is our belief that $x(\omega_0) \in A$, for $A \subseteq X$? It is not an updating rule, contrary to what Fagin and Halpern (1990) apparently claim.

Now let us assume that instead of focusing on the reference class of members of Ω such that $x(\omega) \in S$, we get a piece of evidence that claims that *all* members of Ω satisfy the condition $x(\omega) \in S$. Then we know that if $x(\omega) \in E$, and $E \cap S \neq \emptyset$ we are entiled to let $P_E(S) = 1$. In other words the mass $m(E)$ as a whole can be allotted to $E \cap S$. Then (2) becomes

$$Bel_S^+(A) = \sum_{F \subseteq A} \frac{\sum_{E:E\cap S = F} m(E)}{\sum_{E:E\cap S \neq \emptyset} m(E)} = 1 - \frac{Pl(\bar{A}\cap S)}{Pl(S)} \tag{6}$$

This is Dempster'rule of conditioning. Again the normalization factor that reallocates $\sum_{E\cap S=\emptyset} m(E)$ in a Bayesian way can be challenged in the scope of updating and must be introduced as an axiom when justifying the Dempster rule (Smets, 1990). Indeed $Bel_S^+(A)$ also provides the answer to the question: what is the proportion of ω's with $x(\omega) \in A$, among those with $x(\omega) \in S$, given that $x(\omega) \in S$, as soon as we know $x(\omega) \in E$, and $E \cap S \neq \emptyset$ for each focal element E? In other words, it is focusing with an optimistic assumption on $P_E(S)$. No surprise that the interval $[Bel_S^+(A),\ Pl_S^+(A)]$ is narrower than $[Bel_S(A),\ Pl_S(A)]$, as noticed by several authors, such as Kyburg (1987).

If the piece of evidence is indeed that $x(\omega) \in S$, for all ω, then it is contradictory with the fact that there exists an ω, $x(\omega) \in E$, and $E \cap S = \emptyset$. Hence, as an updating rule in the frequentist framework, (6) makes sense only if $\sum_{E:E\cap S \neq 0} m(E) = 1$, that is, the piece of evidence S does not contradict the set-valued statistics on Ω. In that case, updating is restricted to a set-theoretic operation (changing E into $E \cap S$, for all E) and does not touch the masses.

Another particular case of (2) is when $P_E(S)$ is assumed to be 0 whenever $E \not\subset S$. It gives the so-called geometric rule of conditioning (Shafer, 1976a):

$$Bel_S^0(A) = \frac{\text{Bel}(A \cap S)}{Bel(S)}; \; Pl_S^0(A) = 1 - Bel_S^0(\bar{A}) \tag{7}$$

This rule is justified by Kruse et al. (1991) in terms of random sets. Namely if ω is an object on a plane and $\Gamma(\omega)$ represents the area of this object, then learning that all objects lie in subset S of the plane leads us to eliminate the focal elements E such that $E \not\subset S$ is viewed as a rigid boundary for the object. Then the corresponding mass m_S^0 is defined by

$$m_S^0(A) = \frac{m(A)}{\sum_{E \not\subset S} m(E)} \tag{8}$$

4. A NEW EXPRESSION OF THE FOCUSING RULE OF CONDITIONING WITH BELIEF FUNCTIONS

Frequentist experiments are not, of course, the regular setting for belief functions. In belief function theory à la Shafer, Ω is a set of answers to a question, X is a set of answers to another question, and there is a compatibility relation that maps $\omega \in \Omega$ to some subset $E = x(\omega)$ of X of answers compatible with ω. There is a subjective probability distribution p on Ω and $m(E) = \sum_{x(\omega)=E} p(\omega)$. Given a piece of evidence $S \subseteq X$ that rules out answers $x \notin S$, the problem is to update p on Ω, that is, define p' such that:

- $p'(\omega) = 0$ if $\mathrm{x}(\omega) \cap S = \emptyset$ (when only S is the possible answer, ω becomes impossible)
- All masses given to E are given to $E \cap S$ if $E \cap S \neq \emptyset$

Adopting the Bayesian updating rule on Ω we have for ω such that $x(\omega) \cap S \neq \emptyset$, $P'(\omega) = P(\omega)/P(S^*)$ where $S^* = \{\omega | x(\omega) \cap S \neq \emptyset\}$ is the set of possible answers in Ω after hearing that $\bar{S}$ is impossible in X. Translated back to X, Bayes' rule justifies Dempster's rule of conditioning. So if we reject Dempster's rule of conditioning on X, we must reject Bayes' rule on Ω.

However, it is clear that in that setting as in the frequentist case, the updating problem and the focusing problem no longer coincide, that is, if one has no idea of the probability that S contains the answer in X, given that E contains the answer, it is not possible to compute the relative probability of ω among the ω' such that $x(\omega') \in S$, because we no longer know the subset $\{\omega | x(\omega) \in S\}$. All we can say on this relative probability is that it lies in the interval $[p(\omega)/P(S^*), p(\omega)/P(S_*)]$ as long as $\omega \in S_*$, where $S_* = \{\omega' | x(\omega') \subseteq S\}$. Again, focusing and updating behave quite differently. The question is whether the focusing rule (4)–(5) can be defined as conditioning a regular probability by means of an ill-defined set squeezed betwen S^* and S_*. The following proposition answers in the affirmative.

Proposition 1: The focusing rule (5) for plausibility functions can be expressed as

$$Pl_S(A) = \sup_{S_* \subseteq C \subseteq S^*,\, C \neq \emptyset} P(A^* | C) \tag{9}$$

where P is a probability measure on Ω, S_* and S^* are the lower and upper inverse images of S, A^* the upper image of A, via a multiple-valued mapping $\Gamma: \Omega \to 2^x$ and (P, Γ) generate the plausibility function.

Proof: Let $\mathbf{P}(Pl) = \{P_X | P_X \leqslant Pl\}$ where P_X denotes a probability measure on X. The extreme points of $\mathbf{P}(Pl)$ (such that $\mathbf{P}(Pl)$ is a convex combination thereof) can be obtained using a selection function s which for any focal element E, selects an element $s(E) \in E$ and assigns the mass $m(E)$ to it. Such a selection function can be represented by means of the multiple-valued mapping Γ. Namely let f be a mapping $\Omega \to X$ such that for all $\omega, f(\omega) \in \Gamma(\omega)$. We shall write $f \in \Gamma$ for short. Then if $\Gamma(\omega) = E$, we define $f(\omega) = s(E)$. The induced probability P_X^f on X from P via f is such that for all $A \subset X$, $P_X^f(A) = P(f^{-1}(A))$. If $\mathbf{P}_\Gamma = \{P_X^f | f \in \Gamma\}$, it is easy to see (from results in Dempster [1967]) that $\mathbf{P}(Pl)$ is the convex hull of $\mathbf{P}_\Gamma$. Now

$$Pl_S(A) = \sup\left\{\frac{P_X(A \cap S)}{P_X(S)} \,|\, P \in \mathbf{P}(Pl)\right\} =$$

$$= \sup\left\{\frac{P_X(A \cap S)}{P_X(S)} \,|\, P_X \in \mathbf{P}_\Gamma\right\} = \sup\left\{\frac{P(f^{-1}(A \cap S))}{P(f^{-1}(S))} \,|\, f \in \Gamma\right\} \tag{10}$$

Now $f^{-1}(A \cap S) = f^{-1}(A) \cap f^{-1}(S)$. Besides, $f^{-1}(A) \subseteq A^*$, and $S_* \subseteq f^{-1}(S) \subseteq S^*$, by definition, since $f \in \Gamma$. Hence

$$Pl_S(A) \leqslant \sup\left\{\frac{P(A^* \cap C)}{P(C)} \,|\, S_* \subseteq C \subseteq S^*\right\} \tag{11}$$

What is left to prove is that for all C, A^* and C can be put under the form $f^{-1}(A)$ and $f^{-1}(S)$, respectively. To see it, note that in order to verify $f^{-1}(S) = C$, what is requested is that for all $\omega \in C$, $f(\omega) \in S$, and for all $\omega \notin C$, $f(\omega) \notin S$. This is possible since for all $\omega \in C$, $\Gamma(\omega) \cap S \neq \emptyset$ because $C \subseteq S^*$, and for all $\omega \notin C$, $\Gamma(\omega) \not\subseteq S$ since $S_* \subseteq C$. The condition $f^{-1}(S) = C$ is thus verified for any $f \in \Gamma_C$, where $\Gamma_C(\omega) = \Gamma(\omega) \cap S$, for all $\omega \in C$; and $\Gamma_C(\omega) = \Gamma(\omega) \cap \bar{S}$ if $\omega \notin C$. The condition $f^{-1}(A) = A^*$ can be simply verified by forcing $f(\omega) \in A$ for all $\omega \in A^*$. Now if $\omega \in A^* \cap C$, it is possible to let $f(\omega) \in A \cap S$ since $\Gamma(\omega) \cap A \cap S \neq \emptyset$ and $f(\omega) \in \Gamma_C(\omega)$ since $\Gamma_C(\omega) \cap A = \Gamma(\omega) \cap A \cap S$. If $\omega \in A^* \cap \bar{C}$, we let $f(\omega) \in A \cap \bar{S}$, and $f \in \Gamma_C$ is again possible. Hence

$$\text{for all C, } \exists\ f \in \Gamma, \frac{P(A^* \cap C)}{P(C)} = \frac{P(f^{-1}(A) \cap f^{-1}(S))}{P(f^{-1}(S))}$$

that is, the supremum in the left-hand side of (10) is attained at $Pl_S(A)$. Note that if choosing $C = \emptyset$ is possible in (11), it implies $S_* = \emptyset$ and then it is possible to choose f such that $f^{-1}(A \cap S) = f^{-1}(S) = \{\bar{\omega}\}$ for some $\bar{\omega} \in \Omega$. To see it, notice that if $A \cap S \neq \emptyset$, then $A_* \cap S^* \neq \emptyset$. Let $\bar{\omega} \in A^* \cap S^*$ and force $f(\bar{\omega}) \in A \cap S$. Now, for all $\omega \neq \bar{\omega}$ it is possible to let $f(\omega) \notin S$ since $S_* = \emptyset$. In that case $f^{-1}(S) = \{\bar{\omega}\}$, $Pl_S(A) = 1$, and the supremum in (10) is attained for $C = \{\bar{\omega}\}$.

In order to exemplify the difference between focusing and updating, let us consider the following example: assume that in the die example of Section 1, the player expects a rather high number (5 or 6), does not believe too much in a medium number (3,4), and almost rules out the posssibility of getting a small number (1,2). He assigns a priori probabilities $m(\{5,6\}) = 0.7$, $m(\{3,4\}) = 0.2$ and $m(\{1,2\}) = 0.1$. If he asks himself what if the outcome were not a six, then he has to focus on the situations where he would get no 6 and compute $Bel_S(A)$, $Pl_S(A)$ for $S = \{1, 2, 3, 4, 5\}$, and $A \subseteq \{1, 2... 5\}$. For instance

$$Bel_S(5) = 0 = Bel(5);\ Pl_S(5) = \frac{0.7}{0.7 + 0.3} = 0.7 = Pl(5)$$

This is because he cannot rule out the situation where his belief in outcome 5 precisely would be zero. But if a friend tells him that the outcome is not a 6, then by Dempster's rule one gets $Bel_S^+(5) = 0.7$.

What happens is that the player keeps his belief that the outcome will be a high number, so outcome 5 receives all the mass while 6 is now definitely ruled out. Note that Levi (1983) has challenged this updating method by suggesting that upon learning that 6 is impossible the player might wish to modify his prior belief that the outcome will be a high number, thus acknowledging that his prior probability was erroneus.

Clearly the focusing rule and the updating rule serve different purposes. The focusing rule is good for question answering of the form "what happens for the elements of some subclass of individuals." The updating rule is meant for combining an a priori knowledge and a piece of evidence claiming that situations where some proposition is not true do not exist.

5. REPRESENTING UNCERTAIN RULES WITH BELIEF FUNCTIONS

In this section we try to consider the problem of representing an uncertain rule "if $x \in A$ then $y \in B$ (with weight α)" by means of belief functions. More specifically, α is an uncertainty coefficient that expresses a lower bound on a degree of belief on the conclusion $y \in B$ when the antecedent $x \in A$ is verified. Several approaches have been proposed in the past.

The simplest one is to interpret the rule by means of the material implication $\bar{A} \cup B$ and interpret the weight as a lower bound $Bel(\bar{A} \cup B) \geqslant \alpha$ on a belief function (Chatalic et al., 1987). Then the uncertain rule can be represented as any belief function on the domain $X \times Y$ of (x,y) that verifies the constraint. If a single belief function is requested to represent the rule, one may apply the minimum specificity principle (Dubois and Prade, 1986) that allocates the masses to the greatest possible subsets. Namely a mass α needs to be committed to $\bar{A} \cup B$ (rather than its subsets) and the remaining mass $1 - \alpha$ being free is allocated to $X \times Y$:

$$m(X \times Y) = 1 - \alpha; \; m(\bar{A} \cup B) = \alpha \tag{12}$$

Variants of this approach have been proposed by Eddy and Pei (1986), Chatalic et al. (1987), and Kämpke (1988). However, some of them are debatable because inducing a priori biases on $Bel(A)$ and $Bel(B)$, and the others are equivalent to more than one rule.

Another approach is proposed by Smets (1988) based on Dempster's rule of conditioning. Namely, the weight is interpreted as the belief in B resulting from combining the evidence Bel and the observation A, that is, $Bel_A^+(B) = \alpha$, which is equivalent to $Pl(A \cap \bar{B}) = (1 - \alpha)Pl(A)$, another constraint on the set of belief functions on $X \times Y$. Again, applying the principle of minimum specificity leads us to assume $Pl(A) = 1$ as long as nothing impinges upon A. Hence $Pl(A \cap \bar{B})\, 1 - \alpha$, which is equivalent to $Bel(\bar{A} \cup B) = \alpha$. In other words we get the same result as with the material conditional.

A third approach can be based on the focusing conditioning. Namely the rule "if $x \in A$ then $y \in B(\alpha)$" is understood as $Bel_A(B) \geqslant \alpha$, which reads: the belief in B is at least α for individuals for which A is true (Dubois and Prade, 1992). It leads to

$$\frac{Bel(A \cap B)}{Bel(A \cap B) + Pl(A \cap \bar{B})} \geqslant \alpha > 0$$

This is equivalent to let $\alpha Pl(A \cap \bar{B}) \leqslant (1 - \alpha) Bel(A \cap B) \neq 0$. Finding a minimum specificity representation is more tricky. First some mass, say $x > 0$, must be allocated to $A \cap B$, but none is requested for its subsets. Then we derive the following two inequalities:

$$Pl(A \cap \bar{B}) \leqslant \frac{(1-\alpha)x}{\alpha};\ Bel(\bar{A} \cup B) \geqslant Bel(A \cap B) \geqslant x$$

Hence $Bel(\bar{A} \cup B) \geqslant \max(1 - \frac{(1-\alpha)x}{\alpha}, x)$. But $Bel(\bar{A} \cup B) = m(A \cap B) + m(\bar{A} \cup B)$ (no other subset of $\bar{A} \cup B$ is requested to receive any mass). Hence $1 - x \geqslant m(\bar{A} \cup B) \geqslant \max(0, 1 - \frac{x}{\alpha})$.

In other words, only if $x < \alpha$ is it necessary to have some mass on $\bar{A} \cup B$. The remaining mass $1 - x - \max(0, 1 - \frac{x}{\alpha}) = \min(1 - x, \frac{x}{\alpha} - x)$ can be allocated to $X \times Y$. When x is fixed, the minimum specificity belief function, obtained by allocating as much mass as possible to $X \times Y$, is defined by $m(A \cap B) = x$; $m(\bar{A} \cup B) = \max(0, 1 - \frac{x}{\alpha})$; $m(X \times Y) = \min(1 - x, \frac{x}{\alpha} - x)$.

Moreover, if $x \geqslant \alpha$, because $m(\bar{A} \cup B) = 0$, the minimum specificity belief function is when $x = \alpha$, which minimizes the mass on $A \cap B$. When $x < \alpha$, the set of belief function Bel_x defined by $\{(A \cap B, x), (\bar{A} \cup B, 1 - \frac{x}{\alpha}), (X \times Y, \frac{x}{\alpha} - x)\}$ cannot be ordered in terms of specificity since if $\alpha > x' > x > 0$ we have $Bel_x(A \cap B) < Bel_{x'}(A \cap B)$ and $Bel_x(\bar{A} \cup B) > Bel_{x'}(\bar{A} \cup B)$ conjointly. To conclude we obtain the following result.

Proposition 2 : The set of least specific belief functions compatible with the constraint $Bel_A(B) \geqslant \alpha$ is defined by $m(A \cap B) =$

$xm(\bar{A}\cup B)=1-\frac{x}{\alpha}, m(X\times Y)=\frac{x}{\alpha}-x$, for $x\in(0,\alpha)$. Each of these belief functions Bel_x verifies $Bel_A(B)=\alpha$.

Proof: Only the second part of the result is still to be established:

$$\frac{Bel(A\cap B)}{Bel(A\cap B)+Pl(A\cap \bar{B})}=\frac{x}{x+(x/\alpha)-x}=\alpha, \text{ for all } x\in(0,\alpha)$$

The set $\{Bel_x, x\in(0,\alpha]\}$ is enough to compute the bounds induced by the rule "if $x\in A$ then $y\in B(\alpha)$" on the belief of other events. Especially it can be checked that $Bel_x(A)=x=Bel_x(B)$ so that inf $\{Bel(A)\mid \mathrm{Bel}_A(B)\geqslant\alpha\}=0$, that is, no constraint is induced on the belief in A or in B by the rule, which is satisfactory. For $x=0$, Bel_x corresponds to the material implication, which appears as a limit case. However, the least specific belief function satisfying $Bel(\bar{A}\cup B)\geqslant\alpha$ is not a solution to the constraint $Bel_A(B)\geqslant\alpha$.

6. BELIEF FUNCTION APPROACHES TO SETS OF UNCERTAIN CONDITIONAL STATEMENTS

In the preceding section three approaches have been laid bare to the modeling of uncertain conditional statements using belief functions. Suppose there are several conditional statements of the form $A_i\rightarrow B_i(\alpha_i)$, each one being respresented by a set of belief functions **B**. Two approaches have been proposed in the literature to handle knowledge bases with belief functions:

i. For each statement, a belief function in $\mathbf{B}_i$ is selected to represent the conditional statement. Then Dempster's rule is used to combine the various belief functions. This approach is, for instance, the one in Chatalic et al. (1987) and seems to be most widely used in belief function–based reasoning models (e.g., Shafer et al., 1987; Shenoy and Shafer, 1986; Zarley et al., 1988; Shenoy, 1989; Saffiotti and Umkehrer, 1991). The selection of the proper belief function for representing $A_i\rightarrow B_i(\alpha)_i$ is usually based on material implication and equation (12).

ii. Select a global belief function *Bel* in the intersection $\bigcap_{i=1,n}\mathbf{B}_i$. In other words, each uncertain statement is viewed as a constraint, and *Bel* must satisfy all the constraints. This methodology was suggested by the authors in a previous paper (Dubois and Prade, 1986).

Although the first approach has been widely studied, we claim that it may lead to counterintuitive results because of the lack of idempotency of the Dempster rule of combination. Indeed it presupposes that the granules of knowledge in a knowledge base are independent, while most of the time they are logically linked. Another point is that the representation of conditional statements using either the material implication or the Dempster rule of conditioning also leads to counterintuitive results when improperly facing cases in nonmonotonic reasoning (Pearl, 1990). It is shown here that only the model of conditional statements based on the focusing rule is capable of solving typical cases in nonmonotonic reasoning, without resorting to a modification of the knowledge base.

Let us consider two examples that will be called the "penguin example (PE)" and the "colibri example (CE)." Informally, the two knowledge bases contain the following information:

(PE): Tweety is a penguin
birds are expected to fly
penguins are birds
flying penguins are very surprising

(CE): Kim is a colibri
birds are expected to fly
colibris are birds
colibris almost certainly fly (unless wounded, etc.)

Let *P* mean a penguin, *B* mean a bird, *C* mean a colibri, and *F* mean a fly. We shall adopt a logic style to deal with the knowledge bases, which now read

(PE): $B\ F(\alpha)$
$P \rightarrow B(\beta)$
$P \rightarrow \neg F(\lambda)$
with $\beta > \lambda > \alpha$

(CE): $B \rightarrow F(\alpha)$
$C \rightarrow B(\beta)$
$C \rightarrow F(\gamma)$
with $\beta > \gamma > \alpha$

The coefficient β is usually equal to 1, but this is not assumed here. Each knowledge base will be treated with each approach alternatively.

6.1. Material implication and Dempster's rule of combination

This example has been considered by the authors previously (Dubois and Prade, 1988b). Anomalies have been pointed out that are recalled here. Rules are represented as follows:

- $B \to F(\alpha)$ translates into $m_1(\neg B \vee F) = \alpha$, $m_1(T) = 1 - \alpha$ (T = tautology)
- $P \to B(\beta)$ translates into $m_2(\neg P \vee B) = \beta$, $m_2(T) = 1 - \beta$
- $P \to \neg F(\lambda)$ translates into $m_3(\neg P \vee \neg F) = \lambda, m_3(T) = 1 - \lambda$

and we assume $m_4(P) = 1$ in order to express that Tweety is a penguin. Table 4.1 summarizes the result of computing $m_1 \oplus m_2 \oplus m_3 \oplus m_4 \oplus$ on (PE):

Table 4.1: The penguin example.

Focal sentences	weight	implies F?
$\perp$ (contradiction)	$\alpha\beta\lambda$	/
$P \wedge B \wedge F$	$\alpha\beta(1-\lambda)$	F
$P \wedge B \wedge \neg F$	$(1-\alpha)\beta\lambda$	$\neg F$
$P \wedge B$	$(1-\alpha)\beta(1-\lambda)$	/
$P \wedge \neg B \wedge \neg F$	$\alpha(1-\beta)\lambda$	$\neg F$
$P \wedge (\neg B \vee F)$	$\alpha(1-\beta)(1-\lambda)$	/
$P \wedge \neg F$	$(1-\alpha)(1-\beta)\lambda$	$\neg F$
P	$(1-\alpha)(1-\beta)(1-\lambda)$	/

It gives $Bel_P^+(F) = \dfrac{\beta\alpha(1-\lambda)}{1-\alpha\beta\lambda}$, $Bel_P^+(\neg F) = \dfrac{\lambda(1-\alpha\beta)}{1-\alpha\beta\lambda}$ after normalization.

The usual case is when $\beta = 1$. Then the conclusion is

$$Bel_P^+(F) = \frac{\alpha(1-\lambda)}{1-\alpha\lambda},\ Bel_P^+(\neg F) = \frac{\alpha(1-\alpha)}{1-\alpha\lambda}$$

We find $Bel_P^+(F) \geqslant Bel_P^+(\neg F)$ as soon as $\alpha \geqslant \lambda$. Especially if $\alpha = \lambda$ we remain in total uncertainty as to whether the penguin Tweety flies or not since $Bel_P^+(F) = Bel_P^+(\neg F)$; on the contrary, the expected result should be $Bel(\neg F) = \lambda$, $Bel(F) = 0$, that is, being surprised at Tweety flying.

Let us consider the other knowledge base with Kim, the colibri. P is changed into C and m_3 into $m'_3(\neg C \vee F) = \gamma$, $m'_3(T) = 1 - \gamma$. It gives $Bel_C^+(F) = \alpha\beta + \gamma(1 - \alpha\beta)$, $Bel_C^+(\neg F) = 0$ (see Table 4.2). When $\beta = 1$ (the usual case) $Bel_C^+(F) = \alpha + \gamma - \alpha\gamma > \gamma$; there is a very unnatural reinforcement effect between two rules, that is, being a bird and a colibri are considered as independent reasons to fly, even when being a colibri implies being a bird ($\beta = 1$). Again we would expect $Bel(F) = \gamma$ in the presence of a colibri. Note that the strange reinforcement effect works whenever $\beta > 0$.

Table 4.2: The colibri example.

Focal sentences	weight	implies F?
$C \wedge B \wedge F$	$\alpha\beta\gamma$	F
$C \wedge B \wedge F$	$(\alpha\beta)(1-\gamma)$	F
$C \wedge B \wedge F$	$(1-\alpha)\beta\gamma$	F
$C \wedge B$	$(1-\alpha)\beta(1-\gamma)$	/
$C \wedge F$	$\alpha(1-\beta)\gamma$	F
$C \wedge (\neg B \vee F)$	$\alpha(1-\beta)(1-\gamma)$	/
$C \wedge F$	$(1-\alpha)(1-\beta)\gamma$	F
C	$(1-\alpha)(1-\beta)(1-\gamma)$	/

If we add to (PE) the fact "Tweety is a bird" ($m_5(B) = 1$) on top of Tweety being a penguin, we get

$$Bel^+_{P \cap B}(F) = \frac{(1-\lambda)\alpha}{1-\alpha\lambda} \qquad Bel^+_{P \cap B}(\neg F) = \frac{\lambda(1-\alpha)}{1-\alpha\lambda}$$

that is, the effect of the rule $P \to B$ (β) is canceled. The same happens in the colibri case.

Note that the facts "tweety is a penguin," "Kim is a colibri" have been entered as $m_4(P) = 1$ and $m'_4(C) = 1$ respectively, that is, we have tackled the question-answering problem using the updating rule. If we use the focusing rule and compute $Bel_P(F)$, $Bel_P(\neg F)$, $Bel_C(F)$, $Bel_C(\neg F)$ using $m_1 \oplus m_2 \oplus m_3$ and $m_1 \oplus m_2 \oplus m'_3$

respecively, we get 0 everywhere; the focusing rule does not work here either. The above anomalies are partly due to a blind use of Dempster's rule of combination on pieces of knowledge that are not logically independent.

6.2. Material implication and constraint-based reasoning

The knowledge base PE is then viewed as the set **B** of belief functions verifying

$$\begin{aligned} &Bel(\neg B \vee F) \geqslant \alpha \\ &Bel(\neg P \vee B) \geqslant \beta \qquad \text{(PE)} \\ &Bel(\neg P \vee \neg F) \geqslant \lambda \end{aligned}$$

The fact "Tweety is a penguin" is again entered as $Bel(P) = 1$. From previous results (Dubois and Prade, 1986), it is easy to derive

$$\frac{Bel(P) = 1 \quad Bel(\neg P \vee B) \geqslant \beta}{Bel(B) \geqslant \beta} \qquad \frac{Bel(B) \geqslant \beta \quad Bel(\neg B \vee F) \geqslant \alpha}{Bel(F) \geqslant \max(0,\alpha+\beta-1)}$$

$$\frac{Bel(\neg P \vee \neg F) \geqslant \lambda \quad Bel(P) = 1}{Bel(\neg F) \geqslant \lambda}$$

Clearly, if $\lambda + \max(0, \alpha + \beta - 1) \geqslant 1$, that is, $\alpha + \beta + \lambda > 2$ the two conclusions on F and $\neg F$ are contradicting each other; the set of constraints becomes inconsistent. Hence updating the PE knowledge base using $Bel(P) = 1$ does not solve the penguin example in a satisfactory way, since most of the time $\beta = 1, \alpha > 0.5$ and $\lambda > 0.5$ in this example. Note that $Bel(P \wedge F)$ and $Bel(\neg P \wedge F)$ can take arbitrarily small values using (PE) as constraints, since the belief function Bel_1 such that

$$\begin{aligned} &m_1((\neg B \vee F) \wedge (\neg P \vee B) \wedge (\neg P \vee \neg F)) = \max(\alpha,\beta,\lambda) \\ &m_1(\Omega) = 1 - \max(\alpha,\beta,\lambda) \end{aligned}$$

satisfies all the constraints (PE), but $(\neg B \vee F) \wedge (\neg P \vee B) \wedge (\neg P \vee \neg F)$ does not imply $P \wedge F$, nor $P \wedge \neg F$. Hence $Bel_P(F) = Bel_P(\neg F) = 0$ using the focusing rule on the belief functions satisfying (PE). Again the modeling of the knowledge base is not satisfactory. Here this is clearly due to the use of material implication. Using the CE knowledge base, similiar computations lead to $Bel_C^+(F) \geqslant \max(\gamma, \alpha + \beta - 1)$, which is appealing when $\gamma > \alpha + \beta - 1$ (there is no longer any reinforcement) but strange if $\gamma < \alpha + \beta - 1$, since the result then seems to contradict the conditional statement $C \to F(\gamma)$. If the focusing rule is applied, it leads once more to $Bel_C(F) = Bel_C(\neg F) = 0$, and this contradicts the rule $C \to F(\gamma)$ again.

6.3. Updating-based representation and constraint-based reasoning

Now the knowledge base PE is interpreted as the set **B** of belief functions verifying the following constraints, expressing the Dempster rule of conditioning for representing each rule:

$$\left.\begin{array}{l} Pl(\neg F \wedge B) \leqslant (1-\alpha)Pl(B) \\ Pl(P \wedge \neg B) \leqslant (1-\beta)Pl(P) \\ Pl(P \wedge F) \leqslant (1-\lambda)Pl(P) \end{array}\right\} \Leftrightarrow \left\{\begin{array}{l} Bel(\neg B \vee F) \geqslant 1-(1-\alpha)Pl(B) \\ Bel(\neg P \vee B) \geqslant 1-(1-\beta)Pl(P) \\ Bel(\neg P \vee \neg F) \geqslant 1-(1-\lambda)Pl(P) \end{array}\right.$$

If we add $Bel(P) = 1$, it easily comes, since $Pl(P) = 1$:

$$Bel_P^+(F) \geqslant \max(o,(\alpha - 1)Pl(B) + \beta) \geqslant \max(0, \alpha + \beta - 1);$$
$$Bel_P^+(\neg F) \geqslant \lambda$$

that is, we meet the same type of problems as with the use of material implication. The use of the focusing rule for question answering, the computation of $Bel_P(F)$ and $Bel_P(\neg F)$, also leads to paradoxical results as in section 6.2.

6.4. Focusing-based representation and constraint-based reasoning

Lastly, the knowledge base PE is interpreted using the focusing rule to represent the conditional statements as

$$\begin{array}{ll} Bel_B(F) \geqslant \alpha & \\ Bel_P(B) \geqslant \beta & \text{(PE')} \\ Bel_P(\neg F) \geqslant \lambda & \end{array}$$

It is easy to prove (Dubois and Prade, 1992) that from $Bel_B(F) \geqslant \alpha$ and $Bel_p(B) \geqslant \beta$, no constraint can be derived on $Bel_P(F)$, nor on $Bel_p(\neg F)$. For instance, consider the feasible assignment

$$m(P \wedge \neg B \wedge \neg F) = (1-\beta)/2 \qquad m(\neg P \wedge B \wedge \neg F) = (1-\alpha)/2$$
$$m(P \wedge B \wedge \neg F) = \beta/2 \qquad m(\neg P \wedge B \wedge F) = \alpha/2$$

and then $Bel(P \wedge F) = 0 = Bel_P(F)$. Another feasible assignment is $m(P \wedge B \wedge F) = 1$, which forces $Bel_P(F) = Bel_P(B) = 1$, hence $Bel_P(\neg F) = 0$. Therefore when Tweety is known to be a penguin, only the third constraint will be productive and the expected answer is provided. When Tweety is merely known to be a bird, only the first constraint is active, and Tweety is expected to fly.

When Tweety is known to be both a bird and a penguin, then we must compute $\bar{Bel}_{P \wedge B}(F)$ and $Bel_{P \wedge B}(\neg F)$. It is easy to check that $Bel_{P \wedge B}(F) = 0$. To see it, consider only conditional belief functions that are probabilities. Then we have solve the inequalities $P(F|B) \geqslant \alpha$, $P(B|P) \geqslant \beta$, $P(\neg F|P) \geqslant \lambda$ and calculate inf $P(F|P \wedge B) = {}_{df} P_*(F|P \wedge B)$. Using a result in Dubois et al. (1990) we can establish:

$$P_*(F|P \wedge B) = \max\left(0, 1 - \frac{1 - P_*(F|B)}{P_*(P|B)}, 1 - \frac{1 - P_*(F|P)}{P_*(B|P)}\right)$$

With $P_*(P|B) = 0$, $P_*(F|B) = \alpha$, $P_*(F|P) = 0$, $P_*(B|P) = \beta$, it gives $P_*(F|B \wedge P) = 0$, hence $Bel_{B \wedge P}(F) = 0$.

Similarly, we can compute $P_*(F|B \wedge P) = 1 - P_*(\neg F|B \wedge P)$ as follows

$$P_*(F|P \wedge B) = \min\left(1, \frac{P_*(F|B)}{P_*(P|B)}, \frac{P_*(F|P)}{P_*(B|P)}\right) = \min\left(1, \frac{1-\lambda}{\beta}\right)$$

since $P_*(F|P) = 1 - \lambda$ and $P_*(B|P) = \beta$. Hence we find $P_*(\neg F|P \wedge B) = \max\left(0, 1 - \frac{1-\lambda}{\beta}\right)$ and we conclude

$$Bel_{P \wedge B}(\neg F) \geqslant \max\left(0, 1 - \frac{1-\lambda}{\beta}\right) \qquad (13)$$

since $Bel_{P \wedge B}(\neg F) = \inf\{P(\neg F|P \wedge B), P \geqslant Bel, Bel \text{ feasible}\}$. The equality in (13) is reached insofar as there is a feasible belief function that saturates the three constraints induced by (PE'), otherwise λ and β in (13) must be changed into higher values, which would cause $Bel_{P \wedge B}(\neg F)$ to be higher. But it is easy to check that the three constraints can be saturated by a probability assignment on $\{P, \neg P\} \times \{F, \neg F\} \times \{B, \neg B\}$. Hence the equality can hold in (13). For $\beta = 1$, we get $P \wedge B = P$ and $Bel_{P \wedge B}(\neg F) \geqslant \lambda$ as expected. In the general case ($\beta \leqslant 1$) we conclude that Tweety has a tendency not to fly which reflects our strength of belief that penguins are birds; if $\lambda + \beta < 1$, we do not know about Tweety flying or not.

In the colibri example, with a similar reasoning we get:

$$Bel_{B \wedge C}(F) \geqslant 1 - \frac{1-\gamma}{\beta}$$

$$Bel_{B \wedge C}(\neg F) \geqslant 0$$

Especially when being a colibri and being a bird are viewed as unrelated properties ($\beta = 0$) there is no certainty that special individuals that are both colibris and birds would fly, while in the usual case ($\beta = 1$) $Bel_{B \wedge C}(F) \geqslant \gamma$ is derived. Clearly, modeling conditional statements by means of the focusing rule seems to produce more natural results than other models, and the constraint-based approach also looks more natural. Especially there seems to be a full agreement between the belief function approach and the one based on conditional probability (Dubois et al., 1990). This is to be expected as long as a set of constraints of the form $\{Bel_{A_i}(B_i) \geqslant \alpha_i, i = 1, n\}$ can be saturated by a belief function that is a probability measure.

In this section question answering and rule representation are done via focusing. On the contrary, if we use an updating approach for question answering, namely if we add $Bel(P \wedge B) = 1$, the knowledge base (PE′) becomes

$$\frac{Bel(F \wedge B \wedge P)}{Bel(F \wedge B \wedge P) + Pl(\neg F \wedge B \wedge P)} \geqslant \alpha; \; Bel(P \wedge B \wedge \neg F) \geqslant \lambda$$

which forces to allocate masses to $P \wedge B$ and its implicants only:

$$m(B \wedge F \wedge P)(1-\alpha) \geqslant \alpha(m(B \wedge \neg F \wedge P) + m(P \wedge B))$$
$$m(B \wedge F \wedge P) + m(B \wedge \neg F \wedge P) + m(B \wedge P) = 1$$
$$m(P \wedge B \wedge \neg F) \geqslant \lambda$$

that is, $m(P \wedge B \wedge F) \geqslant \alpha, m(P \wedge B \wedge \neg F) \geqslant \lambda$. If (as is usually the case) $\alpha + \lambda > 1$, the knowledge base (PE′) becomes inconsistent with $Bel(P \wedge B) = 1$. The difference between focusing and updating is thus again patent in this case. The trouble with the updating mode of question answering is that $Bel(P \wedge B) = 1$ means more than just "Tweety is a bird and a penguin"; it claims that all animals are penguins and are birds.

Remark: Other authors (Smets and Hsia, 1990; Wilson, 1990; Smets, 1992) have dealt with the above type of examples and have advocated

Dempster's rule of conditioning for the modeling of rules. However, they have heavily relied on the introduction of supplementary symbols expressing variants of abnormality predicates so as to cope with logical dependence. For instance, they have tried to model the statement "birds fly" by means of a sure rule of the form $B \wedge TB \rightarrow F$ where TB means "typical bird," a typical bird being a bird that is not abnormal. Then the belief weight, allocated to the rule $B \rightarrow F$ in this paper, is allocated by these authors to the default fact TB (i.e., $Bel(TB) = 0.9$) or to an auxiliary rule claiming that "birds are generally typical" ($Bel(TB|B) = 0.9$). This technique, which has been suggested in the past in default theory (assertion predicates in Froidevaux and Kaiser [1988], and to handle exceptions in possibilistic logic (dafault facts as uncertain facts in Dubois and Prade [1988a] and in Dubois et al. [1989]) actually comes from the circumscription approach (McCarthy, 1980). Hence it is not at all specific to the belief function framework. This technique is difficult to manage in the presence of several rules with exceptions since it requires handling dependencies between the introduced auxiliary predicates. The approach proposed here, based on the focusing rule, seems to obviate the need for auxiliary predicates.

7. CONCLUSION

Beyond the particulars of the examples dealt with in this paper, the validity of the Dempster rules of combination and conditioning as universal tools of knowledge represenation and inference with belief functions is questioned. Moreover, the expression of the focusing rule in terms of upper and lower bounds of a conditional probability conditioned upon an ill-defined event shows that this rule is in the spirit of the problem of the transportation of a probability measure by a multivalued mapping, which led Dempster to introduce upper and lower probabilities, renamed as belief and plausibility functions by Shafer. The literature in belief function propagation relies heavily on Dempster's rules of combination and conditioning, which are presented as a counterpart and a formal generalization of Bayesian nets (Shenoy and Shafer, 1990). Nevertheless, the situation in belief function theory is quite different from the one in probability theory. In the latter, Bayesian nets are often proposed as a very convenient way of representing big joint probability distributions obtained from statistics, under the form of a graph weighted by conditional probabilities. It is computationally efficient, and helps in explaining the data. Hence, Bayesian conditioning is used as a way of cutting a joint distribution into independent components as observed in the data.

On the contrary, in belief function theory, Dempster's rule of combination is used as a way of aggregating pieces of knowledge, supposedly independent. But it seems hopeless to assume that subjective uncertain pieces of knowledge as supplied by experts will be independent – they may especially be inconsistent. What this paper tends to reveal is the lack of a systematic tool for deriving a belief function from dependent, possibly inconsistent pieces of knowledge like uncertain conditional statements. Indeed, these statements seem best modeled via the focusing rule of conditioning, and we are left with a constrained family of belief functions, one of which should be chosen. Despite some past investigation on counterparts of the maximal entropy principle in evidence theory, which would guide this selection (Dubois and Prade, 1986), no satisfactory answer to this problem seems to be available (see Hsia, 1991). Once this problem is solved, there remains the one of splitting a belief function into independent components to be merged by means of the Dempster rule of combination. Only when these two questions are addressed will computational techniques developed by Shafer and his colleagues be safely used in automated reasoning.

ACKNOWLEDGMENTS

The authors wish to thank Serafin Moral and Philippe Smets who partially motivated the contents of this paper. Special thanks are due to Philippe Smets for his extensive comments on a preliminary draft.

BIBLIOGRAPHY

Chatalic, P., Dubois, D. and Prade, H. (1987). An approach to approximate reasoning based on the Dempster rule of combination. *Innt. J. of Expert Systems, Research and Applications* 1: 67–85.

de Campos, L.M., Lamata, M.T., and Moral, S. (1990). The concept of conditional fuzzy measure. *Int. J. of Intelligent Systems* 5: 237–46.

Dempster, A.P. (1967). Upper and lower probabilities induced by a multivaled mapping. *Ann. Math. Stat.* 38: 325–39.

Domotor, Z. (1985). Probability kinematics—Conditionals and entropy principles. *Synthese* 63: 74–115.

Dubois, D. and Prade, H. (1986). The principle of minimum specificity as a basis for evidential reasoning. In B. Bouchon and R.R. Yager (eds.), Uncertainty in knowledge-based systems (*Proc. of the Int. Conf. on Information Processing and Management of Uncertainty in Knowledge-Based Systems* [IPMU], June/July 1986), *Lecture Notes in Computer Science*, Vol. 286, pp. 75–84. Berlin: Springer-Verlag.

Dubois, D. and Prade, H. (1988a). Default reasoning and possibility theory. *Artificial Intelligence* 35: 243–57.

Dubois, D. and Prade, H. (1988b). Representation and combination of uncertainty with belief functions and possibility measures. *Computational Intelligence* 4: 244–64.

Dubois, D. and Prade, H. (1992). Evidence, knowledge and belief functions. *Int. J. of Approximate Reasoning* 6(3): 295–319.

Dubois, D., Lang, J., and Prade, H. (1989). Automated reasoning using possibilistic logic: Semantics, belief revision and variable certainty weights. *Proc. of the Fifth Workshop on Uncertainty in Artificial Intelligence*, Windsor, Ontario, Aug. 18–20, pp. 81–87. Revised version to appear in *IEEE Trans. on Data and Knowledge Engineering.*

Dubois, D., Prade, H., and Toucas, J.M. (1990). Inference with imprecise numerical quantifiers. In Z.W. Ras and M. Zemankova (eds.), *Intelligent systems — State of the art and future directions*, pp. 52–72. Chichester: Ellis Horwood.

Eddy, W.F. and Pei, G.P. (1986). Structure of rule-based belief functions. *IBM J. of Res. and Develop.* 30: 93–101.

Fagin, R. and Halpern, J.Y. (1990). A new approach to updating beliefs. *Proc. of the Sixth Conf. on Uncertainty in Artificial Intelligence*, Cambridge, MA, July 27–93, pp. 317–25.

Froidevaux, C. and Kayser, D. (1988). Inheritance in semantic networks and default logic. In P. Smets, A. Mamdani, D. Dubois, and H. Prade (eds.), *Non-standard logics for automated reasoning*, pp. 179–212. New York: Academic Press.

Gilboa, I. and Schmeidler, D. (1991). Updating ambiguous beliefs. Tech. Report, School of Math. Science, Univ. of Tel-Aviv.

Hsia, Y.T. (1991). Characterizing belief with minimum commitment. *Proc. of the Twelfth Int. Joint Conf. on Artificial Intelligence* (IJCAI-91), Sydney, Australia, Aug. 24–30, pp. 1184–89.

Jaffray, J.Y. (1990). Bayesian updating and belief functions. *Proc. of the Third Int. Conf. on Information Processing and Management of Uncertainty in Knowledge-Based Systems* (IPMU'90), Paris, July: ENSTA, 449–51.

Kämpke, T. (1988). About assessing and evaluating uncertain inferences within the theory of evidence. *Decision Support Systems* 4: 433–39.

Kruse, R., Schwecke E., and Heinsohn, J. (1991). *Uncertainty handling in knowledge based systems – Numerical methods.* Heidelberg: Springer-Verlag.

Kyburg, H.E., Jr. (1987). Bayesian and non-Bayesian evidential updating. *Artificial Intelligence* 31: 271–94.

Levi, F. (1983). Consonance, dissonance and evidentiary mechanisms. In P. Gärdenfors, P. Hansson, and N.E. Sahlin (eds.), *Evidentiary value: Philosphical, judicial and psychological aspects of a theory*, pp. 27–43. Lund, Sweden: C.W.K. Gleerups.

Lewis, D. (1976). Probabilities of conditionals and conditional probabilities. *Philos. Review* 85: 297–315.

McCarthy, J. (1980). Circumscription — A form of nonmonotonic reasoning. *Artificial Intelligence* 27: 27–39.

Moral, S. and de Campos, L.M. (1991). Updating uncertain information. In B. Bouchon-Meunier, R.R. Yager, and L.A. Zadeh (eds.), Uncertainty in knowledge bases (*Proc. of the Third Int. Conf. on Information Processing and Management of Uncertainty in Knowledge-Based Systems* [IPMU'90], Paris, July 1990), *Lecture Notes in Computer Science*, Vol. 521, pp. 58–67. Berlin: Springer-Verlag.

Pearl, J. (1988), *Probabilistic reasoning in intelligent systems*. San Mateo, CA: Morgan Kaufmann.

Pearl, J. (1990). Reasoning with belief functions. An analysis of compatibility. *Int. J. of Approximate Reasoning* 4: 363–89.

Ruspini, E.H. (1986). Approximate deduction in single evidential bodies. *Proc. of the Second Workshop on Uncertainty in Artificial Intelligence*, University of Pennsylvania, Aug. 8–10, pp. 215–22.

Saffiotti, A., and Umkehrer, E. (1991). PULCINELLA: A general tool for propagating uncertainty in valuation networks. *Proc. of the Seventh Conf. on Uncertainty in Artifical Intelligence*, Los Angeles, CA, July 13–15, (B.D. D'Ambrosio, P. Smets, P.P. Bonissone, eds.), pp. 323–31. San Mateo, CA: Morgan Kaufmann.

Shafer, G. (1976a). A theory of statistical evidence. In Harper and Hooker (eds.), *Foundations of probability theory, statistical inference, and statistical theories sciences*. Dordrecht: Reidel.

Shafer, G. (1976b). *A mathematical theory of evidence*. Princeton, NJ: Princeton University Press.

Shafer, G. (1990). Perspectives on the theory and practice of belief functions. *Int. J. Approximate Reasoning* 4(5/6): 323–62.

Shafer, G., Shenoy, P.P., and Mellouli, K. (1987). Propagating belief functions in qualitative Markov trees. *Int. J. of Approximate Reasoning* 1(4): 349–400.

Shenoy, P.P. (1989). A valuation-based language for expert systems. *Int. J. of Approximate Reasoning* 3: 383–411.

Shenoy, P.P. and Shafer, G. (1986). Propagating belief functions using local computations. *IEEE Expert* 1: 43–52.

Shenoy, P.P. and Shafer, G. (1990). Axioms for probability and belief-function propagation. In R.D. Shachter, T.S. Levitt, L.N.. Kanal, and J.F. Lemmer (eds), *Uncertainty in artificial intelligence* 4, pp. 169–98. Amsterdam: North-Holland.

Smets, P. (1987). Upper and lower probability functions versus belief functions. *Proc. of the Symp. on Fuzzy Systems and Knowledge Engineering*, Guangzhou, China, July 10–16, pp. 17–21.

Smets, P. (1988). Belief functions. In P. Smets, E.F. Mamdani, D. Dubois, and H. Prade (eds.), *Non-standard logics for automated reasoning*, pp. 253–86. New York: Academic Press.

Smets, P. (1990). The combination of evidence in the transferable belief model. *IEEE Trans. on Pattern Analysis and Machine Intelligence* 12: 447–58.

Smets, P. (1992). Resolving misunderstandings about belief functions. *Int. J. of Approximate Reasoning* 6: 321–44.

Smets, P. and Hsia, Y.T, (1990). Default reasoning and the transferable belief model. *Proc. of the Sixth Conf. on Uncertainty in Artificial Intelligence*, Cambridge, MA, July 27–29, pp. 529–37.

Walley, P. (1991). *Statistical inference with imprecise probabilities*. London: Chapman and Hall.

Williams, P.M. (1980). Bayesian conditionalisation of the principle of minimum information. *Brit. J. Phil. Sci.* 31: 131–44.

Wilson, N. (1990). Rule, belief functions and default logic. *Proc. of the Sixth Conf. on Uncertainty in Artificial Intelligence*, Cambridge, MA, July 27–29, pp. 443–49.

Zarley, D.K., Hsia, Y.T., and Shafer, G. (1988). Evidential reasoning using DELIEF. Working Paper No. 193, School of Business, University of Kansas, Lawrence.

5 Combination of compatible belief functions and relation of specificity

Alain CHATEAUNEUF

Abstract: Necessary and sufficient conditions are given for two belief functions f_1 and f_2 on a finite set of events $a = 2^S$ to be compatible (i.e., for the nonemptiness of the set P of probability measures on (S, a), which simultaneously dominate f_1 and f_2). Hence for every $X \in \mathbb{R}^S$, a computing method of the infimum over P of the mathematical expectations $E_P(X)$ is deduced. As a result we obtain, in the lower-probability approach, a combination rule for two compatible belief functions. The paper ends with a characterization of the relation of specificity.

Keywords: compatible belief functions, lower probabilities, combination rules, relation of specificity.

1. INTRODUCTION

As emphasized by Shafer (1990) in his prominent paper "Perspectives on the theory and practice of belief functions," it is a well-established point in the literature that "a probability-bound interpretation is incompatible with Dempster's rule for combining belief functions."

However, natural circumstances arise where belief functions defined on a finite set of events $a = 2^S$ should be interpreted as lower bounds on some unknown true probability. Thus, if we assume as in Dempster (1967) that $(X, 2^X, \pi)$ is a finite probability space endowed with a multivalued mapping Γ from X to $a^* = a \backslash \{\emptyset\}$, which informs us that if $x \in X$ occurs then $\Gamma(x)$ obtains (such a space $(X, 2^X, \pi, \Gamma)$ will be called a message space), one can assert that each event $A \in a$ is at least as likely to obtain as any event with probability $f(A) = \sum_{B \subset A} m(B)$ where $m(B) = \sum_{\{x \in X, (x) = B\}} \pi(\{x\})$ and f proves to be a belief function.

Suppose now that two experts $i\,(i = 1, 2)$ only receive partial information $(X_i, 2^{X_i}, \pi_i), \Gamma_i \in a^*(X_i)$ about the foregoing mechanism, where elements of X_i form a partition of X, $\pi_i(\{y\}) = \pi(y)$ for all $x \in X_i$ and $\Gamma_i(y) = \bigcup_{\{x \in X: x \in y\}} \Gamma(x)$ for all $y \in X_i$. Obviously the experts' information will lead to (compatible) belief functions $f_i (i = 1, 2)$, and in such a case (referred to in the sequel as "belief functons f_1 and f_2 are conected with [a same] message space $(X, 2^x, \pi, \Gamma)$"), there is some need to combine belief fuctions f_1 and f_2 in order to get the best possible lower bound for the probability of each event A belonging to a.

Example 1: This example, adapted from Zadeh (1983), may serve as an illustration of the previous considerations: From two successive, exhaustive and anonymous surveys of the students of a college, it follows that 30% are smokers and 80% drink alcohol. How many students both smoke and drink alcohol?

Here the set of states of nature is $S = \{(s, a), (s, na), (ns, a)\ (ns, na)\}$, where s, ns stands for smoker, nonsmoker and a, na stands for "drinks alcohol," "does not drink alcohol." Let X be the set of students, π be the "uniform" probability distribution on $(X, 2^X)$ – i.e., $\pi(\{x\}) = 1/|X|$ for all $x \in X$ where $|X|$ is the cardinal of set X– and Γ be the mapping from X to a^*, which would inform us that for the student x chosen in X the true state of nature is $\Gamma(x)$. Obviously, such a "perfect" message space $(X, 2^x, \pi, \Gamma)$ would give the exact value of the sought-for percentage. In fact, in Example 1 we receive two partial items of information. The first one indicates that there exists a partition X_1 of X in two subsets of probability 0.3 (resp.: 0.7) such that for every x belonging to the first subset (resp.: second subset) you only know – through Γ_1 – that the true state of nature is s (resp.: $S \backslash s$). Similar

[1] It should be noticed that in this paper we consider only message spaces providing exact information about the true state of nature $s \in S$. As a consequence $\Gamma(x) = \emptyset$ is impossible, contrary to Dempster (1967).

conclusions for the second partial information show that the information consists in two belief functions f_1 and f_2 on (S, a) connected with the same message space $(X, 2^X, \pi, \Gamma)$.

In this paper we consider, as above, uncertainty situations where the lower-probability interpretation of belief functions is appropriate. A set of events $a = 2^S$ (S, set of states of nature, is assumed to be finite) is given and the information about the occurrence of events is summarized through two belief functions f_1 and f_2 defined on a. Each belief function f_i can be interpreted as follows: two experts were consulted and the only claim of each expert i is that the lower probability for each event $A \in a$ is $f_i(A)$; in other words, according to **expert i, the probability measure P on (S, a) belongs to $\mathrm{P}_i = \{P \geqslant f_i$, $P \in \alpha$, the set of all probability measures on $(S, a)\}$.**[2]

Then, we are interested in knowing when two belief functions f_1 and f_2 on a are compatible, that is, when the joint information $\mathrm{P} = \mathrm{P}_1 \cap \mathrm{P}_2$ is nonempty. Moreover, in case of compatibility, we would like to summarize the joint information P through the set function $f = \inf\{P \in \mathrm{P}\}$; such a set-function f on a, to be denoted $f_1 \square f_2$, will be called the combination of the compatible belief functions f_1 and f_2.

Therefore, in the first part of this paper we give some characterizations of compatible belief functions. From these we deduce a computing method for solving problems as $\inf_{P \in \mathrm{P}} E_P(X)$,[3] where X is a mapping from S to R and P is the joint information of two compatible belief functions. The aim of this method is to reduce the computational complexity (already underlined by de Campos et al. [1988] that would result from a direct approach by linear programming in considering the whole convex set P; actually, here we show that only some set B of belief functions dominating both f_1 and f_2 has to be considered, since this set B summarizes information P. The combination rule $f_1 \square f_2$ of two compatible belief functions f_1 and f_2 is directly obtained as a result. $f_1 \square f_2$ usually differs from Dempster's rule $f_1 \oplus f_2$, all the more so because $f_1 \square f_2$ need not be a belief function. Links between $f_1 \square f_2$ and $f_1 \oplus f_2$ are examined in some detail. Notice that the examination of the case where f_1 and f_2 are **connected with the same message space has considerably facilitated-all the previous investigations.**

In the third and final part of this paper, we propose a characterization of the relation of specificity originally introduced by Yager

[2] $P \geqslant f_i$ means $P(A) \geqslant f_i(A)$, for all $A \in a$.

[3] $E_P(X)$ is the mathematical expectation of X for the probability measure P.

(1982; 1983) and reexamined by Dubois and Prade (1986) under the denomination of inclusion. More precisely, we give a characterization of uncertainty situations when expert 2 is uniformly at least as precise as another expert 1, that is, when $f_2(A) \geqslant f_1(A)$ for all $A \in a$, with f_1, f_2 belief functions on a.

We turn now to the results.

2. COMPATIBLE BELIEF FUNCTIONS

Let $f_i (i = 1, 2)$ be two belief functions on $a = 2^S$ (S finite), and let P_i be defined by $P_i = \{P \geqslant f_i, P \in \alpha$, the set of all probability measures on $(S, a)\}$; we recall what is meant, in this paper, by compatible belief functons.

Definition 1: Belief functions f_1 and f_2 are compatible if the joint information $P = P_i \cap P_2$ is nonempty.

F_i will denote the plausibility function associated with the belief function f_i: $F_i(A) = 1 - f_i(\bar{A})$ for all $A \in a$; $\bar{A}$ is the complementary set of A in S. Some further definitions are needed before coming to Theorem 1.

A mapping $g: a \to R$ is termed a (normalized) capacity[4] if it satisfies the normalization conditions $g(\emptyset) = 0$ and $g(S) = 1$, and monotonicity, that is, for all A and B in a: $A \subset B$ implies $g(A) \leqslant g(B)$. In the sequel, capacity will be short for normalized capacity. For a mapping $X: S \to R$ with values $x_1 \leqslant \ldots \leqslant x_j \leqslant \ldots \leqslant x_n$, $g(X)$ denotes the Choquet integral (Choquet, 1953) of X with respect to (w.r.t.) capacity g and:

$$g(X) = x_1 + \sum_{j=1}^{n-1} (x_{j+1} - x_j)\, g(X \geqslant x_{j+1}) \tag{1}$$

We can now give a first characterization of compatible belief functions, which states natural, easy to check, necessary, and sufficient conditions.[5]

---

[4] Apart from the trivial normalization, this definition is in accordance with Choquet's (1953) capacities.

[5] Notice that such a characterization has independently been obtained by De Campos (1987).

Theorem 1: The following three conditions are equivalent:

(i) The belief functions f_1 and f_2 are compatible.

(ii) $f_1 \leqslant F_2$ (i.e., $f_1(A) \leqslant F_2(A)$ for all $A \in a$) (2)

(iii) $f_2 \leqslant F_1$ (i.e., $f_2(A) \leqslant F_1(A)$ for all $A \in a$) (3)

Proof: First note that conditions (ii) and (iii) are trivially equivalent.

(i) ⇒ (ii): Let P be a probability measure belonging to $\mathrm{P}_1 \cap \mathrm{P}_2$, hence $P \geqslant f_1$ and $P \geqslant f_2$; $P \geqslant f_2$ implies $P \leqslant F_2$ since $P(\bar{A}) \geqslant f_2(\bar{A})$ for all $A \in a$ entails $1 - P(\bar{A}) \leqslant 1 - f_2(\bar{A})$ for all $A \in a$, therefore $f_1 \leqslant P \leqslant F_2$ and consequently $f_1 \leqslant F_2$.

(ii) ⇒ (i): Let E denote the real linear space of a-measurable real valued functions on S. It is known (e.g., Chateauneuf and Jaffray, 1989) that Choquet integrals (Definition 1) $f_1 : X \in E \rightarrow f_1(X)$ and $F_2 : X \in E \rightarrow F_2(X)$ are respectively concave and convex functions on E since f_1 (resp.: F_2) is a belief function (resp.: a plausibility function).

Condition (ii) entails $f_1(X) \leqslant F_2(X)$ for all $X \in E$. From the "Sandwich Theorem" in Fuchssteiner and Lusky (1981, p. 36), one deduces that there is an affine function P on E with $f_1 \leqslant P \leqslant F_2$. Since $f_1(\varnothing) = F_2(\varnothing) = 0$ and $f_1(S) = F_2(S) = 1$, it follows that there exists a probability measure on a also denoted P such that $f_1(A) \leqslant P(A) \leqslant F_2(A)$ for all $A \in a$, which completes the proof.

The aim of Theorem 2 is mainly to prove that two belief functions are compatible if and only if they can be connected with a same message space. In order to clarify this last notion, formally stated in the introduction, let us consider Example 2, which will be dealt with in the sequel.

Example 2: Assume that two experts receive only partial information about the following Dempster experiment: a perfect die is thrown and according to the outcome a ball is drawn at random from one of four urns. Experts are interested in getting the best possible lower bound for the probability of events of type:

$A = \{\text{The colour of the extracted ball is blue}\}$ denoted $A = \{B\}$.

Let us first give the data in case of perfect information as in (4):

$$
\begin{array}{lll}
 & \Gamma & \\
1,2 & \rightarrow \{\mathrm{B} = \text{blue}\}: & \text{urn I} \\
3 & \rightarrow \{\mathrm{B}, \mathrm{G} = \text{green}\}: & \text{urn II} \\
4,5 & \rightarrow \{\mathrm{R} = \text{red}\}: & \text{urn III} \\
6 & \rightarrow \{\mathrm{G}, \mathrm{R}\}: & \text{urn IV}
\end{array}
\qquad (4)
$$

For example, the first line means that if number one or two appears on the upper side of the die, then a ball will be drawn at random out of urn I, which contains blue balls in unknown quantity, but at least one. Let us add that information as {B, G} for urn II means that urn II contains blue and green balls in unknown quantities but again contains at least one ball.

Obviously here $X = \{1,2,3,4,5,6\}$, $\pi(\{x\}) = \frac{1}{6}$, $x \in X$, $S = \{B, G, R\}$, Γ is defined by $\Gamma(1) = \{B\}, \Gamma(2) = \{B\}, \ldots$, and lower probabilities for events belonging to $a = 2^S$ are given through the belief function f: $f(\{B\}) = \frac{2}{6}$, $f(\{B \cup G\}) = \frac{3}{6}, \ldots$

Assume now that expert i ($i = 1,2$) only gets a less informative message, resulting from a partition X_i of X.

Partial information of expert 1 is as in (5):

$$\begin{array}{ccc} & \Gamma_1 & \\ \{1,2,3\} & \to & \{B \cup G\} \\ \{4,5,6\} & \to & \{R \cup G\} \end{array} \tag{5}$$

The first line of (5) indicates that if 1, 2, or 3 appears on the die, then the color of the drawn ball will be either blue or green. Indeed $\Gamma_1(\{1,2,3\}) = \bigcup_{x \in \{1,2,3\}} \Gamma(x)$.

Here $X_1 = \Big\{\{1,2,3\}, \{4,5,6\}\Big\}$, and lower probabilities for events $A \in a$ are given by the belief function $f_1 : f_1(\{B\}) = 0$, $f_1(\{B \cup G\}) = \frac{3}{6}, \ldots$

Partial information of expert 2 is as below:

$$\begin{array}{ccc} & \Gamma_2 & \\ \{1,2\} & \to & \{B\} \\ \{3,4,5\} & \to & \{B \cup G \cup R\} \\ \{6\} & \to & \{G \cup R\} \end{array}$$

Hence the belief function f_2 of expert 2: $f_2(\{B\}) = 2/6$, $f_2(\{B \cup G\}) = 0, \ldots$

Remark 1: According to the definition, belief function f_1 and f_2 are clearly connected to a same message space. Evidently, it follows that f_1 and f_2 are compatible; actually since they result from poorer information than f's, they satisfy: $f_1 \leqslant f$, $f_2 \leqslant f$. ($P_1 \cap P_2$ is nonempty because every belief function, hence f, is dominated by some probability measure.)

The set of focal elements of a belief function f_i, will be denoted F_i: $F_i = \{A \in a, m_i(A) > 0\}$ where m_i is the Möbius inverse of f_i (e.g., Chateauneuf and Jaffray, 1989), or else the basic probability assignment of f_i in Shafer's (1976) terminology.

We can now prove the following preliminary result.

Lemma 1: Let f be a belief function on (S, a), with Möbius inverse m and F as set of focal elements, and let P be a probability measure on (S, a). The following assertions are equivalent.

(i) $P \geqslant f$

(ii) There exists a mapping $q: S \times a \to R^+$ such that

(a) $q(s,A) > 0 \Rightarrow s \in A$ and $A \in F$ (6)

(b) $P(\{s\}) = \sum_{\{A \in a, A \supset \{s\}\}} q(s,A)$, for all $s \in S$ (7)

(c) $m(A) = \sum_{\{s \in A\}} q(s,A)$, for all $A \in F$ (8)

Proof: First let us recall the known result (Dempster, 1967; Chateauneuf and Jaffray, 1989), that (i) is equivalent to the existence of a mapping $\alpha: S \times a \to R^+$ such that:

(a) $\alpha(s,A) > 0 \Rightarrow s \in A$ (9)

(b) $\sum_{s \in A} \alpha(s,A) = 1$, for all $A \in a$ (10)

(c) $P(\{s\}) = \sum_{\{A \in a, A \supset \{s\}\}} \alpha(s,A).m(A)$, for all $s \in S$ (11)

(i) $\Rightarrow$ (ii): Define $q: S \times a \to R^+$ by $q(s,A) = \alpha(s,A).m(A)$. That q satisfies (6), (7), (8) is immediate.

(ii) $\Rightarrow$ (i): Define $\alpha: S \times a \to R^+$ by $\alpha(s,A) = \dfrac{q(s,A)}{m(A)}$ if $A \in F$, $\alpha(s, A) = 0$ if $s \notin A$ and $\alpha(s, A) \geqslant$ such that $\sum_{s \in A} \alpha(s,A) = 1$ if $A \in F$.

That α satisfies (9), (10), (11) is immediate, which completes the proof.

We can now establish the main result of this section.

Theorem 2: The following three assertions are equivalent:

(i) The belief functions f_1 and f_2 are compatible.

(ii) There exists a mapping $Q: a \times a \to R^+$ such that:

(a) (i) $Q(A,B) > 0 \Rightarrow A \times B \in F_1 \times F_2$ (12)

(ii) $A \cap B \neq \emptyset \Rightarrow Q(A,B) = 0$ (13)

(b) (i) $m_1(A) = \sum_{B \in F_2} Q(A,B)$ for all $A \in F_1$ (14)

(ii) $m_2(B) = \sum_{A \in F_1} Q(A,B)$ for all $B \in F_2$ (15)

(iii) The belief functions f_1 and f_2 can be connected with the same message space.

Remark 2: Notice that assertion (iii) suggests that for compatible belief functions, mappings Q satisfying condition (ii) can be interpreted as the only possible joint probabilities that expert 1 asserts that event A is obtained whereas expert 2 asserts event B, in case of connection of f_1 and f_2 with same message space (or even with two different message spaces). Thus, for Example 1 for all $A,B \in 2^S$, $Q(A,B)$ denotes the unknown percentage of students for whom the true state of nature is declared as being in A through the first survey and in B through the second one.

Such an interpretation strongly supports the present analysis, and in particular will facilitate the achievement of our combination rule.

Proof of Theorem 2:

(i)$\Rightarrow$(ii): Let P be a probability measure dominating f_1 and f_2, and let q_1 and q_2 be corresponding mapping as defined in assertion (ii) of Lemma 1. Denote $S^* = \left\{ s \in S,\ P(\{s\}) > 0 \right\}$, and define $Q: a \times a \to \mathrm{R}^+$ by:

$$Q(A,B) = 0 \quad \text{if} \quad A \cap B = \emptyset \tag{16}$$

$$Q(A,B) = 0 \quad \text{if} \quad \{s \in A \cap B,\ s \in S^*\} = \emptyset \tag{17}$$

$$Q(A,B) = \sum_{\{s \in S^*,\ s \in A \cap B\}} \frac{q_1(s,A) \cdot q_2(s,B)}{P(\{s\})} \quad \text{otherwise} \tag{18}$$

It is readily seen that Q is nonnegative and that (12) and (13) are satisfied. By symmetry, it only remains to check (14).

$$\sum_{B \in F_2} Q(A,B) = \sum_{\{s \in S^*,\ s \in A\}} \frac{q_1(s,A)}{P(\{s\})} \cdot \left(\sum_{\{B \in F_2,\ B \supset \{s\}\}} q_2(s,B) \right)$$

Since $\sum_{\{B \in F_2, B \supset \{s\}\}} q_2(s,B) = P(\{s\})$, we obtain $\sum_{B \in F_2} Q(A,B) = \sum_{\{s \in S^*, s \in A\}} q_1(s,A)$, and from (8) there follows $\sum_{B \in F_2} Q(A,B) = m_1(A)$, because (7) implies that $q_1(s,A) = 0$ if $P(\{s\}) = 0$.

(ii)$\Rightarrow$(iii): Denote $I = \{(A,B) \in a \times a,\ A \cap B \neq \emptyset\}$. Let X be a set with card I elements. Elements of X will be indexed by I: a generic element of X is $x_{(A,B)}$ with $(A,B) \in I$. Define a multivalued mapping Γ from X to a^* by $\Gamma(x_{(A,B)}) = A \cap B$, and a probability measure π on $(X, 2^X)$ by $\pi(x_{(A,B)}) = Q(A,B)$, where Q is a mapping from $a \times a$ to R^+ satisfying condition (ii) of Theorem 2. It remains to find two partitions of X, or roughly speaking, two submessage spaces of message space $(X, 2^X, \pi, \Gamma)$, leading respectively to belief functions f_1 and f_2. Let $\tau_1 = \{x_A,\ A \in a$ such that there exists $B \in a$, $(A,B) \in I\}$ be a first partition of X, where $x_A = \bigcup_{\{(C,B) \in I, C = A\}} x_{(C,B)}$; the induced multivalued mapping Γ_1 satisfies $\Gamma_1(x_A) = \bigcup_{\{(C,B) \in I, C = A\}} \Gamma(x_{(C,B)})$, hence $\Gamma_1(x_A) = A$, and the induced probability measure π_1 clearly satisfies $\pi_1(\{x_A\}) = \sum_{B \in a} Q(A,B)$, therefore $\pi_1(\{x_A\}) = m_1(A)$ for all $A \in a$; it follows that the Möbius inverse of the corresponding belief function is m_1. This entails that f_1 can be connected with the message space $(X, 2^X, \pi, \Gamma)$. A symmetric reasoning would imply the same conclusion for f_2, which completes this part of the proof.

(iii) $\Rightarrow$ (i): As noted in Remark 1, belief functions f_1 and f_2 are clearly compatible because $f_1 \leqslant f$ and $f_2 \leqslant f$, since f_1 and f_2 "benefit" from a lower information if compared to f. For sake of completeness, let us give a formal proof of $f_i \leqslant f$. We use notations given in the introduction. Let A belong to a. $f_i(A) = \pi_i\left\{\{y \in X_i,\ \Gamma_i(y) \subset A\}\right\}$, but $\left\{y \in X_i, \Gamma_i(y) \subset A\right\}$ is included in $\left\{x \in X, \Gamma(x) \subset A\right\}$ hence $\pi_i\left\{\{y \in X_i, \Gamma_i(y) \subset A\}\right\} \leqslant \pi\left\{\{x \in X, \Gamma(x) \subset A\}\right\}$ and therefore $f_i(A) \leqslant f(A)$, $i = 1, 2$.

Note that if two belief functions f_1 and f_2 are connected with two *independent* message spaces, then the joint probability Q must satisfy $Q(A,B) = m_1(A) \cdot m_2(B)$ for all $A, B \in a$, hence the compatibility of f_1 and f_2 (which results from our definition of message spaces, see footnote 1 in the beginning of this paper) entails:

$$[A, B \in a,\ A \cap B = \varnothing] \Rightarrow m_1(A) \cdot m_2(B) = 0 \tag{19}$$

Condition (19) will be referred to, in the following, as an independence condition. In fact, we obtain a sufficient condition for compatibility:

Corollary 1: If the Möbius inverses m_1, m_2 of two belief functions f_1, f_2 satisfy independence condition (19), then f_1 and f_2 are compatible.

Proof: It is sufficient to check that $Q : a \times a \to \mathrm{R}^+$ defined by $Q(A,B) = m_1(A) \cdot m_2(B)$ satisfies condition (ii) of Theorem 2.

Remark 3: Clearly condition (19) is not a necessary condition. (See Example 1 where $m_1(\{R \cup G\}) = 1/2$ and $m_2(\{B\}) = 1/3$).

In order to study links between combination rules $f_1 \square f_2$ and $f_1 \oplus f_2$, let us recall that $f_1 \square f_2$ denotes inf $\{P \in \alpha, P \geqslant f_1, P \geqslant f_2\}$ and is obviously defined if and only if f_1 and f_2 are compatible. As for Dempster's rule $f_1 \oplus f_2$, also called the "orthogonal sum of belief functions f_1 and f_2" (Shafer, 1976), it is defined if and only if:

$$\sum_{\{(A,B)\in a \times a, A \cap B \neq \varnothing\}} m_1(A) \times m_2(B) < 1 \tag{20}$$

In such a case $f_1 \oplus f_2$ is the belief function by which the Möbius inverse m is defined:

$$m(\varnothing) = 0 \text{ and } m(A) = \frac{\sum_{\{(B,C)\in a \times a, B\cap C = A\}} m_1(B) \times m_2(C)}{1 - \sum_{\{(B,C)\in a \times a, B\cap C = \varnothing\}} m_1(B)m_2(C)} \text{ for all } A \in a^* \tag{21}$$

We get the following corollary:

Corollary 2: If the belief functions f_1 and f_2 are compatible (i.e., if $f_1 \square f_2$ exists) then $f_1 \oplus f_2$ exists.

Proof: Since $\sum_{\{(A,B)\in a \times a\}} m_1(A) \times m_2(B) = \left(\sum_{A\in a} m_1(A)\right)\left(\sum_{B\in a} m_2(B)\right) = 1$, it suffices to prove that $\sum_{\{(A,B)\in a \times a, A\cap B \neq \varnothing\}} m_1(A) \times m_2(B) = 0$ is impossible. Otherwise, one gets $m_1(A) \times m_2(B) = 0$ for all $(A,B) \in a \times a$, $A \cap B \neq \varnothing$. Let $(A,B) \in a \times a$, $A \cap B \neq \varnothing$, and let Q satisfy condition (ii) of Theorem 2; we obtain: $m_1(A) \times m_2(B) = \left(\sum_{C\in a} Q(A,C)\right)\left(\sum_{D\in a} Q(D,B)\right)$; $m_1(A) \times m_2(B) = 0$, entails $(Q(A,B))^2 = 0$, hence $Q(A,B) = 0$. We deduce $Q(A,B) = 0$, for all $(A,B) \in a \times a$, a contradiction, which completes the proof.

Remark 4: Example 3 illustrates the well-known fact that the converse of Corollary 2 need not be true.

Example 3: $S = \{s_1, s_2\}$. Let f_1, f_2 be two belief functions on $(S, 2^S)$ – in fact, two probability measures – by which the Möbius inverses m_1, m_2 are respectively defined: $m_1(\{s_1\}) = \frac{1}{4}$, $m_1(\{s_2\}) = \frac{3}{4}$, $m_2(\{s_1\}) = \frac{3}{4}$, $m_2(\{s_2\}) = \frac{1}{4}$, $\sum_{\{(A,B)\in a^2; A\cap B \neq \varnothing\}} m_1(A) \times m_2(B) = \frac{6}{16} < 1$, hence

$f_1 \oplus f_2$ exist. Clearly $f_1 \square f_2$ does not exist, since no probability measure P on (S, a) simultaneously majorizes f_1 and f_2.

3. COMBINATION OF COMPATIBLE BELIEF FUNCTIONS

Assume now that f_1 and f_2 are two compatible belief functions on (S, a) and let Q be a mapping defined as in (ii) of Theorem 2. f_Q will denote the belief function whose Möbius inverse is m_Q:

$$m_Q(A) = \sum_{\{(B,C)\in a^2,\, B\cap C = A\}} Q(B,C) \quad \text{for all } A \in a \tag{22}$$

Q will denote the set of mappings Q satisfying conditions (ii) of Theorem 2.

Before giving a computing method of the infimum of the mathematical expectations $E_P(X)$ over the joint information $P = \{P \in \alpha, P \geqslant f_i, i = 1,2\}$ for a given $X \in \mathrm{R}^S$, we establish the following lemma:

Lemma 2: If two belief functions f_1 and f_2 are compatible, then $f_Q \geqslant f_i$, $i = 1,2$, for all $Q \in \mathrm{Q}$.

Proof: This can be seen directly through the proof of (ii)⇒(iii) in Theorem 2, since f_Q is generated by the message space $(X, 2^X, \pi, \Gamma)$, whereas f_i, $i = 1,2$ is generated by the submessage space $(X_i, 2^{X_i}, \pi_i, \Gamma)$. Let us give a simple direct proof. By symmetry, $f_Q \geqslant f_1$ suffices to be proved:

$$A \in a, f_Q(A) = \sum_{\{B\in a,\, B\subset A\}} m_Q(B) \geqslant \sum_{\{B\in a,\, B\subset A)} \left(\sum_{C\in a} Q(B,C) \right) \geqslant$$
$$\geqslant \sum_{\{B\in a,\, B\subset A\}} m_1(B) = f_1(B).$$

Lemma 3: Let f_1, f_2 be two compatible belief functions on (S, a), and let P be a probability measure on (S, a). Then the two assertions are equivalent:

(i) $P \in \mathrm{P}$

(ii) $\exists Q \in \mathrm{Q}$ such that $P \geqslant f_Q$

Proof:

(ii)⇒(i): Directly results from Lemma 2.

(i)⇒(ii): Let $P \geqslant f$, and let q_1, q_2, Q be defined as in the proof of (i)⇒(ii) in Theorem 2. Let $q : S \times a \to \mathrm{R}^+$ be defined by:

$$q(s,A) = \sum_{\{(B,C)\in a^2, B\cap C = A\}} \frac{q_1(s,B)\, q_2(s,C)}{P(\{s\})} \text{ if } s \in S^* \cap A \tag{23}$$

$$q(s,A) = 0 \qquad \text{otherwise.}$$

From Lemma 1, we deduce that only equalities (7) and (8) remain to be checked. If $s \notin S^* = \{s \in S, P(\{s\}) > 0\}$, (7) is trivially satisfied.

Now let s be a fixed element of S^*:

$$\begin{aligned}
\sum_{\{A\in a, A\supset \{s\}\}} q(s,A) &= \frac{1}{P(\{s\})} \sum_{\{A\supset\{s\}\}} \left(\sum_{\{B\cap C = A\}} q_1(s,B)\, q_2(s,C) \right) \\
&= \frac{1}{P(\{s\})} \sum_{\{B\supset\{s\}\}} q_1(s,B). \left(\sum_{\{C\subset\{s\}\}} q_2(s,C) \right) \\
&= \frac{1}{P(\{s\})} \times P(\{s\})^2 \\
&= P(\{s\})
\end{aligned}$$

Hence (7) is satisfied.

Let A be chosen in F:

$$\begin{aligned}
\sum_{\{s\in A\}} q(s,A) &= \sum_{\{s\in S^*, \cap A\}} \left(\sum_{\{B\cap C = A\}} \frac{q_1(s,B)\cdot q_2(s,C)}{P(\{s\})} \right) \\
&= \sum_{\{(B,C)\in a^2, B\cap C = A\}} \left(\sum_{\{s\in S^*, s\in B\cap C\}} \frac{q_1(s,B)\, q_2(s,C)}{P(\{s\})} \right) \\
&= \sum_{\{(B,C)\in a^2,\, B\cap C = A\}} Q(B,C) \\
&= m_Q(A)
\end{aligned}$$

Hence (8) is satisfied.

We can now state the main result of this section.

Theorem 3: Let f_1 and f_2 be two compatible belief functions and let Q be the set of mappings Q satisfying (ii) of Theorem 2, then:

$$\text{for all } X \in \mathbf{R}^S, \qquad \min_{P\in \mathrm{P}} E_P(X) = \min_{Q\in \mathrm{Q}} f_Q(X) \tag{24}$$

where P is the joint information of f_1 and f_2.

Corollary 3: The combination $f_1 \square f_2$ of two compatible belief functions f_1 and f_2 is given by:

$$f_1 \square f_2\, (A) = \min_{Q\in \mathrm{Q}} f_Q(A) \text{ for all } A \in a \tag{25}$$

Remark 5: It is worth noticing that in the two previous propositions, "min" has been substituted to "inf," since the infimum is reached.

Proof of Theorem 3: Let $X \in \mathrm{R}^S$. Compactness of P entails $\inf_{P \in \mathrm{P}} E_P(X) = \min_{P \in \mathrm{P}} E_P(X) = E_{P_0}(X)$ for some $P_0 \in \mathrm{P}$. Let Q_0 be a joint probability measure associated with P_0 as in Lemma 3; it follows: $P_0 \geqslant f_{Q_0}$, hence from the definition of the Choquet integral (1) it results $E_{P_0}(X) \geqslant f_{Q_0}(X)$. $f_{Q_0} \geqslant f_i$, $i = 1, 2$ (see Lemma 2) entails $E_{P_0}(X) = \inf_{\{P \in a, P \geqslant f_{Q_0}\}} E_P(X)$ but it is well known (Dempster, 1967; Huber and Strassen, 1973) that "f_{Q_0} belief function" implies $\inf_{\{P \in a, P \geqslant f_{Q_0}\}} E_P(X) = f_{Q_0}(X)$; therefore $E_{P_0}(X) = f_{Q_0}(X)$.

Now let $Q \in \mathrm{Q}; f_Q \geqslant f_i$, $i = 1, 2$, implies $\inf_{\{P \in a, P \geqslant f_Q\}} E_P(X) \geqslant \inf_{P \in \mathrm{P}} E_P(X)$, from the result just recalled above it follows $f_Q(X) \geqslant E_{P_0}(X)$ for all $Q \in \mathrm{Q}$, hence since $E_{P_0}(X) = f_{Q_0}(X)$, it comes $f_{Q_0}(X) = \min_{Q \in \mathrm{Q}} f_Q(X)$, which gives the desired result: $\min_{P \in \mathrm{P}} E_P(X) = \min_{Q \in \mathrm{Q}} f_Q(X)$.

Proof of Corollary 3: Applying Theorem 3 to characteristic functions $X = A$ of events A in a directly gives the result.

Remark 6: It is worth noticing that $f_1 \square f_2$ need not be a belief function, as shown by Example 4.

Example 4: $S = \{s_1, s_2, s_3, s_4\}$, f_1, f_2 belief functions with the Möbius inverses m_i, defined by: $m_1\left(\{s_1, s_3\}\right) = \frac{7}{24}$, $m_1\left(\{s_2, s_4\}\right) = \frac{17}{24}$, $m_2\left(\{s_1, s_2\}\right) = \frac{1}{2}$, $m_2\left(\{s_3, s_4\}\right) = \frac{1}{2}$. Independence condition (19) is satisfied, hence $f_1 \square f_2$ does exist. Simple calculations give the set Q, and the Möbius inverse m_Q of f_Q for $Q \in \mathrm{Q}$:

$$m_Q(\{s_1\}) = \frac{1}{2} - \lambda,\ m_Q\{s_2\}) = \lambda,\ m_Q(\{s_3\}) = \lambda - \frac{5}{24},\ m_Q(\{s_4\}) = \frac{17}{24} - \lambda,\ \frac{5}{24} \leqslant \lambda \leqslant \frac{12}{24}$$

Hence $f_1 \square f_2$ is deduced, whose Möbius inverse m satisfies $m(\{s_1, s_2, s_3\}) = -\frac{7}{24}$, therefore $f_1 \square f_2$ is not a belief function.

Remark 7: Even if $f_1 \square f_2$ proves to be a belief function, it may differ from Dempster's rule $f_1 \oplus f$ as shown by Example 5.

Example 5: Here we consider belief functions f_1 and f_2, which appeared in Example 2. $S=\{B, G, R\}$; $m_1(B\cup G)=m_1(G\cup R)=\frac{1}{2}$; $m_2(B)=\frac{1}{2}$, $m_2(G\cup R)=\frac{1}{6}$, $m_2(B\cup G\cup R)=\frac{1}{2}$.

Denote $A_1=\{B\cup G\}$, $A_2=\{G\cup R\}$, $B_1=\{B\}$, $B_2=\{G\cup R\}$, $B_3=\{B\cup G\cup R\}$. Simple calculations give the set Q of possible joint probabilities Q_λ:

$$Q_\lambda(A_1,B_1)=\frac{1}{3},\quad Q_\lambda(A_1,B_2)=\frac{1}{6}-\lambda,\quad Q_\lambda(A_1,B_3)=\lambda,$$

$$Q_\lambda(A_2,B_2)=\lambda,\quad Q_\lambda(A_2,B_3)=\frac{1}{2}-\lambda,\quad 0\leqslant\lambda\leqslant\frac{1}{6}.$$

Hence we can deduce f_{Q_λ}, $Q_\lambda\in\mathrm{Q}$, and $f_1\,\square\, f_2$, the results of which are summarized in Table 5.1, adding $f_1\oplus f_2, f_1, f_2$.

Table 5.1

	B	R	G	$B\cup G$	$B\cup R$	$G\cup R$	S
f_{Q_λ}	$\frac{1}{3}$	0	$\frac{1}{6}-\lambda$	$\frac{1}{2}$	$\frac{1}{3}$	$\frac{2}{3}-\lambda$	1
$f_1\,\square\, f_2$	$\frac{1}{3}$	0	0	$\frac{1}{2}$	$\frac{1}{3}$	$\frac{1}{2}$	1
$f_1\oplus f_2$	$\frac{1}{5}$	0	$\frac{1}{10}$	$\frac{3}{5}$	$\frac{1}{5}$	$\frac{1}{2}$	1
f_1	0	0	0	$\frac{1}{2}$	0	$\frac{1}{2}$	1
f_2	$\frac{1}{3}$	0	0	$\frac{1}{3}$	$\frac{1}{3}$	$\frac{1}{6}$	1

Clearly $f_1\,\square\, f_2$ is a belief function since $f_1\,\square\, f_2$ equals f_{Q_λ} for $\lambda=\frac{1}{6}$, but $f_1\,\square\, f_2$ differs from $f_1\oplus f_2$. In this example $f_1\,\square\, f_2=\max(f_1,f_2)$, but indeed:

Remark 8: $f_1\,\square\, f_2$ need not be equal to $\max(f_1,f_2)$ even if $f_1\,\square\, f_2$ proves to be a belief function, as shown by Example 6.

Example 6: $S=\{s_1,s_2,s_3,s_4\}$, f_1,f_2 belief functions with the Möbius inverse m_i: $m_1(\{s_1\})=\frac{1}{3}$, $m_1(\{s_2,s_3\})=\frac{2}{3}$, $m_2(\{s_2,s_4\})=\frac{1}{4}$, $m_2(\{s_1,s_2,s_3\})=\frac{3}{4}$.

Here Q reduces to a single element $Q : Q(\{s_1\}, \quad \{s_1, s_2, s_3\}) = \frac{4}{12}$, $Q(\{s_2, s_3\}, \{s_2, s_4\}) = \frac{3}{12}$, $Q(\{s_2, s_3\}, \{s_1, s_2, s_3\}) = \frac{5}{12}$; hence $f_1 \square f_2$ is a belief function. $f_1 \square f_2(\{s_2\}) = \frac{3}{12}$, $f_1(\{s_2\}) = f_2(\{s_2\}) = 0$, therefore $f_1 \square f_2 \neq \max(f_1, f_2)$.

Remark 9: For the sake of completeness let us point out that in the case of Example 1, it happens that $f_1 \square f_2(\{(s, a)\}) = 0{,}1$.

Remark 10 (on the use of available information): Obviously if the given belief functions f_i, $i = 1, 2$ are known to be connected to some message spaces $(X_i, 2^{X_i}, \pi_i, \Gamma_i)$, and if some additional information is available, this may allow us to quickly get a lower bound g for the probability of each event A at least as good as $f_1 \square f_2(A)$.

An important case is when the true joint probability Q can be obtained, all the more so because in such a case the resulting lower bound $g = f_Q$ is again a belief function. This may happen if the sources (i.e., message spaces) are known to be independent, because this entails that Q must necessarily be defined by: $Q(A, B) = m_1(A) \times m_2(B)$ for all $A, B \in a$; and then g coincides with Dempster's rule $f_1 \oplus f_2$.[6] This may also happen either when $Q(A, B)$ can be estimated through repeated experiments or when $(X_i, 2^{X_i}, \pi_i, \Gamma_i)$ are known. As for an example of this last assertion, consider experts $i (i = 1, 2)$ in Example 2, who were informed of "mechanisms" $(X_i, 2^{X_i}, \pi_i, \Gamma_i)$: they knew more than $f_1 (i = 1, 2)$; in fact, their joint information allowed them to determine their proper joint probability[7] $Q : Q(\{B \cup G\}, \{B\}) = \pi(\{1, 2, 3\} \cap \{1, 2\}) = \pi(\{1, 2\}) = \frac{1}{3}, \ldots$, which proves to be Q_λ with $\lambda = \frac{1}{6}$ (see Example 5). Therefore, they could rapidly get lower bound $f_{Q_{1/6}}$, which in this particular case equals $f_1 \square f_2$.

4. RELATION OF SPECIFICITY

Definition 2: Let f_1 and f_2 be belief functions on (S, a), then f_2 is at least as specific as f_1 if $f_2(A) \geqslant f_1(A)$ for all $A \in a$.

---

[6] According to our definition of message spaces (see footnote 1), this follows from $\sum_{\{A, B \in a, A \cap B \neq 0\}} m_1(A) \times m_2(B) = 0$.

[7] Let us mention that the additional knowledge of probability π on (S, a) was also useful.

Remark 11: This notion introduced by Yager (1982; 1983) and reexamined by Dubois and Prade (1986), when applied in our setting to a pair of experts $i = 1, 2$ – supposed to provide correct information – expresses that expert 1 is at least as precise as expert. 2. As it has been underlined by the above-cited authors, this happens in the meaningful circumstances[8] when f_1 and f_2 are connected with a same message space and when elements of X_1 form a partition of X_2 – in other words, when expert 1 can only "observe" a portion of what is observed by expert 2.

Unfortunately, such nice situations do not characterize relation of specificity, as can be proved by the following theorem:

Theorem 4: Let f_1 and f_2 be two belief functions on (S, a) the Möbius inverses of which are respectively m_1 and m_2; then the three following assertions are equivalent:

(i) f_2 is at least as specific as f_1 (i.e., $f_2(A) \geqslant f_1(A)$ for all $A \in a$

(ii) $m : a \to \mathrm{R}$ such that:

(a) $\sum_{A \in a} m(A) = 1$ for all $A \in a$

(b) $0 \leqslant \sum_{\{B \in a, B \subset A\}} m(B) \leqslant 1$ (26)

for all $A \in a$

(c) $m_1(A) = \sum_{\{(B,C) \in a^2, B \cup C = A\}} m_2(B)\, m(C)$ for all $A \in a$ (27)

(iii) There exists $Q : a \times a \to \mathrm{R}$ satisfying:

(a) $Q(A,B) \neq 0 \Rightarrow A \supset B$, for all $(A,B) \in a^2$ (28)

(b) i. $m_1(A) = \sum_{B \in a} Q(A,B)$, for all $A \in a$ (29)

ii. $m_2(A) = \sum_{A \in a} Q(A,B)$, for all $B \in a$ (30)

(c) for all $(B,C) \in a^2$, $B \subset C : 0 \leqslant \sum_{\{A \in a, B \subset A \subset C\}} Q(A,B) \leqslant m_2(B)$ (31)

Proof: (i)$\Rightarrow$(ii) : $f_2(A) \geqslant f_1(A)$ for all $A \in a$ implies that there exists a mapping $f : a \to \mathrm{R}^+$ such that $f_1(A) = f(A).f_2(A)$ for all $A \in a$. Let us recall that the Möbius inverse m of a mapping $g : a \to \mathrm{R}$ is the unique mapping $m : a \to \mathrm{R}$ such that $f(A) = \sum_{\{B \in a,\, B \subset A\}} m(B)$, for all $A \in a$ (for further details see Rota, 1964; Chateauneuf and Jaffray, 1989). Now let f be a chosen element of $\mathrm{R}+^a$ satisfying $f_1 = f.f_2$, the Möbius inverse of which is denoted m. That m satisfies (26) is immediate.

[8] Called "strong inclusion" by Dubois and Prade (1986).

$D \in a, f_1(D) = f(D).f_2(D)$ entails $\sum_{A \subset D} m_1(A) = \left(\sum_{B \subset D} m(B)\right)$ $\left(\sum_{C \subset D} m_2(C)\right)$, hence $\sum_{A \subset D} m_1(A) = \sum_{A \subset D}\left(\sum_{\{B,C \in a, B \cup C = A\}} m(B).m_2(C)\right)$. Therefore the unicity of the Möbius inverses give (27): $m_1(A) = \sum_{\{(B,C) \in a^2, B \cup C = A\}} m_2(B).m(C)$ for all $A \in a$, which completes this part of proof.

(ii)$\Rightarrow$(iii): Define $Q : a \times a \to \mathrm{R}$ by:

$$Q(A,B) = \sum_{\{C \in a,\, B \cup C = A\}} m_2(B).m(C) \text{ for all } (A,B) \in a,\ A \supset B$$
$$Q(A,B) = 0 \qquad \text{otherwise.}$$

Hence (28) is trivially satisfied. Let us come now to (29) and (30): Let A be chosen in a: $\sum_{B \in a} Q(A,B) = \sum_{\{(B,C) \in a^2,\, B \cup C = A\}} m_2(B).m(C)$, hence (27) gives (29): $\sum_{B \in a} Q(A,B) = m_1(A)$.

Let B be chosen in a: $\sum_{A \in a} Q(A,B) = m_2(B)\left(\sum_{C \in a} m(C)\right)$, hence (26) gives (30): $\sum_{A \in a} Q(A,B) = m_2(B)$.

Only (31) remains to be checked. Let (B,C) be fixed in a^2 with B included in C: $\sum_{\{A \in a,\, B \subset A \subset C\}} Q(A,B) = m_2(B)\left(\sum_{\{D \in a,\, D \subset C\}} m(D)\right)$ hence (30) is satisfied through (26) and $0 \leqslant m_2(B) \leqslant 1$.

(iii)$\Rightarrow$(i):

$A \in a, f_1 = \sum_{\{B \in a,\, B \subset A\}} m_1(B) = \sum_{B \subset A}\left(\sum_{\{C \in a,\, C \subset B\}} Q(B,C)\right)$, hence $f_1(A) =$ $\sum_{C \subset A}\left(\sum_{\{B \in a,\, C \subset B \subset C\}} Q(B,C)\right)$, therefore (31) implies $f_1(A) \leqslant \sum_{C \subset A} m_2(C)$, that is, $f_1(A) \leqslant f_2(A)$ which completes the proof.

Remark 12: Similarity of conditions (ii) (b) in Theorem 2 and (iii) (b) in Theorem 4 can be seen. Actually, if Q appearing in Theorem 4 is assumed to be nonnegative, Q can again be interpreted (as in Remark 2) as a joint probability, and then conditions (28), (29), and (30) characterize circumstances of strong inclusion evocated in Remark 10. Unfortunately, in the general case, interpretation of conditions (iii) seems much more delicate.

5. CONCLUSION

In this paper only the case of two belief functions has been dealt with. Let us underline, however, that our results about compatible belief functions and their combination extend naturally to the case of any finite number n by merely considering joint probabilities Q of order n.

ACKNOWLEDGMENT

I wish to thank J.Y. Jaffray for numerous helpful suggestions and comments.

BIBLIOGRAPHY

Chateauneuf, A. and Jaffray, J. Y. (1989). Some characterizations of lower probabilities and other monotone capacities through the use of Möbius inversion. *Math. Soc. Sc.* 17: 263–83.

Choquet, G. (1953). Théorie des capacités. *Ann. Inst. Fourier* (Grenoble) V: 131–295.

De Campos, L. M. (1987). Caracterizacion y estudio de medidas e integrales difusa a partir de probabilidades. Ph.D. Thesis, Universidad de Granada.

De Campos, L. M., Lamata, M. T., and Moral, S. (1988). Logical connectives for combining fuzzy measures. *Methodologies for Intelligent Systems* 3: 11–18.

Dempster, A.P. (1967). Upper and lower probabilities induced by a multivalued mapping. *Ann. Math. Statist.* 38: 325–39.

Dubois, D. and Prade, H. (1986). A set-theoretic view of belief functions. *Int. J. General Systems* 12: 193–226.

Fuchssteiner, B. and Lusky, W. (1981). *Convex cones.* Amsterdam: North-Holland.

Huber, P. J. and Strassen, V. (1973). Minimax tests and the Neyman-Pearson lemma for capacities. *Ann. Statist.* 1: 251–63.

Rota, G. C. (1964). Theory of Möbius functions. *Z. für Wahr. Theorie und Verw. Gebiete* 2: 340–68.

Shafer, G. (1976). *A mathematical theory of evidence.* Princeton, NJ: Princeton University Press.

Shafer, G. (1990). Perspectives on the theory and practice of belief functions. School of Business, University of Kansas, Lawrence.

Yager, R. (1982). Measuring tranquility and anxiety in decision making: An application of fuzzy sets. *Int. J. General Systems* 8: 139–46.

Yager, R. (1983). Entropy and specificity in a mathematical theory of evidence. *Int. J. General Systems* 9: 249–60.

Zadeh, L. A. (1983). A computational approach to fuzzy quantifiers in natural languages. *Computer and Mathematics with Applications* 9: 149–84.

6 Comparative beliefs

S.K.M. WONG, Y.Y. YAO, and P. LINGRAS

Abstract: This paper is a review of current developments in comparative beliefs. The discussion focuses on the axiomatization, interpretation, and combination of these beliefs. Axiomatization studies the comparative belief structure, which provides a justification for the use of quantitative belief measures. Two different views on the interpretation of qualitative belief, a special class of comparative beliefs, are discussed. Rules for combining belief relations are suggested. These combination rules are crucial in the design of inference networks for qualitative reasoning.

Keywords: comparative belief, belief function, axiomatization and combination of beliefs, qualitative belief, probability and necessity.

1. INTRODUCTION

There are important practical and theoretical reasons to study comparative beliefs as humans frequently reason in qualitative rather than quantitative terms. The qualitative representation of beliefs therefore seems to be a more realistic model of uncertainty particularly when the available information is limited. Savage (1972) analyzed the structure of qualitative probability in the development of an expected utility model for decision making with probability functions. Dubois (1986) studied qualitative necessity and possibility to justify the usage of necessity and possibility functions in the theory of fuzzy sets. More recently, the structure of qualitative belief and plausibility has been established, which strengthens the basis for modeling uncertainty with belief and plausibility functions (Wong, Lingras, and Yao, 1991). If belief functions are considered as a generalization of probability functions, the understanding of qualitative belief becomes as important as that of qualitative probability in the development of probability theory (Fine, 1973; Smets, 1988). Furthermore, the close relationship that exists between consonant belief functions and necessity functions (Dubois and Prade, 1986; Klir and Folger, 1988) provides additional reasons for studying qualitative belief.

Qualitative probability, necessity, and belief are also referred to as probability, necessity, and belief relations, respectively. The qualitative probability and necessity are subclasses of qualitative belief, which in turn is a special case of comparative beliefs. This paper discusses axiomatization, interpretation, and combination of comparative beliefs. Axiomatization studies the structure of comparative beliefs, which provides a justification for the use of quantitative belief measures. By introducing appropriate axioms, one can characterize those comparative beliefs that are fully or partially compatible with belief functions. Two different views on the interpretation of qualitative belief are discussed (Shafer, 1986; Lingras and Wong, 1990). The allocation view demands belief relations to be directly defined on the propositions of the frame of discernment. On the other hand, belief relations in the compatibility view are the results of propagating probability relations (Savage, 1972) from one frame to the frame of interest. This relationship between qualitative probability and belief leads to useful applications of belief structures in decision-making. Finally, we introduce rules to combine belief relations. The combination rules are essential in the design of inference networks for qualitative reasoning (Wong, Lingras, and Yao, 1991).

Although our discussion is focused on belief functions, the same framework can be used to investigate the issues of representation and propagation of other uncertainty measures.

2. AXIOMATIZATION OF COMPARATIVE BELIEFS

2.1. Representations of beliefs

Let $\Theta = \{\theta_1,...,\theta_n\}$ be a finite set of possible answers to a question. This set is referred to as the *frame of discernment* or simply the *frame* defined by the question. Following the convention of representing a proposition by a subset of Θ, the powerset 2^Θ denotes the set of all propositions discerned by frame Θ. With a given frame, there are essentially two approaches to represent beliefs based on available evidence.

In the quantitative approach, a number is associated with each proposition to indicate the degree to which one believes in that proposition. That is, we express our belief in a proposition by a numeric value. To make the quantitative representation of beliefs consistent and meaningful, certain axioms or rules should be observed in expressing one's beliefs. For example, if beliefs are measured by a probability function, the Kolmogorov axioms for probability should be satisfied in order to maintain consistency (Fine, 1973).

In the qualitative approach, it is assumed that one is able to express one's preference on any two propositions. In other words, qualitative judgments can be described in terms of a comparative belief relation $>$ on 2^Θ. By $A > B$, we mean that *A is more believable than B*. In the absence of strict preference, that is, $\neg(A > B)$ and $\neg(B > A)$, we say that A and B are *indifferent*, written $A \sim B$. We also write $A \geqslant B$, if $A > B$ or $A \sim B$. As in quantitative measures of beliefs, such a relation must be consistently defined. For example, if a person believes more in proposition A than in proposition B, and also believes more in B than in C, then it is reasonable to assume that he would believe more in A than in C.

Both the quantitative and qualitative approaches are very useful for the management of uncertainty. In fact, probability theory has been extensively studied within the quantitative as well as the qualitative frameworks (Fishburn, 1970; Savage, 1972; Fine, 1973). Given a belief measure and a comparative belief relation, it is natural to ask whether they are compatible with each other. This is indeed one of the fundamental issues in measurement theory for modeling preferences and beliefs (French, 1986). The relationship between the quantitative and qualitative representations of beliefs can be formally stated as follows. Suppose Θ is a frame, f is a function mapping the elements of 2^Θ into real numbers, and $>$ is a comparative belief relation on 2^Θ. We say that f and $>$ are *fully compatible* with each other if for $A, B \in 2^\Theta$,

$$A > B \Leftrightarrow f(A) > f(B) \tag{1}$$

A function f is said to *represent* a comparative belief relation $>$ if it is fully compatible with $>$. On the other hand, we say that a function f

is *partially compatible with* $>$ if it satisfies the following weaker condition: for $A, B \in 2^{\Theta}$,

$$A > B \Rightarrow f(A) > f(B) \tag{2}$$

A partially compatible function may be viewed as an inexact representation of a comparative belief relation. Both the exact and inexact quantitative representations are useful depending on the applications (Fishburn, 1970).

Clearly, whether a comparative belief relation is compatible with a particular quantitative belief measure depends very much on the preference structure of the qualitative judgments. In subsequent discussions, we will study those comparative beliefs related to belief functions (Shafer, 1976).

2.2. Belief functions and qualitative belief

A belief function, $Bel: 2^{\Theta} \rightarrow [0, 1]$, is a mapping from 2^{Θ} to the interval $[0, 1]$, which satisfies the following axioms:

(S1) $Bel(\emptyset) = 0$,
(S2) $Bel(\Theta) = 1$,
(S3) For every positive integer n and every collection $A_1, A_2, \ldots, A_n$ of subsets of Θ,

$$Bel(A_1 \cup A_2 \ldots . \cup A_n) \geqslant$$

$$\sum_i Bel(A_i) - \sum_{i<j} Bel(A_i \cap A_j) \pm \ldots + (-1)^{n+1} Bel(A_1 \cap A_2 \ldots \cap A_n).$$

Axioms (S1) and (S2) state that the proposition $\emptyset$ is believed to be false and the proposition Θ is believed to be true. Axiom (S3) indicates that belief functions are superadditive, which become additive in the special case. Belief functions can thus be viewed as a generalization of additive probalility functions. For a given belief function, one can define a plausibility function, $Pl: 2^{\Theta} \rightarrow [0, 1]$, as:

$$Pl(A) = 1 - Bel(A^c) \tag{3}$$

where A^c denotes the complement of A. A belief function can be equivalently defined by a mapping, $m: 2^{\Theta} \rightarrow [0, 1]$, called a basic probability assignment, which satisfies the following axioms:

(M1) $m(\emptyset) = 0$,

(M2) $\sum_{A \in 2^{\Theta}} m(A) = 1$,

(M3) $Bel(A) = \sum_{A \supseteq B} m(B)$.

An element $F \in 2^{\Theta}$ is called a *focal* element if $m(F) > 0$. Conversely, by the Möbius inversion one can construct the basic probability assignment from a belief function. Therefore, a belief function can be defined by the axioms (S1)–(S3) or (M1)–(M3).

The qualitative counterpart of a belief function was studied by Wong, Lingras, and Yao (1991). A class of comparative beliefs satisfying the following axioms:

(B1) asymmetry: $A > B \Rightarrow \neg(B > A)$,
(B2) negative transitivity: $(\neg(A > B), \neg(B > C)) \Rightarrow \neg(A > C)$,
(B3) dominance: $A \supseteq B \Rightarrow \neg(B > A)$,
(B4) partial monotonicity:
$(A \supset B, A \cap C = \emptyset) \Rightarrow (A > B \Rightarrow A \cup C > B \cup C)$,
(B5) nontriviality: $\Theta > \emptyset$,

is called a *qualitative belief*. Axiom (B1) says that if one commits more belief in A than in B, one should not at the same time commit more belief in B than in A. Axiom (B2) demands that if one does not believe more in A than in B, nor believes more in B than in C, one should not believe more in A than in C. Axioms (B1) and (B2) ensure that the comparative belief relation is a weak order which guarantees the existence of a quantitative representation (Fishburn, 1970). Axiom (B3) specifies the relationship between two propositions when one is a subset of the other, which says that the belief in a subset should not be more than the belief in the set itself. Axiom (B4) is a much weaker form of the monotonicity axiom (Fishburn, 1970; Savage, 1972). Axiom (B5) eliminates the trivial relation, namely, $A \sim B$ for all $A, B \in 2^{\Theta}$.

Note that (B1)–(B5) form a set of independent axioms. These axioms can be viewed in two ways. The *prescriptive* or *normative* interpretation looks at axioms as conditions of rationality. A second interpretation is that axioms are *descriptive*. They impose conditions on the qualitative judgments which, if satisfied, allow measurement. Both interpretations are useful in practical situations (see Krantz [1968] for a more detailed discussion of this issue).

If $>_{Bel}$ is a belief relation, a relation $>_{Pl}$ defined by:

$$A >_{Pl} B \Leftrightarrow B^c >_{Bel} A^c, \text{ for all } A, B \in 2^{\Theta} \quad (4)$$

is called a *plausibility* relation. This definition is consistent with that of a plausibility function.

The following theorem establishes an important link between a belief function and a belief relation (Wong, Lingras, and Yao, 1991).

Theorem 1: Let Θ be a frame and $>$ a comparative belief relation on 2^Θ. There exists a belief function, $Bel: 2^\Theta \to [0,1]$, which is fully compatible with $>$, if and only if $>$ is a belief relation.

A detailed proof of this theorem is given in Wong, Lingras, and Yao (1991). The *only if* part follows directly from the properties of belief functions. The *if* part can be proved by explicitly constructing a belief function fully compatible with a given belief relation. We outline the proof as follows. Axioms (B1) and (B2) imply that the induced indifference relation $\sim$ is an equivalence relation (Fishburn, 1970). Since axiom (B5) holds, based on the relation $\sim$, we can partition 2^Θ into at least two equivalence classes $E_0,\ldots,E_k$ $(k \geqslant 1)$. Moreover, these equivalence classes are arranged such that $A > B \Leftrightarrow (A \in E_i, B \in E_j, i > j)$. Obviously, the dominance axiom (B3) implies that $\emptyset \in E_0$ and $\Theta \in E_k$. An equialence E_i is also denoted as $[A]$ if $A \in E_i$. For example, E_0 may be written as $[\emptyset]$ and E_k as $[\Theta]$. We can recursively construct a function f on the equivalence classes of $\sim$ as follows:

(i) $f(E_0) = 0$,
(ii) $f(E_{n+1}) = \max\{f'(E_{n+1}), f(E_n) + 1\}$

where

$$f'(E_{n+1}) = \max_{A \in G_{n+1}} \{-\sum_{A \supset B} (-1)^{|A-B|} f([B])\}$$

if $G_{n+1} = \{A \in E_{n+1} \mid A \supset B \Rightarrow B \notin E_{n+1}\}$ is not empty; otherwise $f'(E_{n+1}) = f(E_n) + 1$. The symbol $|.|$ denotes the cardinality of a set. The function f satisfies the condition that $A > B \Leftrightarrow f([A]) > f([B])$ for $A, B \in 2^\Theta$. Let $m'(A) = \Sigma_{A \supseteq B}(-1)^{|A-B|} f([B])$. It can be shown that $m'(A) \geqslant 0$, for all $A \in 2^\Theta$. By the Möbius inversion, $f([A]) = \Sigma_{A \supseteq B} m'(B)$ and $f([\Theta]) = \Sigma_{\Theta \supseteq B} m'(B)$. Thus, the function $Bel(A) = f([A])/f([\Theta])$ has the desired properties.

The following example is adopted from Wong, Lingras, and Yao (1991) to illustrate the procedure for constructing a belief function from a belief relation. Let $\Theta = \{\theta_1, \theta_2, \theta_3\}$. Consider a preference relation $>$ on 2^Θ defined by:

$$\{\theta_1, \theta_2, \theta_3\} > \begin{matrix}\{\theta_1, \theta_3\} \\ \{\theta_2, \theta_3\}\end{matrix} > \begin{matrix}\{\theta_1\} \\ \{\theta_1, \theta_2\}\end{matrix} > \begin{matrix}\emptyset \\ \{\theta_2\} \\ \{\theta_3\}\end{matrix}$$

We use the notation that $A > B > C$ implies $A > C$. This preference relation $>$ indeed satisfies axioms (B1)–(B5); hence, it is a belief relation. The corresponding relation $\sim$ divides 2^{Θ} into four equivalence classes: $E_0 = [\varnothing, \{\theta_2\}, \{\theta_3\}]$, $E_1 = [\{\theta_1\}, \{\theta_1, \theta_2\}]$, $E_2 = [\{\theta_1. \theta_3\}, \{\theta_2, \theta_3\}]$, and $E_3 = [\{\theta_1, \theta_2, \theta_3\}]$.

First, we construct a function f based on formulas (i) and (ii):

E_0: According to formula (i), let $f(E_0) = 0$.

E_1: Since $G_1 = \{\{\theta_1\}\}, f'(E_1)$
$= -\sum_{\{\theta\} \subset B}(-1)^{|\{\theta_1\} - B|} f([B]) = f([\varnothing]) = 0$. Thus,
$f(E_1) = \max\{0, f(E_0) + 1)\} = \max\{0, 1\} = 1$.

E_2: In this case, the set G_2 is the entire equivalence class E_2. According to formula (ii), we compute $-\sum_{A \supset B}(-1)^{|A - B|} f([B])$ for every $A \in E_2$ as follows:

$$- \sum_{\{\theta_1, \theta_3\} \supset B} (-1)^{|\{\theta_1, \theta_3\} - B|} f([B])$$
$$= f([\{\theta_1\}]) + f([\{\theta_3\}]) - f([\varnothing])$$
$$= f(E_1) + f(E_0) - f(E_0) = 1 + 0 - 0 = 1,$$

$$- \sum_{\{\theta_2, \theta_3\} \supset B} (-1)^{|\{\theta_2, \theta_3\} - B|} f([B]) =$$
$$= f([\{\theta_2\}]) + f([\{\theta_3\}]) - f([\varnothing])$$
$$= f(E_0) + f(E_0) - f(E_0) = 0 + 0 - 0 = 0.$$

From these values, we obtain $f'(E_2) = \max\{1, 0\} = 1$. Hence, $f(E_2) = \max\{f'(E_2), f(E_1) + 1\} = \max\{1, 2\} = 2$.

E_3: Since E_3 has only one element, we have:

$$f'(E_3) = - \sum_{\{\theta_1, \theta_2, \theta_3\} \supset B} (-1)^{|\{\theta_1, \theta_2, \theta_3\} - B|} f([B])$$
$$= f([\{\theta_1 . \theta_2\}]) + f([\{\theta_1 . \theta_3\}]) + f([\{\theta_2 . \theta_3\}])$$
$$+ f([\{\theta_1\}]) - f([\{\theta_2\}]) - f([\{\theta_3\}]) + f([\{\varnothing\}])$$
$$= f([\{E_1\}]) + f([\{E_2\}]) + f([\{E_2\}]) - f([\{E_1\}])$$
$$- f([\{E_0\}]) - f([\{E_0\}]) + f([\{E_0\}])$$
$$= 1 + 2 + 2 - 1 - 0 - 0 + 0 = 4.$$

This implies that $f(E_3) = \max\{f'(E_2), f(E_2) + 1)\}$
$= \max\{4, 3\} = 4$.

We can now compute the values of the function m' for every $A \in 2^{\Theta}$ based on the formula $m'(A) = \Sigma_{A \supseteq B}(-1)^{|A - B|} f([B])$. Since $f([\Theta]) = f(E_3) = 4$, the values of the basic probability assignment can be computed by $m(A) = m'(A)/f([\Theta])$. Finally, the belief $Bel(A)$ can be obtained by formula $Bel(A) = \Sigma_{A \supseteq B} m(B)$. Table 6.1 summarizes these results. It can be easily verified that this belief function is fully compatible with the given belief relation.

Table 6.1

A	m'	m	Bel
$\emptyset$	0	0	0
$\{\theta_1\}$	1	$\frac{1}{4}$	$\frac{1}{4}$
$\{\theta_2\}$	0	0	0
$\{\theta_3\}$	0	0	0
$\{\theta_1, \theta_2\}$	0	0	$\frac{1}{4}$
$\{\theta_1, \theta_3\}$	1	$\frac{1}{4}$	$\frac{2}{4}$
$\{\theta_2, \theta_3\}$	2	$\frac{2}{4}$	$\frac{2}{4}$
$\{\theta_1, \theta, \theta_2\}$	0	0	1

There are obviously many different kinds of comparative beliefs that are not fully compatible with belief functions. However, in many situations it is useful to consider those relations that are partially compatible with belief functions. Such relations, for example, play an important role in the design of information retrieval systems (Wong and Yao, 1990). This type of relations is also useful in other decision problems (Fishburn, 1970). A set of sufficient conditions, which guarantees the existence of a belief function partially compatible with a comparative belief relation, is given in the following theorem (Wong, in press).

Theorem 2: Let Θ be a frame and $>$ a comparative belief relation on 2^{Θ}. If $>$ satisfies axioms (B1)–(B3), there exists a belief function, $Bel: 2^{\Theta} \rightarrow [0, 1]$, partially compatible with $>$.

A comparative belief relation satisfying axioms (B1)–(B3) is referred to as a *weak* belief relation.

2.3. Qualitative probability and necessity

In this section, two important subclasses of qualitative belief, qualitative probability and necessity, are analyzed.

2.3.1. Qualitative probability and monotonic belief function

A comparative belief relation $>$ on 2^{Θ} is called a probability relation if for $A, B, C \in 2^{\Theta}$,

(P1) asymmetry: $A > B \Rightarrow \neg(B > A)$,
(P2) negative transitivity: $(\neg(A > B), \neg(B > C)) \Rightarrow \neg(A > C)$,
(P3) monotonicity:
$((A \cup B) \cap C = \theta) \Rightarrow (A > B \Leftrightarrow A \cup C > B \cup C)$,
(P4) improbability of impossibility and nontriviality:
$\neg(\emptyset > A)$, $\Theta > \emptyset$.

Obviously, a probability relation is a belief relation (Wong, Yao, and Lingras, 1991).

The set of axioms for defining qualitative probability was used by de Finetti (1937) to study the qualitative counterpart of probability functions. Savage (1972) in his study of expected utility emphasized the importance of qualitative probability. It was shown by Kraft, Pratt, and Seidenberg (1959) that the axioms of qualitative probability are not sufficient to guarantee the existence of an additive probability measure. Fine (1973) and Dubois (1986) showed that axioms (P1)–(P5) are in fact *sufficient* to imply the existence of the class of functions called *decomposable functions*. However, Fine and Dubois did not identify the class of functions for which the qualitative probability axioms are both necessary and sufficient. Moreover, their proofs of the existence of decomposable functions are not *constructive* and it is therefore not clear how to compute such a function from a probability relation. Recently, Wong, Yao, and Lingras (1991) introduced the notion of *monotonic belief functions* defined by axioms (S1)–(S3) and the following quantitative monotonicity axiom: for A, B, $C \in 2^{\Theta}$ with $(A \cup B) \cap C = \emptyset$,

$$Bel(A) > Bel(B) \Leftrightarrow Bel(A \cup C) > Bel(B \cup C) \tag{5}$$

It has been shown that the qualitative probability axioms are both necessary and sufficient for the existence of a monotonic belief function fully compatible with a probability relation (Wong, Yao, and Lingras, 1991).

Theorem 3: Let Θ be a frame and $>$ a comparative belief relation on 2^{Θ}. There exists a monotonic belief function, $Bel: 2^{\Theta} \rightarrow [0, 1]$, fully compatible with $>$, if and only if $>$ is a probability relation.

Based on the constructive proof of Theorem 1, one can easily construct a monotonic belief function from a probability relation.

2.3.2. Qualitative necessity and consonant belief function

Consonant belief functions are belief functions whose focal elements are nested (Shafer, 1976). In other words, the focal elements can be arranged such that $F_1 \supset F_2 \supset \dots \supset F_s$. In this case:

$$Bel(A \cap B) = \min\{Bel(A), Bel(B)\} \tag{6}$$
$$Pl(A \cup B) = \max\{Pl(A), Pl(B)\} \tag{7}$$

Such *Bel* and *Pl* functions are referred to respectively as necessity and possibility functions, which were introduced independently within the framework of fuzzy sets (Dubois and Prade, 1985; Smets, 1988).

The qualitative counterpart of the consonant belief (necessity) functions was studied by Dubois (1986). A comparative belief relation $>$ on 2^Θ is called a *necessity* relation if for $A, B, C \in 2^\Theta$,

(N1) asymmetry: $A > B \Rightarrow \neg(B > A)$,
(N2) negative transitivity: $(\neg(A > B), \neg(B > C)) \Rightarrow \neg(A > C)$,
(N3) nontriviality: $\Theta > \emptyset$,
(N4) $\neg(A > B) \Rightarrow A \cap B \sim A$.

It can be easily seen that a necessity relation is a belief relation. The following theorem shows that the axioms for qualitative necessity are both necessary and sufficient for the existence of a consonant belief function fully compatible with a necessity relation (Dubois, 1986).

Theorem 4: Let Θ be a frame and $>$ a comparative belief relation on 2^Θ. There exists a consonant belief function, $Bel: 2^\Theta \rightarrow [0, 1]$, fully compatible with $>$, if and only if $>$ is a necessity relation.

Theorem 4 can be considered as a special case of Theorem 1. Thus, one can easily construct a consonant belief function from a necessity relation.

3. INTERPRETATIONS OF QUALITATIVE BELIEF

Similar to belief functions, there are two views to interpret qualitative belief (Lingras and Wong, 1990). In the allocation view, the belief relation satisfying axioms (B1)–(B5) is *directly* defined on the propositions of the frame of interest. This view is straightforward and does not require much explanation. In contrast, the belief relation in the compatibility view is derived from a probability relation defined on another frame. This is similar to the process of deriving a belief function from a probability function as discussed by Dempster (1967).

Consider two frames T and Θ. An element $t \in T$ is said to be *compatible* with an element $\theta \in \Theta$, written $t\,c\,\theta$, if the proposition $\{t\}$ does not contradict the proposition $\{\theta\}$. That is, the answer t to the question that defines T does not exclude the possibility that θ is the answer to the question that defines Θ. Compatibility is symmetric: t is compatible with θ if and only if θ is compatible with t. A *compatibility relation* c between two frames T and Θ is a subset of pairs (t, θ) in the Cartesian product $T \times \Theta$ such that $T c \theta$. This relation provides a qualitative description of the relationships between the elements of two distinct frames. For example, in the context of probability theory, $t c \theta$ describes the assertion $P(\theta, t) > 0$. Similarly, the assertion $P(\theta, t) = 0$ can be described by the fact that t is not compatible with θ, written $\neg(t\, c\, \theta)$.

A compatibility relation c between two frames T and Θ is *complete* if for any $t \in T$ there exists a $\theta \in \Theta$ such that t c θ, and vice versa. Hereafter, we will consider only complete compatibility relations, as one can always obtain a reduced frame by deleting those elements in one of the frames that are not compatible with any element in the other frame. Given a compatibility relation c between T and Θ, one can define a mapping Γ that assigns a subset $\Gamma(t) \subseteq \Theta$ to every $t \in T$ as follows:

$$\Gamma(t) = \{\theta \in \Theta \mid t\, c\, \theta\} \tag{8}$$

Conversely, for any subset $A \subseteq \Theta$, one can define the lower and upper *preimages* of A, written $\underline{\omega}(A)$ and $\bar{\omega}(A)$, as:

$$\underline{\omega}(A) = \{t \in T \mid \Gamma(t) \subseteq A\} \tag{9}$$
$$\bar{\omega}(A) = \{t \in T \mid \Gamma(t) \cap A \neq 0\} \tag{10}$$

Let P be a probability function defined on 2^{Θ}. Based on the notion of compatibility relation, Dempster (1967) defined the following lower and upper probabilities induced by the multivalued mapping (8) as:

$$P_*(A) = P(\underline{\omega}(A)) \tag{11}$$
$$P^*(A) = P(\bar{\omega}(A)) \tag{12}$$

The lower probability function is in fact a belief function and the upper probability function is a plausibility function (Shafer, 1976). By usng the same framework, Dubois and Prade (1985) introduced the lower and upper necessity and possibility functions. These lower and upper belief (plausibility) functions were also studied in Dubois and Prade (1985, 1990), and Yao and Wong (1991).

The framework proposed by Dempster can be used to propagate comparative belief relations (Yao and Wong, 1991). Let $>_p$ be a probability relation defined on 2^T. The lower and upper probability relations, $_*>_p$ and $^*>_p$, on 2^{Θ} are defined as: for A, $B \in 2^{\Theta}$,

$$A\, {_*}{>_p}\, B \Leftrightarrow \underline{\omega}(A) >_p \underline{\omega}(B)$$

and

$$A^* >_p B \Leftrightarrow \bar{\omega}(A) >_p \bar{\omega}(B)$$

The following theorem says that the lower and upper probability relations defined above are indeed the respective qualitative belief and plausibility relations (Yao and Wong, 1991).

Theorem 5: Let T and Θ be two frames, and let **c** be a compatibility relation between T and Θ. If a relation $>_p$ on 2^T satisfies axioms (P1)–(P4), namely, $>_p$ is a probability relation, the propagated relation $_* >_p$ satisfies axioms (B1)–(B5), that is, $_* >_p$ is a belief relation. Moreover, $^* >_p$ is the plausibility relation of $_* >_p$.

The notion of qualitative probability follows naturally from Savage's seven postulates of a personalistic theory of decision (Savage, 1972). The connection between qualitative probability and belief as stated in Theorem 5 thus provides further arguments in favor of our axiomatization of qualitative belief. This in turn provides additional justification for introducing belief functions in the mathematical theory of evidence (Shafer, 1976).

4. PROPAGATION AND COMBINATION OF QUALITATIVE BELIEF RELATIONS

In many practical situations of decision making, we are often interested in a number of related *questions*. We can formulate a frame of discernment for each question, and build a qualitative inference network based on the relationships, represented by compatibility relations, between these frames. If we want to evaluate the comparative beliefs in a particular frame, we have to consider the propagation of information from one frame to another (Yao and Wong, 1991), and the combination of beliefs based on different sources of evidence (Wong, Lingras, and Yao, 1991).

4.1. Propagation of belief relations

We can use the framework introduced in Section 3 to propagate a belief relation between distinct but related frames. The following theorem shows that such a propagation of information has a desirable property (Yao and Wong, 1991).

Theorem 6: Let T and Θ be two frames, and $\mathbf{c}$ a compatibility relation between T and Θ. If $>_{Bel}$ is a belief relation and $>_{Pl}$ is its plausibility relation, the propagated relation $_{*}>_{Bel}$ is also a belief relation and $^{*}>_{Pl}$ is a plausibility relation.

Theorem 6 indicates that the propagation of belief relations is in fact a closed process. This desirable property is essential for the design of a qualitative inference network.

4.2. Sequential combination

Sequential combination deals with propagating information from a frame S to another frame T, from T to Θ, and so on, in a sequential manner. It is sufficient to study the sequential combination involving only three distinct frames.

Consider three different frames S, T, and Θ. Let $\mathbf{c}_1$ be a compatibility relation between S and T, and $\mathbf{c}_2$ a compatibility relation between T and Θ. Let $>$ be a belief relation defined on 2^S. One can first propagate this relation to the frame T. According to Theorem 6, the induced relation $_{*}>$ on 2^T is a belief relation. By using the same procedure, one can construct a belief relation $_{**}>$ on 2^Θ from the belief relation $_{*}>$ on 2^T. The belief relation $_{**}>$ on 2^Θ is the result of the two-step propagations from S to T, and from T to Θ. One can propagate a plausibility relation in a similar way.

The sequential combination can be expressed in terms of the composition of two compatibility relations. A composite relation $\mathbf{c} = \mathbf{c}_1 \circ \mathbf{c}_2$ between S and Θ can be defined as follows: for $s \in S$ and $\theta \in \Theta$,

$$s\, \mathbf{c}_1 \circ \mathbf{c}_2\, \theta \Leftrightarrow \text{there exists a } t \in T \text{ such that } s\, \mathbf{c}_1\, t \text{ and } t\, \mathbf{c}_2\, \theta \quad (13)$$

By using the compatibility relation $\mathbf{c}_1 \circ \mathbf{c}_2$, one may propagate a belief relation $>$ directly from frame S to frame Θ. The following theorem shows that equivalent results are obtained (Wong, Lingras, and Yao, 1991).

Theorem 7: Let S, T, and Θ be three frames, $\mathbf{c}_1$ a compatibility relation between S and T, and $\mathbf{c}_2$ a compatibility relation between T and Θ. For a given belief relation $>$ on frames S, the result of propagating $>$ first from S to T by $\mathbf{c}_1$, and then from T to Θ by $\mathbf{c}_2$, is the same as that of propagating $>$ directly from S to Θ by the composite relation $\mathbf{c}_1 \circ \mathbf{c}_2$.

The sequential combination can also be used to combine quantitative information. Results similar to those of Theorems 6 and 7 can be obtained (Dubois and Prade, 1985, 1990; Yao and Wong, 1991).

4.3. Parallel combination

In parallel combination, one is dealing with a number of belief relations on the same frame, each of which is derived from a different source of evidence. The task is to combine these belief relations to produce a single one.

Given two belief relations $>_1$ and $>_2$, one can combine them by *one* of the following combination rules:

(I) $>_{12} = (>_1 \cup >_2)$;
(II) $>_{12} = (>_1 \cap >_2)$.

The first combination rule (I) attempts to poll all the information provided by $>_1$ and $>_2$ individually, while the second combination rule (II) uses only the information upon which both $>_1$ and $>_2$ agree. These rules represent the two extreme views for combining belief relations.

Rules (I) and (II) are considered well-behaved if the combined relation is a belief relation. In general, they do not guarantee that the combined relation is necessarily a belief relation. Nevertheless, these two combination rules can identify two types of conflicts between belief relations. We say that a type 1 conflict occurs if the combined relation produced by rule (I) is not a belief relation. Likewise, there is a type 2 conflict between two belief relations if the resulting relation produced by rule (II) is not a belief relation. The following lemmas specify the conditions under which there is a type 1 (type 2) conflict between two belief relations.

Lemma 1: Consider two belief relations $>_1$ and $>_2$ defined on 2^{Θ}. There is a type 1 conflict between $>_1$ and $>_2$ if and only if there exists a pair $A, B \in 2^{\Theta}$ such that

$$(A >_1 B) \wedge (B >_2 A) \tag{14}$$

Proof: Let $>_{12}$ be the combined relation of two belief relations $>_1$ and $>_2$. From the combination rule (I), it follows that for any $A, B \in 2^{\Theta}$, $A >_{12} B \Leftrightarrow (A >_1 B) \vee (A >_2 B)$.
($\Longleftarrow$) Assume that there is no type 1 conflict between $>_1$ and $>_2$. This means that $>_{12}$ is a belief relation. Suppose there is a pair $A, B \in 2^{\Theta}$

such that $A > B$ and $B >_2 A$. Then we have $A >_{12} B$ and $B >_{12} A$, which implies that $>_{12}$ is not a belief relation. This is a contradiction. Therefore, there does not exist a pair $A, B \in 2^{\Theta}$ such that $A >_1 B$ and $B >_2 A$.
($\Rightarrow$) Assume that there does not exist a pair $A, B \in 2^{\Theta}$ such that $A >_1 B$ and $B >_2 A$. Under this assumption, we can show that $>_{12}$ satisfies axioms (B1)–(B5), and hence it is a belief relation. Suppose $A >_{12} B$. This means that $A >_1 B$ or $A >_2 B$ holds. From our assumption, it follows that either $(A >_1 B, \neg(B >_2 A))$ or $(A >_2 B, \neg(B >_1 A))$. Since $>_1$ and $>_2$ are belief relations, we can immediately conclude that $(\neg(B >_1 A), \neg(B >_2 A))$. That is, $\neg(B >_{12} A)$ holds. Therefore, $>_{12}$ satisfies axiom (B1). Similarly, we can prove that $>_{12}$ satisfies axioms (B2)–(B5). Thus, $>_{12}$ is a belief relation and there exists no conflict between $>_1$ and $>_2$.

Lemma 2: Consider two belief relations $>_1$ and $>_2$ defined on 2^{Θ}. There is a type 2 conflict between $>_1$ and $>_2$ if and only if there exist $A, B, C \in 2^{\Theta}$ such that

$$(A >_1 B) \wedge (A >_2 B) \wedge (C \geqslant_1 A) \wedge (B \geqslant_2 C) \tag{15}$$

or

$$(A >_1 B) \wedge (A >_2 B) \wedge (B \geqslant_1 C) \wedge (C \geqslant_2 A) \tag{16}$$

Proof: Let $>_{12}$ be the combined relation of two belief relations $>_1$ and $>_2$. From the combination rule (II), it follows that for any $A, B \in 2^{\Theta}$, $A >_{12} B \Leftrightarrow (A >_1 B) \wedge (A >_2 B)$.
($\Leftarrow$) Assume that there is no type 2 conflict between $>_1$ and $>_2$. This means that $>_{12}$ is a belief relation. Suppose there are $A, B, C \in 2^{\Theta}$ such that condition (15) or (16) holds. Then we have $\neg(A >_{12} C)$ and $\neg(C >_{12} B)$. On the other hand, $A >_{12} B$ is true, which implies that $>_{12}$ does not satisfy negative transitivity, and hence it is not a belief relation. This is a contradiction. Therefore, there do not exist $A, B, C \in 2^{\Theta}$ satisfying the condition (15) or (16).
($\Rightarrow$) Assume that there do not exist A, $B, C \in 2^{\Theta}$ satisfying condition (15) or (16). Under this assumption, we can show that $>_{12}$ satisfies axioms (B1)–(B5), and hence it is a belief relation. Therefore, there is no type 2 conflict between $>_1$ and $>_2$. It can be easily verified that $>_{12}$ satisfies axioms (B1) and (B3)–(B5). Now suppose $\neg(A >_{12} C)$ and $\neg(C) >_{12} B)$. This means that $[\neg(A >_1 C) \vee \neg(A >_2 C) \wedge [\neg(C >_1 B) \vee \neg(C >_2 B)]$, which can be conveniently expressed as four different cases:

(i) $\neg(A >_1 C) \wedge \neg(C >_1 B)$,
(ii) $\neg(A >_1 C) \wedge \neg(C >_2 B)$,
(iii) $\neg(A >_2 C) \wedge \neg(C >_1 B)$,
(iv) $\neg(A >_2 C) \wedge \neg(C >_2 B)$.

Based on the property of negative transitivity, we have $\neg(A >_1 B)$ and $\neg(A >_2 \mathrm{B})$ for cases (i) and (iv), respectively. Therefore, $\neg(A >_{12} B)$ holds in these two cases. We now want to show that $\neg(A >_{12} B)$ holds in case (ii). Suppose $A >_{12} B$. This means that $(A >_1 B) \wedge (A >_2 B)$. On the other hand, $\neg(A >_1 C) \wedge \neg(C >_2 B) \Leftrightarrow (C \geqslant_1 A) \wedge (B \geqslant_2 C)$. These results suggest that A, B, C satisfy condition (15). This contradicts the assumption. Therefore, $\neg(A >_{12} B)$ is true in case (ii). Similarly, we can show that $\neg(A >_{12} B)$ holds in case (iii). Therefore, $>_{12}$ satisfies axiom (B2).

From Lemmas 1 and 2, it is clear that the type 1 conflict can be considered as a *direct* conflict, while the type 2 conflict represents an *indirect* conflict between two belief relations. It is interesting to note that combination rule (I) resolves type 2 conflicts, whereas combination rule (II) resolves type 1 conflicts. In general, combination rules (I) and (II) cannot be used to combine belief relations when conflicts exist. To design a parallel combination rule for resolving conflicts remains an important issue, although some progress has been made (Wong, Lingras, and Yao, 1991).

5. CONCLUSION

We have studied the axiomatic structure of different comparative beliefs with an emphasis on a special case called qualitative belief or or belief relation. It is shown that belief relations are compatible with belief functions. The understanding of the structure of qualitative belief facilitates the use of belief functions in decision making. We believe that the results reported here are useful in the development of a generalized expected utility model for belief functions (Jaffray, 1986; Yager, 1986).

Similar to a belief function, a belief relation can be defined directly on the frame of interest or obtained by propagating a probability relation on a different but related frame. For qualitative reasoning, combination rules for belief relations are crucial in the design of inference networks. Our preliminary results on sequential and parallel rules for combining belief relations may serve as a first step toward developing satisfactory combination rules.

BIBLIOGRAPHY

de Finetti, B. (1937). La prévision: ses lois logiques, ses sources subjectives. *Ann. Inst. Poincaré* 7: 1–68. English translation in H.E. Kyburg, Jr., and H.E. Smokler (eds., 1964), *Studies in subjective probability*. New York: Wiley.

Dempster, A.P. (1967). Upper and lower probabilities induced by a multivalued mapping. *Ann. Math. Statist.* 38: 325–39.

Dubois, D. (1986). Belief structures, possibility theory and decomposable confidence measures on finite sets. *Comput. Artif. Intell.* (Czechoslovakia) 5: 403–16.

Dubois, D. and Prade, H. (1985). Evidence measure based on fuzzy information. *Automatica* 21: 547–62.

Dubois, D. and Prade H. (1986). A set-theoretic view of belief functions: Logical operations and approximations by fuzzy sets. *Int. J. General Systems* 12: 193–226.

Dubois, D. and Prade, H. (1990). Rough fuzzy sets and fuzzy rough sets. *Int. J. General Systems*, 17: 191–209.

Fine, T.L. (1973). *Theories of probability: An examination of foundations*. New York: Academic Press.

Fishburn, P.C. (1970). *Utility theory for decision making*. New York: Wiley.

French, S. (1986). *Decision theory – An introduction to the mathematics of rationality*. Chichester: Ellis Horwood.

Jaffary, J.Y. (1986). Linear utility theory for belief functions. *Oper. Res. Lett.* 8: 107–12.

Klir, G.J. and Folger, T.A. (1988). *Fuzzy sets, uncertainty, and information*. Englewood Cliffs, NJ: Prentice Hall.

Kraft, C.H., Pratt, J.W., and Seidenberg, A. (1959). Intuitive probability on finite sets. *Ann. Math. Statist.* 30: 408–19.

Krantz, D.H. (1968). A survey of measurement theory. In G.B. Dantzig and Jr., A.F. Veinott (eds.), *Mathematics of the decision sciences*, Part 2, Vol. 12, pp. 314–50. Providence: Lectures in Applied Mathematics, American Mathematical Society.

Lingras, P. and Wong, S.K.M. (1990). Two perspectives of the Dempster-Shafer theory of belief functions. *Int. J. Man-Machine Studies* 33: 467–87.

Savage, L.J. (1972). *The foundations of statistics*. New York: Dover.

Shafer, G. (1976). *A mathematical theory of evidence*. Princeton, NJ: Princeton University Press.

Shafer, G. (1986). Belief function and possibility measures. In J.C. Bezdek (ed.), *Analysis of fuzzy information*, Vol. I, pp. 51–84. Boca Raton, FL: CRC Press.

Smets, P. (1988). Belief functions (with discussions). In P. Smets, A. Mamdani, D. Dubois, and H. Prade (eds.), *Non-standard logics for automated reasoning*, pp. 252–86. New York: Academic Press.

Wong, S.K.M., and Yao, Y.Y. (1990). Query formulation in linear retrieval models. *J. Am. Soc. Inf. Sci.* 41: 334–41.

Wong, S.K.M., Lingras, P., and Yao, Y.Y. (1991). Propagation of preference relations in qualitative networks. *Proceedings of the Twelfth International Joint Conference on Artificial Intelligence*, pp. 1204–1209.

Wong, S.K.M., Yao, Y.Y., and Lingras, P. (1991). Compatibility of quantitative and qualitative representations of belief. *Uncertainty in Artificial Intelligence: Proceedings of the Serenth Conference*, pp. 418–24.
Wong, S.K.M., Yao, Y.Y., Bollmann, P., and Bürger, H.C. (1991). Axiomatization of qualitative belief structure. *IEEE Trans. Sys. Man Cybern.* 21: 726–35.
Wong, S.K.M., Bollmann, P., and Yao, Y.Y. (In press). Characterization of qualitative belief structure. *Int. J. Man-Machine Studies.*
Yager, R.R. (1986). A general approach to decision making with evidential knowledge. In J.N. Kanal and J.F. Lemmer (eds.), *Uncertainty in artificial intelligence*, pp. 317–27. New York: North-Holland.
Yao, Y.Y. and Wong, S.K.M. (1991). Propagation of uncertain information. Submitted for publication.

7 Calculus with linguistic probabilities and beliefs*

Maria T. LAMATA and Serafin MORAL

Abstract: This paper studies the problem of calculus with probabilities and beliefs that are not expressed by means of real numbers, but by means of linguistic values. Different types of linguistic labels are considered. The approach has been to determine the desirable properties for a close generalization of probabilities and beliefs. Then it is shown which properties are not satisfied by the different sets of labels, the consequences of this lack of some properties, and how the consequences may be minimized by means of heuristic rules or "ad hoc" methods. One of the main objectives has been to produce a calculus with no greater complexity than the classical real valued. Sometimes, mathematical purity has been sacrified to get an efficient and simpler calculus.

Keywords: linguistic probablities, linguistic beliefs, conditioning, Dempster's rule.

1. INTRODUCTION

If we read a medical textbook, we shall find expressions such as

- "The incidence of disease D on population P is verly low"
- "Except in rare occasions, symptom S is present on disease D"
- "If symptom S is observed, then almost surely, the patient will have one of the diseases D1, D2, or D3"

* This work has been supported by the Commission of the European Communities under ESPRIT BRA 3085: DRUMS.

This is the basic a priori knowledge, together with personal past experience, with which doctors make decisions.

The type of knowledge expressed by these assertions is mainly of "probabilistic" or "evidential" nature, but the values are not given by numbers. Most of the effort in the theory of probability has been directed to the numerical point of view. However, it is clear that the above pieces of information are useful and it is possible to do some kind of reasoning with them. One possible solution would be to translate these assertions into numerical probabilities. But this would be unrealistic, because numbers express a degree of precision that is not present in original information.

The approach given in this paper is to develop a calculus for probabilities and beliefs directly for linguistic labels. Different types of labels representations will be considered:

1. *Infinitesimal values.* These are appropriate to represent "low" values of probability or belief: "The probability of A is very low."
2. *Interval probabilities or beliefs.* Here imprecision is represented by an interval of values.
3. *Fuzzy numbers.* This set is similar to the former one. The only difference is that instead of using intervals we use trapezoidal fuzzy numbers and fuzzy arithmetic (see Dubois and Prade [1980] and Bonissone [1982])
4. *Finite set of linguistic values.* In this case a finite set of possible values is enumerated and operations are defined by means of tables.

In all these sets there are two basic operations defined: addition and multiplication. For belief calculus there is also defined a partial ordering relation. These operations are assumed to verify some "desirable" properties in order to do a generalization of the corresponding theories. However, when particularizing to concrete sets of labels some of the properties will not be satisfied. That is, we will have simpler structures than those necessary to reproduce probability or belief calculus. The approach will not be to complicate these structures, but to determine which are the main points that are affected by the lack of some properties and to try to minimize the effects by providing heuristic rules.

Zadeh (1979) introduced the use of numerical quanitifiers represented by means of fuzzy sets to express relative cardinalities or conditional probabilities. Some other authors have studied how to transform linguistic expressions about uncertainty in fuzzy sets probabilities (Zimmer, 1986; Wallsten et al., 1986; Bonissone and Decker, 1986).

Amarger (1991) have considered the representation of imprecise probabilities by means of intervals. The main difference with our methodology is that our approach is simpler but at the expense of being less exact.

Jain and Agonino (1990) study the propagation of linguistic probabilities in influence diagrams. The probabilities are represented by fuzzy sets, and classical arithmetic for triangular fuzzy numbers is used to generalize probability calculus. This model will be included in our approach in the case in which labels are fuzzy numbers. The only difference will be in the normalization associated to conditioning. We propose a normalization procedure that is not based on fuzzy number division.

This paper is divided in three main sections. In the first one, the structure of the set of labels necessary to generalize probability calculus is studied. The four examples of sets of labels are introduced, specifying which properties are not satisfied in each case. In the second section, the study of probabilities taking values on a set of linguistic labels is considered. The main concepts of probability theory are introduced: probability distribution, conditional distributions, marginalization of probabilities, and conditioning. Independence is considered as a primitive concept and defined in an axiomatic way, following Pearl (1989). Finally, in the last section, the calculus with linguistically expressed beliefs is considered (see Dempster, 1967; Shafer, 1976; Smets, 1988). After introducing the appropriate properties to generalize belief functions calculus, the main concepts of this theory are considered: mass assignment, belief-plausibility functions, and Dempster's rule.

2. CALCULUS WITH LINGUISTIC LABELS

We assume that the set of possible labels for probabilities are given by a set L, which may be finite or infinite. The elements of L will be the mathematical representations of linguistic expressions. To define probabilities and to operate with them we need two operations: addition $(+)$ and multiplication $(\times)$. These operations should verify the following properties:

(P1) *Commutative*
for all $l_1, l_2 \in L$, $l_1 + l_2 = l_2 + l_1$, $l_1 \times l_2 = l_2 \times l_1$
(P2) *Associative*
for all $l_1, l_2, l_3 \in L$, $(l_1 + l_2) + l_3 = l_1 + (l_2 + l_3)$,
$(1_1 \times 1_2) \times l_3 = l_1 \times (l_2 \times l_3)$
(P3) *Neutral Element*
- For addition – $\exists 0 \in L$ such that for all $l \in L$, $0 + l = l$.
- For multiplication – $\exists 1 \in L$ such that for all $ll \in L$, $l \times 1 = l$.

(P4) *Distributive*
for all $l_1, l_2, l_3 \in L$, $l_1 \times (l_2 + l_3) = (l_1 \times l_2) + (l_1 \times l_3)$
(P5) *Complementary with respect to 1*
for all $l \in L$, $\exists l' \in L$, such that $l + l' = 1$
(P6) *Inverse Element for Normalization*
for all $l_1, l_2 \in L$, if $\exists l_3 \in L$ such that $l_1 + l_3 = l_2$, then
$\exists l_4 \in L$ such that $l_2 \times l_4 = l_1$ and thus l_4 is unique.

These properties are desirable to define probabilities in a proper way. Addition is necessary to define probabilities of disjoint sets. Multiplication is necessary to build multidimensional distributions from marginal and conditional distributions. It is also used to relate probability values with the concept of independence.

In the following we are going to consider four examples of linguistic labels.

Example 1: Let $L_1 = \{0, 1\} \cup \{l_i \mid i \geqslant 1\}$, where addition is defined as

- $0 + l = l$, for all $l \in L_1$
- $1 + l = 1$, for all $l \in L_1$
- $l_i + l_j = l_{\min\{i,j\}}$, for all $i, j \geqslant 1$

and multiplication is

- $l \times 1 = l$, for all $l \in L_1$
- $l \times 0 = 0$, for all $l \in L_1$
- $l_i \times l_j = l_{i+j}$, for all $i, j \geqslant 1$

When assigned to an event, a value of 1 means that there is no limitation of the probability of this event. A value of 0 means that this event is impossible. A value of l_i means that the probability of this event is of the order ρ^i, where ρ is a "small" number. This semantic establishes a direct relationship with the Spohn conditionals (Spohn, 1988; 1990), which have the same interpretation.

In this case, all the properties are satisfied.

Example 2: Consider now $L_2 = \{[a,b] \mid a,b \in R;\ a \leqslant b;\ a,b \geqslant 0\}$, with the operations:

$$[a_1,b_1] + [a_2,b_2] = [a_1 + a_2, b_1 + b_2]$$
$$[a_1,b_1] \times [a_2,b_2] = [a_1 \cdot a_2, b_1 \cdot b_2]$$

In this case there are some properties that are not satisfied:

- The existence of complementary with respect to 1: There is no interval $[a,b]$ such that $[a,b] + [0.4, 0.5] = 1$.
- The existence of the inverse element. For example, we have

$$[0.1, 0.2] + [0.2, 0.5] = [0.3, 0.7]$$

and if

$$[0.3, 0.7] \times [a,b] = [0.1, 0.2],$$

then $a = 1/3$ and $b = 2/7$, being $a > b$.

Example 3: Consider $L_3 = \{(a,b,\alpha,\beta) | 0 \leqslant a \leqslant b;\ \alpha,\beta \geqslant 0\}$ where (a,b,α,β) is a trapezoidal fuzzy number (Figure 7.1) and operations are defined in the usual way (Bonissone and Decker, 1986):

- $(a_1,b_1,\alpha_1,\beta_1) + (a_2,b_2,\alpha_2,B_2) = (a_1 + a_2, b_1 + b_2, \alpha_1 + \alpha_2, \beta_1 + \beta_2)$
- $(a_1,b_1,\alpha_1,\beta_1) \times (a_2,b_2,\alpha_2,\beta_2) = (a_1 \cdot a_2, b_1 \cdot b_2, a_1 \cdot \alpha_2 + a_2 \cdot \alpha_1 - \alpha_1 \cdot \alpha_2,\ b_1 \beta_2 + b_2 \cdot \beta_1 - \beta_1 \cdot \beta_2)$

This set of labels verifies exactly the same properties as L_2. In fact, trapezoidal fuzzy numbers are a generalization of intervals.

Example 4: In this case L_4 is a finite set with elements that are a direct translation of linguistic labels. For example $L_4 = \{0, AI, LP, LF, F, MF, VP, AS, 1\}$, where: 0 – Impossible, AI – Almost Impossible, LP – Very Little Probability, LF – Something Less than Fair, F – Fair ($\simeq$ 0.5), MF – Something More than Fair, VP – Very Probable, AS – Almost Sure, 1 – Sure.

Operations are defined by means of tables describing the results of the operations. To build these tables, we may follow Bonissone and Decker's (1986) approach consisting in assigning a fuzzy number to each one of the labels. Then the operations are carried out in terms of these fuzzy number. The result is rarely a fuzzy number corresponding to one of the existing labels, and the most similar is selected by an approximation process.

struction of the associated tabels, but considering the constraints associated with the a priori properties we want to impose (see Delgado et al., 1988; López de Mántaras et al., 1990). Consider Tables 7.1 and 7.2 for the addition and multiplication, respectively.

Table 7.1: Addition

+	0	*AI*	*LP*	*LF*	*F*	*MF*	*VP*	*AS*	1
0	0	*AI*	*LP*	*LF*	*F*	*MF*	*VP*	*AS*	1
AI	*AI*	*AI*	*LP*	*LF*	*F*	*MF*	*VP*	1	1
LP	*LP*	*LP*	*LF*	*F*	*MF*	*VP*	1	1	1
LF	*LF*	*LF*	*F*	*MF*	*VP*	1	1	1	1
F	*F*	*F*	*MF*	*VP*	1	1	1	1	1
MF	*MF*	*MF*	*VP*	1	1	1	1	1	1
VP	*VP*	*VP*	1	1	1	1	1	1	1
AS	*AS*	1	1	1	1	1	1	1	1
1	1	1	1	1	1	1	1	1	1

Table 7.2: Multiplication

+	0	*AI*	*LP*	*LF*	*F*	*MF*	*VP*	*AS*	1
0	0	0	0	0	0	0	0	0	0
AI	0	*AI*	*AI*	*AI*	*AI*	*AI*	*AI*	*AI*	*AI*
LP	0	*AI*	*AI*	*AI*	*LP*	*LP*	*LP*	*LP*	*LP*
LF	0	*AI*	*AI*	*LP*	*LP*	*LP*	*LP*	*LF*	*LF*
F	0	*AI*	*LP*	*LP*	*LP*	*LF*	*LF*	*F*	*F*
MF	0	*AI*	*LP*	*LP*	*LF*	*F*	*F*	*MF*	*MF*
VP	0	*AI*	*LP*	*LP*	*LF*	*F*	*MF*	*VP*	*VP*
AS	0	*AI*	*LP*	*LF*	*F*	*MF*	*VP*	*AS*	*AS*
1	0	*AI*	*LP*	*LF*	*F*	*MF*	*VP*	*AS*	1

Two remarks with respect to these operations: first, the part of the addition table that is below the inverse diagonal (all the elements equal to 1) is unrealistic. It has been put there to make the operation closed but, in fact, 1 plus 1 should be undefined or we should extend the set of labels to allow us to consider two times 1. We have preferred this simpler solution. In fact, additions are used to calculate the probability of one event that is equal to the disjoint union of two events. But we cannot have two disjoint events, each one of them with a probability equal to 1. From this point of view, it would be enough to impose that properties are satisfied when the results of the operations are not in this part of the table.

The second remark is that some of the required properties are very difficult to verify and, then, we have to discard them from the beginning. These are:

- *Inverse with respect to the product.* Consider the folowing natural order defined on the set of labels:

$$0 < AI < LP < LF < F < MF < VP < CS < 1$$

Then the result of multiplying a label, for example F (fair), by a label different from 0 should be a label less than or equal to F and different from 0. In our case, multiplying by all the nonzero labels we get

$$AI - LP - LP - LP - LF - LF - F - F$$

As we have a finite granularity, and we multiply more labels than the number of possible results, then some of them have to be repeated. The inverse of one repeated label with respect to F is not well defined: there are several such labels, that, multiplied by that label, give F as a result.

- *Distributive.* If we assume that $AI + AI = AI$ and there exists a label l such that $l \times l = AI$, and $\underbrace{l + \ldots + l}_{i\ times} = 1$ (LP verifies these conditions in our case), then distributive property cannot be satisfied. In effect, we have

$$l \times (\underbrace{l + \ldots + l}_{i\ times}) = l \times 1 = l$$

and

$$\underbrace{(l \times l) + \ldots + (l \times l)}_{i\ times} = \underbrace{AI + \ldots + AI}_{i\ times} = AI.$$

Formally, a simple way of verifying this property would be to do

$$l + l' = Msx(l, l')$$
$$l \times l' = Min(l, l')$$

but this would be more appropriate for possibilities than for probabilities.

In our case, we would accept that these properties are not satisfied. To solve the first one we will propose "ad hoc" methods to normalize probability distributions after conditioning. The effects of the lack of distributivity will be reduced giving heuristic rules to do the calculus.

On the other hand, it should be good that the distributivity be "almost satisfied" meaning that if $l_1 \times (l_2 + l_3) \neq (l_1 \times l_2) + (l_1 \times l_3)$, this is due to lack of granularity, but there should not be a very big difference between these values. For example, we may impose that there is not a difference between them bigger than one step in the above ordering of labels. The same could be said for associativity property. We could relax it, by considering an "approximate associative" property, in the same sense as before.

3. PROBABILITIES WITH LINGUISTIC LABELS

In this section, we shall consider the calculus of probabilities when they belong to a set of labels, L. First, we shall consider that L verifies all the desirable properties. The problems caused by the nonfulfilment of some of them will be pointed out.

The language expressing this theory will not be based on events, but in variables. The reason is that we find it easier to introduce concepts as independence and to adapt the calculus to the case in which some of the properties are not satisfied.

Assume that we have a variable X taking values on a finite set U. A probability distribution about X with respect to the set of labels L, is a mapping

$$p : U \rightarrow L$$

verifying

$$\sum_{u \in U} p(u) = 1$$

where 1 is the neutral element for multiplication on L.

A probability distribution, p, always defines a probability measure, P, which is defined as a mapping

$$P : \mathbf{P}(U) \rightarrow L$$

given by

$$P(A) = \sum_{a \in A} p(a)$$

where $\mathbf{P}(U)$ is the power set of U.

This mapping P verifies the classical properties of probability measures:

1. $P(\emptyset) = 0$
2. $P(U) = 1$
3. If $A \cap B = \emptyset$, $\quad P(A \cup B) = P(A) + P(B)$

These properties are satisfied by all the different types of labels, except $P(U) = 1$ in sets L_2 and L_3, because complementarity with respect to 1 is not satisfied. For L_2 we shall consider a weaker version of this property: $1 \in P(U)$ (remember that $P(U)$ is an interval). That is, we are not requiring $P(U)$ to be 1 exactly, but that 1 is a possible value for $P(U)$. The condition $P(U) = 1$ could be imposed as a high-level restriction, but then other methods have to be considered (see Cano, Moral, and Verdegay-López, 1991) and the calculus is very complicated. Analogously, in L_3, $P(U)$ is a fuzzy set, and we shall require that $\mu_{P(U)}(1) = 1$. That is, 1 belongs to $P(U)$ with degree 1.

Assume now that $X = (X_1, \ldots, X_n)$ is an n-dimensional variable, each one of the X_i taking values on a finite set U_i. If $J \subseteq \{1, \ldots, n\}$, by X_J we shall denote the set of variables $(X_j)_{j \in J}$ and by U_J the set $\Pi_{j \in J} U_j$.

If $J, K \subseteq \{1, \ldots, n\}$ and $J \cap K = \emptyset$, that is, we have two disjoint sets of variables, we shall call a conditional probability of X_J given X_K to a mapping

$$p^{J|K} : U_{J \cup K} \to L$$

such that

$$\text{for all } v \in V, \quad \sum_{u \in U_J} p^{J|K}(u, v) = 1$$

As above, this condition may not be satisfied in L_2 and L_3. To define conditional information in these sets of labels we shall change it to

$$1 \in \sum_{u \in U_J} p^{J|K}(u, v)$$

for the set L_2.

In L_3 we shall impose that 1 belongs to the fuzzy set $\Sigma_{u \in U_J} p^{J|K}(u,v)$ with degree 1.

If we have a probability distribution, p^K, for X_K and a conditional distribution $p^{J|K}$ for X_J given X_K, then these distributions define a global distribution $p^{J \cup K}$, on $U_{J \cup K}$ given by

$$p^{J \cup K}(u, v) = p^K(v) \times p^{J|K}(u, v)$$

If we have a probability p defined on $U_{J \cup K}$, we shall call marginal distribution of p, defined on U_J to the distribution

$$p^{\downarrow J} : U_J \rightarrow L$$

given by

$$p^{\downarrow J}(u) = \sum_{v \in U_K} p(u,v)$$

A first comment is that if either complementarity with respect to one or distributivity are satisfied the following may happen: we start with a probability p^K and a conditional distribution $p^{J|K}$ and build the global $p^{J \cup K}$. If we now calculate the marginal of $p^{J \cup K}$ on U_K, we do not obtain the same probability distribution, p_K.

Example 5: Assume that X_1 and X_2 are variables taking values on $U_1 = \{u_1, v_1\}, U_2 = \{u_2, v_2\}$ and a probability distribution, p, defined on U_1 and with values on L_2, given by

$$p(u_1) = [0.3, 0.5], \quad p(v_1) = [0.5, 0.7]$$

and the following conditional distribution of X_2 given X_1

$$p^{2|1}(u_2, u_1) = [0.1, 0.2], \quad p^{2|1}(v_2, u_1) = [0.8, 0.9]$$
$$p^{2|1}(u_2, v_1) = [0.6, 0.7], \quad p^{2|1}(v_2, v_1) = [0.3, 0.4]$$

Then, a global probability, $p^{\{1,2\}}$, is calculated by multiplication

$$p^{\{1,2\}}(u_1, u_2) = [0.03, 0.10] \qquad p^{\{1,2\}}(u_1, v_2) = [0.24, 0.45]$$
$$p^{\{1,2\}}(v_1, u_2) = [0.30, 0.49] \qquad p^{\{1,2\}}(v_1, v_2) = [0.15, 0.28]$$

If we now calculate the marginal on U_1, we get

$$(p^{\{1,2\}})^{\downarrow 1}(u_1) = [0.27, 0.55]$$

$$(p^{\{1,2\}})^{\downarrow 1}(v_1) = [0.45, 0.77]$$

As we can observe, the intervals have become more imprecise, because we have not taken into account that $p^{2/1}(u_2, u_1) + p^{2/1}(v_2, u_1)$ should be exactly 1. We have forgotten these high-level interactions to get a simpler calculus. But we have to be conscious of this loss of precision when we enlarge the frame of definition of probabilities. From this, we take out our first heuristic rule: *If distributive or complementary properties are not satisfied, then keep frames as small as possible.*

To introduce independence, we follow Pearl (1989) and consider it as a primitive concept defined in an axiomatic way. Thus, we think that is a point of view closer to reality than the approach of classical probability. Independence is usually defined in terms of decomposition of associated probabilities, but the way it is used in practice is: independence is preceived directly from the problem and then global information is built by the product rule.

An independence relation for variables $(X_1, \ldots, X_n)$ is defined (see Pearl [1989] for a more detailled study) as a relation $I(J,K,L)$ where J, K, L are disjoint subsets of $\{1, \ldots, n\}$, meaning that variable X_J is independent of X_L given X_K, and verifying the following axioms:

1. *Symmetry*

   $$I(J,K,L) \Rightarrow I(L,K,J)$$

2. *Decomposition*

   $$I(J,K,L \cup M) \Rightarrow I(J,K,L) \& I(J,K,M)$$

3. *Weak Union*

   $$I(J,K,L \cup M) \Rightarrow I(J,K \cup M,L)$$

4. *Contraction*

   $$I(J,K \cup L,\mathrm{M}) \& I(J,K,L) \Rightarrow I(J,K,L \cup M)$$

Independence relationships allow us to build new conditional distributions from known ones. The rule is as follows: If $p^{J/K}$ is a conditional distribution and $I(J,K,L)$ then the distribution $p^{J|K \cup L}$ given by

$$p^{J|K \cup L}(u.\,v,z) = p^{J|K}(u,v), \quad \text{for all } u \in U_J,\ v \in U_K,\ z \in U_L$$

is a conditional distribution of X_J given $X_{K \cup L}$.

The meaning is that if X_J is independent of X_L given X_K, then if we have conditional information of X_J given X_L, this is also conditional information if we know any value of X_L.

This property implies the decomposition rule of independence.

Proposition 1: *If X_1 and X_2 are independent, that is, $I(\{1\}, 0, \{2\})$ and if p_1 and p_2 are probability distributions for X_1 and X_2, then $p(u_1, u_2) = p_1(u_1) \times p_2(u_2)$ is a global probability distribution for X_1 and X_2.*

The proof is very simple and will be omitted.

To finish the calculus with linguistic probabilities we need the concept of conditioning. We have distinguished the a priori conditional distributions, which are pieces of information given for all the population, but organized by cases, from calculated conditional probabilities, which are deduced from a priori probabilities and observations for a particular element. In classical probability theory, if we have a variable X taking values on U with probability distribution p and we observe '$X \in A$' where A is a subset of U, then the conditional probablity p_A is calculated in two steps:

1. The function h_A, in which all the values assigned to elements that are not in A are changed to 0, is calculated:

$$h_A(u) = \begin{cases} \mathrm{p}(u) & \text{if } u \in A \\ 0 & \text{if } u \notin A \end{cases}$$

2. This function h_A is normalized by $k = \Sigma_{u \in A} h_A(u)$, calculating

$$p_A(u) = \begin{cases} \mathrm{p}(u)/k & \text{if } u \in A \\ 0 & \text{if } u \notin A \end{cases}$$

with which $\Sigma_{u \in A} p_A(u) = 1$.

If all the properties are satisfied, then the two steps can be generalized in a straightforward way. Considering the concrete examples, where some of the properties are not satisfied, step 1 is easily generalized in all systems of labels. However, step 2 is more difficult, because the inverse element is only satisfied in L_1. We have to design methods to renormalize in each particular case. A first solution could be not to do normalization in an operational way, and give the final results relative to the sum.

Example 6: Assume L_4, $U = \{u_1, u_2, u_3\}$ and p given by

$$p(u_1) = LP, \quad p(u_2) = MF, \quad p(u_3) = LP$$

and that we want to condition on $A = \{u_1, u_2\}$. The function h_A is given by

$$h_A(u_1) = LP, \quad h_A(u_2) = MF, \quad h_A(u_3) = 0$$

Then the conditional probabilities are

- $p_A(u_1) = LP$ with respect to VP
- $p_A(u_2) = MF$ with respect to VP

Ad hoc solutions may be also considered for each particular case. For the interval case, L_2, we may calculate the interval

$$[a, b] = \sum_{u \in U} h_A(u)$$

and then normalize by $k = (a + b)/2$:

$$p_A(u) = h_A(u)/k$$

It can be immediately verified that

$$1 \in \sum_{u \in U} p_A(u) = [a/b, b/k]$$

For the case of L_3 we can do a similar normalization, but considering

$$(a,b,\alpha,\beta) = \sum_{u \in U} h_A(u)$$

and $k = (a+b)/2$.

For L_4 the problem is different. If $k = \Sigma_{u \in U} h_A(u)$, then for every $h_A(u)$ we may have several labels such that multiplied by k we get $h_A(u)$. The proposed solution will be to consider all the labels as possible values of conditional probability:

$$p_A(u) = \{l \in L_4 \,|\, l \times k = h_A(u)\}$$

As L_4 is totally ordered and multiplication is increasing, this set may be given as an interval.

Example 7: In above example we had

$$h_A(u_1) = LP, \quad h_A(u_2) = MF, \quad h_A(u_3) = 0$$

and $k = VP$. Then,

$$p_A(u_1) = [LP, LF], \quad p_A(u_2) = [VP], \quad p_A(u_3) = [0]$$

One final remark about the calculus of conditional information: If X_1 and X_2 are independent variables and we observe '$X_2 \in B$' and we want to calculate the conditional probability associated to X_1, then if we calculate the bidimensional probability

$$p(u_1, u_2) = p_1(u_1) \times p_2(u_2)$$

and do the conditioning, and later marginalize X_1, then the probability p_1 may change because distributive property or inverse element is not satisfied. It should not change, because X_1 and X_2 are independent, but because of the lack of properties of the calculus we are using, this may happen. One heuristic rule to avoid this is the following: *Assume that we have variables $(X_1, \ldots, X_n)$, that we have obervations $\{O_i\}_{i \in K}$, (O_i for variable X_i), and that we want to calculate the conditional probability for X_j given all these observations, then:*

1. *Consider $K' = \{i \in K \,|\, O_i$ represents an exact value for $X_i : X_i = u_i\}$.*
2. *Determine a maximal set of variables $J \subseteq K - K'$ such that $I(J, K', \{j\})$.*
3. *Calculate the conditional probability by using the global distribution for variables, $\{j\} \cup (K - J)$.*

That is, we eliminate:

- The variables that are not in the set of observations (K) and are different from the variable in which we are interested.
- A maximal set of variables independent of X_j given K'.

4. BELIEF FUNCTIONS WITH LINGUISTIC LABELS

If we have a variable X taking values on a finite set U, we may have some knowledge about X that does not fit well with the representation provided by probability theory. In particular, the so-called Dempster-Shafer Theory (Dempster, 1967; Shafer, 1976) allows us a more direct representation of personal subjective beliefs, without assuming additivity. Here we shall consider some ideas about the calculus associated with this theory when beliefs belong to a particular set of labels, L. We shall follow Smets' (1988) interpretation, in which this model is distinguished from upper and lower probabilities (see Cano, Moral, and Verdegay-López, 1991). It is not assumed that belief-plausibility intervals represent the possible values of some underlying but unknown probability, but they try only to represent subjective credibility values.

Following Smets (1988) the open-world assumption will be considered and then the empty set can have a possitive mass. In this way, the normalization problem will be avoided.

Assume that we have a set of labels L and two operations, addition $(+)$ and multiplication $(\times)$, defined on it. It will be assumed that properties $P1 - P4$ of Section 2 are satisfied. Furthermore it will be assumed that there is a partial order relation, $\leqslant$, defined on L and verifying the following properties:

(O1) Reflexive, Antisymmetric, Transitive
(O2) for all $l_1, l_2 \in L$, $\quad l_1 \leqslant l_1 + l_2$
(O3) If $l_1 \leqslant l_2$, then there exists one and only one label $l_3 \in L$, such that $l_1 + l_3 = l_2$. In this case, l_3 will be denoted as $l_2 - l_1$.

Evidently, not all the properties are satisfied by the considered label systems. In L_1, L_2, and L_3 we do not have an order relation. This may be defined in the following way.

- L_1 $\quad - \; 0 \leqslant l_i \leqslant 1, \quad$ for all $i \geqslant 1$
  $\quad - \; l_i \leqslant l_j, \quad$ if $i \geqslant j$

- $L_2\,[a_1,b_1] \leqslant [a_2,b_2] \Leftrightarrow (a_1 \leqslant a_2)$ and $(b_1 \leqslant b_2)$
- $L_3\,(a_1,b_1,\alpha_1,\beta_1) \leqslant (a_2,b_2,\alpha_2,\beta_2) \Leftrightarrow (a_1 \leqslant a_2)$ and $(b_1 \leqslant b_2)$ and $(a_1 - \alpha_1 \leqslant a_2 - \alpha_2)$ and $(b_1 + \beta_1 \leqslant b_2 + \beta_2)$

L_1 verifies all the properties except (O3) in the "only" part. For example, we may have $l_2 \leqslant l_2$ and there exist infinite labels $l_i (i = 2, 3, 4, \ldots)$ such that $l_i + l_2 = l_2$.

L_2 and L_3 verify all the properties except (O3). The problem here is different. We may have $l_1 \leqslant l_2$ and for all $l \in L$, $l_1 + l \neq l_3$.

L_4 does not verify distributive property. In general, it does not verify (O3) either. We may impose that there exists one, but not a unique label verifying the given condition.

Now we are going to consider the Dempster-Shafer theory when belief values are expressed by means of linguistic values. The basic concept of this theory is the concept of a mass assignment. This is a mapping

$$m : \mathbf{P}(U) \rightarrow L$$

verifying

$$\sum_{A \subseteq U} m(A) = 1$$

As before, this property cannot be imposed on L_2 and L_3. It is replaced by the corresponding weaker versions.

A mass assignment defines two mappings:

- A belief function

$$Bel : \mathbf{P}(U) \rightarrow L$$
$$Bel(A) = \sum_{\emptyset \neq B \subseteq A} m(B)$$

- A plausibility function

$$Pl : \mathbf{P}(U) \rightarrow L$$
$$Pl(A) = \sum_{B \cap A \neq 0} m(B)$$

This immediately shows the following properties:

1. $Bel(\emptyset) = 0$, $Pl(\emptyset) = 0$
2. $Bel(U) = Pl(U) = 1 - m(\emptyset)$
3. $Bel(A) \leqslant Pl(A)$
4. $Pl(A) + Bel(\bar{A}) = 1 - m(\emptyset)$
5. for all $A_1, \ldots, A_n$,

$$Bel(A_1 \cup \dots \cup A_n) \geqslant \sum_i Bel(A_i) - \sum_{i<j} Bel(A_i \cap A_j) + \dots$$
$$+ (-1)^n Bel(A_1 \cap \dots \cap A_n)$$

In the last property the right part of the inequality has to be understood in the following way. First the positive and negative terms are added separately giving rise to l_1 and l_2 respectively. Then this property says that $l_2 \leqslant l_1$ being $l_1 - l_2 \leqslant Bel(A_1 \cup \dots \cup A_n)$.

For the calculus of mass assignment, m, from belief functions, we may state the following equalities:

- $m(A) = \sum_{\emptyset \neq B \subseteq A} (-1)^{|B-A|} Bel(B)$

- $m(\emptyset) = 1 - \sum_{\emptyset \neq A \subseteq U} m(A)$

where these expressions have to be interpreted as above.

This calculus is totally analogous to numerical belief functions theory; however, property (O3) is never totally satisfied and then it has to be adapted. For L_1 and L_4 it may be done in an easy way:

$$\text{If } l_1 \leqslant l_2, l_2 - l_1 = \max\{l \in L \mid l + l_1 = l_2\}$$

We do not have any special reason to choose the maximum in the above expression. We could have chosen any other element of the nonempty set $\{l \in L \mid l + l_1 = l_2\}$. It is only a way of selecting one element from it.

For L_2 and L_4 the problem is not the same: the set $\{l \in L \mid l + l_1 = l_2\}$ may be empty. However, it can be satisfied that this only happens in expression:

$$m(\emptyset) = 1 - \sum_{\emptyset \neq A \subseteq C} m(A)$$

In the case of intervals, $1 - [a, b]$ may be defined as $[1 - b, 1 - a]$. In the case of fuzzy numbers, we may do $1 - (a, b, \alpha, \beta) = (1 - b, 1 - a, \beta, \alpha)$. For the expression

$$m(A) = \sum_{\emptyset \neq B \subseteq A} (-1)^{|B-A|} Bel(B)$$

if Bel has been defined from a mass assignment, then the operation in the right side of the equality may be always carried out.

Example 8: Assume $U = \{u_1, u_2\}$, $L = L_2$ and

$$Bel(\{u_1\}) = [0.1, 0.2], \quad Bel(\{u_2\}) = [0.2, 0.3], \quad Bel(\{u_1, u_2\}) = 1$$

In this case

$$m(\{u_1\}) = [0.1, 0.2], \quad m(\{u_2\}) = [0.2, 0.3]$$

but

$$m(\{u_1, u_2\}) = Bel(\{u_1, u_2\}) - Bel(\{u_1\}) - Bel(\{u_2\}) = 1 - [0.3, 05]$$

Then, there is not any m associated with this function *Bel.* If we want to use basic probability assignments, we could consider

$$m(\{u_1, u_2\}) = 1 - [0.3, 0.5] = [0.5, 0.7]$$

but then some information is lost: if we recalculate $Bel(U)$ we get [0.8, 1.2].

Finally the nonnormalized Dempster's rule (Smets [1988]):

$$m_1 \oplus m_2(A) = \sum_{A = B_1 \cap B_2} m_1(B_1) \times m_2(B_2)$$

may be easily generalized. It is important to remark that to verify $\Sigma_{A \subseteq U} m_1 \oplus m_2(A) = 1$ we need the distributive property. If this property is not verified as in the case of L_4, some heuristic rule should be applied to recover this equality. As distributivity is "almost satisfied" then the difference between 1 and $\Sigma_{A \subseteq U} m_1 \oplus m_2(A)$ could never be very big. Then we propose the following rule: *the result is modified to add 1, by increasing or decreasing the masses assigned to the different focal elements. To do it, we start with the sets having greater mass (in these sets the relative change of mass is smaller).*

The combination is commutative and associative. However, associativity is not exactly satisfied in L_4 case, because we need the distributive property.

Another remark is that the combination of a mass m with mass,

- $m'(\emptyset) = l_1$
- $m'(U) = l_2$

where $l_1 + l_2 = 1$,

should produce in m an addition of l_1 to the empty set, while reducing all the other masses in a proportional way. However, it may also produce a loss of the relative information of the other masses. For this case we shall consider the following rule: *if we have to combine a mass m with a mass assignment with the total set U as the only focal nonempty element (m') then it is better not to do the combination, and to count the mass l_1 assigned to the empty set as an additional parameter of the resulting mass,* that is, *not to combine with low quality ($m'(\emptyset)$ different from O) and uninformative masses (all the other mass assigned to the total set, U).*

Example 9: Consider $L = L_4$, $U = \{u_1, u_2, u_3\}$, and m given by

$$m(\{u_1, u_2\}) = MF, \quad m(\{u_3\}) = F, \quad m(\{u_2, u_3\}) = LP$$

If we combine it with m':

$$m'(\emptyset) = CS, \quad m'(U) = AI$$

we get

- $m \oplus m'(\emptyset) = 1$
- $m \oplus m'(\{u_1, u_2\}) = AI$
- $m \oplus m'(\{u_3\}) = AI$
- $m \oplus m'(\{u_2, u_3\}) = AI$

with which relative credibilities among the other elements of U are lost. The application of the heuristic rule should imply leaving $m \oplus m'$ equal to m with an additional value of CS for the empty set.

In short, for belief functions with linguistic labels we have the following points:

- In general it is better to start from a mass assignment. If we start with a belief function and we calculate the associated mass assignment, then some information is lost.
- We have to reorganize the masses, after applying Dempster's rule, so that they add to one.
- Some criterion has to be designed to eliminate uninformative pieces of information of low quality. This may be a strong version of the above one. For example, we could eliminate pieces of information that are *almost uninformative*, after defining an information measure.

5. CONCLUSIONS

Probabilites and belief functions taking values on general linguistic labels sets may be studied but, in general, the problems are greater than in classical numerical theories. The main problem is that we are using sets with fewer properties than the real numbers. For example, in the case of L_4 we are using a very narrow scale. In the case of L_2 we are using intervals and forgetting high-level interactions to decrease the complexity of the calculus. We have tried to solve the lack of properties by means of heuristic rules and ad hoc methods. However, we think that more work is necessary to discover a more complete set of heuristic rules. We feel that the work with belief functions is less finished than the probability case.

Future work will include the propagation of these probabilities and beliefs on causal networks, taking as a basis the axiomatic framework given in Cano, Delgado, and Moral (1991). We shall study also the case of a nonperfect specification of the initial labels. Although linguistic labels have some implicit degree of imprecision, it may be considered the ignorance about these values that gives rise to a generalization analogous to upper and lower probabilities with respect to probabilities.

BIBLIOGRAPHY

Amarger, S., Dubois, D. and Prade H. (1991). Constraint propagation with imprecise conditional probabilities. In B. D'Ambrosio, Ph. Smets, and P. P. Bonissone (eds.), *Proceedings of the Seventh Conference on Uncertainty in A.I.*, pp. 26–34. San Mateo, CA: Morgan Kaufmann.

Bonissone, P. P. (1982). A fuzzy set based linguistic approach: Theory and applications. In M. M. Gupta and E. Sanchez (eds.), *Approximate reasoning in decision analysis*, pp. 329–39. New York: North-Holland.

Bonissone, P. P. and Decker, K. S. (1986). Selecting uncertainty calculi and granularity: An experiment in trading-off precision and complexity. In L. N. Kanal and J. F. Lemmer (eds.), *Uncertainty in artificial intelligence*, pp. 217–247. Amsterdam: North-Holland.

Cano, J. E., Delgado, M., and Moral, S. (1991). An axiomatic framework for the propagation of uncertainty in directed acyclic networks. Submitted to *International Journal of Approximate Reasoning*.

Cano, J. E., Moral, S. and Verdegay-López, J. F. (1991). Combination of upper and lower probabilities. In B. D'Ambrosio, Ph. Smets, and P. P. Bonissone (eds.), *Proceedings of the Seventh Conference Uncertainty in A.I.*, pp. 61–68. San Mateo, CA: Morgan Kaufmann.

Delgado, M., Verdegay, J.L., and Vila, M.A. (1988). Ranking linguistic outcomes under fuzziness and randomness. *Proceedings of the Eighteenth International Symposium on Multiple-Valued Logic*, pp. 352–356. Computer Society Press.

Dempster, A. P. (1967). Upper and lower probabilities induced by a multivalued mapping. *Ann. Math. Stat.* 38: 325–39.

Dubois, D. and Prade, H. (1980). *Fuzzy sets and systems: Theory and applications.* New York: Academic Press.

Jain, P. and Agogino, A.M. (1990). Stochastic sensitivity analysis using fuzzy influence diagrams. In R.D. Shacter, T. S. Levitt, L. N. Kanal, and J. F. Lemmer (eds.), *Uncertainty in artificial intelligence* 4, pp. 79–92. Amsterdam: North-Holland.

López de Mántaras, R., Godor, L., and Sanguesa, R. (1990). Connective operators elicitation for linguistic term sets. *Proc. Inter. Conference on Fuzzy Logic and Neural Networks*, pp. 729–733. Iizuka, Japan.

Pearl, J. (1989). *Probabilistic reasoning with intelligent systems*. San Mateo, CA: Morgan Kaufman.

Shafer, G. (1976). *A mathematical theory of evidence*. Princeton, NJ: Princeton University Press.

Smets, Ph. (1988). Belief functions. In Ph. Smets, E. H. Mamdani, D. Dubois, and H. Prade (eds.), *Non-standard logics for automated reasoning*, pp. 253–86. London: Academic Press.

Spohn W. (1988). Ordinal conditional functions: A dynamic theory of epistemic states. In. W. L. Harper and B. Skyrms (eds.), *Causation in decision, belief change, and statistics*, pp. 105–134. Dordrecht: Kluwer.

Spohn, W. (1990). A general non-probabilistic theory of inductive reasoning. In R. D. Shacter, T. S. Levitt, L. N. Kanal, and J. F. Lemmer (eds.), *Uncertainty in artificial intelligence* 4, pp. 149–58. Amsterdam: North-Holland.

Wallsten, T. S., Budescu, D. V., Rapoport, A., Zwick, R., and Forsyth, B. (1986). Measuring the vague meaning of probability terms. *Journal of Experimental Psychology*: General 115: pp. 348–65.

Zadeh, L. A. (1979). A theory of approximate reasoning. *Machine Intelligence* 9: 149–94.

Zimmer, A. C. (1986). What uncertainty judgments can tell about the underlying subjective probabilities. In L. N. Lanal and J. F. Lemmer (eds.), *Uncertainty in artificial intelligence* 4, pp. 249–58. Amsterdam: North-Holland.

8 Steps toward efficient implementation of Dempster-Shafer theory

Hong XU and Robert KENNES

Abstract: We present some steps toward efficient implementation of Dempster-Shafer theory. More explicitly, we have implemented the belief functions propagation using the local computation method due to Shenoy and Shafer. Our implementation has the following two interesting features. First, our implementation reduces the number of computations of Dempster's rule as much as possible. Second, our implementation represents belief functions by bit-arrays. The latter feature speeds up the computation of Dempster's rule and simplifies the computations of projections and extensions required by the local computation method. We also present a fast method for computing Dempster's rule of combination based on commonality functions and the fast Möbius transformation.

Keywords: Dempster-Shafer theory, belief functions, Dempster's rule of combination, local computation, evidential system (belief function network).

1. INTRODUCTION

Dempster-Shafer theory of belief function (Shafer, 1976; Smets, 1988) is an intuitively appealing formalism used for reasoning with uncertainty. However, a problem of using this theory to handle uncertainty lies in the computational complexity of Dempster's rule of combination, the main inference mechanism of Dempster-Shafer theory. In order to reduce the complexity of the Dempster-Shafer theory, several algorithms suitable for some specific cases were proposed in the last decade (Barnett, 1981; Gordon and Shortiffe, 1985; Shafer and Logan, 1987).

The objective of this paper is to present some other steps toward a more efficient implementation of Dempster-Shafer theory. First, we will use the technique of local computation applied to belief functions propagation (Shafer et al., 1987) and we will show how to implement this technique efficiently. In this scheme, some intermediate results are proposed to be stored during propagation. We will show that the number of computations of Dempster's rule of combination can be reduced to the smallest amount by using these stored intermediate results. Moreover, when one or more inputs are changed after propagation has been completed, the intermediate results that are not influenced by the changed inputs can be reused directly in the repropagation, which avoids repeated computations.

The second step for improving this in implementation is to speed up Dempster's rule of combination itself. As the set-intersection and set-comparison needed in Dempster's combination is computationally involved, we propose using bit-arrays for storing belief functions and their combination to avoid them. Besides Dempster's combination, the projection and extension of subsets from one frame to another are also simplified by using bit-arrays.

Another way to speed up the computation of Dempster's rule of combination is via commonality functions (Kennes, 1991). We will show why the transformation from a basic probability assignment (bpa) to its commonality function can be seen as a generalized Fourier transformation, also known as Möbius transformation. Then, we will use a fast algorithm for computing this generalized Fourier transformation, which provides a fast method for computing Dempster's rule of combination.

The remainder of this paper is organized as follows. Section 2 reviews some basic concepts of belief functions and belief function networks. Section 3 describes belief function propagation using local computation and its efficient implementation. Section 4 shows the benefits by using bit-arrays. Section 5 presents commonality function and the Möbius transformation. Finally, some conclusions are given in section 6.

2. BASIC CONCEPTS OF BELIEF FUNCTION NETWORKS

Dempster-Shafer theory, also called theory of belief functions (Shafer, 1976; Smets, 1988), is concerned with the problem of representing and manipulating uncertain knowledge. In this section, we review some basic concepts and definitions of belief functions and belief functions networks. This presentation follows Shafer and Shenoy (1988).

Variables and Configurations. We use the symbol $\mathbf{W}_X$ for the set of possible values of a variable X, and we call $\mathbf{W}_X$ the *frame for X*. Given a finite nonempty set h of variables, let $\mathbf{W}_h$ denote the Cartesian product of $\mathbf{W}_X$ for X in h: $\mathbf{W}_h = \times\{\mathbf{W}_X \mid X \in h\}$. We call $\mathbf{W}_h$ the *frame for h*. We refer to elements of $\mathbf{W}_h$ as *configurations of h*.

Projection and Extension (of configurations and sets of configurations). If g and h are sets of variables $h \subseteq g$, and $\mathbf{x}$ is a configuration of g, then we let $\mathbf{x}^{\downarrow h}$ denote the projection of $\mathbf{x}$ to $\mathbf{W}_h$. $\mathbf{x}^{\downarrow h}$ is always a configuration of h. If $\mathbf{g}$ is a nonempty subset of $\mathbf{W}_g$, then the *projection of* $\mathbf{g}$ *to h*, denoted by $\mathbf{g}^{\downarrow h}$, is obtained by projecting elements of $\mathbf{g}$ to $\mathbf{W}_h$, i.e., $\mathbf{g}^{\downarrow h} = \{\mathbf{x}^{\downarrow h} \mid \mathbf{x} \in \mathbf{g}\}$. If g and h are sets of variables, $h \subseteq g$, and $\mathbf{h}$ is subset of $\mathbf{W}_h$, then the *extension of* $\mathbf{h}$ to g, denoted by $\mathbf{h}^{\uparrow g}$, is $\mathbf{h}^{\times}\mathbf{W}_{g-h}$ (called the cylinder set extension of h into g).

Basic Probability Assignment. A *basic probability assignment (bpa)* — also called *basic belief assignment (bba)* — m on h, is a function that assigns a value in [0, 1] to every subset $\mathbf{a}$ of $\mathbf{W}_h$ and satisfies the following axioms:

(i) $m(\varnothing = 0$; and
(ii) $\sum\{m(\mathbf{a}) \mid \mathbf{a} \subseteq \mathbf{W}_h\} = 1$

Belief Function. The *belief function* Bel_m associated with the bpa m is a function that assigns a value in [0, 1] to every nonempty subset $\mathbf{a}$ of $\mathbf{dW}_h$; called "degree of belief in $\mathbf{a}$," it is defined by

$$Bel_m(\mathbf{a}) = \sum\{m(\mathbf{b}) \mid \mathbf{b} \subseteq \mathbf{a}\}$$

A subset $\mathbf{a}$ for which $m(\mathbf{a}) > 0$ is called a *focal element of* Bel_m. The belief function defined by $m(\mathbf{W}_h) = 1$ is called the vacuous belief function on h.

Dempster's Rule of Combination. Consider two bpa's m_1, m_2 on g, h, let $m = m_1 \oplus m_2$ be the bpa on $g \cup h$. By Dempster's rule of combination, m is defined by:

$$m(\emptyset) = 0 \text{ and}$$
$$m(\mathbf{c}) = K^{-1}\sum\{m_1(\mathbf{a})m_2(\mathbf{b}) \mid (\mathbf{a}^{\uparrow(g\cup h)} \cap \mathbf{b}^{\uparrow(g\cup h)}) = \mathbf{c}\}$$

where

$$K = 1 - \sum\{m_1(\mathbf{a})m_2(\mathbf{b}) \mid (\mathbf{a}^{\uparrow(g\cup h)} \cap \mathbf{b}^{\uparrow(g\cup h)}) = \emptyset\}$$

K is a normalizing factor, which intuitively measures how much m_1 and m_2 are conflicting. In $K=0$, then we say that dm_1 and m_2 are not combinable. In this paper we will discard the normalization factor of Dempster's rule of combination.

Marginalization. Suppose m is a bpa on g, $h \subseteq g$, and $h \neq \emptyset$. *The marginal of m for h*, denoted by $m^{\downarrow h}$, is the bpa defined by

$$m^{\downarrow h}(\mathbf{a}) = \sum\{m(\mathbf{b}) \mid \mathbf{b} \subseteq \mathbf{W}_g, \mathbf{b}^{\downarrow h} = \mathbf{a}\} \text{ for all subsets } \mathbf{a} \text{ of } \mathbf{W}_h$$

Belief Function Network. *A belief function network*, also called an *evidential system*, consists of a finite set of variables **X**, of a set of subsets of **X:H**, and of a finite collection of independent belief functions (Bel_1, Bel_2, ..., Bel_k) where each belief function Bel_i is the prior belief function on some subset h.

Intuitively, the set of variables formalizes different aspects of the situation to consider; the elements of $\mathbf{W}_X$ associated with each variable X are mutually exclusive and exhaustive. The set of belief functions formalizes knowledge about the relations among the variables.

Evaluation of a Belief Function Network. To evaluate a belief function network, we have to proceed as follows:

(i) combine all Bel_i's in the network (the resulting belief function is called *a global belief function*),

(ii) compute the marginal of the global belief function for each variable in the network.

3. THE IMPLEMENTATION OF BELIEF FUNCTION PROPAGATION

Because the computational complexity of Dempster's combination is exponential with the size of the frame of belief functions being combined, it is not feasible to compute the global belief function when there is a large number of variables. Thus, an alternative way for evaluating belief function is needed. Recently, a number of researchers have developed network-based propagation techniques to improve the efficiency of belief function computations. Among them, Shafer and Shenoy have proposed a general technique for local computation that may easily be applied to the belief function case (Shafer et al., 1987; Shafer and Shenoy, 1988). In this section, we first describe this technique, then give an approach for applying it to belief function network efficiently. Normalization of combination is not considered during the propagation process; it can be done after the marginals have been computed.

3.1. Belief function propagation using local computation

It was shown in (Shafer et al., 1987) that if the belief function network can be represented by a certain kind of tree, called Markov tree, the belief functions can be "propagated" in the Markov tree by a local message-passing scheme, producing as a result the marginals of the global belief function for each of the nodes.

Markov tree is a kind of tree whose nodes are the subsets of **X** with the property that when a variable belongs to two distinct nodes, then every node lying on the path between these two nodes contains the variables. For **H** and **X** defined in the previous section, in the language of graph theory, **H** is called a *hypergraph on* **X** and each element of **H** is called a *hyperedge*. In order to use local computation for propagation, the hypergraph should be arranged in a Markov tree. We can always find a method to arrange a hypergraph in a Markov tree. Algorithms for constructing a Markov tree for a hypergraph can be found in Mellouli (1987) and Zhang (1988).

We now discuss the belief funcion propagation scheme using local computation (Shafer and Shenoy, 1988). Suppose we have already arranged the hypergraph in a Markov tree $G=(\mathbf{M},\mathbf{E})$. For each node v, let $\mathbf{N}_v=\{v_k \mid (v_k, v)\in \mathbf{E}\}$ be the set of neighbors of v, Bel_v the prior belief function on v, and $Bel^{\uparrow v}$ the marginal of the global belief function for v. Let $L(G)$ be the set of leaves of G given some designated node as the root of the tree. In the propagation process, each node sends a belief function to each of its neighbors. The belief function sent by v to v_i is referred as a "message" and is denoted by $M^{v\to v_i}$. We define it as:

$$M^{v \to v_i} = ((Bel_v \oplus (\oplus \{M^{v_k \to v} \mid v_k \in (\mathbf{N}_v - \{v_i\})\}))^{\downarrow(v \cap v_i)})^{\uparrow v_i} \qquad (1)$$

Because a leaf v has only one neighbor, say v_i, then the above expression reduces to:

$$M^{v \to v_i} = ((Bel_v)^{\downarrow(v \cap v_i)})^{\uparrow v_i}$$

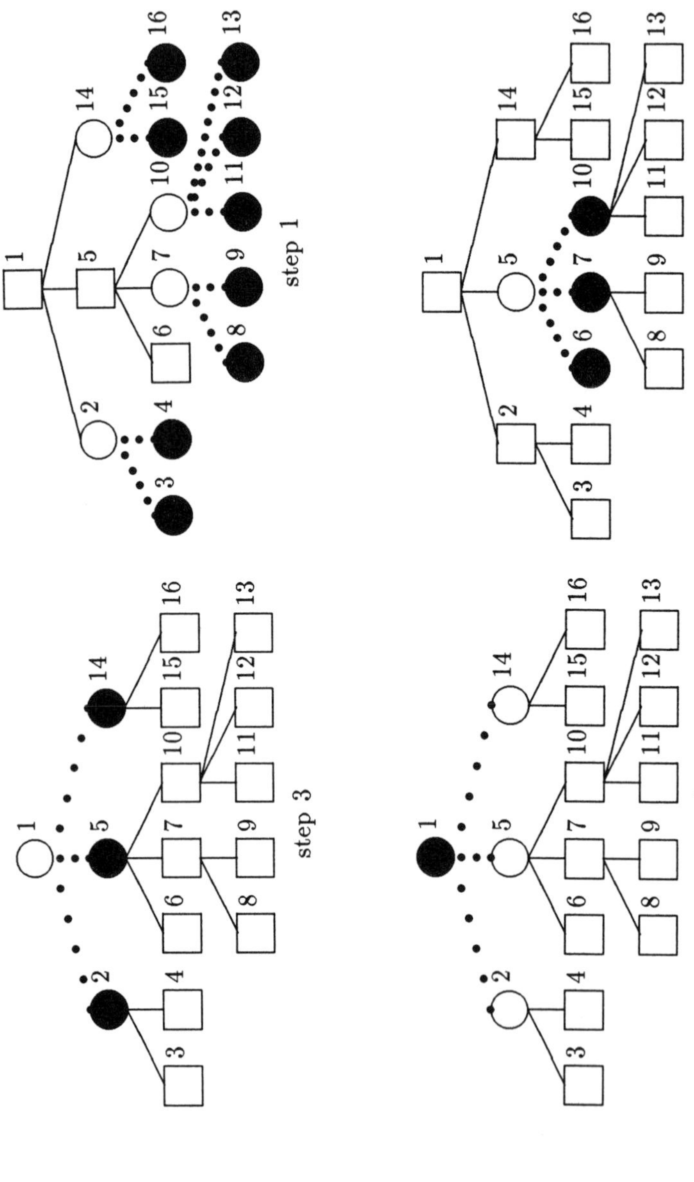

Figure 8.1. The message-passing scheme for belief function propagation.

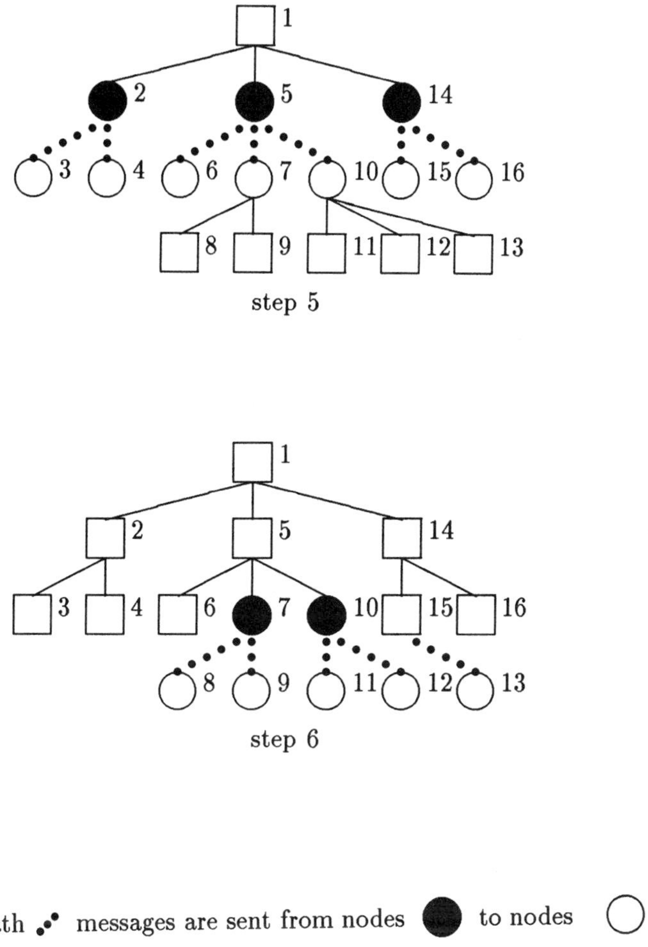

Figure 8.1. (continued)

After v has received the messages from all of its neighbors, the marginal $Bel^{\uparrow v}$ for v is given by

$$Bel^{\uparrow v} = Bel_v \oplus \left(\oplus \{M^{v_i \to v} \mid v_i \in \mathbf{N}_v\}\right) \tag{2}$$

Thus, when the propagation starts, the leaves of the Markov tree can send messages to their neighbors right away. The others send a message to one neighbor after they have received messages from all but that one neighbor. And when a node receives a message from that one neighbor, it apropriately (i.e., by using (1)) sends messages back to the remaining neighbors. All the messages can be transmitted through the Markov tree in this way. This belief function propagation process can be illustrated as in Figure 8.1. For more details about this scheme, see Shafer et al. (1987) and Shafer and Shenoy (1988).

3.2. An efficient implementation

The computation of Dempster's combination involves the most computational expense during the whole propagation process. So the number of applications of the combination during propagation should be reduced as much as possible. In this section, we present a scheme for belief function propagation using local computation that reduces the number of applications of Dempster's combination to the fewest.

In our scheme, it is assumed that once a Markov tree representation $G = (\mathbf{M}, \mathbf{E})$ is chosen, it will not change unless the belief function network that it represents is changed. We choose one node of G, say v_r, to be the root of the tree, thus the edges in Gd can be seen as direct edges: we say that an edge (v, v_i) in G is directed from v to v_i whenever node v_i is on the path between node v and v_r. In other words, we can define the parent-children relationship for each node v: let $\mathbf{Ch}_v$ be the children of v and $\mathbf{P}_v$ be the parent of v. We also assume that there is an order (arbitrary but fixed) for the elements in $\mathbf{Ch}_v$, and let $\mathbf{Ch}'_v$ denote the same set as $\mathbf{Ch}_v$ but with reverse order; let $\mathbf{Lsb}_v$ be the left-hand siblings of v, and $\mathbf{dRsb}_v$ the right-hand siblings of v, where a sibling of v is a node whose parent is the same as v. Futhermore, we can associate three intermediate variables $\mathbf{Cur}_v$, $\mathbf{Intm}_v$ and R_v with each node v. Suppose that for a given node v, it is $\mathbf{Ch}_v = \{c_1, c_2, \ldots, c_m\}$. The formulas computing these variables are:

$$\mathbf{Cur}_v = Bel_v \oplus \{\oplus M^{c_k \to v} \mid c_k \in \mathbf{Ch}_v\} \tag{3}$$

$$\mathbf{Intm}_{c_i} = Bel_v \oplus \{\oplus M^{c_k \to v} \mid c_k \in \mathbf{Lsb}_{c_i}\} \tag{4}$$

$$R_{c_i} = M^{P_v \to v} \oplus \{\oplus M^{c_k \to v} \mid c_k \in \mathbf{Rsb}_{c_i}\} \tag{5}$$

After the parent-children relationship has been defined for the nodes, the propagation process can be described as follows: first, each node receives the messages from all of its children, combines them with its own belief function, and sends the result with proper projection to its parent; as the messages are sent starting from the leaf nodes until the root of G is reached, we call this "propagation-up." Then, after having received the message from its parent, each node sends messages back to its children and computes the marginal; as the messages are sent back from the root until the leaves of G are reached, we call this "propagation-down."

By using the intermediate variables, this propagation process can be implemented as follows: during "propagation-up," $\mathbf{Intm}_{c_i}$ are computed iteratively and thus $\mathbf{Cur}_v$ and $M^{v \to P_v}$ are computed by:

$$\mathbf{Intm}_{c_1} = Bel_v$$

$$\mathbf{Intm}_{c_i} = \mathbf{Intm}_{c_{i-1}} \oplus M^{c_{i-1} \to v},\ i=2,\ldots m$$

$$\mathbf{Cur}_v = \mathbf{Intm}_{c_m} \oplus M^{c_m \to v}$$

$$M^{v \to P_v} = ((\mathbf{Cur}_v)^{\downarrow(v \cap P_v)})^{\uparrow P_v}$$

During "propagation-down," node v can send the messages back to its children and the marginal for it can be computed as follows:

$$R_{c_m} = M^{P_v \to v}$$

$$M^{v \to c_m} = ((\mathbf{Intm}_{c_m} \oplus R_{c_m})^{\downarrow(v \cap c_m)})^{\uparrow c_m}$$

$$R_{c_i} = R_{c_{i+1}} \oplus M^{c_{i+1} \to v},\ i = m-1, \ldots, 1$$

$$M^{v \to c_i} = ((\mathbf{Intm}_{c_i} \oplus R_{c_i})^{\downarrow(v \cap c_i)})^{\uparrow c_i}$$

$$Bel^{\downarrow v} = \mathbf{Cur}_v \oplus M^{P_v \to v}$$

For example, the computations at node 5 of step 2 and step 5 in Figure 8.1 are as follows:

Step 2:

$$\mathbf{Intm}_6 = Bel_5,$$

$$\mathbf{Intm}_7 = \mathbf{Intm}_6 \oplus M^{6 \to 5},$$

$$\mathbf{Intm}_{10} = \mathbf{Intm}_7 \oplus M^{7 \to 5},$$

$$\mathbf{Cur}_5 = \mathbf{Intm}_{10} \oplus M^{10 \to 5},$$

$$M^{5 \to 1} = ((\mathbf{Cur}_5)^{\downarrow(5 \cap 1)})^{\uparrow 1}.$$

Step 5:

$$R_{10} = M^{1 \to 5},$$

$$M^{5 \to 10} = ((\mathbf{Intm}_{10} \oplus R_{10}{}^{\downarrow(5 \cap 10)})^{\uparrow 10},$$

$$R_7 = R_{10} \oplus M^{10 \to 5},$$

$$M^{5\to7} = ((\mathbf{Intm}_7 \oplus R_7)^{\downarrow(5\cap7)})^{\uparrow7},$$
$$R_6 = R_7 \oplus M^{7\to5},$$
$$M^{5\to6} = ((\mathbf{Intm}_6 \oplus R_6)^{\downarrow(5\cap6)})^{\uparrow6},$$
$$Bel^{\downarrow5} = \mathbf{Cur}_5 \oplus M^{1\to5}.$$

Remark: According to the above computation, $\mathbf{Intm}_i$ and $\mathbf{Cur}_i$ should be stored at node v during the propagation to avoid being recomputed. This is not necessary for R_i, as it is used only once during the propagation.

This implementation scheme is optimal in the sense that it uses the combination least during propagation by using $\mathbf{Cur}_i$, $\mathbf{Intm}_i$ and R_i (Xu, 1991). Table 8.1 illustrates the number of applications of Dempster's combination at each node v when using the intermediate variables and when not using them.

Table 8.1: Comparison of computation between using and not using intermediate variables.

Number of neighbors	Number of combinations at each node	
	using intermediate variables	not using intermediate variables
$\mid\{\mathbf{P}_v\}\mid=1, \mid\mathbf{Ch}_v\mid=0$	1	1
$\mid\{\mathbf{P}_v\}\mid=1, \mid\mathbf{Ch}_v\mid=n(>0)$	$3n$	$(n+1)^2$
$\mid\{\mathbf{P}_v\}\mid=0, \mid\mathbf{Ch}_v\mid=n(>0)$	$3n-3$	n^2-n+1

3.3. Updating messages

Suppose we have already computed the marginals for all the nodes and the Markov tree G is still the same, and we now want to change one or more of the prior belief functions for some reason. Because some of the previous computed intermediate information is stored at each node, we can update the marginals for all the nodes without redoing all the work during repropagation.

For the sake of simplicity, we use number i to refer to node v_i in the Markov tree. Suppose that one input Bel_i is changed. According to (1), all the messages $M^{k\to\mathbf{P}_k}$(if $\mathbf{P}_k$ exists) from any k on the path between node i and r (the root), including i, will be discarded. So will all the messages $M^{\mathbf{P}_j\to j}$ (if $\mathbf{P}_j$ exists) for all j not lying on the path between i and r. The remaining half of the messages could be retained.

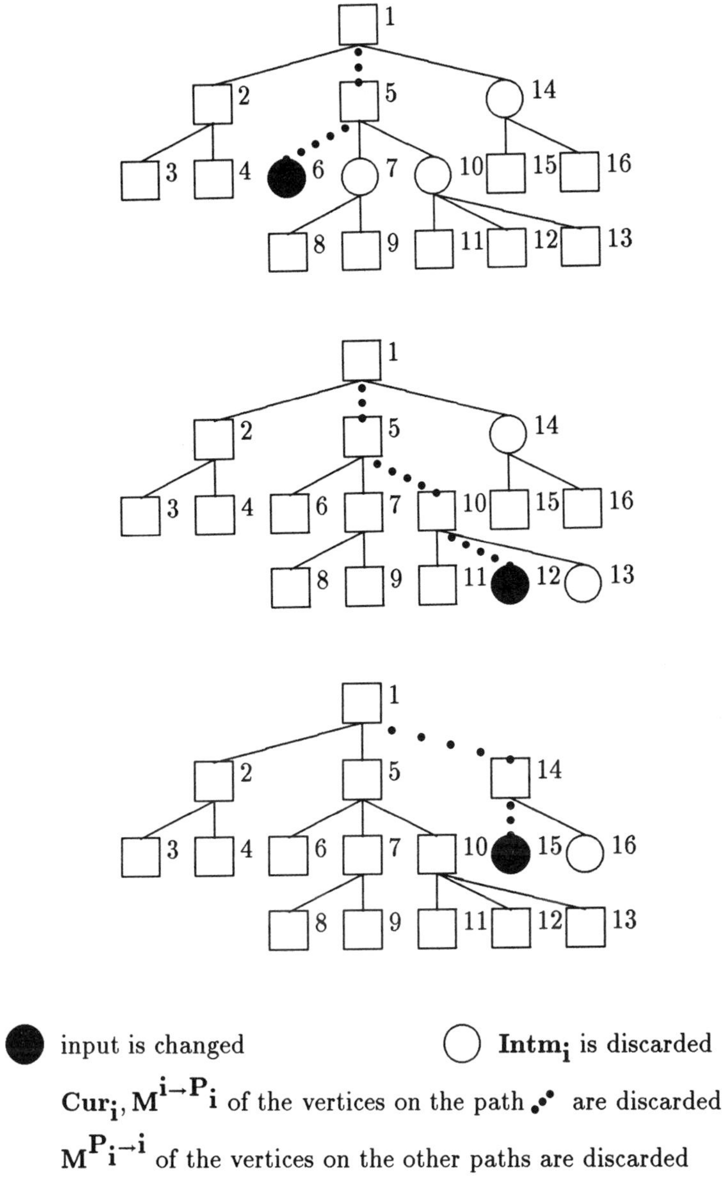

Figure 8.2. Cases for the changes of the messages.

According to (3), $\mathbf{Cur}_k$ is the combination of all the messages sent from the children of k with its own belief function. So only $\mathbf{Cur}_k$ of

k lying on the path between i and r, including i and r, will be discarded. According to (4), $\mathbf{Intm}_j$ depends on Bel_{P_j} and $M^{k \to \mathrm{P}_j}(k \in \mathbf{Lsb}_j)$, so for any k on the path between i and r, including i, if $j \in \mathbf{Rsb}_k$, then $\mathbf{Intm}_j$ will be discarded; others can be retained. This fact is illustrated in Figure 8.2 by showing some cases when one prior belief function is changed.

Now suppose we need to recompute the marginals for all nodes again. If we have stored all the previous messages, then only the changed messages should be recomputed, while the unchanged ones can be retained. As an illustration, let's now focus on the computation of $\mathrm{M}^{5 \to 1}$, a message that has been discarded by the change in Bel_{12}. By using the stored $\mathbf{Intm}_{10}$, we compute $M^{5 \to 1}$ as:

$$\mathbf{Cur}_5 = \mathbf{Intm}_{10} \oplus M^{10 \to 5} \text{ (because } \mathbf{Intm}_{10} \text{ is not changed)}$$

$$M^{5 \to 1} = ((\mathbf{Cur}_5)^{\downarrow (5 \cap 1)})^{\uparrow 1}$$

that is, just one combination is needed here.

Suppose that for the node i, $\mathbf{Cur}_i$ is not changed; as a consequence, all $\mathbf{Intm}_k(k \in \mathbf{Ch}_i)$ are not changed. So we can skip the "propagation-up" part for i during repropagation. But in "propagation-down," those stored $\mathbf{Cur}_i$ and $\mathbf{Intm}_k(k \in \mathbf{Ch}_i)$ can still be used. For instance, we want to compute $Bel^{\downarrow 14}$. Because $M^{14 \to 1}$ is not changed, it is desirable not to recompute $Bel_{14} \oplus M^{15 \to 14} \oplus M^{16 \to 14}$ for computing $Bel^{\downarrow 14}$. This computation can be easily avoided by using $\mathbf{Cur}_{14}$.

4. USING BIT-ARRAYS

We have discussed previously how to apply Dempster's combination as little as possible. In this section, we will discuss how to reduce the complexity of Dempster's combination itself and the projection and extension operations during the propagation. This can be done by using bit-arrays to represent the focal elements of belief functions. The storage can also get the benefit of efficiency from this method.

4.1. Representing subsets based on the bit-arrays

There are at least two ways to represent subsets: Given a frame θ, a subset of θ can be represented as a list of elements it contains or as a n-bit bit-array altenatively, where n is the size of θ. A bit in the bit-array is either 1 or 0, depending on whether its corresponding element is in the subset or not. The order of the elements in θ should be fixed.

Given a frame $\theta = (s_0, s_1, ..., s_{n-1})$, let $\mathbf{Pos}(s_j, \theta) = i$, where $0 \leqslant i < n$. For any $\mathbf{a} \subseteq \theta$, *the bit-array representation of* $\mathbf{a}$, is denoted by $Bit_\theta(\mathbf{a}) = \#^* b_0 b_1 ... b_{n-1}$. For each b_i, where $0 \leqslant i < n$

$$b_i = \begin{cases} 0 & s_i \notin \mathbf{a} \\ 1 & s_i \in \mathbf{a} \end{cases}$$

We use $\#0$ to represent $Bit_\theta(\emptyset)$ and $\#1$ to represent $Bit_\theta(\theta)$. Let $\mathbf{Dim}(Bit)$ denote the size of the bit-array Bit, so for any subset $\mathbf{a}$ of θ, $\mathbf{Dim}(Bit_\theta(\mathbf{a})) = |\theta|$. For example, given a frame $\theta = \{$blue, green, red, yellow$\}$, a basic color set $\mathbf{a} = \{$blue, red, yellow$\}$ is a subset of θ. According to the definition above, we have $Bit_\theta(\mathbf{a}) = \#^*1011$. It is obvious that using bit-arrays to represent subsets takes less space than using a list of elements.

Let $\mathbf{W}$ be a finite nonempty set of frames. For any subset S of $\mathbf{W}$, there is a corresponding product frame $\Theta = \times\{\theta_i \mid \theta_i \in S\}$. For any θ_i, $\theta_j \in S$, $\mathbf{Pos}(\theta_i, S) < \mathbf{Pos}(\theta_j, S)$ if $\mathbf{Pos}(\theta_i, \mathbf{W}) < \mathbf{Pos}(\theta_j, \mathbf{W})$, we assume that the elements in Θ are also in a fixed order, because the elements in each θ_i are in a fixed order. It is easy to see that for any subset s of Θ, $\mathbf{Dim}(Bit_\Theta(s)) = |\Theta| = \Pi\{|\theta_i|$ such that $\theta_i \in S\}$. According to the definition of the position of the element in each θ_i, the position of element $s = (s_{i_j} \mid s_{i_j} \in \theta_i)$ in a product frame Θ can be obtained by:

$$\mathbf{Pos}(s, \Theta) = \sum_{\theta_i \in S} \left(\mathbf{Pos}(s_{i_j}, \theta_i)^* \prod_{\theta_k \in S,\, k > i} |\theta_k| \right) \tag{6}$$

If θ_k in $\Pi|\theta_k|$ does not exist, then $\Pi|\theta_k| = 1$.

Suppose $\mathbf{W} = \{(ab), (xy), (mnp), (st)\}$, $S = \{(ab), (mnp), (st)\}$, $\Theta = (ab) \times (mnp) \times (st)$. Let θ_i, i = 0, 1, 2 be (ab), (mnp) and (st) respectively. Then the position of the element $s = (ant)$ of Θ is computed as:

$$\begin{aligned} \mathbf{Pos}(s, \Theta) &= 6^*\mathbf{Pos}(a, \theta_0) + 2^*\mathbf{Pos}(n, \theta_1) + 1^*\mathbf{Pos}(t, \theta_2) \\ &= 6^*0 + 2^*1 + 1^*1 = 3 \end{aligned}$$

4.2. Basic operations on the subsets based on the bit-arrays

Consider two bit-arrays Bit_1 and Bit_2, $\mathbf{Dim}(Bit_1) = \mathbf{Dim}(Bit_2)$. Let $\mathbf{AND}(Bit_1, Bit_2)$ denote the operation that perfoms bit-wise logic operations "and" on bit-arrays, $\mathbf{OR}(Bit_1, Bit_2)$ denote the operation that performs bit-wise logic operations "inclusive or" on bit-arrays. Suppose **a** and **b** are two subsets of Θ, $Bit_\Theta(\mathbf{a})$ and $Bit_\Theta(\mathbf{b})$ are the bit-array representations, respectively. According to the definition of the bit-array representation, we have:

$$Bit_\Theta(\mathbf{a}) = Bit_\Theta(\mathbf{b}) \text{ iff } \mathbf{a}=\mathbf{b}$$
$$Bit_\Theta(\mathbf{a}\cap\mathbf{b}) = \mathbf{AND}(Bit_\Theta(\mathbf{a}), Bit_\Theta(\mathbf{b}))$$
$$Bit_\Theta(\mathbf{a}\cup\mathbf{b}) = \mathbf{OR}(Bit_\Theta(\mathbf{a}), Bit_\Theta(\mathbf{b}))$$

Noting that the operations described above are both commutative and associative, we can use $\mathbf{op}(Bit_i \mid i=1, \ldots, n)$ to represent the operation **op** on an arbitrary number of bit-arrays, where **op** can be **AND** or **OR**.

Finally, we introduce another operation on a single bit-array: **Subseq**(*Bit, start, length*). This operation gets a sub-bit array of the bit-array *Bit*. Indexing is zero-origin, with *start* (a nonnegative integer) designating the first element of the sub-bit-array, and with *length* (a nonnegative integer) designating the dimension of the sub-bit-array. For example: **Subseq(#*101001, 2, 3)=#*100.**

4.3. Projection and extension of subsets based on the bit-arrays

In this subsection, we will present the algorithms for computing projection and extension of a subset from one frame to another directly through their bit-array representation. These algorithms are applicable to the cases where **W**, *S*, and θ are the nonempty sets.

4.3.1. Projection

Consider two nonempty subsets S_1 and S_2 *of* **W**, where $S_1 \subseteq S_2$. Let $S_1=(\theta_{1_0}, \ldots, \theta_{1_p})$, $S_2=(\theta_{2_0}, \ldots, \theta_{2_q})$, and let Θ_1 and Θ_2 be their corresponding product frames, respectively. For any subset **a** of Θ_2, there is a corresponding projection $\mathbf{a}^{\downarrow\Theta_1}$, which maps **a** from Θ_2 to Θ_1. Our objective is to obtain $Bit_{\Theta_1}(\mathbf{a}^{\downarrow\Theta_1})$, the bit-array representation of $\mathbf{a}^{\downarrow\Theta_1}$, by using $\mathrm{Bit}_{\Theta_2}(\mathbf{a})$, the bit-array representation of **a**.

To this end, we first consider a special case where S_2 has only one different element from S_1, i.e., $|S_2-S_1|=|(\theta_{2_r})|=1$; suppose $|\Theta_1|=m, |\Theta_{2_r}|=n$, then $|\Theta_2|=mn$. Thus, $Bit_{\Theta_2}(\mathbf{a})$ can be represented as $\#{*}a_0a_1\ldots a_{mn-1}$, and we can let $Bit_{\Theta_1}(\mathbf{a}^{\downarrow\Theta_1})=\#{*}c_0c_1\ldots c_{m-1}$. According to the definition of projection, if $\mathbf{s}=(s_0, \ldots, s_{r-1}, s_r, s_{r+1})\in\mathbf{a}$, where $s_i\in\theta_{2_i}$, then $\mathbf{s}'=(s_0, \ldots, s_{r-1}, s_{r+1}, \ldots, s_q)\in\mathbf{a}^{\downarrow\Theta_1}$. Thus, if $a_{pos(s,\Theta_2)}=1$ for any $s_r \in \mathbf{s}$ $s_r \in \theta_{2_r}$, then $c_{pos(s,\Theta_1)}=1$, i.e.,

$$c_{pos(s',\Theta 1)}=\text{bit-or } (a_{pos(s,\Theta_2)} \mid \mathbf{s} \in \mathbf{a}, s_r \in s, s_p \in \theta_{2_r}) \tag{7}$$

Formally, let $u=\Pi\{|\theta_{2_j}| \text{ for } 0 \leqslant j < r\}$, and $v=\Pi\{|\theta_{2_i}| \text{ for } r < i \leqslant q\}$, (if $r=0$, then $u=1$; if $r=q$, then $v=1$), thus, $|\Theta_1|=uv$, $|\Theta_2| = nuv$. From (6) and (7), $Bit_{\Theta_1}(\mathbf{a}^{\downarrow\Theta_1})$ is obtained by:

$$\mathbf{Subseq}(Bit_{\Theta_1}(\mathbf{a}^{\downarrow\Theta_1}), vi, v) = \mathbf{OR}(\mathbf{Subseq}(Bit_{\Theta_2}(\mathbf{a}), nvi+vj, v) \mid 0 \leqslant j < n)), \; i=0, 1 \ldots, \text{u-1}$$

For example, let $S_1=((ab)(st))$, $S_2=((ab)(xy)(st))$, $\mathbf{a}=((axs)(ays)(bxs)(bys)(byt)$ is a subset of Θ_2. Then we have: $Bit_{\Theta_2}(\mathbf{a})=$#*10101011. According to the above formula, let $Bit_{\Theta 2}(\mathbf{a})$ and $Bit_{\Theta 1}(\mathbf{a}^{\downarrow\Theta_1})$ be separated into two groups, each group in $Bit_{\Theta_2}(\mathbf{a})$ consists of two 2-bit sub-bit-arrays, each group in $Bit_{\Theta 1}(\mathbf{a}^{\downarrow\Theta_1})$ consists one 2-bit sub-bit-array. Perfoming **OR** on every **two 2-bit sub-bit-array of each group in** $Bit_{\Theta 2}(\mathbf{a})$ constructs every 2-bit sub-bit-array of $Bit_{\Theta 1}(\mathbf{a}^{\downarrow\Theta_1})$ sequentially, i.e., **OR**(#*10, #*10) = #*10 and **OR**(#*10, #*11) = #*11. Thus $Bit_{\Theta_1}(\mathbf{a}^{\downarrow\Theta_1})$ = #*1011.

If $|S_2 - S_1| \neq 1$, we can use the above method iteratively to obtain $Bit_{\Theta_1(\mathbf{a}^{\downarrow\Theta_1})}$ as follows: Let $S=S_2$, $Bit=Bit_{\Theta}(\mathbf{a})$, then:

1. Find θ_{2_r} in S such that $\theta_{2_r} \notin S_1$ and for $r<i\leqslant q$, $\theta_{2_i} \in S_1$. If found, then go to 2, else Bit is what we want.
2. Let $S=S-(\theta_{2r})$. Construct a bit-array Bit' such that $\mathbf{Dim}(Bit')=\mathbf{Dim}(Bit)/\theta_{2r}|(|\theta_{2r}|$ divides $\mathbf{Dim}(Bit))$, and $\mathbf{Subseq}(Bit', vi, v)=\mathbf{OR}(\mathbf{Subseq}(Bit, nvi+vj) \mid 0 \leqslant j \leqslant n$, $i=0,1, \ldots, u\text{-}1$ where $n=|\theta_{2r}|$, $u=\prod_{0<j<r}|\theta_{2j}|$, and $v=\prod_{r<i<q}|\theta_{2r}|$, (if $r=0$, then $u=1$; if $r=q$, then $v=1$). Let $Bit=Bit'$, go to 1.

4.3.2. Extension

Consider S_1, S_2 and Θ_1, Θ_2 defined in the previous subsection, suppose $S_1 \neq S_2$. For any subset $\mathbf{a}$ of Θ_1, there is also a corresponding extension $\mathbf{a}^{\uparrow\Theta_2}$, which maps $\mathbf{a}$ from Θ_1 to Θ_2. Our objective here is to obtain $Bit_{\Theta_2}(\mathbf{a}^{\uparrow\Theta_2})$, the bit-array representation of $\mathbf{a}^{\uparrow\Theta_2}$, by using $Bit_{\Theta_1}(\mathbf{a})$, the bit-array representation of $\mathbf{a}$.

To this end, we first consider a special case where $|S_2 - S_1|=|(\theta_{2_r})|=1$, i.e., $S_1=(\theta_{2_0}, \ldots, \theta_{2_{r-1}}, \theta_{2_{r+1}}, \ldots, \theta_{2_q})$. Suppose $|\Theta_1|=m$, $|\theta_{2_r}|=n$, then $|\Theta_2|=mn$. Thus, $Bit_{\Theta}(\mathbf{a})$ can be represented as #*$a_0 a_1 \ldots a_{m-1}$, and we can let $Bit_{\Theta}(\mathbf{a}^{\uparrow\Theta_2})$, = #*$c_0 c_1 \ldots c_{mn-1}$.

According to the definition of extension, if $\mathbf{s}=(s_0, ..., s_{r-1}, s_{r+1}, ..., s_p) \in \mathbf{a}$, where $s_1 \in \theta_{2_i}$, then $\mathbf{b}=((s_0, ..., s_{r-1})) \times \theta_{2_r} \times ((s_{r+1}, ..., s_p)) \subseteq \mathbf{a}^{\uparrow\Theta_2}$. Thus, if $a_{pos(s,\Theta_1)}=1$ then $c_{pos(s',\Theta_2)}=1$ for any $\mathbf{s}' \in \mathbf{b}$, i.e.,

$$c_{pos(s'\Theta_2)}=a_{pos(s,\Theta_1)}, \text{ where } \mathbf{s} \in \mathbf{a},\ s_r \in \mathbf{s}', s_r \in \theta_{2_r} \tag{8}$$

Formally, let $u=\Pi\{|\theta_{2_j}| \text{ for } 0 \leqslant j < r\}$, and $v=\Pi\{|\theta_{2_i}| \text{ for } r < i \leqslant q\}$, (if $r=0$, then $u=1$; if $r=q$, then $v=1$), thus, $|\Theta_1|=nv$, $|\Theta_2|=nuv$, then from (6) and (8), $Bit_{\Theta_2}(\mathbf{a}^{\uparrow\Theta_2})$ is obtained by:

$$\mathbf{Subseq}(Bit_{\Theta_2}(\mathbf{a}^{\uparrow\Theta_2}), vi, v)=\mathbf{Subseq}(Bit_{\Theta_1}(\mathbf{a}), v^*[i/n], v), i=0, 1, ..., nu-1$$

where $[number]$ denotes the largest integer less than or equal to *number*.

If $|S_2-S_1|>1$, we can use the above method iteratively to obtain $Bit_{\Theta_2}(\mathbf{a}^{\uparrow\Theta_2})$, as follows: Let $S=S_1$, $Bit=Bit_{\Theta_1}(\mathbf{a})$, then:

1. Find θ_{2_r} in S_2 such that $\theta_{2_r} \notin S$ and for $r<i \leqslant q$, $\theta_{2_i} \in S$. If found, go to 2, else *Bit* is what we want.
2. Let $S=S-(\theta_{2_{r+1}}, ..., \theta_{2_q})+(\theta_{2_r}, \theta_{2_{r+1}}, ... \theta_{2_q})$. Construct a bit-array Bit' such that $\mathbf{Dim}(Bit')=\mathbf{Dim}(Bit)^*|\theta_{2_r}|$, and $\mathbf{Subseq}(Bit', vi, v)=\mathbf{Subseq}(Bit, v^*[i/n], v), i=0, 1, ..., nu-1$, where $n=|\theta_2|$, $u=\prod_{0 \leqslant j<r}|\theta_{2_j}|$, and $v=\prod_{r<i \leqslant q}|\theta_{2_i}|$, (if $r=0$, then $u=1$; if $r=q$, then $v=1$). Let $Bit=Bit'$, go to 1.

Remark: In order to avoid the set-comparisons during finding θ_{2_r} in step 1 of both algorithms, S_i can be the set of the position of the frame θ_j in $\mathbf{W}$ instead of the frame itself in the implementation, because the position of the frame in $\mathbf{W}$ is unique and θ_j used during projection or extension can always be substituted by $\mathbf{pos}(\theta_i, \mathbf{W})$. Then, step 1 is to find the position of θ_{2_r}. In this way, all the set-comparisons can be substituted by the comparison of the integers.

4.4. Applying bit-arrays to belief function storage and computation

In general, a belief function over the frame of a subset is stored as a set of pairs $(\mathbf{a}, v)$ where $\mathbf{a}$ is a focal element and $v=m(\mathbf{a})$ is the value assigned on $\mathbf{a}$. It is obvious that most of the space is used for storing subsets information. As the number of focal elements depends on the problem at hand, we cannot change the number of pairs associated with a belief function, and the space required will depend on the compactness of the subsets stored correspondingly. In fact, applying bit-arrays to belief function storage will require less space. For example, suppose we have a belief of 0.9 that the true value of a variable A with frame {red, green, yellow} is in {red}. Using the bit-arrays, the belief function is stored as ((#*100 0.9) (#*111 0.1)), instead of (((red) 0.9) (*red, gren, yellow*) 0.1)). For any focal element in a belief function over the frame, only one *n-bit* bit-array is needed, where n is the size of the frame.

For a belief function network defined earlier, if we let $\mathbf{W} = (W_{Xi} | X_i \in \mathbf{X})$, then for any subset $h = \{X_i | X_i \in h\}$, $\theta_i = W_{X_i}$, $S = \{W_{X_i} | X_i \in h\}$ and $\Theta_h = W_h$, the above computational methods based on the bit-arrays can be used for the belief function computation, that is, combination and marginalization.

The large number of set-intersection and set-comparison computations needed to perform Dempster's combination is a factor that strongly impacts the complexity of computation. Suppose n is the size of the frame over which two belief functions are combined. In the worst case, there are n^2 comparisons of focal elements. If we consider each configuration of the frame as a set with size m, the comparison of the focal elements is the set-equal comparison; it thus needs m^*n^2 atomic comparisons. If we use bit-arrays to represent the subsets, the interesection of two focal elements just needs one **AND** operation on the two n-bit bit-arrays, thus the computational complexity of combination is greatly reduced.

It has been described in section 3 that in using local computation for belief function propagation, the operations of projection and extension that require a lot of set-manipulations are frequently used during the computation. These set-manipulations can be avoided by using bit-arrays, which results in a much faster computation of propagation.

5. COMMONALITY FUNCTIONS AND THE MÖBIUS TRANSFORMATION

Another method to speed up the computation of Dempster's rule of combination is based on firmly established theoretical reasons. This method rests on two facts. The first one is based on a *generalized Fourier transformation* and the second one is based on a *fast algorithm* for computing this generalized Fourier transformation.

The first fundamental fact, which has been proved by Shafer (1976), can be stated as follows. There exists a representation of belief functions (or equivalently of basic belief masses) in which Dempster's rule of combination is turned into a pointwise product. This representation is called the commonality function representation and is defined in the next definition.

In this section we will consider one fixed finite set Ω and its powerset denoted by $\mathbf{P}\Omega$. The inclusion relation in the powerset will be denoted by $A \subseteq B$ or equivalently by $B \supseteq A$.

Commonality Function (Shafer, 1976, p. 40 and Smets, 1988, p. 262): If m: $\mathbf{P}\Omega \rightarrow [0,1]$ is a basic belief assignment, then the *commonality function associated to m* is the function Q_m: $\mathbf{P}\Omega \rightarrow [0,1]$ where

$$\text{for all } A \in \mathbf{P}\Omega : Q_m(A) = \sum_{X \supseteq A} m(X)$$

$Q^m(A)$ is called the commonality number of A induced by the basic belief assignment m.

The usefulness of the commonality is due to the following simple formula (Shafer 1976, p. 61):

$$\text{for all } A \in \mathbf{P}\Omega : \; Q_{m_1 \oplus m_2}(A) = Q_{m_1}(A) \cdot Q_{m_2}(A)$$

Thoma (1989) showed that the transformation $m \rightarrow Q_m$, called the Möbius transformation (Kennes, 1991), is in fact a generalized Fourier transformation.

The usual Fourier theory deals with functions defined on a group. The Fourier transformation transforms each function (defined on the group) into another function (defined on the same group) in such a way that the convolution product of functions (induced by the group operation) is mapped on the pointwise product of functions. The situation here is fundamentally the same except that the functions are not defined on a group but on the semigroup $<\mathbf{P}\Omega, \cap>$. Dempster's rule of combination — without normalization — is none other than the convolution product (induced by the semigroup operation $\cap$) on a space of functions defined on $<\mathbf{P}\Omega, \cap>$.

The secound fundamental fact is that there also exists a *fast Fourier transformation* in this generalized setting (Thoma, 1989, 1991; Kennes, 1991). Kennes (1991) proved that this fast algorithm for computing the generalized Fourier transformation is a runtime optimal transformation of m into Q_m. We now explain the algorithm for the set $\Omega = \{a,b,c\}$ on the network diagram, shown in Figure 8.3.

This network must be looked at from top to bottom. The first row gets the initial basic belief assignment (masses). Then the masses are transferred to the second row according to the arrows. So, e.g., $\{b,c\}$ in the second row gets the sum of the masses from $\{b,c\}$ and $\{a,b,c\}$. We

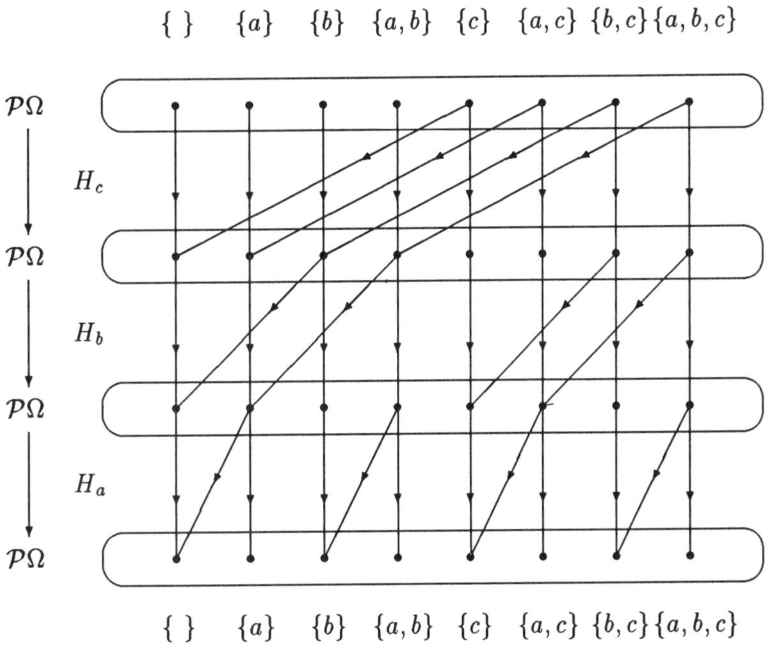

Figure 8.3. Diagram of: $m \rightarrow Q_m$.

will end up in the last row with a series of numbers that are the commonality numbers.

The inverse transformation $Q \rightarrow m_Q$ is given by the formula (Smets, 1988; p. 263):

$$\text{for all } A \in \mathbf{P}\Omega : m_Q(A) = \textstyle\sum_{X \supseteq A} (-1)^{\#(X-A)} Q(X)$$

It can be computed by the network diagram, shown in Figure 8.4. This time the masses transferred by the arrows with label (−1) must be multiplied by −1.

Now, for computing the Dempster product of two bpa $m1$ and $m2$ we can proceed as follows:

1. Compute the commonality functions Q_{m1} and Q_{m2} using the fast Fourier algorithm explained above,

2. Multiply Q_{m1} and Q_{m2} pointwise,

3. Compute the bpa corresponding to $Q_{m1} \cdot Q_{m2}$ using the fast inverse Fourier algorithm explained above.

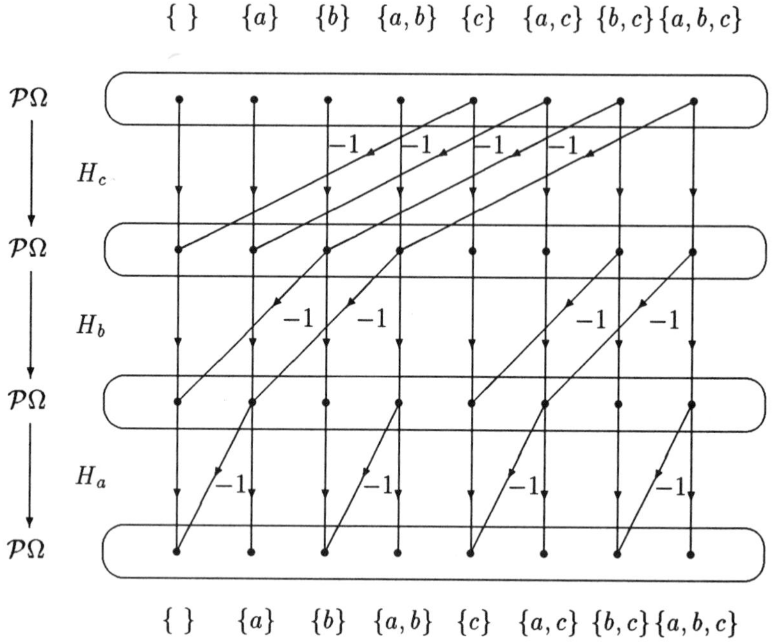

Figure 8.4. Diagram of: $Q \rightarrow m_Q$.

The procedure can be summarized by the commutative diagram, shown in Figure 8.5.

This detour appears to be computationally very efficient. For more details, the reader is referred to Kennes (1991), and Kennes and Smets (1990).

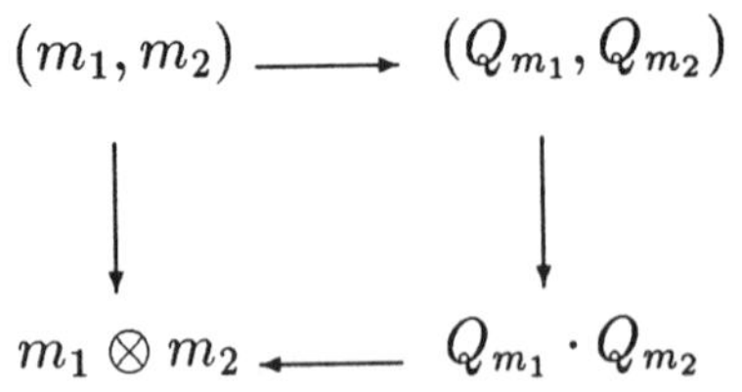

Figure 8.5.

6. CONCLUSION

In this paper, three techniques to improve the implementation of Dempster-Shafer theory are proposed. First, it was shown that, for belief function propagation using local computation, we can reduce the applications of Dempster's rule of combination as much as possible by storing intermediate results. We can also avoid repeated computations during repropagation by using unchanged intermediate results.

Next, it is shown how to speed up Dempster's rule of combination using bit-arrays for representing belief functions. Another benefit of using bit-arrays is the simplification of projection and extension required in belief function propagation.

Finally, a faster method for computing Dempster's rule of combination based on commonality function and Möbius transformation is proposed. The usefulness of commonality functions comes from two facts: first, commonality functions are Fourier transforms (they multiply pointwise); second, there are fast algorithms for transforming between basic belief assignments and commonalities.

The techniques discussed here have been implemented in LISP at IRIDIA, Université Libre de Bruxelles.

ACKNOWLEDGMENTS

The authors are grateful to Professor Philippe Smets for valuable suggestions. Many thanks to Alessandro Saffiotti, Yen-Teh Hsia, and Youbin Peng for their careful reading of the paper and their worthy comments.

BIBLIOGRAPHY

Barnett, J.A. (1981). Computational methods for a mathematical theory of evidence. *Proc. Seventh IJCAI*, pp. 868–75.

Gordon, J. and Shortliffe, E.H. (1985). A method for managing evidential reasoning in a hierarchical hypothesis space. *Artificial Intelligence* 26: 323–58.

Hsia, Y. and Shenoy, P.P. (1989). MacEvidence: A visual environment for constructing and evaluating evidential systems. Working Paper No. 211, School of Business, University of Kansas, Lawrence.

Kennes, R. (1991). Computational aspects of the Möbius transformation of graphs. *IEEE Transactions on Systems, Man, and Cybernetics.* In press.

Kennes, R. and Smets, Ph. (1990). Computational aspects of the Möbius transform. *Proceedings of the Sixth Conference on Uncertainty in Artificial Intelligence*, Cambridge, MA, USA, July 27–29, 1990, pp. 344–51.

Mellouli, K. (1987). On the propagation of beliefs in network using the Dempster-Shafer theory of evidence. Ph.D dissertation, School of Business, University of Kansas, Lawrence.

Shafer, G. (1976). *A mathematical theory of evidence*. Princeton, NJ: Princeton University Press.

Shafer, G. and Logan, R. (1987). Implementing Dempster's rule for hierarchical evidence. *Artificial Intelligence* 33: 271–98.

Shafer, G. and Shenoy, P.P. (1988). Local computation in hypertrees. Working Paper No. 201, School of Business, University of Kansas, Lawrence.

Shafer, G., Shenoy, P.P., and Mellouli, K. (1987). Propagating belief functions in qualitative Markov trees. *International Journal of Approximate Reasoning* 1: 349–400.

Shenoy, P.P. (1989). A valuation-based language for expert systems. *International Journal of Approximate Reasoning* 3: 383–411.

Smets, Ph. (1988). Belief functions. In Smets, Ph., Mamdani, A., Dubois, D. and Prade, H. (eds.), *Nonstandard logics for automated reasoning*, pp. 253–86. London: Academic Press.

Thoma, H.M. (1989). Factorization of belief functions. Ph.D. Thesis, Department of Statistics, Harvard University, Cambridge, MA.

Thoma, H.M. (1991). Belief functions computations. In Goodman, I.R., Gupta, M.M., Nguyen, H.T., Roger, G.S. (eds.), *Conditional logic in expert systems*, pp. 269–308. New York: North-Holland.

Xu, H. (1991). An efficient implementation of belief function propagation. In D'Ambrosio, B.D., Smets, Ph., and Bonissone, P.P. (eds.), *Proceedings of the Seventh Conference of Uncertainty in Artificial Intelligence*, pp. 425–32. San Mateo, CA: Morgan Kaufmann.

Zarley, D., Hsia, Y., and Shafer, G. (1988). Evidential reasoning using DELIEF. In *Proceedings of the Seventh National Conference on Artificial Intelligence*, vol. 1, pp. 205–209. St. Paul, MN.

Zhang, L. (1988). Studies on finding hypertree covers of hypergraphs. Working Paper No. 198, School of Business, University of Kansas, Lawrence.

9 Monte-Carlo methods make Dempster-Shafer formalism feasible

Vladik Y. KREINOVICH, Andrew BERNAT, Walter BORRETT, Yvonne MARISCAL, and Elsa VILLA

Abstract: One of the main obstacles to the application of Dempster-Shafer formalism is its computational complexity. If we combine m different pieces of knowledge, then in general we have to perform up to 2^m computational steps, which for large m is infeasible. For several important cases algorithms with smaller running time have been proposed. We prove, however, that if we want to compute the belief $bel(Q)$ in any given query Q, then exponential time is inevitable. It is still inevitable, if we want to compute $bel(Q)$ with given precision ε. This restriction corresponds to the natural idea that since initial masses are known only approximately, there is no sense in trying to compute $bel(Q)$ precisely. A futher idea is that there is always some doubt in the whole knowledge, so there is always a probability p_0 that the expert's knowledge is wrong. In view of that it is sufficient to have an algorithm that gives a correct answer a probability $> 1 - p_0$. If we use the original Dempster's combination rule, the possibility diminishes the running time, but still leaves the problem infeasible in the general case. We show that for the alternative combination rules proposed by Smets and Yager feasible methods exist. We also show how these methods can be parallelized, and what parallelization model fits this problem best.

Keywords: Dempster-Shafer formalism, combination rules, Monte-Carlo methods, feasible, parallel.

1. FORMULATION OF THE PROBLEM

Dempster-Shafer formalism in brief. Dempster-Shafer (DS) formalism, proposed in Shafer (1976), is very promising and is already widely used. In this formalism knowledge is described by a finite set of statements $E_1, ..., E_n$, to each of which a number (*mass*) $m(E_i)$ is asigned so that $\Sigma_i m(E_i)=1$. Then, if someone asks a query Q, we must produce as an answer the belief $bel(Q)$ that Q is true. This belief is defined as a sum of masses $m(E_i)$ of all the statements E_i that imply Q (i.e., for which $E_i \rightarrow Q$ is true). In addition to belief in Q one can also ask for the plausibility $pl(Q)$ of Q.

Comment. From the computational viewpoint the problems of computing *bel* and *pl* are equivalent, because $bel(Q)=1-pl(\neg Q)$ and $pl(Q)=1-bel(\neg Q)$. Therefore in the following text we'll analyze only the problem of computing beliefs. In Yager (1987) a slightly different definition of plausibility is given; our negative theorems and algorithm can be easily applied to this definition as well.

If we have several pieces of knowledge that are represented in the Dempster-Shafer form, then we can combine them into a single knowledge base. Several combination rules have been proposed. The original Dempster's rule is as follows: if we are given two pieces $(E_i, m_1(E_i))$ and $(F_i, m_2(F_i))$, then for the statements of the resulting knowledge base we take all consistent combinations $E_i \& F_j$, and to each of these statements X we assign the mass

$$m(X) = \frac{\sum_{i,j:\, X \rightarrow (E_i \& F_j)} m_1(E_i)m(F_j)}{\sum_{i,j:\, Consis(E_i \& F_j)} m(E_i)m(F_j)}$$

where *Consis* means consistent and $\sum_{i,j:\, A}$ means the sum over all i, j, for which A is true.

Comment. Informally speaking, this means that we neglect all the inconsistent combinations and "divide" our belief between the consistent ones.

It was shown (Zadeh, 1984) that this rule sometimes contradicts our intuition. Following Smets (1988), let us briefly describe this contradiction. Suppose we have three suspects in a murder case, Peter, Paul, and Mary, and two witnesses. The first witness is almost sure that Peter is a murderer, and his degrees of belief are: 0.99 that Peter murdered, 0.01 that Paul murdered, and 0 that Mary did it. The second witness has a 0.99 belief that Mary is the murderer, 0.01 that Paul is the murderer, and 0 that Peter is the one. From commonsense viewpoint, this means that we have strong suspicions against Peter and Mary. However, the original Dempster's rule leads to a different conclusion. Indeed, let us denote "Peter is the murderer" by E_1, "Paul is the murderer" by E_2, and "Mary is the murderer" by E_3. Then, the beliefs m_1, m_2 of the two witnesses are $m_1(E_1) = m_2(E_3) = 0.99$, $m_1(E_3) = m_2(E_1) = 0$, and $m_1(E_2) = m_2(E_2) = 0.01$. The original Dempster's combination rule then leads to $m(E_2) = 1$ and $m(E_1) = \mathrm{m}(E_3) = 0$, that is, to the conclusion that Paul is certainly the murderer.

Because of this contradiction, alternative combination rules were proposed by Yager (1985, 1987) and Smets (1988). Smets proposed the formula

$$m(X) = \sum_{i,j:\, X \to (E_i \& F_j)} m_1(E_i) m_2(F_j)$$

for all X (in particular for identically false $X = f$, that corresponds to the case when the statements E_i and F_j are inconsistent). For the case when we have to combine $k > 2$ pieces of knowledge, he proposed a similar formula

$$m(X) = \sum_{i,\ldots,j:\, X \to (E_i \& \ldots \& F_j)} m_1(E_i) \ldots m_k(F_j)$$

Yager applies this rule only for X'_s different from t ("identically true") and f ("identically false"), and assigns $m(f) = 0$ and

$$m(t) = \sum_{i,\ldots,j:\, \neg\, \mathit{Consis}(E_i \& \ldots \& F_j) \vee t \to (E_i \& \ldots \& F_j)} m_1(E_i) \ldots m_k(F_j)$$

Computational complexity is the main obstacle to the application of Dempster-Shafer formalism. Although this formalism is widely used, there are some obstacles to its application, the main of which is its computational complexity (Bonissone, 1987; Dempster and Kong, 1987; Kyburg, 1987; Paass, 1988; Pearl, 1988; Hsia, 1989; Phillips, 1990). Indeed, when we apply one of the above combination rules to combine m pieces of knowledge, and each of them consists of at least two different statements, then we have to analyze at least 2^m different combinations of statements. Therefore, we must make at least 2^m computational steps. For large m this is **infeasible** (e.g., for $m = 200$ it takes $> 10^{60}$ steps). So it is difficult to compute masses. But even if we manage to compute them, there is still a problem to compute beliefs from masses. If we directly apply the above formula for $bel(Q)$, and the number of statements in the resulting knowledge base is exponentially large, we must undertake exponentially many computational steps. The running time remains exponentially big even if we use the computationally optimal "fast Möbius" algorithm (Kennes, 1990; Kennes and Smets, 1990). So *what to do?*

For some cases faster algorithms are known that compute $bel(Q)$ for different Q in $<2^m$ steps (Barnett, 1981; Gordon and Shortliffe, 1985; Shafer, 1985; Shenoy and Shafer, 1986; Shafer and Logan, 1987; Wilson, 1989, 1991). These methods are applicable in many important cases, but still the problem remains: *what to do in the general case?*

General case: negative result. Orponen (1990) proved that exponential time is inevitable in the following sense: even for the propositional case the problem of computing beliefs is $\#P$-complete (Garey and Johnson, 1979). The majority of computer scientists believe that $P \neq NP$; so from their viewpoint no feasible algorithm is possible for computing beliefs (likewise results are proved in Maung and Paris [1990] for different uncertainty formalisms).

Is this negative result really tragic? To answer this question let's look at the usual logic, without any masses or degrees of belief. In this case knowledge consists of statements $E_1,\ldots,E_n$, and for every query Q the possible answers are "yes" (if $E_1 \& E_2 \& \ldots \& E_n \rightarrow Q$), "no" (if $E_1 \& E_2 \& \ldots \& E_n \rightarrow \neg Q$), and "unknown" in all other cases. For this case many negative results are known, starting from the famous Godel's theorem. However, efficient inference engines and theorem provers exist and are successfully applied. In other words, theoretically the logical case is infeasible, but in practice it is feasible.

So the natural question is: is the Dempster-Shafer case practically feasible (in some reasonable sense) or not?

Feasible: in what sense? The natural formulation of this question is as follows: suppose that we already have an inference engine for logical statements, and we can use it as an additional tool while computing beliefs $bel(Q)$. In this case the running time is equal to the weighted sum of the number of real computational steps and the number of calls of this inference engine. Will this new computational time still be exponentially large?

If it is small, then we can quickly compute beliefs, and therefore DS approach is feasible. If this running time turns out to be exponentially large, this would mean that even the usage of the existing inference engines does not help, and therefore DS approach is infeasible.

The purpose of this paper is to analyze whether DS approach is practically feasible (in the above sense) or not. Our answer will be: "yes" it's feasible." In Section 2 we give precise definitions and formulate a negative result: that the problem of computing beliefs precisely is practically infeasible. Since the initial masses express our degree of belief and are therefore only approximately known, there is no sense in trying to compute the beliefs precisely. However, as we show in Section 3, the problem of computing the beliefs with a given precision is also infeasible. In Section 4 we take into consideration that human experts may not only be slightly uncertain about their degrees of belief, but may also have doubts in their whole knowledge. Therefore, since there is a probability that what an expert says is absolutely wrong, it is reasonable to allow the algorithms for computing $bel(Q)$ to err with some (very small) probability. For Dempster's rule the resulting problem is still infeasible, but for two other rules it is already feasible! In Section 5 we show that the methods from Section 4 can be parallelized, and what parallelization model fits this problem best. All the proofs are given in Section 6. Our main results first appeared in Borrett and Kreinovich (1990a, b).

2. ALGORITHMS THAT COMPUTE BELIEFS PRECISELY ARE PRACTICALLY INFEASIBLE

Inference engine: general definition. Assume that some alphabet is given that includes the symbols & and F; assume also that two sets of words from this alphabet are given. The words from the first set will be called *statements*, words from the second set *queries*. We assume that the word f (meaning *false*) belongs to both sets, and that if S_1 and S_2 are statements, then $S_1 \& S_2$ is also a statement. Assume also that an algorithm I is given, which transforms every pair (S,Q) where S is a statement and Q is a query, into one of the words "*yes*" or "*no.*" When $I(S,Q)=$"*yes*," we say that Q *follows from* S, or S *implies* Q and denote it by $S \rightarrow Q$. We say that the statements S_1 and S_2 are equivalent and denote it by $S_1 \leftrightarrow S_2$ if $S_1 \rightarrow S_2$ and $S_2 \rightarrow S_1$. We demand that this algorithm is consistent in the sense that if $A \leftrightarrow B$, then $I(A,Q)=\mathrm{I}(B,Q)$ for all Q. Such consistent algorithms will be called *inference engines*.

Comment. One should bear in mind that in many cases (e.g., in first order logic) no algorithm is posible for which $I(S,Q)=$"*yes*" if and only if Q is a logical consequence of S. Therefore the notion "imply" that stems from the inference engine can be different from the logical implication.

We say that $E_1,\ldots,E_k$ *imply* Q if $E_1 \& E_2 \& \ldots \& E_k$ implies Q. If S implies f, we say that S is *inconsistent*, else that S is *consistent*. The fact that a formula S is consistent will be denoted by *Consis* (S).

Dempster-Shafer knowledge base: definition. By a *piece of knowledge* we mean a pair consisting of the finite set of statements $E_1,\ldots,E_n$ and a function m that assigns to each statement from this set a value $m(E_i)\geqslant 0$ so that $\Sigma m(E_i)=1$. For every query Q we define the *belief* $bel(Q)$ in Q as the sum of $m(E_i)$ for all E_i; for which $I(E_i,Q)=$"*yes*" (i.e., for which E_i implies Q).

By a *Dempster-Shafer knowledge base* (or simply *knowledge base* for short) we mean a finite list of pieces of knowledge. For every knowledge base we can define the resulting piece of knowledge by applying one of the above-defined combination rules: Dempster's, Smets' and Yager's (we'll denote them by D, S and Y). For every query Q by a *belief* $bel(Q)$ in Q with respect to a knowledge base we mean its belief with respect to the resulting piece of knowledge.

Comment. In the combination formulas we must understand $\rightarrow$, $\leftrightarrow$, and *Consis* in the sense of the inference engine I.

In the present section we'll consider algorithms that combine normal computational steps with calls of an inference engine I.

Comment. In more theoretical terms, we can say that we consider algorithms that use I as an oracle (Garey and Johnson, 1979).

Assume that two positive real numbers are fixed: t_0 and t_c. t_0 will be called the *time of one computational step* and t_c *the time of one call*. For every input by a *running time* of an algorithm we mean the total number N_0 of normal computational steps, multiplied by t_0, plus the total number N_c of calls, multiplied by t_c. By the *length of the input* we mean the total length of the knowledge base and the query. By a *computational complexity* $t_U(n)$ of algorithm U we mean the maximum of its running time on all the inputs of length $\leqslant n$.

We say that an algorithm *computes the beliefs precisely* if for every inference engine I, for every knowledge base and every query Q it computes $bel(Q)$.

THEOREM 1 (D, S, Y). *If an algorithm U computes the beliefs precisely, then* $t_U(n) \geqslant ca^n$ *for some* $a > 1$.

Comment. So, whatever combination rule we use, it takes exponetially many computational steps to compute beliefs precisely. Therefore the problem "to compute beliefs precisely" is infeasible.

3. ALGORITHMS THAT COMPUTE BELIEFS WITH GIVEN PRECISION ARE PRACTICALLY INFEASIBLE

Initial masses express our degree of belief. It is very difficult to express one's degree of belief with great precision: e.g., who can boast that he is 84% and not 83% sure in something? So these initial degrees of belief are only approximately known, and therefore there is no sense in trying to compute the resulting beliefs with bigger precision than the precision of the input data. So the natural idea is to fix some precision $\varepsilon > 0$ and compute beliefs only with this precision. Alas, the resulting problem is also infeasible. Let us give precise definitions.

Definition. Assume that a positive number ε is fixed. We say that an algorithm *U computes the beliefs with precision* ε if for every inference engine *I*, for every knowledge base and every query *Q* it generates a real number $U(Q)$, for which $|U(Q) - bel(Q)| \leqslant \varepsilon$.

Comment. If $\varepsilon \geqslant 1/2$, then we can take an algorithm that always generates 1/2, and thus satisfy this inequality for all possible values of belief. Therefore this definition makes sense only when $\varepsilon < 1/2$.

THEOREM 2 (D, S, Y). *If an algorthm U computes the beliefs with precision* $\varepsilon < 1/2$, *then* $t_U(n) \geqslant ca^n$ *for some* $a > 1$.

So this computation also demands exponential time and is therefore infeasible.

4. MONTE-CARLO METHODS: FEASIBLE FOR SMETS' AND YAGER'S RULES, STILL INFEASIBLE FOR DEMPSTER'S RULE

Why probabilistic methods? Let us now take into consideration the fact that human experts may not only be slightly uncertain about their degrees of belief, but may also have doubts in their whole knowledge. In other words, there is a probability p_0 (small but positive) that what an expert says is absolutely wrong. If this is the case, then no matter what algorithm we apply the resulting values of belief will be absolutely inadequate. In view of that it is not necessary to achieve 100% correctness of the algorithm. The only thing that is reasonable to demand is that the probability that an algorithm errs must be smaller than this p_0, so that the resulting probability of an error (due both to the possible errors of the algorithm and the errors in the initial data) is not much greater than p_0.

So we arrive at the following definitions:

Definitions. By a *standard random number generator* we mean a program or device that generates real numbers that are uniformly distributed on the interval [0,1]. By a *probabilistic algorithm* we mean an algorithm that in addition to normal computational steps and calling I calls a standard random number generator. The result of applying an algorithm U to the data x will be denoted by $U(x)$.

In addition to t_0 *and* t_c let us fix a number $t_r > 0$ (called *the time of one call of this random number generator*); let us define a *running time* of a probabilistic algorithm U on any input data as $N_0 t_0 + N_c t_c + N_r t_r$ where N_0 is the total number of normal computational steps, N_c is the total number of calls of I, and N_r is the total number of calls of a generator. Let us now define the *computational complexity* $t_U(n)$ of an algorithm U as a maximum running time for all inputs of length n and for all possible values of the random number generator. If $t_U(n)$ is bounded by some polynomial of n, we call U a *polynomial-time algorithm*. If it is limited by a linear function, we call U a *linear-time* algorithm.

Comment. By definition a probabilistic algorithm uses a random number generator; therefore its output is not uniquely determined by the inputs: for every input it is a random variable.

Definition. Assume that positive numbers ε and p_0 are given. We say that a statement is *reliably true* if it is true with probability $1 - p_0$ or greater. We say that a probabilistic algorithm U *computes the beliefs with precision* ε *and reliability* $1 - p_0$ if for every knowledge base, for every inference engine I, and for every query Q it is reliably true that $|U(Q) - bel(Q)| \leqslant \varepsilon$.

In other words, $P(|U(Q) - bel(Q)| \leqslant \varepsilon) \geqslant 1 - p_0$.

Comment. In order to formulate the related negative result we must recall the denotation *RP*: it is the class of problem that can be solved (with reliability $1 - p_0$) in polynomial time. The majority of computer scientists believe that $RP \neq NP$ (for details see, e.g., Maung and Paris, 1990).

THEOREM 3 (D). *If* $\varepsilon < 1/4$, $p_0 < 1$, and $RP \neq NP$, *then there is no polynomial-time algorithm that computes beliefs with precision* ε *and reliability* $1 - p_0$.

Comment. So if we use Dempster's combination rule, the problem of computing beliefs is still infeasible.

THEOREM 4 (S, Y). *For every* $\varepsilon < 1/4$ *and* $p_0 < 1$ *there exists a linear-time algorithm that computes beliefs with precision* ε *and reliability* $1 - p_0$.

Comments.

1. So the problem is feasible!
2. Linear-time means that when the size of the problem increases (i.e., the number of pieces of knowledge increases, and/or the number of statements in every piece), then the number of calls of the inference engine I grows linearly or more slowly. What this time is equal to in absolute units, that is, whether it is reasonably small or really big, depends on how quickly the inference engine works.

Description of the algorithm. Let us describe the algorithm from Theorem 4. For that we need an auxiliary algorithm that given a piece of knowledge $(E_1,\ldots,E_n), m$, generates a statement E_i with probability $m(E_i)$. To get it we first compute the values $r_1 = m(E_1)$, $r_2 = m(E_1) + m(E_2)$, $r_3 = r_2 + m(E_3)$, ..., $r_n = r_{n-1} + m(E_n) = m(E_1) + \ldots + m(E_n) = 1$. Then we call a standard random number generator and compare the result r consequently with $r_1, r_2, \ldots, r_n = 1$. If $r \leqslant r_1$, generate E_1; if $r_{i-1} < r \leqslant r_i$, generate E_i.

Comments.

1. One can easily check that the probability of generating E_i is precisely $m(E_i)$.
2. This auxiliary algorithm is already a linear-time one. We can, however, further diminish its running time if we use bisection search instead of a linear search.

As a second auxiliary step we must find an integer N depending on ε and p_0; in the general case we can take $N = 2\varepsilon^{-2}\ln(2/p_0)$. For small ε and p_0 we can take smaller values of N: e.g., to get 10% precision and 95% reliability it is sufficient to take $N = 100$.

Now the main algorithm is as follows. Suppose we are given a knowledge base that consists of several pieces of knowledge $P_1, \ldots, P_k$. We do the following:

- *In case of Smets' combination rule*: Reserve an integer variable M for a counter, and set its initial value to 0. Then N time repeat the following:
  Apply the auxiliary algorithm to each piece of knowledge P_i, and get a random statement E_1; then apply I to check whether Q follows from all these statements, that is, whether $I(E_1 \& E_2 \& \ldots \& E_k, Q) =$ "*yes.*" If "*yes*", add 1 to the counter M; if not, leave M unchanged.
  As a desired estimate for $bel(Q)$ we take M/N, where M is the value of the counter N iterations.
- *In case of Yager's combination rule*: Same algorithm; the only difference is that we add 1 if $I(E_1 \& E_2 \& \ldots \& E_k, Q) =$ "*yes*" and the set $\{E_1, E_2, \ldots, E_k)$ is consistent, that is, $I(E_1 \& E'_2 \& \ldots \& E'_k, f)$ = "*no*".

Comments

1. This algorithm belongs to the class of Monte-Carlo methods. Such methods were proposed for Dempster-Shafer formalism (Pearl, 1988; Kampke, 198; Laskey and Lerner, 1989). If we use this algorithm with the original Dempster's combination rule, then for the case when conflicts between the pieces of knowledge are in some reasonable sense restricted, we also get linear-time estimates (Wilson, 1989, 1991).
2. Our result that Smets and Yager's rules are better than Dempster's rule because they are feasible and Dempster's is not in good accordance with the abovementioned fact that the original Dempster's rule, unlike the other two, contradicts our intuition (Zadeh, 1984).

5. PARALLEL COMPUTATION OF BELIEFS

Parallelization: possible advantages. Monte-Carlo methods can be easily implemented in parallel (Pearl, 1988); indeed, they consist of applying the inference engine to several randomly chosen sets of statements. If we have several processors at our disposal, then we can make each of them choose and process one set of statements. So each processor applies the inference engine only once, and the resulting running time of this parallel algorithm equals the running time of the inference engine. So we compute the beliefs precisely in the same time as we apply the inference engine, and adding masses and beliefs does not increase the running time!

How to implement it. Theoretically the more processors we have, the quicker the results. But in real parallel systems a lot of time is consumed on communication protocols, information exchange, waiting in the queues, etc. The more processors we have, the more time-consuming all these communication procedures become, and they seriously impact the whole computation process. So if we implement our parallelized algorithms on real parallel systems with many processors, this additional time will add to our running time and thus worsen our theoretical estimates.

In our case, however, during the main stage ("call inference engine") no communication is necessary, so we don't need to waste time on protocols. As a result each processor generates one bit ("yes" or "no"), and to estimate a belief we must send these bits to one processor and process them there. This can be done also without any protocols, by using a small shared memory of N bits, where N is the number of processors. Such an architecture was produced by Septor Electronics for use in machinery control applications (Roberts, 1989; Hardin and Taylor, 1990) and was efficiently used to parallelize Monte-Carlo algorithms (Kreinovich et al., 1991).

6. PROOFS

Comment. Some of the ideas that we use in these proofs appeared first in Dantsin (1990) and Dantsin and Kreinovich (1990).

Proofs of Theorems 1 and 2. If an algorithm computes beliefs precisely, then, of course, it also computes beliefs with precision ε. Therefore, if we prove Theorem 2, we get Theorem 1 as a corollary. So it is sufficient to prove Theorem 2. Let's do it.

Since we are proving a negative result, it is sufficient to construct a case in which the algorithm must work for a long time. Suppose that

U is an algorithm that computes beliefs with precision ε. Let's take a knowledge base that consist of n pieces of knowledge $P_1, P_2, \ldots, P_n$. The ith piece of knowledge consists of two statements E_i and $\neg E_i$, with $mi(E_i) = m_i(\neg E_i) = 0.5$. For Q let us take a statement that is different from any Boolean combination of these E_i. We'll use the denotations E_i^+ for E_i and E_i^- for $\neg E_i$.

Let us consider only such I, that for Boolean formulas, formed from E_i, coincide with logical implication. So, for example, $E_1 \& E_2 \rightarrow E_1$, but $E_1 \& \neg E_2 \not\rightarrow E_3$. In particular, for every sequence $\vec{\varepsilon} = (\varepsilon_1, \ldots, \varepsilon_n)$ of + and − symbols $I(E_1^{\varepsilon_1} \& E_2^{\varepsilon_2} \& \ldots \& E_n^{\varepsilon_n}, f) =$ "*no*." In other words, all possible combinations of E_i and $\neg E_i$ are consistent.

Three combination rules differ only in case of inconsistent knowledge. Therefore for the abovementioned case, when all the combinations are consisent, all three rules lead to the same combined knowledge. This knowledge consists of 2^n statements $E = E_1^{\varepsilon_1} E_2^{\varepsilon_2} \& \ldots \& E_n^{\varepsilon_n}$, and the mass of each statement equals to $m_1(E_1^{\varepsilon_1}) m_2(E_2^{\varepsilon_2}) \ldots m(E_n^{\varepsilon_n}) = (1/2)^n = 2^{-n}$. So for every query Q the belief $bel(Q)$ equals to the sum of the masses of all the statements that imply Q, that is, to $2^{-n}N(Q)$, where by $N(Q)$ we denoted the total number of statements E that imply Q.

Let us denote the numer of times during which our algorithm U called the inference engine I to know whether E implies Q for some E, by N. If $N < 2^n$, this means that for some of 2^n combinations E we did not ask whether $E \rightarrow Q$. So, if we take an inference engine J that coincides with I on all Boolean combinations of E_i and on all the pairs (E,Q), for which the algorithm U called I, and apply the same algorithm to this J instead of I, U will not feel the difference, because whenever it asks an inference engine something, it still gets the same results. So the result $U_J(Q)$ of applying this algorithm to J will be the same, as in case of I: $U_J(Q) = U_I(Q)$. Let's take two such J: J_1 says "yes" for all pairs (E,Q), for which U did not ask I; and J_2 answers "*no*" on all such pairs. Let us denote the number of statements for which $J_i(E,Q) =$ "*yes*," by $N_i(Q)$. The difference between $N_1(Q)$ and $N_2(Q)$ consists precisely of $2^n - N_c$ statements E, for which U did not ask I, i.e., $N_1(Q) - N_2(Q) = 2^n - N$. Since in our case $bel(Q) = 2^{-n}N(Q)$, we conclude that the values of belief $bel_i(Q)$ that correspond to J_i satisfy the equality $bel_1(Q) - bel_2(Q) = 2^{-n}(2^n - N) = 1 - 2^{-n}N$. But we took an algorithm that computes beliefs with precision ε, therefore the result $U(Q)$ of this algorithm must differ from both of these beliefs by no more than ε: $|bel_1(Q) - U(Q)| \leqslant \varepsilon$ and $|bel_2(Q) - U(Q)| \leqslant \varepsilon$. From these inequalities we conclude that $|bel_1(Q) - bel_2(Q)| \leqslant |bel_1(Q) - U(Q)| +$

$|bel_2(Q)| - U(Q)| \leqslant 2\varepsilon$, and so $1-2^{-n}N \leqslant 2\varepsilon$. So $2^{-n}N \geqslant (1-2\varepsilon)$ and therefore $N \geqslant 2^n(1-2\varepsilon)$. Since $\varepsilon < 1/2$, this difference $1-2\varepsilon$ is positive.

So the total running time is $\geqslant t_c N \geqslant 2^n(1-2\varepsilon)$, that is, it is really exponentially increasing with the length of the input.

Proof of Theorem 3. Let's prove this theorem by reductio ad absurdum: we'll suppose that such a polynomial algorithm U exists, and conclude that $RP = NP$, that is, that there exists a polynomial-time probabilistic algorithm that solves one of NP–complete problems. Namely, we'll construct such an algorithm for the propositional satisfiability problem. Indeed, suppose that U exists, and we have a propositional formula P with n propositional variables $x_1, \ldots, x_n$. Let's figure out whether this formula is satisfiable or not. For that purpose let's introduce a new propositional variable x_{n+1} and consider the knowledge base that consists of the following $n+1$ pieces of knowledge $P_1, \ldots, P_{k+1}$. When $i \leqslant k$, then P_i consists of two statements x_i and $\neg x_i$ with equal masses. P_{k+1} consists of two statements $P \& \neg x_{n+1}$ and $x_1 \& x_2 \& \ldots \& x_n \& x_{n+1}$, also with equal masses.

Statements of the combined knowledge base are formed as follows: for every i from 1 to n we must choose either x_i or $\neg x_i$, and then we must choose either $P \& \neg x_{n+1}$, or $x_1 \& x_2 \& \ldots \& x_n \& x_{n+1}$. In other words, we must first choose an n-dimensional Boolean vector $\vec{x} = (x_1, \ldots, x_n)$, and then choose one of the statements with which it is consistent: $P \& \neg x_{n+1}$ or $x_1 \& x_2 \& \ldots \& x_n \& x_{n+1}$. For each vector $\vec{x}$ consistency is easy to check: if P is true for this $\vec{x}$ (and this can be checked in polynomial time), then the first is consistent, if $x_1 = x_2 = \ldots = x_n =$ "*true*," then the second one is consistent. So we can easily implement logical consistency checking for these cases.

The resulting masses are as follows: If P is not satisfiable, then the combinations with $P \& \neg x_{n+1}$ are inconsistent, and therefore the only consistent combination is $x_1 \& x_2 \& \ldots \& x_n \& x_{n+1}$; therefore it gets the mass 1. If P is satisfiable, and N is the number of Boolean vectors that satisfy it, then we have $N+1$ consistent combinations. Since all the masses in all the pieces of knowledge are equal, the masses assigned to these consistent combinations are also equal, so we assign $1/(N+1)$ to each of them.

Let us take $Q = x_{n+1}$. For every statement E from the combined knowledge base we already know x_{n+1}, so the trivial algorithm will work as I in this case. The resulting belief $bel(Q)$ is as follows: if P is satisfiable, then $bel(Q) = 1$. If P is not satisfiable, then $bel(Q) = 1/(N+1)$, where $N \geqslant 1$, so $bel(Q) \leqslant 1/2$.

If $|U(Q)-bel(Q)|<1/4$, then in case $bel(Q)=1$ we have $U(Q)>1-1/4=3/4$, and in case $bel(Q)\leqslant 1/2$ we have $U(Q)<1/2+1/4=3/4$. So if we apply U to this knowledge base and compare $U(Q)$ with 3/4, we can tell whether P is satisfiable or not: if $U(Q)<3/4$, it is satisfiable; when $U(Q)>3/4$, it is not. So, using U, we constructed an algorithm that checks whether a formula is satisfiable with reliability $\geqslant 1-p_0$. So our assumption that a polynomial-time algorithm U can compute beliefs with given precision and reliability contradicts the assumption that $RP\neq NP$. Therefore such an algorithm U is impossible.

Proof of Theorem 4. That the algorithm described in Section 4 is linear-time can be easily seen: the number N_c of calls for I equals either to N (in Smets' case) or to $2N$ (in Yager's case); in both cases it does not depend on the input length at all. Likewise the number of times during which this algorithm calls the random-number generator is limited by N. As for additional computations, for each of N iterations they demand looking through all the pieces of the knowledge base N times, that is, the necessary running time is $\leqslant const\cdot Nn$ and is therefore linear in n.

Let us now prove that these linear-time algorithms really work. Let's first consider Smets' rule. By definition $bel(Q)=\sum_{E:E\to Q}m(E)$, where E runs over all combinations $E_i\&...\&F_j$ of statements from different pieces of knowledge. And the masses $m(E)$ are equal to $m(E)=\sum_{i,j:E\leftrightarrow(E_i\&...\&F_j)}m_1(E_i)...m_k(F_j)$. Substituting this expression for $m(E)$ into the formula for $bel(Q)$, we conclude that $bel(Q)=\sum_{E:E\to Q}\sum_{i,j:E\leftrightarrow(E_i\&...\&F_j)}m_1(E_i)...m_k(F_j)$. We defined an inference engine as a consistent algorithm, that is, an algorithm for which $A\leftrightarrow B$ implies that $I(A,Q)=I(B,Q)$. In particular, if $E\leftrightarrow(E_i\&...\&F_j)$, then $E\leftrightarrow Q$ if and only if $(E_i\&...\&F_j)\to Q$. Therefore the above expression for $bel(Q)$ can be simplified:

$$bel(Q)=\sum_{i,j:(E_i\&...\&F_j)\to Q} m_1(E_i)...m_k(F_j)$$

Let us now prove that this expression equals some probability. We say that a statement is *randomly chosen* from a piece of knowledge $((E_1,...,E_k),m)$ if it coincides with E_i with probability $m(E_i)$. We suppose that the choices from different pieces of knowledge are independent. In this case the probability that a sequence $E_i,...,F_j$ is chosen, equals to $m_1(E_i)...m_k(F_j)$. Therefore the right-hand side of the above formula for $bel(Q)$ is the sum of the probabilities of all cases in which the chosen sequence implies Q, that is, $bel(Q)$ equals the probability that a random sequence implies Q.

Comment. This fact does not mean that we interpret masses as probabilities: it is a purely formal equality that may have nothing to do with semantics of masses, but that turns out to be useful for computing beliefs.

This probability can be computed as follows: we make several (N) simulations of the random event, and estimate probability p by a ratio M/N, where M is the number of cases in which the event happened (in our case in which the randomly chosen sequence implied Q). The precision of these estimates is known from mathematical statistics: to get a precision ε with reliability $1-p_0$, we must take $N=2\varepsilon^{-2}\ln(2/p_0)$ (so-called Hoefding theorem; see also Dantsin and Kreinovich, 1990; Wilson, 1989, 1991).

For big N the distribution for the difference $p-M/N$ is close to Gaussian, so we can use the estimates for the Gaussian distribution. In particular, we get $N=100$ for $\varepsilon=0.1$ and $p_0=0.05$.

For Yager's case the arguments are the same, with the only difference that $bel(Q)$ is equal to the probability that the randomly chosen sequence is consistent and implies Q.

ACKNOWLEDGMENTS

This research was supported by NSF grant No. CDA-9015006, NASA Research grant NAG 9-482, a grant from the Institute for Manufacturing and Materials Management, and an equipment donation from Septor Electronics. The authors are also thankful to E. Dantsin (Leningrad), D. Dubois (Toulouse), M. Gelfond (El Paso), J. Paris (Manchester), J. Pearl (Los Angeles), H. Prade (Toulouse), Ph. Smets (Brussels), and P. Suppes (Stanford) for valuable discussions.

BIBLIOGRAPHY

Barnett, J.A. (1981). Computational methods for a mathematical theory of evidence. In *Proceedings of the Seventh International Joint Conference on Artificial Intelligence* (IJCAI-81), Vancouver, pp. 868–75.

Bonissone, P.P. (1987). Reasoning, plausible. In S.C. Shapiro (ed.), *Encyclopedia of Artificial Intelligence*. New York: Willey.

Borrett, W. and Kreinovich, V. (1990a). *Monte-Carlo methods allow us to avoid exponential time in Dempster-Shafer formalism*. Technical Report UTEP-CS-90-05, University of Texas at El Paso.

Borrett, W. and Kreinovich, V. (1990b). Monte-Carlo methods allows us to avoid exponential time in Dempster-Shafer formalism. *Abstracts Amer. Math. Soc.* 11: 473.

Dantsin, E. (1990). Algorithms for probabilistic inference. In *Springer Lecture Notes in Computer Science* 417: 67–75.

Dantsin, E. and Kreinovich, V. (1990). Probabilistic inference in prediction systems. *Soviet Math. Doklady* 40: 8–12.

Dempster, A.P. and Kong, A. (1987). A discussion of G. Shafer, Probability judgement in artificial intelligence and expert systems. *Statisical Science* 2: 3–44.

Dubois, D. and Prade, H. (1988). Representation and combination of uncertainty with belief functions and possibility measures. *Computational Intelligence* 4: 244–64.

Garey, M.R. and Johnson, D.S. (1979). *Computers and intractability — A guide to the theory of* NP-*completeness*. New York: Freeman.

Gordon, J. and Shortliffe, E.H. (1985). A method for managing evidential reasoning in a hierarchical hypothesis space. *Artificial Intelligence* 26: 323–57.

Hardin, J. and Taylor, J. (1990). A distributed parallel processing system can solve today's complex automated machine control problems. In *Proceedings Nineteenth Annual International Programmable Controllers Conference*.

Hsia, Y.-T. (1989). *Valuation invariance, epistemic irrelevance and the use of the Dempster-Shafer theory for reasoning*. Université Libre de Bruxelles, IRIDIA Technical Report No. 89–9.

Kampke, T. (1988). About assessing and evaluating uncertain inferences within the theory of inference. *Decision Support Systems* 4: 433–39.

Kennes, R. (1990). *Computational aspects of the Möbius transform of a graph*. Université Libre de Bruxelles, IRIDIA Technical Report No. 90–13.

Kennes, R. and Smets, P. (1990). Computational aspects of the Möbius transform. In *Proceedings of the Sixth Conference on Uncertainty in Artificial Intelligence*, Cambridge, MA, pp. 344–51.

Kreinovich, V., Bernat, A., Villa, E., and Mariscal, Y. (1991). Parallel computers estimate errors caused by imprecise data. *Proc. Fourth ISMM (International Society on Mini and Micro Computers) International Conference on Parallel and Distributed Computing and Systems*, Washington, Vol. 1, pp. 386–90.

Kyburg, H.E., Jr. (1987). Bayesian and non-Bayesian evidential updating. *Artificial Intelligence* 31: 271–93.

Laskey, K.B. and Lerner, P.E. (1989). Assumptions, beliefs and probabilities. *Artificial Intelligence* 41: 65–77.

Maung, I. and Paris, J.B. (1990). A note on the infeasibility of some inference processes. *International Journal of Intelligent Systems* 5: 595–603.

Orponen, P. (1990). Dempster's rule of combination is #*P-complete*. *Artificial Intelligence* 44: 245–53.

Paass, G. (1988). A discussion on Dempster-Shafer formalism. In Smets et al., 1988, pp. 279–80.

Pearl, J. (1988). *Probabilistic reasoning in intelligent systems*. San Mateo, CA: Morgan Kaufmann.

Phillips, D. (1990). Belief maintenance using the Dempster-Shafer theory of evidence. *C Users Journal* 3: 67–78.
Roberts, R. (1989). AI enhanced transfer lines. *Programmable Controls*, May, 105–108.
Shafer, G. (1976). *A mathematical theory of evidence*. Princeton, NJ: Princeton University Press.
Shafer, G. (1985). Hierarchical evidence. In *Proceedings of the Second Conference on Artificial Ingelligence Applications*, IEEE Press, pp. 16–21.
Shafer, G. and Logan, R. (1987). Implementing Dempster's rule for hierarchical evidence. *Artificial Intelligence* 33: 271–98.
Shenoy, P.P. and Shafer, G. (1986). Propagating belief functions with local computations. *IEEE Expert* 1: 43–52.
Smets, P. (1988). *Belief functions*. In Smets et al., 1988, pp. 253–86.
Smets, P. et al., (eds.). (1988). *Nonstandard logics for automated reasoning*. London: Academic Press.
Wilson, N. (1989). *Justification, computational efficiency and generalization of the Dempster-Shafer theory*. Oxford Polytechnic Dept. of Computing and Math. Sci. Technical Report No. 15, 1989.
Wilson, N. (1991). A Monte-Carlo algorithm for Dempster-Shafer belief. In *Proceedings of the Seventh Conference on Uncertainty in Artificial Intelligence*, Los Angeles, CA.
Yager, R.R. (1985). On the relationships of methods of aggregation evidence in expert systems. *Cybernetics and Systems* 16: 1–21.
Yager, R.R. (1987). On the Dempster-Shafer framework and new combination rules. *Information Sciences* 41: 93–137.
Zadeh, L. (1984). A mathematical theory of evidence. *AI Magazine* 5: 81–83.

10 From rough set theory to evidence theory

Andrzej SKOWRON
and Jerzy GRZYMAŁA-BUSSE

Abstract: The rough set approach is objective in the sense that the values of uncertainty measures are computable. In the case of the evidence theoretic approach those values are expected to be given by an expert. The aim of the paper is to show that the rough set approach can be treated as a basis for evidence theory. We interpret the basic notions of evidence theory in the framework of rough set theory. In particular we give an interpretation of the **belief and plausibility** functions in terms of the lower and upper approximations of sets. It seems to us that the relationships between the rough set approach and evidence theory will stimulate practical growth of applications based on those approaches.

Keywords: reasoning with incomplete information, rough sets, evidence theory.

1. INTRODUCTION

One fundamental feature in deciding about the behavior of living creatures is their ability to classify objects (Pawlak, 1991; Kodratoff and Michalski, 1990). In the simplest case the classification process has two stages. In the first stage some properties of objects are measured by sensors (represented by attributes). In the second stage, on the basis of the results (values of attributes) of those measurements living creatures are able to somehow classify objects very efficiently. In many cases, because of missing or inexact information, it is only possible to give a rough classification of objects.

The classification problems are central for the rough set approach (Pawlak, 1991) as well as for the evidence theoretic approach (Shafer, 1976).

To show that, in some sense, the rough set approach can be treated as a basis for evidence theory we will consider this central problem for both theories.

Every classification problem is related to a partition of a universe U_∞ (finite or infinite) of objects. We restrict our considerations to the case when the following assumptions related to the incomplete information about U_∞, objects and partition are satisfied:

1. Two kinds of incomplete information about U_∞ are accessible. In the first case the information about U_∞ is represented by a special kind of information system (data table, attribute-value system) called a *decision table* (condition-action table) (Pawlak, 1982, 1991). In the second case the information is given by a finite set of partial dependencies defining the family of decision tables.
2. The incomplete information about an object s from the universe U_∞ is obtained by "measuring" (computing) values of all accessible attributes (in the case of decision tables they are called conditions) on the object s.
3. Incomplete information about partition of U_∞ is given by the so-called frame of discernment (Shafer, 1976), a finite set of names of sets (or predicate names) $\Theta = \{\theta_1, \ldots, \theta_k\}$. The objects from U_∞ are classified into sets corresponding to those names $\theta_1, \ldots, \theta_k$ on the basis of information about them and values of (expert) decisions that appear in the decision tables.

The fundamental assumption in the rough set approach (Pawlak, 1991) is the following one: the objects from the universe are perceived only through the accessible information about them, that is, the values of attributes that can be evaluated on these objects. Objects with the same information are indiscernible. In consequence, the classification of objects is based on the accessible information about them, not on objects themselves.

The above two cases of classification can be described on the basis of rough set approach in the following ways.

In the first case, together with the information about objects from a finite set of objects, the expert classification of them is given. The classification problem in this case is related to the question of to what extent it is possible to reflect by accessible (condition) attributes the classification done by an expert.

One can represent the results of evaluations of attributes on objects by means of information systems (data tables). The information system consists of a data table with the number of rows equal to the number of objects and the number of columns equal to the number of different attributes. In that table, in the position corresponding to a given object and given attribute, there is the result of evaluation of that attribute on the object. Information systems with distinguished columns representing the results of an expert's classification are called decision tables. The distinguished attributes are called decisions.

In the second case a finite set of (partial) dependencies (Pawlak, 1991) between attributes are used to describe possible information about objects from the universe U_∞. Those dependencies describe some constraints on rows that can appear in the decision tables. This kind of description determines a family of decision tables rather than a single decision table. The classification problem is related to all decision tables from that family.

In the evidence theory (Shafer, 1976) the information about sets creating a given partition is included directly in some numerical functions called the basic probability assignment, belief function, and plausibility function, whereas in the case of rough set approach the information about classified sets and objects is included in decision table(s).

In both the abovementioned cases, we show how it is possible to compute the basic probability assignment function. We obtain belief functions properties compatible with the intuition encoded in the evidence theory (Shafer, 1976, Bhatnager and Kanal, 1986). Some initial results about relationships between the rough set theory and evidence theory are presented in Grzymała-Busse (1989, 1991) and Skowron (1989a, 1989b, 1990, 1991).

The relationships between rough set theory and evidence theory allow us also to put some new light on the Dempster combination rule. We formulate a notion of the independent product of decision tables. We prove (Theorem 3) the validity of the Dempster combination rule for such products. We also show that it is possible to represent by decision tables all basic probability assignments taking rational values.

We hope that strong connections between the rough set and Dempster-Shafer approaches presented in this paper will stimulate further practical applications of both theories.

2. EVIDENCE THEORY

Evidence theory, also called the "Dempster-Shafer theory" or the "belief function theory," is treated as a promising method of dealing with uncertainty in expert systems.

The first ideas of evidence theory were presented by Hooper and Bernoulli in the seventeenth century. The basic notions we present in this section are due to Shafer (1976).

The evidence theory approach is based on the idea of placing a number from the interval [0, 1], given by an expert, to indicate a degree of belief for a given proposition on the basis of a given evidence.

We will now introduce the following basic notions: *frame of discernment, basic probability assignment, belief function,* and *plausibility function.*

A frame of discernment Θ is a finite nonempty set.

The basic probability assignment (bpa) on Θ is any function

$$m:\mathbf{P}(\Theta) \rightarrow \mathbf{R}_+$$

where $\mathbf{P}(\Theta)$ is the powerset of Θ and $\mathbf{R}_+$ is the set of nonnegative reals, satisfying the following conditions:

1. $m(\emptyset) = 0$
2. $\sum_{\Delta \subseteq \Theta} m(\Delta) = 1$

For a given bpa m two functions are defined.

- A function $Bel:\mathbf{P}(\Theta) \rightarrow \mathbf{R}_+$ is called the belief function over Θ (generated by m) iff for any $\theta \subseteq \Theta$

$$Bel(\theta) = \sum_{\Delta \subseteq \theta} m(\Delta)$$

- A function $Pl:\mathbf{P}(\Theta) \rightarrow \mathbf{R}_+$ is called the plausibility function over Θ (generated by m) iff for any $\theta \subseteq \Theta$

$$Pl(\theta) = \sum_{\Delta \cap \theta \neq \emptyset} m(\Delta)$$

In the literature (Shafer, 1976) one can find several interesting properties of the functions defined above. Let us note some of them:

$$Bel(\emptyset) = Pl(\emptyset) = 0;$$
$$Bel(\Theta) = Pl(\Theta) = 1;$$
$$\text{If } \Delta \subseteq \theta, \text{ then } Bel(\Delta) \subseteq Bel(\theta) \text{ and } Pl(\Delta) \subseteq Pl(\theta);$$
$$Bel(\theta) \leqslant Pl(\theta);$$
$$Bel(\theta) + Bel(\Theta - \theta) \leqslant 1 \text{ and } Pl(\theta) + Pl(\Theta - \theta) \geqslant 1,$$

where $\theta, \Delta \subseteq \Theta$.

Let us observe that the inequality $Bel(\theta) + Bel(\Theta - \theta) \leqslant 1$ cannot in general be reduced to the equality $Bel(\theta) + Bel(\Theta - \theta) = 1$ ($P(\theta) + P(\Theta - \theta) = 1$ for any probability function on $P(\Theta)$). This allows us to take into account ignorance; for example, if we have no evidence at all for or against θ, then $Bel(\theta) = Bel(\Theta - \theta) = 0$.

The *plausibility function* Pl is definable by the belief function:

$$Pl(\theta) = 1 - Bel(\Theta - \theta), \text{ for } \theta \subseteq \Theta$$

From a given belief function, a basic probability assignment can be reconstructed:

$$m(\theta) = \sum_{\Delta \subseteq \theta} (-1)^{|\theta - \Delta|} Bel(\Delta), \text{ for } \theta \subseteq \Theta$$

The union of all subsets $\theta \subseteq \Theta$ that are focal (i.e., have the following property: $m(\theta) > 0$) is called the *core of* Θ.

A belief function Bel is called *Bayesian belief function* iff $Bel(\theta) + Bel(\Theta - \theta) = 1$ for $\theta \subseteq \Theta$. The following conditions are equivalent:

1. Bel is Bayesian:
2. $Bel(\theta \cup \Delta) = Bel(\theta) + Bel(\Delta)$ for θ, $\Delta \subseteq \Theta$ and $\theta \cap \Delta = \emptyset$;
3. $Bel = Pl$;
4. All focal elements are singletons (i.e., one-element subsets of Θ).

The basic probability assignment m corresponding to a Bayesian belief function Bel has the following properties:

$$\sum_{\Delta \in \Theta} m(\{\Delta\}) = 1 \text{ and } Bel(\theta) = \sum_{\Delta \in \theta} m(\{\Delta\})$$

where $\theta \subseteq \Theta$.

The Bayesian belief function satisfies all three of Kolmogorov's axioms while a belief function satisfies only two of them. In fact, we have

$$Bel(\theta) = \sum_{\Delta \subseteq \theta} m(\Delta) = \sum_{\Delta \in \theta} m(\{\Delta\}) + \sum_{\substack{\Delta \subseteq \theta \\ |\Delta| > 1}} m(\Delta) =$$

$$= \sum_{\Delta \in \theta} Bel(\{\Delta\}) + \sum_{\substack{\Delta \subseteq \theta \\ |\Delta| > 1}} m(\Delta)$$

Hence, in general, $Bel(\theta) \neq \sum_{\Delta \in \theta} Bel(\{\Delta\})$.

In this paper we will describe how these functions can be defined and interpreted on a basis of rough set approach. This interpretation seems to be helpful for practical applications of the evidence theory in systems dealing with uncertainty.

3. INFORMATION SYSTEMS AND DECISION TABLES

Information systems are used for representing knowledge. The notion of an information system presented here is due to Pawlak and was investigated by several researchers (see, e.g., the bibliography in Pawlak, 1991). Among research topics related to information systems are: rough set theory, problems of knowledge representation, problems of knowledge reduction, dependencies in knowledge bases.

In this section we present basic notions related to information systems. An *information system* is a pair $\mathbf{A} = (U, A)$, where

- U is a nonempty, finite set called the universe;
- A is a nonempty, finite set of attributes, i.e., a: $U \rightarrow V_a$ for $a \in A$, where V_a is called the domain of a.

Elements of U are called objects. There are various possible interpretations of objects in practical applications, for example, cases, states, processes, patients, observations. Attributes can be interpreted as features, variables, characteristic conditions, etc.

In this paper we consider a special case of information systems called *decision* tables. In any decision table together with the set of attributes a partition of that set into conditions and decisions is given. For our purposes it will be enough to consider decision tables with one decision because by simple coding one can always transform any decision table with more than one decision into a decision table with exactly one decision. One can interpret a decision attribute as a kind of classification of the universe of objects given by an expert decision maker, operator, physician, etc. Eventually, we adopt the following definition of the decision table (sometimes also called condition-actions table):

A *decision table* is any information system of the form $A = (U, A \cup \{d\})$, where $d \notin A$ is a distinguished attribute called *decision*. The elements of A are called *conditions*.

The cardinality of the image $d(U) = \{k \in \mathbf{N}: d(s) = k$ for some $s \in U\}$ is called the ***rank*** of d and is denoted by $r(d)$.

We say that two decision tables $\mathbf{A} = (U, A \cup \{d\})$ and $\mathbf{A}' = (U', A' \cup \{d'\})$ are *isomorphic* iff there exist bijections $h: U \to U'$, $g: A \to A'$, and $t_a: V_a \to V_{g(a)}$, for any $a \in A$ such that $t_a(a(s)) = g(a)(h(s))$ for any $s \in U$ and $a \in A$.

In the sequel we do not distinguish between isomorphic decision tables. In particular, without loss of the generality, one can assume that the set V_d of values of the decision d is equal to $\{1, \ldots, r(d)\}$.

Let us observe that the decision d determines the partition

$$CLASS_{\mathbf{A}}(d) = \{X_1, \ldots, X_{r(d)}\}$$

of the universe U, where $X_k = d^{-1}(\{k\})$ for $1 \leqslant k \leqslant r(d)$. $CLASS_{\mathbf{A}}(d)$ will be called the classification of objects in $\mathbf{A}$ determined by the decision d.

Any decision table $\mathbf{A} = (U, A \cup \{d\})$ can be represented by a data table with the number of rows equal to the cardinality of the universe U and the number of columns equal to the cardinality of the set $A \cup \{d\}$. In the position corresponding to the row s and column a there is the value $a(s)$.

Example 1. Let us consider the example of a decision table defined by the data presented in Table 10.1.

In the example we have $U = \{1, \ldots, 28\}$, $A = \{a, b, c, e, f\}$. The decision is denoted by d. The possible values of conditions from A equal 0 or 1 and the rank of the decision d, that is, $r(d)$ is equal to 3. The decision d defines in U the classification

$$CLASS_{\mathbf{A}}(d) = \{X_1, X_2, X_3\}$$

where

$$X_1 = \{1, 2, 4, 8, 10, 15, 22, 25\}$$
$$X_2 = \{3, 5, 11, 12, 16, 18, 19, 21, 23, 24, 27\}$$
$$X_3 = \{6, 7, 9, 13, 14, 17, 20, 26, 28\}$$

Table 10.1

U	*a*	*b*	*c*	*e*	*f*	*d*
1	0	0	1	0	0	1
2	1	1	1	0	0	1
3	0	1	0	0	0	2
4	1	0	0	0	1	1
5	0	1	0	0	0	2
6	1	0	0	0	1	3
7	0	0	0	1	1	3
8	1	1	1	1	1	1
9	0	0	0	1	1	3
10	0	0	1	0	0	1
11	1	1	1	0	0	2
12	1	1	1	1	1	2
13	1	1	0	1	1	3
14	1	1	0	0	1	3

U	*a*	*b*	*c*	*e*	*f*	*d*
15	0	0	1	1	1	1
16	1	1	0	1	1	2
17	0	0	0	1	1	3
18	0	0	0	0	0	2
19	0	0	0	0	0	2
20	1	1	1	0	0	3
21	1	1	0	0	1	2
22	0	0	1	0	1	1
23	1	1	1	0	0	2
24	0	0	1	1	1	2
25	1	0	1	0	1	1
26	1	0	1	0	1	3
27	1	0	1	0	1	2
28	1	1	1	1	0	3

4. LOWER AND UPPER APPROXIMATIONS OF SETS

Rough sets have been introduced by Pawlak (1982) as a tool to deal with inexact, uncertain, or vague knowledge in AI applications such as knowledge-based systems in medicine, natural language processing, pattern recognition, decision systems, and approximate reasoning. Since 1982 rough sets have been intensively studied and many practical applications have been implemented based on developed theory of rough sets.

Let $\mathbf{A} = (U, A)$ be an information system. With every subset of attributes $B \subseteq A$, a binary relation, denoted by $IND_{\mathbf{A}}(B)$ or $IND(B)$ (when no confusion arises), called the *B-indiscernibility relation*, is associated and defined as follows:

$$IND(B) = \{(s, s') \in U^2 \colon \text{for every } a \in B,\ a(s) = a(s')\}$$

$IND(B)$ is an equivalence relation and $IND(B) = \bigcap_{a \in B} IND(a)$. Objects s, s' satisfying relation $IND(B)$ are indiscernible by attributes from B.

Every subset $B \subseteq A$ may be considered as a name of the relation $IND(B)$, or in other words, as a name of knowledge represented by an equivalence relation $IND(B)$. For simplicity, if it does not cause confusion, we shall identify B and the corresponding relation $IND(B)$.

The value a(s) assigned by the attribute a to the object s can be viewed as a name (or a description) of the primitive category of a to which s belongs, that is, $a(s)$ is the name of $[s]_{IND(a)}$. The name (description) of a category of $B \subseteq A$ containing object s is the set of pairs

$$\{(a, a(s)) \colon a \in B\}$$

Example 2. For the decision table presented in Example 1 we have: $U/IND_{\mathrm{A}}(d) = \{X_1, X_2, X_3\}$, where X_1, X_2, X_3 are defined in Example 1 and $X_i = d^{-1}(\{i\}) = \{k \in U \colon d(k) = i\}$ for $i = 1, 2, 3$. Then, $U/IND_{\mathrm{A}}(A) = \{[1], [2], [3], [4], [7], [8], [13], [14], [15], [18], [22], [25], [28]$. For simplicity of notation we omit the subscript $IND_{\mathrm{A}}(A)$ in equivalence classes of $IND_{A}(A)$ and $[1] = \{1, 10\}$, $[2] = \{2, 11, 20, 23\}$, $[3] = \{3, 5\}$, $[4] = \{4, 6\}$, $[7] = = \{7, 9, 17\}$, $[8] = \{8, 12\}$, $[13] = \{13, 16\}$, $[14] = \{14, 21\}$, $[15] = \{15, 24\}$, $[18] = \{18, 19\}$, $[22] = \{22\}$, $[25] = \{25, 26, 27\}$, $[28] = \{28\}$.

Sets that are unions of some classes of the indiscernibility relation $IND(B)$ are called definable by B. Some subsets (categories) of objects in an information system cannot be expressed exactly by employing available attributes but they can be roughly defined.

If $\mathbf{A} = (U, A)$ is an information system, $B \subseteq A$ set of attributes and $X \subseteq U$ a set of objects, then the sets

$$\{s \in U \colon [s]_B \subseteq X\} \text{ and } \{s \in U \colon [s]_B \cap X \neq \emptyset\}$$

are called B-lower and B-upper approximation of X in $\mathbf{A}$, and they are denoted by $\underline{B}X$ and $\bar{B}X$, respectively. One can interpret $\underline{B}X$ and $\bar{B}X$ as the interior and closure of the set X in the topology generated by equivalence classes of the indiscernibility relation $IND(B)$.

The set $BN_B(X) = \bar{B}X - \underline{B}X$ will be called the B-boundary of X. When $B = \underline{A}$ we will write also $BN_{\mathrm{A}}(X)$ instead of $BN_{A}(X)$.

The set X is B-definable if $\bar{B}X = \underline{B}X$. It is easy to observe also that $\underline{B}X$ is the greatest B-definable set contained in X, whereas $\bar{B}X$ is the smallest B-definable set containing X.

The set $\underline{B}X$ is the set of all elements of U that can be with certainty classified as elements of X having the knowledge represented by attributes from B; set $\bar{B}X$ is the set of elements of U that can be possibly classified as elements of X employing the knowledge represented by attributes from B; set $BN_B(X)$ is the set of elements that cannot be classified either to X or to $-X$ having knowledge B.

Example 3. Let us consider the decision table from Example 1. We obtain the following lower and upper approximations of sets X_1, X_2, X_3 for the classification determined by decision d:

$$\underline{A}X_1 = [1] \cup [22] = \{1, 10, 22\},$$
$$\underline{A}X_2 = [3] \cup [18] = \{3, 5, 18, 19\},$$
$$\underline{A}X_3 = [7] \cup [28] = \{7, 9, 17, 28\},$$
$$\bar{A}X_1 = \underline{A}X_1 \cup [2] \cup [4] \cup [8] \cup [15] \cup [25] = \\ = \{1, 2, 4, 6, 8, 10, 11, 12, 15, 20, 22, 23, 24, 25, 26, 27\},$$
$$\bar{A}X_2 = \underline{A}X_2 \cup [2] \cup [8] \cup [13] \cup [14] \cup [15] \cup [25] = \\ = \{2, 3, 5, 8, 11, 12, 13, 14, 15, 16, 18, 19, 20, 21, 23, 24, 25, 26, 27\},$$
$$\bar{A}X_3 = \underline{A}X_3 \cup [2] \cup [4] \cup [13] \cup [14] \cup [25] = \\ = \{2, 4, 6, 7, 9, 11, 13, 14, 16, 17, 20, 21, 23, 25, 26, 27, 28\},$$

An arbitrary object with the information $\{(a,0), (b,0), (c,1), (e,0), (f, 0)\}$ is classified as element of X_1 and objects with the information $\{(a,1), (b,1), (c,1), (e,0), (f,0)\}$ belong to the boundary region of every set X_1, X_2, X_3, whereas all objects with information $\{(a, 1), (b,1), (c, 0), (e, 1), (f, 1)\}$ belong to the boundary region of X_2 and X_3 but not to the boundary region of X_1.

From the last example it follows that objects from the boundary regions can be classified on the basis of knowledge represented by condition attributes.

5. APPROXIMATION OF EXPERT CLASSIFICATION

In this section we introduce an approximation of the classification made by an expert.

A decision d determines in the decision table $\mathbf{A} = (U, A \cup \{d\})$ two sets

$$\Theta_{\mathbf{A}} = \{1, \dots, r(d)\} \text{ and } CLASS_{\mathbf{A}}(d) = \{X_1, \dots, X_{r(d)}\}$$

called the frame of discernment defined by d in **A** and the classification determined by d in **A**, respectively.

We say that the frame of discernment Θ is compatible with **A** if $r(d) = |\Theta|$ (i.e., $|\Theta_{\mathbf{A}}| = |\Theta|$). If $\Theta = \{\theta_1,...,\theta_k\}$ is compatible with $\Theta_{\mathbf{A}}$, then by χ we denote the bijection between Θ and $\Theta_{\mathbf{A}}$ defined in the following way: $\chi(\theta_i) = i$ for $i = 1,...,k$. We extend χ on subsets of Θ in the following way: $\chi(\theta) = \{i: \theta_i \in \theta\}$, where $\theta \subseteq \Theta$. The objects from the universe U of **A** can be classified employing the knowledge represented by conditions from A. This allows the answer that either an object belongs to the lower approximation of a given set $X \subseteq$ U or it is in the complement of the upper approximation of X or belongs to the boundary region corresponding to X. The last example shows that we can do more; we can, in some sense, better classify objects from the boundary regions. This is based on the following observation:

Proposition 1. Let $\mathbf{A} = (U, A \cup \{d\})$ be a decision table. The family of all nonempty sets from

$$\{\underline{A}X_1,...,\underline{A}X_{r(d)}\} \cup \{Bd_{\mathbf{A}}(\theta): \theta \subseteq \Theta_{\mathbf{A}} \text{ and } |\theta| > 1\}$$

where $Bd_{\mathbf{A}}(\theta) = \bigcap_{i \in \theta} BN_A(X_i) \cap \bigcap_{i \notin \theta} - BN_A(X_i)$, is a partition of the universe U. Moreover, the following equality holds:

$$\bigcup_{i \in \theta} \underline{A}X_i \cup \bigcup_{\Delta \subseteq \theta, |\Delta| > 1} Bd_{\mathbf{A}}(\Delta) = \underline{A}\bigcup_{i \in \theta} X_i, \text{ for } \theta \subseteq \Theta_{\mathbf{A}} \text{ with } |\theta| > 1$$

The classification (partition) of the universe U described in Proposition 1 is called the standard classification of U approximating in **A** the classification ($CLASS_{\mathbf{A}}(d)$) of U defined by the decision d (or in other words, by an expert). By $APP\_CLASS_{\mathbf{A}}(d)$ we denote the family:

$$\{\underline{A}X_1,..., \underline{A}_{r(d)}\} \cup \{Bd_{\mathbf{A}}(\theta): \theta \subseteq \Theta_{\mathbf{A}} \text{ and } |\theta| > 1\}$$

Example 4. In Example 3 we obtained the lower and upper approximations of sets X_1, X_2, X_3. In this case we have the following partition of boundary sets:

$$Bd_{\mathbf{A}}(\{1,2\}) = BN_{\mathbf{A}}(X_1) \cap BN_{\mathbf{A}}(X_2) \cap (U - BN_{\mathbf{A}}(X_3)) = \{8, 12, 15, 24\}$$

$$Bd_{\mathbf{A}}(\{1,3\}) = BN_{\mathbf{A}}(X_1) \cap (U - BN_{\mathbf{A}}(X_2)) \cap BN_{\mathbf{A}}(X_3) = \{4, 6\}$$

$$Bd_{\mathbf{A}}(\{2,3\}) = (U - BN_{\mathbf{A}}(X_1)) \cap BN_{\mathbf{A}}(X_2) \cap BN_{\mathbf{A}}(X_3) = \{13, 14, 16, 21\}$$

$$Bd_{\mathbf{A}}(\{1,2,3\}) = BN_{\mathbf{A}}(X_1) \cap BN_{\mathbf{A}}(X_2) \cap BN_{\mathbf{A}}(X_3) = \{2, 11, 20, 23, 25, 26, 27\}$$

An illustration of the partition of the universe U defined by the lower approximations of sets X_1, X_2, X_3 and the partition of boundary regions is depicted in Figure 10.1.

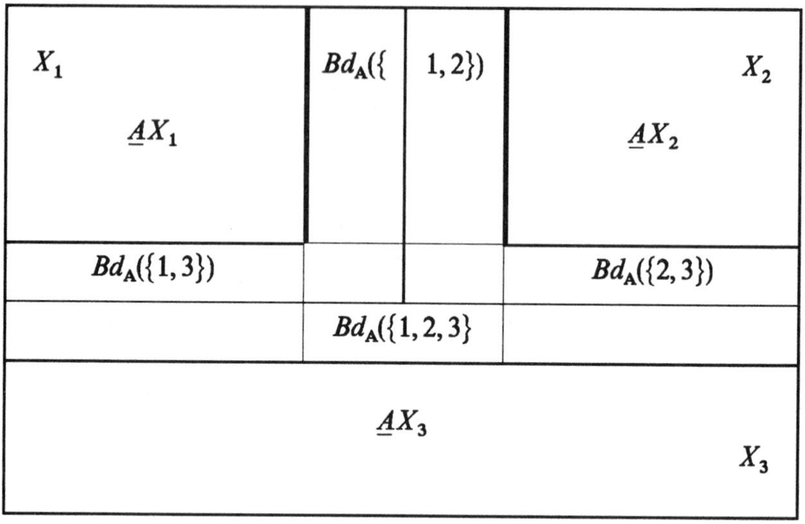

Figure 10.1

We now have a clear interpretation of the new classification. Objects from the universe U of **A** represented by an information (from $\{(A, v_a)): a \in A \text{ and } v_a \in V_a\})$ appearing in the rows of **A** can be classified exactly on the basis of that information only when the category (i.e., the equivalence class of the indiscernibility relation $IND_A(A)$) corresponding to that information is included in X_i for some i. Otherwise, that category is included in a boundary region of the form $Bd_A(\theta)$, for some θ and objects from U represented by a given information belong to the boundary region of all sets X_i, where $i \in \theta$ and do not belong to sets X_j, where $j \notin \theta$ (i.e., they are in the union $\bigcup_{i \in \theta} X_i$ but we do not have enough information to say in which of the sets X_i they occur!).

Let us observe that our information system (data table) is representing only a partial information about some objects from the universe U_∞ of all classified objects.

The following question arises: how to classify new objects from U_∞? First of all let us note that very often the exact description of the sets corresponding to names θ_i from the frame of discernment Θ is unknown. The sets from $CLASS_A(d) = \{X_1, ..., X_{r(d)}\}$ are images of some subsets of sets corresponding to $\theta_1, ..., \theta_{r(d)}$, respectively. One can make the classification of new objects from the universe U_∞ on the basis of experience that has been encoded in the information system. Simply, one can follow the previous rules; we classify an object s on the basis of the information $Inf_{\mathbf{A}}(s) = \{a, a(s)): a \in A\}$.

In this way we obtain the following rules:

- If we get the information $Inf_A(s)$ about a classified object s from the universe U_∞ and all objects with that information have so far been classified to the lower approximation $\underline{A}X_i$ of the set X_i then the object s is classified to the set corresponding to θ_i.
- If we get the information $Inf_A(s)$ about an object s from the universe U_∞ and all objects with that information have been classified so far to the boundary region $Bd_{\mathbf{A}}(\theta)$ then the object s is classified to the union of subsets (of U_∞) corresponding to names included in θ but we do not have enough information to say exactly to which of those sets s belongs.

We will not discuss here problems of correctness of such approximation and necessity of interaction with an expert to improve the quality of classification.

For further consideration it is important to observe that for any decision table $\mathbf{A} = (U, A \cup \{d\})$ and the frame of the discernment $\Theta_{\mathbf{A}}$ we have defined a new decision table $\mathbf{A}' = (U, A \cup \{\partial_{\mathbf{A}}\})$, where $\partial_{\mathbf{A}}(s)$ denotes the unique subset θ of $\Theta_{\mathbf{A}}$ such that either $s \in \underline{A}X_i$ if $\theta = \{i\}$ for some i or $s \in Bd_{\mathbf{A}}(\theta)$ if $|\theta| > 1$. We will explain this later in detail.

6. QUALITY OF APPROXIMATION

Inexactness of a set (category) is due to the existence of a boundary region.

The following qualities of the lower approximation of X by B in $\mathbf{A}$ and upper approximation of X by B in $\mathbf{A}$ were introduced in Pawlak (1982):

$$\underline{\gamma}_B(X) = \frac{|\underline{B}X|}{|U|} \quad \text{and} \quad \overline{\gamma}_B(X) = \frac{|\overline{B}X|}{|U|}$$

Thus, the quality of lower approximation of X by B in $\mathbf{A}$ is the ratio of the number of all certainly classified objects by attributes from B as being in X to the number of all objects in the system. $\overline{\gamma}_B(X)$ is intended to capture the degree of completeness of our knowledge about the set X. It is a kind of relative frequency. The quality of upper approximation of X by B in A is the ratio of the number of all possibly classified objects by attributes from B as being in X to the number of all objects in the system. It is also a kind of relative frequency.

Example 5. From Example 4 we have the following qualities of lower and upper approximations of sets X_1, X_2, X_3 (with respect to the set of attributes A):

$$\underline{\gamma}_A(X_1) = \frac{3}{28}; \quad \bar{\gamma}_A(X_1) = \frac{4}{7};$$
$$\underline{\gamma}_A(X_2) = \frac{1}{7}; \quad \bar{\gamma}_A(X_2) = \frac{19}{28};$$
$$\underline{\gamma}_A(X_3) = \frac{1}{7}; \quad \bar{\gamma}_A(X_3) = \frac{17}{28}.$$

In Grzymała-Busse (1989, 1991) and Skowron (1989a, 1989b, 1990) it was proved that $\underline{\gamma}_B$ is a belief function according to the Dempster-Shafer theory.

Let $\{U_1, \ldots, U_n)$ be a classification of U generated by B in A. The basic probability assignment m that corresponds to $\underline{\gamma}_B$ is given by

$$m(U_i) = \frac{|U_i|}{|U|}$$

where $i = 1, \ldots, n$, and $m(Y) = 0$ for all other $Y \subseteq U$. Therefore, focal elements (Shafer, 1976) of $\underline{\gamma}_B$ are equivalence classes of the indiscernibility relation $IND_{\mathrm{A}}(B)$, and the core of $\underline{\gamma}_B$ is the set U. The quality of upper approximation of X by B in A is a plausibility function from viewpoint of the Dempster-Shafer theory (Shafer, 1976). In fact, we have

$$\bar{\gamma}_B(X) = \frac{|\bar{B}X|}{|U|} = 1 - \frac{|U| - |\bar{B}X|}{|U|} = 1 - \frac{U - \bar{B}X}{U} = 1 - \frac{|\underline{B}X|}{|U|}$$
$$= 1 - \gamma_B(-X)$$

We extend the results presented in Grzymała-Busse (1989, 1991) and Skowron (1989, 1989a, 1989b, 1990) showing more deep relationships between the two approaches.

7. THE BASIC PROBABILITY ASSIGNMENT GENERATED BY THE CLASSIFICATION APPROXIMATING EXPERT DECISIONS

In the previous section we have observed some similarities between qualities of approximation considered in rough set theory and belief functions generated by basic probability assignments in evidence theory. Now we present a definition of the basic probability assignment function generated by the classification approximating expert decisions. This is a kind of a standard basic probability assignment that seems to capture the basic intuitions encoded in the evidence theory (Shafer, 1976; Bhatnagar and Kanal, 1986).

Let $\Theta_A = \{1,...,r(d)\}$ be the frame of discernment defined by the decision d in the decision table $\mathbf{A} = (U, A \cup \{d\})$ and let $CLASS_A(d) = \{X_1,...,X_{r(d)}\}$ be the classification determined by decision d. Let $APP\_CLASS_A(d)$ be the family of sets defined in Proposition 1.

There is a natural correspondence between subsets of Θ_A and elements of $APP\_CLASS_A(d)$, which can be expressed by the following function:

$$F_A(\theta) = \begin{cases} \underline{A}X_i & \text{if } \theta = \{i\} \text{ for some i } (1 \leqslant \text{i} \leqslant r(d)) \\ \varnothing & \text{if } \theta = \varnothing \\ Bd_A(\theta) & \text{if } |\theta| > 1 \end{cases}$$

Now we can define the injection $\partial_A: U \rightarrow \mathbf{P}(\Theta)_A)$ such that $\partial_A(s)$ is the unique subset θ of Θ_A such that $s \in F_A(\theta)$, where $\mathbf{P}(\Theta_A)$ is the powerset of Θ_A.

The function ∂_A can be treated as a new decision attribute defined by conditions in **A**. The values of ∂_A for the decision table from Example 1 are presented in Table 10.2.

Let $\Theta = \{\theta_1,...,\theta_k\}$ be a frame of discernment compatible with **A** and let $\chi:\Theta \rightarrow \Theta_A$ be the standard bijection between Θ and Θ_A i.e., $\chi(\theta_i) = i$ for $i = 1,...,k$.

The function $m_A:\mathbf{P}(\Theta) \rightarrow \mathbf{R}_+$, called the standard basic probability assignment (defined by Θ, **A** and χ), is defined as follows:

$$m_A(\theta) = \frac{|F_A(\chi(\theta))|}{|U|}$$

where $\theta \subseteq (\theta) = \{i: \theta_i \in \theta\}$.

Proposition 2. The function m_A defined above is a basic probability assignment (in the sense of evidence theory).

The above definition has a natural interpretation:

- If $\theta = \{\theta_i\}$ then $m_A(\theta)$ is the ratio of the number of all objects from the universe U (of **A**) certainly classified by attributes from A as being in X_i to the number of all objects in U.

- If $|\theta| > 1$ then $m_{\mathbf{A}}(\theta)$ is the ratio of the number of all objects from the universe U (of **A**) certainly classified by attributes from A as being in the boundary region $Bd_{\mathbf{A}}(\theta)$ to the number of all objects in U.

Table 10.2

U	a	b	c	e	f	$\partial_{\mathbf{A}}$	U	a	b	c	e	f	$\partial_{\mathbf{A}}$
1	0	0	1	0	0	{1}	15	0	0	1	1	1	{1,2}
2	1	1	1	0	0	{1,2,3}	16	1	1	0	1	1	{2,3}
3	0	1	0	0	0	{2}	17	0	0	0	1	1	{3}
4	1	0	0	0	1	{1,3}	18	0	0	0	0	0	{2}
5	0	1	0	0	0	{2}	19	0	0	0	0	0	{2}
6	1	0	0	0	1	{1,3}	20	1	1	1	0	0	{1,2,3}
7	0	0	0	1	1	{3}	21	1	1	0	0	1	{2,3}
8	1	1	1	1	1	{1,2}	22	0	0	1	0	1	{1}
9	0	0	0	1	1	{3}	23	1	1	1	0	0	{1,2,3}
10	0	0	1	0	0	{1}	24	0	0	1	1	1	{1,2}
11	1	1	1	0	0	{1,2,3}	25	1	0	1	0	1	{1,2,3}
12	1	1	1	1	1	{1,2}	26	1	0	1	0	1	{1,2,3}
13	1	1	0	1	1	{2,3}	27	1	0	1	0	1	{1,2,3}
14	1	1	0	0	1	{2,3}	28	1	1	1	1	0	{3}

Example 6. We can calculate the values of the function $F_{\mathbf{A}}$ for the decision table considered in the previous examples. The results are presented in Table 10.3, where the sets occurring in the second row of the table were computed in Example 3 and Example 4.

Table 10.3

{1}	{2}	{3}	{1,2}	{1,3}	{2,3}	{1,2,3}
$\underline{A}X_1$	$\underline{A}X_2$	$\underline{A}X_3$	$Bd_{\mathbf{A}}(\{1,2\})$	$Bd_{\mathbf{A}}(\{1,3\})$	$Bd_{\mathbf{A}}(\{1,3\})$	$Bd_{\mathbf{A}}(\{1,2,3\})$

Let $\Theta = \{\theta_1, \theta_2, \theta_3\}$ be a frame of discernment. The values of the standard probability assignment $m_{\mathbf{A}}$ (defined by Θ, **A** and χ) are presented in Table 10.4.

Table 10.4

θ	$\{\theta_1\}$	$\{\theta_2\}$	$\{\theta_3\}$	$\{\theta_1,\theta_2\}$	$\{\theta_1,\theta_3\}$	$\{\theta_2,\theta_3\}$	$\{\theta_1,\theta_2,\theta_3\}$
$\chi(\theta)$	$\{1\}$	$\{2\}$	$\{3\}$	$\{1,2\}$	$\{1,3\}$	$\{2,3\}$	$\{1,2,3\}$
$m_{\mathbf{A}}(\theta)$	$\frac{3}{28}$	$\frac{1}{7}$	$\frac{1}{7}$	$\frac{1}{7}$	$\frac{1}{14}$	$\frac{1}{7}$	$\frac{1}{4}$

8. THE BELIEF AND PLAUSIBILITY FUNCTIONS FOR THE STANDARD BASIC PROBABILITY ASSIGNMENT

The belief function $Bel_{\mathbf{A}}$ for the frame of discernment Θ and decision table **A** compatible with Θ is defined as follows:

$$Bel_{\mathbf{A}}(\theta) = \sum_{\Delta \subseteq \theta} m_{\mathbf{A}}(\Delta)$$

where $\theta \subseteq \Theta$ and $m_{\mathbf{A}}$ is the standard probability assignment for Θ and **A**.

The interpretation of the above definition is obtained from the following theorem:

Theorem 1. Let Θ be the frame of discernment compatible with the decision table $\mathbf{A} = (U, A \cup \{d\})$ and let χ be the standard bijection between Θ and $\Theta_{\mathbf{A}}$. For arbitrary $\theta \subseteq \Theta$ the following equality holds:

$$Bel_{\mathbf{A}}(\theta) = \frac{\left|\underline{A} \bigcup_{i \in \chi(\theta)} X_i\right|}{|U|}$$

The belief function $Bel_{\mathbf{A}}$ is Bayesian iff all sets from $CLASS_{\mathbf{A}}(d)$ are definable by the set A of conditions. In particular the belief function $Bel_{\mathbf{A}'}$ where $\mathbf{A}' = (U, A \cup \{\partial_{\mathbf{A}}\})$, is Bayesian.

Proof. From the definitions of $Bel_{\mathbf{A}}$ we have:

$$Bel_{\mathbf{A}}(\theta) = \sum_{\Delta \subseteq \theta} m_{\mathbf{A}}(\Delta) = \sum_{i \in \chi(\theta)} \frac{|\underline{A}X_i|}{|U|} + \sum_{\Delta \subseteq \theta |\Delta| > 1} \frac{|Bd_{\mathbf{A}}(\chi(\Delta))|}{|U|} = $$

$$= \frac{\left|\underline{A} \bigcup_{i \in \chi(\theta)} X_i\right|}{|U|}$$

The last equality follows from Proposition 2. The proof of the other parts of the theorem we leave to the reader.

We obtain a natural interpretation of the belief function $Bel_{\mathbf{A}}$ (defined by Θ, $\mathbf{A}$ and χ). The value $Bel_{\mathbf{A}}(\theta)$ is the ratio of the number of objects in the lower approximation of the union of sets X_i for $i \in \chi(\theta)$, i.e., the number of objects from U certainly classified to the union $\bigcup_{i \in \chi(\Theta)} X_i$ to the number of elements in the universe U.

Corollary 1. Let Θ be the frame of discernment compatible with the decision table $\mathbf{A} = (U, A \cup \{d\})$. For arbitrary $\theta \subseteq \Theta$ the following equality holds:

$$Pl_{\mathbf{A}}(\theta) = \frac{\left|\bar{A} \bigcup_{i \in \chi(\theta)} X_i\right|}{|U|}$$

Proof. Follows from the definition of $Pl_{\mathbf{A}}$ and Theorem 3. We have

$$Pl_{\mathbf{A}}(\theta) = 1 - Bel_{\mathbf{A}}(\Theta - \theta) = 1 - = \frac{\left|\underline{A} \bigcup_{i \in \chi(\Theta - \theta)} X_i\right|}{|U|} =$$

$$= \frac{|U| - \left|\underline{A} \bigcup_{i \in \chi(\Theta - \theta)} X_i\right|}{|U|} = \frac{\left|\bar{A} \bigcup_{i \in \chi(\theta)} X_i\right|}{|U|}$$

The value $Pl_{\mathbf{A}}(\theta)$ is the ratio of the number of objects in the upper approximation of the union of sets X_i for $i \in \chi(\theta)$, i.e., of the number of objects from U possibly classified to the union $\bigcup_{i \in \chi(\theta)} X_i$ to the number of elements in the universe U.

Example 7. The values of belief function $Bel_{\mathbf{A}}$ are given in Table 10.5. For example, $Bel_{\mathbf{A}}(\{2,3\}) = m_{\mathbf{A}}(\{2\}) + m_{\mathbf{A}}(\{3\}) + m_{\mathbf{A}}(\{2,3\}) = 1/7 + 1/7 + 1/7 = 12/28 = 3/7$. In the example, the belief in $\{\theta_2, \theta_3\}$ is equal to 12/28, that is, 12 out of 28 objects are in $X_2 \cup X_3$. Among them four are in X_2, four in X_3 and four can be classified to $X_2 \cup X_3$. Incomplete information represented by the values of attributes a,b,c,e,f about the last four elements mentioned do not allow us to classify them exactly, that is, to say which of them are in X_2 and which in X_3.

Table 10.5

θ	$\{\theta_1\}$	$\{\theta_2\}$	$\{\theta_3\}$	$\{\theta_1, \theta_2\}$	$\{\theta_1, \theta_3\}$	$\{\theta_2, \theta_3\}$	$\{\theta_1, \theta_2, \theta_3\}$
$\chi(\theta)$	$\{1\}$	$\{2\}$	$\{3\}$	$\{1,2\}$	$\{1,3\}$	$\{2,3\}$	$\{1,2,3\}$
$Bel_{\mathbf{A}}(\theta)$	$\frac{3}{28}$	$\frac{1}{7}$	$\frac{1}{7}$	$\frac{11}{28}$	$\frac{9}{28}$	$\frac{3}{7}$	1

9. DECISION TABLE REPRESENTATION OF THE BASIC PROBABILITY ASSIGNMENT

The main problem studied in this section is finding a representation or a given basic probability assignment $m: \mathbf{P}(\Theta) \to \mathbf{Q}_+$, in the form of a decision table $\mathbf{A} = (U, A \cup \{d\}$, such that the standard basic probability assignment, defined on $\mathbf{A}$, is equal to m, where $\mathbf{Q}_+$ is the set of nonnegative rational numbers. Obviously, the necessary condition is that the frame of discernment Θ is compatible with $\mathbf{A}$, that is, that $r(d) = |\Theta|$. For the sake of simplicity, we assume that $\Theta = \Theta_{\mathbf{A}} = \{1,...,k\}$. Moreover, for $CLASS_{\mathbf{A}}(d) = \{X_1, X_2,..., X_k\}$, the A-lower approximation $\underline{A}X_i$ will be denoted $\underline{A}(i)$ and the A-boundary set $BN_{\mathbf{A}}(X_i)$ of X_i will be denoted $BN(i)$, where $i = 1,...,k$.

In general there exist infinitely many representations in the form of a deision table for a given basic probability assignment $m: \mathbf{P}(\Theta) \to \mathbf{Q}_+$. One of them will be described in this section. First, let us observe that

$$BN(i) = \bigcup_{j \in \Theta - \{i\}} BN(i) \cap BN(j)$$

where i = 1,2,...,k. Moreover, for $\theta \subseteq \Theta$, $1 < |\theta| \leqslant k$, the following formula

$$Bd_{\mathbf{A}}(\theta) = \bigcap_{i \in \theta} BN(i) - \bigcup_{j \notin \theta} \bigcap_{i \in \theta 8 \cup \{j\}} BN(i)$$

gives the same result as the corresponding formula for $Bd_{\mathbf{A}}(\theta)$ from Section 5.

The following Lemma is based on the two preceding observations:

Lemma 1. Let m be a function of $\mathbf{P}(\Theta)$ to $\mathbf{Q}_+$. There exists a decision table $\mathbf{A} = (U, A \cup \{d\})$ such that for the standard basic probability assignment $m_{\mathbf{A}}$ of $\mathbf{P}(\Theta)$ to $\mathbf{Q}_+$, defined on A, $m_{\mathbf{A}}(\theta) > 0$ if and only if $m(\theta) > 0$ where $\theta \subseteq \Theta$.

Proof. This proof is the first part of the construction of the decision table that is the representation of the given basic probability assignment m.

Let $\Theta_m = \{\theta \subseteq \Theta \mid m(\theta) > 0\}$. Let $|\Theta_m| = l$. Let us assume that members of Θ_m are $\theta_1, \theta_2, ..., \theta_l$.

A decision table $\mathbf{A} = (U, A \cup \{d\})$ is constructed in the following way. The set A consists of one attribute a. The domain of attribute a is $(1,2,...,l\}$, the domain of the decision d is $\{1,2,...,k\} = \Theta$. The universe U is the set of pairs (i,j) of integers such that $(i,j) \in U$ if and only if $\theta_i \in \Theta_m$ and $j \in \theta_i$, where $i \in \{1,2,...,l\}$and $j \in \{1,2,...,k\}$. For a member (i,j) of U the value of attribute a is i and the value of decision d is j.

Fot the decision table **A**, defined above, the set $Bd_{\mathbf{A}}(\theta) \neq \emptyset$ if and only if $m(\theta) > 0$, for any $\theta \subseteq \Theta$. The proof of this statement is based on the staightforward computation of the set $Bd_{\mathbf{A}}(\theta)$, since from the above definition of **A** it follows that: for any $\theta_i = \{j\}, \underline{A}(i) = \{(i,j)\}$; for any $\theta_i = \{i_1, i_2, ..., i_j\} \in \Theta_m, j > 0, Bd_{\mathbf{A}}(\theta_i) = \{(i, i_1) \{i, i_2), ..., (i, i_j)\}$; and for any $\theta \notin \Theta_m$, $|\theta| > 1$, $Bd_{\mathbf{A}}(\theta) = \emptyset$.

Example 8. The frame $\Theta = \{1,2,3\}$ of discernment is given. We will construct a decision table **A** such that $m(\theta) > 0$ if and only if $\theta \in \Theta_m$, where $\Theta_m = \{\theta_1, \theta_2, \theta_3\}$, $\theta_1 = \{2\}$, $\theta_2 = \{1,3\}, \theta_3 = \{1,2,3\}$. Table 10.6 presents the decision table **A** constructed according to the proof of Lemma 1.

Table 10.6

	a	d
(1, 2)	1	2
(2, 1)	2	1
(2, 3)	2	3
(3, 1)	3	1
(3, 2)	3	2
(3, 3)	3	3

As follows from Table 10.6, $\underline{A}(2) = \{(1,2)\}$, $Bd_{\mathbf{A}}(\{1,3\}) = \{(2,1), (2,3)\}$, and $Bd_{\mathbf{A}}(\{1,2,3\}) = \{(3,1), (3,2), (3,3)\}$. Thus $m(\theta_1) = 1/6$, $m(\theta_2) = 1/3$, $m(\theta_3) = 1/2$, and $m(\theta) = 0$ if and only if $\theta \notin \Theta_m$.

The standard basic probability assignment m_A, defined for the decision table **A** in the proof of Lemma 5, is, in general, different from the given function m of $\mathbf{P}(\Theta)$ to $\mathbf{Q}_+$. The following result shows that it is always possible to modify **A** in such a way that the standard basic probability assignment, defined for a modified decision table, will be identical with m.

Theorem 2. Let m be a function of $\mathbf{P}(\Theta)$ to $\mathbf{Q}_+$. There exists a decision table $\mathbf{B} = (V, A \cup \{d\})$ such that the standard basic probability assignment $m_B: \mathbf{P}(\Theta) \to \mathbf{Q}_+$, defined on **B**, is identical with m.

Proof. In this proof we will use definitions and notation from the proof of Lemma 1. Assume that $\mathbf{A} = (U, A \cup \{d\})$ is the decision table as defined in the proof of Lemma 1. Let $n = \sum_{\theta \in \Theta_m} |\theta|$. Then for the standard basic probability assignment m_A, defined on **A** and for any $\theta \in \Theta_m$, $m_A(\theta) = \dfrac{|\theta|}{n, |\Theta|/n}$ and $m_A(\theta) = 0$ if $\theta \notin \Theta_m$. Let us assume that **m is defined as follows:** $m(\theta) = p_\theta/q$ where p_θ and q are positive integers, q is fixed and p_θ depends on the choice of θ. Let us observe that any object $(i,j) \in U$ can be split into two objects (i,j') and (i,j''); the values of attribute a and decision d for both (i,j') and (i,j'') remain the same as for (i,j). Let $(i,j) \in \theta_i$ and θ_i' be equal to θ_i except that (i,j) is substituted by (i,j') and (i,j''). Then the standard basic probability assignment, defined on a new decision table **A**$'$, will be defined as follows: if $\theta \neq \theta_i'$ then $m_A(\theta) = \dfrac{|\theta|}{n+1}$ and $m_A(\theta_i') = \dfrac{|\theta_i'|}{n+1} = \dfrac{|\theta_i|+1}{n+1}$.

Conversely, if we wish to modify the original standard basic probability assignment m_A, defined on A, in such a way that the value of m_A is modified to $\dfrac{|\theta|+1}{n+1}$ for the set $\theta \in \Theta_m$, then it may be accomplished by splitting any object from θ into two objects.

Thus, a decision table $\mathbf{B} = (V, A \cup \{d\})$ may be constructed by splitting original objects of the decision table $\mathbf{A} = (U, A \cup \{d\})$ so that $P_\theta \cdot n - |\theta|$ additional objects are created by splitting for any set $\theta \in \Theta_m$. The value of the standard basic probability assignment becomes

$$m_B(\theta) = \frac{|\theta| + (p_\theta \cdot n - |\theta|)}{n + \sum_{\theta \in \Theta_m} (p_\theta \cdot n - |\theta|)} = \frac{n \cdot p_\theta}{n + (q-1) \cdot n} = \frac{p_\theta}{q} = m(\theta)$$

Example 8 (continued). Say that we want to modify the original basic probability assignment m to a function m', where $m'(\theta_1) = 3/5$, $m'(\theta_2) = 1/5$, $m'(\theta_3) = 1/5$, and $m'(\theta) = 0$ if and only if $\theta \notin \Theta_m$.

Objects in θ_1, θ_2 and θ_3 should be split, according to the proof of Theorem 6. Table 10.7 presents one of the resulting decision tables.

Table 10.7

	a	d
$(1, 2^{(1)})$	1	2
$(1, 2^{(2)})$	1	2
$(1, 2^{(3)})$	1	2
$(1, 2^{(4)})$	1	2
$(1, 2^{(5)})$	1	2
$(1, 2^{(6)})$	1	2
$(1, 2^{(7)})$	1	2
$(1, 2^{(8)})$	1	2
$(1, 2^{(9)})$	1	2
$(1, 2^{(10)})$	1	2
$(1, 2^{(11)})$	1	2
$(1, 2^{(12)})$	1	2
$(1, 2^{(13)})$	1	2
$(1, 2^{(14)})$	1	2
$(1, 2^{(15)})$	1	2
$(1, 2^{(16)})$	1	2
$(1, 2^{(17)})$	1	2
$(1, 2^{(18)})$	1	2
$(1, 2^{(1)})$	2	1
$(1, 2^{(2)})$	2	1
$(1, 2^{(3)})$	2	1
$(2, 3^{(1)})$	2	3
$(2, 3^{(2)})$	2	3
$(2, 3^{(3)})$	2	3
$(3, 1^{(1)})$	3	1
$(3, 1^{(2)})$	3	1
$(3, 2^{(1)})$	3	2
$(3, 2^{(2)})$	3	2
$(3, 3^{(1)})$	3	3
$(3, 3^{(2)})$	3	3

$$\underline{A}(2) = \{(1, 2^{(1)}), (1, 2^{(2)}), (1, 2^{(3)}), (1, 2^{(4)}), (1, 2^{(5)}), (1, 2^{(6)}), (1, 2^{(7)}), (1, 2^{(8)}), (1, 2^{(9)}), (1, 2^{(10)}), (1, 2^{(11)}), (1, 2^{(12)}), (1, 2^{(13)}), (1, 2^{(14)}), (1, 2^{(15)}), (1, 2^{(16)}), (1, 2^{(17)}), (1, 2^{(18)})\},$$

$$Bd(\{1, 3\}) = \{(2, 1^{(1)}), (2, 1^{(2)}), (2, 1^{(3)}), (2, 3^{(1)}), (2, 3^{(2)}), (2, 3^{(3)})\},$$

$$Bd(\{1, 2, 3\} = \{(3, 1^{(1)}), (3, 1^{(2)}), (3, 2^{(1)}), (3, 2^{(2)}), (3, 3^{(1)}), (3, 3^{(2)})\},$$

and $m'(\theta_1) = 18/30 = 3/5$, $m'(\theta_2) = 6/30 = 1/5$, and $m'(\theta_3) = 6/30 = 1/5$.

As follows from Theorem 2, for any given basic probability assignment m of evidence theory, provided that values are nonnegative rational numbers, there exists a representation in the form of a decision table such that its standard basic probability assignment is identical with m. Obviously, if the values of m are nonnegative real numbers, it is possible to approximate m by a decision-table representation of m with arbitrary small error.

10. BASIC PROBABILITY ASSIGNMENTS GENERATED BY DECISION SUBTABLES OF A GIVEN DECISION TABLE

Up to now we have not discussed how to introduce into our considerations different sources of information or evidence. In fact, we have discussed only one kind of information obtained by the evaluation of all conditions in a considered decision table. In consequence, we have defined only one standard basic probability assignment related to a given decision table **A**, namely $m_{\mathbf{A}}$. In this section we extend our approach and with any decision table **A** we associate a family of (standard) basic probability assignments $\{m_{\mathbf{A},\alpha}\}_{\alpha \in \mathbf{C}}$, where **C** is a set of information about **A**, called the set of condition formulas. Any element $\alpha \in \mathbf{C}$ defines for a given **A** a decision subtable $\mathbf{A}_\alpha$ of **A** and $m_{\mathbf{A},\alpha}$ is related to that table. We show that the previous properties of standard probability assignments and belief functions can be extended on the standard basic probability assignments to be defined here and to their corresponding belief functions.

By A and d we denote a fixed set of condition names and decision name, respectively. Let V_a be a finite set of value names for $a \in A$ and V_d the set of value names for d. (We will use the same notation for condition and condition name, decision and decision name, value and value name. This will not lead to confusion because the meaning will always be clear from the context.) Let $V = \bigcup_{a \in A} V_a \cup V_d$.

The atomic formulas over $B \subseteq A \cup \{d\}$ and V are expressions of the form (a, v), called descriptors over B, where $a \in B$ and $v \in V_a$. The set $\mathbf{F}(B, V)$ of formulas over B is the least set containing all atomic formulas over B and closed with respect to the classical propositional connectives $\vee$ (disjunction), $\wedge$ (conjunction) and $\neg$ (negation).

If $\mathbf{A} = (U, A \cup \{d\})$ is a decision table and $\alpha \in \mathbf{F}(B, V)$ (where $B \subseteq A$) then by $\alpha_{\mathbf{A}}$ we denote the meaning of α in **A**, i.e., the set of all objects in U with property α, defined inductively as follows:

1. if α is of the form (a, v) then $\alpha_{\mathbf{A}} = \{s \in U: a(s) = v\}$;
2. $(\alpha \wedge \beta)_{\mathbf{A}} = \alpha_{\mathbf{A}} \cap \beta_{\mathbf{A}}$; $(\alpha \vee \beta)_{\mathbf{A}} = \alpha_{\mathbf{A}} \cup \beta_{\mathbf{A}}$; $(\neg\alpha)_{\mathbf{A}} = U - \alpha_{\mathbf{A}}$.

The set $\mathbf{F}(A, V)$ is called the set of condition formulas in **A** and is denoted by $\mathbf{C}_{\mathbf{A}}$. The set $\mathbf{F}(\{d\}, V)$ is called the set of decision formulas in **A** and is denoted by $\mathbf{D}_{\mathbf{A}}$. We omit subscripts (if no confusion will arise).

Now we can extend our definition of the standard basic probability assignment. Let Θ be the frame of discernment and $\mathbf{A} = (U, A \cup \{d\})$ be a decision table compatible with **A**. For every $\alpha \in \mathbf{C}_{\mathbf{A}}$ (with $\alpha_{\mathbf{A}} \neq \emptyset$) there is a natural correspondence between subsets of the frame of the discernment $\Theta_{\mathbf{A}}$ and intersection of the meaning $\alpha_{\mathbf{A}}$ of α in **A** with some sets in $APP\_CLASS_{\mathbf{A}}(d)$, which can be expressed by the following function:

$$F_{\mathbf{A},\alpha}(\theta) = \begin{cases} \underline{A}X_i \cap \alpha_{\mathbf{A}} & \text{if } \theta = \{i\} \text{ for some i } (1 \leqslant \text{i} \leqslant r(d)) \\ \emptyset & \text{if } \theta = \emptyset \\ Bd_{\mathbf{A}}(\theta) \cap \alpha_{\mathbf{A}} & \text{if } |\theta| > 1 \end{cases}$$

The function $m_{\mathbf{A},\alpha}$, called the α-standard basic probability assignment (defined by $\Theta, \mathbf{A}, \alpha$, and χ), is defined as follows:

$$m_{\mathbf{A},\alpha}(\theta) = \frac{|F_{\mathbf{A},\alpha}(\chi(\theta))|}{|\alpha_{\mathbf{A}}|}$$

where $\theta \subseteq \Theta$ and $\chi(\theta) = \{i: \theta_i \in \theta\}$.

Proposition 3. For every formula $\alpha \in \mathbf{C}_{\mathbf{A}}$ the function $m_{\mathbf{A},\alpha}$ defined above is a basic probability assignment (in the sense of evidence theory). Moreover, $m_{\mathbf{A},\alpha}(\theta) = m_{\mathbf{A}_\alpha}(\theta)$ for any $\theta \subseteq \Theta$, where $\mathbf{A}_\alpha$ is the restriction of the decision table **A** to $\alpha_{\mathbf{A}}$ (i.e., the universe of $\mathbf{A}_\alpha$ is equal to $\alpha_{\mathbf{A}}$ and the conditions and decision of $\mathbf{A}_\alpha$ are obtained by restriction of corresponding conditions and decision in **A** to $\alpha_{\mathbf{A}}$, respectively). The above definition has the following interpretation:

- If $\theta = \{\theta_i\}$ then $m_{\mathbf{A},\alpha}(\theta)$ is the ratio of the number of all certainly classified objects from $\alpha_{\mathbf{A}}$ by attributes from A as being in X_i to the number of all objects in the set $\alpha_{\mathbf{A}}$.
- If $|\theta| > 1$ then $m_{\mathbf{A},\alpha}(\theta)$ is the ratio of the number of all objects from $\alpha_{\mathbf{A}}$ classified by attributes from A as being in the boundary region $Bd_{\mathbf{A}}(\chi(\theta))$ to the number of all objects in the set $\alpha_{\mathbf{A}}$.

The situation is depicted in Figure 10.2.

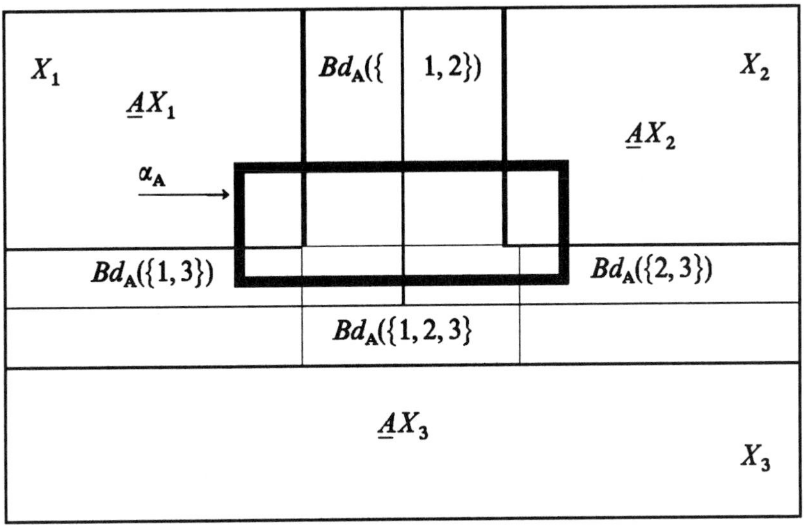

Figure 10.2

Example 9. Let A be the information system considered in the previous examples and let $\alpha = (a = 0) \vee (b = 1)$. We have:

$$\alpha_A = (a = 0)_A \cup (b = 1)_A = \{s \in U: a(s) = 0\} \cup \{s \in U: b(s) = 1\} =$$
$$= \{1,3,5,7,9,10,15,17,18,19,22,24\} \cup \{2,3,5,8,11,12,13,$$
$$14,16,20,21,23,28\} = U - \{4,6,25,26,27\}.$$

The values of function $F_{A,\alpha}$ are the following:

$$F_{A,\alpha}(\{1\}) = \underline{A}X_1 \cap \alpha_A =$$
$$= \{1,10,22\} \cap (U - \{4,6,25,26,27\}) =$$
$$= \{1,10,22\};$$
$$F_{A,\alpha}(\{2\}) = \underline{A}X_2 \cap \alpha_A =$$
$$= \{3,5,18,19\} \cap (U - \{4,6,25,26,27\}) =$$
$$= \{3,5,18,19\};$$
$$F_{A,\alpha}(\{3\}) = \underline{A}X_3 \cap \alpha_A =$$
$$= \{7,9,17,28\} \cap (U - \{4,6,25,26,27\}) =$$
$$= \{7,9,17,28\};$$
$$F_{A,\alpha}(\{1,2\}) = Bd_A(\{1,2\}) \cap \alpha_A =$$
$$= Bd_A(X_1) \cap Bd_A(X_2) \cap (U - Bd_A(X_3)) \cap \alpha_A =$$
$$= \{8,12,15,24\} \cap (U - \{4,6,25,26,27\}) =$$
$$= \{8,12,15,24\};$$

$$F_{A,\alpha}(\{1,3\}) = Bd_A(\{1,3\}) \cap \alpha_A =$$
$$= BN_A(X_1) \cap (U - BN_A(X_2)) \cap BN_A(X_3) \cap \alpha_A =$$
$$= \{4,6\} \cap (U - \{4,6,25,26,27\}) = \emptyset;$$
$$F_{A,\alpha}(\{2,3\}) = Bd_A(\{2,3\}) \cap \alpha_A =$$
$$= (U - BN_A(X_1)) \cap BN_A(X_2) \cap BN_A(X_3)) \cap \alpha_A =$$
$$= \{13,14,16,21\} \cap (U - \{4,6,25,26,27\}) =$$
$$= \{13,14,16,21\};$$
$$F_{A,\alpha}(\{1,2,3\}) = Bd_A(\{1,2,2\}) \cap \alpha_A =$$
$$= BN_A(X_1) \cap BN_A(X_2) \cap BN_A(X_3) \cap \alpha_A =$$
$$= \{2,11,20,23,25,26,27\} \cap (U - \{4,6,25,26,27\}) =$$
$$= \{2,11,20,23\};$$

Let $\Theta = \{\theta_1, \theta_2, \theta_3\}$ be a frame of discernment. The values of the α-standard basic probability assignment $m_{A,\alpha}$ (defined by Θ, A, α and χ) are presented in Table 10.8.

Table 10.8

θ	$\{\theta_1\}$	$\{\theta_2\}$	$\{\theta_3\}$	$\{\theta_1,\theta_2\}$	$\{\theta_1,\theta_3\}$	$\{\theta_2,\theta_3\}$	$\{\theta_1,\theta_2,\theta_3\}$
$\chi(\theta)$	$\{1\}$	$\{2\}$	$\{3\}$	$\{1,2\}$	$\{1,3\}$	$\{2,3\}$	$\{1,2,3\}$
$m_{A,\alpha}(\theta)$	$\frac{3}{23}$	$\frac{4}{23}$	$\frac{4}{23}$	$\frac{4}{23}$	0	$\frac{4}{23}$	$\frac{4}{23}$

Example 10. Let us consider Example 1 from Gordon and Shortliffe (1984, p. 276). In the example the frame of discernment $\Theta = \{hep, cirr, gall, pan\}$. Every element of Θ is an abbreviation of the disease name. Let A be a decision table representing knowledge about the diseases from Θ. In general we could have 15 regions corresponding to the possibly nonempty subsets of Θ into which objects could be classified:

> I: $\underline{A}X_{hep}$, II: $\underline{A}X_{cirr}$, III: $\underline{A}X_{pan}$, *IV:* $\underline{A}X_{gall}$, V: $Bd_A(\{cirr, hep\})$, VI: $Bd_A(\{cirr, pan\})$, VII: $Bd_A(\{cirr, gall\})$, VIII: $Bd_A(\{hep, pan\})$, IX: $Bd_A(\{hep, gall\})$, X: $Bd_A(\{pan, gall\})$, XI: $Bd_A(\{cirr, hep, pan\})$, XII: $Bd_A(\{cirr, pan, gall\})$, XIII: $Bd_A(\{cirr, hep, gall\})$, XIV: $Bd_A(\{hep, pan, gall\})$, and XV: $Bd_A(\{cirr, hep, pan, gall\})$,

In general for the frame of discernment with k elements it is necessary to consider 2^k sets. A skepticism related to possible practical applications of evidence theory is based on the claim that the number 2^k is very large even for relatively small k, as for $k = 600$ for some medical applications (Buchanan and Shortliffe, 1984). Fortunately, for most of the sets from the powerst $\mathbf{P}(\Theta)$ the value of the standard basic probability assignment is 0 and is not represented in the decision table (the decision table $\mathbf{A}$ contains only $|U|$ objects and $|U| \ll 2^k$). Moreover, using hierarchical representation we can divide a large decision table into samaller ones that can be separately analyzed. To explain this better let us consider a decision table $\mathbf{A}$ with the decision d of the rank k. Suppose that it is possible to find a partition $\{I, J\}$ of the set $\{1,\ldots k\}$ such that the sets $U_1 = \{s \in U\colon d(s) \in I\}$ and $U_2 = \{s \in U\colon d(s) \in J\}$ are definable, that is, there exists a formula $\alpha \in \mathbf{C}_{\mathbf{A}}$ such that $\alpha_{\mathbf{A}} = U_1$ and $\neg\alpha_{\mathbf{A}} = U_2$, and the absolute value of the difference $|U_1| - |U_2|$ is "small" (e.g., less than a given $\varepsilon > 0$). Then it is possible to divide the decision table $\mathbf{A}$ into two decision tables $\mathbf{A}_1 = (U_1, A_1 \cup \{d_1\})$ and $\mathbf{A}_2 = (U_2, A_2 \cup \{d_2\})$ where for $i = 1, 2$ the conditions A_i and decisions d_i are the restrictions of conditions from A to U_i and the values of decisions to I and J, respectively. If the evidence α about a classified object is given, then it is enough to consider $\mathbf{A}_1$ (to find the proper decision from I), otherwise $\mathbf{A}_2$ (to find the proper decision from J).

11. THE BELIEF FUNCTIONS CORRESPONDING TO BASIC PROBABILITY ASSIGNMENTS GENERATED BY DECISION SUBTABLES OF A GIVEN DECISION TABLE

Let Θ be the frame of discernment compatible with the decision table $\mathbf{A} = (U, A \cup \{d\})$ and let $\alpha \in \mathbf{C}_{\mathbf{A}}$.

The α-belief function $Bel_{\mathbf{A},\alpha}$ for $\mathbf{A}$ is defined as follows:

$$Bel_{\mathbf{A},\alpha}(\theta) = \sum_{\Delta \subseteq \theta} m_{\mathbf{A},\alpha}(\Delta), \text{ where } \theta \subseteq \Theta$$

The interpretation of the above definition is obtained from the following theorem:

Theorem 3. Let Θ be the frame of discernment compatible with the decision table $A = (U, A \cup \{d\})$ and let χ be the standard bijection between Θ and $\Theta_{\mathbf{A}}$. For arbitrary $\theta \subseteq \Theta$ and $\alpha \in \mathbf{C}_{\mathbf{A}}$ (with $\alpha_{\mathbf{A}} \neq \emptyset$) the following equality holds:

$$Bel_{\mathbf{A},\alpha}(\theta) = \frac{\left|\alpha_{\mathbf{A}} \cap \underline{A} \bigcup_{i \in \chi(\theta)} X_i\right|}{|\alpha_{\mathbf{A}}|}$$

Moreover we have $Bel_{\mathbf{A},\alpha}(\theta) = Bel_{\mathbf{A}_\alpha}(\theta)$ for any $\theta \subseteq \Theta$.

Proof. Analogous to the proof of Theorem 1. The last equality in the theorem is true because $\alpha_{\mathbf{A}}$ is a definable set.

We obtain a natural interpretation of the α-belief function $Bel_{\mathbf{A},\alpha}$ for **A** (defined by the α-standard basic probability assignment for **A**). The value $Bel_{\mathbf{A},\alpha}(\theta)$ is the ratio of the number of objects in the intersection of the $\alpha_{\mathbf{A}}$ with the lower approximation of the union of sets X_i for $i \in \chi(\theta)$ (i.e., the number of objects from $\alpha_{\mathbf{A}}$ certainly classified to the union $\bigcup_{i \in \chi(\theta)} X_i$) to the number of elements in $\alpha_{\mathbf{A}}$.

Corollary 2. Let Θ be the frame of discernment compatible with the decision table $\mathbf{A} = (U, A \cup \{d\})$. For arbitrary $\theta \subseteq \Theta$ and $\alpha \in \mathbf{C_A}$ (with $\alpha_{\mathbf{A}} \neq \emptyset$) the following equality holds:

$$Pl_{\mathbf{A},\alpha}(\theta) = \frac{\left|\alpha_{\mathbf{A}} \cap \bar{A} \bigcup_{i \in \chi(\theta)} X_i\right|}{|\alpha_{\mathbf{A}}|}$$

Moreover, $Pl_{\mathbf{A},\alpha}\theta) = PL_{\mathbf{A}_\alpha}(\theta)$ for any $\theta \subseteq \Theta$.

Proof. Follows from the definition of $Pl_{\mathbf{A},\alpha}$ (see Corollary 1 and Theorem 3). The last equality in the corollary is true because $\alpha_{\mathbf{A}}$ is definable set in **A**.

The value $Pl_{\mathbf{A},\alpha}(\theta)$ is the ratio of the number of objects in the intersection of $\alpha_{\mathbf{A}}$ with the upper approximation of the union of sets X_i for $i \in \chi(\theta)$ (i.e., the number of objects from $\alpha_{\mathbf{A}}$ possibly classified to the union $\bigcup_{i \in \chi(\theta)} X_i$) to the number of elements in $\alpha_{\mathbf{A}}$.

Example 11. The values of α-belief function $Bel_{\mathbf{A},\alpha}$ for **A**, where α and **A** are defined as in the previous example, are given in Table 10.9. In the example, the belief in $\{\theta_1, \theta_2\}$ is equal to 11/23; 11 out of 23 objects are in $X_1 \cup X_2$; three of them in X_1, four of them in X_2 and four that can be classified to $X_1 \cup X_2$. Imcomplete information represented by conditions *a, b, c, e, f* about the last four elements mentioned does not allow us to classify them exactly, that is, to say which of them are in X_1 and which in X_2.

Table 10.9

θ	$\{\theta_1\}$	$\{\theta_2\}$	$\{\theta_3\}$	$\{\theta_1, \theta_2\}$	$\{\theta_1, \theta_3\}$	$\{\theta_2, \theta_3\}$	$\{\theta_1, \theta_2, \theta_3\}$
χ	$\{1\}$	$\{2\}$	$\{3\}$	$\{1,2\}$	$\{1,3\}$	$\{2,3\}$	$\{1,2,3\}$
$Bel_{\mathbf{A},\alpha}$	$\frac{3}{23}$	$\frac{4}{23}$	$\frac{4}{23}$	$\frac{11}{23}$	$\frac{7}{23}$	$\frac{12}{23}$	1

Example 12. Let us consider Example 1 from Gordon and Shortliffe (1984, p. 276). In the example, the frame of discernment $\Theta = \{hep, cirr, gall, pan\}$. Every element of Θ is an abbreviation of the disease name. The vacuous basic probability assignment representing ignorance assigns 1 to Θ and 0 to every other subset of Θ. The interpretation of vacuous standard probability assignment we can obtain from the definition $m_{A,\alpha}(\Theta) = 1$ and $m_{A,\alpha}(\theta) = 0$ for $\theta \subset \Theta$, where the decision table **A** can be treated as a knowledge representation about considered diseases.

Let us assume $\chi(hep) = 1$, $\chi(cirr) = 2$, $\chi(\text{gall}) = 3$, $\chi(pan) = 4$. We have $m_{A,\alpha}(\Theta) = 1$ and $m_{A,\alpha}(\theta) = 0$ for $\theta \subset \Theta$. Hence $Bel_{A,\alpha}(\Theta) = m_{A,\alpha}(\Theta) = 1$. From Theorem 3 we have $|\alpha_A| Bel_{A,\alpha}(\Theta) = = |\alpha_A \cap \underline{A}(X_1 \cup X_2 \cup X_3 \cup X_4)|$. Hence $|\alpha_A| = |\alpha_A \cap \underline{A}(X_1 \cup X_2 \cup X_3 \cup X_4)|$, so $\alpha_A = \alpha_A \cap \underline{A}(X_1 \cup X_2 \cup X_3 \cup X_4)$ (because $\alpha_A \cap \underline{A}(X_1 \cup X_2 \cup X_3 \cup X_4) \subseteq \alpha_A$ and both sets are finite). Also $|\alpha_A| m_{A,\alpha}(\Theta) = |\alpha_A \cap Bd_A(\{1,2,3,4\})| = |\alpha_A \cap BN_A(X_1) \cap BN_A(X_2\}) \cap BN_A(X_3) \cap BN_A(X_4)|$, where $X_i = \{s \in a_A : d(s) = i\}$ for $i = 1, 2, 3, 4$. Hence $|\alpha_A| = |\alpha_A \cap BN_A(X_1) \cap BN_A(X_2\}) \cap BN_A(X_3) \cap BN_A(X_4)|$, so $\alpha_A = \alpha_A \cap BN_A(X_1) \cap BN_A(X_2\}) \cap BN_A(X_3) \cap BN_A(X_4)$.

Eventually we have $\alpha_A \cap \underline{A}(X_1 \cup X_2 \cup X_3 \cup X_4) = \alpha_A \cap BN_A(X_1) \cap BN_A(X_2\}) \cap BN_A(X_3) \cap BN_A(X_4)$.

The above equality states that every object in A_α that is certainly classified to $X_1 \cup X_2 \cup X_3 \cup X_4$ belongs to the intersection of the set α_A defined in **A** by the evidence α with the boundary region $Bd_A(1,2,3.4\})$, so on the basis of that evidence it is not possible to classify any such object to the union of any proper subfamily of $\{X_1, X_2, X_3, X_4\}$.

A given evidence α is extracting from our knowledge represented in **A** a subdecision table A_α. In this situation we have in A_α only the objects that can be classified on the basis of evidence α as being in the boundary region $Bd_{A,\alpha}(\chi(\Theta))$; we can only say that the given evidence α is extracting from our knowledge represented in **A** a sub-decision table A_α with elements classified to one of the diseases *hep, cirr, gall, pan,* but we do not know to which.

Example 13. We can interpret the discussion from Example 2 (Gordon and Shortliffe, 1984, p. 276) in the following way:

$$m_{A,\alpha}(\{hep, cirr\}) = 0.6 \; m_{A,\alpha}(\Theta) = 0.4 \text{ and } m_{A,\alpha}(\theta) = 0$$
$$\text{for } \theta \neq \{hep, cirr\}, \Theta$$

On the basis of the evidence α we extract from **A** the sub-decision table A_α in which 60% of objects are classified to the boundary region

$Bd_{\mathbf{A}}(\{1,2\})$ and 40% to the boundary region $Bd_{\mathbf{A}}(\Theta)$. Having the evidence α we can say that it is a 60% chance that the classified object belongs to one of the sets X_1 or X_2 (but we cannot say to which! – see the explanation given below) and a 40% chance that it is an object belonging to one of the sets X_1, X_2, X_3, X_4 (but we do not know to which!).

Let us observe that $Bel_{\mathbf{A},\alpha}(\{hep, cirr\}) = m_{\mathbf{A},\alpha}(\{hep, cirr\}) = 0.6$, $Bel_{\mathbf{A},\alpha}(\Theta) = m_{\mathbf{A},\alpha}(\{hep, cirr\}) + m_{\mathbf{A},\alpha}(\Theta) = 06 + 0.4 = 1$, and, e.g., $Bel_{\mathbf{A},\alpha}(\{hep, pan\}) = 0$.

From the first equality in the above list it follows (Theorem 3) that $|\alpha_{\mathbf{A}} \cap \underline{A}(X_1 \cup X_2)| = |\alpha_{\mathbf{A}} \cap Bd_{\mathbf{A}}(\{1,2\})|$. Because (see Proposition 1) $Bd_{\mathbf{A}}(\{1,2)\}) \subseteq \underline{A}(X_1 \cup X_2)$ and the sets $\underline{A}(X_1 \cup X_2)$, $Bd_{\mathbf{A}}(\{1,2\}$ are finite, we obtain $\alpha_{\mathbf{A}} \cap \underline{A}(\mathrm{X}_1 \cup \mathrm{X}_2) = \alpha_{\mathbf{A}} \cap Bd_{\mathbf{A}}(\{1,2\})$.

From that equality it follows that all objects that can be with certainty classified to the union $X_1 \cup X_2$ on the basis of the evidence α are objects that are in the boundary region $Bd_{\mathbf{A}}(\{1,2\})$; we cannot say to which of the sets X_1 or X_2 they belong.

The last equality from the above ones means that among objects in **A** with evidence α there does not exist an object that can be with certainty classfied to the union of sets corresponding to $\{hep, pan\}$, that is, an object about which with certainty it is possble to say on the basis of evidence α that it has property represented by *hep* or *pan* but we do not know which.

We have also $Pl_{\mathbf{A}}(\{hep, cirr\}) = 1 - Bel_{\mathbf{A}}(\{gal, pan\}) = 1$. On the other hand, $Pl(\{hep, cirr\}) = \dfrac{|\alpha_{\mathbf{A}} \cap \bar{A}(X_1 \cup X_2)|}{|\alpha_{\mathbf{A}}|}$. Hence $\alpha_{\mathbf{A}} = \alpha_{\mathbf{A}} \cap \bar{A}(X_1 \cup X_2)$.

From the last equality we conclude that on the basis of the evidence α each object from **A** can be possibly classfied to the union $X_1 \cup X_2$. If we receive the evidence α about a new object (not necessarily registered already in **A**) we can classify it as having possibly property *hep* or *cirr* but we do not have enough information to say which of these properties (or even others, i.e., *gall* or *pan*) it can have.

Example 14. Let us now consider Example 3 from Gordon and Shortliffe, (1984, p. 276). In this case for an evidence β and a decision table **A** we have: $m_{\mathbf{A},\beta}(\{cirr, gall, pan\}) = 0.7$, $m_{\mathbf{A},\beta}(\Theta) = 0.3$ and $m_{\mathbf{A},\beta}(\theta) = 0$ for $\theta \neq \{cirr, gall, pan\}, \Theta$. On the basis of the evidence β we extract from **A** the sub-decision table $\mathbf{A}_\beta$ in which 70% of objects are classified to the boundary region $Bd_{\mathbf{A}}(\{2,3,4\})$ and 30% to the boundary region $Bd_{\mathbf{A}}(\Theta_{\mathbf{A}})$. Having the evidence β we can say that it is a 70% chance that the classified object belongs to one of the sets

X_2 or X_3 or X_4 (but we cannot say to which! – see the explanation given below) and a 30% chance that it is an object belonging to one of the sets X_1, X_2, X_3, X_4 (but we do not know to which!).

Again it is easy to calculate from the equality $Bel_{A,\beta}(\{cirr, gall, pan\}) = m_{A,\beta}(\{cirr, gall, pan\})$ that $\beta_A \cap \underline{A}(X_2 \cup X_3 \cup X_4) = \beta_A \cap Bd_A(\{2,3,4\})$.

Hence we conclude that among objects from A classified with certainty to the union $X_2 \cup X_3 \cup X_4$ on the basis of the evidence β there are only objects in the boundary region $Bd_A(\{2,3,4\})$; the evidence β does not allow us to classify objects to the union of a proper subfamily of $\{X_2, X_3, X_4\}$.

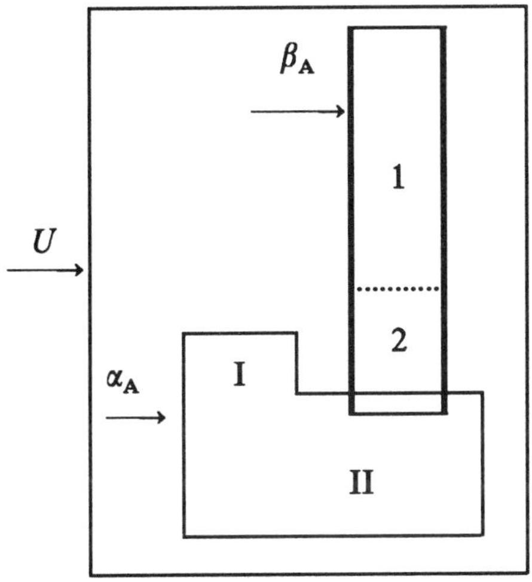

I: $\alpha_A \cap Bd_A(\{\chi(hep), \chi(cirr)\})$ II: $\alpha_A \cap Bd_A(\chi(\Theta))$
1: $\beta_A \cap Bd_A(\{\chi(cirr), \chi(gall), \chi(pan)\})$ 2: $\beta_A \cap Bd_A(\chi(\Theta))$

Figure 10.3

In Figure 10.3 some possible intersections of different boundary regions for the different evidences α and β are shown.

12. INDEPENDENT SOURCES OF EVIDENCE

The Dempster rule of combination allows us to compute a new belief function from the combined evidence of several belief functions over the same frame of discernment if they are based on entirely distinct (independent) sources of evidence. The general formulation is due to Dempster (1967). In the special case of a frame of discernment containing only two elements Dempster's rule was used by Johanann Heinrich Lambert in 1764 (Shafer, 1976).

The aim of this section is to show that for the belief functions based on standard basic probability assignment it is possible to formulate precisely the meaning of "independent sources of information" and on that basis to prove the compatibility of our approach with the Dempster combination rule. Some preliminary results in this direction are presented in Skowron (1990).

Let Θ be a frame of discernment compatible with the decision tables

$$\mathbf{A}_1 = (U_1, A_1 \cup \{d_1\}) \text{ and } \mathbf{A}_2 = (U_2, A_2, \cup \{d_2\})$$

The decision table $\mathbf{A} = (U, A \cup \{d\})$ is called a Θ-independent product of decision tables $\mathbf{A}_1$ and $\mathbf{A}_2$ iff the following conditions hold:

1. $U = U_1 \times U_2 - U_1 \otimes U_2$, where $U_1 \otimes U_2 = \{(s_1, s_2) \colon U_1 \times U_2 \colon \partial_{\mathbf{A}_1}(s_1) \cap \partial_{\mathbf{A}_2}(s_2) = \emptyset$;
2. For any $(s_1, s_2) \in U \, d(s_1, s_2) = \partial_{\mathbf{A}_1}(s_1) \cap \partial_{\mathbf{A}_2}(s_2)$;
3. $A = A_1 \bar{\cup} A_2$ (i.e., A is the disjoint union of A_1 and A_2 defined by $A_1 \times \{1\} \cup A_2 \times \{(2\}$);
4. For $(a, i) \in A$, $i = 1, 2$ and $(s_1, s_2) \in U$

   $(a, i)(s_1, s_2) = a(s_i)$

The independent product of decision tables $\mathbf{A}_1$, $\mathbf{A}_2$ is denoted by $\mathbf{A}_1 \odot \mathbf{A}_2$. The decision in $\mathbf{A}_1 \odot \mathbf{A}_2$ has values in $\mathbf{P}(\Theta)$. We take $\Theta_0 = \mathbf{P}(\Theta)$ as the frame of discernment for $\mathbf{A}_1 \odot \mathbf{A}_2$ and we consider the standard basic probability assignment

$$m_{\mathbf{A}_1 \odot \mathbf{A}_2} \colon \mathbf{P}(\Theta_0) \to \mathbf{R}_+$$

We have the following property:

$$m_{\mathbf{A}_1 \odot \mathbf{A}_2}(\Delta) = 0 \text{ if } (|\Delta| > 1 \text{ and } \Delta \subseteq \Theta_0) \text{ or } \Delta = \{\emptyset\}$$

so the belief function corresponding to $m_{\mathbf{A}_1 \odot \mathbf{A}_2}$ is Bayesian.

Hence, the classification determined by the decision d in $\mathbf{A}_1 \odot \mathbf{A}_2$ is definable by conditions of $\mathbf{A}_1 \odot \mathbf{A}_2$.

The theorem formulated below gives the rule for computing the values

$$m_{\mathbf{A}_1 \odot \mathbf{A}_2}(\Delta) \text{ for } |\Delta| = 1 \text{ and } \Delta \subseteq \Theta_0, \Delta \neq \{\emptyset\}$$

Theorem 4. Let $\mathbf{A}_1 \odot \mathbf{A}_2$ be a Θ-independent product of decision tables $\mathbf{A}_1$ and $\mathbf{A}_2$. Then for every $\varnothing \neq \theta \subseteq \Theta$ we have the following equality, called *Dempster's combination rule:*

$$m_{\mathbf{A}_1 \odot \mathbf{A}_2}(\{\theta\}) = \frac{\sum_{\theta_1 \cap \theta_2 = \theta} m_{\mathbf{A}_1}(\theta_1) m_{\mathbf{A}_2}(\theta_2)}{1 - \sum_{\theta_1 \cap \theta_2 = \varnothing} m_{\mathbf{A}_1}(\theta_1) m_{\mathbf{A}_2}(\theta_2)}$$

Proof. From the definition of the standard basic probability assignment we have:

$$m_{\mathbf{A}_1 \odot \mathbf{A}_2}(\{\theta\}) = \frac{|F_{\mathbf{A}_1 \odot \mathbf{A}_2}(\{\theta\})|}{|U_1 \times U_2 - U_1 \otimes U_2|} = \frac{|\underline{A}X_\theta|}{|U_1 \times U_2| (1 - \frac{|U_1 \otimes U_2|}{|U_1 \times U_2|})}$$

$$= \frac{\dfrac{|\underline{A}\{(s_1, s_2) \in U : \partial_{\mathbf{A}_1}(s_1) \cap \partial_{\mathbf{A}_2}(s_2) = \theta\}|}{|U_1 \times U_2|}}{1 - \dfrac{|\{(s_1, s_2) \in U : \partial_{\mathbf{A}_1}(s_1) \cap \partial_{\mathbf{A}_2}(s_2) = \varnothing\}|}{|U_1 \times U_2|}}$$

Let us observe that $|\{(s1, s_2) \in U : \partial_{\mathbf{A}_1}(s_1) \cap \partial_{\mathbf{A}_2}(s_2) = \varnothing\}| =$
$= | \bigcup_{\theta_1 \cap \theta_2 = \varnothing} \partial_{\mathbf{A}_1}^{-1}(\{\theta_1\}) \times \partial_{\mathbf{A}_2}^{-1}(\{\theta_2\})| = | \sum_{\theta_1 \cap \theta_2 = \varnothing} |\partial_{\mathbf{A}_1}^{-1}(\{\theta_1\}) \times \partial_{\mathbf{A}_2}^{-1}(\{\theta_2\})|$
$= | \sum_{\theta_1 \cap \theta_2 = \varnothing} |\partial_{\mathbf{A}_1}^{-1}(\{\theta_1\})| \cdot |\partial_{\mathbf{A}_2}^{-1}(\{\theta_2\})|.$

Moreover

$$|\underline{A}\{(s_1, s_2) \in U : \partial_{\mathbf{A}_1}(s_1) \cap \partial_{\mathbf{A}_2}(s_2) = \theta\}| =$$
$$= |\underline{A} \bigcup_{\theta_1 \cap \theta_2 = \theta} \partial_{\mathbf{A}_1}^{-1}(\{\theta_1\}) \times \partial_{\mathbf{A}_2}^{-1}(\{\theta_2\})| =$$
$$= | \sum_{\theta_1 \cap \theta_2 = \theta} |\underline{A}(\partial_{\mathbf{A}_1}^{-1}(\{\theta_1\}) \times \partial_{\mathbf{A}_2}^{-1}(\{\theta_2\}))| =$$
$$= | \sum_{\theta_1 \cap \theta_2 = \theta} |\partial_{\mathbf{A}_1}^{-1}(\{\theta_1\}) \times \partial_{\mathbf{A}_2}^{-1}(\{\theta_2\})| =$$
$$= | \sum_{\theta_1 \cap \theta_2 = \theta} |\underline{A}_1 \partial_{\mathbf{A}_1}^{-1}(\{\theta_1\}) \times \underline{A}_2 \partial_{\mathbf{A}_2}^{-1}(\{\theta_2\}))| =$$
$$= | \sum_{\theta_1 \cap \theta_2 = \theta} |\underline{A}_1 \partial_{\mathbf{A}_1}^{-1}(\{\theta_1\})| \cdot |\underline{A}_2 \partial_{\mathbf{A}_2}^{-1}(\{\theta_2\}))|$$

Hence

$$m_{\mathbf{A}_1 \odot \mathbf{A}_2}(\{\theta)\} = \frac{\displaystyle\sum_{\theta_1 \cap \theta_2 = \theta} \frac{|\underline{A}_1\, \partial_{\mathbf{A}_1}^{-1}(\{\theta_1\})|}{|U_1|} \cdot \frac{|\underline{A}_2\, \partial_{\mathbf{A}_2}^{-1}(\{\theta_2\})|}{|U_2|}}{1 - \displaystyle\sum_{\theta_1 \cap \theta_2 = \varnothing} \frac{|\partial_{\mathbf{A}_1}^{-1}(\{\theta_1\})|}{|U_1|} \cdot \frac{|\partial_{\mathbf{A}_2}^{-1}(\{\theta_2\})|}{|U_2|}} =$$

$$= \frac{\displaystyle\sum_{\theta_1 \cap \theta_2 = \theta} m_{\mathbf{A}_1}(\theta_1)\, m_{\mathbf{A}_2}(\theta_2)}{1 - \displaystyle\sum_{\theta_1 \cap \theta_2 = \varnothing} m_{\mathbf{A}_1}(\theta_1)\, m_{\mathbf{A}_2}(\theta_2)}$$

Example 15. We shall consider two decision tables $\mathbf{A}_1$ and $\mathbf{A}_2$, which are described in Tables 10.10 and 10.11.

Table 10.10

$\mathbf{A}_1$:

U_1	a	b	c	d_1
1	1	1	0	1
2	0	1	0	2
3	0	1	0	1
4	0	0	1	2

Table 10.11

$\mathbf{A}_2$:

U_2	e	f	g	d_2
5	1	1	1	2
6	1	1	1	2
7	0	0	1	2
8	0	0	1	1

We have:

$$X_1^1 = \{s \in U_1 : d_1(s) = 1\} = \{1, 3\}$$
$$X_2^1 = \{s \in U_1 : d_1(s) = 2\} = \{2, 4\}$$
$$\underline{A}_1\, X_1^1 = \{1\};\ \underline{A}_1\, X_2^1 = \{4\};\ \overline{A}_1\, X_1^1 = \overline{A}_1\, X_2^1 = \{1, 2, 3, 4\}$$
$$BN_{\mathbf{A}_1}(X_1^1) = \{2, 3, 4\};\ BN_{\mathbf{A}_1}(X_2^1) = \{1, 2, 3\}$$
$$Bd_{\mathbf{A}_1}(\{1, 2\}) = BN_{\mathbf{A}_1}(X_1^1) \cap BN_{\mathbf{A}_1}(X_2^1) = \{2, 3\}$$
$$m_{\mathbf{A}_1}(\{1\}) = \frac{1}{4};\ m_{\mathbf{A}_1}(\{2\}) = \frac{1}{4};\ m_{\mathbf{A}_1}(\{1, 2\}) = \frac{1}{2}$$
$$X_1^2 = \{s \in U_2 : d_2(s) = 1\} = \{8\}$$
$$X_2^2 = \{s \in U_2 : d_2(s) = 2\} = \{5, 6, 7\}$$
$$\underline{A}_2 X_1^2 = \varnothing;\ \underline{A}_2 X_2^2 = \{5, 6\};\ \overline{A}_1 X_1^2 = \overline{A}_1 X_2^2 = \{5, 6, 7, 8\}$$
$$BN_{\mathbf{A}_2}(X_1^2) = \{5, 6, 7, 8\};\ BN_{\mathbf{A}_2}(X_2^2) = \{7, 8\}$$
$$Bd_{\mathbf{A}_2}(\{1, 2\}) = BN_{\mathbf{A}_2}(X_1^2) \cap BN_{\mathbf{A}_2}(X_2^2) = \{7, 8\}$$
$$m_{\mathbf{A}_2}(\{1\}) = 0;\ m_{\mathbf{A}_2}(\{2\}) = \frac{1}{2};\ m_{\mathbf{A}_2}(\{1, 2\}) = \frac{1}{2}$$

We obtain two new decision tables $\mathbf{A}'_2$ and $\mathbf{A}'_2$ (defined by Tables 10.12 and 10.13) from $\mathbf{A}_1$ and $\mathbf{A}_2$ (defined by Tables 10.10 and 10.11) by substituting $\partial_{\mathbf{A}_1}$ and $\partial_{\mathbf{A}_2}$ instead of decisions d_1 and d_2, respectively.

Table 10.12

$\mathbf{A}'_1$:

U_1	a	b	c	$\delta_{\mathbf{A}_1}$
1	1	1	0	{1}
2	0	1	0	{1,2}
3	0	1	0	{1,2}
4	0	0	1	{2}

Table 10.13

$\mathbf{A}'_2$:

U_2	a	b	c	$\partial_{\mathbf{A}_2}$
5	1	1	1	{2}
6	1	1	1	{2}
7	0	0	1	{1,2}
8	0	0	1	{1,2}

Table 10.14

$\mathbf{A}_1 \odot \mathbf{A}_2$:

$U_1 \odot U_2$	$a1$	$b1$	$c1$	$e2$	$f2$	$g2$	$\partial_{\mathbf{A}_1 \odot \mathbf{A}_2}$
(1, 7)	1	1	0	0	0	1	{1}
(1, 8)	1	1	0	0	0	1	{1}
(2, 5)	0	1	0	1	1	1	{2}
(2, 6)	0	1	0	1	1	1	{2}
(2, 7)	0	1	0	0	0	1	{1, 2}
(2, 8)	0	1	0	0	0	1	{1, 2}
(3, 5)	0	1	0	1	1	1	{2}
(3, 6)	0	1	0	1	1	1	{2}
(3, 7)	0	1	0	0	0	1	{1, 2}
(3, 8)	0	1	0	0	0	1	{1, 2}
(4, 5)	0	0	1	1	1	1	{2}
(4, 6)	0	0	1	1	1	1	{2}
(4, 7)	0	0	1	0	0	1	{2}
(4, 8)	0	0	1	0	0	1	{2}

From Tables 10.12 and 10.13 we obtain $U_1 \odot U_2 \{(s_1, s_2): \partial_{A_1}(s_1) \cap \partial_{A_2}(s_2) = \emptyset\} = \{1\} \times \{5,6\}$.Hence the universe of the independent product $\mathbf{A}_1 \odot \mathbf{A}_2$ of $\mathbf{A}_1$ and $\mathbf{A}_2$ is equal to $U_1 \times U_2 - \{1\} \times \{5,6\}$ and has 14 elements. The decision table $\mathbf{A}_1 \odot \mathbf{A}_2$ is presented in Table 10.14. The partition defined by the decision attribute $\partial_{A_1 \odot A_2}$ in Table 10.14 is definable by the set A of conditions in that table, that is, set of pairs $(a, 1)$, $(b, 2)$, $(c, 1)$ $(e, 2)$, $(f, 2)$ $(g, 2)$.

Let $Y_i = \{(s, s') \in U_1 \odot U_2 : \partial_{A_1 \odot A_2}(s, s') = \{i\}\}$ for $i = 1, 2$ and $Y_3 = \{(s, s') \in (U_1 \odot U_2 : \partial_{A_1 \odot A_2}(s, s') = \{1, 2\}\}$.

From the definition of $\mathbf{A}_1 \odot \mathbf{A}_2$ we obtain:

$$\underline{A}Y_1 = Y_1\{1\} \times \{7,8\}$$
$$\underline{A}Y_2 = Y_2\{2,3\} \times \{2,3\} \times \{5,6\} \cup \{4\} \times \{5,6,7,8\}$$
$$\underline{A}Y_3 = Y_3\{2,3\} \times \{7,8\}$$

Hence

$$\mathrm{m}_{A_1 \odot A_2}(\{\{1\}\}) = \frac{1}{7};\ m_{A_1 \odot A_2}(\{\{2\}\}) = \frac{4}{7};\ m_{A_1 \odot A_2}(\{\{1,2\}\}) = \frac{2}{7}.$$

We obtain the same results by applying Dempster's combination rule. First let us compute

$$K = 1 - \sum_{\theta_1 \cap \theta_2 = \emptyset} m_{A_1}(\theta_1) m_{A_2}(\theta_2) =$$
$$= 1 - m_{A_1}(\{1\}) m_{A_2}(\{2\}) - m_{A_1}(\{2\}) m_{A_2}(\{1\}) = \frac{7}{8}$$

We have:

$$m_{A_1 \odot A_2}(\{\{1\}\}) = K^{-1}(\sum_{\theta_1 \cap \theta_2 = \{1\}} m_{A_1}(\theta_1) m_{A_2}(\theta_2) =$$
$$= \frac{8}{7}\Big\{ m_{A_1}(\{1\}) m_{A_2}(\{1\}) + m_{A_1}\{(1\}) m_{A_2}(\{1,2\}) +$$
$$+ m_{A_1}(\{1,2\} m_{A_2}(\{1\})\Big\} = \frac{8}{7}(\frac{1}{4}.0 + \frac{1}{4}\frac{1}{2} + \frac{1}{2}.0) = \frac{1}{7}$$

$$m_{A_1 \odot A_2}(\{\{2\}\}) = K^{-1}(\sum_{\theta_1 \cap \theta_2 = \{2\}} m_{A_1}(\theta_1) m_{A_2}(\theta_2) =$$
$$= \frac{7}{8}\Big\{ m_{A_1}(\{2\}) m_{A_2}(\{2\}) + m_{A_1}(\{2\}) m_{A_2}(\{1,2\})$$
$$+ m_{A_1}(\{1,2\}) m_{A_2}(\{2\})\Big\} = \frac{8}{7}(\frac{1}{4}\frac{1}{2} + \frac{1}{4}\frac{1}{2} + \frac{1}{2}\frac{1}{2})$$
$$= \frac{4}{7}$$

$$m_{A_1 \odot A_2}(\{\{1,2\}\}) = K^{-1}(\sum_{\theta_1 \cap \theta_2 = \{1,2\}} m_{A_1}(\theta_1) m_{A_2}(\theta_2) =$$
$$= \frac{8}{7} m_{A_1}(\{1,2\}) m_{A_2}(\{1,2\}) = \frac{8}{7}\frac{1}{2}\frac{1}{2} = \frac{2}{7}$$

Let us consider again a frame of discernment Θ compatible with decision tables $A_1 = (U_1, A_1 \cup \{d_1\})$ and $A_2 = (U_2, A_2 \cup \{d_2\})$, and Θ-independent product $A_1 \odot A_2 = (U, A \cup \{d\}$ of decision tables A_1 and A_2. Any decision table $A = (U, A \cup \{d^*\}$ satisfying the following conditions:

1. $\bigcup_{s \in U} d(s) = \bigcup_{s \in U} \{d^*(s)\};$
2. $d^*(x) \stackrel{df}{=} \{d^*(s): s \in x\} = \theta$ for any $\theta \subseteq \Theta$ and any abstract class x of the indiscernibility relation $IND_A(A)$ included in $\partial^{-1}_{A_1 \odot A_2}(\{\theta\});$

is called the realization of $A_1 \odot A_2$ and is denoted by $d^*[A_1 \odot A_2]$. We have the following property:

Corollary 3. Let $d^*[A_1 \odot A_2]$ be a realization of $A_1 \odot A_2$. Then for any $\emptyset \neq \theta \subseteq \Theta$ the following equality holds:

$$m_{A_1 \odot A_2}(\{\theta\}) = m_{d^*[A_1 \odot A_2]}(\theta)$$

Proof. Follows from the definition of realization of $A_1 \odot A_2$. From Theorem 4 and Corollary 3 we obtain:

Corollary 4. Let $A_1 \odot A_2$ be a Θ-independent product of decision tables A_1 and A_2 and let $d^*[A_1 \odot A_2]$ be a realization of $A_1 \odot A_2$. Then for every $\emptyset \neq \theta \subseteq \Theta$ we have the following equality, called Dempster's combination rule:

$$m_{d^*[A_1 \odot A_2]}(\theta) = \frac{\sum_{\theta_1 \cap \theta_2 = \theta} m_{A_1}(\theta_1) m_{A_2}(\theta_2)}{1 - \sum_{\theta_1 \cap \theta_2 = \emptyset} m_{A_1}(\theta_1) m_{A_2}(\theta_2)}$$

13. DEPENDENCIES IN DECISION TABLES

The aim of this section is to show that the approach presented can be extended to the case when only partial information about possible decision tables is accessible. We consider the partial information about the universe U_∞, which can be expressed using dependencies. We illustrate our considerations discussing examples from Shafer (1986).

Dependencies in a decision table are basic tools for drawing conclusions from basic knowledge. They express some of the relationships between basic categories described in the decision tables. A process of building theories is based on discovering inference rules of the form "if ... then ..." or how from a given knowledge another knowledge can be induced (Pawlak, 1991).

In our further considerations we will need the notion of partial dependency. Let A be a finite nonempty set called the set of condition names and let d be the decision name. A partial dependency over (A, d) is any expression of the form $\alpha \xrightarrow{\lambda} \beta$ where $\alpha \in \mathbf{C}_A$, $\beta \in \mathbf{D}_A$ and $0 \leqslant \lambda \leqslant 1$. if $\lambda = 1$ the partial dependency $\alpha \xrightarrow{\lambda} \beta$ is called simply the dependency and is denoted by $\alpha \to \beta$.

A partial dependency $\alpha \xrightarrow{\lambda} \beta$ over (A, d) is valid in the decision table $\mathbf{A} = (U, A \cup \{d\})$ iff

$$\alpha_{\mathbf{A}} \neq \emptyset$$

and

$$\lambda = \frac{|\alpha_{\mathbf{A}} \cap \beta_{\mathbf{A}}|}{|\alpha_{\mathbf{A}}|}$$

By $\mathbf{A} \models \alpha \xrightarrow{\lambda} \beta$ we denote the fact that the partial dependency $\alpha \xrightarrow{\lambda} \beta$ is true in $\mathbf{A}$, and by $\mathbf{A} \models \alpha -\!\backslash\!\xrightarrow{\lambda} \beta$ the fact that $\alpha \xrightarrow{\lambda} \beta$ is not true in $\mathbf{A}$:

$$|\alpha_{\mathbf{A}} \cap \beta_{\mathbf{A}}| \neq \lambda\, |\alpha_{\mathbf{A}}|$$

For a given finite set D of partial dependencies over (A, d) by $\mathbf{DT}(D)$ we denote the family of all decision tables $\mathbf{A}$ in which all partial dependencies from D are true:

$$\mathbf{DT}(D) = \{\mathbf{A} : \mathbf{A} \models \alpha \xrightarrow{\lambda} \beta \text{ and } \alpha \xrightarrow{\lambda} \beta \in D\}$$

The intuitive meaning of the above definition is the following: the partial dependency $\alpha \xrightarrow{\lambda} \beta$ is valid in a decision table $\mathbf{A}$ iff λ*100 percent of objects from $\mathbf{A}$ with property described by α in $\mathbf{A}$ also have property described by β in $\mathbf{A}$.

Some other definitions of partial dependency semantics can be found (see, e.g., Pawlak, 1991) but we restrict our considerations to the one presented above. We would like to show that it is possible to extend the previous approach to the case when a partial information about the universe U_∞ is given as a list of (partial) dependencies.

We will discuss Examples 1–3 from Shafer (1986, pp. 129–33).

Example 16. In Example 1 from Shafer (1986) it is assumed that Fred's announcements are truthful reports on what he knows about 80% of the time and are careless statements the other 20% of the time. We assume that Fred's announcement turns out to be, "The streets outside are slippery." The question is how to compute the belief in Fred's answer. We distinguish the following set of conditions:

> $A = \{Fred, streets\}$,
> where $V_{Fred} = \{truthful, \; careless\}$; and $V_{Streets} = \{slippery, not\_slippery\}$
> and the decision: *Fred_Answer* with the set of possible values $V_{Fred\_Answer} = \{yes, no\}$. The frame of discernment is $\Theta = \{yes, no\}$.

The following dependencies are assumed:

$(Fred\_Answer = yes) \xrightarrow{0.8} (Fred = truthful)$;
$(Fred\_Answer = no) \xrightarrow{0.8} (Fred = truthful)$;
$(Fred = truthful) \wedge (Fred\_Answer = yes) \rightarrow (Streets = slippery)$;
$(Fred = careless) \wedge (Streets = slippery) -/\rightarrow (Fred\_Answer = yes)$;
$(Fred = careless) \wedge (Streets = slippery) -/\rightarrow (Fred\_Answer = no)$;
$(Fred = careless) \wedge (Streets = not\_slippery) -/\rightarrow (Fred\_Answer = no)$;
$(Fred = careless) \wedge (Streets = not\_slippery) -/\rightarrow (Fred\_Answer = yes)$;

The first two dependencies state that in 80% of situations (objects are interpreted here as situations) Fred's announcements are *truthful*. From that it follows that in 20% of situations Fred's announcements are *careless*. The last four dependencies describe in some sense the meaning of *careless*. When Fred is *careless* then there exists a situation when the streets are *slippery* and Fred's answer will be *no* and there exists a situation when streets are *not slippery* but Fred's answer will be *yes*. Moreover, he may not always answer *no* when the streets are *slippery* and he may not always answer *yes* when the streets are *not_slippery* (in the opposite case we cannot treat him as *careless* because he is taking care not to give us a true value in every situation).

The problem is how to compute the values $Bel_A(\{yes\})$ and $Bel_A(\{no\})$ for **A** satisfying the above dependencies. Taking into account the above dependencies we have:

$$Bel_{\mathbf{A}}(\{yes\}) = m_{\mathbf{A}}(\{yes\}) = \frac{|\{Fred, Streets\}\, X_{Yes}|}{|U|} =$$
$$= \frac{0.8\,|U|}{|U|} = 0.8 \text{ and } Bel_{\mathbf{A}}(\{no\}) = m_{\mathbf{A}}(\{no\}) = 0$$

Let us observe that the computation gives the same results for any decision table satisfying the considered set of dependencies.

Example 17. Let us now take Example 2 from Shafer (1986). We consider the following set of condition names: $A' = \{Thermometer, Temp = 31\}$ and the decision *Answer*. We assume:

$$V_{Thermometer} = \{working, wrong\};\ V_{TEMP=31} = \{yes, no\};$$
$$\text{and } V_{Answer} = \{yes, no\}.$$

We take the following set of dependencies:

$$1 \rightarrow (Temp = 31)$$
$$1 \xrightarrow{0.99} (Thermometer = working);$$
$$1 \xrightarrow{0.99} (Thermometer = wrong);$$
$$(Thermometer = working) \wedge (Temp = 31) \rightarrow (Answer = no);$$
$$(Thermometer = wrong) \wedge (\text{Temp} = 31) -/\rightarrow (Answer = no);$$
$$(Thermometer = wrong) \wedge (Temp = 31) -/\rightarrow (Answer = yes),$$

where 1 denotes any logical tautology, e.g., $(Thermometer = working) \vee (Thermometer = wrong)$.

The first dependency restricts situations to cases when the temperature is 31 degrees (Fahrenheit). The next two express that in 99% of situtations the thermometer is *working* and only in 1% of situations is *wrong*. The next dependency states that if the thermometer is working and the temperature is 31 degreees Fahrenheit then the answer is *no* (the streets are not slippery: because of the traffic ice could not form on the streets at this temperature). The last two dependencies express the fact that when the thermometer is not working and showing 31 degrees Fahrenheit then there are some situations when the answer is *yes* and others when the answer is *no*.

We now compute the values $Bel_{\mathbf{A}'}(\{yes\})$ and $Bel_{\mathbf{A}'}(\{no\})$ for any $\mathbf{A}'$ satisfying the above dependencies.

Taking into account the above dependencies we have:

$$Bel_{\mathbf{A}'}(\{no\}) = m_{\mathbf{A}'}(\{no\}) = \frac{|\{Thermometer, Temp = 31\}X_{no}|}{|U|} =$$
$$= \frac{0.99\,|U|}{|U|} = 0.99. \text{ and } Bel_{\mathbf{A}'}(\{yes\}) = m_{A'}(\{yes\}) = 0$$

Moreover, in this case we have $m_{\mathbf{A}'}(\{yes, no\}) = \dfrac{0.01\,|U|}{|U|} = 0.01.$

Let us observe that the computation gives the same results for any decision table satisfying the considered set of dependencies.

Example 18. We can apply the Dempster combination rule to compute the standard basic probability assignment of the independent product $\mathbf{A} \odot \mathbf{A}'$ of arbitrary decision tables $\mathbf{A}$ and $\mathbf{A}'$ satisfying respectively the dependencies from Examples 16 and 17. We have:

$$Bel_{\mathbf{A}\odot\mathbf{A}'}(\{\{yes\}\}) = m_{\mathbf{A}\odot\mathbf{A}'}(\{\{yes\}\}) =$$
$$= \frac{m_{\mathbf{A}}\{yes\}m_{\mathbf{A}'}\{yes\} + m_{\mathbf{A}}\{yes,no\}m_{\mathbf{A}'}\{yes\} + m_{\mathbf{A}}\{yes\}m_{\mathbf{A}'}\{yes,no\}}{1 - m_{\mathbf{A}}\{no\}m_{\mathbf{A}'}\{yes\} - m_{\mathbf{A}}\{yes\}m_{\mathbf{A}'}\{no\}}$$
$$= 1/26 \approx 0.04.$$
$$Bel_{\mathbf{A}\odot\mathbf{A}'}(\{\{no\}\}) = m_{\mathbf{A}\odot\mathbf{A}'}(\{\{no\}\}) =$$
$$= \frac{m_{\mathbf{A}}\{no\}m_{\mathbf{A}'}\{no\} + m_{\mathbf{A}}\{yes,no\}m_{\mathbf{A}'}\{no\} + m_{\mathbf{A}}\{no\}m_{\mathbf{A}'}\{yes,no\}}{1 - m_{\mathbf{A}}\{no\}m_{\mathbf{A}'}\{yes\} - m_{\mathbf{A}}\{yes\}m_{\mathbf{A}'}\{no\}}$$
$$= 99/104 \approx 0.95$$

Hence $m_{\mathbf{A}\odot\mathbf{A}'}(\{\{yes, no\}\}) \approx 0.01$

Example 19. In the third example from Shafer (1986, p. 132) it is assumed that Fred's judgments are not independent from the thermometer state. This leads to the new dependency, which should be added to the lists of dependencies from two previous examples:

$$(Thermometer = wrong) \xrightarrow{0.9} (Fred = careless)$$

Taking a decision table $\mathbf{A}$ satisfying the received list of dependencies one can calculate the values of the belief function $Bel_{\mathbf{A}}$.

As we observed in the examples the specification of a problem is correct if the computed values of the standard basic probability assignment are independent from a choice of a decision table satisfying the considered set of dependencies. This can be used as a correctness request in the specification of the considered type of problems.

14. CONCLUSIONS

By linking two approaches, namely the rough set theory and evidence theory, we have obtained (at least partial) answers for several questions related to the evidence theory:

1. What is the evidence?
2. How do we compute in practical applications the values of the basic probability assignments?
3. Is it true that the large cardinality of the powerset $\mathbf{P}(\Theta)$ of the frame of discernment Θ does not allow practical applications of evidence theory?
4. Is it possible to formulate precisely the notion of independent sources of information?
5. Is it possible to prove the validity of the Dempster combination rule?
6. How do we interpret the belief and plausibility functions?

On the basis of rough set approach it was possible to better understand basic ideas underlying fundamental concepts of evidence theory. We presented a semantical basis for the evidence approach with computable uncertainty measures.

Our investigations turned out to be fruitful also for the rough set approach. In particular, it was possible to describe the approximation of the expert classification using a partition of boundary regions. Moreover, it was possible to observe an interesting application of partial dependencies for specification of belief functions.

Let us observe that our results are obtained by taking into consideration some specific numerical uncertainty measures determined on the basis of the rough set approach. The rough set approach is not restricted to those measures only (Pawlak and Skowron, 1991) and several problems have been solved in the rough set approach without applying uncertainty measures (Pawlak, 1991).

We believe that the results presented in this paper as well as the further investigation of relationships between the evidence theory and rough set theory, will stimulate theoretical research related to them as well as new practical applications.

BIBLIOGRAPHY

Bhatnagar, R.K. and Kanal, L.N. (1986). Handling uncertain information: A review of numeric and non-numeric methods. In Kanal, L.N.. and Lemmer, J.F. (eds.), *Uncertainty in artificial intelligence*. Amsterdam: North-Holland.

Buchanan, B.G. and Shortliffe, E.H. (1984). *Rule-based expert systems: The MYCIN experiments of the Stanford heuristic programming project*. Reading, MA: Addison-Wesley.

Dempster, A.D. (1976). Upper and lower probabilities induced by multi-valued mapping. *Annals of Mathematical Statistics* 38: 325–39.

Dubois, D. and Prade, H. (1985). Combination and propagation of uncertainty with belief functions: A reexamination. *Proc. Ninth IJCAICA 85,* Aug.18–23, Los Angeles, pp. 111–13.

Fagin, R. And Halpern, J.Y. (1988). Reasoning about knowledge and probability. *Proc. Second Conf. on Theoretical Aspects of Reasoning about Knowledge.* San Mateo, CA: Morgan Kaufmann, pp. 277–93.

Grzymała-Busse, J.W. (1989). Manuscript.

Grzymała-Busse, J.W. (1991). *Managing uncertainty in expert systems.* San Mateo, CA: Morgan Kaufmann.

Gordon, J. and Shortliffe, E.H. (1984). The Dempster-Shafer theory of evidence. In Buchanan, B.G. and Shortliffe, E.H. (eds.), *Rule-based expert systems: The MYCIN experiments of the Stanford heuristic programming project.* Reading, MA: Addison-Wesley.

Henrion, M., Shachter, R.D., Kanal, L.N., and Lemmer, J.F. 1990. *Uncertainty in artificial intelligence* 5. Amsterdam: North-Holland.

Kanal, L.N. and Lemmer, J.F. (1986). *Uncertainty in artificial intelligence.* Amsterdam: North-Holland.

Kanal, L.N. and Lemmer, J.F. (1988). *Uncertainty in artificial intelligence* 2. Amsterdam: North-Holland.

Kanal, L.N., Levitt, T.S., and Lemmer, J.F. (1989). *Uncertainty in artificial intelligence* 3. Amsterdam: North-Holland.

Kodratoff, Y. and Michalski, R. (1990). *Machine learning: An artificial intelligence approach,* Vol. 3. San Mateo, CA: Morgan Kaufmann.

Kruse, R., Schwecke, E., and Heinsohn, J. (1991). *Uncertainty and vagueness in knowledge based systems: Numerical methods.* Berlin, Heidelberg: Springer-Verlag.

Pawlak, Z. (1982). Rough sets: Basic notions. Report #431, Institute of Computer Science, Polish Academy of Sciences, 1981. Also in *International Journal of Computer and Information Sciences* 11: 344–56.

Pawlak, Z. (1985). Rough sets and decision tables. *Lecture Notes in Computer Science* 208, pp. 186–96. Berlin, Heidelberg: Springer-Verlag.

Pawlak, Z. (1991). *Rough sets: Theoretical aspects of reasoning about data.* Dordrecht: Kluwer.

Pawlak, Z. and Skowron, A. (1991). *Rough membership functions.* ICS Research Report 10/91, pp. 1–24. Warsaw University of Technology.

Shachter, R.D., Levitt, T.S., Kanal, L.N., and Lemmer, J.F. (1990). *Uncertainty in artificial intelligence* 4. Amsterdam: North-Holland.

Shafer, G. (1976). *A mathematical theory of evidence.* Princeton, NJ: Princeton University Press.

Shafer, G. (1981). Constructive probability. *Synthese* 48: 1–60.

Shafer, G. (1986). Probability judgement in artificial intelligence. In Kanal, L.N. and Lemmer, J.F. (eds.), *Uncertainty in artificial intelligence,* pp. 127–35. Amsterdam: North-Holland.

Shafer, G. and Pearl, J. (1990). *Readings in uncertain reasoning.* San Mateo, CA: Morgan Kaufmann.

Skowron, A. (1989a). The relationship between rough set theory and evidence theory. *Bull. Polish. Acad. Sci. Math.* 37: 87–90.

Skowron, A. (1989b). The evidence theory and decision tables. *Bulletin of the European Association for Theoretical Computer Science* 39: 199–204.

Skowron, A. (1990). The rough sets theory and evidence theory. *Fundamenta Informaticae* 13: 245–62.

Skowron, A. (1991). *The rough set theory as a basis for the evidence theory*. ICS Research Report 2/91, pp. 1–53. Warsaw University of Technology.

Skowron, A. and Grzymała-Busse, J.W. (1991). *From the rough set theory to the evidence theory*. ICS Report 8/91, pp. 1–49. Warsaw University of Technology.

Smets, P. (1988). Belief functions. In Smets, P., Mamdami, E.H., Dubois, D., and Prade, H. (eds.), *Non-standard logics for automated reasoning*, pp. 235–86. London: Academic Press.

Yager, R.R. (1987). On the Dempster-Shafer framework and new combination rules. *Information Sci.* 41: 93–137.

Zadeh, L.A. (1986). A simple view of the Dempster-Shafer theory of evidence and its implication for the rule of combination. *AI Magazine* 7: 85–90.

2

FUZZIFICATION OF DEMPSTER-SHAFER THEORY OF EVIDENCE

11 Mass distributions on *L*-fuzzy sets and families of frames of discernment

Rudolf KRUSE and Frank KLAWONN

Abstract: In this paper mass distributions (basic probability assignments) are understood as representations of vague knowledge provided by a weighted set of sensors, subexperts, or contexts that specify imprecise information. By investigating the semantics of mass distributions in this sense, we are able to distinguish updating schemes like revision (Dempster's rule of conditioning) and conditioning (strong conditioning) by the treatment of sensors or subexperts that specified (partially) contradicting information. Considering all possible updatings in a refined space, we introduce the concept of specialization. In opposition to updating Dempster's rule of combination is a method for the aggregation of mass distributions. We discuss the aggregation of mass distributions on various characteristics in an appropriate product space, and describe the role of Dempster's rule of combination in this framework using our semantics of mass distributions. Finally, we generalize these ideas to mass distributions on *L*-fuzzy sets and show how problems in the context of *L*-fuzzy sets can be solved by using the concept of specialization.

Keywords: mass distributions, specialization, *L*-fuzzy sets, Dempster's rule of combination.

1. INTRODUCTION

Shafer (1976) introduced basic probability assignments for the representation of vague information. The corresponding belief functions can be interpreted as lower probabilities, if the framework under consideration is of probabilistic nature. But other interpretations of basic probability assignments given, for example, by Smets' transferable belief model (1988, 1990) are possible.

In section 2 we describe our nonprobabilistic view of mass distributions (the name we prefer to "basic probability assignments" in order to avoid any confusion with probabilistic notions) induced by a weighted set of experts, sensors, or contexts, each of them giving vague information. This interpretation leads to the concepts of revision and conditioning and the more general term of flow of evidence masses in the form of specializations.

Section 3 deals with the aggregation of knowledge of various characteristics specified by mass distributions on the coordinate spaces of a product space.

In section 4 the notions introduced in the previous sections are generalized for mass distributions on L-fuzzy sets.

2. MASS DISTRIBUTIONS AND SPECIALIZATIONS

Belief functions aim to model a human decision maker's subjective evaluation of evidence. For this purpose we consider a (usually inaccessible) nonempty, finite space Θ of sensors, "subexperts," or contexts, which is assumed to be weighted according to the importance and reliability of the sensors, subexperts, or contexts, respectively. Without loss of generality, we may assume that the weights sum up to one, that is, we have a function:

$$w : \Theta \to [0,1], \text{s.t.} \sum_{\theta \in \Theta} w(\theta) = 1$$

Each sensor/subexpert $\theta \in \Theta$ specifies a certain subset $S_\theta \subseteq \Omega$ in our finite sample space Ω, also called universe of discourse. We always presuppose the closed world assumption for our universe of discourse (for a discussion of the closed and the open world assumption see, e.g., Smets, 1988). This does not impose any restrictions on our model, since in the case of the open world assumption for the sample space Ω, we can always consider the space $\Omega' = \Omega \cup \{u\}$, $u \notin \Omega$, where the element u represents the unknown, but possible elements not contained in Ω and, therefore, the closed world assumption for Ω' holds.

According to the closed world assumption each sensor/subexpert $\theta \in \Theta$ should be able to specify a *nonempty* subset $S_\theta \subseteq \Omega$ of possible elements $\omega \in S_\theta$. However, some sensors might be faulty or subexperts could refuse to choose any subset. We will neglect these sensors or subexperts and normalize the weights of the remaining sensors/subexperts.

The evidence induced by the weighted sensor/subexpert space Θ and the specified subsets S_θ is represented in the universe of discourse by a function

$$m : 2^\Omega \to [0,1], \quad A \to \sum_{\theta \in \Theta : S_\theta = A} \omega(\theta)$$

This motivates the following definition.

Definition 2.1. *A function* $m : 2^\Omega \to [0,1]$ *is called a mass distribution, if*

(i) $m(\theta) = 0$, *and*
(ii) $\sum_{A : A \subseteq \Omega} m(A) = 1$

hold.

The mass $m(A)$ attached to the set $A \subseteq \Omega$ is understood as the measure of belief that is committed exactly to A and corresponds to the support given to A, but not to any proper subset of A. The corresponding belief, plausibility, and commonality functions of the mass distribution M are defined in the usual way:

$$\mathrm{bel}_m : 2^\Omega \to [0,1], \quad A \to \sum_{B : B \subseteq A} m(B)$$

$$\mathrm{pl}_m : 2^\Omega \to [0,1], \quad A \to \sum_{B : B \cap A \neq \theta} m(B)$$

$$\mathrm{q}_m : 2^\Omega \to [0,1], \quad A \to \sum_{B : A \subseteq B} m(B)$$

We now consider a new evidence given by a subset $E \subseteq \Omega$ that contains the true element of Ω with certainty. There are two approaches to the updating of a mass distribution on Ω with respect to the new evidence E. In any case we have to neglect those sensors/subexperts $\theta \in \Theta$ that specified a set S_θ, s.t. $S_\theta \cap E = \emptyset$. On the other hand, all sensors/subexperts whose corresponding sets S_θ

are contained in E are, of course, correct and must be taken into account. But those sensors/subexperts θ with a set S_θ s.t. $S_\theta \cap E \neq \emptyset$ and $S_\theta \cap (\Omega - E) \neq \emptyset$ can be treated in two different ways.

The first possibility is to assume that those sensors/subexperts θ were correct, although they specified some incorrect elements $\omega \in S_\theta \cap (\Omega - E)$ due to some lack of information. This leads to a data revision, which corresponds to Dempster's rule of conditioning.

Definition 2.2. *Let m be a mass distribution on* Ω *and let* $E \subseteq \Omega$, *s.t.* $\mathrm{pl}_m(E) > 0$. *The mass distribution*

$$m_E : 2^\Omega \to [0,1], \quad A \to \begin{cases} \dfrac{\sum_{B: B \cap E = A} m(B)}{\mathrm{pl}_m(E)} & \text{if } A \neq \emptyset \\ 0 & \text{otherwise} \end{cases}$$

is called revised mass distribution.

In the other case we consider those sensors/subexperts to be contradictory, which implies that we have to neglect them. This concept is called strong conditioning (Dubois and Prade, 1986a).

Definition 2.3. *Let m be a mass distribution on* Ω *and let* $E \subseteq \Omega$, *s.t.* $\mathrm{bel}_m(E) > 0$. *The mass distribution*

$$m(.|E) : 2^\Omega \to [0,1], \quad A \to \begin{cases} \dfrac{m(A)}{\mathrm{bel}_m(E)} & \text{if } A \subseteq E \\ 0 & \text{otherwise} \end{cases}$$

is called conditional mass distribution.

Before we introduce the concept of specialization, we have to recall the notion of refinement (Shafer, 1976). An element $\omega \in \Omega$ of the universe of discourse might stand for a set of indistinguishable elements $\omega'_1, \ldots, \omega'_k$. Therefore, Ω would only be a coarse representation of a refined universe of discourse Ω'.

Definition 2.4. *Let* Ω *and* Ω' *be two universes of discourse and let* $\hat{\Pi}$ *be a mapping* $\hat{\Pi} : 2^\Omega \to 2^{\Omega'} - \{\emptyset\}$, *s.t.*

(*i*) for all $\omega \in \Omega : \hat{\Pi}(\{\omega\}) \neq \emptyset$

(*ii*) for all $\omega_1, \omega_2 \in \Omega : \left(\hat{\Pi}(\{\omega_1\}) \cap \hat{\Pi}(\{\omega_2\}) \neq \emptyset \Rightarrow \omega_1 = \omega_2 \right)$

(*iii*) $\bigcup \{\hat{\Pi}(\{\omega\}) | \omega \in \Omega\} = \Omega'$

(*iv*) for all $A \subseteq \Omega : \hat{\Pi}(A) = \bigcup \{\hat{\Pi}(\{\omega\}) | \omega \in A\}$.

Then $\hat{\Pi}$ *is called a refinement mapping and* Ω' *is a refinement of* Ω.

Definition 2.5. *Let Ω' be a refinement of Ω with refinement mapping $\hat{\Pi}$. The mapping*

$$\Pi : 2^{\Omega'} \to 2^{\Omega}, \quad A' \to \{\omega \in \Omega \mid \hat{\Pi}(\{\omega\}) \cap A' \neq \emptyset\}$$

is called the outer reduction induced by $\hat{\Pi}$.

A mass distribution on a refined space Ω' induces a mass distribution Ω in the following way.

Definition 2.6. *Let Ω' be a refinement of Ω with refinement mapping $\hat{\Pi}$ and let m' be a mass distribution on Ω'. The projection $\Pi(m')$ of m' to Ω is defined by*

$$\Pi(m'): 2^{\Omega} \to [0,1], \quad A \to \sum_{A' \subseteq \Omega' : \Pi(A') = A} m'(A').$$

It is also possible to extend a mass distribution on Ω to a mass distribution on a refined space Ω'.

Definition 2.7. *Let Ω' be a refinement of Ω with refinement mapping $\hat{\Pi}$ and let m be a mass distribution on Ω. The mass distribution*

$$\hat{\Pi}(m): 2^{\Omega'} \to [0,1], \quad A' \to \begin{cases} m(A) & \text{if } A' = \hat{\Pi}(A) \\ 0 & \text{otherwise} \end{cases}$$

is called the vacuous extension of m.

Note that $\Pi(\hat{\Pi}(m)) = m$ holds, but not necessarily $\hat{\Pi}(\Pi(m')) = m'$.

We now consider the situation where the sensors/subexperts observe an inaccessible refinement Ω' of the universe of discourse Ω, that is, we have a weighted sensor/subexpert–space Θ and subsets $S_\theta \subseteq \Omega'$ specified by the sensors/subexperts. This induces a mass distribution m' on Ω' by

$$m'(A') = \sum_{\theta \in \Theta : S_\theta = A'} \omega(\theta), \quad \text{for all } A' \subseteq \Omega'$$

For us, only the projection $\Pi(m')$ on Ω is accessible.

$$(\Theta, \omega) \xrightarrow{S_\theta} (\Omega', m') \xrightarrow{\Pi} (\Omega, \Pi(m'))$$

Consider a mass distribution t' on Ω', which induces a mass distribution $t = \Pi(t')$ on Ω, and an evidence $E' \subseteq \Omega'$. Thus we obtain a mass distribution $s' = t'_{E'}$ inducing a mass distribution $s = \Pi(s')$ on Ω. s is a mass distribution carrying more information than t and is therefore called a specialization of t (Kruse and Schwecke, 1990; Kruse, Schwecke, and Heinsohn, 1991). This important concept is formalized in the following definition.

Definition 2.8. *Let s and t be two mass distributions on* Ω. *s is a specialization of t* ($s \sqsubseteq t$), *if there is a refinement* Ω' *of* Ω *with refinement mapping* $\hat{\Pi}$ *and two mass distribution* s' *and* t' *on* Ω', *s.t.*

(i) $\exists E' \subseteq \Omega' : s' = t'_{E'}$
(ii) $s = \Pi(s')$
(iii) $t = \Pi(t')$

The specializations of a mass distribution are all possible updating w.r.t. an evidence E' in a refined space Ω'. Specializations can be characterized in the following way.

Theorem 2.1. *Let s and t be two mass distributions on* Ω. *The following three statements are equivalent:*

(i) $s \sqsubseteq t$

(ii) for all $A \subseteq \Omega$: $\left(q_t(A) = 0 \Rightarrow q_s(A) = 0 \right)$

(iii) $\exists h : 2^{\Omega} \times 2^{\Omega} \rightarrow [0, 1]$, *s.t.*

(a) for all $A \subseteq \Omega : t(A) = \sum_{B : B \subseteq \Omega} h(A, B)$

(b) for all $A, B \subseteq \Omega : \left(h(A, B) > 0 \Rightarrow B \subseteq A \right)$

(c) for all $\emptyset \neq B \subseteq \Omega : s(B) = \dfrac{\sum_{A : A \subseteq \Omega} h(A, B)}{1 - \sum_{A : A \subseteq \Omega} h(A, \emptyset)}$

For a proof see Kruse and Schwecke (1990).

Part (iii) of this theorem leads to an interpretation of specialization as a flow of evidence masses from supersets to subsets. $h(A, B)$ specifies the amount of belief committed to A by t that in the light of new evidence flows to the set B. Condition (a) assures that no evidence mass is lost, whereas condition (b) requires that the masses flow only to subsets. Masses flowing to the empty set represent partial contradictions and have to be neglected due to our treatment of faulty sensors/subexperts, described in the beginning of this section. This forces the normalization in condition (c).

Yager (1988) and Dubois and Prade (1986b) introduced a stronger notion of specialization called strong inclusion, denoted $<$. $s < t$ holds, if the normalization in (iii.c) can be avoided; no mass flows to the empty set. Obviously we have $s < t \Rightarrow s \sqsubseteq t$ but not vice versa. $<$ is a (partial) ordering on the set of mass distributions on Ω, whereas $\sqsubseteq$ is only a preordering. But any preordering induces a (partial) ordering on the set of equivalence classes w.r.t. the equivalence relation $\approx$, defined by $s \approx t$, if $s \subseteq t$ and $t \subseteq s$. In both orderings the infimum of two elements does not exist in general. However, the supremum of two elements exists always only in the case of $\subseteq$. This property will be useful for the generalization to mass distributions on L-fuzzy sets when we consider product spaces.

3. AGGREGATION OF MASS DISTRIBUTIONS

Until now we only considered (data) revision and conditioning, where one mass distribution was involved. In this section we deal with the problem of how a universe of discourse Ω can be treated, if it is composed of various characteristics, that is, Ω corresponds to a product space $\Omega = \Omega_1 \times \ldots \times \Omega_n$.

Given two mass distributions m_1 and m_2 on Ω_1 and Ω_2, respectively, which mass distribution should be chosen on the product space $\Omega_1 \times \Omega_2$ for the representation of the combined knowledge given by m_1 and m_2, if we assume m_1 and m_2 to be "independent"? Usually Dempster's rule of combination is applied to the vacuous extensions of m_1 and m_2, yielding a mass distribution $m = \hat{\Pi}_1(m_1) \otimes \hat{\Pi}_2(m_2)$ on $\Omega_1 \times \Omega_2$, where

$$\hat{\Pi}_1 : 2^{\Omega_1} \to 2^{\Omega_1 \times \Omega_2}, \quad A \to A \times \Omega_2,$$
$$\hat{\Pi}_2 : 2^{\Omega_2} \to 2^{\Omega_1 \times \Omega_2}, \quad A \to \Omega_1 \times A.$$

The mass distribution m has the following properties:

(M1) $\Pi_1(m) = m_1$ and $\Pi_2(m) = m_2$

(M2) If s is a mass distribution on $\Omega_1 \times \Omega_2$, s.t. $\Pi_1(s) = m_1$ and $\Pi_2(s) = m_2$, then $s < m$ and $s \subseteq m$ hold.

That means m is the least specific mass distribution on $\Omega_1 \times \Omega_2$ whose projections are m_1 and m_2. More general formulations of (M1) and (M2) in terms of $\subseteq$ and $<$ are the following:

(M1′) $\Pi_1(m) \subseteq m_1$ and $\Pi_2(m) \subseteq m_2$

(M2′) If s is a mass distribution on $\Omega_1 \times \Omega_2$, s.t. $\Pi_1(s) \subseteq m_1$ and $\Pi_2(s) \subseteq m_2$, then $s \subseteq m$.

And for strong inclusion:

(M1″) $\Pi_1(m) < m_1$ and $\Pi_2(m) < m_2$

(M2″) If s is a mass distribution on $\Omega_1 \times \Omega_2$, s.t. $\Pi_1(s) < m_1$ and $\Pi_2(s) < m_2$, then $s < m$.

These results also hold for a universe of discourse composed of more than two characteristics.

4. MASS DISTRIBUTIONS ON L-FUZZY SETS

As described in section 2, we assume that each sensor/subexpert specifies a certain subset of possible elements in the universe of discourse. This "crisp" concept forces the sensor/subexper to decide, for each element of the universe of discourse, if he thinks that it might be the "true" element or not. But in some cases the sensor/subexpert does not specify a certain subset, but describes the set of possible elements in vague terms.

Example. Let $\Omega = \{1, \ldots, 100\}$ – the set of ages measured in years – be the universe of discourse. Translating a subexpert's statement like "*The age of the person is young*" into a crisp set is not adequate.

Example. Let $\Omega = \{\text{position}_1, \ldots, \text{position}_k\}$ – the set of possible locations of a large ship – be the universe of discourse. A certain radar sensor shows two points on the screen – a big one and a smaller one. So there are two possible locations of the ship under consideration. But the position indicated by the larger point should be preferred to the position indicated by the other point.

In order to represent vague knowledge as in the above examples we allow the sensors/subexperts to specify more than one set of possible elements. Let $(L, \leqslant)$ be a linear ordering with the least element 0 and the greatest element $1 \neq 0$. L is the set of levels of speculation. A sensor/subexpert $\theta \in \Theta$ specifies a subset of possible elements on each level of speculation $\alpha \in L$; the greater α the more speculative is the specified subset, that is, it contains less elements, because those elements that the subexpert considers nearly impossible will be left out in a more speculative level.

Formally, this concept can be described as a mapping

$$S_\theta : L \to 2^\Omega, \text{ s.t. for all } \alpha, \beta \in L : (\alpha \leqslant \beta \Rightarrow S_\theta(\beta) \subseteq S_\theta(\alpha))$$

This formal definition corresponds to the representation of an L-fuzzy set by level cuts; S_θ represents the L-fuzzy set

$$\mu_\theta : \Omega \to L, \quad \omega \to \sup\{\alpha \mid \omega \in S_\theta(\alpha)\}$$

Therefore, each sensor/subexpert specifies an L-fuzzy set on Ω. Straightforward generalization of Definition 2.1 yields:

Definition 4.1. *A function $m : L^{\Omega} \to [0,1]$, where $L^{\Omega} = \{\mu \mid \mu : \Omega \to L\}$ is the set of L-fuzzy sets on Ω, is called generalized mass distribution, if*

(i) $m(0_{\Omega}) = 0$ *(where $O_{\Omega} : \Omega \to L,\quad \omega \to 0$), and*
(ii) $\sum_{\mu : \mu \in L^{\Omega}} m(\mu) = 1$

hold.

Condition (i) could be replaced by the stronger condition

$$(i') \text{ for all } \mu \in L^{\Omega} : \left(m(\mu) > 0 \Rightarrow \sup\{\mu(\Omega) \mid \omega \in \Omega\} = 1 \right)$$

which would lead to some modifications that we will not discuss here.

Many of the results, obtained for mass distributions, belief functions, etc., make use of the fact that the universe of discourse Ω is finite, which implies that also the powerset 2^{Ω} is finite. To preserve these results for generalized mass distributions, we have to restrict ourselves to finite linear orderings L, which we presuppose in the following.

Taking an infinite ordering L like the unit interval $[0, 1]$ would lead to certain difficulties. Additional assumptions have to be made then; for example, the support $\mathbf{C}_m = \{\mu \in L^{\Omega} \mid m(\mu) > 0\}$ of m has to be at most countable, in order to assure that $\Sigma_{\mu:\mu \in L^{\Omega}} m(\mu)$ exists. If we required that $\mathbf{C}_m$ is finite, we would have to prove for each operation on generalized mass distributions that we obtain again a generalized mass distribution with finite support. But even if the support of the generalized mass distribution is finite, this property is not inherited to the corresponding generalized belief, plausibility, and commonality functions.

Thus we only consider finite orderings L. This is not a severe restriction, since the number of elements in L can be chosen to be arbitrarily large.

Now we define revision of a generalized mass distribution with respect to an L-fuzzy set η to be understood as a fuzzy evidence. Thus we obtain a definition analogous to 2.2.

Definition 4.2. *Let m be a generalized mass distribution on Ω and let $\eta \in L^{\Omega}$, s.t.* $\mathrm{pl}_m(\eta) > 0$. *The generalized mass distribution*

$$m_{\eta} : L^{\Omega} \to [0,1], \quad \mu \to \begin{cases} \dfrac{\sum_{\nu:\nu \cap \eta = \mu} m(\nu)}{\mathrm{pl}_m(\eta)} & \text{if } \mu \neq 0_{\Omega} \\ 0 & \text{otherwise} \end{cases}$$

is called a revised generalized mass distribution.

Definition 4.3. *Let Ω' be a refinement of Ω with refinement mapping $\hat{\Pi}$ and let m' be a generalized mass distribution on Ω'. The projection* $\Pi(m')$ of m' *to Ω is defined by*

$$\Pi(m') : L^{\Omega} \to [0,1], \quad \mu \to \sum_{\mu' \in L^{\Omega'} : \Pi(\mu') = \mu} m'(\mu'),$$

where the L-fuzzy set $\Pi(\mu')$ on Ω is defined by

$$\Pi(\mu')(\omega) = \sup\left\{\mu(\omega') \mid \omega' \in \hat{\Pi}(\{\omega\})\right\}.$$

The definition of the concept of specialization for generalized mass distributions is now straightforward.

Definition 4.4. *Let s and t be two generalized mass distributions on Ω. s is a specialization of t ($s \subseteq t$), if there is a refinement Ω' of Ω with refinement mapping $\hat{\Pi}$ and two generalized mass distributions s' and t' on Ω', s.t.*

(i) $\exists \eta' \in L^{\Omega'} : s' = t'_{\eta'}$
(ii) $s = \Pi(s')$
(iii) $t = \Pi(t')$

An analogous version of Theorem 2.1. holds also for generalized mass distributions.

Theorem 4.1. *Let s and t be two generalized mass distributions on Ω. The following three statements are equivalent:*

(i) $s \subseteq t$

(ii) for all $\mu \in L^{\Omega} : \left(q_t(\mu) = 0 \Rightarrow q_s(\mu) = 0 \right)$

(iii) $\exists h : L^{\Omega} \times L^{\Omega} \to [0,1]$, *s.t.*

(a) for all $\mu \in L^{\Omega} : t(\mu) = \sum_{\eta : \eta \in L^{\Omega}} h(\mu, \eta)$

(b) for all $\mu, \eta \in L^{\Omega} : \left(h(\mu, \eta) > 0 \Rightarrow \eta \subseteq \mu \right)$

(c) for all $\eta \in L^{\Omega} - \{0_{\Omega}\} : s(\eta) = \dfrac{\sum_{\mu : \mu \in L^{\Omega}} h(\mu, \eta)}{1 - \sum_{\mu : \mu \in L^{\Omega}} h(\mu, 0_{\Omega})}$

Considering the aggregation of knowledge on various characteristics as was done in section 3 for ordinary mass distributions, we encounter some difficulties if we have to deal with generalized mass distributions. If m_i is a generalized mass distribution on Ω_i $(i = 1, 2)$, then there is in general no generalized mass distribution m on $\Omega_1 \times \Omega_2$, s.t. $\Pi_1(m) = m_1$ and $\Pi_2(m) = m_2$.

Example. Let $\Omega_1 = \Omega_2 = \{\omega\}$, $L = \{0, \frac{1}{2}, 1\}$,

$$m_1(\mu) = \begin{cases} 1 & \text{if } \mu(\omega) = 1 \\ 0 & \text{otherwise} \end{cases} \quad \text{and } m_2(\mu) = \begin{cases} 1 & \text{if } \mu(\omega) = 1/2 \\ 0 & \text{otherwise.} \end{cases}$$

Then for all generalized mass distributions m on $\Omega_1 \times \Omega_2$

$$\Pi_1(m) \neq m_1 \quad \text{or} \quad \Pi_2(m) \neq m_2$$

holds.

Thus condition (M1) described in section 3 cannot be satisfied in the case of generalized mass distributions. But we are able to characterize the aggregation of two generalized mass distributions in terms of (M1′) and (M2′).

Theorem 4.2. *Let m_i be generalized mass distributions on Ω_i ($i = 1,2$). Let*

$$m : L^{\Omega_1 \times \Omega_2} \to [0,1], \quad \mu \to \sum_{\substack{\mu_1 \in L^{\Omega_1},\, \mu_2 \in L^{\Omega_2} \\ \mu_1 \times \mu_2 = \mu}} m_1(\mu_1) \cdot m_2(\mu_2).$$

Then we have

(i) $\Pi_1(m) \subseteq m_1$ and $\Pi_2(m) \subseteq m_2$

(ii) *If s is a generalized mass distribution on $\Omega_1 \times \Omega_2$, s.t. $\Pi_1(s) \subseteq m_1$ and $\Pi_2(s) \subseteq m_2$, then $s \subseteq m$.*

Again, the generalized mass distribution obtained by applying Dempster's rule of combination to the vacuous extensions of m_1 and m_2 turns out to be the appropriate aggregation of the generalized mass distributions m_1 and m_2 in the product space $\Omega_1 \times \Omega_2$.

5. CONCLUSIONS

The concept of specialization represents the possible updatings of a given (generalized) mass distribution. Considering a product space in which each characteristic of the domain is represented by a coordinate space, the aggregation of knowledge on single characteristics can be carried out by applying Dempster's rule of combination to the vacuous extensions of the (generalized) mass distributions on the coordinate spaces.

A tool for the efficient computation of knowledge propagation with mass distributions in a product space was implemented on TI-Micro Explorer under KEE in cooperation with the German company Dornier and can be used in the field of data fusion (Kruse, Schwecke, and Heinsohn, 1991; Kruse, Schwecke, and Klawonn, 1991). Although the generalization to *L*-fuzzy sets is not yet implemented, the results of this paper guarantee that no problems are encountered in the case of generalized mass distributions.

We emphasized the strict use of the semantics, described for (generalized) mass distributions in this paper, in order to motivate and clarify the introduced concepts. Mass distributions are understood as representations of vague knowledge in the form of subsets provided by a weighted set of sensors, subexperts, or contexts. A more general view of this context model is described by Gebhardt and Kruse (1991).

BIBLIOGRAPHY

Dubois D., and Prade H. (1986a). On the unicity of dempster's rule of combination. *Int. J. Intelligent Systems* 1: 133–42.

Dubois D, and Prade H. (1986b). A set theoretic view of belief functions. *Int. J. General Systems* 12: 193–226.

Gebhardt, J. and Kruse R. (1991). The context model – A uniform approach to vagueness and uncertainty. In R. Lowen and M. Roubens (eds.), *Proceedings of the Fourth IFSA Congress: Computer, Management & System Science, IFSA*, Brussels, pp. 82–85.

Kruse, R. and Schwecke E. (1990). Specialization – A new concept for uncertainty handling with belief functions. *Int. J. General Systems* 18: 49–60.

Kruse, R., Schwecke E., and Heinsohn, J. (1991). *Uncertainty and vagueness in knowledge based systems: Numerical methods.* Berlin: Springer-Verlag.

Kruse R., Schwecke, E. and Klawonn, F. (1991). On a tool for reasoning with mass distributions. In J. Mylopoulos and R. Reiter (eds.), *Proceedings of the Twelfth International Joint Conference on Artificial Intelligence (IJCAI-91)*, Vol. 2, pp. 1190–95. San Mateo, CA: Morgan Kaufmann.

Shafer, G. (1976). *A mathematical theory of evidence.* Princeton, NJ: Princeton University Press.

Smets, P. (1988). Belief functions. In P. Smets, E. H. Mamdani, D. Dubois, and H. Prade (eds.), *Non-standard-logics for automated reasoning*, pp. 253–86. London: Academic Press.

Smets, P. (1990). The transferable belief model and possibility theory. *Proc. NAFIPS-90*, pp. 215–18.

Yager R. (198). Non-monotonic compatibility relations in the theory of evidence. *Int. J. Man-Machine Studies* 29: pp. 517–37.

12 Rough membership functions

Zdzisław PAWLAK and Andrzej SKOWRON

Abstract: A variety of numerical approaches for reasoning with uncertainty have been investigated in the literature. We propose *rough membership functions* (or *rm-functions*, for short) as a basis for such a reasoning. These functions have values in the interval [0, 1] of the real numbers and they are computable on the basis of the observable information about the objects rather than on the basis of the objects themselves. We investigate properties of the *rm*-functions. In particular we show that our approach is intensional with respect to the class of all information systems (Pawlak, 1991). As a consequence we point out some differences between the *rm*-functions and the fuzzy membership functions (Zadeh, 1965); the *rm*-function values for $X \cup Y (X \cap Y)$ cannot be computed in general by applying the operation max (min) to the *rm*-function values for X and Y. We propose the algorithm for computing the *rm*-functions for the sets from a given field of sets.

Keywords: reasoning with incomplete information, rough sets, fuzzy sets, evidence theory.

1. INTRODUCTION

One of the fundamental problems studied in artificial intelligence is related to the object classification that is the problem of associating a particular object to one of many predefined sets. In studing that problem, our approach is based on the observation that the classification of objects is performed on the basis of the accessible information about them. Objects with the same accessible information will be considered as indiscernible (Pawlak, 1991). Therefore we are faced with the problem of determining whether or not an object belongs to a given set when only some properties (i.e., attribute values) of the object are accessible.

We introduce the concept of a *rough membership function* (*rm*-functions, for short), which allows us to measure the degree with which any object with given attribute values belongs to a given set X. The information about objects is stored in data tables called information systems (Pawlak, 1991). Any *rm*-function $\mu_X^{\mathbf{A}}$ is defined relatively to a given information system **A** and a given set X of objects.

The paper is structured as follows. Section 2 contains a brief discussion of information systems (Pawlak, 1991), information functions (Skowron, 1991b), and rough sets (Pawlak, 1991). In Section 3 we define a partition of boundary regions (Skowron, 1991a) and we present some basic properties of this partition, which we apply later. In Section 4 we define the *rm*-functions and we study their basic properties. In Section 5 we present formulas for computing the *rm*-function values $\mu_{X\cup Y}^{\mathbf{A}}(x)$ and $\mu_{X\cap Y}^{\mathbf{A}}(x)$ from the values $\mu_X^{\mathbf{A}}(x)$ and $\mu_Y^{\mathbf{A}}(x)$ (when it is possible, i.e., when classified objects are not in a particular boundary region) if information encoded in the information system **A** is accessible. In the construction of those formulas we apply a partition of boundary regions related to X and Y defined in Section 3. One can interpret that result as follows: the computation of *rm*-function values $\mu_{X\cup Y}^{\mathbf{A}}(x)$ and $\mu_{X\cap Y}^{\mathbf{A}}(x)$ (if one excludes a particular boundary region!) is *extensional* under the condition that the information system is fixed.

We also show, in Section 5, that our approach is *intensional* with respect to the set of all information systems (with a universe including sets X and Y); namely it is not possible, in general, to compute the *rm*-function values $\mu_{X\cup Y}^{\mathbf{A}}(x)$ and $\mu_{X\cap Y}^{\mathbf{A}}(x)$ from the values $\mu_X^{\mathbf{A}}(x)$ and $\mu_Y^{\mathbf{A}}(x)$ when information about **A** is not accessible (Theorem 3). Also in Section 5, we specify the maximal classes of information systems such that the computation of *rm*-function values for union and intersection is extensional when related to those classes, and is defined by the operations *min* and *max* as in the fuzzy set approach (Zadeh, 1965; Duois and Prade, 1980), that is, the values $\mu_{X\cup Y}^{\mathbf{A}}(x)$ and $\mu_{X\cap Y}^{\mathbf{A}}(x)$ are obtained by applying the operation *min* and the operation *max* to the values $\mu_X^{\mathbf{A}}(x)$ and $\mu_Y^{\mathbf{A}}(x)$, respectively (if **A** belongs to those maximal classes).

In Section 6 we present an algorithm for computing the *rm*-function values $\mu_X^A(x)$ for $x \in X$, where X is any set generated by the set theoretical operations $\cup$, $\cap$, - from a given family of finite sets.

2. INFORMATION SYSTEMS AND ROUGH SETS

Information systems (sometimes called data tables, attribute-value systems, condition-action tables etc.) are used for representing knowledge. The information system notion presented here is due to Pawlak (1991) and was investigated by several researchers (see the references in Pawlak, 1991).

Rough sets have been introduced as a tool to deal with inexact, uncertain, or vague knowledge in artificial intelligence applications as, for example, knowledge-based systems in medicine, natural language processing, pattern recognition, decision systems, approximate reasoning. Rough sets have been intensively studied since 1982 and many practical applications based on the theory of rough sets have already been implemented.

In this section we present some basic notions related to information systems and rough sets that will be necessary for understanding our results.

An information system is a pair $\mathbf{A} = (U, A)$, where

U – a nonempty, finite set called the *universe* and
A – a nonempty, finite set of *attributes*, i.e.,
$a : U \to V_a$ for $a \in A$,
where V_a is called the *value set* of a.

With every subset of attributes $B \subseteq A$ we associate a binary relation $IND(B)$, called *B-indiscernibility relation*, and defined as:

$$IND(B) = \{(x, y) \in U^2 : \text{for every } a \in B,\ a(x) = a(y)\}$$

By $[x]_{IND(B)}$ or $[x]_B$ we denote the equivalence class of the equivalence relation $IND(B)$ generated by x, i.e., the set $\{y \in U : xIND(B)y\}$.

We have that

$$IND(B) = \bigcap_{a \in B} IND(a)$$

If $xIND(B)y$, then we say that the objects x and y are indiscernible with respect to attributes from B. In other words, we cannot distinguish x from y in terms of attributes in B.

Some subsets of objects in an information system cannot be expressed exactly in terms of the available attributes; they can be only roughly defined.

If $\mathbf{A} = (U, A)$ is an information system, $B \subseteq A$ and $X \subseteq U$, then the sets

$$\underline{B}X = \{x \in U : [x]_B \subseteq X\} \text{ and } \bar{B}X = \{x \in X : [x]_B \cap X \neq \emptyset\}$$

are called the *B-lower* and the *B-upper approximation of X* in $\mathbf{A}$, respectively.

The set $BN_B(X) = \bar{B}X - \underline{B}X$ will be called the *B-boundary of X*.

Clearly, $\underline{B}X$ is the set of all elements of U, which can be with certainty classified as elements of X with respect to the values of attributes from B; and $\bar{B}X$ is the set of those elements of U that can be possibly classified as elements of X with respect of the values of the attributes from B; finally, $BN_B(X)$ is the set of elements that can be classified neither in X nor in $-X$ on the basis of the values of attributes from B.

A set X is said to be *B-definable* if $\bar{B}X = \underline{B}X$. It is easy to observe that $\underline{B}X$ is the greatest B-definable set contained in X, whereas $\bar{B}X$ is the smallest B-definable set containing X. One can observe that a set is B-definable iff it is the union of some equivalence classes of the indiscernibility relation $IND(B)$.

By $\mathbf{P}(X)$ we denote the powerset of X.

Every information system $\mathbf{A} = (U, A)$ determines an *information function*

$$Inf_{\mathbf{A}} : U \to \mathbf{P}(A \times \bigcup_{a \in A} V_a)$$

defined as

$$Inf_{\mathbf{A}}(x) = \{(a, a(x)) : a \in A\}$$

Hence, $xIND(A)y$ iff $Inf_{\mathbf{A}}(x) = Inf_{\mathbf{A}}(y)$.

We restrict our considerations in the paper to the information functions related to information systems but our results can be extended to the case of more general information functions (Skowron, 1991b). One can consider as *information function* an arbitrary function f defined on the set of objects U with values in some computable set C.

For example, one may take as the set U of objects the set $Tot_{\mathbf{A}}$ of total elements in the Scott information system $\mathbf{A}$ (Scott, 1982) and as

C a computable (an accessible) subset of the set D of sentences in $\mathbf{A}$. The information function f related to C can be defined as follows:

$$f(x) = x \cap C \text{ for } x \in Tot_{\mathbf{A}}$$

Every such general information function f defines the indiscernibility relation $IND(f) \subseteq U \times U$ as follows:

$$x IND(f) y \quad \text{iff} \quad f(x) = f(y)$$

3. AN APPROXIMATION OF CLASSIFICATIONS

In this section we introduce and study the notion of approximation of classification. It was preliminarily considered in Skowron (1991a) and Skowron and Grzymała-Busse (1991). The main idea is based on observation that it is possible to classify boundary regions corresponding to sets from a given classification, that is, a partition of object universe.

Let $\mathbf{A} = (U, A)$ be an information system and let $\mathbf{X}$ and $\mathbf{Z}$ be families of subsets of U such that $\mathbf{Z} \subseteq X$ and $|\mathbf{Z}| > 1$, where $|\mathbf{Z}|$ denotes the cardinality of $\mathbf{Z}$. The set

$$\bigcap_{X \in \mathbf{Z}} BN_A(X) \cap \bigcap_{X \in \mathbf{X} - \mathbf{Z}} (U - BN_A(X))$$

is said to be the $\mathbf{Z}$-boundary region defined by $\mathbf{X}$ and $\mathbf{A}$ and is denoted by $Bd_{\mathbf{A}}(\mathbf{Z}, \mathbf{X})$.

By $CLASS\_APPR_{\mathbf{A}}(\mathbf{X})$ we denote the set family

$$\{\underline{A}X: X \in \mathbf{X}\} \cup \{Bd_{\mathbf{A}}(\mathbf{Z}, \mathbf{X}): \mathbf{Z} \subseteq \mathbf{X} \text{ and } |\mathbf{Z}| > 1\}$$

From the above definitions we get the following proposition (Skowron, 1991):

Proposition 1. Let $\mathbf{A} = (U, A)$ be an information system and let $\mathbf{X}$ be a family of pairwise disjoint subsets of U such that $\bigcup \mathbf{X} = U$. Let $\mathbf{Z} \subseteq \mathbf{X}$ and $|\mathbf{Z}| > 1$. Then

(i) The set $Bd_{\mathbf{A}}(\mathbf{Z}, \mathbf{X})$ is definable in $\mathbf{A}$;
(ii) $CLASS\_APPR_{\mathbf{A}}(\mathbf{X}) - \{\varnothing\}$ is a partition of $\mathbf{U}$;
(iii) If $x \in Bd_{\mathbf{A}}(\mathbf{Z}, \mathbf{X})$ then $[x]_A \subseteq \bigcup \mathbf{Z}$;
(iv) If $x \in Bd_{\mathbf{A}}(\mathbf{Z}, \mathbf{X})$ then for every $X \in \mathbf{X}$ the following equivalence is true:

$$[x]_A \cap X \neq \varnothing \quad \text{iff} \quad X \in \mathbf{Z};$$

(v) The following equality holds:

$$\underline{A}(\bigcup \mathbf{Y}) = \bigcup_{X \in \mathbf{Y}} \underline{A}X \cup \bigcup_{|\mathbf{Z}|>1, \mathbf{Z} \subseteq \mathbf{Y}} Bd_{\mathbf{A}}(\mathbf{Z},\mathbf{X}), \text{ where } \mathbf{Y} \subseteq \mathbf{X}.$$

Proof. (i) If $x \in Bd_{\mathbf{A}}(\mathbf{Z},\mathbf{X})$ then $x \in BN_{\mathbf{A}}(X)$ for any $X \in \mathbf{Z}$ and $x \in U - BN_{\mathbf{A}}(X)$ for any $X \in \mathbf{X} - \mathbf{Z}$. From the definability in **A** of sets $BN_{\mathbf{A}}(X)$ and $U - BN_{\mathbf{A}}(X)$ for $X \subseteq U$ we have $[x]_A \subseteq BN_{\mathbf{A}}(X)$ for any $X \in \mathbf{Z}$ and $[x]_A \subseteq U - BN_{\mathbf{A}}(X)$ for any $X \in \mathbf{X} - \mathbf{Z}$. Hence $[x]_A \subseteq Bd_{\mathbf{A}}(\mathbf{Z},\mathbf{X})$. We proved that $Bd_{\mathbf{A}}(\mathbf{Z},\mathbf{X}) \subseteq \underline{A}(Bd_{\mathbf{A}}(\mathbf{Z},\mathbf{X}))$. Since $Bd_{\mathbf{A}}(\mathbf{Z},\mathbf{X}) \supseteq \underline{A}(Bd_{\mathbf{A}}(\mathbf{Z},\mathbf{X})$ we get $Bd_A(\mathbf{Z},\mathbf{X}) = \underline{A}(Bd_A(\mathbf{Z},\mathbf{X}))$.

(ii) It is easy to observe that $CLASS\_APPR_{\mathbf{A}}(\mathbf{X})$ is a family of pairwise disjoint sets. We prove that $\bigcup CLASS\_APPR_{\mathbf{A}}(\mathbf{X}) = U$. If $x \in U$ then $x \in X$ for some $X \in \mathbf{X}$. If $x \in \underline{A}X$ then $x \in CLASS\_APPR_{\mathbf{A}}(\mathbf{X})$, otherwise $x \in \bar{A}X - \underline{A}X$. In the latter case let $\mathbf{Z}_x = \{X \in \mathbf{X} : [x]_A \cap X \neq \emptyset\}$. Then we have $|\mathbf{Z}_x| > 1$ and $x \in Bd_{\mathbf{A}}(\mathbf{Z}_x,\mathbf{X})$.

(iii) Let $x \in Bd_{\mathbf{A}}(\mathbf{Z},\mathbf{X})$. Suppose that $y \notin \bigcup \mathbf{Z}$ for some $y \in [x]_A$. Since $\bigcup \mathbf{X} = U$, we have $y \in \bigcup \mathbf{X} - \bigcup \mathbf{Z}$. Hence $y \in X_0$ for some $X_0 \in \mathbf{X} - \mathbf{Z}$. In the consequence $X_0 \cap [y]_A = X_0 \cap [x]_A \neq \emptyset$. If $x \in Bd_A(\mathbf{Z},\mathbf{X})$ then $x \in U - BN_A(X)$ for $X \in \mathbf{Z} - \mathbf{Z}$. Since $U - BN_A(X)$ is definable in **A** we obtain $[x]_A \subseteq U - BN_A(X) = (U - \bar{A}X) \cup \underline{A}X$. Hence $[x]_A \subseteq \underline{A}X_0$ or $[x]_A \subseteq U - \bar{A}X_0$. Since $X_0 \cap [x]_A \neq \emptyset$ we get

(*) $[x]_A \subseteq \underline{A}X_0$

From the assumption $x \in Bd_{\mathbf{A}}(\mathbf{Z},\mathbf{X})$ we have also $x \in BN_A(X)$ for any $X \in \mathbf{Z}$, so

(**) $[x]_A \cap X \neq \emptyset$ for any $X \in \mathbf{Z}$

From (*) and (**) we would have $X \cap X_0 \neq \emptyset$ for any $X \in \mathbf{Z}$ but this contradicts the assumption that **X** is a family of pairwise disjoint sets.

(iv) Let $x \in Bd_{\mathbf{A}}(\mathbf{Z},\mathbf{X})$ and $X \in \mathbf{X}$. Suppose that $[x]_A \cap X \neq \emptyset$, i.e., $x \in BN_A(X)$. Hence from the definition of $Bd_A(\mathbf{Z},\mathbf{X})$ we have $X \in \mathbf{Z}$. If $X \in \mathbf{Z}$ then we have $x \in BN_A(X)$. Hence $[x]_A \cap X \neq \emptyset$.

(v) ($\subseteq$) If $x \in Bd_{\mathbf{A}}(\mathbf{Z},\mathbf{X})$ we have from (iii) that $x \in \underline{A} \bigcup \mathbf{Z} \subseteq \underline{A} \bigcup \mathbf{Y}$. We also have $\underline{A}X \subseteq \underline{A} \bigcup \mathbf{Y}$ for any $X \in \mathbf{Y}$.

($\supseteq$) Let $x \in \underline{A} \bigcup \mathbf{Y}$, i.e., $[x] \subseteq \bigcup \mathbf{Y}$. If $x \notin \underline{A}X$ for a certain $X \in \mathbf{Y}$ then let $\mathbf{Z}_x = \{X \in \mathbf{Y} : [x]_A \cap X \neq \emptyset\}$. Hence $|\mathbf{Z}_x| > 1$ and $[x]_A \subseteq \bigcup \mathbf{Z}_x$. Thus, we have $x \in Bd_{\mathbf{A}}(\mathbf{Z}_x,\mathbf{X})$.

4. ROUGH MEMBERSHIP FUNCTIONS: DEFINITION AND BASIC PROPERTIES

One of the fundamental notions of set theory is the membership relation, usually denoted by $\in$. When one considers subsets of a given universe it is possible to apply the characteristic functions for expressing the fact whether or not a given element belongs to a given set. We discuss the case when only partial information about objects is accessible. In this section we show it is possible to extend characteristic function notion to that case.

Let $\mathbf{A} = (U, A)$ be an information system and let $\emptyset \neq X \subseteq U$. The *rough* **A**-*membership function of the set X* (or *rm*-function, for short) denoted by $\mu_X^{\mathbf{A}}$, is defined as follows:

$$\mu_X^{\mathbf{A}}(x) = \frac{|[x]_A \cap X|}{|[x]_A|}, \text{ for } x \in U, \ \mu_\emptyset \equiv 0.$$

The above definition is illustrated in Figure 12.1.

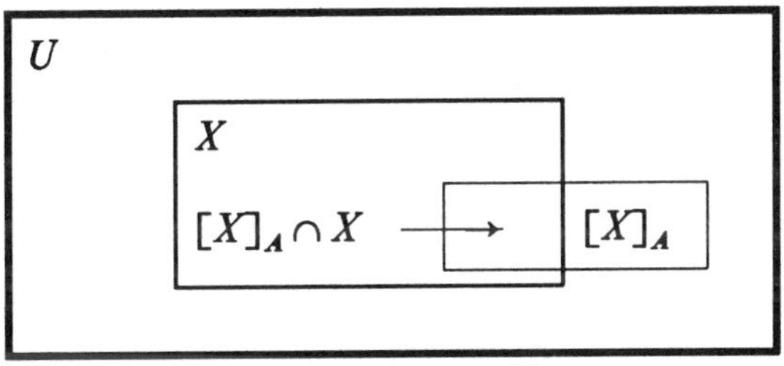

Figure 12.1

One can observe a similarity between the expression on the right-hand side of the above definition and that expression used to define the conditional probability.

From the definition of $\mu_X^{\mathbf{A}}$ we have the following proposition characterizing some basic properties of *rm*-functions.

Proposition 2. Let $\mathbf{A} = (U, A)$ be an information system and let $X, Y \subseteq U$.

The rm-functions have the following properties:

(i) $\mu_X^{\mathbf{A}}(x) = 1$ iff $x \in \underline{A}X$;
(ii) $\mu_X^{\mathbf{A}}(x) = 0$ iff $x \in U - \bar{A}X$;

(iii) $0 < \mu_X^{\mathbf{A}}(x) < 1$ iff $x \in BN_{\mathbf{A}}(X)$;
(iv) If $IND(A) = \{(x,x): x \in U\}$ then $\mu_X^{\mathbf{A}}$ is the characteristic function of X;
(v) If $xIND(A)y$ then $\mu_X^{\mathbf{A}}(x) = \mu_X^{\mathbf{A}}(y)$;
(vi) $\mu_{U-X}^{\mathbf{A}}(x) = 1 - \mu_X^{\mathbf{A}}(x)$ for any $x \in X$;
(vii) $\mu_{X \cup Y}^{\mathbf{A}}(x) \geqslant \max(\mu_X^{\mathbf{A}}(x), \mu_Y^{\mathbf{A}}(x))$ for any $x \in U$;
(viii) $\mu_{X \cap Y}^{\mathbf{A}}(x) \leqslant \min(\mu_X^{\mathbf{A}}(x), \mu_Y^{\mathbf{A}}(x))$ for any $x \in U$;
(ix) If $\mathbf{X}$ is a family of pairwise disjoint subsets of U then

$$\mu_{\cup \mathbf{X}}^{\mathbf{A}}(x) = \sum_{X \in \mathbf{X}} \mu_X^{\mathbf{A}}(x) \text{ for any } x \in U.$$

Proof.

(i) We have $x \in \underline{A}X$ iff $[x]_A \subseteq X$ iff $\mu_X^{\mathbf{A}}(x) = 1$.
(ii) We have $x \in U - \bar{A}X$ iff $[x]_A \cap X = \emptyset$ iff $\mu_X^{\mathbf{A}}(x) = 0$.
(iii) We have $x \in BN_{\mathbf{A}}(X)$ iff ($[x]_A \cap X \neq \emptyset$ and $[x]_A \cap (U - X) \neq \emptyset$) iff ($\mu_X^{\mathbf{A}}(x) > 0$ and $\mu_X^{\mathbf{A}}(x) < 1$).
(iv) If $IND(A) = \{(x,x) : x \in U\}$ then $|[x]_A| = 1$ for any $x \in X$. Moreover $|[x]_A \cap X| = 1$ if $x \in X$ and $|[x]_A \cap X| = 0$ if $x \in U - X$.
(v) Since $[x]_A = [y]_A$ we have $\mu_X^{\mathbf{A}}(x) = \mu_X^{\mathbf{A}}(y)$.
(vi) $\mu_{U-X}^{\mathbf{A}}(x) = \dfrac{|[x]_A \cap (U - X)|}{|[x]_A|} = 1 - \dfrac{|[x]_A \cap X|}{|[x]_A|} = 1 - \mu_X^{\mathbf{A}}(x)$.
(vii) $\mu_{X \cup Y}^{\mathbf{A}}(x) = \dfrac{|[x]_A \cap (X \cup Y)|}{|[x]_A|} \geqslant \dfrac{|[x]_A \cap X)|}{|[x]_A|} = \mu_X^{\mathbf{A}}(x)$. In a similar way one can obtain $\mu_{X \cup Y}^{\mathbf{A}}(x) \geqslant \mu_Y^{\mathbf{A}}(x)$.
(viii) Proof runs as in case (vi).
(ix) $\mu_{\cup \mathbf{X}}^{\mathbf{A}}(x) = \dfrac{|[x]_A \cap \bigcup \mathbf{X}|}{|[x]_A|} = \dfrac{|\bigcup \{[x]_A \cap X : X \in \mathbf{X}|}{|[x]_A|} = \sum_{X \in \mathbf{X}} \mu_X^{\mathbf{A}}(x)$

The last equality follows from the assumption that $\mathbf{X}$ is a family of pairwise disjoint sets.

The set $\{Inf_{\mathbf{A}}(x): x \in U\}$ is called the A-information set and it is denoted by INF(A). For every $X \subseteq U$ we define the rough A-information function, denoted by $\hat{\mu}_X^{\mathbf{A}}$, as:

$$\hat{\mu}_X^{\mathbf{A}}(u) = \mu_X^{\mathbf{A}}(x), \text{ where } u \in \mathrm{INF}(\mathbf{A}) \text{ and } Inf_{\mathbf{A}}(x) = u$$

The correctness of the above definition follows from (v) in Proposition 1.

If $\mathbf{A} = (U, A)$ is an information system then we define rough $\mathbf{A}$-inclusion of subsets of U in the standard way:

$$X \leqslant_{\mathbf{A}} Y \quad \text{iff} \quad \mu_X^{\mathbf{A}}(x) \leqslant \mu_Y^{\mathbf{A}}(x) \text{ for any } x \in U$$

Proposition 3. If $X \leqslant_{\mathbf{A}} Y$ then $\underline{A}X \subseteq \underline{A}Y$ and $\bar{A}X \subseteq \bar{A}Y$.

Proof. Follows from Proposition 2 (see (i) and (ii)).

The above definition of the rough $\mathbf{A}$-inclusion is not equivalent to the one in Pawlak (1991). Indeed, in Pawlak (1991) the reverse implication to that formulated in Proposition 2 is not valid.

One can show that they are equivalent for any information system $\mathbf{A}$ only if $\bar{A}X \subseteq \underline{A}Y$. This is a consequence of our definition taking into account some additional information about objects from the boundary regions.

5. ROUGH MEMBERSHIP FUNCTIONS FOR UNION AND INTERSECTION

Now we present some results obtained as a consequence of our assumption that objects are observable by means of partial information about them represented by attribute values. In this section we prove that the inequalities in (vii) and (viii) of Proposition 1 cannot be in general substituted by the equalities.

We also prove that for some boundary regions it is not possible to compute the values of the *rm*-functions for union $X \cup Y$ and intersection $X \cap Y$ knowing the values of *rm*-functions for X and Y only (if information about information systems is not accessible and does not hold some special relations between sets X and Y). These results show that the assumptions about properties of the fuzzy membership functions (Dubois and Prade, 1980, p. 11) related to the union and intersection should be modified if one would like to take into account that objects are classified on the basis of a partial information about them. We present also the necessary and sufficient conditions for the following equalities (which are the ones used in fuzzy set theory) to be true for any $x \in U$.

$$\mu_{X \cup Y}^{\mathbf{A}}(x) = \max(\mu_X^{\mathbf{A}}(x), \mu_Y^{\mathbf{A}}(x))$$

$$\mu_{X \cap Y}^{\mathbf{A}}(x) = \min(\mu_X^{\mathbf{A}}(x), \mu_Y^{\mathbf{A}}(x))$$

These conditions are expressed by means of the boundary regions of a partition of U defined by sets X and Y or by means of some relationships that should hold for the sets X and Y. In particular we show that the above equalities are true for arbitrary information system **A** iff $X \subseteq Y$ or $Y \subseteq X$.

First we prove the following two lemmas.

Lemma 1. Let $\mathbf{A} = (U, A)$ be an information system, $X, Y \subseteq U$ and $\mathbf{X} = \{X \cap Y, X \cap -Y, -X \cap Y, -X \cap -Y\}$.

If $x \in U - Bd_A(\mathbf{X}, \mathbf{X})$, then

$\mu^{\mathbf{A}}_{X \cap Y}(x) =$

if $x \in Bd_{\mathbf{A}}(\{X \cap -Y, -X \cap Y\}, \mathbf{X}) \cup Bd_{\mathbf{A}}(\{X \cap -Y, -X \cap Y, -X \cap -Y\}, \mathbf{X})$

then 0

else if $x \in Bd_{\mathbf{A}}(\{X \cap Y, X \cap -Y, -X \cap Y)$ then $\mu^{\mathbf{A}}_X(x) + \mu^{\mathbf{A}}_Y(x) - 1$

else $\min(\mu^{\mathbf{A}}_X(x), \mu^{\mathbf{A}}_Y(x))$

Proof. In the proof we apply property (iii) from Proposition 1. Let $x \in Bd_{\mathbf{A}}(\{X \cap -Y, -X \cap Y\} \cup Bd_{\mathbf{A}}(\{X \cap -Y, -X \cap Y, -X \cap -Y\}$. Hence $[x]_A \subseteq (X \cap -Y) \cup (-X \cap Y) \cup (-X \cap -Y)$, so $[x]_A \cap (X \cap Y) = \varnothing$ and $\mu^{\mathbf{A}}_{X \cap Y}(x) = 0$.

If $x \in Bd_{\mathbf{A}}(\{X \cap Y, X \cap -Y, -X \cap Y\}, \mathbf{X})$ then $[x]_A \subseteq (X \cap Y \cup X \cap -Y \cup -X \cap Y)$. Hence, $[x]_A = [x]_A \cap (X \cap Y) \cup [x]_A \cap (X \cap -Y) \cup [x]_A \cap (-X \cap Y)$, so $[x]_A = [x]_A \cap X \cup [x]_A \cap Y$.

We obtain $|[x]_A| = |[x]_A \cap X| + |[x]_A \cap Y| - |[x]_A \cap (X \cap Y)|$. Hence $\mu^{\mathbf{A}}_{X \cap Y}(x) = \mu^{\mathbf{A}}_X(x) + \mu^{\mathbf{A}}_Y(x) - 1$.

If $x \in \underline{A}(X \cap Y)$, then $[x]_A \subseteq X \cap Y$. Hence $\mu^{\mathbf{A}}_{X \cap Y}(x) = 1$. We have also $[x]_A \subseteq X$ and $[x]_A \subseteq Y$ because $X \cap Y \subseteq X$ and $X \cap Y \subseteq Y$. Hence $\mu^{\mathbf{A}}_X(x) = \mu^{\mathbf{A}}_Y(x) = 1$.

If $x \in \underline{A}(X \cap -Y)$ then $[x]_A \subseteq X \cap -Y$. Hence $[x]_A \cap (X \cap Y) = \varnothing$ and $[x]_A \cap Y \subseteq (X \cap -Y) \cap Y = \varnothing$, so $\mu^{\mathbf{A}}_{X \cap Y}(x) = \min(\mu^{\mathbf{A}}_X(x), \mu^{\mathbf{A}}_Y(x))$.

If $x \in \underline{A}(-X \cap Y)$ the proof is analogous to the latter case.

If $x \in \underline{A}(-X \cap -Y)$ we obtain $\mu^{\mathbf{A}}_{X \cap Y}(x) = \mu^{\mathbf{A}}_X(x) = \mu^{\mathbf{A}}_Y(x) = 0$.

If $x \in Bd_{\mathbf{A}}(\{X \cap Y, X \cap -Y\}, \mathbf{X})$ we have $[x]_A = [x]_A \cap (X \cap Y) \cup [x]_A \cap (X \cap -Y)$. Hence $[x]_A \cap (X \cap Y) = [x]_A \cap Y$ and $[x]_A = [x]_A \cap X \subseteq X$. Hence $\mu^{\mathbf{A}}_{X \cap Y}(x) = \mu^{\mathbf{A}}_Y(x) \leqslant \mu^{\mathbf{A}}_X(x) = 1$.

If $x \in Bd_{\mathbf{A}}(\{X \cap Y, -X \cap Y\}, \mathbf{X})$ the proof is analogous to the latter case.

If $x \in Bd_{\mathbf{A}}(\{X \cap -Y, -X \cap -Y), \mathbf{X})$ one can calculate $\mu^{\mathbf{A}}_{X \cap Y}(x) = \mu^{\mathbf{A}}_Y(x) = 0 \leqslant \mu^{\mathbf{A}}_X(x)$. Similarly, in the case when $x \in Bd_{\mathbf{A}}(\{-X \cap Y, -X \cap -Y\}, \mathbf{X})$ one can calculate that $\mu^{\mathbf{A}}_{X \cap Y}(x) = \mu^{\mathbf{A}}_X(x) = 0 \leqslant \mu^{\mathbf{A}}_Y(x)$.

If $x \in Bd_{\mathbf{A}}(\{X \cap Y, -X \cap -Y\}, \mathbf{X})$ we have $\mu^{\mathbf{A}}_{X \cap Y}(x) = \mu^{\mathbf{A}}_{X}(x) = \mu^{\mathbf{A}}_{Y}(x)$.

Lemma 2. Let $\mathbf{A} = (U, A)$ be an information system, $X, Y \subseteq U$ and $\mathbf{X} = \{X \cap Y, X \cap -Y, -X \cap Y, -X \cap -Y\}$. If $x \in U - Bd_{\mathbf{A}}(\mathbf{X}, \mathbf{X})$ then

If $x \in U - Bd_A(\mathbf{X}, \mathbf{X})$, then

$\mu^{\mathbf{A}}_{X \cup Y}(x) =$

if $x \in Bd_{\mathbf{A}}(\{X \cap -Y, -X \cap Y\}, \mathbf{X}) \cup Bd_{\mathbf{A}}(\{X \cap -Y, -X \cap Y, -X \cap -Y\}, \mathbf{X})$

then $\mu^{\mathbf{A}}_{X}(x) + \mu^{\mathbf{A}}_{Y}(x)$

else if $x \in Bd_{\mathbf{A}}(\{X \cap Y, X \cap -Y, -X \cap Y\}, \mathbf{X})$ **then** 1

else $\max(\mu^{\mathbf{A}}_{X}(x), \mu^{\mathbf{A}}_{Y}(x))$

Proof. In the proof we apply property (iii) from Proposition 1.

If $x \in Bd_{\mathbf{A}}(\{X \cap -Y, -X \cap Y\}$ then $[x]_A = [x]_A \cap (X \cap -Y) \cup [x]_A \cap (-X \cap Y)$. Hence $[x]_A \cap X = [x]_A \cap X \cap -Y$, $[x]_A \cap Y = [x]_A \cap -X \cap Y$.

Since $[x]_A \cap (X \cup Y) = ([x]_A \cap X) \cup ([x]_A \cap Y)$ and $([x]_A \cap X) \cap ([x]_A \cap Y) = [x]_A \cap X \cap -Y \cap -X \cap Y = \emptyset$, we get $\mu^{\mathbf{A}}_{X \cup Y}(x) = \mu^{\mathbf{A}}_{X}(x) + \mu^{\mathbf{A}}_{Y}(x)$.

If $x \in Bd_{\mathbf{A}}(\{X \cap -Y, -X \cap Y, -X \cap -Y\}, \mathbf{X})$, then $[x]_A = [x]_A \cap (X \cap -Y) \cup [x]_A \cap (-X \cap Y) \cup [x]_A \cap (-Y \cap -Y)$.

Since $[x]_A \cap (X \cup Y) = ([x]_A \cap X) \cup ([x]_A \cap Y)$ and $([x]_A \cap X) \cap ([x]_A \cap Y) = [x]_A \cap X \cap -Y \cap -X \cap Y = \emptyset$, we get $\mu^{\mathbf{A}}_{X \cup Y}(x) = \mu^{\mathbf{A}}_{X}(x) + \mu^{\mathbf{A}}_{Y}(x)$.

If $x \in Bd_{\mathbf{A}}(\{X \cap Y, X \cap -Y, -X \cap Y\}, \mathbf{X})$ then $[x]_A = [x]_A \cap (X \cap Y) \cup [x]_A \cap (X \cap -Y) \cup [x]_A \cap (-X \cap Y)$. Hence $[x]_A \cap (X \cup Y) = [x]_A$, so $\mu^{\mathbf{A}}_{X \cup Y}(x) = 1$.

If $x \in \underline{A}(-X \cap -Y)$ then $[x]_A = [x]_A \cap (-X \cap -Y)$. Hence $[x]_A \cap (X \cup Y) = [x]_A \cap X = [x]_A \cap Y = \emptyset$.

If $x \in \underline{A}(X \cap Y)$, then $[x]_A = [x]_A \cap X \cap Y$. Hence $[x]_A \cap (X \cup Y) = [x]_A = [x]_A \cap X = [x]_A \cap Y$.

If $x \in \underline{A}(-X \cap Y)$, then $[x]_A = [x]_A \cap (-X \cap Y)$. Hence $[x]_A \cap (X \cup Y) = [x]_A \cap Y \neq \emptyset$ and $[x]_A \cap X = \emptyset$.

If $x \in \underline{A}(-X \cap Y)$, the proof is analogous as in the latter case.

If $x \in Bd_{\mathbf{A}}(\{X \cap Y, X \cap -Y\}, \mathbf{X})$ then $[x]_A = [x]_A \cap (X \cap Y) \cup [x]_A \cap (X \cap -Y)$. Hence $[x]_A \cap (X \cup Y) = [x]_A \cap X \supseteq [x]_A \cap (X \cap Y) = [x]_A \cap Y$.

If $x \in Bd_{\mathbf{A}}(\{X \cap Y, -X \cap Y\}, \mathbf{X})$, then the proof is analogous as in the latter case.

If $x \in Bd_A(\{X \cap Y, -X \cap -Y\}, \mathbf{X})$, then $\mu^{A}_{X \cup Y}(x) = \mu^{A}_{X}(x) = \mu^{A}_{Y}(x)$.

If $x \in Bd_{\mathbf{A}}(\{X \cap -Y, -X \cap -Y\}, \mathbf{X})$, then $\mu^{\mathbf{A}}_{X \cup Y}(x) = \mu^{\mathbf{A}}_{X}(x)$ and $\mu^{\mathbf{A}}_{Y}(x) = 0$.

If $x \in Bd_{\mathbf{A}}(\{-X \cap Y, -X \cap -Y\}, \mathbf{X})$, then $\mu^{\mathbf{A}}_{X \cup Y}(x) = \mu^{\mathbf{A}}_{X}(x)$ and $\mu^{\mathbf{A}}_{X}(x) = 0$.

If $x \in Bd_{\mathbf{A}}(\{X \cap -Y, X \cap Y, -X \cap -Y\}, \mathbf{X})$, then $\mu^{\mathbf{A}}_{X \cup Y}(x) = \mu^{\mathbf{A}}_{X}(x) \geqslant \mu^{\mathbf{A}}_{Y}(x)$.

If $x \in Bd_{\mathbf{A}}(\{-X \cap Y, X \cap Y, -X \cap -Y\}, \mathbf{X})$, then $\mu^{\mathbf{A}}_{X \cup Y}(x) = \mu^{\mathbf{A}}_{Y}(x) \geqslant \mu^{\mathbf{A}}_{X}(x)$.

Theorem 1. Let $\mathbf{Z}$ be a (nonempty) class of information systems with the universe including sets X and Y. The following conditions are equivalent:

(i) $\mu^{\mathbf{A}}_{X \cap Y}(x) = \min(\mu^{\mathbf{A}}_{X}(x), \mu^{\mathbf{A}}_{Y}(x))$ for any $x \in U$ and $\mathbf{A} = (U, A) \in \mathbf{Z}$.

(ii) $Bd_{\mathbf{A}}(\mathbf{Y}, \mathbf{X}) = \emptyset$ for any $\mathbf{X} \supseteq \mathbf{Y} \supseteq \{X \cap -Y, -X \cap Y\}$ and $\mathbf{A} = (U, A) \in \mathbf{Z}$, where $\mathbf{X} = \{X \cap Y, -X \cap Y, X \cap -Y, -X \cap -Y\}$.

Proof. (ii) → (i) Follows from Lemma 1.

(i) → (ii) Suppose that $Bd_{\mathbf{A}}(\mathbf{Y}, \mathbf{X}) \neq \emptyset$ for some $\mathbf{Y} \supseteq \{X \cap -Y, -X \cap Y\}$ and $\mathbf{A} \in \mathbf{Z}$.

If $x \in Bd_{\mathbf{A}}(\{X \cap -Y, -X \cap Y\}, \mathbf{X}) \neq \emptyset$ for some $\mathbf{A} \in \mathbf{Z}$, then $[x]_A \cap (X \cap -Y) \neq \emptyset$ and $[x]_A \cap (-X \cap Y) \neq \emptyset$. Hence $\mu^{\mathbf{A}}_{X}(x) > 0$ and $\mu^{\mathbf{A}}_{Y}(x) > 0$. We also have from Lemma 1 $\mu^{\mathbf{A}}_{X \cap Y}(x) = 0$. Thus we have $\mu^{\mathbf{A}}_{X \cap Y}(x) \neq \min(\mu^{\mathbf{A}}_{X}(x), \mu^{\mathbf{A}}_{Y}(x))$, i.e., a contradiction with (i).

If $x \in Bd_{\mathbf{A}}(\{X \cap -Y, -X \cap Y, -X \cap -Y\}, \mathbf{X})$ for some $\mathbf{A} \in \mathbf{Z}$ and $x \in U$ then one can see that it contradicts (i) in the same manner as before.

If $x \in Bd_{\mathbf{A}}(\{X \cap -Y, -X \cap Y, X \cap Y\}, \mathbf{X}) \neq \emptyset$ for some $\mathbf{A} \in \mathbf{Z}$ then we have $[x]_A = [x]_A \cap (X \cap -Y) \cup [x]_A \cap (-X \cap Y) \cup [x]_A \cap (X \cap Y)$. Hence $[x]_A \cap X = [x]_A \cap (X \cap -Y) \cup [x]_A \cap (X \cap Y)$ and $[x]_A \cap Y = [x]_A \cap (-X \cap Y) \cup [x]_A \cap (X \cap Y)$.

Since $[x]_A \cap (X \cap -Y) \neq \emptyset$ and $[x]_A \cap (-X \cap Y) \neq \emptyset$, we would have $\mu^{\mathbf{A}}_{X}(x) > \mu^{\mathbf{A}}_{X \cap Y}(x)$ and $\mu^{\mathbf{A}}_{Y}(x) > \mu^{\mathbf{A}}_{X \cap Y}(x)$ but this contradicts assumption (i).

If $x \in Bd_{\mathbf{A}}(\{X \cap -Y, -X \cap Y, -X \cap -Y, X \cap Y\}, \mathbf{X})$ for some $\mathbf{A} \in \mathbf{Z}$, then $[x]_A = [x]_A \cap (X \cap -Y) \cup [x]_A \cap (-X \cap Y) \cup [x]_A \cap (X \cap Y) \cup [x]_A \cap (-X \cap -Y)$.

Again we would have $[x]_A \cap X = [x]_A \cap (X \cap -Y) \cup [x]_A \cap (X \cap Y)$ and $[x]_A \cap Y = [x]_A \cap (-X \cap Y) \cup [x]_A \cap (X \cap Y)$.

Since $[x]_A \cap (X \cap -Y) \neq \emptyset$ and $[x]_A \cap (-X \cap Y) \neq \emptyset$, we would have $\mu^{\mathbf{A}}_{X}(x) > \mu^{\mathbf{A}}_{X \cap Y}(x)$ and $\mu^{\mathbf{A}}_{Y}(x) > \mu^{\mathbf{A}}_{X \cap Y}(x)$ but this contradicts assumption (i).

This completes the proof of (i) → (ii).

Theorem 2. Let $\mathbf{Z}$ be a (nonempty) class of information systems with the set of objects including sets X and Y. The following conditions are equivalent:

(i) $\mu^{\mathbf{A}}_{X \cup Y}(x) = \max(\mu^{\mathbf{A}}_X(x), \mu^{\mathbf{A}}_Y(x))$ for any $x \in U$ and $\mathbf{A} = (U, A) \in \mathbf{Z}$.

(ii) $Bd_{\mathbf{A}}(\mathbf{Y}, \mathbf{X}) = \emptyset$ for any $\mathbf{X} \supseteq \mathbf{Y} \supseteq \{X \cap -Y, -X \cap Y\}$ and $\mathbf{A} = (U, A) \in \mathbf{Z}$, where $\mathbf{X} = \{X \cap Y, -X \cap Y, X \cap -Y, -X \cap -Y\}$.

Proof. (ii) $\to$ (i) Follows from Lemma 2.

(i) $\to$ (ii) Suppose that $Bd_{\mathbf{A}}(\mathbf{Y}, \mathbf{X}) \neq \emptyset$ for some $\mathbf{Y} \supseteq \{X \cap -Y, -X \cap Y\}$ and $\mathbf{A} \in \mathbf{Z}$.

If $x \in Bd_{\mathbf{A}}(\{X \cap -Y, -X \cap Y\}, \mathbf{X}) \neq \emptyset$ for some $\mathbf{A} \in \mathbf{Z}$, then $[x]_A \cap (X \cap -Y) \neq \emptyset$ and $[x]_A \cap (-X \cap Y) \neq \emptyset$. Hence $\mu^{\mathbf{A}}_X(x) > 0$ and $\mu^{\mathbf{A}}_Y(x) > 0$. We have also from Lemma 2 that $\mu^{\mathbf{A}}_{X \cup Y}(x) = \mu^{\mathbf{A}}_X(x) + \mu^{\mathbf{A}}_Y(x)$. This gives $\mu^{\mathbf{A}}_{X \cup Y}(x) > \mu^{\mathbf{A}}_X(x)$ and $\mu^{\mathbf{A}}_{X \cup Y}(x) > \mu^{\mathbf{A}}_Y(x)$, contrary to (i).

If $x \in Bd_{\mathbf{A}}(\{X \cap -Y, -X \cap Y, -X \cap -Y\}, \mathbf{X})$ for some $\mathbf{A} \in \mathbf{Z}$ and $x \in U$ then one can see that it contradicts (i) in the same manner as before.

If $x \in Bd_{\mathbf{A}}(\{X \cap -Y, -X \cap Y, X \cap Y\}, \mathbf{X}) \neq \emptyset$ for some $\mathbf{A} \in \mathbf{Z}$ then we have $[x]_A = [x]_A \cap (X \cap -Y) \cup [x]_A \cap (-X \cap Y) \cup [x]_A \cap (X \cap Y)$ and $[x]_A \cap Z \neq \emptyset$ for $Z \in \{X \cap -Y, -X \cap Y, X \cap Y\}$. Hence $|[x]_A| > |[x]_A \cap X|$ and $|[x]_A > |[x]_A \cap Y|$. Thus $\mu^{\mathbf{A}}_X(x) < 1$ and $\mu^{\mathbf{A}}_Y(x) < 1$. However $\mu^{\mathbf{A}}_{X \cup Y}(x) = 1$ from Lemma 2. This contradicts our assumption (i).

Now let us assume that $x \in Bd_{\mathbf{A}}(\{X \cap -Y, -X \cap Y, -X \cap -Y, X \cap Y\}, \mathbf{X})$ for some $\mathbf{A} \in \mathbf{Z}$. Then $[x]_A = [x]_A \cap (X \cap -Y) \cup [x]_A \cap (-X \cap Y) \cup [x]_A \cap (X \cap Y) \cup [x]_A (-X \cap -Y)$ and $[x]_A \cap Z \neq \emptyset$ for $Z \in \{X \cap -Y, -X \cap Y, -X \cap -Y, X \cap Y\}$. Hence $[x]_A \cap (X \cup Y) = [x]_A \cap \mathrm{X} \cup [x]_A \cap (-X \cap Y)$ and $[x]_A \cap (X \cup Y)$ $[x]_A \cap Y \cup [x]_A \cap (X \cap -Y)$.

Consequently $\mu^{\mathbf{A}}_{X \cup Y}(x) > \mu^{\mathbf{A}}_X(x)$ and $\mu^{\mathbf{A}}_{X \cup Y}(x) > \mu^{\mathbf{A}}_Y(x)$. This contradicts our assumption (i), which completes the proof of (i) $\to$ (ii).

Now we would like to characterize the conditions related to the boundary regions occurring in Theorems 1 and 2.

Lemma 3. Let $\mathbf{Z}$ be a class of information systems with the set of objects including sets X and Y. The following conditions are equivalent for arbitrary $\mathbf{A} = (U, A) \in \mathbf{Z}$:

(i) $Bd_{\mathbf{A}}(\mathbf{Y}, \mathbf{X}) = \emptyset$ for any $\mathbf{X} \supseteq \mathbf{Y} \supseteq \{X \cap -Y, -X \cap Y\}$, where $\mathbf{X} = \{X \cap Y, -X \cap Y, X \cap -Y, -X \cap -Y\}$;

(ii) $\alpha \vee \beta \vee \gamma \vee \delta \vee \varepsilon$ where

$\alpha := (X \subseteq Y \text{ or } Y \subseteq X)$;

$\beta := (X - Y \neq \emptyset \text{ and } Y - X \neq \emptyset \text{ and } X \cup Y = U \text{ and } X \cap Y = \emptyset \text{ and } Bd_{\mathbf{A}}(\{X \cap -Y, -X \cap Y\}, \mathbf{X}) = \emptyset)$;

$\gamma := (X - Y \neq \emptyset \text{ and } Y - X \neq \emptyset \text{ and } X \cup Y = U \text{ and } X \cap Y = \emptyset \text{ and } Bd_{\mathbf{A}}(\{X \cap -Y, -X \cap Y\}, \mathbf{X}) = \emptyset \text{ and } Bd_{\mathbf{A}}(\{X \cap -Y, -X \cap Y, X \cap Y\}, \mathbf{X}) = \emptyset)$;

$\delta := (X - Y \neq \emptyset \text{ and } Y - X \neq \emptyset \text{ and } X \cup Y \neq U \text{ and } X \cap Y \neq \emptyset \text{ and } Bd_{\mathbf{A}}(\{X \cap -Y, -X \cap Y\}, \mathbf{X}) = \emptyset \text{ and } Bd_{\mathbf{A}}(\{X \cap -Y, -X \cap Y, -X \cap -Y\}, \mathbf{X}) = \emptyset)$;

$\varepsilon := (X - Y \neq \emptyset \text{ and } Y - X \neq \emptyset \text{ and } X \cup Y \neq U \text{ and } X \cap Y \neq \emptyset \text{ and } Bd_{\mathbf{A}}(\{X \cap -Y, -X \cap Y\}, \mathbf{X}) = \emptyset \text{ and } Bd_{\mathbf{A}}(\{X \cap -Y, -X \cap Y, -X \cap -Y\}, \mathbf{X}) = \emptyset \text{ and } Bd_{\mathbf{A}}(\{X \cap -Y, -X \cap Y, X \cap Y\}, \mathbf{X}) = \emptyset \text{ and } Bd_{\mathbf{A}}(\{X \cap -Y, -X \cap Y, X \cap Y, -X \cap -Y\}, \mathbf{X}) = \emptyset)$.

Proof. We have the following equivalencies:

$Bd_A(\{X \cap -Y, -X \cap Y\}) = \emptyset$ iff $X \subseteq Y$ or $Y \subseteq X$ or $X - Y \neq \emptyset$ and $Y - X \neq \emptyset$ and $Bd_A(\{X \cap -Y, -X \cap Y\}, X) \neq \emptyset$;

$Bd_{\mathbf{A}}(\{X \cap -Y, -X \cap Y, -X \cap -Y\}, \mathbf{X}) = \emptyset$ iff $X \subseteq Y$ or $Y \subseteq X$ or $X \cup Y = U$ or $(X - Y \neq \emptyset$ and $Y - X \neq \emptyset$ and $X \cup Y \neq U$ and $Bd_{\mathbf{A}}(\{X \cap -Y, -X \cap Y, -X \cap -Y\}, \mathbf{X}) = \emptyset)$;

$Bd_{\mathbf{A}}(\{X \cap -Y, -X \cap Y, X \cap Y\}, \mathbf{X}) = \emptyset$ iff $X \subseteq Y$ or $Y \subseteq X$ or $X \cap Y = \emptyset$ or $(X - Y \neq \emptyset$ and $Y - X \neq \emptyset$ and $X \cap Y \neq \emptyset$ and $Bd_{\mathbf{A}}(\{X \cap -Y, -X \cap Y, X \cap Y\}, \mathbf{X}) = \emptyset)$;

$Bd_{\mathbf{A}}(\{X \cap -Y, -X \cap Y, -X \cap -Y, X \cap Y\}, \mathbf{X}) = \emptyset$ iff $X \subseteq Y$ or $Y \subseteq X$ or $X \cap Y = \emptyset$ or $X \cup Y = U$ or $(X - Y \neq \emptyset$ and $Y - X \neq \emptyset$ and $X \cap Y \neq \emptyset$ and $X \cup Y \neq U$ and $Bd_{\mathbf{A}}(\{X \cap -Y, -X \cap Y, -X \cap -Y, X \cap Y\}, \mathbf{X}) = \emptyset)$.

Hence, taking the conjunction of above equivalencies, we obtain: $Bd_{\mathbf{A}}(\mathbf{Y}, \mathbf{X}) = \emptyset$ for any $\mathbf{Y} \supseteq \{X \cap -Y, -X \cap Y\}$ iff one of the conditions α, β, γ, δ, ε from (ii) is satisfied.

Let us remark that only when condition α holds, that is, when $X \subseteq Y$ or $Y \subseteq X$, condition (ii) is independent from the properties of boundary regions in the information systems.

In Figure 12.2 we illustrate the conditions formulated in (ii) of Lemma 3.

Now we prove that the assumptions from Lemmas 1 and 2 related to the boundary region $Bd_{\mathbf{A}}(\mathbf{X}, \mathbf{X})$ cannot be removed because otherwise it will not be possible to compute the values of $\mu^{\mathbf{A}}_{X \cup Y}(x)$ and $\mu^{\mathbf{A}}_{X \cap Y}(x)$ knowing the values $\mu^{\mathbf{A}}_{X}(x)$ and $\mu^{\mathbf{A}}_{Y}(x)$ only.

α :

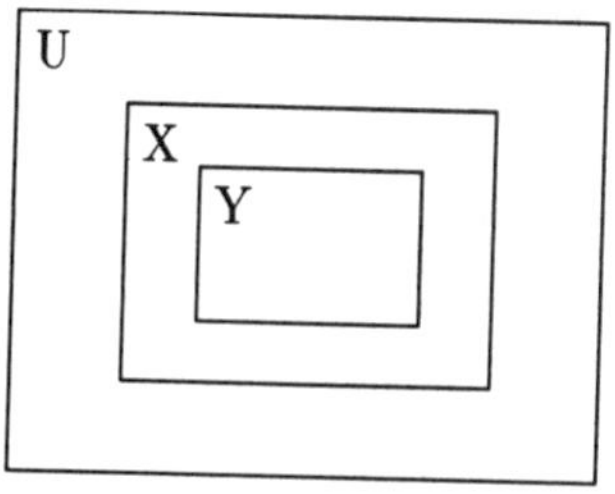

β :

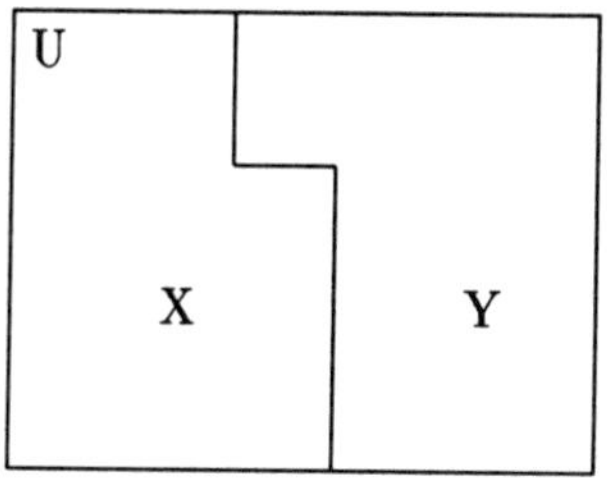

X and Y form a partition of U
The condition for the boundary regions is:
$Bd_{\mathbf{A}}(\{X \cap -Y, -X \cap Y\} \neq \emptyset)$

γ :

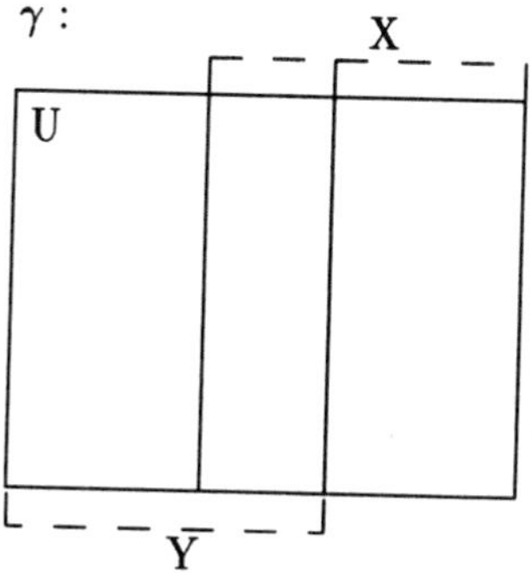

The conditions for the boundary regions are:
$Bd_{\mathbf{A}}(\{X \cap -Y, X \cap Y\}, \mathbf{X}) \neq \emptyset)$
$Bd_{\mathbf{A}}(\{X \cap -Y, X \cap Y, -X \cap Y\}, \mathbf{X}) \neq \emptyset)$

δ :

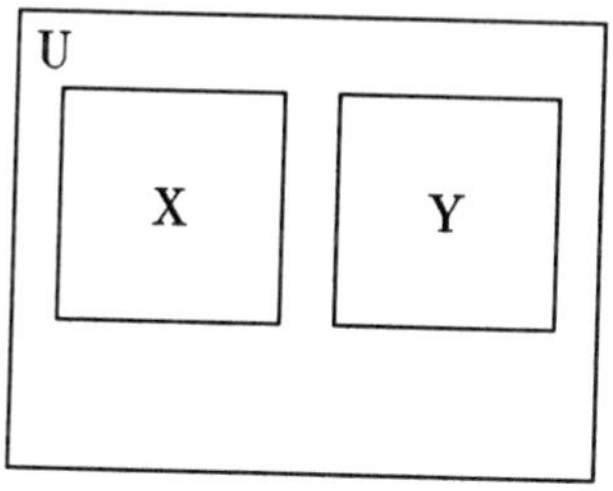

The conditions for the boundary regions are:
$Bd_{\mathbf{A}}(\{X \cap -Y, -X \cap Y\}, \mathbf{X}) \neq \emptyset)$
$Bd_{\mathbf{A}}(\{X \cap -Y, -X \cap Y, -X \cap -Y\}, \mathbf{X}) \neq \emptyset)$

ε :

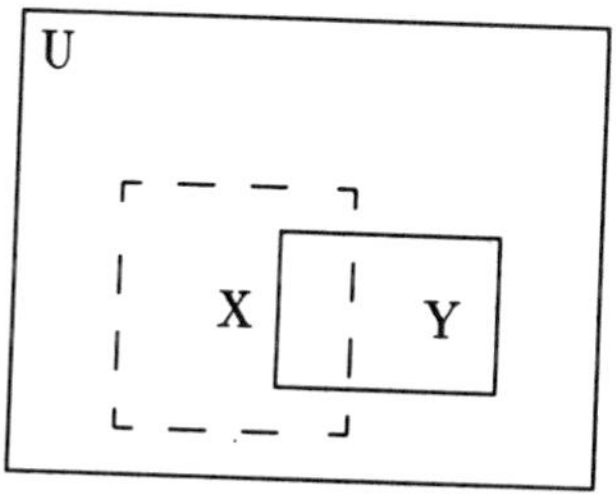

The conditions for the boundary regions are:
$Bd_{\mathbf{A}}(\{X \cap -Y, -X \cap Y\}, \mathbf{X}) \neq \emptyset)$
$Bd_{\mathbf{A}}(\{X \cap -Y, -X \cap Y, X \cap Y\}, \mathbf{X}) \neq \emptyset)$
$Bd_{\mathbf{A}}(\{X \cap -Y, -X \cap Y, -X \cap -Y\}, \mathbf{X}) \neq \emptyset)$
$Bd_{\mathbf{A}}(\{X \cap -Y, -X \cap Y, X \cap Y, -X \cap -Y\}, \mathbf{X}) \neq \emptyset)$

Figure 12.2

Theorem 3. There is no function

$$F : [0,1] \times [0,1] \rightarrow [0,1]$$

such that for any finite sets X and Y and any information system $\mathbf{A} = (U, A)$ such that $X, Y \subseteq U$ the following equality holds:

$$\mu_{X \cup Y}^{\mathbf{A}}(x) = F(\mu_X^{\mathbf{A}}(x), \quad \mu_Y^{\mathbf{A}}(x)), \text{ for any } x \in U.$$

Proof. Let us take $X = \{1, 2, 3, 5\}$ and $Y = \{1, 2, 3, 4\}$. Let $U = \{1, \ldots, 8\}$. It is easy to construct atrribute sets A and A' such that $[1]_A = U$ and $[1]_{A'} = \{1, 4, 5, 6\}$. Thus we have $\mu_X^{\mathbf{A}}(1) = \mu_Y^{\mathbf{A}}(1) = 1/2$ and $\mu_{X \cup Y}^{\mathbf{A}}(1) = 5/8$, where $\mathbf{A} = (U, A)$ and $\mu_X^{\mathbf{B}}(1) = \mu_Y^{\mathbf{B}}(1) = 1/2$ and $\mu_{X \cup Y}^{\mathbf{B}}(1) = 3/4$, where $\mathbf{B} = (U, A')$.

Similarly one can prove:

Theorem 4. There is no function

$$F : [0,1] \times [0,1] \rightarrow [0,1]$$

such that for any finite sets X and Y and any information system $\mathbf{A} = (U, A)$ such that $X, Y \subseteq U$ the following equality holds:

$$\mu_{X \cap Y}^{\mathbf{A}}(x) = F(\mu_X^{\mathbf{A}}(x), \quad \mu_Y^{\mathbf{A}}(x)), \text{ for any } x \in U.$$

6. AN ALGORITHM FOR COMPUTING THE ROUGH MEMBERSHIP FUNCTION VALUES

In the previous section we proved that it is not possible, in general, to construct a function such that it can be used for computing values of the *rm*-function corresponding to the $X \cup Y$ or $X \cap Y$ from the values of the *rm*-functions corresponding to X and Y. Hence any particular functions, for example, *min or max* applied for computing the values of *rm*-functions, will give incorrect values. This shows a major drawback of some approaches in fuzzy set theory.

We present an efficient algorithm for computing values of *rm*-functions based on the properties of the atomic components of the sets.

Let $\mathbf{X}$ be a (nonempty) family of subsets of a given finite set U. By $\mathbf{B}(\mathbf{X})$ we denote the field set generated by $\mathbf{X}$, that is, $\mathbf{B}(\mathbf{X})$ is the least family of sets satisfying the following two conditions:

(i) $\mathbf{X} \subseteq \mathbf{B}(\mathbf{X})$;
(ii) if $X, Y \in \mathbf{B}(\mathbf{X})$ then $X \cup Y$, $X \cap Y$, $-X \in \mathbf{B}(\mathbf{X})$.

If $X \subseteq U$ then we define $X^0 = X$ and $X^1 = U - X$. By $\mathrm{AT}(\mathbf{A},\mathbf{X})$ we denote the set of all nonempty atoms generated by $\mathbf{X} = \{X_1, \dots, X_k\}$, i.e., $\mathrm{AT}(\mathbf{A},\mathbf{X}) = \{X_1^{i1} \cap \dots \cap X_k^{ik} : i1, \dots, ik \in (0,1\}$ and $X_1^{i1} \cap \dots \cap X_k^{ik} \neq \emptyset\}$.

We will apply the well-known properties of atoms.

Proposition 4. Let $\mathbf{X}$ be a (nonempty) family of subsets of a given set U. The following properties hold:

(i) If $Y, Y' \in \mathrm{AT}(\mathbf{A},\mathbf{X})$ and $Y \neq Y'$ then $Y \cap Y' = \emptyset$.

(ii) If $\emptyset = Y \in \mathbf{B}(\mathbf{X})$ then there exists a uniquely determined set of (nonempty) atoms $\mathbf{Y} \subseteq \mathrm{AT}(\mathbf{A},\mathbf{X})$ such that $Y = \bigcup_{X \in \mathbf{Y}} X$.

Let $\mathbf{A} = (U, A)$ be an information system and let $\mathbf{X}$ be a family of subsets of U. For every $u \in \mathrm{INF}(\mathbf{A})$ we define the set $\mathrm{AT}(\mathbf{A},\mathbf{X},u)$ of all atoms $Y \in \mathrm{AT}(\mathbf{A},\mathbf{X})$ such that

$$Y \cap u_{\mathbf{A}} \neq \emptyset, \text{ where } u_{\mathbf{A}} = \{x \in U: \mathit{Inf}_{\mathbf{A}}(x) = u\}.$$

Moreover, let $f(\mathbf{A},\mathbf{X},u)$ be a function from $\mathrm{AT}(\mathbf{A},\mathbf{X})$ into nonnegative reals such that

$$f(\mathbf{A},\mathbf{X},u)(Y) = \frac{|u_{\mathbf{A}} \cap Y|}{|u_{\mathbf{A}}|} \text{ for any } Y \in \mathrm{AT}(\mathbf{A},\mathbf{X})$$

From the definition we have the following equality:

$$f(\mathbf{A},\mathbf{X},\mathit{Inf}_{\mathbf{A}}(x))(Y) = \mu_Y^{\mathbf{A}}(x), \text{ for any } x \in U \text{ and } Y \in \mathrm{AT}(\mathbf{A},\mathbf{X})$$

There is a simple method for computing all functions from the family $\{f(\mathbf{A},\mathbf{X},u)\}_{u \in \mathrm{INF}(\mathbf{A})}$ for a given information system $\mathbf{A}$. We represent the family $\{f(\mathbf{A},\mathbf{X},u)\}_{u \in \mathrm{INF}(\mathbf{A})}$ in a table $\mathrm{T}(\mathbf{A},\mathbf{X})$ in which rows correspond to different information $u \in \mathrm{INF}(\mathbf{A})$ and the columns correspond to different atoms from $\mathrm{AT}(\mathbf{A},\mathbf{X})$. In the table $\mathrm{T}(\mathbf{A},\mathbf{X})$ the position corresponding to an information u and to an atom $Y \in \mathrm{AT}(\mathbf{A},\mathbf{X})$ is empty if $Y \notin \mathrm{AT}(\mathbf{A},\mathbf{X},u)$ and contains the value $f(\mathbf{A},\mathbf{X},u)(Y)$ if $Y \in \mathrm{AT}(\mathbf{A},\mathbf{X},u)$.

Example 1. Let us consider the following information system. Let $U = \{1, \dots, 20\}$, $A = \{a,b,c,d,e\}$, $\mathbf{X} = \{X_1, X_2\}$, $X_1 = (5, \dots, 15)$, $X_2 = \{10, \dots, 20\}$ and the attributes are defined as in Table 12.1.

Table 12.1

	a	*b*	*c*	*d*	*e*
1	1	1	0	0	0
2	0	0	1	0	1
3	1	0	1	0	1
4	1	1	1	1	1
5	0	0	1	0	1
6	1	1	1	1	1
7	1	0	1	0	1
8	1	1	0	0	0
9	0	1	0	1	0
10	0	0	1	1	1

	a	*b*	*c*	*d*	*e*
11	0	0	1	0	1
12	0	0	0	0	0
13	0	0	1	1	1
14	1	1	0	0	0
15	0	0	0	0	0
16	1	1	1	0	0
17	0	0	1	0	1
18	1	1	1	1	1
19	1	1	1	1	1
20	0	0	0	0	0

From the above definitions we get:

$\mathrm{AT}(\mathbf{A},\mathbf{X}) = \{Y_1, Y_2, Y_3, Y_4\}$, where $Y_1 = X_1 \cap X_2 = \{10,\dots,15\}$, $Y_2 = X_1 \cap -X_2 = \{5,\dots,9\}$, $Y_3 = -X_1 \cap X_2 = \{16,\dots,20\}$, $Y_4 = -X_1 \cap -X_2 = \{1,\dots,4\}$;

$\mathrm{INF}(\mathbf{A}) = \{11000, 00101, 10101, 11111, 01010, 00111, 0000, 11100\}$;
$11000_{\mathbf{A}} = \{1,8,14\}$; $00101_{\mathbf{A}} = \{2,5,11,17\}$; $10101_{\mathbf{A}} = \{3,7\}$;
$11111_{\mathbf{A}} = \{4,6,18,19\}$; $01010_{\mathbf{A}} = \{9\}$; $00111_{\mathbf{A}} = \{10,13\}$;
$00000_{\mathbf{A}} = \{12,15,20\}$; $11100_{\mathbf{A}} = \{16\}$;
$\mathrm{AT}(\mathbf{A},\mathbf{X},11000) = \{Y_1, Y_2, Y_4\}$; $\mathrm{AT}(\mathbf{A},\mathbf{X},00101) = \{Y_1, Y_2, Y_3, Y_4\}$;
$\mathrm{AT}(\mathbf{A},\mathbf{X},10101) = \{Y_2, Y_4\}$; $\mathrm{AT}(\mathbf{A},\mathbf{X},11111) = \{Y_2, Y_3, Y_4\}$;
$\mathrm{AT}(\mathbf{A},\mathbf{X},01010) = \{Y_2\}$; $\mathrm{AT}(\mathbf{A},\mathbf{X},00111) = \{Y_1\}$;
$\mathrm{AT}(\mathbf{A},\mathbf{X},00000) = \{Y_1, Y_3\}$; $\mathrm{AT}(\mathbf{A},\mathbf{X},11100) = \{Y_3\}$;

Thus, we have $\mathrm{T}(\mathbf{A},\mathbf{X})$ as in Table 12.2 specifying the functions $f(\mathbf{A},\mathbf{X},u)$ for $u \in \mathrm{INF}(\mathbf{A})$.

Let us denote by $[\mathbf{A},\mathbf{X}]$ the extension of the data table corresponding to **A** by the columns corresponding to the characteristic functions of sets from **X**.

One can show that the tabel $\mathrm{T}(\mathbf{A},\mathbf{X})$ can be constructed from $[\mathbf{A},\mathbf{X}]$ in the number of steps of order $0(\mathrm{n}^2(\mathrm{m} + \mathrm{k}))$, where $\mathrm{n} = |U|$, $\mathrm{m} = |A|$, and $\mathrm{k} = |\mathbf{X}|$.

Table 12.2

u	Y_1	Y_2	Y_3	Y_4
11000	1/3	1/3		1/3
00101	1/4	1/4	1/4	1/4
10101		1/2		1/2
11111		1/4	1/2	1/4
01010		1		
00111	1			
00000	2/3		1/3	
11100		1		

Let us observe that by a slight modification of the construction of the table $T(\mathbf{A},\mathbf{X})$ one can obtain a table for computing the belief and plausibility functions of the information systems (Skowron, 1991; Skowron and Grzymała-Busse, 1991). This modification can be realized by adding to $T(\mathbf{A},\mathbf{X})$ one additional column in which in the position corresponding to u the cardinality of $u_{\mathbf{A}}$ is stored.

After such a modification one can easily compute the A-basic probability assignment $m_{\mathbf{A}}(\theta)$ for any nonempty set θ of atoms. It is sufficient, in fact, first to find all rows with nonempty entries corresponding exactly to elements of θ, second, to compute the sum s of all numbers appearing in the last column of these rows, and third to put $m_{\mathbf{A}}(\theta) = s/|U|$.

Now we are ready to present a simple method for computing the rm-function values.

We assume that the family $\{f(\mathbf{A},\mathbf{X},u)\}_{u\in \mathrm{INF}(\mathbf{A})}$ is represented by its data table $T(\mathbf{A},\mathbf{X})$ in the way described before. We also assume that the information system $\mathbf{A}$ is represented in the standard way by its data table. The data table of a given information system $\mathbf{A}$ is extended by one additional column containing for any $x \in U$ a pointer to the row labeled by $Inf_{\mathbf{A}}(x)$ in the table $T(\mathbf{A},\mathbf{X})$. A set X of objects is represented by marking all columns in the table $T(\mathbf{A},\mathbf{X})$ corresponding to atoms included in X.

ROUGH MEMBERSHIP FUNCTION PROCEDURE:

INPUT: representations of $\mathbf{X}$, $\mathbf{A}$, $\{f(\mathbf{A},\mathbf{X},u)\}_{u\in \mathrm{INF}(\mathbf{A})}$ and $X \in \mathbf{B}(\mathbf{X})$ in the form described above.

OUTPUT: $\mu_X^{\mathbf{A}}$.

1. For any $x \in U$ perform the following steps:
    1.1. For a given x find in the table $\mathrm{T}(\mathbf{A}, \mathbf{X})$ the row corresponding to $u = Inf_{\mathbf{A}}(x)$;
    1.2. Compute $\mu_X^{\mathbf{A}}(x) = \sum f(\mathbf{A}, \mathbf{X}, u)(Y)$, where the above sum is taken for all $\mathbf{Y}$ such that, first, the entry in $\mathrm{T}(\mathbf{A}, \mathbf{X})$ corresponding to the column labeled Y and the row labeled u is nonempty, and second, Y corresponds to a marked column in $\mathrm{T}(\mathbf{A}, \mathbf{X})$.

The correctness of this method follows from Proposition 2 (part (ix)) and from the construction of the table $\mathrm{T}(\mathbf{A}, \mathbf{X})$. One can see that the sum in Step 1.2 is taken for all $Y \in \mathbf{Y} \cap \mathrm{AT}(\mathbf{A}, \mathbf{X}, u)$, where $\mathbf{Y}$ is a set of atoms such that $X = \bigcup \mathbf{Y}$.

The number of steps to realize Step 2 is of order $0(\mathrm{n}^2)$ (at most n additions for each u), where $n = |U|$.

Example 2. (continuation of Example 1). Let $X = X_1 \cup X_2$. We have $X = X_1 \cap X_2 \cup X_1 \cap -X_2 \cup -X_1 \cap X_2 = Y_1 \cup Y_2 \cup Y_3$. Hence $\mathbf{Y} = \{Y_1, Y_2, Y_3\}$.

Let $x = 7$. Then $Inf_{\mathbf{A}}(7) = 10101$, $\mathbf{Y} \cap \mathrm{AT}((\mathbf{A}, \mathbf{X}, 10101) = \{Y_2\}$, and $\mu_X^{\mathbf{A}}(7) = f(\mathbf{A}, \mathbf{X}, 10101)(Y_2) = 1/2$.

Let $x = 6$. Then $Inf_{\mathbf{A}}(6) = 11111$, $\mathbf{Y} \cap \mathrm{AT}((\mathbf{A}, \mathbf{X}, 11111) = \{Y_2, Y_3\}$, and $\mu_X^{\mathbf{A}}(6) = f(\mathbf{A}, \mathbf{X}, 11111)(Y_2) + f(\mathbf{A}, \mathbf{X}, 11111)(Y_3) = 1/4 + 1/2 = 3/4$.

7. CONCLUSIONS

We introduced the rough membership functions (*rm*-functions) as a new tool for reasoning with uncertainty. The definition of those functions is based on the observation that objects are classified by means of partial information that is available. That definition allows us to overcome some problems that may be encountered if we use other approaches (like the ones mentioned in Section 5). We have investigated the properties of the *rm*-functions, and in particular, we have shown that the *rm*-functions are computable in an algorithmic way so that their values can be derived without the help of an expert.

We would also like to point out one important topic for further research based on the results presented here. Our *rm*-functions are defined relative to information systems. We will look for a calculus with rules based on properties of *rm*-functions and also on belief and plausibility functions for information systems. One important problem to be studied is the definition of strategies that can allow us to reconstruct those rules when the information systems are modified by environment. In some sense we would like to embed a nonmonotonic reasoning on our *rm*-functions approach as well as the belief and plausibility functions related to the information systems (Shafer, 1976; Skowron, 1991; Skowron and Grzymała-Busse, 1991).

ACKNOWLEDGMENTS

The authors wish to express their thanks to Professor Alberto Pettorossi for his helpful comments and for suggesting several corrections to the previous version.

BIBLIOGRAPHY

Dubois, D. and Prade, H. (1980). *Fuzzy sets and systems: Theory and applications.* London: Academic Press.

Pawlak, Z. (1991). *Rough sets: Theoretical aspects of reasoning about data.* Dordrecht: Kluwer.

Scott, D. (1982). Domains for denotational semantics. A corrected and expanded version of a paper presented at ICALP'82, Aarhus, Denmark.

Shafer, G. (1976). *A mathematical theory of evidence.* Princeton, NJ: Princeton, University Press.

Skowron, A. (1991a). *The rough set theory as a basis for the evidence theory.* ICS Research Report 2/91.

Skowron, A. (1991b). Numerical uncertainty measures. Lecture delivered at S. Banach Mathematical Center's Semester: *Algebraic methods in logic and their computer science applications,* Warsaw.

Skowron, A. and Grzymała-Busse, J. (1991). *From the rough set theory to the evidence theory.* ICS Research Report 8/91.

Zadeh, L. A. (1965). Fuzzy sets. *Information and Control* 8: 338–53.

3

DEMPSTER-SHAFER THEORY IN DECISION MAKING AND OPTIMIZATION

13 Decision analysis using belief functions

Thomas M. STRAT

Abstract: A primary motivation for reasoning under uncertainty is to derive decisions in the face of inconclusive evidence. Shafer's theory of belief functions, which explicitly represents the underconstrained nature of many reasoning problems, lacks a formal procedure for making decisions. Clearly, when sufficient information is not available, no theory can prescribe actions without making additional assumptions. Faced with this situation, some assumption must be made if a clearly superior choice is to emerge. In this paper we offer a probabilistic interpretation of a simple assumption that disambiguates decision problems represented with belief functions. We prove that it yields expected values identical to those obtained by a probabilistic analysis that makes the same assumption. We maintain a strict separation between evidence that carries information about a situation and assumptions that may be made for disambiguation of choices. In addition, we show how the decision analysis methodology frequently employed in probabilistic reasoning can be extended for use with belief functions. This generalization of decision analysis allows the use of belief functions within the familiar framework of decision trees.[1]

Keywords: decision analysis, uncertainty, belief function, decision tree.

[1] This research was partially supported by the Defense Advanced Research Projects Agency under Contract No. N00030-88-C-0248 in conjunction with the U.S. Navy Space and Naval Warfare Systems Command.

1. INTRODUCTION

Decision analysis provides a methodological approach for making decisions. Uncertain states of nature are represented by probability distributions, and each possible state is assigned a value or *utility*. The best decision is the one that yields the greatest *expected utility*. By enumerating in a *decision tree* all available choices and assessing the probabilities and utilities of the states of nature that may result, one can mechanically determine the optimal sequence of actions he should take (Howard, 1966; Lapin, 1981; La Valle, 1970; Raiffa, 1970).

In practice, these simple requirements are difficult to satisfy (Horvitz et al., 1988). Sometimes, reliable estimates of the probabilities involved are hard to come by. For example, few statistics are available for determining the probability of a nuclear reactor core meltdown. Assessing the utility of many-faceted states of nature is equally challenging. How should one give a unique value to the anticipated quality of married life? These limitations have hindered the more widespread application of decision analysis.

Shafer's theory of *belief functions* (Lowrance et al., 1986; Ruspini, 1986; Shafer, 1976; Smets, 1988) allows one to express partial beliefs when it is impossible or impractical to assess complete probability distributions confidently. Using belief functions, one can bound the probabilities of events for which the assignment of a precise probability would be misleading. The theory provides a facility to express one's beliefs only to the degree to which there is supporting evidence, thereby resulting in an appropriate description of an uncertain event. For example, there might be reason to assign a probability to a reactor malfunction, without saying what the chance is that it may lead to a core meltdown.

Despite its representational advantages, the theory of belief functions lacks a formal basis upon which decisions can be made in the face of ambiguity (Barnett, 1981). Computing the expected utility of a random event that has been represented with belief functions results in an *expected utility interval* (EUI). To choose between two actions one must compare their respective EUIs. If they don't overlap, the choice is clear. But when the EUIs overlap, the decision maker is confronted with a dilemma — the available evidence does not support either choice. Ideally, one should collect more information until the intervals no longer overlap and the choice becomes clear. However, sometimes one is forced to choose without benefit of additional information. What should be done?

In this situation there is no recourse except to make an assumption to eliminate the ambiguity. Various authors have expressed preference for different assumptions such as renormalization, generalized insufficient reason (Dubois and Prade, 1982; Smets and Kennes, 1990), minimax (Wald, 1950), and optimism/pessimism (Hurwicz, 1952), etc. More elaborate schemes have been suggested, but they also amount to the introduction of unfounded assumptions (Loui et al., 1985; Pittarelli, 1988; Yager 1989). Here we advocate the interpolation of a point-valued utility within the EUI. We make no claim that it leads to superior decisions, but do claim that it is no less viable than the alternative assumptions. We show that it gives the same expected utility (and hence leads to the same decisions) as would be obtained by assuming that there is some probability that ambiguity will be resolved in one's favor.

We further show how decision analysis can be generalized to accommodate a belief function representation of uncertainty. This involves two modifications: allowing an interval as the utility of a state or set of states, and allowing a belief function in place of a probability distribution. The result is a complete decision analysis procedure compatible with either probabilistic or belief function representations of uncertainty.

We should point out that decision theory (and its associated utility theory) is not the only approach for making decisions under uncertainty. For example, Lesh has proposed a model based on an ignorance-preference coefficient that is empirically derived (Lesh, 1986). Shafer has advocated a "constructive" decision theory that seeks support for actions that achieve goals (Shafer, 1982). Loui et al. suggest representing beliefs not by one distribution, but by a sequence of progressively more decisive distributions (Loui et al., 1985). In this paper we are concerned with providing for the use of belief functions within the general framework of decision analysis.

It is worth noting that none of the material described in this paper depends on the use of Dempster's rule, which is commonly used in Shafer's theory to combine independent bodies of evidence (Shafer, 1976). The computation of expected utility interval, and the procedure for using EUIs in decision analysis, only requires that a belief function representation of the problem be available. Dempster's rule *could* be used to construct that belief function, but it is not required for decision analysis.

In the sections that follow we develop the theory and illustrate its use with simple examples. In Section 2 we derive the expected utility interval that results from the use of belief functions. We then show

how making an assumption about the probability of nature's cooperation leads to the same expected utility as interpolation within the EUI. In Section 3, this result is used to generalize decision analysis and is illustrated within a decision problem concerning whether or not to drill for oil. We conclude with a discussion of the benefits and limitations of our approach, and compare its use with other approaches to decision making under uncertainty.

2. EXPECTED VALUE

Decision analysis provides a methodological approach for making decisions. The crux of the method is that one should choose the action that will maximize the expected utility. In this section we review the computation of expected utility using a probabilistic representation of a simple example and show how a belief function gives rise to a range of expected utilities. We then show how a simple assumption about the inclination of nature leads to a means for choosing a single-point expected utility for belief functions.

2.1. Expected value using probabilities

Example 1 (Carnival Wheel # 1): A familiar game of chance is the carnival wheel pictured in Figure 13.1. This wheel is divided into 10 equal sectors, each of which is labeled with a dollar amount as shown. For a \$6 fee, the player gets to spin the wheel and receives the amount shown in the sector that stops at the top. Should we be willing to play?

The analysis of this problem lends itself readily to a probabilistic representation. From inspection of the wheel (assuming each sector really is equally likely), we can construct the following probability distribution:

$$p(\$1) = 0.4 \quad p(\$5) = 0.3 \quad p(\$10) = 0.2 \quad p(\$20) = 0.1$$

The expected value $E(x)$ is computed from the formula

$$E(x) = \sum_{x \in \Theta} x \cdot p(x) \tag{1}$$

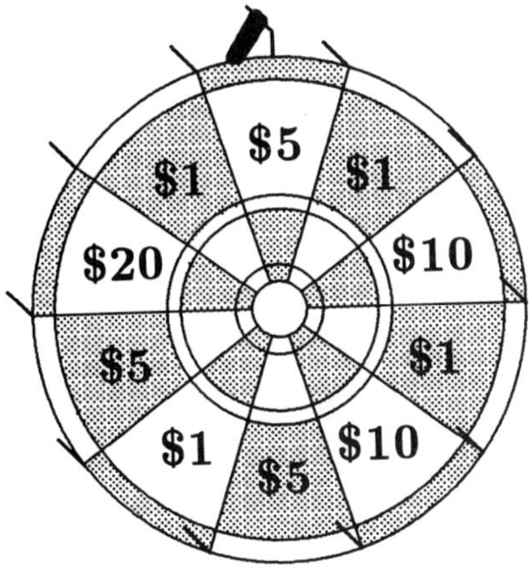

Figure 13.1: Carnival Wheel # 1

where Θ is the set of possible outcomes. The expected value of the carnival wheel is \$5.90 as shown in Table 13.1. Therefore, we should refuse to play, because the expected value of playing the game is less than the \$6 cost of playing.[2] Let us now modify the problem slightly in order to motivate a belief function approach to the problem.

Table 13.1: Expected value of Carnival Wheel # 1.

x	$p(x)$	$x \cdot p(x)$
1	0.4	0.4
5	0.3	1.5
10	0.2	2.0
20	0.1	2.0
	$E(x) =$	5.90

[2] We assume that the monetary value is directly proportional to utility because of the small dollar amounts involved. We could instead have chosen to work with utilities to account for nonlinearities in one's preferences for money.

2.2. Expected value intervals

Example 2 (Carnival Wheel # 2): Another carnival wheel is divided into 10 equal sectors, each having \$1, \$5, \$10, or \$20 printed on it (Figure 13.2). However, one of the sectors is hidden from view. How much are we willing to pay to play this game?

Figure 13.2: Carnival Wheel # 2.

This problem is ideally suited to an analysis using belief functions. In a belief function representation, a unit of belief is distributed over the space of possible outcomes (comonly called the *frame of discernment*). Unlike a probability distribution, which distributes belief over *elements* of the outcome space, this distribution (called a *mass function*) attributes belief to *subsets* of the outcome space. Belief attributed to a subset signifies that there is reason to believe that the outcome will be among the elements of that subset, without committing to any preference among those elements. Formally, a mass distribution m_Θ is a mapping from subsets of a frame of discernment Θ into the unit interval:

$$m_\Theta : 2^\Theta \rightarrow [0,1]$$

such that $m_\Theta(\emptyset) = 0$ and $\sum_{A_i \subseteq \Theta} m_\Theta(A_i) = 1$

Any subset to which nonzero mass has been attributed is called a *focal element.* One of the ramifications of this representation is that the belief in a hypothesis $A (A \subseteq \Theta)$ is constrained to lie within an interval $[Spt(A), Pls(A)]$, where

$$Spt(A) \sum_{A_i \subseteq A} m_\Theta(A_i); \quad Pls(A) = 1 - Spt(\neg A) \tag{2}$$

These bounds are commonly referred to as *support* and *plausibility*.

The frame of discernment Θ for Wheel # 2 is {\$1, \$5, \$10, \$20}. The mass function for Wheel # 2 is shown below,

$$\begin{aligned} m(\{\$1\}) &= 0.4 \\ m(\{\$5\}) &= 0.2 \\ m(\{\$10\}) &= 0.2 \\ m(\{\$20\}) &= 0.1 \\ m(\{\$1, \$5, \$10, \$20\}) &= 0.1 \end{aligned}$$

and its associated belief intervals are

$$\begin{aligned} [Spt(\{\$1\}), Pls(\{\$1\})] &= [0.4, 0.5] \\ [Spt(\{\$5\}), Pls(\{\$5\})] &= [0.2, 0.3] \\ [Spt(\{\$10\}), Pls(\{\$10\})] &= [0.2, 0.3] \\ [Spt(\{\$20\}), Pls(\{\$20\})] &= [0.1, 0.2] \end{aligned}$$

Before we can compute the expected value of the wheel represented by this belief function, we must somehow assess the value of the hidden sector. We know that there is a 0.1 chance that the hidden sector will be selected, but what value should we attribute to that sector? If the carnival hawker were allowed to assign a dollar value to that sector, he would surely have assigned \$1. On the other hand if we (or a cooperative friend) were allowed to do so, it would have been \$20. Any other assignment method would result in a value between \$1 and \$20, inclusive. Therefore, if we truly do not know what assignment method was used, the strongest statement that we can make is that the value of the hidden sector is between \$1 and \$20. Using interval arithmetic we can apply the expected value formula of (1) to obtain an *expected value interval* (EVI):

$$E(x) = [E_*(x), E^*(x)] \tag{3}$$

where[3]

$$E_*(x) = \sum_{A_i \subseteq \Theta} \inf(A_i) \cdot m_\Theta(A_i)$$

[3] We use $\inf(A_i)$ or $\sup(A_i)$ to denote the smallest or largest element in the set $A_i \subseteq \Theta$. Θ is assumed to be a set of scalar values (Strat, 1984).

$$E^*(x) = \sum_{A_i \subseteq \Theta} \sup(A_i) \cdot m_\Theta(A_i)$$

The expected value interval of Wheel # 2 is

$$E(x) = [0.4(1) + 0.2(5) + 0.2(10) + 0.1(20) + 0.1(1), \\ 0.4(1) + 0.2(5) + 0.2(10) + 0.1(20) + 0.1(20)] = [5.50, 7.40]$$

2.3. Expected value using belief functions

As many researchers have pointd out, an interval of expected values is not very satisfactory when we have to make a decision. Sometimes it provides all the information necessary to make a decision — if the game costs $5 to play, then clearly we should be willing to play regardless of who gets to assign a value to the hidden sector. Sometimes we can defer making the decision until we have collected more evidence — if we could peek at the hidden sector and then decide whether or not to play. But the need to make a decision based on the currently available information is often inescapable; should we spin Wheel # 2 for a $6 fee? We will present our methodology for decision making using belief functions after pausing to consider a Bayesian analysis of the same situation.

If we are to use the probabilistic definition of expected value from (1), we are forced to assess probabilities of all possible outcomes. To do this, we must make additional assumptions before proceeding further. One possible assumption is that all four values of the hidden sector ($1, $5, $10, $20) are equally likely, and we could evenly distribute among those four values the 0.1 chance that the hidden sector is chosen. This is an example of the generalized insufficient reason principle advanced by Dubois and Prade (1982) and by Smets (Smets and Kennes, 1990). The resulting computation of expected value with this assumption is shown in Table 13.2; the expected value is $6.30.

Table 13.2: Expected value of Carnival Wheel # 2, assuming equal likelihood.

x	$p(x)$	$x \cdot p(x)$
1	0.425	0.425
5	0.225	1.125
10	0.225	2.250
20	0.125	2.500
	$E(x) =$	6.30

An alternative assumption is that the best estimate of the probability distribution for the value of the hidden sector is the same as the known distribution of the visible sectors. Using this assumption, the result is $6 (*cf.* Table 13.3).

Table 13.3: Expected Value of Carnival Wheel # 2, assuming normalized probabilities.

x	$p(x)$	$x \cdot p(x)$
1	4/9	4/9
5	2/9	10/9
10	2/9	20/9
20	1/9	20/9
	$E(x) =$	6.00

Rather than making one of these assumptions, we may wish to parameterize by an unknown probability ρ our belief that either we get to choose the value of the hidden sector or the carnival hawker does. Let ρ be the probability that the value assigned to the hidden sector is the one that we would have assigned, if given the opportunity, so $(1 - \rho)$ is the probability that the carnival hawker chose the value of the hidden sector. That is,

p(hidden sector is labeled \$20) $= \rho$
p(hidden sector is labeled \$1) $= 1 - \rho$

The expected value of Wheel # 2 can then be recomputed using probabilities and (1) as illustrated in Table 13.4:

Table 13.4: Expected value of Carnival Wheel # 2, parameterized by ρ.

x	$p(x)$	$x \cdot p(x)$
1	$0.4 + 0.1(1 - \rho)$	$0.5 - 0.1\rho$
5	0.2	1.0
10	0.2	2.0
20	$0.1 + 0.1\rho$	$2.0 + 2\rho$
	$E(x) =$	$5.50 + 1.90\rho$

To decide whether to play the game, we need only assess the probability ρ. For the carnival wheel it would be wise to allow that the hawker has hidden the value from our view; thus we might assume that $\rho = 0$. So $E(x) = 5.50$, and we should not be willing to pay more than $5.50 to spin the wheel.

Example 3 (Carnival Wheel # 3): A third carnival wheel is divided into 10 equal sectors, each having $1, $5, $10, or $20 printed on it (Figure 13.3). This wheel has 5 sectors hidden from view. However, we do know that none of these sectors is a $20, that the first hidden sector is either a $5 or a $10, and that the second hidden sector is either a $1 or a $10. How much are we willing to pay to spin Wheel # 3?

Figure 13.3: Carnival Wheel # 3.

A probabilistic analysis of Wheel # 3 requires one to make additional assumptions. Estimating the conditional probability distribution for each hidden sector would provide enough information to compute the expected value of the wheel. Alternatively, estimating just the expected value of each hidden sector would suffice as well. However, doing so can be both tedious and frustrating: tedious because there may be many hidden sectors, and frustrating because we're being asked to provide information that, in actuality, we do not have. (If we knew the conditional probabilities or the expected values, we would have used them in our original analysis.) What is the minimum information necessary to establish a single expected value for Wheel #3?

The probability, ρ, that we used to analyze Wheel #2 can be used here as well.

Definition 1. *Let ρ = the probability that ambiguity will be resolved as favorably as possible; $(1-\rho)$ = the probability that ambiguity will be resolved as unfavorably as possible.*

Estimating ρ is sufficient to restrict the expected value of a belief function to a single point. It is easy to see that expected value derived from this analysis as ρ varies from 0 to 1 is exactly the value obtained by linear interpolation of the EVI that results from using belief functions. The following derivation shows that this is true in general.

Theorem 1. *Given a mass function m_Θ defined over a scalar frame Θ of utilities, and an estimate of ρ (the probability that all residual ambiguity will turn out favorably), the expected utility given m_Θ is*

$$E(x) = E_*(x) + \rho\cdot(E^*(x) - E_*(x)) \tag{4}$$

Proof: Consider a mass function m_Θ defined over a frame of discernment Θ. Now consider any focal element $A \subseteq \Theta$, such that $m_\Theta(A) > 0$. Since ρ is the probability that a cooperative agent will control which $x \in A$ will be selected, and $(1-\rho)$ is the probability that an adversary will be in control, then the probability that x will be chosen given that focal element A occurs is

$$p_\Theta(x|A) = \begin{cases} \rho & \text{if } x = \sup(A) \\ (1-\rho) & \text{if } x = \inf(A) \\ 0 & \text{otherwise} \end{cases}$$

Considering all focal elements in m_Θ, we can construct a probability distribution $p_\Theta(x)$ as follows:

$$p_\Theta(x) = \sum_{A_i \subseteq \Theta} p_\Theta(x|A_i)\cdot p_\Theta(A_i)$$

$$p_\Theta(x) = \sum_{A:\sup(A)=x} \rho\cdot m_\Theta(A) + \sum_{A:\inf(A)=x} (1-\rho)\cdot m_\Theta(A)$$

Using (1), we have

$$E(x) = \sum_{x\in\Theta} x\cdot p_\Theta(x)$$

$$= \sum_{x \in \Theta} x \cdot \left(\sum_{A:\sup(A)=x} \rho \cdot m_\Theta(A) + \sum_{A:\inf(A)=x} (1-\rho) \cdot m_\Theta(A) \right)$$

$$= \sum_{x \in \Theta} \left(\sum_{A:\sup(A)=x} \sup(A) \cdot \rho \cdot m_\Theta(A) + \sum_{A:\inf(A)=x} \inf(A) \cdot (1-\rho) \cdot m_\Theta(A) \right)$$

The double summations can be collapsed to a single summation because every $A \subseteq \Theta$ has a unique $\sup(A) \in \Theta$ and a unique $\inf(A) \in \Theta$.

$$E(x) = \sum_{A \subseteq \Theta} \sup(A) \cdot \rho \cdot m_\Theta(A) + \inf(A) \cdot (1-\rho) \cdot m_\Theta(A)$$

$$= \sum_{A \subseteq \Theta} \inf(A) \cdot m_\Theta(A) + \rho \cdot \sum_{A \subseteq \Theta} [\sup(A) - \inf(A)] \cdot m_\Theta(A)$$

$$= E_*(x) + \rho \cdot (E^*(x) - E_*(x))$$

The important point of the proof is that the probabilistic analysis provides a meaningful way to choose a distinguished point within an EVI that results from the use of belief functions. That distinguished point can then be used as the basis for comparison of several choices when their respective EVIs overlap.

2.4. Discussion

Because of its interval representation of belief, Shafer's theory poses difficulties for a decision maker who uses it. Lesh has proposed a different method for choosing a distinguished point to use in the ordering of overlapping choices (Lesh, 1986). Lesh makes use of an empirically derived "ignorance preference coefficient," τ, that is used to compute the distinguished point called "expected evidential belief" (EEB):

$$EEB(A) = \frac{Spt(A) + Pls(A)}{2} + \tau \frac{(Pls(A) - Spt(A))^2}{2}$$

A choice is made by choosing the action that maximizes the "expected evidential value" (EEV):

$$EEV = \sum_{A_i \subseteq \Theta} A_i \cdot EEB(A_i)$$

There are some important differences between Lesh's approach and the present approach for evidential decision making. The ignorance preference parameter τ can be seen as a means for interpolating a distinguished value within a *belief* interval $[Spt(A), Pls(A)]$, while the cooperation probability, ρ, is used to interpolate within an interval of *expected utilities* $[E_*(x), E^*(x)]$. Secondly, Lesh's parameter τ is empirically derived and has no theoretical underpinning. In contrast, the cooperation parameter ρ has been explained as a probability of a comprehensible event—that the residual ambiguity will be favorably resolved. It leads to a simple procedure involving linear interpolation between bounds of expected utility, and is derived from probability theory.

The use of a single parameter to choose a value between two extremes is similar in spirit to the approach taken by Hurwicz with a probabilistic formulation (Hurwicz, 1952). Hurwicz suggested that rather than computing the expected utility of a variable for which a probability distribution is known, one could interpolate a decision index between two extremes by estimating a single parameter related to the disposition of nature. When this parameter is zero, one obtains the Wald minimax criterion – the assumption that nature will act as strongly as possible against the decision maker (Wald, 1950). In contrast to the Hurwicz approach in which one ignores the probability distribution and computes a decision index on the basis of the parameter only, in our approach the expected utility interval is computed, and interpolation between extremes occurs only within the range of residual ambiguity allowed by the focal elements of a belief function. Thus our approach is identical to the use of expected utilities when a probability distribution is available; it is identical to Hurwicz's approach when there are known constraints on the distribution; and it combines elements of both when the distribution is a belief function.

There may be circumstances in which a single parameter is insufficient to capture the underlying structure of a decision problem. In these cases it would be more appropriate to use a different probability to represent the attitude of nature for each source of ambiguity. Let ρ_i be the probability that ambiguity within each focal element A_i will be decided favorably, (for all A_i)$A_i \subseteq \Theta$. Then we obtain

$$E(x) = \sum_{A_i \subseteq \Theta} \inf(A_i) \cdot m_\Theta(A_i) + \sum_{A_i \subseteq \Theta} \rho_i [\sup(A_i) - \inf(A_i)] \cdot m_\Theta(A_i) \quad (5)$$

in place of (4).

3. DECISION ANALYSIS

In the preceding section we have defined the concept of an expected utility interval for belief functions and we have shown that it bounds the expected utility that would be obtained with any probability distribution consistent with that belief function. Furthermore, we have proposed a parameter (the probability that residual ambiguity will be decided in our behalf) that can be used as the basis for computing a unique expected utility when the available evidence warrants only bounds on that expected utility. In this section we will show how the expected utility interval can be used to generalize probabilistic decision analysis.

Decision analysis was first developed as a means by which one could organize and systematize one's thinking when confronted with an important and difficult choice (Howard, 1966; Raiffa, 1970). Its formal basis has made it adaptable as a computational procedure by which computer programs can choose actions when provided with all relevant information. Simply stated, the analysis of a decision problem under uncertainty entails the following steps:

- List the viable options available for gathering information, for experimentation, and for action.
- List the events that may possibly occur.
- Arrange the information you may acquire and the choices you may make in chronological order.
- Decide the value to you of the consequences that result from the various courses of action open to you.
- Judge the chances that any particular uncertain event will occur.

3.1. Decision analysis using probabilities

First we will illustrate the use of decision analysis on a problem that can be represented with probabilities to acquaint the reader with the method and terminology.

Example 4 (Oil Drilling # 1): A wildcatter must decide whether or not to drill for oil. He is uncertain whether the hole will be dry, have a trickle of oil, or be a gusher. Drilling a hole costs $70,000. The payoffs for hitting a gusher, a trickle, or a dry hole are $270,000, $120,000, and $0, respectively. At a cost of $10,000 the wildcatter could take seismic soundings that would help determine the underlying geologic structure. The soundings will determine whether the terrain has no structure, open structure, or closed structure. The experts have provided us with the joint probabilities shown in Table 13.5. We are to determine the optimal strategy for experimentation and action (Lapin, 1981).

Table 13.5: Probabilities for Oil Drilling # 1.

State	No struct	Open	Closed	Marginal
Dry	0.30	0.15	0.05	0.50
Trickle	0.09	0.12	0.09	0.30
Gusher	0.02	0.08	0.10	0.20
Marginal	0.41	0.35	0.24	1.00

In decision analysis, a decision tree is constructed that captures the chronological order of actions and events (Lapin, 1981; La Valle, 1970). A square is used to represent a decision to be made, and its branches are labeled with the alternative choices. A circle is used to represent a chance node, and its branches are labeled with the conditional probability of each event, given that the choices and events along the path leading to the node have occurred.

To compute the best strategy, the tree is evaluated from its leaves toward its root.

- The value of a leaf node is the utility of the state of nature it represents.
- The value of a chance node is the expected utility of the probability distribution represented by its branches as computed using (1).
- The value of a choice node is the maximum of the utilities of each of its sons. The best choice for the node is denoted by the branch leading to the son with the greatest utility. Ties are broken arbitrarily.

This procedure is repeated until the root node has been evaluated. The value of the root node is the expected utility of the decision problem; the branches corresponding to the maximal value at each choice node give the best *strategy* to follow (i.e., choices to make in each situation).

The evaluated decision tree for the oil drilling example is portrayed in Figure 13.4. It can be seen that the expected value is \$22,500 and that the best strategy is to take seismic soundings, to drill for oil if the soundings indicate open or closed structure, and not to drill if the soundings indicate no structure.

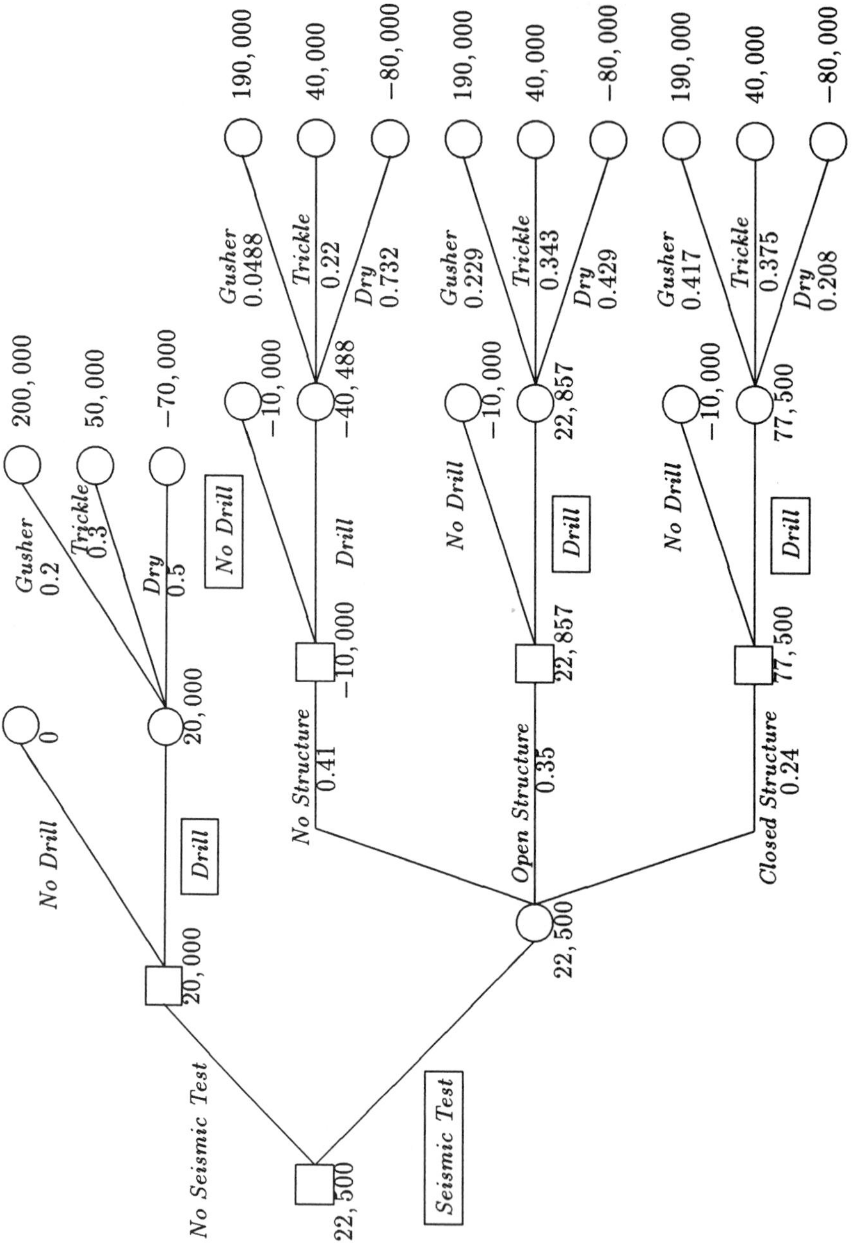

Figure 13.4: Decision tree for the first oil-drilling example.

3.2. Decision analysis using belief functions

To use the decision procedure just described, it must be possible to assess the probabilities of all uncertain events. That is, the set of branches emanating from each chance node in the decision tree must depict a probability distribution. In many scenarios, however, estimating these probability distributions is difficult or impossible, and the decision maker is forced to assign probabilities even though he knows they are unreliable. Using belief functions, one need not estimate any probabilities that are not readily available. The representation better reflects the evidence at hand, but the decision analysis procedure canot be used with the resulting interval representation of belief. In this section we describe a generalization of decision analysis that accommodates belief functions.

Example 5 (Oil Drilling #2): As in the first oil-drilling example, a wildcatter must decide whether or not to drill for oil. His costs and payoffs are the same as before: drilling costs $70,000, and the payoffs for hitting a gusher, a trickle, or a dry well are $270,000, $120,000, and $0, respectively. However, at this site, no seismic soundings are available. Instead, at a cost of $10,000, the wildcatter can make an electronic test that is related to the well capacity as shown in Table 13.6. We are to determine the optimal strategy for experimentation and action.

Table 13.6: Probabilities for Oil Drilling # 2.

Prob	Test result	Capacity
0.5	red	dry
0.2	yellow	dry or trickle
0.3	green	trickle or gusher

Several issues arise that prevent one from constructing a well-formed decision tree for this example. First, consider the branch of the tree in which the test is conducted and the result is green (Figure 13.5). If we drill for oil, then we know we will find either a trickle or a gusher, but we cannot determine the probability of either from the given information. We are tempted to label the branch with the disjunction (Trrickle V Gusher) with probability 1.0. But what should be the payoff of that branch? All we can say is that the payoff will be either $40,000 (if a trickle) or $190,000 (if a gusher). Ordinary decision analysis requires a unique value to be assigned, but we have

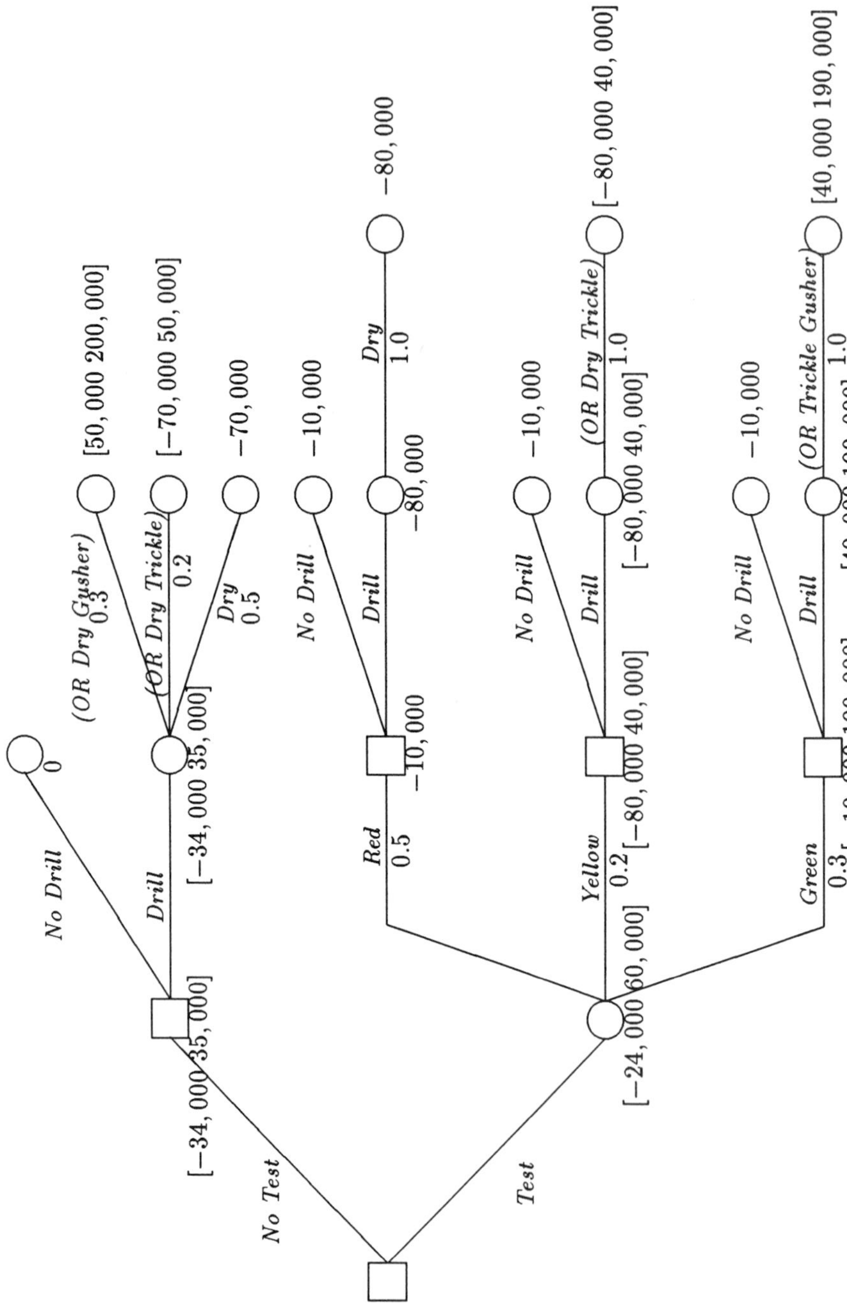

Figure 13.5: Modified decision tree for the second oil-drilling example.

no basis for computing one. So the first modification we make to the construction of decision trees is to allow disjunctions of events on branches emanating from chance nodes, and to allow intervals as the payoffs for leaf nodes. We will discuss later how to evaluate such a tree.

To see the second issue, consider the branch of the tree in which the test is not conducted. If we drill for oil, there is a chance that we will hit a gusher, a trickle, or a dry well, but what is the probability distribution? We know only that

$$\begin{array}{ll} \mathrm{p(Dry \mid Red)} = 1.0 & \mathrm{p(Red)} = 0.5 \\ \mathrm{p(Dry \vee Trickle \mid Yellow)} = 1.0 & \mathrm{p(Yellow)} = 0.2 \\ \mathrm{p(Trickle \vee Gusher \mid Green)} = 1.0 & \mathrm{p(Green)} = 0.3 \end{array}$$

There is not enough information to use Bayes' rule to compute the probability distribution for the well capacity. Without adding a new assumption at this point, the strongest statement that can be made is

$$\begin{array}{l} 0.5 \leqslant p(\mathrm{Dry}) \leqslant 0.7 \\ 0.0 \leqslant p(\mathrm{Trickle}) \leqslant 0.5 \\ 0.0 \leqslant p(\mathrm{Gusher}) \leqslant 0.3 \end{array}$$

Using belief functions, this can be represented as

$$\begin{array}{l} m(\{\mathrm{Dry}\}) = 0.5 \\ m(\{\mathrm{Dry, Trickle}\}) = 0.2 \\ m(\{\mathrm{Trickle, Gusher}\}) = 0.3 \end{array}$$

which yields the required belief intervals

$$\begin{array}{ll} [Spt(\{\mathrm{Dry}\}), Pls(\{\mathrm{Dry}\})] & = [0.5, 0.7] \\ [Spt(\{\mathrm{Trickle}\}), Pls(\{\mathrm{Trickle}\})] & = [0.0, 0.5] \\ [Spt(\{\mathrm{Gusher}\}), Pls(\{\mathrm{Gusher}\})] & = [0.0, 0.3] \end{array}$$

The second modification we make to decision trees is to allow the branches emanating from a chance node to represent a mass function. The masses must still sum to one, but the events need not be disjoint.[4] The completed decision tree for Example 4 is shown in Figure 13.5.

The tools of Section 2 can be used to evaluate a decision tree modified in this manner.

- The value of a leaf node is the utility of the state of nature it represents. This may be a unique value or, in the case of a disjunction of states, an interval of values.

---

[4] Recall that a probability distribution is an assignment of belief over mutually exclusive elements of a set, whereas a mass function is a distribution over possibly overlapping subsets.

- A chance node represents a belief function. Its value is the expected utility interval computed with (3):

$$E(x) = [E_*(x), E^*(x)]$$

- A decision node represents a choice of the several branches emanating from it. The utility of each branch may be a point value or an interval. The value of a decision node is the expected utility computed using (4) and an estimate of ρ:

$$E(x) = E_*(x) + \rho \cdot (E^*(x) - E_*(x))$$

  The action on the branch that yields the greatest $E(x)$ is chosen. Ties are broken arbitrarily.

In summary, a decision tree and decision analysis procedure for belief functions have been described. Two modifications were made to adapt ordinary decision trees: intervals are allowed where utilities occur; and belief functions are allowed where probability distributions occur. A unique strategy can be obtained by estimating the probability ρ.[5]

3.3 Generalized decision tree examples

Figures 13.6, 13.7, and 13.8 show the evaluated decision tree for several values of ρ each node is labeled with its expected value or expected value interval. In the cases where the expected value is an interval, the evidential expected value $E(x)$ is also shown (using the assumed ρ). Preferred decisions are highlighted with a black background.

If we opt not to test, then our choice is either to not drill (expected value 0) or to drill (expected value interval [−34,000 35,000]). The better choice depends on what value of ρ is assumed. As can be seen in the figures, if $\rho = 0.0$, then it is better to not drill, but if $\rho = 0.5$ or $\rho = 1.0$, then drilling is the better choice.

If we choose to test and the result is yellow, then our choice is to not drill (expected value −10,000) or to drill (expected value interval [−80,000 40,000]). In this case it is better to not drill if either $\rho = 0.0$ or $\rho = 0.5$ and to drill if $\rho = 1.0$.

[5] When all utilities are point-valued and all belief functions are true probability distributions, no assumption is required and the strategy will be identical to that prescribed by ordinary decision analysis.

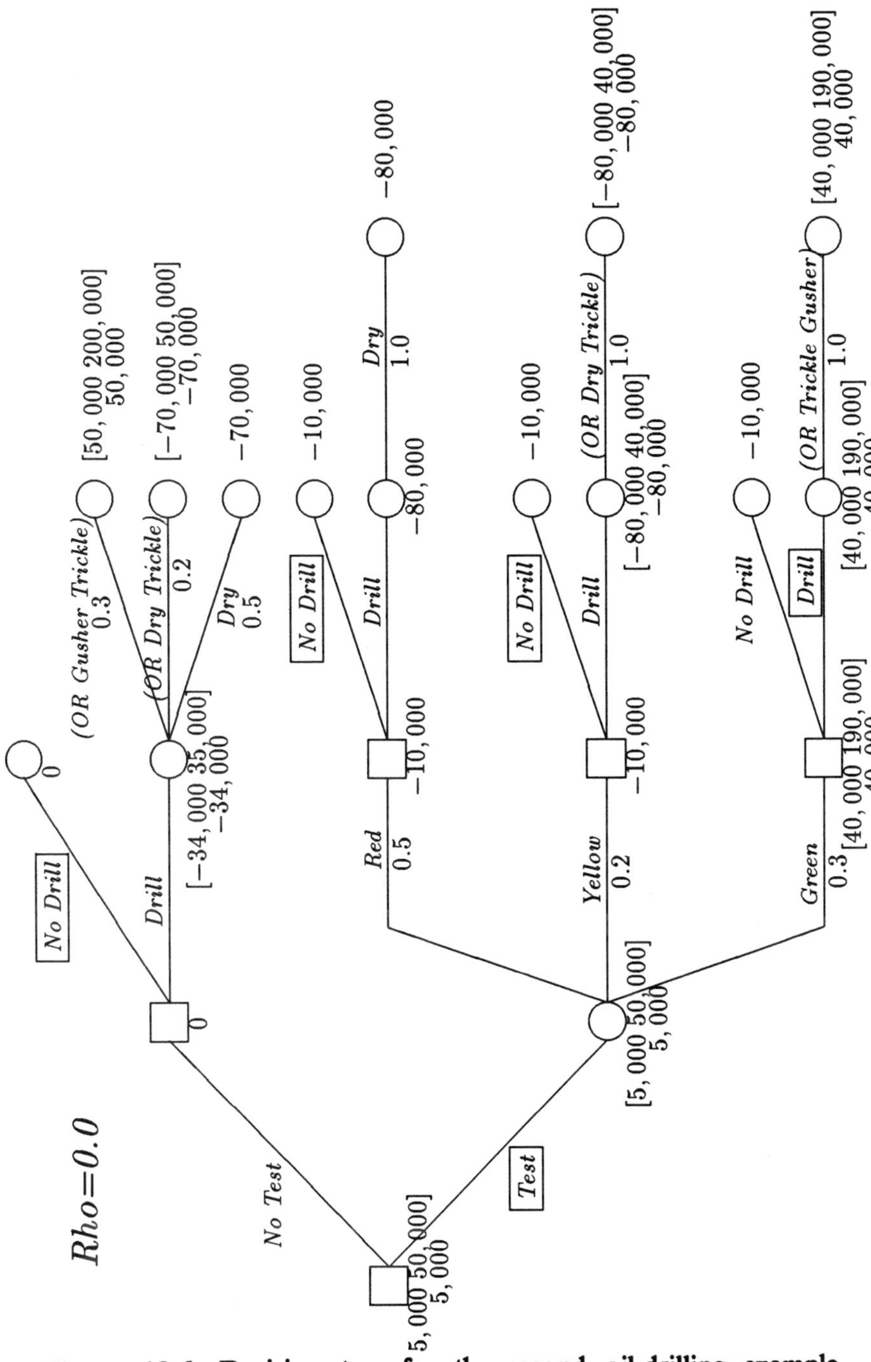

Figure 13.6: Decision tree for the second oil-drilling example (assuming $\rho = 0.0$).

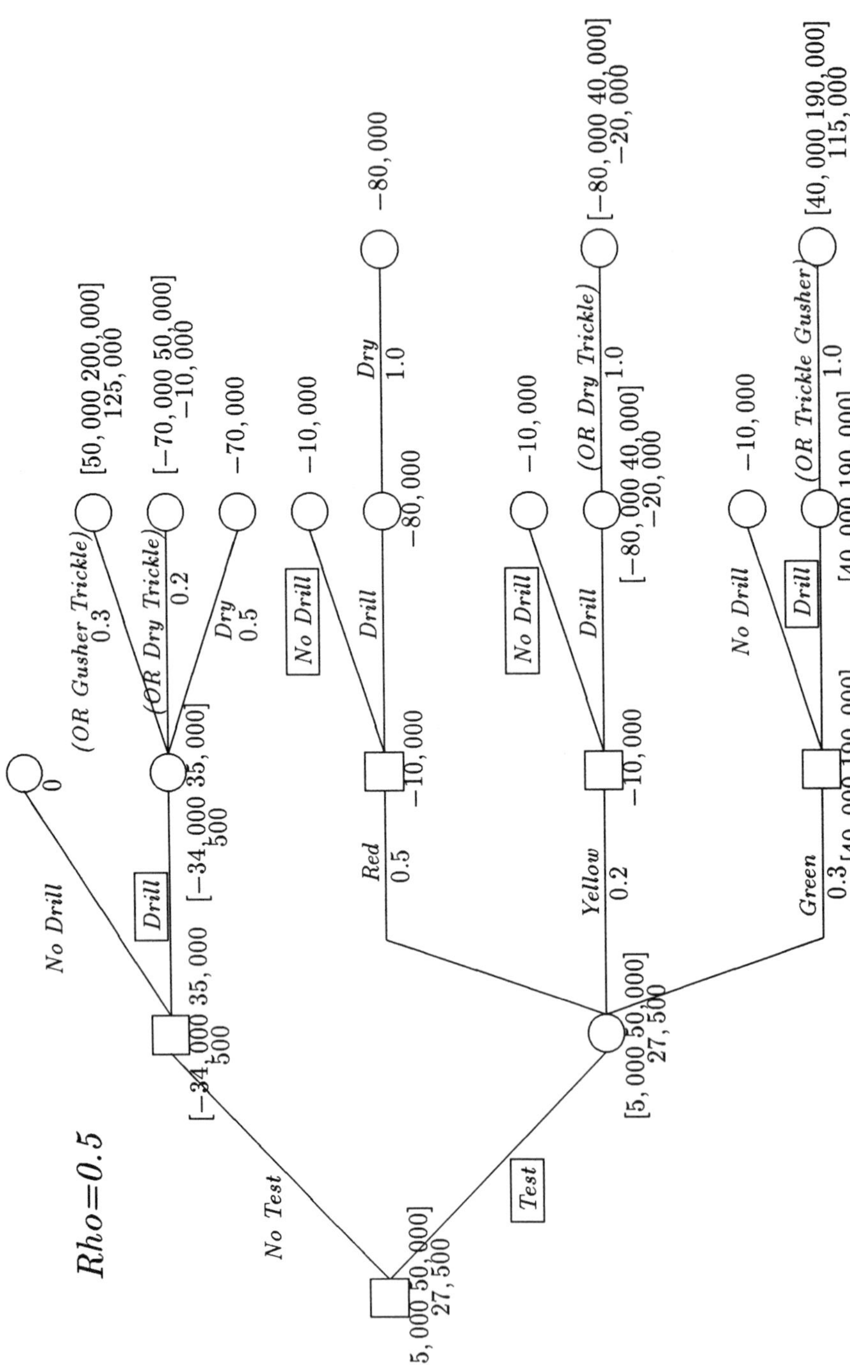

Figure 13.7: Decision tree for the second oil-drilling example (assuming $\rho = 0.5$).

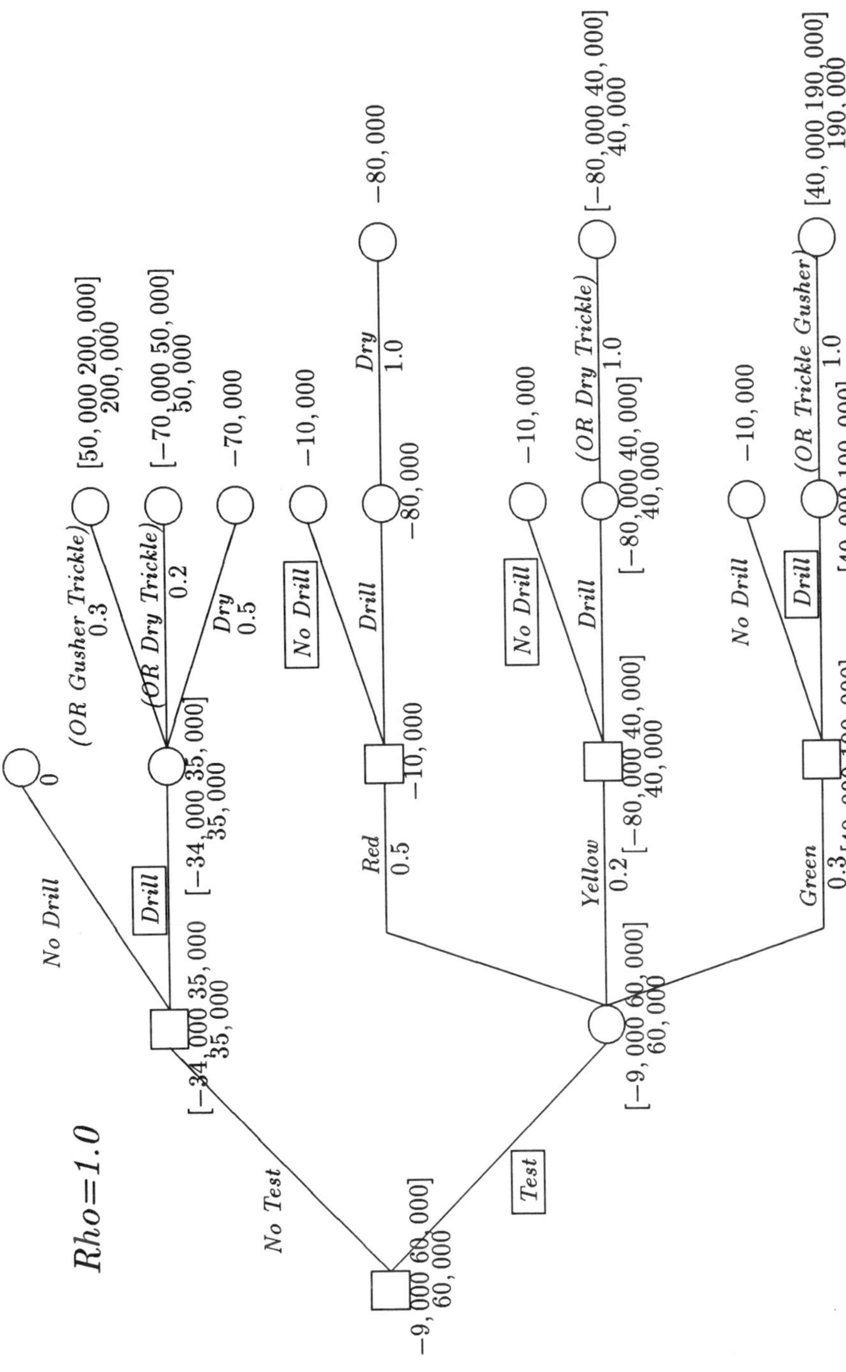

Figure 13.8: Decision tree for the second oil-drilling example (assuming $\rho = 1.0$).

If the test result is red, then one should not drill regardless of ρ (−10,000 is never as good as the interval [40,000 190,000]).

3.4. Comparing two choices

Instead of assuming a value for ρ first, and calculating the choices that result, one may ask the reverse question. At what value of ρ would I change my decision? This can be answered in general by examining a choice between two states having expected utility intervals.

Theorem 2: *Let the expected utility intervals of two choices be as follows:*

Choice 1: $[E_{1*}(x), E_1^*(x)]$
Choice 2: $[E_{2*}(x), E_2^*(x)]$

Assume without loss of generality that Choice 1 has the smaller interval, i.e., $(E_2^*(x) - E_{2*}(x)) > (E_1^*(x) - E_{1*}(x))$. *Then Choice 2 is preferred over Choice 1 iff*

$$\rho > \frac{E_{1*}(x) - E_{2*}(x)}{E_2^*(x) - E_1^*(x) + E_{1*}(x) - E_{2*}(x)} \tag{6}$$

Proof: Using Theorem 1 and solving for ρ gives the point ρ_c at which one is indifferent between Choice 1 and Choice 2:

$$\begin{aligned} E_1(x) &= E_{1*}(x) + \rho\cdot(E_1^*(x) - E_{1*}(x)) \\ E_2(x) &= E_{2*}(x) + \rho\cdot(E_2^*(x) - E_{2*}(x)) \\ \rho_c &= \frac{E_{1*}(x) - E_{2*}(x)}{(E_2^*(x) - E_1^*(x)) + (E_{1*}(x) - E_{2*}(x))} \end{aligned} \tag{7}$$

The expected value of both choices at ρ_c is

$$E_c(x) = \frac{E_{1*}(x)\cdot E_2^*(x) - E_1^*(x)\cdot E_{2*}(x)}{E_{1*}(x) - E_{2*}(x) + E_2^*(x) - E_1^*(x)}$$

Now consider the choice at $\rho = \rho_c + \delta$ where $\delta > 0$:

$$E_1(x) = E_c(x) + \delta\cdot(E_1^*(x) - E_{1*}(x)) \tag{8}$$
$$E_2(x) = E_c(x) + \delta\cdot(E_2^*(x) - E_{2*}(x)) \tag{9}$$

Since $(E_2^*(x) - E_{2*}(x)) > (E_1^*(x) - E_{1*}(x))$ and $\delta > 0$, it must be the case that $E_2(x) > E_1(x)$. Therefore, Choice 2 is preferred. Similar argument shows that Choice 1 is preferred whenever $\rho < \rho_c$.

Letting

$$a = E_{1*}(x) - E_{2*}(x) \text{ and } b = E_2^*(x) - E_1^*(x)$$

gives

$$\rho_c = \frac{a}{a+b} \tag{10}$$

Thus, Choice 1 is preferable if

$$\rho < \frac{a}{a+b}$$

and Choice 2 is preferable if

$$\rho > \frac{a}{a+b}$$

If $a/(a+b) > 1.0$ then Choice 1 is always preferred (no assumption of ρ is necessary). If $a/(a+b) < 0.0$ then Choice 2 is always preferred. It follows that whenever one EUI is slightly "higher" than another,

$$E_{1*}(x) > E_{2*}(x) \quad \text{and} \quad E_1^*(x) > E_2^*(x)$$

then the action that gives rise to it is always preferred.

Returning to the second oil-drilling example (Figure 13.5), the decision of whether or not to drill when the test result is yellow involves a choice between

No Drill: $E(x) = [-10{,}000 \ \ -10{,}000]$
Drill: $E(x) = [-80{,}000 \ \ 40{,}000]$

By Theorem 2, $\rho_c = 0.583$, and one should drill only if $\rho > 0.583$.

When $\rho > 0.583$, the decision as to whether or not to conduct the test involves a choice between

No Test: $E(x) = [-34{,}000 \ \ 35{,}000]$
Test: $E(x) = [-9{,}000 \ \ 60{,}000]$

Here, Test is the preferred choice because its EUI is higher.

4. DISCUSSION

The value of the result of an action is frequently measured in money (e.g., in dollars), but people often exhibit preferences that are not consistent with maximization of expected monetary value. The theory of *utility* accounts for this behavior by associating for an individual decision maker a value (measured in *utiles*) with each state s, $u = f(s)$, such that maximization of expected utility yields choices consistent with that individual's behavior (Howard, 1966). Utility theory can satisfactorily account for a person's willingness to expose himself to risk and should be used whenever one's preferences are not linearly related to value. This attitude toward risk should not be confused with one's attitude toward ambiguity, which is the quality that is modeled by ρ.

4.1. On making assumptions

It is interesting to compare the types of assumptions made in a probabilistic analysis with the ρ assumption proposed here for belief functions. When using probability, a maximum entropy assumption is often made. Sometimes, this assumption is justified, and it should properly be considered part of the evidence, not as an assumption. When this is the case, a maximum entropy belief function can be used as well (Dubois and Prade, 1982). At other times, the maximum entropy assumption is not justified, but is used simply because *some* assumption must be made, and maximum entropy has some desirable properties (Smets and Kennes, 1990). In these cases, the choice of elements in the sample space (the set of possibilities) introduces distortion into the expected value that will result. That is, adding a few more possibilities into the sample space will change the expected value of the maximum entropy distribution over that sample space. For example, if we choose to allow for the possibility of $2 being among the possibilities for the hidden sector of Carnival Wheel #2, the sample space would be $\{1,2,5,10,20\}$ instead of $\{1,5,10,20\}$, and the expected value of the maximum entropy distribution of that wheel would be $6.16 instead of $6.30. On the other hand, for any choice of ρ, the evidential expected value using either of the two preceeding sample spaces would be identically $(5.50 + 1.90\rho)$ dollars. Of course, adding possibilities outside the interval $[1, 20]$ would change the evidential expected value. For example, allowing for the possibility of $50 in the hidden sector would change the maximum entropy expected value to $7.12 and would change the evidential expected value to $(5.50 + 4.90\rho)$ dollars. The point is that both assumptions introduce bias into the decision criteria. This should not be surprising because *both* are unjustified assumptions. There is no basis on which to prefer one over the other; both assumptions are entirely plausible.

Having made this point, there are some consequently weak arguments for recommending the use of the assumption of the probability of nature's cooperation ρ. Because the EUI spans the range of all expected utilities that could be obtained by adding *any* assumption to a probabilistic analysis, there always exists some value of ρ, $0 \leqslant \rho \leqslant 1$ that yields the same expected utility $E(x)$ as probabilistic analysis. Therefore, the decisions that are prescribed depend only on one's ability to estimate ρ, not on his election to use (3). Furthermore, the use of a single parameter means that the decision maker is asked to provide only one additional piece of information.

The parameter ρ has been explained as a probability, giving it a formal grounding that earlier decision schemes for belief functions have lacked. Furthermore, we believe that it is the probability of a meaningful event. Selecting $\rho = 0$ is appropriate when an adversary controls the situation (as in game playing, for example) or when a decision maker wishes only to minimize his expected loss, and is equivalent to the maximin criteria of Wald. An optimistic decision maker would prefer to choose $\rho = 1$ to maximize his chance of realizing the greatest possible expected payoff without worrying about what losses might be possible. Intermediate values of ρ can be used to compromise between these extremes.

4.2. On the limitations of the approach

Despite the appeal of a computationally efficient decision analysis procedure for belief functions, there remain some issues that are not addressed. As in classical decision analysis, it remains necessary to enumerate the potential states of nature and to assign utilities (actually utility intervals, which should be easier to assign in practice). This task can be overwhelming when complex scenarios are considered. Furthermore, it should not be forgotten that the assignment of value to ρ (when it is necessary) remains an assumption unwarranted by the evidence at hand, just as maximum entropy or any other assumption is unwarranted when insufficient information is available.

It is inherent in the methodology described that the determination of what is best or worst is considered *after* the decision maker's choice is postulated. That is, the reaction of nature is allowed to depend on the decision that is to be taken. This is sometimes reasonable, and sometimes not. For example, conducting a regional test market for a new product may affect the national demand by virtue of publicity or increased competition. As a result, there may be no single underlying probability distribution that can simultaneously give rise to the expected utilities obtained for each choice. This should not be particularly worrisome as long as this consideration suits the problem at hand. If not, the expected utility intervals computed with the method described here may be wider than prescribed by the evidence. In that case, it is necessary to conduct a more complicated case-based analysis that is analogous to the linear-programming problems that arise in game theory. See Jaffray (1988) for further discussion of this approach.

4.3. On the automation of decision analysis

A probabilistic analysis of a decision problem (e.g., the second oil-drilling example) follows the paradigm: assess, assume, combine, decide. An *assessment* of a probability distribution is made for each piece of evidence; *assumptions* are made about the distributions of missing pieces of evidence; the assumptions and evidence are *combined* to obtain a distribution of payoffs, and a *decision* is made on the basis of the expected utility of the payoff. In contrast, a belief function analysis follows the paradigm: assess, combine, assume, decide. An *assessment* of a belief function is made for each piece of evidence; these pieces of evidence are then *combined* to obtain a belief function over the possible payoffs; then an *assumption* is made (about the benevolence of nature); and a *decision* is made using that assumption and the expected utility interval of the payoffs.

While the same decisions will be reached whether one makes assumptions first and then combines or combines evidence and then adds those assumptions, the difference in paradigms has important implications for automating the procedure. First, in some decision problems the EUI of the top choice will not overlap the EUI of any other choice, the decision follows from what is truly known, and in no way depends upon the accuracy of any assumption that might be made. Using belief functions, the best decision in this case is immediately determinable without additional assumptions. Because Bayes' rule requires a prior distribution, this situation cannot be recognized without a more complex sensitivity analysis when a purely probabilistic representation is used. Second, when an assumption must be made becase intervals do overlap, making it as late as possible allows one to maintain the assumption-free intermediate calculations for use in other computations. This is not an issue when the evidence will be used once and discarded, but affords a considerable computational savings when other decisions must be based on the original evidence plus new evidence as it comes along. Third, consider what must be computed if one chooses to use a different assumption (as needed for sensitivity analysis, for example). In a probabilistic analysis the assumptions and all evidence must be recombined before a decision can be made because the assumptions are needed to combine the evidence. Using belief functions, one need only combine the new assumption with the already combined evidence before selecting the decision. This separation of evidence and assumption is similar in spirit to the distinction between credal and pignistic beliefs described by Smets (1989).

5. CONCLUSION

We have proposed a decision analysis methodology for Shafer's theory of belief functions. We started by defining the notion of expected utility interval (EUI) and showed it to properly bound the expected utility of any probability distribution that could be obtained by introducing additional assumptions. Because an expected utility interval is often insufficient for decision making, we recognize that a point-value must be chosen to compare alternative choices. We then showed how a linear interpolation of a distinguished value within the EUI is equivalent to making an assumption of the benevolence or maleficence of nature. Letting ρ be the probability that ambiguity will be resolved favorably, we derived that distinguished point.

We have also shown how the theory can be used to generalize the decision trees used in probabilistic decision analysis. These tools allow a decision maker to defer unwarranted assumptions until the latest possible moment. In so doing he can sometimes avoid making any assumptions at all. Otherwise, he is forced to provide only enough additional information to allow a clear choice, and has the benefit of all available information to selectively decide where he would like to make that assumption.

We have implemented the techniques and have used that software to generate the decision trees shown in the figures in this paper. In addition a new evidential operator for decision making has been added to the repertoire of the evidential reasoning technology developed at SRI International (see Appendix B). Decision analysis has been incorporated into Gister,[6] SRI's evidential reasoning system, which uses the Dempster-Shafer theory of belief functions as its underlying representation.

What we have described is by no means a full theory of decision making for belief functions. Rather, we hope it may provide some insight that will someday lead to a better understanding of decision making with incomplete information.

ACKNOWLEDGMENT

I thank John Lowrance, Tom Garvey, Leonard Wesley, and Enrique Ruspini for their contributions to the ideas presented in this paper. I am also grateful for the close scrutiny provided by Philippe Smets, who called attention to the difference between this approach and the assumption of a single underlying probability distribution.

BIBLIOGRAPHY

Barnett, Jeffrey A. (1981). Computational methods for a mathematical theory of evidence. *Preceedings Seventh IJCAI,* Vancouver, Canada, pp. 868–75.

Dubois, Didier, and Prade, Henri. (1982). On several representations of an uncertain body of evidence. In Gupta, M.M., and Sanchez, E. (eds.), *Fuzzy information and decision processes,* pp. 167–81. Amsterdam: North-Holland.

Horvitz, Eric J., Breese, John S., and Henrion, Max. (1988, July). Decison theory in expert systems and artificial intelligence. *International Journal of Approximate Reasoning* 2(3): 247–302.

Howard, Ronald A. (1966). Decision analysis: Applied decision theory. In *Proceedings of the Fourth International Conference on Operational Research,* D. B. Hertz and J. Melese (eds.), pp. 55–77.

Howard, Ronald A. (1984). The science of decision-making. In Howard, R. A., Matheson, J. E., and Miller, K. L. (eds.), *Readings in decision analysis,* Chapter 6, pp. 147-164. Menlo Park, CA: SRI International.

Hurwicz, Leonid. (1952). A criterion for decision-making under uncertainty. Technical Report 355, Cowles Commission.

Jaffray, Jean-Yves. Application of utility theory to belief functions. In Bouchon, B., Saitta, L. and Yager, R. R. (eds.), *Uncertainty and Intelligence Systems,* pp. 1–8. Berlin: Springer-Verlag.

Lapin, Lawrence L. (1981). *Quantitative methods for business decisions.* New York: Harcourt Brace Jovanovich.

---

[6] Gister is a trademark of SRI International.

La Valle, Irving H. (1970). *An introduction to probability, decision, and inference*. New York: Holt, Rinehart, and Winston.
Lesh, Stephen A. (1986, December). An evidential theory approach to judgment-based decision making. Ph.D. Thesis, Department of Forestry and Environmental Studies, Duke University.
Loui, Ronald P., Feldman, Jerome A., and Kyburg, Henry G. E. Jr. (1985, August). Interval-based decisions for reasoning systems. *Proceedings of the Worksop on Uncertainty and Probability in Artificial Intelligence*, UCLA, pp. 193–99.
Lowrance, John D., Garvey, Thomas D., and Strat, Thomas M. (1986). A framework for evidential-reasoning systems. *Proceedings of AAAI-86*, Philadelphia.
Pittarelli, Michael. (1988). Decision making with linear constraints on probabilities. *Proceedings of the Fourth Workshop on Uncertainty in Artificial Intelligence*, University of Minnesota, pp. 283–90.
Raiffa, Howard. (1970). *Decision analysis: Introductory lectures on choices under uncertainty*. Reading, MA: Addison-Wesley.
Ruspini., Enrique H. (1986). The logical foundations of evidential reasoning. SRI International Technical Note 408.
Shafer, Glenn A. (1976). *A mathematical theory of evidence*. Princeton, NJ: Princeton University Press.
Shafer, Glenn A. (1982). Constructive decision theory. University of Kansas Department of Mathematics Working Paper.
Smets, Philippe. (1988). Belief functions. In Smets, P., Mamdani, E., Dubois, D., and Prade, H. (eds.), *Non-standard logics for automated reasoning*. London: Academic Press.
Smets, Philippe. (1989). Decision under uncertainty. *Proceedings of the Workshop on Uncertainty in Artificial Intelligence*.
Smets, Philippe, and Kennes, Robert. (1990). The transferable belief model: Comparison with Bayesian models. In Press.
Strat, Thomas M. (1984). Continuous belief functions for evidential reasoning. *Proceedings of AAAI-84*, Austin, TX.
Wald, Abraham. (1950). *Statistical decision functions*. New York: Wiley.
Yager, Ronald R. (1989). Decision making under Dempster-Shafer uncertainties. Iona College Machine Intelligence Institute Tech. Report #MII-915.

APPENDIX A. SUMMARY OF NOTATION

$p_\Theta(x)$	– Probability distribution over sample space Θ, $x \in \Theta$
$m_\Theta(A)$	– Mass function defined over frame of discernment Θ, $A \subseteq \Theta$
$Spt(A)$	– Support: $Spt(A) = \sum_{A_i \subseteq A} m_\Theta(A_i)$
$Pls(A)$	– Plausibility: $Pls(A) = 1 - Spt(\neg A)$

$E(x)$ – Expected value of random variable whose outcome is governed by a probability distribution:

$$E(x) = \sum_{x \in \Theta} x \cdot p_{\Theta}(x)$$

– Evidential expected value – the expected value of a variable governed by a belief function assuming that any residual ambiguity will be decided favorably with probability ρ:

$$E(x) = (1 - \rho) \cdot E_*(x) + \rho \cdot E^*(x)$$

$E^*(x)$ – Upper bound of expected value:

$$E^*(x) = \sum_{A_i \subseteq \Theta} \sup(A_i) \cdot m_{\Theta}(A_i)$$

$E_*(x)$ – Lower bound of expected value:

$$E_*(x) = \sum_{A_i \subseteq \Theta} \inf(A_i) \cdot m_{\Theta}(A_i)$$

EVI – Expected value interval: $[E_*(x), E^*(x)]$

EUI – Expected utility interval: Same as EVI, when Θ is a frame of utilities

ρ – The probability that any residual ambiguity will be decided favorably

$1 - \rho$ – The probability that any residual ambiguity will be decided unfavorably

ρ_c – The value of ρ at which one would be indifferent between two choices

APPENDIX B. DECISION MAKING WITH EVIDENTIAL REASONING

In this section we reanalyze the second oil-drilling example within the framework of evidential reasoning. First we review some of the tools of evidential reasoning and then introduce a decision operator for belief functions based on the theory described earlier.

In evidential reasoning, domain-specific knowledge is defined in terms of *compatibility relations* that relate one frame of discernment to another. A compatibility relation simply describes which elements from the two frames can simultaneously be true. A compatibility relation $\Theta_{A,B}$ between two frames Θ_A and Θ_B is a set of pairs such that

$$\Theta_{A,B} \subseteq \Theta_A \times \Theta_B$$

where every element of Θ_A and every element of Θ_B is included in at least one pair.

Evidential reasoning provides a number of formal operations for assessing evidence, including:

- **Fusion** – to determine a consensus from several bodies of evidence obtained from independent sources. Fusion is accomplished through Dempster's rule of combination:

$$m^3_\Theta(A_h) = \frac{1}{1-k} \sum_{A_i \cap A_j = A_h} m^1_\Theta(A_i) m^2_\Theta(A_j) \tag{11}$$

$$k = \sum_{A_i \cap A_j = \emptyset} m^1_\Theta(A_i) m^2_\Theta(A_j)$$

Dempster's Rule is both commutative and associative (meaning evidence can be fused in any order) and has the effect of focusing belief on those propositions that are held in common.

- **Translation** – to determine the impact of a body of evidence upon elements of a related frame of discernment. The *translation* of a belief function from frame Θ_A to frame Θ_B using the compatibility relation $\Theta_{A,B}$ is defined by

$$m_{\Theta_B}(B_j) = \sum_{\substack{C_{A\to B}(A_k) = B_j \\ A_k \subseteq \Theta_A,\ B_j \subseteq \Theta_B}} m_{\Theta_A}(A_k) \tag{12}$$

where $C_{A\to B}(A_k) = \{b_j | (a_i, b_j) \in \Theta_{A,B}, a_i \in A_k\}$

Several other evidential operations have been defined and are described elsewhere (Lowrance et al., 1986).

We now describe a new evidential operation for making decisions. Its operation is analogous to the evaluation of a choice node in probabilistic decision analysis, except that it is defined for belief functions and substitutes the notion of evidential expected utility for the probabilistic expected utility.

- **Decision** – to choose an action based on a body of evidence representing the states of nature believed at the time of the decision and a body of evidence representing the beliefs resulting from any particular decision. Let m_{Θ_A} represent the beliefs in frame Θ_A about the state of nature at the time a decision is to be made. Let frame Θ_D be the possible actions that can be taken. Let $m_{\Theta_U}(U|A,D)$ represent the beliefs over the utility frame Θ_U that result from making decision D when A is true. The mass function representing the best *policy* is

$$m_{\Theta_A \times \Theta_D}(A,D) = \begin{cases} m_\Theta(A) \text{ if } E(m_{\Theta_U}(U|A,D)) > E(m_{\Theta_U}(U|A,D_i)) \\ \qquad \text{for all } D_i \in \Theta_D,\ D_i \neq D \\ 0 \qquad \text{otherwise} \end{cases} \tag{13}$$

Ties are broken arbitrarily. The optimal policy computed by the decision node is given by the focal elements (A,D) in $m_{\Theta_A \times \Theta_D}$ (A,D_o) such that if A is the most precise statement known to be true, then the best decision is D.

Within Gister, a decision node is represented by a square. An evidence node leading into the decision node represents what would be known at the time a decision is to be made. The output of the decision node is the optimal policy (as defined above), and is represented as a belief function over the cross-product frame of states of nature and alternative decisions ($\Theta_A \times \Theta_D$). That belief function is then available to other evidential reasoning operations: it may be discounted, translated to a dependent frame, fused with additional evidence that would only be available after the decision is taken, etc. With this definition, a decision node represents a primitive operation that can be included in the data flow represented by an analysis. Figure 13.9 illustrates the analysis that was constructed for representing the second oil-drilling example within Gister.

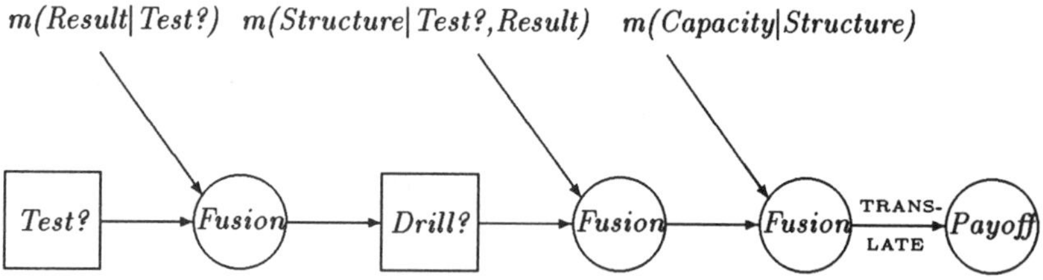

Figure 13.9: Evidential decision analysis of the second oil-drilling example.

The optimal policies computed by the Test? and Drill? nodes are summarized in Table 13.7 (assuming that $\rho = 0.5$). The result is identical to the strategy computed using a decision tree as can be verified by comparison with Figure 13.7.

Table 13.7: Contents of Test? and Drill? nodes.

Decision Test?:	Expected value: 27500	Rho = 0.5
1.0 = m((No Test Test))	-- Test	
E(x) = 27500	EVI = [5000 50000]	Test
E(x) = 500	EVI = [−34000 35000]	No Test
Decision Drill?:	Expected value: 27500	Rho = 0.5
1.50 = m((Test & Red))	-- No Drill	
E(x) = −10000	EVI = [−10000 −10000]	No Drill
E(x) = −80000	EVI = [−80000 −80000]	Drill
0.20 = m((Test & Yellow))	-- Drill	
E(x) = −10000	EVI = [−10000 −10000]	No Drill
E(x) = 20000	EVI = [−80000 40000]	No Drill
0.30 = m((Test & Green))	-- Drill	
E(x) = 115000	EVI = [40000 190000]	Drill
E(x) = − 10000	EVI = [−10000 −10000]	No Drill

14 On decision making using belief functions

Hung T. NGUYEN and Elbert A. WALKER

Abstract: We present an investigation into the problem of decision making based on numerical utilities in the context of expert systems, where partial knowledge is modeled by Dempster-Shafer's belief functions. In view of current approaches to this problem, we show that (i) the Choquet integral, that is, expected utility with respect to belief functions, leads to the pessimistic strategy of minimizing expected utilities, (ii) a more general framework can be established by considering expectations of functions of random sets, and (iii) the so-called (Laplace) insufficient reason principle can be properly generalized as a form of the maximum entropy principle. Algorithms for maximizing entropy are presented.

Keywords: belief functions, Choquet integral, evidence, expected utility, maximum entropy distributions, random sets.

1. INTRODUCTION

The theory of evidence developed by Shafer (1976) seems useful in modeling incomplete knowledge in various situations in artificial intelligence. Recently, there has been considerable interest in pursuing the possbility of decision making with belief functions from a numerical utility standpoint, for example, in Strat (1990), Yager (1990), Smets and Kennes (1990), and Shafer (1990). The time seems ripe for providing tools for decision making when the probabilistic information is incomplete. So far, belief functions have been used in modeling incomplete information, with Dempster's rule of combination as a counterpart for Bayes' formula in updating procedures. The problem of choosing a "best" course of action in the context of numerical utilities requires a counterpart of expected value of random variables. Since the information about a probability measure on the set of states of nature is incomplete, one is forced to deal with multi-valued random elements, that is, random sets, rather than with random variables, so that it is not clear what the counterpart of expectation of random variables is. Of course, from a mathematical viewpoint, one can consider expected values of random sets in the context of the theory of integration of random elements with values in separable Banach spaces. However, from the decision analysis standpoint, where it is necessary to compare expected utilities, such an approach is not feasible due to the lack of a total ordering of the set of values of random sets. Thus, all current approaches to this problem have been directed toward ways of extracting a single expected value from among a set of possible expected values, and providing a rationale for the one extracted. As we will see, since the problem is much less structured than a statistical decision problem, some form of additional, though subjective, information will be used in the extracting process. Most of these procedures are ad-hoc. In this paper, after presenting the problem of belief modeling through simple examples, we first consider the generalized expected utility values through the use of the Choquet integral. This is a natural attack in which no additional information is required. We show that this procedure leads to a pessimistic strategy in decision making, namely that of choosing a probability density minimizing the expected utility.

Next, it is shown that all current approaches can be put in a unified framework in which expectations of functions of random sets are used. Finally, we take the principle of maximum entropy as a reasonable way of selecting a particular density function in view of the available evidence. The classical Laplace principle of insufficient reason is generalized in this spirit. Some algorithms for entropy maximization are given.

2. BELIEF FUNCTION MODELING

In its simplest form, a decision problem consists of choosing an action among a collection of relevant actions **A** in such a way that utility is maximized. Specifically, if Θ denotes the collection of possible "states of nature," the true state θ_0 being unknown, then a utility function

$$u: \mathbf{A} \times \Theta \to \mathbf{R}$$

is specified, where $u(a, \theta)$ is the "payoff" when action a is chosen and nature presents θ. In the Bayesian framework, the knowledge about Θ is described by a probability P on Θ. Then the expected value $E_P u(a, \ )$ of the utility function $u(a, \theta)$ is used to make a choice as to which action a to take. When P is specified, the "optimal" action is the one that maximizes $E_P u(a, \ )$ over $a \in \mathbf{A}$. In practical problems in statistics, one can even gather more information about θ_0 through experimentation. In evidential knowledge problems, this luxury is not available.

The following examples illustrate the case where P is not known completely. To focus on the modeling of incomplete information, we leave aside the space of actions **A**, but will return to it in Section 7.

Example 1. Let $\Theta \ \Theta \{\theta_1, \theta_2 \ \theta_3\}$. The "true" probability measure P_0 is known only up to the extent that $P_0\{\theta_1\} = 1/3$ and then of course, $P_0\{\theta_2, \theta_3\} = 2/3$. Let **P** denote the class of probability measures on Θ having this property. Then it follows that $\mathbf{P} = \{P: F \leqslant P\}$, where F is defined on 2^Θ by $F(A) = \inf\{P(A): P \in \mathbf{P}\}$. Moreover, it is easily checked that $F(A) = \Sigma_{B \subseteq A} m(B)$, where $m\{\theta_1\} = 1/3$, $m\{\theta_1, \theta_3\} = 2/3$, and $m(A) = 0$ for all other subsets of Θ. Thus, F is a belief function in the sense of Shafer (1976). Note that the mass function m is a density on 2^Θ. For a density f on Θ, P_f is its associated probability. That is, $P_f(A) = \Sigma_{\theta \in A} f(\theta)$. The class **P** consists of those probability measures associated with the densities $\mathbf{F}_m = \{f: F \leqslant P_f\}$.

In Pfanzagl (1971), the following situation is considered. A box contains 30 red balls and 60 black and yellow balls in unknown proportions. A ball is going to be drawn from the box. Suppose the payoff of getting a red, black, and yellow ball are \$5, \$10, and \$20, respectively. What is the expected payoff?

Let $\Theta = \{\theta_1, \theta_2, \theta_3\}$, with θ_1 specifying red, θ_2 black, and θ_3 yellow. The density on Θ is not known, but is one of

Θ	θ_1	θ_2	θ_3
f	1/3	k/90	$(60 - k)/90$

where $k \in \{0, 1, \ldots, 60\}$. This model is strictly smaller than **F** above since the mass $m\{\theta_2, \theta_3\} = 2/3$ can only be distributed to θ_2 and θ_3 in discrete proportions of the form $k/90$ and $(60 - k)/90$, rather than in any proportions.

Example 2. Let $\Theta = \{1, 5, 10, 20\}$. Suppose that the information about the true probability is that $P\{1\} \geqslant 0.4$, $P\{5\} \geqslant 0.2$, $P\{10\} \geqslant 0.2$, and $P\{20\} \geqslant 0.1$. Let $\mathbf{P}$ denote the collection of all P satisfying these conditions. Then we can describe the "model" by $\mathbf{P} = \{P : F \leqslant P\}$, where for $A \in 2^{\Theta}$, $F(A) = inf\{P(a) : P \in \mathbf{P}\}$. If we let $m\{1\} = 0.4, m\{5\} = 0.2, m\{10\} = 0.2$, and $m\{20\} = 0.1$, then it can be checked that $F(A) = \Sigma_{B \subseteq A} m(B)$, so that F is a belief function.

This example is inspired by Strat (1990). However, Strat's example cannot be modeled by a belief function. His example is this. Consider a carnival wheel with ten equal sectors, four of which are labeled \$1, two \$5, two \$10, one \$20, and one sector is hidden from view. It is known, however, that the label in this hidden sector is among \$1, \$5, \$10, and \$20. The question is how much one is willing to pay to spin the wheel, receiving the amount shown in the sector that comes up.

Here, $\Theta = (1, 5, 10, 20\}$ and $u(\theta) = \theta$. There are four possible densities, given by the following table.

Θ	1	5	10	20
f_1	0.5	0.2	0.2	0.1
f_2	0.4	0.3	0.2	0.1
f_3	0.4	0.2	0.3	0.1
f_4	0.4	0.2	0.2	0.2

The "model" of this situation is $\mathbf{F} = \{f_1, f_2, f_3, f_4\}$. If $F(A) = \text{Min}_i\{P_{f_i}(A)\}$, then it is easy to check that $F(A) = \Sigma_{B \subseteq A} m(B)$ where m is given as above. However, $\mathbf{F}$ is strictly contained in $\mathbf{F}_m$. Indeed, the density

Θ	1	5	10	20
g	0.425	0.225	0.225	0.125

is clearly in $\mathbf{F}_m$ but not in $\mathbf{F}$. Also, for $\rho \in (0, 1)$, a density f_ρ of the form

Θ	1	5	10	20
f_ρ	$0.4 + 0.1(1 - \rho)$	0.2	0.2	$0.1 + 0.1\rho$

is in $\mathbf{F}_m$ but not in $\mathbf{F}$. The point is this. If we seek a density to "approximate" the unknown true one, then it should be in the model $\mathbf{F}$. The model $\mathbf{F}_m$ should not be substituted for the model $\mathbf{F}$ unless they are the same.

Example 3. This example generalizes Example 1. Let $\{\Theta_1, \Theta_2,...,\Theta_k\}$ be a partition of the finite set Θ. Suppose that the information about the true probability measure is that $P_0(\Theta_i) = \alpha_i$. Then this model $\mathbf{P} = \{P: P(\Theta_i) = \alpha_i\}$ can be described by a belief function. That is,

(i) $F(A) = inf\{P(A): P \in \mathbf{P}\}$ for $A \in 2^\Theta$ is a belief function, and
(ii) $\mathbf{P} = \{P: F \leqslant P\}$.

Indeed, let $A \in 2^\Theta$. The "best" lower approximation of A by the Θ_i is

$$\underline{A} = \cup_{\Theta_i \subseteq A} \Theta_i$$

Now it is clear that all the $P \in \mathbf{P}$ agree on $\underline{A}$ and so we may define $G: 2^\Theta \to [0,1]$ by $G(A) = P(\underline{A})$ for any $P \in \mathbf{P}$. We are going to show that

(i) F is an infinite monotone capacity, that is, a belief function.
(ii) $\mathbf{P} = (P: G \leqslant P\}$.
(iii) $G = F$.

For (i), use the obvious facts that

$$\cup \underline{A_i} \leqslant (\underline{\cup A_i})$$

and

$$\cap \underline{A_i} = (\underline{\cap A_i})$$

Now, $F(\Phi) = P(\Phi) = P(\underline{\Phi}) = 0$, and $F(\Theta) = P(\Theta) = P(\underline{\Theta}) = 1$. Now it follows that

$$G(\cup \underline{A_i}) \geqslant \sum_{I \subseteq \{1,...,n\}} (-1)^{|I|+1} G(\underline{\cap A_i})$$

For (ii), since $\underline{A} \subseteq$ A, $G \leqslant P$ for all $P \in \mathbf{P}$. Conversely, if Q is a probability mearure on Θ such that $G \leqslant Q$, then in particular, $G(\Theta_i) = P(\underline{\Theta_i}) = P(\Theta_i) = \alpha_i \leqslant Q(\Theta_i)$. Since P and Q are probabilities and $\{\Theta_1, \Theta_2,...,\Theta_k\}$ is a partition, it follows that $Q(\Theta_i) = \alpha_i$ for all i.

For (iii), it suffices to show that for $A \in 2^\Theta$ there is a $P_A \in \mathbf{P}$ such that $P_A(A) = P_A(\underline{A})$. But this is obvious.

Example 4. In expert systems, a typical situation is this. The "evidence" is represented mathematically as a density m on 2^Θ, or equivalently, since Θ is finite, as a belief function F. As we will see in Section 3, the class **F** is not empty, but it might be immaterial. Besides the situation in this example where the model is given directly by a mass function m on 2^Θ, the belief function modeling of a probabilistic model such as in Examples 1, 2, and 3 has some advantages. First, when we know only that the true probability P_0 is in **P**, a lower bound for $P_0(A)$ is $F(A) = inf\{A\}: P \in \mathbf{P}\}$. Also, if $u: \Theta \to \mathbf{R}$ is a utility function, a lower bound for the expected utility $E_{P_0}(u)$ is $inf \{E_P(u): P \in \mathbf{P}\}$. In general, these quantities are hard to compute. As we will see in Section 4, when $\mathbf{P}$ can be modeled by m, $\inf\{E_P(u): P \in \mathbf{P}\}$ turns out to be fairly easy to compute.

Second, when the maximum entropy principle is used as a way of obtaining a cononical distribution on Θ, the constraint **F** turns out to be easier to handle than the orignal model **P**. This is due essentially to the fact that densities in **F** can be related to m in a more "visual" way.

Finally, for decision analysis, where the concept of expected utilities is essential, a model of the form (Θ, m, u) is convenient. Indeed, as shown in Section *s*, the most general way for defining an expected utility is to select a set-function $\varphi: 2^{\Theta} \to \mathbf{R}$, depending on u, and take

$$E_m(\varphi) = \sum_{A \subseteq \Theta} \varphi(A) m(A)$$

which is an ordinary expectation of a function of a random set.

After reviewing belief functions in Section 3, we look in Section 4 at a concept of expected value with respect to a belief function (which is not to be confused with Strat's "expected value using belief functions") and show that this leads to picking a density in $\mathbf{F}_m$, depending on the utility function u, and minimizing expected utility over $\mathbf{F}_m$. In Section 5, we point out that all current approaches to this problem are nothing more than choosing some function of a random set. The Choquet integral approach in Section 4, as well as the maximum entropy principle, are no exceptions.

3. BELIEF FUNCTIONS

The following elementary exposition of the basic concepts of belief functions in the finite case is sufficient for our purposes here. The reader might want to consult the excellent work of Wasserman (1990a, b) for the continuous case.

Let Θ be a finite set and **P** any set of probability measures on Θ. We take the algebra of subsets of Θ to be 2^{Θ}. Then, since Θ is finite, the density f associated with $F \in \mathbf{P}$ is given by $f(\theta) = F(\{\theta\})$. If f is a density on Θ, then its associated measure P_f is defined by $P_f(A) = \Sigma_{\theta \in A} f(\theta)$. The set function defined on 2^{Θ} by

$$F(A) = \inf\{P(A): P \in \mathbf{P}\}$$

has the following properties:

(i) $F(\Phi) = 0, F(\Theta) = 1$,
(ii) if $A \subseteq B$, then $F(A) \leqslant F(B)$.

For Θ finite, such a set function is called a (Choquet) capacity. For example, if **P** is the set of all probability measures on Θ, it P_0 is a probability measure on Θ and $0 < \varepsilon < 1$, then the capacity associated with

$$\mathbf{P} = \{(1-\varepsilon)P_0 + \varepsilon Q : Q \in \mathbf{P}\}$$

is of a special type called *infinitely monotone*. This means that for any family $A_1, A_2,..., A_n$ of subsets of 2^{Θ}, it satisfies

$$F(\cup_J \mathrm{A}_i) \geqslant \sum_{\Phi \neq J \subseteq I} (-1)^{|J|+1} F(\cap_J A_i)$$

where $I = \{1, 2,...., n\}$. To see this, note first that for $A \neq \Theta$, $F(A) = (1-\varepsilon)P_0(A)$ since there is a Q in **P** with $Q(A) = 0$. Thus

$$F(\cup_I A_i) \geqslant \sum_{\Phi \neq J \subseteq I} (-1)^{|J|+1} F(\cap_J A_i)$$

for $\cup_I A_i \neq \Theta$. For $\cup_I A_i = \Theta$, $F(\cup_I A_i) = 1$ and $\Sigma_{\Phi \neq J \subseteq I} (-1)^{|J|+1}$ $F(\cap_J A_i) = (1-\varepsilon)P_0(\cup_I A_i) \leqslant 1 - \varepsilon$, unless each $A_i = \Theta$, in which case $\Sigma_{\Phi \neq J \subseteq I}(-1)^{|J|+1} F(\cap_J A_i) = 1$. In any case, the desired inequality holds.

Now for an infinitely monotone capacity F, m defined on 2^{Θ} by $m(A) = \Sigma_{B \subseteq A}(-1)^{|A/B|} F(B)$ is nonnegative, $\Sigma\, m(A) = 1$, $m(\Phi) = 0$, and $m(\Theta) = 1$. By Möbius inversion (see, for example, Aigner, 1979), $F(A) = \Sigma_{B \subseteq A}\, m(B)$. If we view $m: 2^{\Theta} \rightarrow [0,1]$ as a probability density, then F plays the role of a distribution function of some *random set* $S: (\Omega, \mathrm{A}, P) \rightarrow 2^{\Theta}$, where $m(A) = P\{\omega : S(\omega) = A\}$, and $F(A) = P\{\omega\} : S(\omega) \subseteq A$, with $P(S = \Phi) = 0$. (See, for example, Hestir et al., 1991.) The distribution function F, which is an infinitely monotone capacity, is called a *belief function*. In the example above, the class **P** of probability measures on Θ is described as $\mathbf{P} = \{P : F \leqslant P\}$, with F being a belief function. Indeed, if $P \in \mathbf{P}$ and $F \leqslant P$, then

$$f(\theta) = P(\{\theta\}) - F(\{\theta\}) = [P(\{\theta\}) - (1-\varepsilon)P_0\{\theta\}]/\varepsilon \geqslant 0.$$

Moreover, f is a density on Θ. Thus

$$P = (1-\varepsilon)P_0 + \varepsilon P_f$$

is in **P**.

If F is a belief function on Θ, then the class $\{P : F \leqslant P\}$ is not empty, and $F(A) = \mathit{inf}\{P(A) : F \leqslant P\}$. In fact, for each A, define for $\theta \in A$,

$$f_A(\theta) = \sum_{\theta \in B \subseteq A} m_F(B)/|A|$$

and for $\theta \notin A$,

$$f_A(\theta) = \sum_{\theta \in B} m_F(B)/|B \backslash AB|$$

Then $P_{f_A} \geqslant F$ and

$$P_{f_A}(A) = \sum_{\theta \in A} f_A(\theta) = \sum_{\theta \in A} \sum_{B:\theta \in B \subseteq A} m(B)/|B| =$$
$$= \sum_{B \subseteq A} m(B)/|B| \sum_{\theta \in B} 1 = \sum_{B \subseteq A} m(B) = F_m(A)$$

Not all classes P of probability measures can be represented as $\{P:F \leqslant P\}$ with $F = \inf\{P:P \in \mathbf{P}\}$ with F a belief function. See Wasserman and Kadane (1990) for examples.

Another example where a class **P** is described by a belief function is that arising from a partition $\Theta_1, \Theta_2,\ldots,\Theta_n$ of Θ. Define m on 2^Θ by $m(\Theta_i) = \alpha_i$ and $m(A) = 0$ for all other elements of 2^Θ, where $\alpha_i \geqslant 0$ and $\Sigma\, \alpha_i = 1$. Then $\mathbf{P}\{P:F_m \leqslant P\}$. (See Section 2.) The α_i could arise from a probability space (Ω, E Q) and a mapping $Y:\Omega \rightarrow \{\Theta_1, \Theta_2,\ldots,\Theta_n\}$ such that $Y^{-1}(\Theta_i) \in$ E, and defining m by $m(\Theta_i) = Q(Y^{-1}(\Theta_i))$. More generally, if $\{\Theta_1, \Theta_2,\ldots,\Theta_n\}$ is replaced by any finite set Γ, then m is always a density on Γ. When $\Gamma = \Theta$, this is the familiar situation in probability where m induces only one density on Θ. When $\Gamma = 2^\Theta$, the density m induces a class $\mathbf{F}_m$ of densities on Θ, namely those compatible with it, which is the set $\{f:F_m \leqslant P_f\}$. By a density being compatible with m, we mean that $f(\theta) = \Sigma_{\theta \in A}\, \alpha_A(\theta)$, where $m(A) = \Sigma_{\theta \in A}\, \alpha_A(\theta)$ with $\alpha_A(\theta) \geqslant 0$. (See Dempster, 1967.) For example, setting $\alpha_A(\theta) = m(A)/|A|$ yields a density compatible with m.

In Example 2, the "naive density" is obtained by calculating $m(A)/|A|$ for each A for which $m(A) \neq 0$. These are $m(\{1\})/1 = 0.4$, $m(\{5\})/1 = 0.2$, $m(\{10\})|1 = 0.2$ $m(\{20\})/1 = 0.1$, and $m(1, 5, 10, 20\})/4 = 0.025$. Thus the naive density f is given by

$$f(1) = 0.425, f(5) = 0.225, f(10) = 0.225, f(20) = 0.125$$

4. EXPECTATION WITH RESPECT TO A BELIEF FUNCTION

If u is an integrable random variable defined on a probability space (Θ, E, P), then its expected value can be written as

$$E_P(u) = \int_0^\infty P(u^+ > t)dt - \int_0^\infty P(u^- > t)dt =$$

$$= \int_0^{\infty} P(u > t)dt + \int_{-\infty}^{0} (P(u > t) - 1)dt$$

Here, u^+ and u^- are the positive and negative parts of u, respectively. If P is replaced by a capacity F, then E_P is generalized as a Choquet integral by

$$E_F(u) = \int_0^{\infty} F(u > t)dt + \int_{-\infty}^{0} (F(u > t) - 1)dt$$

If $u \geqslant 0$, then the second term in this definition vanishes. It should be noted that this definition is obtained just by replacing P by F in

$$\int_0^{\infty} P(u > t)dt + \int_{-\infty}^{0} (P(u > t) - 1)dt$$

rather than defining it for $u \geqslant 0$ and then using $u = u^+ - u^-$. This is necessary because E_F is not an additive operator.

When Θ is finite, the computation of $E_F(u)$ is simple (Wakker, 1989). Suppose that $\Theta = \{\theta_1, \theta_2, \ldots, \theta_n\}$. We may as well take

$$u(\theta_1) \leqslant u(\theta_2) \leqslant \ldots \leqslant u(\theta_n)$$

It is easy to check that

$$E_F(u) = \sum_1^n u(\theta_i)\,[F(\{\theta_i, \theta_{i+1}, \ldots, \theta_n\}) - F(\{\theta_{i+1}, \theta_{i+2}, \ldots, \theta_n\})]$$

Now

$$g(\theta_i) = F(\{\theta_i, \theta_{i+1}, \ldots, \theta_n\}) - F(\theta_{i+1}, \theta_{i+2}, \ldots, \theta_n\})$$

is a probability density on Θ, so that the Choquet integral $E_F(u)$ is an ordinary probabilistic expectation, but the density used for this ordinary expectation depends not only on F but on the ordering given Θ via u. When our probabilistic knowledge about Θ is modeled by a belief function F, then $E_F(u)$ can be used as a generalized expected value of the utility function u. This seems attractive since our criteria for decision should involve u rather than other more subjective factors. The theorem below shows that, using $E_F(u)$ for decision making leads to the pessimistic strategy of minimizing probabilistic expected values.

Theorem. *Let* Θ *be finite,* $u: \Theta \to \mathbf{R}$, *and* F *a belief function on* Θ. *Then there exists a density* $g \in \mathbf{E}_{m_F}$ *such that*

$$E_F(u) = E_{P_g}(u) = \inf\{E_{P_f}(u) : f \in \mathbf{E}_{m_F}\}$$

Proof. As above, let

$$g(\theta_i) = F(\{\theta_i, \theta_{i+1},\dots,\theta_n\}) - F(\{\theta_{i+1}, \theta_{i+2},\dots,\theta_n\})$$

For $A_i = \{\theta_i, \theta_{i+1},\dots,\theta_n\}$,

$$g(\theta_i) = F(A_i) - F(A_i\backslash\{\theta_i\}) = \textstyle\sum_{B\subseteq A_i} m(B) - \sum_{B\subseteq(A_i\backslash\{\theta_i\})} m(B)$$
$$= \textstyle\sum_{\theta_i\in B\subseteq A_i} m(B)$$

which shows that g is in $\mathbf{F}_{m_F}$.

For the rest, it suffices to show that for any $t\in\mathbf{R}$ and for all $f\in\mathbf{F}_{m_F}$, we have

$$E_{P_f}(u) = \int_0^\infty P_f(u) > t)dt + \int_{-\infty}^0 (P(u > t) - 1)dt \geqslant E_{P_g}(u)$$

Indeed, let $(u > t) = \{\theta_i, \theta_{i+1},\dots,\theta_n\}$. Then by construction of g, we have

$$P_g(u > t) = \sum_{i=1}^n g(\theta_k) = \sum m(B)$$

where the summation is over all subsets of $\{\theta_i, \theta_{i+1},\dots,\theta_n\}$. If $f\in\mathbf{F}_{m_F}$, then $P_f(u > t) = \sum_{i=1}^n f(\theta_k)$, where the set of A's for which $m(A)$ can be distributed to the θ_k for $k \geqslant i$ is at least as large as that of the set of B's above.

In Example 2, g turns out to be f_1 as seen from

$$g(1) = F\{1, 2, 3, 4\} - F\{2, 3, 4\} = 1 - 0.5 = 0.5$$
$$g(2) = F\{2, 3, 4\} - F\{3, 4\} = 0.5 - 0.3 = 0.2$$
$$g(3) = F\{3, 4\} - F\{4\} = 0.3 - 0.1 = 0.2$$
$$g(4) = F\{4\} = 0.1$$

$E_F(u) = \Sigma\, u(i)g(i) = 5.5$. Further, this expected value is the smallest of all those whose densities are compatible with m_F. This is clear since all the mass to be distributed is assigned to the smallest utility. Namely $m_F\{1, 2, 3, 4\} = 0.1$, it is all assigned to 1, and $u(1)$ is smaller than all the other values of u. This holds in general. Namely, $E_F(u) = E_{P_g}(u)$ where g is a density compatible with m_F with the resulting expectation the smallest.

The fact that the Choquet integral of u is equal to $inf\{E_P(u): P\in\mathbf{P}\}$ when $\mathbf{P}$ is modeled by $\mathbf{P}_m$ is known from the work of Wasserman (1987) even in the general case. However, the computation of $inf\{E_P(u): P\in\mathbf{P}\}$ seems to relate to another integral rather than directly to the Choquet integral. Also, it is not clear whether in Wasserman the $inf\{E_P(u): P \in \mathbf{P}\}$ is actually attained. Wasserman worked in Dempster's scheme of multivalued mappings, where his proof of the result above was much less direct than ours. He first showed that the Choquet integral is equal to an ordinary integral of some associated function, and then, using selectors of a multivalued mapping, he showed that this ordinary integral is in fact $inf\{E_P(u\}: P \in \mathbf{P}\}$.

5. EXPECTATION OF A FUNCTION OF A RANDOM SET

Current approaches to decision making based on numerical utilities, such as those of Yager, Smets and Kennes, and Strat (1990), are all centered around the idea of extracting a single value from the evidence to form a reasonable concept of expected utility. To do this, they all rely heavily on various additional subjective assumptions. In discussing the Transferable Belief Model, Smets and Kennes (1990) argue the use of a probability density compatible with the mass function *m*, namely the *naive density*

$$f(\theta) = \sum_{\theta \in A} m(A)/|A|$$

(See also Dubois and Prade, 1982.)

Note that the transformation $m \to P_f$ above is *not* of the form $h \circ m$ for some $h: [0,1] \to [0,1]$. Such a form is what Lindley (1982) required for "admissibility" of an uncertainty measure (see Goodman et al., 1991). This is opposed to the case of Sugeno measure. If

$$\mu: 2^{\Theta} \to [0,1]$$

is such that $\mu(\Phi) = 0$, $\mu(\Theta) = 1$, and $\mu(A \cup B) = \mu(A) + \mu(B) + \lambda\mu(A)\mu(B)$ for some $\lambda > -1$, then μ can be transformed into a probability measure on 2^{Θ}. Indeed, take

$$h(x) = log_{1+\lambda}(1 + \lambda x)$$

for x in [0,1]. Then $h \circ \mu$ is a probability measure. (See, for example, Wierzchoń, 1987.)

The rationale behind the choice of the naive distribution f above is the so-called *Laplace insufficient reason principle* (Jaynes, 1979). We will elaborate further on this principle in the next section in connection with the maximum entropy principle.

The approach of Section 4 as well as that of Section 6, based on maximum entropy, leads to the selection of a density $f \in \mathbf{F}_m$ in order to come up with an expected utility $E_f(u)$. Now it is clear that, for an $f \in \mathbf{F}_m$, one can find many set functions $\varphi : 2^{\Theta} \to \mathbf{R}$ such that

$$E_f(u) = E_m(\varphi) = \sum_{A \in 2^{\Theta}} \varphi(A)m(A)$$

In fact, define φ arbitrarily on every element of 2^{Θ} except for some A for which $m(A) \neq 0$, and define $\varphi(A) = [E_f(u) - \Sigma_{B \neq A} \varphi(B) m(B)]/m(A)$. The point is this. Selecting φ and considering $E_m(\varphi) = \sum \varphi(a)m(a)$ as expected utility seems to be a more general procedure.

In Strat (1990), a set function φ is selected for decision making as follows. For $\rho \in [0,1]$, define

$$\varphi_\rho(A) = \rho \max\{u(\theta) : \theta \in A\} + (1 - \rho) \min\{u(\theta) : \theta \in A\}$$

It turns out that $E_m(\varphi_\rho) = E_f(u)$, where the density f is constructed as follows. Suppose that $\Theta = \{\theta_1, \theta_2,\ldots,\theta_3\}$ is ordered so that

$$u(\theta_1) \leqslant, u(\theta_2) \leqslant,\ldots, \leqslant u(\theta_n)$$

Now f is defined by

$$f(\theta_i) = \rho \textstyle\sum_{\mathbf{A}} m(A) + (1 - \rho) \sum_{\mathbf{B}} m(A)$$

where

$$\mathbf{A} = \{A : \theta_i \in A \subseteq \{\theta_1,\ldots,\theta_i\}\}$$

and

$$\mathbf{B} = \{A : \theta_i \in A \subseteq \{\theta_i,\ldots,\theta_n\}\}$$

The interpretation of this density is this. For each θ_i, subsets A containing θ_i and made up of elements θ_j with $j \leqslant i$ get the proportion ρ of their mass $m(A)$ given to $f(\theta_i)$, and subsets A containing θ_i and made up of elements θ_j with $j \geqslant i$ get the proportion $1 - \rho$ of their mass $m(A)$ given to $f(\theta_i)$. If $\rho = 0$, then $E_f(u) = \min\{E_h(u) : h \in \mathbf{F}_m\}$ as in Section 4. At the set-function level, we see that the set of values $\{u(\theta) : \theta \in A\}$ is transformed into the single number

$$\rho \max\{u(\theta) : \in A\} + (1 - \rho) \min\{u(\theta) : \theta \in A\}$$

Two remarks are in order here: (i) This number is a function only of the *max* and *min* of u. (ii) The transformation depends on the parameter ρ supplied by the decision maker.

In his recent work, Yager (1990) proceeded in precisely this direction and considered the selection of φ in a more general fashion.

For each A for which $m(A) > 0$, the decision maker decides subjectively on a vector $(w_1(A), w_2(A),...,w_{|A|}(A))$, with $w_i(A) \geqslant 0$ and $\Sigma w_i(A) = 1$. Then $\varphi(A)$ is taken to be $\Sigma u_i w_i(A)$, where the u_i are the values of the $u(\theta)$ for $\theta \in A$ arranged in increasing order of magnitude. the choice of the vector of w's can be done by the decision maker giving a "degeree of optimism" α and relying on some principle such as maximum entropy to specify this vector. For example, choose $(w_1(A), w_2(A),...,w_{|A|}(A))$ to maximize $\Sigma w_1(A) \, log(w_i(A))$ subject to $w_i(A) \geqslant 0$ and $\sum w_i(A) = 1$, and $\Sigma(|A|) - i)/(|A| - 1)w_i(A) = \alpha$. (For $|A| = 1$, there is nothing to do; $\varphi(A) = u(\theta)$, where $A = \{\theta\}$.)

As in Strat (1990), once φ is chosen, the ordinary expectation $E_m(\varphi)$ is used as an expected utility for decision purposes. In all the above, the selection of φ depends on an additional parameter, ρ in the case of Strat, and α in the case of Yager. It all boils down to using some additional subjective opinion of the decision maker to transform sets of values of utilities to numbers, that is, to considering functions of random sets. This leads to strategies different from the extremes ones, either pessimistic or optimistic. the justification of the parameters involved in this process remains.

A very general way to define the concept of expected utility in the framework (Θ, m, u) is to select a set function $\varphi: 2^{\Theta} \to \mathbf{R}$ and to form $E_m(\varphi)$. But there should be some rationale for the process used to select φ. As far as the latter is concerned, the maximum entropy principle seems to be a reasonable one in some decision-making problems. That is the topic of the next section.

6. MAXIMUM ENTROPY DISTRIBUTIONS

In this section, we investigate in some detail a commonly used rationale for selecting a canonical probability distribution from among a set of relevant ones. When there is no information about a finite set of states of nature Θ, it makes sense to put the elements of Θ on an equal footing, that is, to endow Θ with a uniform distribution. This is Laplace's *insufficient reason principle* (Jaynes, 1979). If the occurence of elements of Θ are governed by a probability density f on Θ, then a measure of the uncertainty of the phenomenon is the *entropy* of f, that is,

$$H(f) = \sum_{\theta} f(\theta) \, log(f(\theta))$$

The entropy of f does not involve the utility function. Since the uniform distribution has the highest entropy among all densities on

Θ, the *insufficient reason principle* is equivalent to the *principle of maximum entropy*. Motivated by the success of statistical mechanics, the principle of maximum entropy has been formalized as an inference procedure (Jaynes, 1957). The postulated density of Laplace is one that maximizes $H(f)$ over all densities f on Θ. More generally, if **F** is any set of densities on Θ, determined by constraints or evidence on the possible laws governing Θ, then we are led to seek an $f \in \mathbf{F}$ with maximum $H(f)$. A familiar situation is when **F** is a collection of densities with a given expected utility value, and in that case, such a density can be found (see, for example, Guiasu, 1977). In the decision problem under the evidence, the constraint set is $\mathbf{F}_m$. The case of total ignorance corresponds to the m with $m(\Theta) = 1$, and then $\mathbf{F}_m$ is the set of all densities on Θ. Laplace's insufficient reason principle is to select the f having the greatest entropy from the set of all densities on Θ. A generalization of this principle in the context of evidence is to select a density f having the greatest entropy from $\mathbf{F}_m$ where the "evidence" is presented through m. In Example 1,

X	θ_1	θ_2	θ_3
f	1/3	$k/90$	$(60 - k)/90$

with $k \in \{0, 1, 2, \ldots, 60\}$. The density in F_m with maximum entropy is the uniform density, that is, with each color occurring with probability 1/3. That this density is actually in the model is somewhat of an accident. The mass of θ_1 has been fixed at 1/3, and the mass of the other two elements can be equally distributed between them, making the situation as uncertain as possible.

If m is a density on 2^{Θ}, and the focal elements of m are *disjoint*, then the density in $\mathbf{F}_m$ with maximum entropy is given by $f(\theta) = \Sigma_{\theta \in A} m(A)/|A|$. That is, the mass of A is distributed equally to the elements of A. In Example 2, where the focal elements are not mutually disjoint, assigning the remaining mass .1 equally to each of 1, 5, 10, and 20 yields an entropy of 1.2948, while the maximum entropy density is given by $f(1) = 0.4$, $f(5) = 0.2$, $f(10) = 0.2$, and $f(20) = 0.2$. The mass $m\{1, 5, 10, 20\} = 0.1$ can be distributed in any proportion, but to make the uncertainty maximum, the whole mass 0.1 should be assigned to 20 in view of the other masses 0.4, 0.2, of 1, 5, and 10, respectively. The utility function is irrelevant in this process. To achieve maximum entropy, the mass of (1, 5, 10, 20} is not distributed equally amongst its elements. The correct generalization of Laplace's insufficient reason principle is to maximize the entropy of the $f \in \mathbf{F}_m$, not simply to distribute the mass of a subset of Θ equally among its elements. In the rest of this section, we will concentrate on algorithms for this maximum entropy problem.

The first situation that we will consider is this. Let $\Theta = \{\theta_1, \theta_2, \ldots, \theta_n\}$, and m be a density on 2^Θ with $m(\{\theta_i\}) = \alpha_i$ and $m(\Theta) = 1 - \Sigma\alpha_i = \varepsilon$. The problem here is to apportion ε among the α_i so that the resulting density on Θ has the largest possible entropy. That is, write $\varepsilon = \Sigma\varepsilon_i$ with $\varepsilon_i \geqslant 0$ so that the entropy of the density f given by $f(\theta_i) = \alpha_i + \varepsilon_i$ is maximum. Here is a precise statement of the problem.

Problem. *For $i = 1, 2, \ldots, n$ let $\alpha_i \geqslant 0$, $\varepsilon_i \geqslant 0$, and $\Sigma\alpha_i + \Sigma\varepsilon_i = 1$. Determine the ε_i which maximize*

$$H(\varepsilon_1, \varepsilon_2, \ldots, \varepsilon_n) = -\sum(\alpha_i + \varepsilon_i)\, log\,(\alpha_i + \varepsilon_i)$$

Offhand, this problem looks like a nonlinear programming problem. The constraint on the variables ε_i is linear, but the function H to be maximized is nonlinear. However, nonlinear programming techniques are not needed. The essence of the matter lies in the following simple lemma whose repeated use will effect a solution.

Lemma. *Let x and $c - x$ be positive. Then $L(x) = -[(c-x)\, log\,(c-x) + x\, log(x)]$ is increasing in x if $c - x > x$.*

Proof. The derivative $L'(x) = 1 + log(c - x) - 1 - log(x) = log(c - x) - log(x)$ is positive as long as $c - x > x$.

Now suppose that we have α_i's and ε_i's satisfying the conditions of the Problem. We are interested in maximizing the quantity

$$H(\varepsilon_1, \varepsilon_2, \ldots, \varepsilon_n) = -\sum(\alpha_i + \varepsilon_i)\, log(\alpha_i + \varepsilon_i)$$

Suppose that $\alpha_i + \varepsilon_i < \alpha_j + \varepsilon_j$ with $\varepsilon_j > 0$. (We may as well take $i < j$ here.) Let δ be such that $\delta > 0$, $\varepsilon_j - \delta > 0$, and $\alpha_i + \varepsilon_i + \delta < \alpha_j + \varepsilon_j - \delta$. Now apply the Lemma with $c = \alpha_i + \varepsilon_i + \alpha_j + \varepsilon_j$ and $x = \alpha_i + \varepsilon_i$. Then the Lemma asserts that

$$-[(\alpha_i + \varepsilon_i)\, log(\alpha_i + \varepsilon_i) + \sum(\alpha_j + \varepsilon_j)\, log(\alpha_j + \varepsilon_j)] <$$
$$-[(\alpha_i + \varepsilon_i + \delta)\, log(\alpha_i + \varepsilon_i + \delta) + \sum(\alpha_j + \varepsilon_j - \delta)\, log(\alpha_j + \varepsilon_j - \delta)].$$

Thus

$$H(\varepsilon_1, \varepsilon_2, \ldots, \varepsilon_i + \delta, \ldots, \varepsilon_j - \delta, \ldots, \varepsilon_n) > H(\varepsilon_1, \varepsilon_2, \ldots, \varepsilon_n)$$

The upshot of this is that if an apportionment $\varepsilon_1, \varepsilon_2, \ldots, \varepsilon_n$ of ε to the α_i's maximizes H, then whenever $\alpha_i + \varepsilon_i < \alpha_j + \varepsilon_j$, we must have $\varepsilon_j = 0$. Now let the α_i's be indexed so that $\alpha_1 \leqslant \alpha_2 \ldots \leqslant \alpha_n$. Thus to maximize H, we must have

$$(*) \qquad \alpha_1 + \varepsilon_1 = \alpha_2 + \varepsilon_2 = \ldots = \alpha_k + \varepsilon_k \leqslant \alpha_{k+1} \leqslant \ldots \leqslant \alpha_n$$

with $\varepsilon_{k+i} = 0$ for $i > 0$. Of course, k may be n. There is at most one assignment of the ε_i like this. For any other apportionment $\gamma_1, \gamma_2, \ldots, \gamma_n$ of ε, some $\varepsilon_1 < \gamma_i$ and some $\varepsilon_j > \gamma_j$, and in that case, $\alpha_j + \gamma_j < \alpha_i + \gamma_i$ with $\gamma_i > 0$. But (*) does not have this property, so there is at most one apportionment satisfying (*).

To get ε_i's satisfying (*), simply let $\delta_i = \alpha_k - \alpha_i$, $i = 1, 2, \ldots, k$ with k maximum such that $\Sigma\,\delta_i \leqslant \varepsilon$. Now let $\varepsilon_i = \delta_i + (\varepsilon - \Sigma\,\delta_i)/k$, $i = 1, 2, \ldots, k$, and $\varepsilon_i = 0$ for $i > k$. Then

$$\sum_{i=1}^{n} \varepsilon_i = \sum_{i=k}^{k} (\delta_i + (\varepsilon - \sum_{i=1}^{k} \delta_i)/k) = \varepsilon$$

and for $i < k$,

$$\begin{aligned} \alpha_i + \varepsilon_i &= \alpha_i + \delta_i + (\varepsilon - \textstyle\sum \delta_i)/k = \\ &= \alpha_i + \alpha_k - \alpha_i + (\varepsilon - \textstyle\sum \delta_i)/k = \\ &= \alpha_k + (\varepsilon - \textstyle\sum \delta_i)/k = \alpha_k + \varepsilon_k \end{aligned}$$

Thus there is a unique set of ε_i's satisfying (*) and it is the only set of ε_1's which could maximize H. We call this apportionment the *standard apportionment*. At this point we do not know that this apportionment does indeed maximize H. It maximizes H if any apportionment does. That one exists maximizing H follows from a general theorem. The set of points $\{(\varepsilon_1, \varepsilon_2, \ldots, \varepsilon_n) : \varepsilon_i \geqslant 0, \Sigma\,\varepsilon_i = c\}$ for any constant c is a closed and bounded subset of $\mathbf{R}^n$, and thus its image in $\mathbf{R}$ under the continuous function

$$H(\varepsilon_1, \varepsilon_2, \ldots, \varepsilon_n) = -\sum (\alpha_i + \varepsilon_i)\, log\,(\alpha_i + \varepsilon_i)$$

has a maximum.

Thus the standard apportionment maximizes H, and this is the only apportionment that does so. Further, calculating this apportionment as spelled out above is routine, and can be programmed easily. Just put the α_i in increasing order, set $\delta_i = \alpha_k - \alpha_i$, $i = 1, 2, \ldots, k$ with k maximum such that $\sum \delta_i \leqslant \varepsilon$, let $\varepsilon_i = \delta_i + (\varepsilon - \sum \delta_i)/k$, $i = 1, 2, \ldots, k$, and $\varepsilon_i = 0$ for $i > k$.

There is some merit in providing a constructive proof that there is an apportionment maximizing H. We showed that there is at most one such apportionment, and showed how to construct it. But to show that some apportionment provided a maximum for H, we appealed to a general existence theorem. Here is a constructive proof that the standard configuration

$$\alpha_1 + \varepsilon_1 = \alpha_2 + \varepsilon_2 = \ldots = \alpha_k + \varepsilon_k \leqslant \alpha_{k+1} \leqslant \ldots \leqslant \alpha_n$$

maximizes H. First, we remark that the fact that $\sum \alpha_i + \sum \varepsilon_i = 1$ is not crucial in any of the discussion above, but only that the sum is some positive number. Suppose that $\gamma_1, \gamma_2, \ldots, \gamma_n$ is an apportionment of ε, always with $\alpha_1 \leqslant \alpha_2 \ldots \leqslant \alpha_n$. Let i be the smallest index such that $\varepsilon_i \neq \gamma_1$. If $\varepsilon_i > \gamma_i$ then the indices $i_1, i_2, \ldots, i_m$ such that $\gamma_{i_j} > \varepsilon_{i_j}$ satisfy $\Sigma_j \gamma_{i_j} - \Sigma_j \varepsilon_{i_j} \geqslant \varepsilon_i - \gamma_i$. (Some ε_{i_j} may be 0.) This is simply because $\Sigma \gamma_j = \Sigma \varepsilon_j$. Thus we have $\alpha_{i_j} + \gamma_{i_j} > \alpha_{i_j} + \varepsilon_{i_j} \geqslant \alpha_i + \varepsilon_i > \alpha_i + \gamma_i$. Let δ_{i_j} be such that $\gamma_{i_j} - \delta_{i_j} \geqslant 0, \alpha_{i_j} + \gamma_{i_j} - \delta_{i_j} \geqslant \alpha_i + \varepsilon_i$, and $\alpha_i + \varepsilon_i = \alpha_i + \gamma_i + \Sigma_j \delta_{i_j}$. By the Lemma above, the apportionment obtained from the γ's by replacing γ_{i_j} by $\gamma_{i_j} - \delta_{i_j}$ and γ_i by $\gamma_i + \Sigma_j \delta_{i_j}$ has larger entropy. But now this new apportionment has the first i terms $\varepsilon_1, \varepsilon_2, \ldots, \varepsilon_i$.

The argument is entirely similar for $\varepsilon_i < \gamma_i$. Thus we may transform in at most n steps any apportionment into our standard one, each step increasing entropy. Thus we have a constructive proof that our standard apportionment yields maximum entropy. We sum up the discussion above in the following theorem.

Theorem. *Let* $\Theta = \{\theta_1, \theta_2, \ldots, \theta_n\}$, *and* m *be a density on* 2^Θ *with* $m\{\theta_i\} = \alpha_i$, *and* $m(\Theta) = 1 - \Sigma \alpha_i$. *Then there is exactly one density* f *on* Θ *that is compatible with* m *and that has the largest entropy*

$$H(f) = -\sum f(\theta_i) \log(\theta_i)$$

if $\alpha_1 \leqslant \alpha_2 \leqslant \ldots \leqslant \alpha_n$, *then that density is given by* $f(\theta_i) = \alpha_i + \varepsilon_i$, *where* $\varepsilon_i \geqslant 0$, $\Sigma_{i=1}^{k} \varepsilon_i = m(\Theta)$, *and*

$$\alpha_1 + \varepsilon_1 = \alpha_2 + \varepsilon_2 = \ldots = \alpha_k + \varepsilon_k \leqslant \alpha_{k+1} \leqslant \ldots \leqslant \alpha_n$$

This density is constructed by putting the α_i *in increasing order, setting* $\delta_i = \alpha_k - \alpha_i$, $i = 1, 2, \ldots, k$ *with* k *maximum such that* $\Sigma \delta_i \leqslant m(\Theta)$, *letting* $\varepsilon_i = \delta_i + (\varepsilon - \sum \delta_i)/k$, $i = 1, 2, \ldots, k$, and *letting* $\varepsilon_i = 0$ for $i > k$.

The discussion above generalizes to the case where instead of having $m\{\theta_i\} = \alpha_i$, we have $m(\Theta) = \alpha_i$, where $\Theta_1, \Theta_2, \ldots, \Theta_n$ is a partition of Θ. First we observe that there is an assignment yielding maximum entropy. The set of possible assignments is a closed and bounded subset of $\mathbf{R}^{2^{|\Theta|}}$, and entropy is a continuous function of those assignments into $\mathbf{R}$, and hence achieves a maximum. Maximum entropy is achieved by assigning each θ in Θ_i the mass $m\{\theta\} = m(\Theta_i)/|\Theta_i|$, and proceeding as before. To see this, note first that two points in Θ_i must wind up with the same probability. If two points in Θ_i are assigned probabilities $\alpha + \varepsilon$ and $\beta + \gamma$, where α and β come from $m(\Theta_i)$ and ε and γ come from $m(\Theta)$, and $\alpha + \varepsilon < \beta + \gamma$, then one of β and γ is positive, and by the Lemma above, a part of that one may be shifted to $\alpha + \varepsilon$ so that entropy is increased. So for entropy to be maximized, $a + \varepsilon = \beta + \gamma$, and clearly we may take $\alpha = \beta$ and $\varepsilon = \gamma$. So to maximize entropy, we may as well begin by assigning the mass $m(\Theta_i)$ equally among its elements. This puts us in the situation of the Theorem. So there is an assignment yielding maximum entropy, and we have an algorithm for getting it.

7. CONCLUDING REMARKS

Let $u: \mathbf{A} \times \Theta \to \mathbf{R}$ be a utility function in a decision problem. Optimal actions in terms of expected utility value require certain information about Θ. The concept of expected utility value is well formulated as a mathematical expectation when occurrences of states of nature, the elements of Θ, are specified by a probability density f. Then the decision problem consists of maximizing $E_f u(a, \theta)$ over a in $\mathbf{A}$.

If the probabilistic information about Θ is less precise, for example, that the density on Θ is known only to be in some collection $\mathbf{F}$ of densities, then some rationale is needed in order to select some density in this collection and proceeding as in the case where the density is known. For example, from a minimax viewpoint, one might take α_0 to be the best course of action if

$$E_f u(a_0, \theta) = sup_{a \in \mathbf{A}} inf_{f \in \mathbf{F}} E_f u(a, \theta)$$

The set function

$$F(A) = inf_{f \in \mathbf{F}} P_f(A)$$

need not be a belief function. That is, it need not be of the form F_m for some density m on 2^Θ. The domain of applicability of belief functions consists of situations in which knowledge about Θ is of the form F_m, with m arising from an underlying density on 2^Θ as in the examples in Section 2, or from F_m being given directly. In the latter case, first m is formally a probability density of some random set on 2^Θ, and second, the "constraint" F_m exists as a mathematical entity.

We summarize the potential recipes as follows.

(i) Because the law governing Θ is a belief function F rather than a probability measure, one can generalize the concept of integral with respect to an additive measure to the case of Choquet's capacities. This is

$$E_F u(a, \,) = \int_0^{\infty} F(\theta : u(a, \theta) > t)\, dt + \int_{-\infty}^{0} [F(\theta) : u(a, \theta) > t) - 1]\, dt$$

As we have seen, the computation in the finite case is simple, and

$$E_F u(a, \,) = inf_{f \in \mathbf{F}_{m_F}} E_f u(a, \,)$$

In fact, the *inf* is attained by g_a in $\mathbf{F}_{m_F}$ as we constructed in the previous section.

(ii) If additional information is available, or the decision maker is willing to incorporate some subjective view into the process, the most general way to formalize this opinion is in the form of set functions. Specifically, since the mass function m on 2^{Θ} is a probability density, we imagine a random set S, defined one some probability space (Ω, E, P) with values in 2^{Θ}, having m as density. Also, let X be a random variable with values in Θ with density $f_0 \in \mathbf{F}_m$. Since f_0 is unknown, the expected utility $E_{f_0} u(A, X)$ is replaced by $E_m \varphi_A(S)$, where φ_A is a set function $2^{\Theta} \to \mathbf{R}$ depending on $u(A, \,)$, and possibly on some other parameters. The optimal action is the one that maximizes $E_m \varphi_A(S)$ over $A \in \mathbf{A}$.

(iii) If the choice of a canonical h in $\mathbf{F}_m$ is desired, the maximum entropy principle can be called upon. Maximize $H(f)$ over the f in $\mathbf{F}_m$, yielding h, and then maximize $E_h u(a, \,)$ over a in $\mathbf{A}$.

ACKNOWLEDGMENTS

We thank the two anonymous referees for their helpful comments.

BIBLIOGRAPHY

Aigner, M. (1979). *Combinatorial theory.* Berlin: Springer-Verlag.

Dempster, A.P. (1967). Upper and Lower probabilities induced by a multi--valued mapping. *Ann. Math. Statist.* 38: 325–39.

Dubois, D. and Prade, H. (1982). On several representations of an uncertain body of evidence. In M. Gupta and E. Sanchez (eds.), *Fuzzy information in decision processes,* pp. 167–81. North-Holland.

Goodman, I.R.., Nguyen, H.T., and Rogers, G.S. (1991). On scoring approach to the admissibility of uncertainty measures in expert systems. To appear in *J. Math Anal. and Appl.*

Guiasu, S. (1977). *Information theory with applications.* New York: McGraw-Hill.

Hestir, K., Nguyen, H.T., and Rogers, G.S. (1991). A random set formalism for evidential reasoning. I.R. Goodman, M. Gupta, H.T. Nguyen, and G.S. Rogers (eds.), *Conditional logic in expert systems*, pp. 309–77. Amsterdam: North-Holland.
Jaynes, E.T. (1957). Information theory and statistical mechanics. *Phys. Rev.* 106: 620–30; 108: 171–82.
Jaynes, E.T. (1979). Where do we stand on maximum entropy? In R.D. Levine and M. Tribus (eds.), *The maximum entropy formalism*, pp. 15–118. Cambridge, MA: MIT Press.
Lindley, D.V. (1982). Scoring rules and the inevitability of probability. *Intern Statist. Rev.* 50: 1–26.
Pfanzagl, J. (1971). *Theory of measurement*. Würzburg-Wien: Physica-Verlag.
Shafer, G. (1976). *A mathematical theory of evidence*. Princeton: Princeton University Press.
Shafer, G. (1990). Perspectives on the theory of belief functions. *Intern. J. Approximate Reasoning* 4: 323–62.
Smets, P. and Kennes, R. (1990). The transferable belief model. Technical Report IRIDIA-ULB, Belgium.
Strat, T.M. (1990). Decision analysis using belief functions. *Intern. J. Approximate Reasoning* 4: 391–417.
Wakker, P. (1989). *Additive representations of inferences*. Dordrecht: Kluwer.
Wasserman. L.A. (1987). Some applications of belief functions to statistical inference. Ph.D. Thesis, University of Toronto.
Wasserman, L.A. (1990a). Prior envelopes based on belief functions. *Ann. Statist.* 18: 454–64.
Wasserman, L.A. (1990b). Belief functions and statistical inference. *Can. J. Statist.* 18(3): 183–96.
Wasserman, L.A. and Kadane, J.B. (1990). Bayes' theorem for Choquet capacities. *Ann. Statist.* 18(3): 1328–29.
Wierzchoń, S.T. (1987). An inference rule based on Sugeno measure. In J. Bezdek (ed.), *Analysis of fuzzy information*, Vol. I, pp. 85–96. Boca Raton, FL: CRC Press.
Yager, R.R. (1990). Decision making under Dempster-Shafer uncertainties. Technical Report MII-915, Iona College, New Rochelle, N.Y.

15 Dynamic decision making with belief functions

Jean-Yves JAFFRAY

Abstract: A prescriptive decision model for situations of uncertainty representable by a belief function, interpreted as a lower probability, is proposed. A reinforcement of the axioms of linear utility theory is shown to reduce the class of rational criteria to the subclass of Hurwicz criteria. Problems posed, in a dynamic context, by the evaluation of conditional decisions are shown to have a simple solution for these criteria. The question of the dynamic inconsistency of non-expected-utility models is raised and discussed.[1]

Keywords: belief function, lower probability, linear utility theory, Hurwicz criterion, decision theory.

1. INTRODUCTION

Decision models are generally presented in a static version, designed for the resolution of one-stage choice problems. Most applications, however, involve multistage – sequential and/or conditional – decision making and require the use of a dynamic extension of the model.

[1] I wish to thank A. Chateauneuf and P. Wakker for their helpful comments.

In decision making under uncertainty, the derivation of a dynamized version from the static one is not, in general, straightforward: first the question of knowledge updating must be clarified, and, if necessary, the model must be adapted to cover new types of situations created by conditioning; second, the problem of dynamic consistency necessarily leads to a reappraisal of the model from the normative point of view.

In this paper, we consider situations of uncertainty where the knowledge concerning the events is represented by a belief function (Dempster, 1967; Shafer, 1976). Specific situations require specific models. Furthermore, the suitability of a given model will depend on the interpretation given to belief functions. It has been shown by Jaffray (1989, 1991) that, in the lower probability interpretation of belief functions, the axioms of von Neumann-Morgenstern linear utility theory could be justified with the same arguments as in the case of risk (probabilized uncertainty). We shall undertake here to extend the resulting criterion to a dynamic setting.

The main difficulty to overcome is the fact that the new uncertainty situation, after an event has been observed, is no longer properly described by the conditional lower probabilities. We shall circumvent this obstacle by restricting the class of criteria considered to the particular subclass of Hurwicz criteria – a restriction backed up by normative arguments. For Hurwicz criteria, as we shall show, the evaluation of a decision in a conditional situation can nearly be reduced to a related evaluation in the original unconditional situation.

Finally, we shall discuss this model from the point of view of dynamic consistency and compare it with other models that have been proposed.

2. BELIEF FUNCTIONS AS LOWER PROBABILITIES AND DECISION MAKING

2.1. The lower probability interpretation of belief functions

Let $\mathbf{X}_0$ be the set of states of nature, $\mathbf{A}_0 = 2^{\mathbf{X}_0}$ be the algebra of events, and $\mathbf{L}_0$ and $\mathbf{F}_0$ be, respectively, the set of all probability measures and the set of all belief functions on $\mathbf{A}_0$.

In the lower probability interpretation, belief function f_0 is used to describe the situation of uncertainty where: (i) a true probability measure P_0 exists on the events, but (ii) all one knows about P_0 is that it belongs to

$$\mathbf{P}_0 = \{P_0 \in \mathbf{L}_0 : P_o \geqslant f_o\} \tag{1}$$

where $P_0 \geqslant f_0$ is short for: $P_0(A_0) \geqslant f_0(A_0)$, for all $A_0 \in \mathbf{A}_0$.

All the arguments in this paper are based on the lower probability interpretation. Other interpretations are considered in the discussion section only.

2.2. Decisions and knowledge about their outcomes

In one-stage decision making under uncertainty, the outcome of a decision is determined by the state of nature that prevails. Thus a decision δ is conveniently identified with a mapping $\delta : \mathbf{X}_0 \rightarrow \mathbf{X}$, where $\mathbf{X}$ is the outcome set – a finite set. $\mathbf{L}$ and $\mathbf{F}$ will denote, respectively, the set of all probability measures and the set of all belief functions $\mathbf{A} = 2^{\mathbf{X}}$.

In a random environment, with probability P_0 on $\mathbf{A}_0$, the outcome of decision δ is itself random, with probability $P = P_0 \circ \delta^{-1}$ on $\mathbf{A}$ (i.e., $P(A) = P_0(\delta^{-1}(A))$ for all $A \in \mathbf{A}$). Thus, when the knowledge about the events is described by the belief function f, the probability on $\mathbf{A}$ generated by decision δ may be any member of the image of $\mathbf{P}_0$ by δ, which is

$$\mathbf{P} = \{\mathrm{P} = \mathrm{P}_0 \circ \delta^{-1} : \mathrm{P}_0 \in \mathbf{P}_0\} = \{\mathrm{P} = \mathrm{P}_0 \circ \delta^{-1} : \mathrm{P}_0 \in \mathrm{L}_0 \text{ and } \mathrm{P}_0 \geqslant \mathrm{f}_0\} \tag{2}$$

It can be shown (Jaffray, 1989, 1991) that $f = f_0 \circ \delta^{-1}$ (defined by $f(A) = f_0(\delta^{-1}(A))$, for all $A \in \mathbf{A}$) is a belief function and characterizes $\mathbf{P}$ since

$$\mathbf{P} = \{Q \in \mathbf{L} : Q \geqslant f\} \tag{3}$$

Thus the knowledge about the possible outcomes of a decision is perfectly described by a belief function. We shall see below (Section 4) that this property does not extend to contingent decisions in multistage problems.

3. LINEAR UTILITY THEORY FOR BELIEF FUNCTIONS

As shown by Jaffray (1989), a static decision model for situations of uncertainty describable by belief functons can be directly derived from von Neumann and Morgenstern (1947) linear utility theory. The validity of its axioms in this framework is fully discussed in Jaffray (1991). These results can be summarized as follows.

3.1. The axioms and their justification

It is assumed that the decision maker (d.m.) bases his or her judgment on the sole comparison of the belief functions on the outcome set associated with each decision. Thus the d.m.'s preference ordering can be defined directly on the set **F** of belief functions on **A**. The convex linear combination (c.l.c.) operation which, for f and g in **F** and λ in $[0, 1]$, defines $h = \lambda f + (1 - \lambda)g$ by $h(A) = \lambda f(A) + (1 - \lambda)g(A)$, for all $A \in \mathbf{A}$, is a mixture operation, and the axioms of linear utility theory apply formally. Denoting the d.m.'s preference ordering by $\succsim$ (and its asymmetric and symmetric part by $>$ and $\sim$, respectively), these axioms can be expressed as follows (Jensen, 1967):

A1 (Transitivity and Completeness) – $\succsim$ *is a transitive and complete relation (i.e., a weak order) on* **F**.
A2 (Independence) – *For all* f_1, f_2 g *in* **F** *and* λ *in* (0,1),

$$f_1 > f_2 \Rightarrow \lambda f_1 + (1 - \lambda)g > \lambda f_2 + (1 - \lambda)g$$

A3 (Continuity) – *For* f, g, k *in* **F** *such that* $f > k > g$, *there exist* λ, μ *in* (0,1) *such that*

$$\lambda f + (1 - \lambda)g > k > \mu f + (1 - \mu)g$$

A1 is a standard axiom in decision theory. The justification of A2 and A3, in the lower probability interpretation, relies on the fact that, when $h = \lambda f + (1 - \lambda)g$, sets $\mathbf{P}_h = \{R \in \mathbf{L}: R \geqslant h\}$, $\mathbf{P}_f = \{P \in \mathbf{L}: P \geqslant f\}$ and $\mathbf{P}_g = \{Q \in \mathbf{L}: Q \geqslant g\}$ are themselves linked by relation $\mathbf{P}_h = \lambda \mathbf{P}_f + (1 - \lambda)\mathbf{P}_g$: in other words, $R \geqslant h$ if and only if there exist $P \geqslant f$ and $Q \geqslant g$ such that $R = \lambda P + (1 - \lambda) Q$ (the validity of the "only if" statement is due to the monotonicity properties of belief functions).

Thus, the d.m. is faced with the situation of uncertainty about outcomes characterized by h (the true R belongs to $\mathbf{P}_h$) when, depending on a random device, he or she expects to be in uncertainty situation f, with probability λ, or in situation g, with probability $(1 - \lambda)$.

It then becomes possible to present the following justification of A2, which is simply the transposition of the traditional argument in the case of risk: Situations $h_1 = \lambda f_1 + (1 - \lambda)g$ and $h_2 = \lambda f_2 + (1 - \lambda)g$ can, in particular, be generated by a common random device, so that alternatives h_1 and h_2 lead, with probability $(1 - \lambda)$, to the same situation g and, with probability λ, to situations f_1 and f_2, respectively. Since the latter is strictly preferred to the former, and the choice is irrelevant in the other event, h_1 should be strictly preferred to h_2.

Standard arguments in favor of A3, in the case of risk, can also be adapted.

3.2. Expression of the linear utility criterion

According to von Neumann and Morgenstern's theorem (in its modern version) A1, A2, and A3 are necessary and sufficient conditions for the existence of a linear utility V on $\mathbf{F}$ representing $\gtrsim$, i.e., for the existence of $V : \mathbf{F} \to \mathbf{R}$ satisfying

$$V(f) \geqslant V(g) \Leftrightarrow f > g \tag{4}$$

and

$$V(\lambda f + (1 - \lambda)g) = \lambda V(f) + (1 - \lambda)\, V(g) \tag{5}$$

for all f, g in $\mathbf{F}$ and all λ in $[0,1]$.

Moreover, these properties uniquely determine V up to a strictly increasing affine transformation.

The linearity property (5) has interesting implications. Let e_B be the elementary belief function focused on B, defined for every B in $\mathbf{A}^* = \mathbf{A} \setminus \{\emptyset\}$ by

$$e_B(A) = 1 \text{ for } A \supseteq B,\ e_B(A) = 0 \text{ otherwise}$$

Since f is linked with its Möbius transform, the basic probability assignment (b.p.a.) Φ, by

$$f(A) = \sum_{B \subseteq A} \Phi(B) \text{ for all } A \in \mathbf{A} \tag{6}$$

which is equivalent to

$$f = \sum_{B \in A^*} \Phi(B)\, e_B \tag{7}$$

f is a c.l.c. of the e_B's, and it follows from repeated applications of (5) that

$$V(\mathrm{f}) = \sum_{B \in \mathbf{A}^*} \Phi(B)\ V(e_B) \tag{8}$$

3.3. The addition of a dominance axiom and its implications

Let us admit that the d.m.'s preference relation under certainty (also denoted by $\gtrsim$) is identical to its preference relation under almost certainty, i.e., that

$$x \gtrsim y \Leftrightarrow e_{\{x\}} \gtrsim e_{\{y\}} \text{ for all } x, y \in \mathbf{X} \tag{9}$$

A natural rationality requirement is that a decision which yields a better outcome than another decision with certainty should be preferred to it:

$$[\delta_1(x_o) \gtrsim \delta_2(x_o) \text{ for all } x_0 \in \mathbf{X}_0] \Rightarrow f_0 \circ \delta_1^{-1} \gtrsim f_0 \circ \delta_2^{-1} \tag{10}$$

However, this property is not secured by the previous axioms. Denoting by m_B and M_B respectively, the worst and the best outcomes in B (i.e., m_B, $M_B \in B$ and $x \in B \Rightarrow M_B \gtrsim x \gtrsim m_B$), a nonstandard additional assumption can be stated as follows:

A4 (Dominance) – *For all B', B'' in* $\mathbf{A}^*$,

$$[m_{B'} \gtrsim m_{B''} \textit{ and } M_{B'} \gtrsim M_{B''}] \Rightarrow e_{B'} \gtrsim e_{B''}$$

Under A4, the expression (8) of the criterion takes the simpler form

$$V(f) = \sum_{B \in \mathbf{A}^*} \Phi(B)\, v(m_B, M_B) \tag{11}$$

where v is a real function on $\mathbf{M} = \{(m, M) \in \mathbf{X}^2 : M \gtrsim m\}$.

Since (11), applied to the particular case $f = P \in \mathbf{L}$, gives

$$V(P) = \sum_{x \in \mathbf{X}} P(\{x\})\, v(x, x) \tag{12}$$

the criterion is a generalization of the EU criterion, and v is related to the von Neumann-Morgenstern utility u of the d.m. by

$$v(x, \mathbf{x}) = u(\mathbf{x}),\ x \in \mathbf{X} \tag{13}$$

Other important properties of v are inequalities

$$u(m) \leqslant v(m, M) \leqslant u(M) \tag{14}$$

and, more generally, its decomposition as

$$v(m, M) = \bar{v}(u(m), u(\mathbf{M})) \tag{15}$$

where $\bar{v}$ is an increasing function on its domian.

3.4. Further axiomatic requirements: A characterization of Hurwicz criteria

3.4.1. The mixed uncertainty approach

The fact that the general criterion (11) reduces to the EU criterion on L suggests an alternative description of the possible effects of a decision δ, which consists in saying that δ offers an expected utility that is not exactly known but belongs to $\{E_P u : P \in \mathbf{P}\}$, where E_P denotes the expectation of u with respect to the measure P and $\mathbf{P}$ is the image of $\mathbf{P}_0$ by δ given by (2).

Rationality axioms adapted to this view have been proposed by Cohen and Jaffray (1985) in the more general framework of "mixed uncertainty" situations, which do not make any requirement about the structure of P_0 and $\mathbf{P}$. These axioms express:

(i) that there is complete ignorance on the location of P_0 in $\mathbf{P}_0$ and that the d.m. behaves rationally in that situation, in the sense of Cohen and Jaffray (1980, 1983);
(ii) that the d.m. is an expected utility maximizer under risk; and
(iii) that the d.m. must prefer decision δ_1 to decision δ_2 when he or she prefers, for every P_0 in $\mathbf{P}_0$, the situation of risk described by $P_1 = P_0 \circ \delta_1^{-1}$ to that described by $P_2 = P_0 \circ \delta_2^{-1}$ (i.e., according to (ii), when $E_{P1} u \geqslant E_{P2} u$).

Under these assumptions preference approximately (in a sense defined in Cohen and Jaffray, 1983) only depends on the set of probabilities $\mathbf{P} = \{P_0 \circ \delta^{-1} : P_0 \in \mathbf{P}_0\}$ associated with each decision δ and is representable by a utility function W of the form

$$W(\mathbf{P}) = w(\inf\{E_P u : P \in \mathbf{P}\}, \sup\{E_P u : P \in \mathbf{P}\}) \qquad (16)$$

where w is an increasing function of two variables and W and w are unique up to a common strictly increasing transformation.

3.4.2. Consistency with linear utility theory

In the particular case of situations representable by belief functions, the question arises whether the rationality requirements of the mixed uncertainty approach are consistent with those of linear utility theory.

We shall formulate this question as follows:

Are there preference orderings on **F** that are simultaneously representable by V of the form (11) and by $\bar{W}$, defined on **F** by $f \to \bar{W}(f) = W(\mathbf{P})$, where $\mathbf{P} = \{P \in \mathbf{L} : P \geqslant \mathrm{f}\}$ and W is of the form (16)?

Let us first show that the answer is affirmative. Consider the case where v, in (11), is of the particular form

$$v(m, M) = \alpha u(m) + (1 - \alpha) u(\mathbf{M}) \qquad (17)$$

for some α in [0,1], and therefore

$$V(f) = \alpha \sum_{B \in \mathbf{A}^*} \Phi(B) u(m_B) + (1 - \alpha) \sum_{B \in \mathbf{A}^*} \Phi(B) u(M_B) \qquad (18)$$

By a well-known property of belief functions (see, e.g., Chateauneuf and Jaffray, 1989, or Appendix 1)

$$\inf\{E_P u : P \in \mathbf{P}\} = \sum_{B \in \mathbf{A}^*} \Phi(B) u(m_B) \qquad (19)$$

and

$$\sup\{E_P u : P \in \mathbf{P}\} = \sum_{B \in \mathbf{A}^*} \Phi(B) u(m_B) \qquad (20)$$

Hence,

$$V(f) = \alpha \inf\{E_P u : P \in \mathbf{P}\} + (1 - \alpha) \sup\{E_P u : P \in \mathbf{P}\} \qquad (21)$$

and V itself is a $\bar{W}$ for $w = \bar{v}$.

Let us now show that, conversely, v must be of the particular form (17) to reconcile the two approaches.

When V and $\bar{W}$ represent the same ordering, there exists a strictly increasing mapping H such that $V = H \circ \bar{W}$. Relation $V(f) = H(\bar{W}(f))$ takes, by (11), (15), (16), (19) and (20), the developed form

$$\sum_{B \in \mathbf{A}^*} \Phi(B)\, v(u(m_B, u(M_B)) = H(w(\sum_{B \in \mathbf{A}^*} \Phi(B)\, u(m_B), \sum_{B \in \mathbf{A}^*} \Phi(B)\, u(M_B))) \tag{22}$$

By applying (22) successively to situations f_0 and decisions δ, such that:

(i) $\Phi(B) = 1$ for $B = \{y, z\}$; and
(ii) $\Phi(B_i) = \lambda_i$ for $B_i = \{y_i, z_i\}$, i = 1,2,

it becomes straightforward:

(i) that $\bar{v}(y, z) = H(w(y, z))$ for all $y, z \in u(\mathbf{X})$ such that $z \geqslant y$; and
(ii) that

$$\lambda_1 \bar{v}(y_1, z_1) + \lambda_2 \bar{v}(y_2, z_2) = \bar{v}(\lambda_1 y_1 + \lambda_2 y_2, \lambda_1 z_1 + \lambda_2 z_2) \tag{23}$$

for all $\lambda_1, \lambda_2 \in [0,1]$ such that $\lambda_1 + \lambda_2 = 1$, and all $y_i, z_i \in u(\mathbf{X})$ such that $z_i \geqslant y_i (i = 1,2)$.

By applying (23) to (y, z) expressed as a c.l.c. of (u^-, u^+), (u^-, u^+), and (u^+, u^+), where $u^- = \inf\{u(x): x \in \mathbf{X}\}$ and $u^+ = \sup\{u(x): x \in \mathbf{X}\}$, it is easily seen that $\bar{v}$ must be an affine function

$$\bar{v}(y, z) = \alpha y + \beta z + \gamma$$

with α, $\beta \geqslant 0$, since $\bar{v}$ is an increasing function as well. Therefore

$$v(m, M) = \alpha\, u(m) + \beta\, u(M) + \gamma$$

and, since u can be replaced by any positive affine transform of it, v is indeed of the form (17).

Thus the combination of the axioms of linear utility theory with the axioms of rational decision making under mixed uncertainty leaves as the only rational criteria the Hurwicz α-criteria

$$V(f) = \alpha \inf\{E_P u : P \in \mathbf{P}\} + (1 - \alpha) \sup\{E_P u : P \in \mathbf{P}\} \tag{24}$$

where α belongs to $[0,1]$ and is generally interpreted as a pessimism index, characterizing the d.m.'s attitude with respect to ambiguity (Luce and Raiffa, 1957).

3.4.3. Extension

Moreover, since the function w in (16) is the same, whether $\mathbf{P}$ is associated with a belief function f by $\mathbf{P} = \{P \in \mathbf{L}: P \geqslant f)$ or $\mathbf{P}$ has no particular structure, the preceding normative argument also supports the adoption of the Hurwicz α-criterion

$$W(\mathbf{P}) = \alpha \inf \{E_P u : P \in \mathbf{P}\} + (1 - \alpha) \sup \{E_P u : P \in \mathbf{P}\}$$

in the more general situations of mixed uncertainty.

4. DECISION MAKING AFTER CONDITIONING

In the lower probability approach, the possibility of characterizing the uncertainty situation $\mathbf{P}_0$ by its lower envelope $f_0 = \inf \{P_0 : P_0 \in \mathbf{P}_0\}$ is due to the fact that $\mathbf{P}_0$ can be retrieved from f_0 as $\mathbf{P}_0 = \{P_0 \in \mathrm{L}_0 : P_0 \geqslant f_0\}$.

Unfortunately, conditioning does not preserve this property. Let E_0 be an event in $\mathbf{A}_0$ such that $f_0(\mathrm{E}_0) > 0$, and $\mathbf{L}_0^{E_0}$ denote the set of probability measures on $\mathbf{A}_0^{E_0} = 2^{E_0}$. In the lower probability interpretation, the observation of E_0 transforms uncertainty situation $\mathbf{P}_0$ into situation $\mathbf{P}_0^{E_0} = \{P_0^{E_0} \in \mathbf{L}_0^{E_0} : P_0 \in \mathbf{P}_0\}$. Although, as shown by Fagin and Halpern (1990), $f_0^{E_0} = \inf\{P_0^{E_0} : P_0^{E_0} \in \mathbf{P}_0^{E_0}\}$ is a belief function, $\mathbf{P}_0^{E_0}$ is, in general, a strict subset of $\{Q \in \mathbf{L}_0^{E_0} : Q_0^{E_0} \geqslant f_0^{E_0}\}$ (Jaffray 1990).

This difficulty extends to the expression of the uncertainty about the outcome of a decision taken after the occurrence of E_0. Such a decision can be identified to a mapping $\delta_{E_0} : E_0 \to \mathbf{X}$. The resulting situation of uncertainty is characterizable by

$$\mathbf{Q} = \{Q \in \mathrm{L} : Q = P_0^{E_0} \circ \delta_{E_0}^{-1} \text{ and } P_0 \in \mathbf{P}_0\} \tag{25}$$

but not by $f_0^{E_0} = f_0^{E_0} \circ \delta_{E_0}^{-1}$.

The general criterion (11), derived from linear utility theory, is thus not relevant to conditional decision making. On the other hand, Hurwicz criteria still make sense and their use is justified by the remarks of Section 3.4.3.

The Hurwicz α-criterion attributes to decision δ_{E_0} the utility level

$$\tilde{W}(\delta_{E_0}) = W(\mathbf{Q}) = \alpha \inf \{W_Q u : Q \in \mathbf{Q}\} + (1 - \alpha) \cdot \sup \{E_Q : Q \in \mathbf{Q}\} \tag{26}$$

with $\mathbf{Q}$ given by (25).

Since data concerning the uncertainty situation consists in a description of $\mathbf{P}_0$, such as its characterization by the lower probability f_0 or its Möbius transform Φ_0, the natural evaluation of $W(\mathbf{Q})$ is based on relation

$$\inf\{E_Q u : Q \in \mathbf{Q}\} = \inf\{E_{P_0} E_0 u \circ \delta_{E_0} : P_0 \in \mathbf{P}_0\} \tag{27}$$

(and the simlar relation between the suprema) and uses the following property:

Proposition 1. *Let* $\mathbf{P}$ *be a set of probability measures on* $\mathbf{A} = 2^X$ *and* $E \in \mathbf{A}$ *be such that* $\inf\{P(E): P \in \mathbf{P}\} > 0$. *Given mapping* $u: E \to \mathbf{R}$, *let mapping* $u_\lambda: \mathbf{X} \to \mathbf{R}$ *be defined, for any* $\lambda \in \mathbf{R}$, *by*

$$u_\lambda(x) = u(x) \text{ for } x \in E; \; u_\lambda(x) = \lambda \text{ for } x \in E^c \tag{28}$$

Then, the value of $\inf\{E_P Eu: P \in \mathbf{P}\}$ *is the unique solution,* $\bar{\lambda}$, *of equation*

$$\lambda = \inf\{E_P u_\lambda : P \in \mathbf{P}\} \tag{29}$$

In particular, if $\mathbf{P} = \{P \in \mathbf{L}: P \geqslant f\}$ *and* f *is a belief function, then*

$$\bar{\lambda} = E^-{}_f u_{\bar{\lambda}} \tag{30}$$

where $E^-{}_f u_\lambda$ *is the Choquet integral of* u_λ *with respect to* f.

(The proof of Proposition 1 is given in Appendix 1, where (43) and (44) recall the expression of the Choquet integral.)

By Proposition 1, applied to f_0, E_0 and $u \circ \delta_{E_0}$, and (27), $\inf\{E_Q u: Q \in \mathbf{Q}\} = \bar{\lambda}$, where $\bar{\lambda}$ is uniquely determined by

$$\bar{\lambda} = \inf\{E_{P_0}(u \circ \delta_{E_0})\bar{\lambda} : P_0 \in \mathbf{P}_0\} \tag{31}$$

and $(u \circ \delta_{E_0})\lambda: \mathbf{X} \to \mathbf{R}$ is defined, for any $\lambda \in \mathbf{R}$, by

$$(u \circ \delta_{E_0})\lambda(x_0) = u(\delta_{E_0}(x_0)) \text{ for } x_0 \in E_0; \; (u \circ \delta_{E_0})\lambda(x_0) = \lambda \text{ for } x_0 \in E_0^c \tag{32}$$

Moreover, f_0 being a belief function,

$$\bar{\lambda} = E^-{}_{f_0}(u \circ \delta_{E_0})\bar{\lambda} \tag{33}$$

which equation can be reexpressed as follows: Let $\mathbf{X}_0$ be enumerated in such a way that

$$E_0 = \{x_0^1, \ldots, x_0^i, \ldots, x_0^{r_0}\} \text{ and } u(\delta_{E_0}(x_0^j)) \geqslant u(\delta_{E_0}(x^{j+1}_0)) \text{ for } 1 \leqslant j \leqslant r_0 - 1$$

let moreover $A_0^j = \{x_0^1, \ldots, x_0^j\}$, $1 \leqslant j \leqslant r_0$. It results then from the definition of the Choquet integral (see (43) in Appendix 1) that

$$\bar{\lambda} = \sum_{j=1}^{k-1} [u(\delta_{E_0}(x_0^j)) - u(\delta_{E_0}(x^{j+1}_0))] f_0(A_0^j) + \\ + [u(\delta_{E_0}(x_0^{\bar{k}})) - \bar{\lambda}] f_0(A_0^{\bar{k}}) + [\bar{\lambda} - u(\delta_{E_0}(x^{\bar{k}+1}_0))] f_0(A_0^{\bar{k}} \cup E_0^c)$$

$$+ \sum_{j=\bar{k}+1}^{r_0-1} [u(\delta_{E_0}(x_0^j)) - u(\delta_{E_0}(x_0^{j+1}))] f_0(A_0^j \cup E_0^c) + u(\delta_{E_0}(x_0^{r_0})) \tag{34}$$

where $\bar{k}$ depends on $\bar{\lambda}$ and satisfies

$$u(\delta_{E_0}(x_0^{\bar{k}})) \geqslant \bar{\lambda} \geqslant u(\delta_{E_0}(x_0^{\bar{k}+1})) \tag{35}$$

The value of $\bar{\lambda}$ can thus easily be found by a tâtonnement method based on (34), (35). Alternatively, one can solve equation (36) below, which uses the expression of the Choquet integral involving the Möbius transform of f_0(see (44) in Appendix 1):

$$\bar{\lambda} = [\sum_{B_0 \cap E_0 \neq \emptyset, B_0 \cap E_0^c \neq \emptyset} \varphi_0(B_0) \inf\{\bar{\lambda}, \inf\{u(\delta_{E_0}(x_0)),\ x_0 \in B_0 \cap E_0\}\} + \\ + \sum_{B_0 \subseteq E_0} \varphi_0(B_0) \inf\{u(\delta_{E_0}(x_0)), x_0 \in B_0\}] [1 - f_0(E_0^c)]^{-1} \tag{36}$$

where φ_0 is the Möbius transform of f_0.

Finally, as shown by the proof of Proposition 1, linear programming offers another approach for calculating $\bar{\lambda}$.

Symmetrically, there is a unique $\bar{\mu} \in \mathbf{R}$ such that

$$\sup\{E_Q u : Q \in \mathbf{Q}\} = \bar{\mu} = \sup\{E_{P_0}(u \circ \delta_{E_0})\bar{\mu} : P_0 \in \mathbf{P}_0\} \tag{37}$$

$\bar{\mu}$ can be determined by resolving equations similar to (34), (35), and (36); hence

$$\tilde{W}(\delta_{E_0}) = W(\mathbf{Q}) = \alpha\bar{\lambda} + (1-\alpha)\bar{\mu} \tag{38}$$

5. DISCUSSION

5.1. Dynamic inconsistencies

The model we have presented is not dynamically consistent: It may happen that the d.m. prefers a decision δ'' to another decision δ' and that, nonetheless, the contingent choices in a dynamic situation will make him or her select δ' although δ'' was also feasible, as in Figure 15.1.

This claim is substantiated by the following example.

Example 1. The information about the colour (R(ed), B(lack) or W(hite)) of the balls in Ellsberg's urn experiment is that 1/3 of the

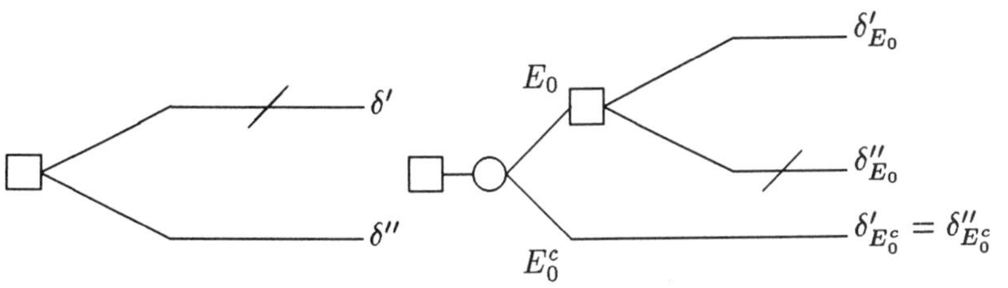

Figure 15.1

Table 15.1

$A_0 : \Phi$	R	B	W	R∪B	R∪W	B∪W	R∪B∪W
$f_o : 0$	1/3	0	0	1/3	1/3	2/3	0
$\Phi_0 : 0$	1/3	0	0	0	0	2/3	0

balls are **R**; thus f_0 and φ_0 are given as in Table 15.1. Suppose that $M > m$ and $v(m, M) = \alpha m + (1 - \alpha)M$ and consider decisions δ' and δ'' defined by:

$$\delta'(R) = M;\ \delta'(B) = \delta'(W) = m;\ \delta''(R) = \delta''(B) = m;\ \delta''(W) = M$$

Information about their outcomes in $\mathbf{X} = \{m, M\}$ is characterized as in Table 15.2. Therefore, $V(f) < V(f'') \Leftrightarrow 2/3m + 1/3M < 1/3m + 2/3\,[\alpha m + (1 - \alpha)M]$, hence $V(f') < V(f'') \Leftrightarrow \alpha > 1/2$.

Table 15.2

A :	ø	{m}	{M}	{m, M}
$f = f_0 \circ \delta'^{-1}$:	0	2/3	1/3	1
Φ' :	0	2/3	1/3	0
$f'' = f_0 \circ \delta''^{-1}$:	0	1/3	0	1
Φ'' :	0	1/3	0	2/3

Suppose now that the decision has to be taken after event $E_0 = R \cup W$ has been observed. Then

$$\tilde{W}(\delta'_{E_0}) = \alpha\lambda' + (1 - \alpha)\mu'$$

where $\lambda' = 1/3M + 2/3 \inf\{m, \lambda'\}$ and $\mu' = 1/3M + 2/3 \sup\{m, \mu'\}$, and thus $\lambda' = 1/3M + 2/3m$ and $\mu' = M$.

Similarly,

$$\tilde{W}(\delta''_{E_0}) = \alpha\lambda'' + (1-\alpha)\mu''$$

where $\lambda'' = 1/3m + 2/3 \inf\{M, \lambda''\}$ and $\mu'' = 1/3m + 2/3 \sup\{M, \mu'\}$, and thus $\lambda'' = m$ and $\mu'' = 1/3m + 2/3M$. Therefore, $\tilde{W}(\delta'_{E_0}) > \tilde{W}(\delta''_{E_0})$ for all $\alpha \in [0,1]$, since

$$\alpha[1/3M + 2/3m] + (1-\alpha)M > \alpha m + (1-\alpha)[1/3m + 2/3M]$$
$$\Leftrightarrow M > m$$

Thus, all optimistic d.m.'s ($\alpha < 1/2$) exhibit dynamic inconsistency in this example.

The reason for the existence of dynamic inconsistencies is the fact that the independence properties of Hurwicz criteria are not sufficient to make them satisfy the full independence requirements expressed by Savage's (1954) Sure Thing Principle (see Jaffray and Wakker, 1992).

Dynamic inconsistency makes some undesirable consequences possible such as opportunities for Dutch Books (Machina, 1989) or a negative value of information (Wakker, 1988).

5.2. Comparison with other models

Strat (1990) advocates the use of Hurwicz criteria for decision analysis, but makes no attempt at providing an axiomatic justification. He also proposes a modification of decision trees that makes the representation more convenient for decisions that generate belief functions on the outcome set. However, although he clearly introduces belief functions as lower probabilities, he does not discuss the question of the representation of contingent decisions by belief functions.

Yager (1990) proposes a criterion that applies to decisions directly. In its spirit, Yager's model is close to linear utility theory proper and departs from ours only by its assumptions concerning behavior under complete ignorance. Yager does not discuss dynamic decision making.

Smets and Kennes (1990) present a complete decision model using belief functions, the transferable belief model (TBM). TBM favors a purely subjective interpretation of belief functions, for which Dempster's rule is the appropriate conditioning rule. At the decision choice level, TBM transforms the beliefs into probabilities and simply compares expected utilities. The transformation used is uniquely determined by axiomatic requirements (in particular, the principle of insufficient reason). As emphasized by Smets and Kennes (1990), the transform of a conditional belief function is not the conditional probability that would be derived from the transform of the original belief function.

Since the respect of Bayes' rule is the only way to avoid dynamic inconsistencies when maximizing expectations (Weller, 1978), they assume that the d.m. can enforce the decision strategy that maximizes the expected utility with respect to the transform of the initial beliefs (commitment).

More generally, it is known that the only dynamically consistent models, other than subjective expected utility, necessarily fail to satisfy other standard requirements, such as consequentialism (Hammond, 1988; Machina, 1989).

Thus the acceptance of dynamic inconsistencies seems to be the price to be paid for making decisions according to one's psychological inclinations, on the sole basis of one's knowledge, with no room left for arbitrariness.

APPENDIX 1

Proof of Proposition 1:

(i) Let $P \in \mathbf{P}$. Since $P(E) > 0$, P^E exists, and

$$E_P u_\lambda = P(E) E_{P_E} u + P(E^c)\lambda, \text{ for all } \lambda \in \mathbf{R} \tag{39}$$

from which it follows that equation

$$E_P u_\lambda = \lambda \tag{40}$$

always has a unique solution $\lambda = E_{P_E} u$.

(ii) Let $\lambda^* = \inf\{E_{P_E} u : P \in \mathbf{P}\}$. By (i) above,

$$\lambda^* = \inf\{\lambda \in \mathbf{R} : E_P u_\lambda = \lambda \text{ for some } P \in \mathbf{P}\} \tag{41}$$

For any $P \in \mathbf{P}$, function $g : \lambda \to g(\lambda) = E_P u_\lambda - \lambda$, being linear with slope $(-P(E))$, is decreasing; there is a unique λ such that $g(\lambda) = 0$ and, by (41), $\lambda \geqslant \lambda^*$, hence $g(\lambda^*) = E_P u_{\lambda^*} - \lambda^* \geqslant 0$. Thus $\lambda^* \leqslant \inf \{E_P u : P \in \mathbf{P}\}$.

Moreover, by (41) again, for any $\varepsilon > 0$, there exists $P \in \mathbf{P}$ such that $E_P u_\lambda = \lambda$ and $\lambda^* \leqslant \lambda < \lambda^* + \varepsilon$, hence that $E_P u_{\lambda^*} \leqslant E_P u_\lambda < \lambda^* + \varepsilon$; therefore

$$\lambda^* = \inf\{E_P u_{\lambda^*} : P \in \mathbf{P}\} \tag{42}$$

(iii) Let μ^* be any solution of equation (42). Then, for all $P \in \mathbf{P}$, $\mu^* \leqslant E_P u_{\mu^*}$, and it follows from (39) (with $\lambda = \mu^*$) that $\mu^* \leqslant E_{P^E} u$, for all $P \in \mathbf{P}$, hence that $\mu^* \leqslant \lambda^*$.

Moreover, for every $\varepsilon > 0$, there exists $P \in \mathbf{P}$ such that $E_P u_{\mu^*} < \mu^* + \varepsilon$, which implies, by (39) again, that $E_{P^E} u < \mu^* + \dfrac{\varepsilon}{P(E)} \leqslant \mu^* + \dfrac{\varepsilon}{f(E)}$.

Thus $\lambda^* \leqslant E_{P^E} u < \mu^* + \dfrac{\varepsilon}{f(E)}$ for all $\varepsilon > 0$, so that $\lambda^* \leqslant \mu^*$.

Together we get $\lambda^* = \mu^*$, which proves that λ^* is the unique solution of equation (42).

(iv) When $\mathbf{P} = \{P \in \mathbf{L} : P \geqslant f\}$, and f is a belief function, it follows from general properties of convex capacities (which include belief functions; see, e.g., Chateauneuf and Jaffray, 1989), that: (i) λ^* is achieved for some $P \in \mathbf{P}$; and (ii) the right member of equation (42) is equal to the Choquet integral of u_{λ^*} with respect to f, which makes the resolution of this equation easy. Let us recall that by definition, the Choquet integral of function $h : \mathbf{X} \to \mathbf{R}$ with respect to f is given, for $\mathbf{X} = \{x_1, x_2, \ldots, x_n\}$ enumerated so that

$$h(x_j) \geqslant h(x_{j+1}),\ 1 \leqslant j \leqslant n-1$$

by

$$E_{-f} h = \sum_{j=1}^{n-1} [h(x_j) - h(x_{j+1})]\, f(\{x_1, \ldots, x_j\}) + h(x_n) \tag{43}$$

and can also be expressed as

$$E_{-f} h = \sum_{B \in \mathbf{A}^*} \Phi(B) \inf\{h(x) : x \in B\} \tag{44}$$

where Φ is the Möbius transform of f.

We shall now give a direct and complete proof of these last results, based on the duality theorem in linear programming.

Alternative proof of Proposition 1 for the case where $\mathbf{P} = \{P \in \mathbf{L} : P \geqslant f\}$ and f is a belief function:

(i) Let the index set of $\mathbf{X} = \{x_1, x_2, \ldots, x_n\}$ be such that $E = \{x_1, \ldots, x_j, \ldots, x_r\}$ and $u(x_j) \geqslant u(x_{j+1})$ for $1 \leqslant j \leqslant r-1$. Let moreover $A_j = \{x_1, \ldots, x_j\}$ for $1 \leqslant j \leqslant r$ and $A_0 = \emptyset$. Let us first identify $\mathbf{P}$ to a subset of $\mathbf{R}^n$, i.e.,

$$\mathbf{P} = \{P = (P(\{x_1\}), \ldots, P(\{x_n\})) : \sum_{x_j \in A} P(\{x_j\}) \geqslant f(A), A \in \mathbf{A}^*;$$
$$\sum_{j=1}^{n} P(\{x_j\}) = 1; \text{ and } P(\{x_j\}) \geqslant 0 \text{ for } 1 \leqslant j \leqslant n\} \tag{45}$$

and note that

$$E_{P^E} u = \sum_{j=1}^{r} u(x_j)\, P_E(\{x_j\}) = [\sum_{j=1}^{r} u(\{x_j\})\, P(\{x_j\})]$$
$$[\sum_{j=1}^{r} P(\{x_j\})]^{-1} \tag{46}$$

Second, let us make the change of variables

$$y_j = P(\{x_j\})\, [\sum_{j=1}^{r} P(\{x_j\})]^{-1}, j = 1, \ldots, n, \tag{47}$$

which defines a one-to-one mapping from $\mathbf{P}$ onto

$$\mathbf{Y} = \{y = (y_1, \ldots, y_n) : \sum_{j \in J(A)} y_j - f(A) \sum_{j=1}^{n} y_j \geqslant 0, A \in \mathbf{A}^*$$
$$\sum_{j=1}^{r} y_j = 1; \text{ and } y_j \geqslant 0, j = 1, \ldots, n\} \tag{48}$$

(where $J(A)$ is defined by $j \in J(A) \Leftrightarrow x_j \in \mathrm{A}$) since, equivalently (note that $P(E) \geqslant f(E) > 0$),

$$P(\{x_j\}) = y_j [\sum_{j=1}^{n} y_j]^{-1}, j = 1, \ldots, n \tag{49}$$

Therefore,

$$\inf\{E_{P^E} u : P \in \mathbf{P}\} = \inf\{\sum_{j=1}^{r} u(x_j)\, y_j : y \in \mathbf{Y}\}$$

which is equivalent to the linear program:

$$\min \sum_{j=1}^{r} u(x_j) y_j$$

subject to:

PL1 $$\sum_{j \in J(A)} y_j - f(A) \sum_{j=1}^{n} y_j \geqslant 0, A \in \mathbf{A}^*$$

$$\sum_{j=1}^{r} y_j = 1$$

$$y_j \geqslant 0, 1 \leqslant j \leqslant n$$

Denoting by $\mu = \{\mu(A), A \in \mathbf{A}^*\}$ and λ the dual variables of the principal constraints of PL1, the dual linear program is

$$\max \lambda$$

subject to:

PL2 $$\sum_{J(A) \supseteq \{j\}} \mu(A) - \sum_{A \in \mathbf{A}^*} \mu(A) f(A) + \lambda \leqslant u(x_j), 1 \leqslant j \leqslant r$$

$$\sum_{J(A) \supseteq \{j\}} \mu(A) - \sum_{A \in \mathbf{A}^*} \mu(A) f(A) \leqslant 0, r+1 \leqslant j \leqslant n$$

$$\mu(A) \geqslant 0, A \in \mathbf{A}^*$$

According to the duality theorem (Dantzig, 1963), a feasible solution y of PL1 and a feasible solution (μ, λ) of PL2 are optimal solutions of PL1 and PL2, respectively, if and only if they satisfy the complementary slackness conditions:

$$\mu(A)\Big[\sum_{j \in J(A)} y_j - f(A) \sum_{j=1}^{n} y_j\Big] = 0, A \in \mathbf{A}^* \tag{50}$$

$$\Big[\sum_{J(A) \supseteq \{j\}} \mu(A) - \sum_{A \in \mathbf{A}^*} \mu(A) \mathrm{f}(A) + \lambda - u(x_j)\Big] y_j = 0, 1 \leqslant j \leqslant r \tag{51}$$

and

$$\Big[\sum_{J(A) \supseteq \{j\}} \mu(A) - \sum_{A \in \mathbf{A}^*} \mu(A) f(A)\Big] y_j = 0, r+1 \leqslant j \leqslant n \tag{52}$$

Let us construct optimal solutions $(\bar{\lambda}, \bar{\mu})$ and $\bar{y}$.

(ii) Define $\Phi : [u(x_1), u(x_r)] \to \mathbf{R}$ as follows: for $u(x_k) \geqslant \lambda \geqslant u(x_{k+1})$, let $\Phi(\lambda)$ be given by

$$\Phi(\lambda) = \sum_{j=1}^{k-1} [u(x_j) - u(x_{j+1})] f(A_j) + [u(x_k) - \lambda] f(A_k) \tag{53}$$

$$+ [\lambda - u(x_{k+1})] f(A_k \cup E^c) + \sum_{j=k+1}^{r-1} [u(x_j) - u(x_{j+1})] f(A_j \cup E^c) + u(x_r)$$

Since Φ is piecewise linear and satisfies $\Phi(x_r) \geqslant u(x_r)$ and $\Phi(x_1) \leqslant u(x_1)$, there exists

$$\bar{\lambda} \in [u(x_r), u(x_1)] \text{ such that } \Phi(\bar{\lambda}) = \bar{\lambda} \tag{54}$$

Moreover, since, by convexity of f,

$$f(A_k \cup E^c) - f(A_k) \leqslant f(\mathbf{X}) - f(E) < 1$$

$\Phi(\lambda)$ increases more slowly than λ, $\bar{\lambda}$ is unique.

We can then define $\bar{k}$ as an index such that

$$u(x_{\bar{k}}) \geqslant \bar{\lambda} \geqslant u(x_{\bar{k}+1}) \tag{55}$$

(iii) Define $\bar{\mu}$ by

$$\begin{aligned}
&\bar{\mu}(A_j) = u(x_j) - u(x_{j+1}),\ 1 \leqslant j \leqslant \bar{k} - 1\\
&\bar{\mu}(A_{\bar{k}}) = u(x_{\bar{k}}) - \bar{\lambda}; \bar{\mu}(A_{\bar{k}} \cup E^c) = \bar{\lambda} - u(x_{\bar{k}+l})\\
&\bar{\mu}(A_j \cup E^c) = u(x_j) - u(x_{j+1}),\ \bar{k} + 1 \leqslant j \leqslant r - 1\\
&\bar{\mu}(A_r \cup E^c) = u(x_r)\\
&\bar{\mu}(A) = 0 \text{ for } A \notin \{A_j, 1 \leqslant \mathrm{j} \leqslant \bar{k}\} \cup \{A_j \cup E^c, \bar{k} + 1 \leqslant j \leqslant r\}
\end{aligned} \tag{56}$$

It is straightforward that, for $j \leqslant \bar{k}$,

$$\sum_{J(A) \supseteq \{j\}} \bar{\mu}(A) = \sum_{k=j}^{\bar{k}} \mu(A_k) + \sum_{k=\bar{k}+1}^{r} \bar{\mu}(A_k \cup E^c) = u(x_j) - \bar{\lambda} + \bar{\lambda} = u(x_j)$$

and for $\bar{k} + 1 \leqslant j \leqslant r$,

$$\sum_{J(A) \supseteq \{j\}} \bar{\mu}(A) = \sum_{k=j}^{r} \bar{\mu}(A_k \cup E^c) = u(x_j)$$

By (53), $\sum_{A \in \mathbf{A}^*} \bar{\mu}(A) f(A) = \bar{\lambda}$; moreover $\sum_{J(A) \supseteq \{j\}} \bar{\mu}(A) = \bar{\lambda}$ for $r + 1 \leqslant j \leqslant n$, and $\bar{\mu}(A) \geqslant 0$ for all $A \in \mathbf{A}^*$. It is then easily checked that $(\bar{\mu}, \bar{\lambda})$ is a feasible solution of PL2.

(iv) Finally consider $\bar{P} \in \mathrm{L}$ such that

$$\bar{P}(A_j) = f(A_j), \text{ for } 1 \leqslant j \leqslant \bar{k} \tag{57}$$

$$\bar{P}(A_j \cup E^c) = f(A_j \cup E^c), \text{ for } \bar{k}+1 \leqslant j \leqslant r \tag{58}$$

and, with $G_i = \{x_{r+1}, \ldots, x_{r+i}\}$

$$\bar{P}(A_{\bar{k}} \cup G_i) = f(A_{\bar{k}} \cup G_i), i = 1, \ldots, n-r \tag{59}$$

Let us show that $\bar{P}$ is uniquely defined and belongs to **P**, i.e., satisfies

$$\bar{P}(B) = \sum_{j \in J(B)} \bar{P}(\{x_j\}) \leqslant f(B) \text{ for all } B \in \mathbf{A}^*$$

Now, by (57) and the convexity of f,

$$\bar{P}(\{x_j\}) = f(A_j) - f(A_{j-1}) \geqslant f(B \cap A_j) - f(B \cap A_{j-1}), \text{ for } 1 \leqslant j \leqslant k$$

hence, since $j \notin J(B) \Rightarrow f(B \cap A_j) = f(B \cap A_{j-1})$, $\bar{P}(B \cap A_{\bar{k}}) \geqslant \sum_{j=1}^{k} [f(B \cap A_j) - f(B \cap A_{j-1})] = f(B \cap A_{\bar{k}})$.

Similarly, it can be shown, by using (59) and (58), that

$$\bar{P}(B \cap E^c) \geqslant \sum_{i=1}^{n-1} [f(B \cap (A_{\bar{k}} \cup G_i)) - f(B \cap (A_{\bar{k}} \cup G_{i-1}))]$$

$$= f(B \cap A_{\bar{k}} \cup E^c)) - f(B \cap A_{\bar{k}})$$

and that

$$\bar{P}(B \cap (E \setminus A_{\bar{k}})) \geqslant \sum_{j=k+1}^{r} [f(B \cap (A_j \cup E^c)) - f(B \cap (A_{j-1} \cup E^c))$$

$$= f(B) - f(B \cap (A_{\bar{k}} \cup E^c)).$$

It is straightforward that $\bar{P}(B) \geqslant f(B)$.

Therefore $\bar{y}$ resulting from $\bar{P}$ by (47) is a feasible solution of PL1, and

$$\sum_{j \in A} \bar{y}_j - f(A) \sum_{j=1}^{n} \bar{y}_j = 0 \text{ for } A = A_j, j \leqslant \bar{k} \text{ and } A = A_j \cup E^c,$$

$\bar{k}+1 \leqslant j \leqslant r$.

(v) It remains only to check that $\bar{y}$ and $(\bar{\mu}, \bar{\lambda})$ satisfy the complementary slackness conditions (50)–(52).

The optimal values of PL1 and PL2 being equal $\sum_{j=1}^{r} u(x_j)\bar{y}_j = \bar{\lambda}$. Thus $\lambda^* = \inf\{E_{P^E}u : P \in \mathbf{P}\} = E_{\bar{P}^E}u = \bar{\lambda}$, where $\bar{\lambda}$ is the unique solution of $\Phi(\lambda) = \lambda$, which (see (43) and (53)) can also be written as $E_{\bar{f}}u_\lambda = \lambda$.

BIBLIOGRAPHY

Chateauneuf, A. and Jaffray, J. Y. (1989). Some characterizations of lower probabilities and other monotone capacities through the use of Möbius inversion. *Math. Social Sciences* 17: 263–83.

Cohen, M. and Jaffray, J. Y. (1980). Rational behavior under complete ignorance. *Econometrica* 48 (5): 1281–99.

Cohen, M. and Jaffray J. Y. (1983). Approximations of rational criteria under complete ignorance and the independence axiom. *Theory and Decision* 15: 121–50.

Cohen, M. and Jaffray J. Y. (1985). Decision making in a case of mixed uncertainty: A normative model. *J. of Math. Psychology* 29 (4): 428–42.

Dantzig, G. (1963). *Linear programming and extension*. Princeton: Princeton University Press.

Dempster, A. (1967). Upper and lower probabilities induced by a multivalued mapping. *Ann. Math. Stat.* 38: 325–39.

Fagin, R. and Halpern, J. H. (1990). A new approach to updating beliefs. *Proc. of Sixth Conf. on Uncertainty in A.I.*

Hammond, P. (1988). Consequentialists foundations for expected utility. *Theory and Decision* 25: 25–78.

Jaffray J. Y. (1989). Linear utility theory for belief functions. *Op. Res. Letters* 8: 107–12.

Jaffray, J. Y. (1990). Bayesian updating and belief functions. Working paper, to appear in *IEEE Trans. on Syst. Man and Cyb.*

Jaffray, J. Y. (1991). Linear utility theory and belief functions: A discussion. In A. Chikan (ed.), *Proc. of FUR IV Conf.* Dordrecht: Kluwer.

Jaffray, J. Y. and Wakker, P. (1992). Decision making with belief functions: Comparability and incompatibility with the sure thing principle. In preparation.

Jensen, N. E. (1967). An introduction to Bernoullian utility theory. I: Utility functions. *Swedish J. of Economics* 69: 163–83.

Luce, D. and Raiffa, H. (1957). *Games and decisions*. New York: Wiley.

Machina, M. (1989). Dynamic consistency and non-expected utility models of choice under uncertainty. *J. of Economic Literature* 27: 1622–68.

von Neumann, J. and Morgenstern, O. (1947). Theory of games and economic behavior. Princeton: Princeton University Press.

Savage, L. J. (1954). *The foundations of statistics*. New York: Wiley.

Shafer, G. (1976), *A mathematical theory of evidence*. Princeton: Princeton University Press.

Smets, Ph. and Kennes, R. (1990). The transferable belief model. Technical Report IRIDIA/90-14.

Strat, T. M. (1990). Decision analysis using belief functions. *Int. J. of Approximate Reasoning* 4–5/6.

Wakker, P. (1988). Non-expected utility as aversion of information, *J. of Behavioral Decision Making* 1: 169–75.

Weller, P. (1978). Consistent intertemporal decision making under uncertainty. *Review of Economic Studies* XLV (2): 263–67.

Yager, R. R. (1990). Decision making under Dempster-Shafer uncertainties. Technical Report MII-915, Iona College, New Rochelle, NY.

16 Interval probabilities induced by decision problems

Thomas WHALEN

Abstract: There are many practical decision problems and information channels whose most natural probability representation involves ranges or regions in probability space. A major source of such problems is team decisions requiring optimal use of limited or costly communication. Probabilities may be communicated in rounded form, or events whose probability exceeds a prespecified threshold may be identified. Another major concern is ordinal information about probability. This ordinal information may come as a summary message from a teammate, or more directly as, for example, by observing a random walk process after an unknown number of steps. All the above cases, and many others, can be expressed by systems of linear constraints on probabilities. Some of them, but not all, can also be represented by the basic probability assignments of Dempster-Shafer's theory. Several methods for decision making with linearly constrained probabilities are introduced and compared in a simulation experiment. On both theoretical and empirical grounds the most promising appears to be the extended Laplace criterion, based on a concept of second-order maximum entropy. An alternative approach using an interactive graphic decision support system for problems of this type is also presented using a simple example.

Keywords: interval probabilities, second-order probabilities, decision analysis

1. RISK AND IGNORANCE

The general problem of decision making under uncertainty involves a set of n states of nature, a set of k alternative actions, and a utility function. The utility function assigns a vector of n values to each alternative action; each element of this vector specifies the value of the action under the corresponding state of nature. The k utility vectors typically take the form of row vectors collected into a k by n utility matrix associating a specific value to each (state, action) pair.

Standard treatments of decision making under uncertainty are divided into two separate branches: decisions under risk and decisions under ignorance (Bunn, 1984; Resnik, 1987). Under risk, the numeric probability of each state of nature is also assumed to be known or estimated. This enables us to reduce the utility vector of each alternative action to a scalar expected utility, by weighting each possible utility by the probability of the corresponding state of nature. The action whose expected utility is highest is selected.

Under ignorance, the decision maker has no knowledge at all about the probabilities of the states of nature. Many criteria exist for making a decision without recourse to probability. Implicitly or explicitly, each of these criteria also reduces an action's vector of possible utilities to a scalar figure of merit to facilitate comparisons between alternative actions. This requires replacing the weighting role of the missing probabilities with some other weighting scheme. The Laplace criterion emphasizes all states of nature equally. The Hurwicz criterion (of which maximax and maximin are special cases) emphasizes the most favorable and/or the most unfavorable states of nature. The minimax regret criterion emphasizes the states of nature for which the decision makes the most difference.

2. INTERMEDIATE CASES

Decisions must very often rely on probability information that falls between the well studied extremes of pure risk and pure ignorance. This is especially true in team decision making (Marschak, 1955; Ho and Chu, 1972) when one team member assesses a probability distribution but because of time or other constraints can only communicate a standard, concise description of the distribution to the actual decision maker. Each message that can be sent corresponds to a region within a probability space with (n-1) dimensions, where n is the number of states of nature. Note that the authors and publishers of handbooks, almanacs, or other sources of potentially useful information can be viewed as generalized "teammates" of everyone who consults their publications.

Sometimes the decision maker has enough information to arrange the possible states of nature in order from most probable to least probable without being able to numerically specify the probabilities of individual states of nature. This ordinal information may come as a summary message from a teammate, or it may come more directly. For example, if a random walk process is observed after a large but unknown number of steps, the most probable direction can be inferred but not how probable it is. This is useful information for implementing a stochastic control system, since it is as important to keep probabilities of opposite discrepancies in balance as it is to keep them small in order to minimize long-run overall drift.

Alternatively, the decision maker may be given information about which states of nature, if any, have a probability above a specified threshold. Another important special case of incomplete probability information arises when probabilities are in rounded form; for example, we may be told that $P(A)=.2$, $P(B)=.3$, and $P(C)=.4$ to the nearest tenth, where A, B, and C are a mutually exclusive exhaustive event set whose unrounded probabilities must sum to 1.

3. LINEARLY CONSTRAINED PROBABILITIES

All the above cases, and many others, can be expressed by systems of linear constraints on probabilities. The true probability distribution (or a teammate's true subjective distribution) is not known in detail, but the decision maker knows that it must lie within a particular region in probability space.

If a decision maker receives enough information to determine a precise (objective or subjective) probability assessment, the probability region is reduced to a single point and the recipient faces a problem of decision making under pure risk. On the other hand, if the recipient can derive no information about the sender's subjective probabilities, the probability region is the whole of probability space, constrained only by the ordinary axioms of probability. In this case, the recipient's problem is equivalent to decision making under pure ignorance.

4. PARTIAL SECOND-ORDER IGNORANCE

In the general case, the decision maker is ignorant about what probability distribution holds within a region of possible probability distributions. Each point in the region specifies an ordinary probability distribution over the original states of nature. This probability distribution together with the utility matrix for (state-action) pairs in turn specifies an expected value for each action. Thus each point in the region of possible probability distributions specifies an expected utility for each action. The decision maker knows that the true probability distribution over states of nature corresponds to one of the points, but has no information about the relative likelihood of the points within the region.

This is equivalent to a second-order problem of decision making under ignorance in which the role of "states of nature" is filled by probability distributions over the original states of nature. In the absence of an appropriate second-order probability distribution, the decision maker must rely on some other considerations to weight the expected return or regret of each probability distribution, just as in ordinary decision making under ignorance.

It is relatively straightforward to find the corner points of a region in probability space defined by a system of linear constraints and to calculate the expected utility arising from each alternative action at each corner point. For any possible probability distribution, the expected utility for an action is a linear combination of the expected utilities of that action at these corner points. Therefore the maximum and minimum expected utility for each alternative action can be found by examining only these corner points.

5. GRAPHICAL ANALYSIS WHEN $n=3$

Suppose that the uncertainty of a decision problem can be expressed using just three possible states of nature. The space of possible probability distributions with respect to these three events forms a plane triangle bisecting the unit cube, as shown in Figure 16.1. This fact enables us to graph any trinomial probability as a point on a set of triangular coordinates. The three corners of the triangle represent respectively the three degenerate probability distributions which assign a probability of 1 to the corresponding states of nature.

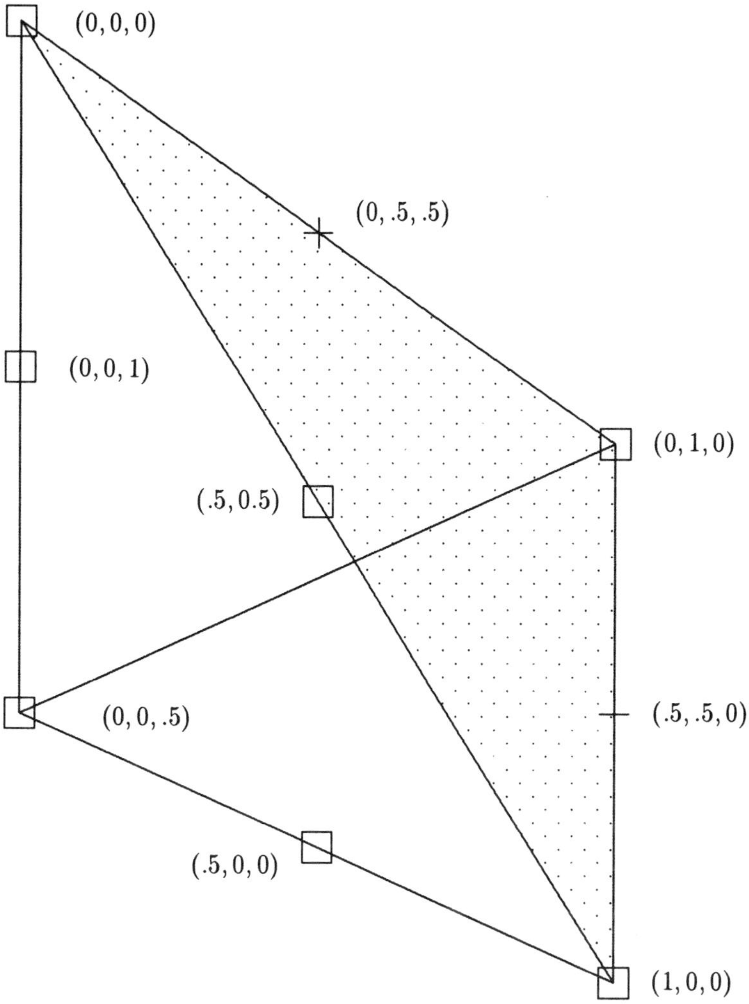

Figure 16.1: Probability space ($n = 3$).

Figure 16.2 shows the partitioning of trinomial probability space corresponding to information that completely orders the three probabilities. The three vertices, labeled (1,0,0), (0,1,0) and (0,0,1) represent degenerate probability distributions in which one of the three states (respectively A, B, or C) is certain. The point labeled (.1,.6,.3) is an example of a probability distribution compatible with the ordinal information that $P(B) \geqslant P(C) \geqslant P(A)$ corresponding to the lower left-hand region of the probability space. Similarly, Figures

16.3, 16.4, and 16.5 show the partitionings for information systems that inform the decision maker which, if any, of the states has a probability greater than a particular threshold probability, denoted L. In Figure 16.3 the threshold is $L=1/2$, in Figure 16.4, $L=1/3$, and in Figure 16.5, $L=1/4$.

Figure 16.6 shows the 166 different regions of probability space that arise from rounding each of the probabilities of three exclusive exhaustive events to the nearest tenth. The hexagonal and trapezoidal regions represent cases where the three rounded probabilities add up to 1.0. The upward-pointing triangles at the three corners represent the cases when one probability is rounded to 1.0 and the other two are rounded to zero. The upward-pointing triangles in the interior of Figure 16.6 contain probability distributions such as (.86,.06,.08), which when rounded add up to more than 1.0. Finally, the downward-pointing triangles contain probability distributions such as (.84,.03,.13) or (.94,.03,.03), which when rounded add up to less than 1.0.

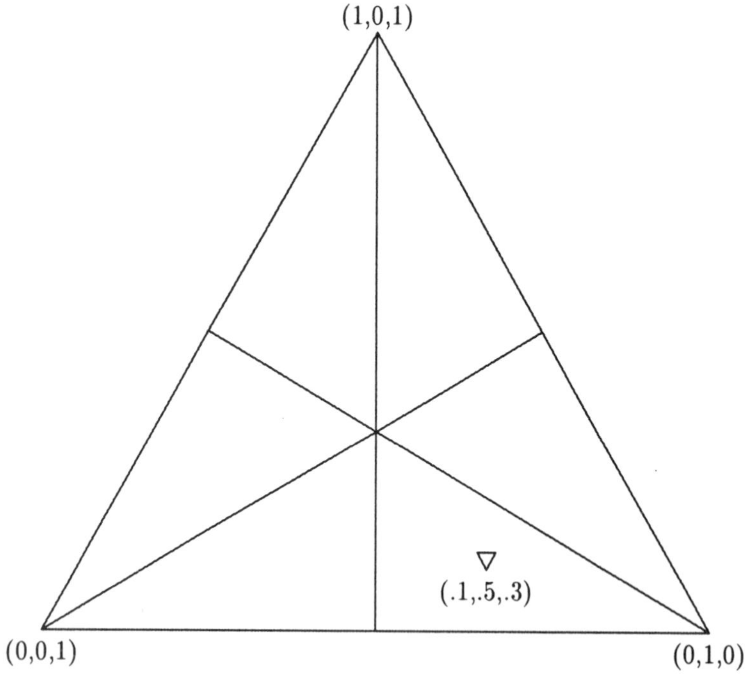

Figure 16.2

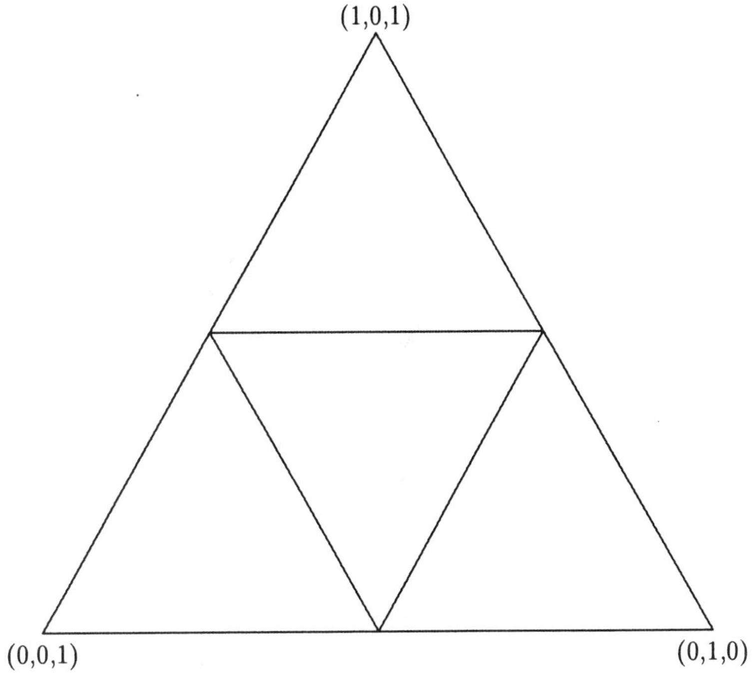

Figure 16.3

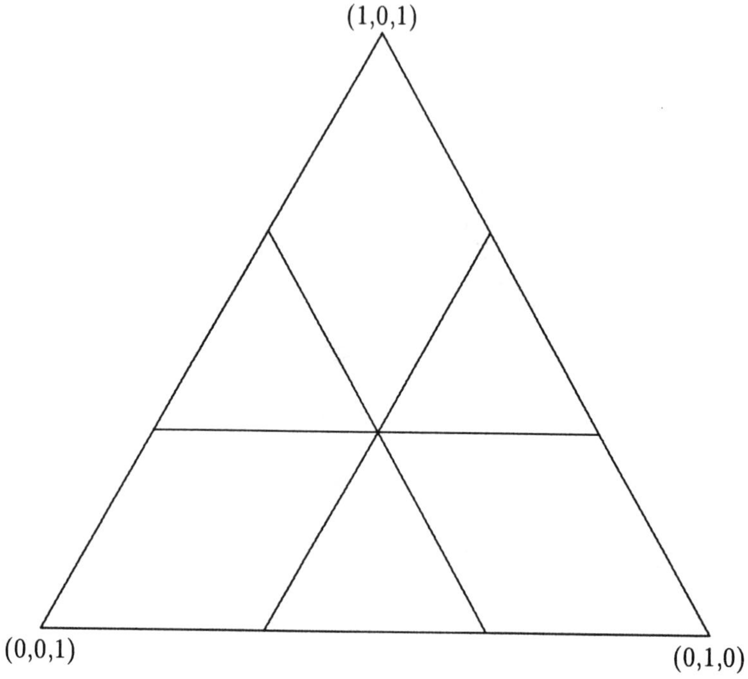

Figure 16.4

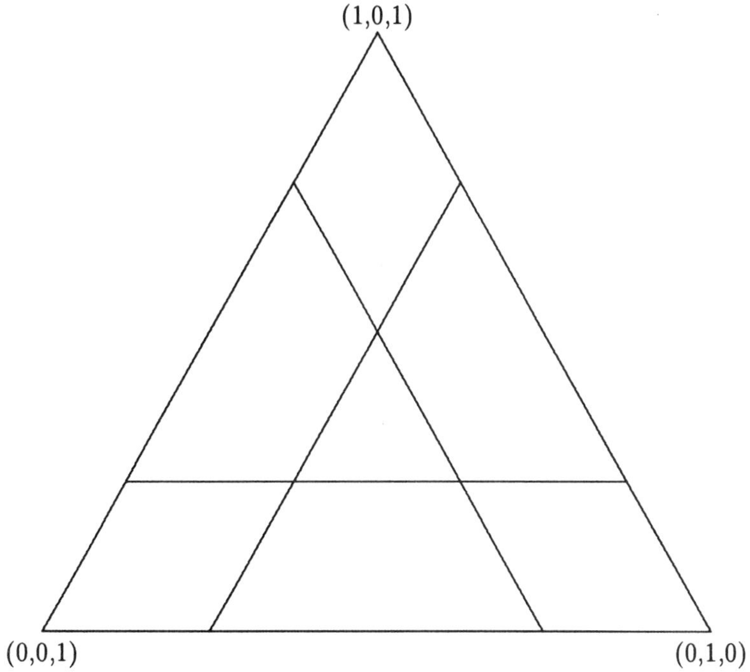

Figure 16.5

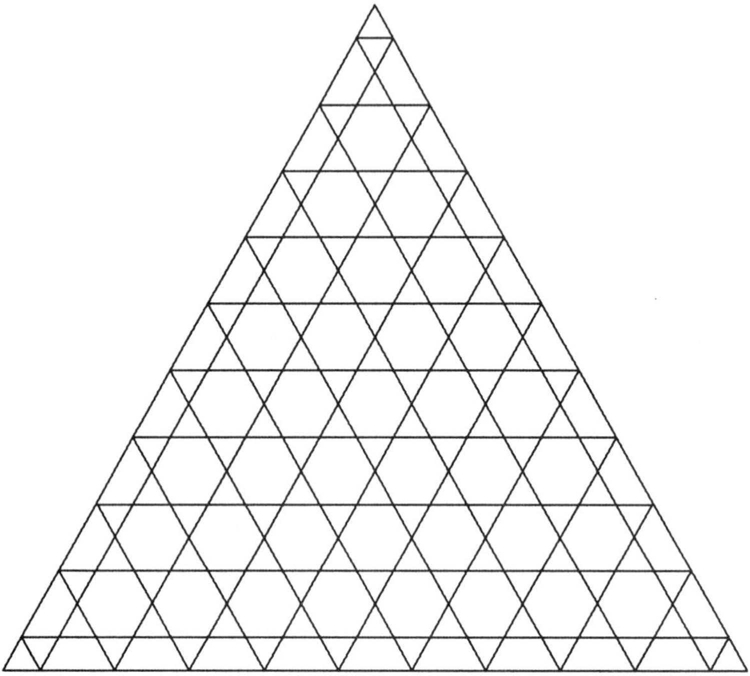

Figure 16.6

6. WHEN DO LINEAR CONSTRAINTS DEFINE DEMPSTER-SHAFER EVIDENCE?

The Dempster-Shafer theory of evidence (Shafer, 1976; Zadeh, 1986) concerns one particular type of incomplete probability knowledge, represented by basic probability assignments. However, this model does not account for some kinds of probability knowledge that are of great practical importance.

An "evidence" (Shafer, 1976) is equivalent to a collection of lower bounds on the probabilities of all the event sets in a universe of discourse. Given a system of linear constraints on probabilities, these lower bounds can be found by linear programming. For example, when there are three possible states of nature, we can find lower bounds on the probability of the six nontrivial event sets using six linear programs all with the same constraints. Let $L1$ be the minimum possible value of $P(s1)$ subject to the constraints (including $P(s1)+P(s2)+P(s3)=1$ and $P(s1), P(s2), P(s3) \geqslant 0$). Similarly, let $L2$ and $L3$ be the minima of $P(s2)$ and $P(s3)$, $L12=\min\{P(s1)+P(s2)\}$, $L13=\min\{P(s1)+P(s3)\}$, $L23=\min\{P(s2)+P(s3)\}$.

Basic probability assignments, if they exist, can then be determined from the lower probabilities: $m1=L1$, $m2=L2$, $m3=L3$, $m12=L12-L1-L2$, $m13=L13-L1-L3$, $m23=L23-L2-L3$, and $m123=1-(m1+m2+m3+m12+m13+m23) = 1-L12-L13-L23+L1+L2+L3$.

It is convenient to compute the final quantity first; if it is nonnegative then a valid basic probability assignment exists and the system of linear constraints constitutes an evidence in the sense of Shafer. If the calculated value for $m123$ is negative this immediately shows that the system of linear constraints does not correspond to any Dempster-Shafer evidence.

When there are only two possible states of nature, the ordinal information that state 1 is more probable than state 2 corresponds to the probability threshold information that $P(s1)>.5$. This can be represented by the basic probability assignment $m(s1)=.5, m(s2)=0$, $m(s1 U s2)=.5$. However, when there are more than two possible states of nature, as in Figure 16.2, ordinal information about probabilities can never be expressed by basic probability assignments.

Probability threshold information does not always correspond to basic probability assignments. In Figure 16.3 (probability threshold$=.5$), each of the three corner regions corresponds to a bpa; the central region is the intersection of three regions all of which have a bpa, but it cannot be represented by any bpa. The information systems shown in Figures 16.4 and 16.5, on the other hand, are entirely describable in Dempster-Shafer's terms.

Rounded probabilities, as in Figure 16.6, can sometimes be represented by basic probability assignments but not when the rounded probabilities add up to less than 1.0. For example, probabilities of .33, .33, and .34 would be rounded to .3, .3, and .3. The latter would be a useful approximation to the true probabilities but it cannot be expressed as a basic probability assignment. The rounded information system (Figure 16.6) contains five types of regions. Let us examine each type in turn to see whether they correspond to a Dempster-Shafer evidence.

The 36 hexagonal regions in Figure 16.6 correspond to the simplest sort of rounded probabilities, in which none of the three rounded values are zero or 1 and the three sum to exactly one. One such rounded distribution is (.6,.3,.1). This defines the following system of linear constraints: $.55 \geqslant P(s1) \leqslant .65, .25 \leqslant P(s2) \leqslant .35, .05 \leqslant P(s3) \leqslant .15$. Six linear programs give us $L1 = .55$, $L2 = .25$, $L3 = .05$, $L12 = .85$, $L13 = .65$, and $L23 = .35$.

$$1 - (L12 - L13 - L23 + L1 + L2 + L3) = 1 - 1.85 + .85 = 0$$

Since $0 \geqslant 0$, the region is an evidence with the following bpa:

$m1 = .55$, $m2 = .25$, $m3 = .05$, $m12 = .05$, $m13 = .05$, $m23 = .05$, $m123 = 0$

Table 16.1 summarizes these calculations for all five types of regions. Note that since $1 - L12 - L13 - L23 + L1 + L2 + L3$ is negative in the last case (downward-pointing triangles), no corresponding basic probability assignment exists.

Converting from a Dempster-Shafer evidence to a system of linear constraints is very straightforward. The lower bound for the probability of each state of nature is equal to its basic probability assignment, and the upper bound is the sum of all the basic probability assignments of sets containing that state of nature.

7. DECISION CRITERIA

A logical first step in making a decision under uncertainty is dominance screening. Potter and Anderson (1980) discuss dominance screening in the context of linearly constrained Bayesian priors. Ordinary linear programming can find the maximum and minimum values of the difference between the expected utility (EU) of one alternative and that of another. One alternative decision dominates another if the maximum and the minimum difference have the same sign. (A common error is to assume that the maximum EU of the dominated act must be less than the minimum EU of the act that dominates it. In fact two utility ranges can overlap even if one action always has higher EU than the other for every particular feasible probability distribution.)

Table 16.1: Are rounded probabilities Dempster-Shafer's evidences?

Shape	Example	Probability Bounds	Lower Probabilities	Calculated m123	Basic Probability Assignment
36 Hexagons	(.6,.3,.1)	$0.55 \leqslant P(s1) \leqslant 0.65$ $0.25 \leqslant P(s1) \leqslant 0.35$ $0.05 \leqslant P(s1) \leqslant 0.15$	$L1 = 0.55$ $L2 = 0.25$ $L3 = 0.05$ $L12 = 0.85$ $L13 = 0.65$ $L23 = 0.35$	0	$m1 = 0.55$ $m2 = 0.25$ $m3 = 0.05$ $m12 = 0.05$ $m13 = 0.05$ $m23 = 0.05$ $m123 = 0$
27 Trapezoids at Edges	(.6,.4,0.)	$0.55 \leqslant P(s1) \leqslant 0.65$ $0.35 \leqslant P(s1) \leqslant 0.45$ $0 \leqslant P(s1) \leqslant 0.05$	$L1 = 0.55$ $L2 = 0.35$ $L3 = 0$ $L12 = 0.95$ $L13 = 0.55$ $L23 = 0.35$	0.05	$m1 = 0.55$ $m2 = 0.35$ $m3 = 0$ $m12 = 0.05$ $m13 = 0$ $m23 = 0$ $m123 = 0.05$
3 Upward- Pointing Triangles at Corners	(1.,0.,0.)	$0.95 \leqslant P(s1) \leqslant 1$ $0 \leqslant P(s1) \leqslant 0.05$ $0 \leqslant P(s1) \leqslant 0.05$	$L1 = 0.95$ $L2 = 0$ $L3 = 0$ $L12 = 0.95$ $L13 = 0.95$ $L23 = 0$	0.05	$m1 = 0.95$ $m2 = 0$ $m3 = 0$ $m12 = 0$ $m13 = 0$ $m23 = 0$ $m123 = 0.05$
45 Upward- Pointing Triangles in Interior	(.6,.4,.1) note sum = 1.1	$0.55 \leqslant P(s1) \leqslant 0.65$ $0.35 \leqslant P(s1) \leqslant 0.45$ $0.05 \leqslant P(s1) \leqslant 0.15$	$L1 = 0.55$ $L2 = 0.35$ $L3 = 0.05$ $L12 = 0.9$ $L13 = 0.6$ $L23 = 0.4$	0.05	$m1 = 0.55$ $m2 = 0.35$ $m3 = 0.05$ $m12 = 0$ $m13 = 0$ $m23 = 0$ $m123 = 0.05$
55 Downward- Pointing Triangles	(.5,.3,.1) note sume = 0.9	$0.45 \leqslant P(s1) \leqslant 0.55$ $0.25 \leqslant P(s1) \leqslant 0.35$ $0.05 \leqslant P(s1) \leqslant 0.15$	$L1 = 0.5$ $L2 = 0.3$ $L3 = 0.1$ $L12 = 0.85$ $L13 = 0.65$ $L23 = 0.45$	0.05	$m1 =$ ERR $m2 =$ ERR $m3 =$ ERR $m12 =$ ERR $m13 =$ ERR $m23 =$ ERR $m123 =$ ERR

Typically, more than one nondominated alternative will remain. To reach a final decision, it is helpful to calculate a figure of merit to represent the attractiveness of each action by a single number. When each state's probability is fully determined, expected utility is the figure state's probability is fully determined, expected utility is the figure of merit. When the probability is undetermined, there are evaluates the range of expected utilities possible for an action and then reduces this range to a single representative expected utility. The other approach first reduces the range of probability distributions to a single distribution and then calculates just one expected utility based on this representative probability distribution.

8. REPRESENTATIVE UTILITY APPROACHES

The two most common ways to reduce a range of utilities to a single figure of merit are the maximin criterion and the midpoint criterion. Both are special cases of the Hurwicz family of criteria, which use a general weighted average of the minimum and maximum possible utility. The maximin criterion expresses conservatism in decision making, while the midpoint criterion seeks to optimize average performance.

The extended Hurwicz criterion selects the action with the greatest value of

$$a^*[\max\{E(\text{utility})\}] + (1-a)^*[\min\{E(\text{utility})\}]$$

taking max and min over the set of admissible probability distributions and taking expectation over states of nature according to each particular distribution. In particular, when the optimism coefficient a equals zero the extended Hurwicz criterion becomes extended maximin. If the constraints on probability are correct and remain constant for many iterations of the decision maker's action, the long-run average utility of the extended maximin criterion's selected action cannot possibly fall below the indicated value, while that of other actions might be below this value for some possible probability distribution. Similarly, when $a = .5$ the extended Hurwicz criterion becomes the extended midpoint criterion, while when $a = 1$ it reduces to the extended maximax criterion.

9. REPRESENTATIVE PROBABILITY APPROACHES

On the other hand, many authors (e.g., Jaynes, 1968; Gottinger, 1990) argue that uncertainties about probabilities ought to be resolved as objectively as possible; in other words, without reference to utilities. Under this assumption, Gottinger has shown that the only reasonable choice for a representative probability distribution from a range is the disribution whose entropy is highest (the Laplace criterion). These arguments are convincing, but their direct application to the probabilities of states of nature can lead to discarding most or all of the available information. For example, the standard maximum entropy (Laplace) form for a complete order over probabilities is equivalent to the maximum entropy form for total ignorance!

This dilemma can be resolved using a second-order maximum entropy concept that preserves more real information while satisfying the requirements that motivate the original maximum entropy concept (Whalen and Brönn, 1990). Rather than considering the probability distribution over the original set of states, we consider a second-order probability distribution over points in probability space (Figures16.2 – 16.6). Applying the maximum entropy principle to this distribution implies that all points in probability space should be considered equally likely. Thus the representative point for a region of probability space is the mean point of that region.

Geometrically, the ordinary maximum entropy distribution for a region in probability space (as in Figures 16.1–16.6) is the point in the region closest to the center of the entire probability space. The second-order maximum entropy distribution for a region is the center of that region itself. Under total ignorance, the region in question is the entire probability space, and both versions of maximum entropy select the same representative point, that is, the center of the space.

10. SIMULATION EXPERIMENTS

A series of simulation experiments compared four methods of determining a figure of merit (maximin, midpoint, standard Laplace, and extended Laplace) using seven different information systems:

1. The null information system in which the decision maker has no information about probability,

2. The ordinal information system of Figure 16.2, which ranks the three probabilities from lowest to highest (six posssible messages),
3. The information system of Figure 16.3, which identifies any state of nature whose probability is greater than .5 (four possible messages),
4. The information system of Figure 16.4, which identifies any state(s) of nature whose probability is greater than 1/3 (six possible messages),
5. The information system of Figure 16.5, which identifies any state(s) of nature whose probability is greater than .25 (seven possible messages),
6. The information system of Figure 16.6, which gives the approximate probability of each of the three events, rounded to the nearest tenth, and
7. The perfect information system in which the decision maker knows the exact probabilities of the three states.

Ten thousand trinomial distributions were generated using a uniform second-order distribution: $p1 = 1 - \sqrt{R}$, $p2 = S^*(1 - p1)$, $p3 = 1 - p1 - p2$ where R and S are uniformly distributed random fractions. (This procedure makes the proportion of generated probability distributions falling in a region proportional to the area of the region in the graph of probability space.) Ten thousand 3×3 utility matrices were randomly generated; the highest utility in each matrix was 100 and the lowest zero, with other utilities uniformly distributed. Each pairing of a criterion with an information system selected an action, and the expected utility of that action was recorded for a total of ten thousand iterations. The lowest mean expected value was 64.255 (maximin criterion, null information system), and the highest mean expected value was 71.748 (perfect information system).

For the "rounded" information system, a fifth decision criterion is also shown. In this criterion, the expected value is simply calculated using the three rounded probabilities, regardless of whether they sum to 0.9, 1.0, or 1.1.

Table 16.2 summarizes the experimental findings. The table shows the mean expected utility of each combination of one of the seven information systems with one of the four decision criterion, expressed as a percentage of the range of mean expected utility from the lowest (64.255) to the highest (71.745). Thus, the percentages represent the proportion of the maximum benefit that can be derived from probability information.

Table 16.2: Results of simulation experiments.

	Number of Messages	Maximin	Midpoint	Standard Laplace	Extended Laplace	As Rounded
None	1	0.0%	33.9%	48.0%	48.0	
Threshold = 1/2	4	78.0%	86.4%	80.9%	88.57%	
Ordinal	6	81.1%	89.7%	48.0%	88.55%	
Threshold = 1/3	6	84.7%	92.4%	48.0%	92.2%	
Threshold = 1/4	7	85.2%	91.6%	79.0%	92.3%	
Rounded	166	98.8%	99.1%	98.6%	99.5%	99.4%
Perfect	10000	100.0%	100.0%	100.0%	100.0%	

Since the results in Table 16.2 are average results, the values for the midpoint criterion are automatically better than the corresponding values for maximin. Similarly, the second-order Laplace criterion is automatically higher than the conservative standard Laplace.

Not surprisingly, there is a general tendency for the performance of the various techniques to increase with increasing richness of information as measured by the number of alternative messages. But there are some noteworthy exceptions.

One very striking finding is the poor performance of the ordinal information system. By the standard Laplace criterion, ordinal information is no better than no information at all. Under the other three criteria, knowing which one of the six ordinal regions contains the true probability is always less useful than knowing which one of the six regions derived from a probability threshold of 1/3 contains it. In the two representative probability approaches (standard Laplace and extended Laplace), the six-message ordinal information system is actually inferior to the four-message information system with probability threshold .5! Furthermore, learning which of the four regions for $L=1/2$ contains the true probability and applying the second-order Laplace criterion obtains 88.57% of the benefit of the perfect information system. This is better than that obtainable by any of the four criteria applied to the six-region ordinal information system.

The additional bandwidth of the seven-message information system in Figure 16.5 versus the six-message system in Figure 16.4 does not guarantee improved performance. Under the midpoint criterion, the seven-message information system with threshold .25 is inferior to the six-message information system with threshold 1/3, while under the standard Laplace criterion the four-message infor-

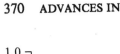

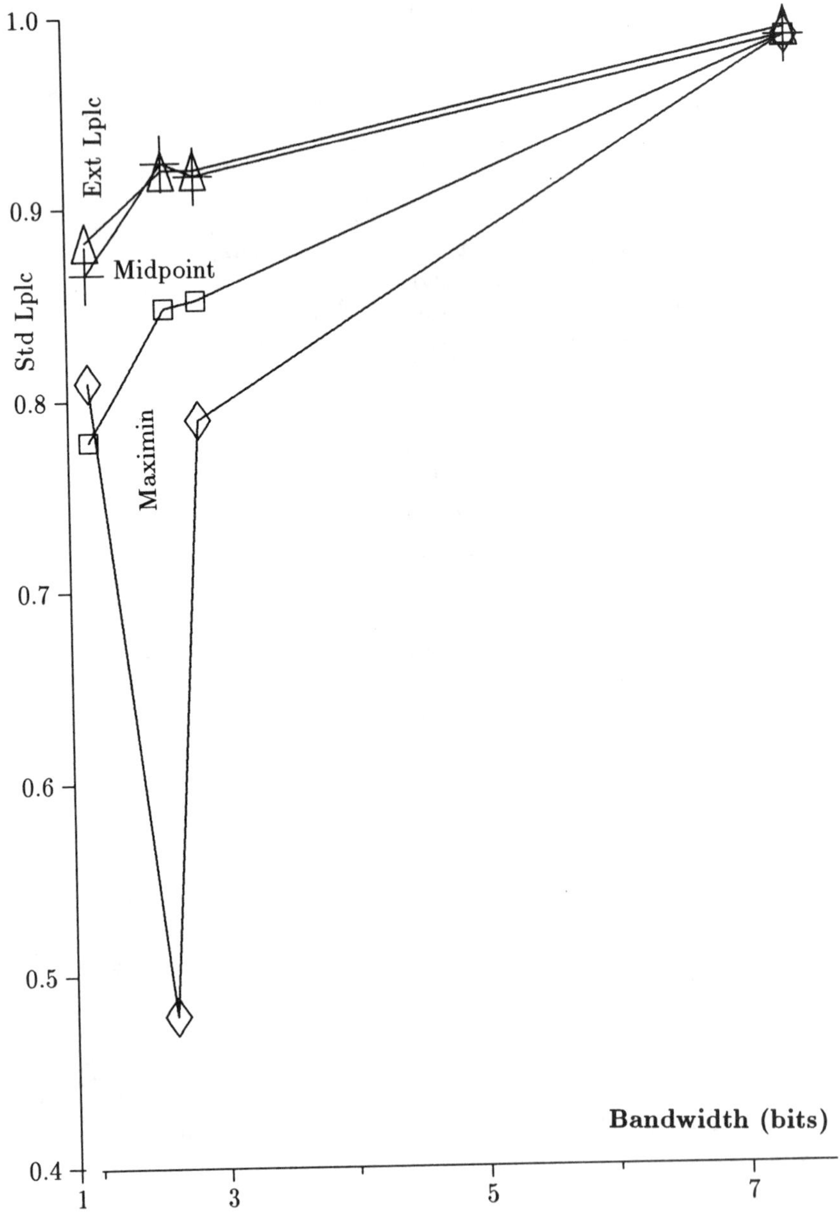

Figure 16.7: Results of simulation experiments

mation system with probability threshold .25 outperforms both six-message information systems and the seven-message information system. The only decision criterion that comes close to consistenly rewarding richer information with better performance is the extended Laplace, although even here the performance with ordinal is very slightly poorer than the performance with threshold .5.

Comparing decision criteria under a given information system, the extended Laplace consistently outperforms the others except in the case of the ordinal information system, in which it is not quite as good as the midpoint criterion. The standard Laplace is consistently the worst except with the information system with probability threshold = .5, in which it is better than the maximin criterion but worse than the midpoint and extended Laplace.

Figure 16.7 compares the decision criteria for the three probability threshold information systems and the rounded probability information system. (The horizontal axis, labeled "bandwidth," is the logarithm to the base 2 of the number of messages in the information sytem, ranging from 2 bits for the four-message system to 7.375 bits for the 166-message system.)

11. APPLICATION TO DECISION SUPPORT SYSTEMS

We are currently designing and implementing a variety of decision support systems (DSS) based on second-order representative utility approaches. These systems will be used to carry out a program of experimentation comparing the actual effectiveness of these competing concepts of decision making under partial ignorance. These decision support systems include a maximin DSS, a maximax DSS, a Hurwicz DSS which combines the latter two, and a minimax regret DSS.

In the maximin DSS, the user picks an alternative action Ai to serve as standard. The first step is to find the minimum and maximum possible expected utilities for Ai subject to the system of linear constraints that define the region of possible probability distributions. The DSS graphs this information in the form of a 45-degree line segment from the point (min($euAi$), min($euAi$)) to the point (max ($euAi$), max($euAi$)).

For each possible expected utility of the standard alternative, min ($euAi$) $\leqslant x \leqslant$ max($euAi$), the DSS then finds the minimum possible expected utility for each of the other alternative actions when $euAi=x$, denoted min($euAj \mid euAi=x$). This is done by adding an additional constraint, $euAi = x$, to the system of linear constraints that define the region of possible probability distributions. The sensitivity analysis features of linear programming make it possible to completely identify min $(euAj \mid euAi = x)$ as a function of x by evaluating a relatively small number of LP problems.

The maximin DSS then graphs the minimum possible expected utility of each alternative action given each possible expected utility $(euAi)$ of the standard alternative. Suppose that action Ai is the standard and x is one possible expected utility for action Ai. $\text{Min}(euAj \mid euAi = x) = x$, so the DSS will plot a point at (x, x) in the 45-degree line corresponding to action Ai. Each of the other alternative actions Aj, $j \neq i$, generates a piecewise linear curve composed of points of the form $(x, \min(euAj \mid euAi = x))$ showing the minimum possible expected utility of action Aj over all possible probability distributions for which the expected utility of action Ai is x.

The maximax DSS differs from the maximin DSS only in plotting points $(x, \max(euAj \mid euAi = x))$ instead of points $(x, \min(euAj \mid eu\,Ai = x))$ for each action Aj other than the standard Ai. The "Hurwicz" DSS plots a linear combination (typically a simple average) of the expected utilities used by the maximin DSS and the maximax DSS.

The minimax regret DSS uses the range of possible expected regrets (erg) for the standard alternative instead of range of possible expected utilities, and plots $\max(ergAj \mid ergAi = x)$ to show the maximum possible expected regret of action A_j for all possible probability distributions for which the expected regret of action Ai is x. (This DSS is based on the extended minimax regret criterion, which selects the act whose $\max(E(regret))$ is least. Thus, the criterion emphasizes those probability distributions where the decision makes the greatest difference to the consequences, measured by the difference between the expected utility of a given action and the expected utility of the optimal action for that probability distribution.)

12. DSS EXAMPLE

Table 16.3: Utility matrix.

	States		
Actions	$s1$	$s2$	$s3$
$A1$	2	1	0
$A2$	1.5	3	1
$A3$	0.5	2	6

Table 16.4: Corner points of probability region.

$p1$	$p2$	$p3$	$euA1$	$euA2$	$euA3$
0.33	0.33	0.33	1	1.83	2.83
0.5	0	0.5	1	1.25	3.25
0.5	0.5	0	1.5	2.25	1.25
1	0	0	2	1.5	0.5

Table 16.3 shows a utility matrix that will be used to illustrate one of the projected decision support systems. Suppose the decision maker's knowledge of the probabilities of the three states of nature is as indicated by the basic probability assignment $m1 = 1/3$, $m2 = 0$, $m3 = 0$, $m12 = 1/6$, $m13 = 1/6$, $m23 = 0$, $m123 = 1/3$. (This is the most restrictive bpa that contains all probability distributions for which s1 is the most likely state.) Table 16.3 gives the corner points of the corresponding probability region along with the expected utilities of the three alternative actions at these points.

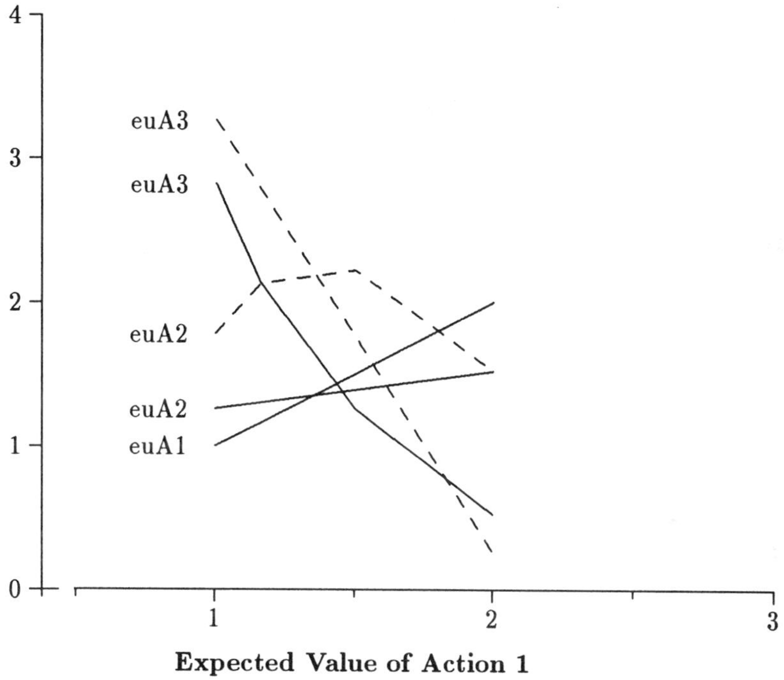

Figure 16.8: Sample DSS display.

Figure 16.8 shows the maximin DSS display for this situation when action $A1$ is used as the standard. Both axes range from 0 to 4 because that is the full range of utilities in Table 16.2. With the given information, the expected utility of action $A1$ ($euA1$) ranges from 1 to 2, so the minimum expected utility function for action $A2$ is a straight line running from (1,1) to (2,2). The dark lines labeled $euA2$ and $euA3$

are found by examining the points in the probability region for which $euA1$ has a given value and taking the minimum value of $euA2$ (resp. $euA3$) over those points. (The lighter lines show the maximum possible expected utilities of $euA2$ and $euA3$ for each possible value of $euA1$. Note that there is only one possible probability distribution for which $euA1 = 2$, so the minimum and maximum values of each action coincide when $euA1 = 2$.)

BIBLIOGRAPHY

Bunn, D. (1984). *Applied Decision Analysis.* New York: MCGraw-Hill.

Gottinger, H.W. (1990). Decision problems under uncertainty based on entropy functionals. *Theory and Decision* 28: 143–72.

Ho, Y-C. and Chu, K.C. (1972). Team decision theory and information structure in optimal control problems Parts I & II. *IEEE Trans. on Autom. Control* AC-17: 18–38.

Jaynes, E.T. (1968). Prior probabilities. *IEEE Transactions on Systems Science and Cybernetics* SSC-4: 227–41.

Marschak, J. (1955). Elements for a theory of teams. *Mgmt. Sci.* 1: 126–37.

Potter, J. and Anderson, B. (1980). Partial prior information and decision-making. *IEEE Transactions on Sytems, Man., and Cybernetics* SMC-10: 125–33.

Resnik, M. (1987). *Choices: An introduction to decision theory.* Minneapolis: University of Minnesota Press.

Shafer, G. (1976). *A mathematical theory of evidence.* Princeton: Princeton University Press.

Whalen, T. and Brönn, C. (1990). Hurwicz and regret criteria extended to decisions with ordinal probabilities. *Proc. of 1990 North Amer. Fuzzy Inform. Proc. Soc. Conference*, pp. 219–22.

Zadeh, L. (1986). A simple view of the Dempster-shafer theory of evidence and its implication for the rule of combination. *AI Magazine*, Summer.

17 Constraint propagation over a restricted space of configurations, and its use in optimization

Sławomir T. WIERZCHOŃ

Abstract: An application of the message-passing algorithm to solving a class of constrained optimization problems is proposed. The method can be used in problems like belief revision or the generation of explanations in expert systems. Procedures for the marginalization and extension of valuations are presented, and a method for generating the Markov trees is proposed.

Keywords: discrete optimization, local computations, belief revision, algorithms.

1. INTRODUCTION

Constraint propagation is widely used in AI systems to perform inferences. A constraint network is a structure which expresses relations between variables or parameters. It consists of a set of nodes (representing variables) connected by constraints (weights attached to different combinations of possible values of the linked variables). Shenoy and Shafer (1990) proposed a very general method for propagating constraints that satisfies a certain set of axioms. Their work was mainly concerned with the propagation of so-called mass assignments being a generalization of the probability distributions. However, the class of problems satisfying Shenoy and Shafer's axioms is much larger. A simple example is discrete optimization discussed by Shenoy (1990). In this paper we show a further application of Shenoy's approach to constrained optimization problems. This approach may be of value when we are interested in problems like belief revision of generation of explanations in expert systems (see Chapter V in Pearl [1988] for more details).

The paper is organized as follows. In Section 2 we introduce basic notions, and in Section 3 the message-passing algorithm is explained. Some implementational issues concerning this algorithm are discussed in Section 4. In Section 5 a class of optimization problems is briefly described and in Section 6 a numerical example is presented.

2. BASIC NOTIONS

Let **X** be a finite set of variables, and Θ_i be a state space (i.e., a set of values) of a variable $X_i \in \mathbf{X}$. Through $\Theta(\mathbf{x})$ we denote a *configuration space* of a set $\mathbf{x} \subseteq \mathbf{X}$ of variables, i.e., $\Theta(\mathbf{x}) = \times \{\Theta_i | X_i \in \mathbf{x}\}$. Following database terminology, an element $\xi \in \Theta(\mathbf{x})$ can be viewed as a tuple $\xi = <x_{i_1},...,x_{i_n}>$, $n = |\mathbf{x}|$, where x_{i_j} is a member of Θ_{i_j} – the state space of j-th variable from the set **x**.

Let **V** be a set whose elements are called values; in **V** we distinguish two special elements: **0** (zero) and **1** (one). A mapping $v: \Theta(\mathbf{x}) \to \mathbf{V}$ is said to be a *valuation.* If $v(\xi) = \mathbf{0}$ for all $\xi \in \Theta(\mathbf{x})$ then v is said to be an improper valuation, otherwise v is a proper valuation. Among proper valuations we distinguish the so-called vacuous valuation such that $v(\xi) = \mathbf{1}$ for all $\xi \in \Theta(\mathbf{x})$. Intuitively, a proper valuation represents knowledge that is consistent in itself, and a vacuous valuation represents total ignorance about all configurations in $\Theta(\mathbf{x})$. In the probabilistic setting a vacuous valuation is exemplified by the potential $v(\xi) = 1$ for all $\xi \in \Theta(\mathbf{x})$, and an improper valuation by the potential $v(\xi) = 0$ for all $\xi \in \Theta(\mathbf{x})$. One must note that the valuations defined here are point valuations contrary to the set valuations $v: 2^{\Theta(\mathbf{x})} \to \mathbf{v}$ used in the Dempster-Shafer theory; in this paper we will consider only point-valuations.

If **H** is a family of subsets of set **X**, then the triplet $(\mathbf{X}, \mathbf{H}, \{v_\mathbf{x}\}_{\mathbf{x} \in \mathbf{H}})$ is a hypergraphical representation of the problem considered.

Suppose **a** and **b** are two subsets of **X** such that $\mathbf{b} \subset \mathbf{a}$. If ξ is a configuration from $\Theta(\mathbf{a})$, then $\xi.\mathbf{b}$ stands for the configuration defined on $\Theta(\mathbf{b})$; $\xi.\mathbf{b}$ consists of only those components which correspond to the variables from **b**. Now if $\nu_{\mathbf{a}}$ is a valuation on $\Theta(\mathbf{a})$, then its projection to $\Theta(\mathbf{b})$, $\mathbf{b} \subset \mathbf{a}$, denoted $\nu_{\mathbf{a}}^{\downarrow \mathbf{b}}$, is defined as follows:

$$\nu_{\mathbf{a}}^{\downarrow \mathbf{b}}(\theta) = \mathrm{GLUE}(\{\nu_{\mathbf{a}}(\xi) | \xi \in \Theta(\mathbf{a}), \xi.\mathbf{b} = \theta\}), \theta \in \Theta(\mathbf{b})$$

Here GLUE is an appropriate "glueing" operator. A well-known example of projection is probabilistic marginalization: if $p_{\mathbf{a}}$ is a joint probability distribution defined on the set **a** of variables, then $p_{\mathbf{a}}^{\downarrow \mathbf{b}}$, $\mathbf{b} \subset \mathbf{a}$, is the marginal probability distribution defined on **b**.

A valuation $\nu_{\mathbf{b}}$ can be extended to the valuation $\nu_{\mathbf{b}}^{\uparrow \mathbf{a}}$ over $\Theta(\mathbf{a})$, $\mathbf{a} \supset \mathbf{b}$, by means of the vacuous embedding defined as below:

$$\nu_{\mathbf{b}}^{\uparrow \mathbf{a}}(\xi) = \nu_{\mathbf{b}}(\theta) \text{ if } \xi.\mathbf{b} = \theta$$

Suppose $\nu_{\mathbf{a}}$ and $\nu_{\mathbf{b}}$ are two valuations; combining them by means of a combining operator $\oplus$ we obtain the valuation $\nu_{\mathbf{a}} \oplus \nu_{\mathbf{b}}$ on $\Theta(\mathbf{a} \cup \mathbf{b})$. If $\nu_{\mathbf{a}} \oplus \nu_{\mathbf{b}}$ is not a proper valuation, then $\nu_{\mathbf{a}}$ and $\nu_{\mathbf{b}}$ are not combinable.

Following Shenoy and Shafer (1990) we introduce the following axioms:

(A1) Commutativity and associativity:
$\nu_{\mathbf{a}} \oplus \nu_{\mathbf{b}} = \nu_{\mathbf{b}} \oplus \nu_{\mathbf{a}'}, (\nu_{\mathbf{a}} \oplus \nu_{\mathbf{b}}) \oplus \nu_{\mathbf{c}} = \nu_{\mathbf{a}} \oplus (\nu_{\mathbf{b}} \oplus \nu_{\mathbf{c}})$.

(A2) Consonance of marginalization:
if $\mathbf{a} \subset \mathbf{b} \subset \mathbf{c}$, then $(\nu_{\mathbf{c}}^{\downarrow \mathbf{b}})^{\downarrow \mathbf{a}} = \nu_{\mathbf{c}}^{\downarrow \mathbf{a}}$.

(A3) Distributivity of marginalization over combination:
$(\nu_{\mathbf{a}} \oplus \nu_{\mathbf{b}})^{\downarrow \mathbf{a}} = \nu_{\mathbf{a}} \oplus \nu_{\mathbf{b}}^{\downarrow \mathbf{a} \cap \mathbf{b}}$.

3. CONSTRAINTS PROPAGATION

An immediate consequence of axioms (A1) – (A3) is the next theorem.

Theorem 1: Suppose a valuation ν is stored in a factorized form $\nu = \oplus\{\nu_{\mathbf{h}} | \mathbf{h} \in \mathbf{H}\}$. Then

$$\nu^{\downarrow(\mathbf{X} \setminus \{X_i\})} = \oplus\{\nu_{\mathbf{h}} | \mathbf{h} \in \mathbf{H}, X_i \notin \mathbf{h}\} \oplus (\oplus\{\nu_{\mathbf{h}} | \mathbf{h} \in \mathbf{H}, X_i \in \mathbf{h}\})^{\downarrow(\mathbf{X} \setminus \{X_i\})}$$

Proof: Let $\nu_1 = \oplus\{\nu_{\mathbf{h}} | \mathbf{h} \in \mathbf{H}, X_i \notin \mathbf{h}\}$ and $\nu_2 = \oplus\{\nu_{\mathbf{h}} | \mathbf{h} \in \mathbf{H}, X_i \in \mathbf{h}\}$. By convention ν_1 is a valuation over $\mathbf{X} \setminus \{X_i\}$ and ν_2 is a valuation over **x**. Using axiom A1 we represent ν as $\nu_1 \oplus \nu_2$ and employing axiom A3 we obtain the result.

The marginalization of v to $\mathbf{X}\backslash\{X_i\}$ is called the elimination of variable X_i.

Applying this procedure to a set $\mathbf{x} \subset \mathbf{X}$ we can obtain a marginal over $\mathbf{x}\backslash\mathbf{x}$. Analyzing the proof we observe that the elimination process can be radically sped up. Namely, let us note that the pair $(\mathbf{X}, \mathbf{H})$ constitutes a hypergraph H in which $\mathbf{X}$ is the set of nodes and $\mathbf{H}$ is the set of hyperedges, $\mathbf{H} \subseteq 2^{\mathbf{X}}$.

Assume for a moment that H is a hypertree, or an acyclic hypergraph, i.e., the set $\mathbf{H}$ can be reduced to the empty set by repeatedly applying the following two operations (Graham's test):

(G1) If X is a node that appears in exactly one hyperedge $\mathbf{h}$, then delete X from $\mathbf{h}$;
(G2) Delete $\mathbf{h}$ if there exists a hyperedge $\mathbf{h}' \in \mathbf{H}$ such that $\mathbf{h}' \neq \mathbf{h}$ and $\mathbf{h}$ is contained in $\mathbf{h}'$.

It is known that for every hypertree $H = (\mathbf{X}, \mathbf{H})$ there exists a join tree $T(H) = (\mathbf{H}, \mathbf{E})$ such that (Maier, 1983):

(a) The set of nodes is identified with the set of hyperedges $\mathbf{H}$;
(b) The set of edges $\mathbf{E}$ consists of pairs $\{\mathbf{x}, \mathbf{y}\}$, $\mathbf{x}, \mathbf{y} \in \mathbf{H}$, such that $\mathbf{x} \cap \mathbf{y} \neq \emptyset$;
(c) For every pair $\mathbf{x}$, $\mathbf{y}$ and for every $X \in \mathbf{x} \cap \mathbf{y}$ each edge along the unique path between $\mathbf{x}$ and $\mathbf{y}$ includes X.

Property (c) can be reinterpreted in two ways. Suppose first that H is a hypertree and $\mathbf{t}$ and $\mathbf{b}$ are such sets from $\mathbf{H}$ that if $X \in \mathbf{t}$ and $X \in \mathbf{h}$, where $\mathbf{h} \in \mathbf{H}$ and $\mathbf{h} \neq \mathbf{t}$, $\mathbf{h} \neq \mathbf{b}$, then $X \in \mathbf{b}$. In other words $\mathbf{b}$ contains every vertex of $\mathbf{t}$ that is contained in a hyperedge of H other than $\mathbf{t}$ and $\mathbf{b}$. The sets $\mathbf{t}$ and $\mathbf{b}$ are referred to as a *twig* and a *branch*, respectively.

The second interpretation refers to the so-called running intersection property. Namely, we can order the hyperedges from set $\mathbf{H}$ in a sequence $\mathbf{h}_1, \mathbf{h}_2, \ldots, \mathbf{h}_n$, such that $\mathbf{h}_1$ is the root of a join tree and $\mathbf{h}_k$ is a twig in the hypergraph $\mathbf{H}_k = (\bigcup_{i=1}^{k} \mathbf{h}_i, \{\mathbf{h}_1, \ldots, \mathbf{h}_k\})$. In other words,

$$\mathbf{h}_k \cap (\mathbf{h}_1 \cup \ldots \cup \mathbf{h}_{k-1}) \subseteq \mathbf{h}_i,\ i < k,\ k \geqslant 2$$

The hyperedge $\mathbf{h}_k$ specified above is just the branch of twig $\mathbf{h}_i$. One observes that every twig of a hypergraph H is a leaf in the corresponding join tree $T(H)$ while a branch of this twig is a father node in tree $T(H)$. This observation allows us to create a join tree for a given hypertree.

Now it is easy to observe that if **t** is a twig and **b** is its branch, then the nodes from **t****b** belong to the twig **t** only. Hence, deleting **t** from hypergraph H means the reduction of H to hypergraph $H\backslash\{\mathbf{t}\} = (\mathbf{X}\backslash(\mathbf{t}\backslash\mathbf{b}), \mathbf{H}\backslash\{\mathbf{t}, \mathbf{b}\})$. This way we obtain the following version of Theorem 1.

Theorem 2: Suppose a valuation ν is stored in a factorized form $\nu = \oplus\{\nu_{\mathbf{h}} | \mathbf{h} \in \mathbf{H}\}$. Let $\mathbf{t} \in \mathbf{H}$ be a twig and $\mathbf{b} \in \mathbf{H}$ be its branch. Let $\mathbf{X}' = \mathbf{X}\backslash(\mathbf{t}\backslash\mathbf{b})$. Then

$$\nu^{\downarrow \mathbf{X}'} = \nu_{\mathbf{b}} \oplus \nu_{\mathbf{a}}^{\downarrow(\mathbf{t}\cap\mathbf{b})} \oplus (\oplus\{\nu_{\mathbf{h}} | \mathbf{h} \in \mathbf{H}\backslash\{\mathbf{t}, \mathbf{b}\}\})$$

Theorem 2 offers a conceptual background for recursive computations of marginal valuations. Suppose a valuation ν is stored in the factorized form over set **H** of belief universes and we wish to find a marginal $\varphi^{\downarrow \mathbf{a}}$ for some $\mathbf{a} \in \mathbf{H}$. To do it we order the sets from **H** into the tree construction sequence $\mathbf{h}_1, \ldots, \mathbf{h}_n$ satisfying the running intersection property and such that $\mathbf{h}_1 = \mathbf{a}$. Next, we fix a join tree and we denote $\beta(\mathbf{h})$ the branch of node **h** in this tree. Define now

$$M^{\mathbf{X} \to \beta(\mathbf{x})} = (\varphi_{\mathbf{x}} \oplus (\oplus\{M^{\mathbf{Y} \to \beta(\mathbf{Y})} | \mathbf{Y} \in \mathbf{H}, \beta(\mathbf{Y}) = \mathbf{x}\}))^{\downarrow \mathbf{x} \cap \beta(\mathbf{x})} \tag{1}$$

to be a message sent from node **h** to its branch $\beta(\mathbf{h})$. We note that if **1** is a leaf in the join tree, then $\beta^{-1}(1) = \emptyset$. In this case formula (1) reduces to

$$M^{1 \to \beta(1)} = \nu_{1}^{\downarrow 1 \cap \beta(1)} \tag{2}$$

and if **r** is the root of the join tree, then since $\beta(\mathbf{r}) = \emptyset$, (1) takes the form

$$\nu^{\downarrow \mathbf{r}} = \nu_{\mathbf{r}} \oplus (\oplus\{M^{\mathbf{y} \to \beta(\mathbf{y})} | \mathbf{y} \in \mathbf{H}, \beta(\mathbf{y}) = \mathbf{R}\}) \tag{3}$$

The process of computing messages can be organized very efficiently as described by Xu (1991).

Of course, to use this method we must convert a given hypergraph into a hypertree. Algorithms for doing this can be found in Mellouli (1987), Zarley (1988), or Shenoy (1990); another method is discussed in the next section.

4. IMPLEMENTATIONAL ISSUES

In this section we present some useful algorithms for the message-passing method.

First, we describe a procedure for finding an optimal acyclic hypergraph covering a given hypergraph $H = (\mathbf{X}, \mathbf{H})$. Suppose H is a list of hyperedges, i.e., each element of the list contains a hyperedge $\mathbf{h} \in \mathbf{H}$, and E is a list of hyperedges of the acyclic hypergraph. Further, assume that GRAHAM is a function which realizes Graham's test on a current list H. A Pascal-like code of the procedure Find Hypertree is given here.

Procedure FindHypertree:

```
begin
  E: =H;
  H: = GRAHAM(H);
  while(H < > NIL) do
  begin
    find {h,h'} s.t. Card(Θ(h\h')) = min{Card(Θ(g\g'))|g,g' ∈ H}; (*
    if there is a tie, choose {h,h'} such that Card(Θ(h ∪ h')) is the
    smallest *)
    e: = h ∪ h';
    E: = E ∪ {e};
    H: = (H\{h,h'}) ∪ {e};
    H: = GRAHAM(H);
  end;
end;
```

This procedure is a variant of Zhang's algorithm described in Zarley (1988). However, using the original algorithm it was found that in some circumstances it produces superfluous hyperedges. For instance, when $H = \{\{A, B\}, \{B, C\}, \{C, D\}, \{A, D\} \{D, E\}, \{E, G\}, \{G, F\}, \{D, F\}\}$, then $E = H \cup \{\{A, B, D\}, \{B, C, D\}, \{D, E, F\}, \{E, F, G\}, \{C, D, E\}\}$ and the hyperedge $\{C, D, E\}$ is superfluous. With our modification – relying upon using the GRAHAM function – we obtain the correct list E.

To see how the algorithm works, let us reconsider the example studied in Almond and Kong (1991). Assume that $\mathbf{X} = \{A, B, C, D, E, F, G, H, I, J\}$ and $H = \{\{A, B\}, \{A, D\}, \{A, E\}, \{B, D\}, \{B, E\}, \{C, D\}, \{C, G\}, \{D, G\}, \{E, F\}, \{E, H\}, \{F, H\}, \{G, H\}, \{G, I\}, \{H, I\}\}$. Assume for simplicity that all the variables $A,\ldots,I$ are binary ones. Note that $\text{GRAHAM}(H) = H$, i.e., no element of the initial list can be reduced. Now we start our **while**-loop:

Step 1. We join $\{A, B\}$ and $\{A, D\}$. Hence
$e = \{A, B, D\}, E = H \cup \{A, B, D\}$,
and GRAHAM$((H \backslash \{\{A, B\}, \{B, D\}\}) \cup \{A, B, D\})$
returns the list $H = \{\{A, B, D\}, \{A, E\}, \{B, E\}, \{C, D\}, \{C, G\}, \{D, G\}, \{E, F\}, \{E, H\}, \{F, H\}, \{G, H\}, \{G, I\}, \{H, I\}\}$.

Step 2. We join $\{A, E\}$ and $\{B, E\}$. Hence
$E = H \cup \{\{A, B, D\}, \{A, B, E\}\}$,
GRAHAM$((H \backslash \{\{A, E\}, \{B, E\}\}) \cup \{A, B, E\}) =$
$= \{\{A, B, D\}, \{A, B, E\}, \{C, D\}, \{C, G\}, \{D, G\}, \{E, F\}, \{E, H\}, \{F, H\}, \{G, H\}, \{G, I\}, \{H, I\}\}$.

Step 3. We join $\{C, D\}$ and $\{C, G\}\}$. Now
$E = H \cup \{\{A, B, D\}, \{A, B, E\}, \{C, D, G\}\}$,
GRAHAM$((H \backslash \{\{C, D\}, \{G, D\}\}) \cup \{C, D, G\}) =$
$= \{\{A, B, D\}, \{A, B, E\}, \{D, G\}, \{E, F\}, \{E, H\}, \{F, H\}, \{G, H\}, \{G, I\}, \{H, I\}\}$.

Step 4. We join $\{E, F\}$ and $\{E, H\}\}$. Now
$E = H \cup \{\{A, B, D\}, \{A, B, E\}, \{C, D, G\}, \{E, F, H\}\}$,
GRAHAM$((H \backslash \{\{E, F\}, \{E, H\}\}) \cup \{E, F, H\}) =$
$= \{\{A, B, D\}, \{A, B, E\}, \{D, G\}, \{E, H\}, \{G, H\}, \{G, I\}, \{H, I\}$

Step 5. We join $\{G, H\}$ and $\{G, I\}$. Now
$E = H \cup \{\{A, B, D\}, \{A, B, E\}, \{C, D, G\}, \{E, F, H\}, \{G, H, I\}\}$,
GRAHAM$((H \backslash \{\{E, F\}, \{E, H\}\}) \cup \{G, H, I\}) =$
$= \{\{A, B, D\}, \{A, B, E\}, \{D, G\}, \{E, H\}, \{G, H\}\}$.

Step 6. We join $\{D, G\}$ and $\{G, H\}$. Now
$E = H \cup \{\{A, B, D\}, \{A, B, E\}, \{C, D, G\}, \{E, F, H\}, \{G, H, I\}, \{D, G, H\}\}$,
GRAHAM$((H \backslash \{\{E, F\}, \{E, H\}\}) \cup \{G, H, I\}) =$
$= \{\{A, B, D\}, \{A, B, E\}, \{D, H\}, \{E, H\}\}$.

Step 7. We join $\{D, H\}$ and $\{E, H\}$. Now
$E = H \cup \{\{A, B, D\}, \{A, B, E\}, \{C, D, G\}, \{E, F, H\}, \{G, H, I\}, \{D, G, H\}\}, \{D, E, H\}\}$
GRAHAM$((H \backslash \{\{E, F\}, \{E, H\}\}) \cup \{G, H, I\}) =$
$= \{\{A, B, D\}, \{A, B, E\}, \{D, H\}\}$.

Step 8. We join $\{D, H\}$ and $\{A, B, D\}$. Now
$E = H \cup \{\{A, B, D\}, \{A, B, E\}, \{C, D, G\}, \{E, F, H\}, \{G, H, I\}, \{D, G, H\}\}, \{D, E, H\}, \{A, B, D, E\}\}$
GRAHAM$((H \backslash \{\{E, F\}, \{E, H\}\}) \cup \{G, H, I\}) =$ NIL

Of course, the acyclic hypergraph obtained by using our procedure must be organized into an appropriate propagation tree, $T = (N, E')$. This can be gained by using the next procedure.

Procedure MakeHypertree:

```
begin
  N: = NIL;
  E': = NIL;
  while E <> NIL do
  begin
    (1) coose an e ∈ E;
    (2) if there exists an e' ∈ E such that
        Card(e'\e) = min{Card(g\e)|g∈E and e ⊆ g}
        then
        begin
          N: = N ∪ {e};
          E': = E' ∪ {e, e'};
          E: = E\{e}
        end else
    (3) begin
          find e' ∈ E such that
          Card(e'∩e) = max{Card(g ∩ e)|g∈E};
          N: =N ∪ {e};
          E': = E' ∪ {e, e'};
          E: = E\{e}
        end;
  end;
  (4) Using the idea of step 2 add the nodes corresponding to the
      variables from set X to set E';
      (* this step is not necessary in the optimization problem
         studied in Section 6 *)
end;
```

When sending messages from node to node we have to marginalize the corresponding valuations or extend them into new spaces of configurations. Below we present fast procedures (in Pascal code) for doing these operations on point-valuations stored in array *Tab*. It is assumed that the nodes *FromNode* and *ToNode* differ in one variable X_i only; if they differ on set **x** of variables, the procedures are repeated for all $X \in \mathbf{x}$. Notice that both the procedures operate on the same array.

```
Procedure Extend (FromNode, ToNode: node; var Tab: array);
var i, i, k, LEN, STEP, CHANGE: integer;
begin
(* Here it is assumed that ToNode-FromNode = {X_i} *)
(* Size (x) computes the cardinality of Θ(x) *)
  LEN: = Size({X_i}) - 1;
  STEP: = max(1, Size({X_j|X_j ∈ ToNode, j > i}));
  CHANGE: = Size({X_j|X_j ∈ ToNode, j ≥ i}) - STEP;
  for i: = Size(FromNode) to 1 do
  begin
    j: = i + ((i - 1) div STEP) *CHANGE;
    for k: = 0 to LEN do Tab[j + k * STEP]: = Tab[i];
  end;
end;

Procedure Marginalize (FromNode, ToNode: node; var Tab:
array);
var i, j, k, k0, LEN, STEP, CHANGE, temp: integer;
begin
(* Here it is assumed that FromNode-ToNode = {X_i} *)
(* Variable k0 allows us to realize all manipulations on the same
   table Tab *)
(* GLUE is a function realizing a "glueing" operation, e.g., the
   summation *)
  LEN: = Size({X_i}) - 1;
  STEP: = max(1, Size({X_j|X_j ∈ FromNode, j > i}));
  CHANGE: = Size({X_j|X_j ∈ FromNode, j ≥ i}) - STEP;
  for i : = 1 to Size(ToNode) do
  begin
    k0: = 0;
    j: = i + ((i - 1) div STEP) *CHANGE;
    for k: = 0 to LEN do
    begin
      temp:j + k*STEP;
      if (temp > i) then
      begin
        if (k0 = 0) then
        begin
          Tab[i]: = Tab[temp];
          k0: = 1;
        end else Tab[i]: = GLUE(Tab[i] + Tab[temp]);
      end else k0: = 1;
```

```
      end;
    end;
  end;
```

5. OPTIMIZATION PROBLEMS

By an optimization problem we shall understand the so-called nonserial problem (see Bertelé and Brioschi [1972] for more details):

$$\min_{\mathbf{X}} v(\mathbf{X}) = \min_{\mathbf{X}} \sum_{i \in N} v_i(\mathbf{x}^i)$$

where $v_i(\mathbf{x}^i)$ is a real-valued function defined over configuration space $\Theta(\mathbf{x}^i)$, $i \in N$, and $N = \{1,...,n\}$ is an index set.

To illustrate the mechanics of finding the minimum of v, assume that we delete variable X from set $\mathbf{X}$. Hence

$$\min_{\mathbf{X}} v(\mathbf{X}) = \min_{\mathbf{X}\backslash\{X\}} \min_{X} \sum v_i(\mathbf{x}^i)$$

$$= \min_{\mathbf{X}\backslash\{X\}} \Big(\sum_{i \in N\backslash N_1} v_i(\mathbf{x}^i) + \min_{\{X\}} \sum_{i \in N_1} v_j(\mathbf{x}^j)\Big)$$

$$= \min_{\mathbf{X}\backslash\{X\}} \Big(\sum_{i \in N\backslash N_1} v_i(\mathbf{x}^i) + v_{\mathbf{y}}\Big)$$

Here $N_1 = \{i \in N | X \in \mathbf{x}^i)$, $\mathbf{y} = (\bigcup_{i \in N} \mathbf{x}^i)\backslash\{X\}$, and $v_{\mathbf{y}}$ is a valuation on $\Theta(\mathbf{y})$.

Taking into account that the min operator acts as the projection operator $\downarrow$, and that Σ corresponds to the combining operator $\oplus$, we state that the above procedure is an instantiation of the procedure proposed in Theorem 1. Again, to find the minimal value of v over set $\mathbf{X}$, we can eliminate variables one by one from $\mathbf{X}$. Such an approach is extensively studied by Bertelé and Brioschi (1972). It is obvious now that the procedure can be sped up by using the result of Theorem 2. The only difference is that now we operate on the so-called rooted Markov tree, i.e., a Markov tree with the empty subset as the root and such that all edges in the tree are directed toward the root.

In the optimization problem, besides the minimum we are also interested in finding a configuration where the minimum of the joint valuation is attained. By a solution for a valuation v we mean a configuration ξ_o such that $\nu(\xi_o) = \nu^{\downarrow\emptyset} = (\square)$. Here $\square$ is the unique element of the frame $\Theta(\emptyset)$. To find a solution for a variable we proceed as follows: let $\mathbf{y}'$ be a set of variables containing the eliminated variable X and let $\nu_{\mathbf{y}'}$ be a valuation for $\mathbf{y}'$. A function $S_X : \Theta(\mathbf{y}) \rightarrow \Theta(\{X\})$ is a solution for X with respect to $\mathbf{y}'$ if

$$\nu_{\mathbf{y}'}^{\downarrow\mathbf{y}}(\theta) = \mathrm{v}_{\mathbf{y}'}(\theta, S_X(\theta)), \; \theta \in \Theta(\mathbf{y})$$

Here $\theta' = <\theta, \mathrm{S}_X(\theta)>$ stands for a configuration from $\Theta(\mathbf{y}')$ such that $\theta'.\mathbf{y} = \theta$ and $\theta'.\{X\} = S_X(\theta)$. A procedure for finding the solution was proposed by Shenoy (1990). It is closely related to the message-passing algorithm and can be summarized as follows. Let $\mathbf{h}$ be a vertex of a Markov tree, Pa($\mathbf{h}$) be the parent of $\mathbf{h}$ and $\mathbf{X}(\mathbf{h})$ denote a set of variables associated to $\mathbf{h}$. Pa($\mathbf{h}$) contains an optimal configuration of the variables belonging to set $\mathbf{X}(\mathbf{h}) \backslash \mathbf{X}(\mathrm{Pa}(\mathbf{h}))$. An optimal configuration σ is computed by

$$\sigma^{\mathrm{Pa}(\mathbf{h}) \rightarrow \mathbf{h}} = (\sigma^{\mathrm{Pa}(\mathrm{Pa}(\mathbf{h})) \rightarrow \mathrm{Pa}(\mathbf{h})}, \mathrm{S}_X(\sigma^{\mathrm{Pa}(\mathbf{h}) \rightarrow \mathbf{h}}))^{\downarrow \mathbf{X}(\mathrm{Pa}(\mathbf{h})) \cap \mathbf{X}(\mathbf{h})}$$

where X is a variable from the $\mathbf{X}(\mathbf{h}) \backslash \mathbf{X}(\mathrm{Pa}(\mathbf{h}))$, and $\sigma^{\mathrm{Pa}(\mathbf{h}) \rightarrow \mathbf{h}}$ stands for the configuration transmitted from father Pa($\mathbf{h}$) to its son $\mathbf{h}$. More details will be shown in an example in the next section.

So far we have considered unconstrained problems only. In practice we are sometimes faced with constrained optimization problems (e.g., in dynamic systems, allocation problems, etc.). This class of problems can be summarized as follows:

$$\min_{\mathbf{X}} \nu(\mathbf{X}) = \min_{\mathbf{X}} \sum_{i \in N'} \nu_i(\mathbf{x}^i)$$

subject to $\theta^i \in F^i \subseteq \Theta(\mathbf{x}^i)$, $i \in N$; $N' \subset N$.

Here F^i represent the set of admissible configurations, so each valuation is defined on the restricted space F^i, $i \in N'$, and the constraints F^i for $i \in N \backslash N'$ further restrict the space of total configurations. Denoting $F = \underset{i \in N}{\times} F^i$ we are looking for the minimal value of ν over the set F of configurations.

It appears that such problems can also be solved by using Theorem 2. The only modifications are:

(1) for each $j \in N \backslash N'$ we define a vacuous valuation; in the case of the Σ combining operator it is $\nu_j(\theta^j) = 0$, $\theta^j \in F^j$;

(2) the summation $\nu_j(\theta^j) + \nu_k(\theta^k)$ can be done if and only if both valuations are defined on the corresponding configurations.

6. EXAMPLE

Consider the constrained problem, taken from Bertelé and Brioschi (1972, pp. 187–188):

$$\min_{\mathbf{X}} v(\mathbf{X}) = \min_{\mathbf{X}} \sum_{i=1}^{5} v_i(\mathbf{x}^i)$$

subject to $\theta^i \in F^i$, $i = 1,\ldots,7$

where: $\mathbf{X} = \{A, B, C, D, E, F\}$, $\mathbf{x}^1 = \{A, B\}$, $\mathbf{x}^2 = \{A, B, C\}$, $\mathbf{x}^3 = \{B, C, E\}$, $\mathbf{x}^4 = \{C, D, F\}$, $\mathbf{x}^5 = \{E, F\}$, $\mathbf{x}^6 = \{A, C, D\}$, $\mathbf{x}^7 = \{B, F\}$, $\Theta_i = \{0, 1, 2\}$, $i = 1,\ldots,6$.

The valuations v_i and admissible sets of configurations are presented in the tables shown in Figure 17.1. To represent constraints F^i, $i = 6,7$, we introduce two vacuous valuations v_6 and v_7. The Markov tree for the problem is shown in Figure 17.2.

In Figure 17.3 details of the computations are presented. The final solution is: $\min v(\mathbf{X}) = 15$. To find the optimal configuration we start from the root: the optimal values $\Theta_E^* = 1$ and $\theta_F^* = 1$ are assigned to the empty element □ (see Stage 9). Returning to Stage 7 we find that this configuration is compatible with $\theta_B^* = 1$ and $\theta_C^* = 1$; moving to Stage 4 we find $\theta_D^* = 1$, and finally (Stage 2) $\theta_A^* = 2$. So, the optimal configuration is $<2, 1, 1, 1, 1, 1>$.

7. CONCLUDING REMARKS

In Pearl (1988, Chapter V) a belief revision problem is defined as follows. Suppose $\mathbf{X}$ is a set of variables and $E \subset \mathbf{X}$ is a set of instantiated variables (representing evidence). The problem is to find a consistent assignment of values of the variables from set $\mathbf{X} \backslash E$ that best explains the evidence $\mathbf{e} = \{X = \theta^*, X \in E\}$. Such a problem can be solved by the message-passing algorithm by setting max as the marginalization operator $\downarrow$, and the product as the combining operator $\oplus$. The same procedure may be applied in generating explanations for a given evidence. Additional constraints (corresponding to the hypothetical assumptions) can be represented by the vacuous valuations as was demonstrated in the previous section.

F^1		v_1
A	B	
0	0	4
0	1	6
0	2	0
1	0	1
1	1	3
1	2	7
2	0	4
2	1	2
2	2	5

F^2			v_2
A	B	C	
0	0	0	1
0	0	2	7
0	1	1	8
0	2	1	1
0	2	2	4
1	0	0	6
1	0	1	8
1	0	2	4
1	1	2	2
1	2	2	7
2	0	2	5
2	1	1	3
2	1	2	9
2	2	2	10

F^3			v_3
B	C	E	
0	0	1	4
0	0	2	7
0	2	0	5
1	0	0	3
1	0	1	2
1	0	2	5
1	1	1	4
1	1	2	9
2	0	0	11
2	0	1	8
2	0	2	13
2	2	0	6
2	2	2	1

F^4			v_4
C	D	E	
0	0	0	15
0	1	0	2
0	1	1	6
0	2	1	9
0	2	2	8
1	1	0	3
1	1	1	0
1	2	0	1
1	2	1	2
2	0	1	4
2	0	2	9
2	1	0	14
2	1	1	15
2	1	2	7
2	2	1	12
2	2	2	11

F^5		v_5
E	F	
0	1	5
0	2	8
1	1	6
2	0	2

F^7	
B	F
0	0
0	2
1	0
1	1
1	2
2	0
2	2

F^6		
A	C	D
0	1	0
0	1	1
0	2	0
0	2	1
1	1	0
1	1	1
1	2	1
2	1	1
2	2	0
2	2	1

Figure 17.1: Valuations and admissible configurations.

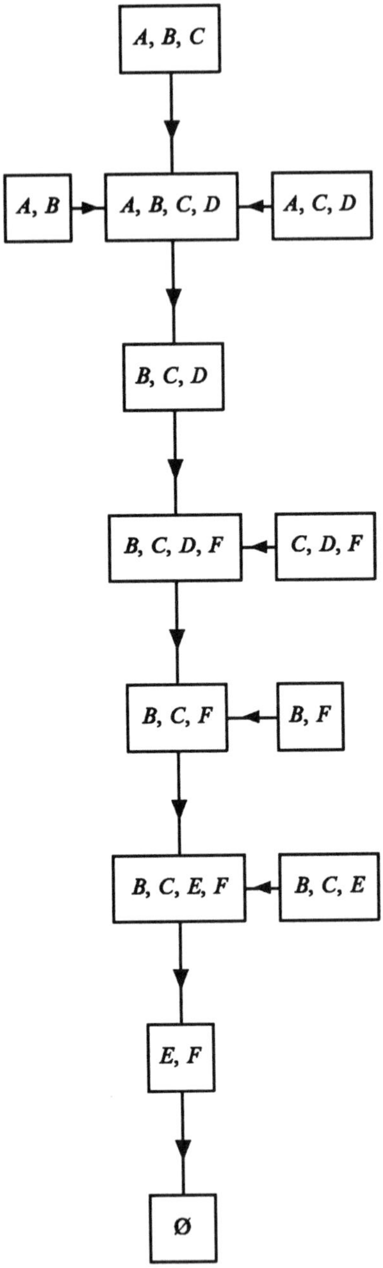

Figure 17.2: Markov tree representation for the optimization problem.

A	B	C	D	$F_1 = v_1 + v_2 + v_6$
0	0	2	0	11
0	0	2	1	11
0	1	1	0	14
0	1	1	1	14
0	2	1	0	1
0	2	1	1	1
0	2	2	0	4
0	2	2	1	4
1	0	1	0	9
1	0	1	1	9
1	0	2	1	5
1	1	2	1	5
1	2	2	1	14
2	0	2	0	9
2	0	2	1	9
2	1	1	1	5
2	1	2	0	11
2	1	2	1	11
2	2	2	0	15
2	2	2	1	15

Stage 1

B	C	D	$F_1{\downarrow}\{B, C, D\}$	S_A
0	1	0	9	1
0	1	1	9	1
0	2	0	9	2
0	2	1	5	1
1	1	0	14	0
1	1	1	5	2
1	2	0	11	2
1	2	1	5	1
2	1	0	1	0
2	1	1	1	0
2	1	1	4	0
2	2	1	4	0

Stage 2

B	C	D	F	$F_2 = F_1^{\downarrow\{B, C, D\}} + v_4$
0	1	1	0	12
0	1	1	1	9
0	2	0	1	13
0	2	0	2	18
0	2	1	0	19
0	2	1	1	20
0	2	1	1	12
1	1	1	0	8
1	1	1	1	5
1	2	0	1	15
1	2	0	2	20
1	2	1	0	19
1	2	1	1	20
1	2	1	2	12
2	1	1	0	4
2	1	1	1	1
2	2	0	1	8
2	2	0	2	13
2	2	1	0	18
2	2	1	1	19
2	2	1	2	11

Stage 3

B	C	F	$F_2{\downarrow}\{B, C, F\}$	S_D
0	1	0	12	1
0	1	1	9	1
0	2	0	19	1
0	2	1	13	0
0	2	2	12	1
1	1	0	8	1
1	1	1	5	1
1	2	0	19	1
1	2	1	15	0
1	2	2	12	1
2	1	0	4	1
2	1	1	1	1
2	2	0	18	1
2	2	1	8	0
2	2	2	11	1

Stage 4

Figure 17.3: Details of computations.

B	C	F	$F_3 = F_2^{\downarrow\{B,C,F\}} + v_7$
0	1	0	12
0	2	0	19
0	2	2	12
1	1	0	8
1	1	1	5
1	2	0	19
1	2	1	15
1	2	2	12
2	1	0	4
2	2	0	18
2	2	2	11

Stage 5

B	C	E	F	$F_4 = F_3 + v_3$
0	2	0	0	24
0	2	0	2	17
1	1	1	0	12
1	1	1	1	9
1	1	2	0	17
1	1	2	1	14
2	2	0	0	24
2	2	0	2	19
2	2	2	0	19
2	2	2	2	14

Stage 6

E	F	$F_4^{\downarrow\{E,F\}}$	S_B	S_C
0	0	24	0,2	2
0	2	17	0,2	2
1	0	12	1	1
1	1	9	1	1
2	0	17	1,2	1
2	1	14	1	1
2	2	14	2	2

Stage 7

E	F	$F_5 = F_4^{\downarrow\{E,F\}} + v_5$
0	2	23
1	1	15
2	0	19

Stage 8

$\Theta(\varnothing)$	$F_5^{\downarrow\varnothing}$	S_E	S_F
□	15	1	1

Stage 9

Figure 17.3: Details of computations (continued).

BIBLIOGRAPHY

Almond, R., and Kong, A. (1991). Optimality issues in constructing a Markov tree from graphical models. Research Report A-3, Harvard University, Department of Statistics.

Bertelé, U., and Brioschi, F. (1972). *Nonserial dynamic programming*. New York: Academic Press.

Maier, D. (1983). *The theory of relational databases*. New York: Computer Science Press.

Mellouli, K. (1987). On the propagation of beliefs in networks using the Dempster-Shafer theory of evidence. Ph. D. dissertation, School of Business, University of Kansas, Lawrence.

Pearl, J. (1988). *Probabilistic reasoning in intelligent systems*. San Mateo, CA: Morgan Kaufmann.

Shenoy, P.P. (1990). Valuation-based system for discrete optimization. School of Business Working Paper No. 221, School of Business, University of Kansas, Lawrence.

Shenoy, P.P., and Shafer, G. (1990). Axioms for probability and belief-function propagation. In R.D. Shachter et al. (eds.), *Uncertainty in artificial intelligence* 4, pp. 169–198. Amsterdam: North-Holland.

Xu, H. (1991). An efficient implementation of belief function propagation. Technical Report TR/IRIDIA/91-4, Université Libre de Bruxelles, Brussels.

Zarley, D.K. (1988). An evidential reasoning system. School of Business Working Paper No. 206, School of Business, University of Kansas, Lawrence.

4

DEMPSTER-SHAFER THEORY FOR THE MANAGEMENT OF UNCERTAINTY IN KNOWLEDGE-BASED SYSTEMS

18 Using Dempster-Shafer's belief-bunction theory in expert systems

Prakash P. SHENOY

Abstract: The main objective of this paper is to describe how Dempster-Shafer's (DS) theory of belief functions fits in the framework of valuation-based systems (VBS). Since VBS serve as a framework for managing uncertainty in expert systems, this facilitates the use of DS belief-function theory in expert systems.

Keywords: Dempster-Shafer's theory of belief functions, valuation-based systems, expert systems.

1. INTRODUCTION

The theory of belief functions was first described by Dempster (1967) and further developed by Shafer (1976). In belief-function theory, the basic representational unit is called a *basic probability assignment* (bpa) function. The two main operations for manipulating bpa functions are marginalization and Dempster's rule of combination.

The framework of VBS was first defined by Shenoy (1989) as a general language for incorporating uncertainty in expert systems. It was further elaborated in (Shenoy, 1990a, b, c, 1991b, c, d, 1992) to include axioms that permit local computation in solving a VBS, and a fusion algorithm for solving a VBS using local computation. VBSs encode knowledge using functions called valuations. VBSs include two operators called *combination* and *marginalization* that operate on valuations. Combination corresponds to aggregation of knowledge. Marginalization corresponds to coarsening of knowledge. The process of reasoning in VBS can be described simply as finding the marginal of the joint valuation for each variable in the system. The joint valuation is the valuation obtained by combining all valuations. In systems with many variables, it is computationally intractable to explicitly compute the joint valuation. However, if combination and marginalization satisfy certain axioms, it is possible to compute the marginals of the joint valuation without explicitly computing the joint valuation.

The framework of VBS is general enough to represent many domains, such as Bayesian probability theory (Shenoy, 1990c, d), Spohn's theory of epistemic beliefs (Spohn, 1988; Shenoy, 1991a), Zadeh's possibility theory (Zadeh, 1979; Shenoy, 1992), discrete optimization (Shenoy 1991b), propositional logic (Shenoy, 1990a, b), constraint satisfaction (Shenoy and Shafer, 1988), and Bayesian decision theory (Shenoy, 1990c, d). Saffiotti and Umkehrer (1991) describe an efficient implementation of VBS called Pulcinella.

The correspondence between belief-function theory and VBS is as follows. Dempster's rule of combination in belief-function theory corresponds to the combination operation in VBS. And the marginalization operation in belief-function theory corresponds to the marginalization operation in VBS. The framework of VBS was inspired by the axiomatic study of the computational theory in Bayesian probability theory and belief-function theory (Shenoy and Shafer, 1990).

An outline of this paper is as follows. Section 2 describes the framework of VBS. Section 3 describes the main features of belief-function theory in terms of the framework of VBS. Section 4 describes a small example illustrating the use of belief-function theory for managing uncertainty in expert systems. Section 5 contains some concluding remarks. Finally, section 6 contains proofs of all results in the paper.

2. VALUATION-BASED SYSTEMS

In this section, we sketch the basic features of VBS. Also, we describe three axioms that permit the use of local computation, and describe a fusion algorithm for solving a VBS using local computation.

2.1. The framework

This subsection describes the framework of valuation-based systems. In a VBS, we represent knowledge by functions called valuations. We make inferences in a VBS using two operators called combination and marginalization. We use these operators on valuations.

Variables and Configurations. We use the symbol $\mathbf{W}_X$ for the set of possible values of a variable X, and we call $\mathbf{W}_X$ the *frame for X*. We assume that one and only one of the elements of $\mathbf{W}_X$ is the true value of X. We are concerned with a finite set $\mathbf{X}$ of variables, and we assume that all the variables in $\mathbf{X}$ have finite frames.

Given a nonempty set s of variables, let $\mathbf{W}_s$ denote the Cartesian product of $\mathbf{W}_X$ for X in s; $\mathbf{W}_s = \times\{\mathbf{W}_X | X \in s\}$. We call $\mathbf{W}_s$ the *frame for s*. We call the elements of $\mathbf{W}_s$ *configurations of s*.

Valuations. Given a subset s of variables, there is a set $\mathbf{V}_s$. We call the elements of $\mathbf{V}_s$ *valuations for s*. Let $\mathbf{V}$ denote the set of all valuations, i.e., $\mathbf{V} = \cup\{\mathbf{V}_s | s \subseteq \mathbf{X}\}$. If σ is a valuation for s, then we say s is the *domain of* σ.

Valuations are primitives in our abstract framework and as such require no definition. But as we shall see shortly, they are objects that can be combined and marginalized. Intuitively, a valuation for s represents some knowledge about the variables in s.

Nonzero valuations. For each $s \subseteq \mathbf{X}$, there is a subset $\mathbf{P}_s$ of $\mathbf{V}_s$ whose elements are called *nonzero valuations for s*. Let $\mathbf{P}$ denote $\cup\{\mathbf{P}_s | s \subseteq \mathbf{X}\}$, the set of all nonzero valuations.

Intuitively, a nonzero valuation represents knowledge that is internally consistent. The notion of nonzero valuations is important as it enables us to constrain the definitions of combination and marginalization to meaningful operators. An example of a nonzero valuation is a basic probability assignment (bpa) function.

Combination. We assume there is a mapping $\oplus : \mathbf{V} \times \mathbf{V} \rightarrow \mathbf{V}$, called *combination*, such that

(i) if ρ and σ are valuations for r and s, respectively, then $\rho \oplus \sigma$ is a valuation for $r \cup s$;

(ii) if either ρ or σ is not a nonzero valuation, then $\rho \oplus \sigma$ is not a nonzero valuation; and

(iii) if ρ and σ are both nonzero valuations, then $\rho \oplus \sigma$ may or may not be a nonzero valuation.

We call $\rho \oplus \sigma$ the *combination of ρ and σ*.

Intuitively, combination corresponds to aggregation of knowledge. If ρ and σ are valuations for r and s representing independent knowledge about variables in r and s, respectively, then $\rho \oplus \sigma$ represents the aggregated knowledge about variables in $r \cup s$. (The definition of independence is given in Shenoy, 1991e). For bpa functions, combination is Dempster's rule of combination (described in section 3).

Marginalization. We assume that for each $s \subseteq \mathbf{X}$, and for each $X \in s$, there is a mapping $\downarrow(s - \{X\}): \mathbf{V}_s \rightarrow \mathbf{V}_{s-\{X\}}$, called *marginalization to $s - \{X\}$* such that

(i) If σ is a valuation for s, then $\sigma^{\downarrow(s-\{X\})}$ is a valuation for $s - \{X\}$; and

(ii) $\sigma^{\downarrow(s-\{X\})}$ is a nonezero valuation if and only if σ is a nonzero valuation.

We call $\sigma^{\downarrow(s-\{X\})}$ the *marginal of σ for $s - \{X\}$*.

Intuitively, marginalization corresponds to coarsening of knowledge. If σ is a valuation for s representing some knowledge about variables in s, and $X \in s$, then $\sigma^{\downarrow(s-\{X\})}$ represents the knowledge about variables in $s - \{X\}$ implied by σ if we disregard variable X. In the case of bpa functions, marginalization is addition.

In summary, a *valuation-based system* consists of a 3-tuple $\{\{\sigma_1, \ldots, \sigma_m\}, \oplus, \downarrow\}$ where $\{\sigma_1, \ldots, \sigma_m\}$ is a collection of valuations, $\oplus$ is the combination operator, and $\downarrow$ is the marginalization operator.

Valuation Networks. A graphical depiction of a valuation-based system is called a *valuation network*. In a valuation network, variables are represented by circular nodes, and valuations are represented by diamond-shaped nodes. Also, each valuation node is connected by an

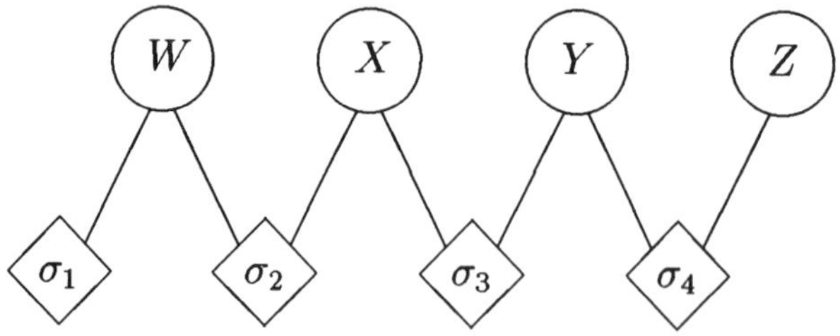

Figure 18.1: A valuation network for a VBS consisting of valuations σ_1 for $\{W\}$, σ_2 for $\{W, X\}$, σ_3 for $\{X, Y\}$, and σ_4 for $\{Y, Z\}$.

undirected edge to each variable node in its domain. Figure 18.1 shows a valuation network for a VBS that consists of valuations σ_1 for $\{W\}$, σ_2 for $\{W, X\}$, σ_3 for $\{X, Y\}$, and σ_4 for $\{Y, Z\}$.

Making Inference in VBS. In a VBS, the combination of all valuations is called the *joint valuation*. Given a VBS, we make inferences by computing the marginal of the joint valuation for each variable in the system.

If there are n variables in the system, and each variable has two configurations in its frame, then there are 2^n configurations of all variables. Hence, it is not computationally feasible to compute the joint valuation when there are a large number of variables. In section 2.3, we describe an algorithm for computing marginals of the joint valuation without explicitly computing the joint valuation, that is, using only local computation. In order to ensure that this algorithm gives us the correct answers, we require combination and marginalization to satisfy three axioms. The axioms and the algorithm are described in the next two subsections, respectively.

2.2. Axioms

In this section, we state three simple axioms that enable local computation of marginals of the joint valuation. These axioms were first formulated by Shenoy and Shafer (1990). The axioms are stated slightly differently here.

Axiom A1 (*Commutativity and associativity of combination*): Suppose ρ, σ, and τ are valuations for r, s and t, respectively. Then

$$\rho \oplus \sigma = \sigma \oplus \rho, \text{ and } \rho \oplus (\sigma \oplus \tau) = (\rho \oplus \sigma) \oplus \tau$$

Axiom A2 (*Order of deletion does not matter*): Suppose σ is a valuation for s, and suppose $X_1, X_2 \in s$. Then

$$(\sigma^{\downarrow(s-\{X_1\})})^{\downarrow(s-\{X_1,X_2\})} = (\sigma^{\downarrow(s-\{X_2\})})^{\downarrow(s-\{X_1,X_2\})}$$

Axiom A3 (*Distributivity of marginalization over combination*): Suppose ρ and σ are valuations for r and s, respectively. Suppose $X \notin r$, and suppose $X \in s$. Then

$$(\rho \oplus \sigma)^{\downarrow((r\cup s)-\{X\})} = \rho \oplus (\sigma^{\downarrow(s-\{X\})})$$

One implication of Axiom A1 is that when we have multiple combinations of valuations, we can write it without using parenthesis. For example, $(\ldots((\sigma_1 \oplus \sigma_2) \oplus \sigma_3) \oplus \ldots \oplus \sigma_m)$ can be written simply as $\oplus \{\sigma_i \mid i = 1,...,m\}$ or as $\sigma_1 \oplus ... \oplus \sigma_m$; we need not indicate the order in which the combinations are carried out.

If we regard marginalization as a coarsening of a valuation by deleting variables, then axiom A2 says that the order in which the variables are deleted does not matter. One implication of this axiom is that $(\sigma^{\downarrow(s-\{X_1\})})^{\downarrow(s-\{X_1,X_2\})}$ can be written simply as $\sigma^{\downarrow(s-\{X_1,X_2\})}$, we need not indicate the order in which the variables are deleted.

Axiom A3 is the crucial axiom that makes local computation possible. Axiom A3 states that the computation of $(\rho \oplus \sigma)^{\downarrow((r\cup s)-\{X\})}$ can be accomplished without having to compute $\rho \oplus \sigma$. The combination operation in $\rho \oplus \sigma$ is on the frame for $r \cup s$, whereas the combination operation in $\rho \oplus (\sigma^{\downarrow(s-\{X\})})$ is on the frame for $(r \cup s) - \{X\}$. In the next subsection, we describe a fusion algorithm that applies this axiom repeatedly resulting in an efficient method for computing marginals.

2.3. A fusion algorithm

In this subsection, we describe a fusion algorithm for making inferences in a VBS using local computation. Suppose $\{\{\sigma_1,...,\sigma_m\}, \oplus, \downarrow\}$ is a VBS with n variables and m valuations. Suppose that combination and marginalization satisfy the three axioms stated in section 2.2. Suppose we have to compute the marginal of the joint valuation for variable X, $(\sigma_1 \oplus ... \oplus \sigma_m)^{\downarrow\{X\}}$. The basic idea of the fusion algorithm is to successively delete all variables but X from the VBS. The variables may be deleted in any sequence. Axiom A2 tells us that all deletion sequences lead to the same answers. But, different deletion sequences may involve different computational costs. We will comment on good deletion sequences at the end of this section.

When we delete a variable, we have to do a "fusion" operation on the valuations. Consider a set of k valuations $\rho_1,...,\rho_k$. Suppose ρ_i is a valuation for r_i. Let $\text{Fus}_X\{\rho_1,...,\rho_k\}$ denote the collection of valuations after fusing the valuations in the set $\{\rho_1,...,\rho_k\}$ with respect to variable X. Then

$$\text{Fus}_X\{\rho_1,...,\rho_k\} = \{\rho^{\downarrow(r-\{X\})}\} \cup \{\rho_i \mid X \notin r_i\}$$

where $\rho = \oplus\{\rho_i \mid X \in r_i\}$, and $r = \cup\{r_i \mid X \in r_i\}$. After fusion, the set of valuations is changed as follows. All valuations that bear on X are combined, and the resulting valuation is marginalized such that X is eliminated from its domain. The valuations that do not bear on X remain unchanged.

We are ready to state the theorem that describes the fusion algorithm.

Theorem 1. Suppose $\{\{\sigma_1,\ldots,\sigma_m\},\oplus,\downarrow\}$ is a VBS, where σ_i is a valuation for s_i and suppose $\oplus$ and $\downarrow$ satisfy axioms A1-A3. Let $\mathbf{X}$ denote $s_1 \cup \ldots \cup s_m$. Suppose $X \in \mathbf{X}$, and suppose $X_1 X_2 \ldots X_{n-1}$ is a sequence of variables in $\mathbf{X} - \{X\}$. Then

$$(\sigma_1 \oplus \ldots \oplus \sigma_m)^{\downarrow\{X\}} = \oplus \{\mathrm{Fus}_{X_{n-1}}\{\ldots \mathrm{Fus}_{X_2}\{\mathrm{Fus}_{X_1}\{\sigma_1,\ldots,\sigma_m\}\}\}\}.$$

Example 1 (Fusion Algorithm). Consider a VBS with four variables: W, X, Y, and Z, and four valuations: σ_1 for $\{W\}$, σ_2 for $\{W, X\}$, σ_3 for $\{X, Y\}$, and σ_4 for $\{Y, Z\}$. Suppose we need to compute the marginal of the joint for Z, $(\sigma_1 \oplus \ldots \oplus \sigma_4)^{\downarrow\{Z\}}$. Consider the deletion sequence WXY. After fusion with respect to W, we have $(\sigma_1 \oplus \sigma_2)^{\downarrow\{X\}}$ for $\{X\}$, σ_3 for $\{X, Y\}$, and σ_4 for $\{Y, Z\}$. After fusion with respect to X, we have $((\sigma_1 \oplus \sigma_2)^{\downarrow\{X\}} \oplus \sigma_3)^{\downarrow\{Y\}}$ for $\{Y\}$, and σ_4 for $\{Y, Z\}$. Finally, after fusion with respect to Y, we have $(((\sigma_1 \oplus \sigma_2)^{\downarrow\{X\}} \oplus \sigma_3)^{\downarrow\{Y\}} \oplus \sigma_4)^{\downarrow\{Z\}}$ for $\{Z\}$. Theorem 1 tells us that $(((\sigma_1 \oplus \sigma_2)^{\downarrow\{X\}} \oplus \sigma_3)^{\downarrow\{Y\}} \oplus \sigma_4)^{\{Z\}} = (\sigma_1 \oplus \ldots \oplus \sigma_4)^{\downarrow\{Z\}}$. Thus, instead of doing combinations on the frame for $\{W, X, Y, Z\}$, we do combinations on the frame for $\{W, X\}$, $\{X, Y\}$, and $\{Y, Z\}$. The fusion algorithm is shown graphically in Figure 18.2.

If we can compute the marginal of the joint valuation for one variable, then we can compute the marginals for all variables. We simply compute them one after the other. It is obvious, however, that this will involve much duplication of effort. Shenoy and Shafer (1990) describe an efficient algorithm for simultaneous computation of all marginals without duplication of effort. Regardless of the number of variables in a VBS, we can compute marginals of the joint valuation for all variables for roughly three times the computational effort required to compute one marginal.

Deletion Sequences. Different deletion sequences may involve different computational efforts. For example, consider the VBS in the above example. In this example, deletion sequence WXY involves less computational effort than, for example, XYW, as the former involves combinations on the frame for two variables only whereas the latter involves combination on the frame for three variables. Finding an optimal deletion sequence is a secondary optimization problem that has shown to be NP-complete (Amborg et al., 1987). But there are several heuristics for finding good deletion sequences (Kong, 1986; Mellouli, 1987; Zhang, 1988; Kjærulff, 1990).

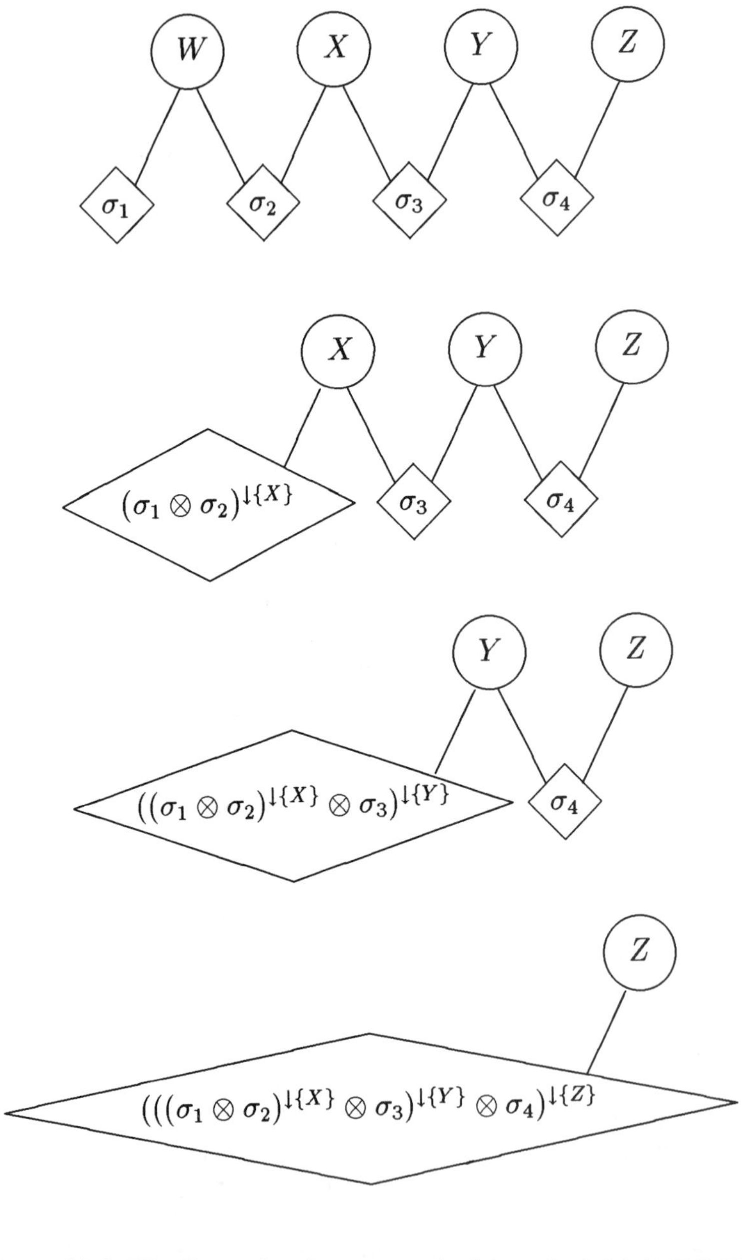

Figure 18.2: The first valuation network shows the initial VBS. The second network is the result after fusion with respect to *W*. The third network is the result after fusion with respect to *X*. The fourth network is the result after fusion with respect to Y.

One such heuristic is called one-step-look-ahead (Kong, 1986). This heuristic tells us which variable to delete next. Per this heuristic, the variable that should be deleted next is one that leads to combination over the smallest frame. For example, in the VBS described above, if we assume that each variable has a frame consisting of two configurations, then this heuristic would pick W over X and Y for first deletion since deletion of W involves combination on the frame for $\{W, X\}$ whereas deletion of X involves combination on the frame for $\{X, X, Y\}$, and deletion of Y involves combination on the frame for $\{X, Y, Z\}$. After W is deleted, for second deletion, this heuristic would pick X over Y. Thus, this heuristic would choose deletion sequence WXY.

3. DS THEORY OF BELIEF FUNCTIONS

In this section, we describe the main features of DS theory of belief functions in terms of the framework of VBS described in the previous section. The basic unit of knowledge representation is called a basic probability assignment (bpa) function.

Definition 1 (Bpa Function). *A basic probability assignment (bpa) function μ for h* is a function $\mu{:}2^{\mathbf{W}'_h} \to [0, 1]$ such that $\Sigma\ \{\mu(\mathbf{a})|(\mathbf{a}) \in 2^{\mathbf{W}'_h}\} = 1$. $2^{\mathbf{W}'_h}$ denotes the set of all nonempty subsets of $\mathbf{W}_h$).

Intuitively, $\mu(\mathbf{a})$ represents the degree of belief assigned exactly to **a** (the proposition that the true configuration of h is in the set **a**) and to nothing smaller. A bpa function is the belief function equivalent of a probability mass function in probability theory. Whereas a probability mass function is restricted to assigning probability masses only to singleton configurations of variables, a bpa function is allowed to assign probability masses to sets of configurations without assigning any mass to the individual configurations contained in the sets.

Consider the following bpa function μ for $h{:}\mu(\mathbf{W}_h) = 1$, and $\mu(\mathbf{a}) = 0$ for all other $\mathbf{a} \in 2^{\mathbf{W}'_h}$. We shall call such a bpa function *vacuous*. It represents a state of complete ignorance.

Belief Functions. The information contained in a bpa function can be expressed in several different ways. One way is in terms of the belief function defined as follows.

Definition 2 (Belief Function). A *belief function β for h* corresponding to bpa function μ for h is a function $\beta{:}2^{\mathbf{W}'_h} \to [0, 1]$ such that

$$\beta(\mathbf{a}) = \Sigma\{\mu(\mathbf{b}) \mid \mathbf{b} \subseteq \mathbf{a}\} \tag{1}$$

for each $\mathbf{a} \in 2^{\mathbf{W}_h}$.

Intuitively, whereas the quantity $\mu(\mathbf{a})$ measures the belief that one commits exactly to **a**, the quantity $\beta(\mathbf{a})$ measures the total belief that one commits to **a**.

It is shown in Shafer (1976, p. 39) that we can recover μ from β:

$$\mu(\mathbf{a}) = \Sigma\{(-1)^{|a-b|}\beta(\mathbf{b}) \mid \mathbf{b} \subseteq \mathbf{a}\}$$

where $|\mathbf{a} - \mathbf{b}|$ denotes the number of elements in the set $\mathbf{a} - \mathbf{b}$.

Plausibility Function. Another way of expressing the information contained in a bpa function μ is in terms of the *plausibility function* π, defined as follows.

Definition 3 (Plausibility Function). A *plausibility function* π *for* h corresponding to bpa function μ for h is a function $\pi: 2^{\mathbf{W}_h} \to [0, 1]$ such that

$$\pi(\mathbf{a}) = \Sigma\{\mu(\mathbf{b}) \mid \mathbf{b} \cap \mathbf{a} \neq 0\} \tag{2}$$

for each $\mathbf{a} \in 2^{\mathbf{W}_h}$.

Since the probability mass $\mu(\mathbf{b})$ can move into **a** if and only if $\mathbf{b} \cap \mathbf{a} \neq \varnothing$, $\pi(\mathbf{a})$ measures the total probability mass that can move into **a**, that is, $\pi(\mathbf{a})$ measures the extent to which one finds **a** plausible. Suppose $\sim\mathbf{a}$ denotes the complement of **a**; $\sim\mathbf{a} = \mathbf{W}_h - \mathbf{a}$. Since

$\{\mathbf{b} \in 2^{\mathbf{W}_h} \mid \mathbf{b} \subseteq \mathbf{a}\} \cup \{\mathbf{b} \in 2^{\mathbf{W}_h} \mid \mathbf{b} \cap \sim\mathbf{a} \neq \varnothing\} = 2^{\mathbf{W}_h}$, $\beta(\mathbf{a}) = 1 - \pi(\sim\mathbf{a})$, and $\pi(\mathbf{a}) = 1 - \beta(\sim\mathbf{a})$

Thus $\pi(\mathbf{a})$ also measures the extent to which the given evidence fails to refute **a**.

Since $\{\mathbf{b} \in 2^{\mathbf{W}_h} \mid \mathbf{b} \subseteq \mathbf{a}\} \subseteq \{\mathbf{b} \in 2^{\mathbf{W}_h} \mid \mathbf{b} \cap \mathbf{a} \neq \varnothing\}$, $\beta(\mathbf{a}) \leqslant \pi(\mathbf{a})$ for every subset **a** of $\mathbf{W}_h$. Both β and π are monotone: $\beta(\mathbf{a}) \leqslant \beta(\mathbf{b})$ and $\pi(\mathbf{a}) \leqslant \pi(\mathbf{b})$ whenever $\mathbf{a} \subseteq \mathbf{b}$.

Although belief functions and plausibility functions are easier to interpret than bpa functions, bpa functions are easier to work with mathematically. Bpa functions correspond to nonzero valutions in VBS.

Before we can define combination and marginalization for bpa functions, we need the concepts of projection of configurations, and projection and extension of subsets of configurations.

Projection of Configurations. Projection of configurations simply means dropping extra coordinates; if (w, x, y, z) is a configuration of $\{W, X, Y, Z\}$, for example, then the projection of (w, x, y, z) to $\{W, X\}$ is simply (w, x), which is a configuration of $\{W, X\}$. If g and h are sets of variables, $h \subseteq g$, and $\mathbf{x}$ is a configuration of g, then $\mathbf{x}^{\downarrow h}$ denotes the projection of $\mathbf{x}$ to h.

Projection and Extension of Sets of Configurations. If g and h are sets of variables, $h \subseteq g$, and $\mathbf{g}$ is a nonempty subset of $\mathbf{W}_g$, then the *projection of* $\mathbf{g}$ *to* h, denoted by $\mathbf{g}^{\downarrow h}$, is the subset of $\mathbf{W}_h$ given by $\mathbf{g}^{\downarrow h} = \{\mathbf{x}^{\downarrow h} \mid \mathbf{x} \in \mathbf{g}\}$. For example, if $\mathbf{a}$ is a subset of $\mathbf{W}_{\{W,X,Y,Z\}}$, then the projection of $\mathbf{a}$ to $\{X, Y\}$ consists of the elements of $\mathbf{W}_{\{X,Y\}}$ which can be obtained by projecting elements of $\mathbf{a}$ to $\mathbf{W}_{\{X,Y\}}$.

By extension of a subset of a frame to a subset of a larger frame, we mean a cylinder set extension. If g and h are sets of variables, h is a proper subset of g, and $\mathbf{h}$ is a nonempty subset of $\mathbf{W}_h$, then the *extension of* $\mathbf{h}$ *to* g is $\mathbf{h} \times \mathbf{W}_{g-h}$. Let $\mathbf{h}^{\uparrow g}$ denote the extension of $\mathbf{h}$ to g. For example, if $\mathbf{a}$ is a nonempty subset of $\mathbf{W}_{\{W,X\}}$, then the extension of $\mathbf{a}$ to $\{W, X, Y, Z\}$ is $\mathbf{a} \times \mathbf{W}_{\{Y,Z\}}$.

Marginalization. Suppose μ is a bpa function for h. Suppose $X \in h$. We may be interested only in propositions about variables in $h - \{X\}$. In this case, we would like to marginalize μ to $h - \{X\}$.

Definition 4 (Marginalization). Suppose μ is a bpa function for h, and suppose $X \in h$. The *marginal of* μ *for* $h - \{X\}$, denoted by $\mu^{\downarrow(h-\{X\})}$, is the bpa function for $h - \{X\}$ defined as follows:

$$\mu^{\downarrow(h-\{X\})}(\mathbf{a}) = \Sigma\{\mu(\mathbf{b}) \mid \mathbf{b} \subseteq \mathbf{W}_h \text{ such that } \mathbf{b}^{\downarrow(h-\{X\})} = \mathbf{a}\}$$

for all nonempty subsets $\mathbf{a}$ of $\mathbf{W}_{h-\{X\}}$.

Theorem 2 states that the marginalization operation for belief function satisfies Axiom A2 stated in section 2.2.

Theorem 2. Suppose μ is a bpa function for h, and suppose $X_1, X_2 \in h$. Then

$$(\mu^{\downarrow(h-\{X_1\})})^{\downarrow(h-\{X_1,X_2\})} = (\mu^{\downarrow(h-\{X_2\})})^{\downarrow(h-\{X_1,X_2\})}$$

Example 2 (Bpa Functions and Marginalization). We would like to determine whether a stranger (about whom we know nothing) is a pacifist or not depending on whether he is a Republican or not, and whether he is a Quaker or not. Consider three variables R, Q, and P. R has two configurations : r (for Republican), and $\sim r$ (not Republican); Q has two configurations: q (Quaker), and $\sim q$ (not Quaker); and P has two configurations: p (pacifist), and $\sim p$ (not pacifist). Our knowledge that most (at least 90 percent) Republicans are not pacifists and that most (at least 99 percent) Quakers are pacifists is represented by the bpa function μ for $\{R, Q, P\}$ shown in Table 18.1. (The construction of this bpa function will be explained later in this section – see Example 3.)

Table 18.1: A bpa function μ for $\{R, Q, P\}$.

$2^{\mathcal{W}}\{R, Q, P\}$	μ
$\{(r, \sim q, \sim p), (\sim r, q, p), (\sim r, \sim q, p), (\sim r, \sim q, \sim p)\}$	0.891
$\{(r, q, \sim p), (r, \sim q, \sim p), (\sim r, q, p), (\sim r, \sim q, p) (\sim r, q, \sim p), (\sim r, \sim q, \sim p)\}$	0.009
$\{(r, q, p), (r, \sim q, p), (r, \sim q, \sim p), (\sim r, q, p) (\sim r, \sim q, p), (\sim r, \sim q, \sim p)\}$	0.099
$\{(r, q, p), (r, q, \sim p), (r, \sim q, p), (r, \sim q, \sim p) (\sim r, q, p), (\sim r, q, \sim p), (\sim r, \sim q, p) (\sim r, \sim q, \sim p)\}$	0.001

Note that the marginal of μ for R is the vacuous bpa function for R, that is, $\mu^{\downarrow\{R\}}(\{r, \sim r\}) = 1$. Thus, we have no knowledge whether the stranger is a republican or not. Similarly, notice that the marginals of μ for $\{Q\}$ and $\{P\}$ are also vacuous. The marginal of μ for $\{R, P\}$ is as follows:

$$\mu^{\downarrow\{R,P\}}(\{(r, \sim p), (\sim r, p), (\sim r, \sim p)\}) = 0.90, \ \mu^{\downarrow\{R,P\}}(\{(r, p), (r, \sim p), (\sim r, p), (\sim r, \sim p)\}) = 0.10$$

Thus the plausibility of a Republican pacifist is only 0.10. Similarly, notice that the marginal of μ for $\{Q, P\}$ is as follows:

$$\mu^{\downarrow\{Q,P\}}(\{(q, p), (\sim q, p), (\sim q, \sim p)\}) = 0.99, \ \mu^{\downarrow\{Q,P\}}(\{(q, p), (q, \sim p), (\sim q, p), (\sim q, \sim p)\}) = 0.01$$

Thus the plausibility of a nonpacifist Quaker is only 0.01. Finally note that the marginal of μ for $\{R, Q\}$ is as follows:

$$\mu^{\downarrow\{R,Q\}}(\{(r, \sim q), (\sim r, q), (\sim r, \sim q)\}) = 0.891, \ \mu^{\downarrow\{R,Q\}}(\{(r, q), (r, \sim q), (\sim r, q), (\sim r, \sim q)\}) = 0.109$$

Thus the plausibility of a Republican Quaker is only 0.109.

Next, we state a rule for combining bpa functions, called Dempster's rule (Dempster, 1967, pp. 335–37).

Definition 5. Consider two bpa functions μ_1 and μ_2 for h_1 and h_2, respectively. Suppose $K = \Sigma\{\mu_1(\mathbf{a})\,\mu_2(\mathbf{b}) \mid (\mathbf{a}^{\uparrow(h_1 \cup h_2)}) \cap (\mathbf{b}^{\uparrow(h_1 \cup h_2)}) \neq \varnothing\}$.

The *combination of* μ_1 *and* μ_2, denoted by $\mu_1 \oplus \mu_2$, is the function for $h_1 \cup h_2$ given by

$$(\mu_1 \oplus \mu_2)(\mathbf{c}) = \begin{cases} K^{-1} \Sigma\{\mu_1(\mathbf{a})\mu_2(\mathbf{b}) \mid (\mathbf{a}^{\uparrow(h_1 \cup h_2)}) \cap (\mathbf{b}^{\uparrow(h_1 \cup h_2)}) = \mathbf{c}\}, & \text{if } K \neq 0 \\ 0, \text{ if K} = 0 \end{cases}$$

for all nonempty $\mathbf{c} \subseteq \mathbf{W}_{h_1 \cup h_2}$.

If $K = 0$, then $\mu_1 \oplus \mu_2$ is not a bpa function. In this case, $\mu_1 \oplus \mu_2$ is not a nonzero valuation. This means that the knowledge in μ_1 and μ_2 is inconsistent. If $K \neq 0$, then K is a normalization constant that ensures that $\mu_1 \oplus \mu_2$ is a bpa function.

Example 3 (Dempster's Rule of Combination). Consider two pieces of independent knowledge as follows:

1. Most Republicans (at least 90 percent) are not pacifists.
2. Most Quakers (at least 99 percent) are pacifists.

If μ_1 is a bpa function representation of the first piece of knowledge, and μ_2 is bpa function representation of the second piece of knowledge, then $\mu_1 \oplus \mu_2$ represents the aggregation of these two pieces of knowledge. The first piece of knowledge can be represented by the bpa function μ_1 for $\{R, P\}$ as follows:

$$\mu_1(\mathbf{W}_{\{R,P\}} - \{(r,p)\}) = 0.90, \ \mu_1(\mathbf{W}_{\{R,P\}}) = 0.10$$

(i.e., the plausibility of pacifist Republicans is only 0.10). Similarly, the second piece of knowledge can be represented by the bpa function μ_2 for {Q,P} as follows:

$$\mu_2(\mathbf{W}_{\{Q,P\}} - \{(q, \sim p)\}) = 0.99, \ \mu_2(\mathbf{W}_{\{Q,P\}}) = 0.01$$

(i.e., the plausibility of nonpacifist Quakers is only 0.01). Then the bpa function $\mu_1 \oplus \mu_2 = \mu$, say, shown in Table 18.1, represents the aggregate knowledge.

Theorem 3 Dempster's rule of combination has the following properties (Shafer, 1976):

C1. (Commutativity) $\mu_1 \oplus \mu_2 = \mu_2 \oplus \mu_1$.

C2. (Associativity) $(\mu_1 \oplus \mu_2) \oplus \mu_3 = \mu_1 \oplus (\mu_2 \oplus \mu_3)$.

C3. If μ_1 is vacuous, then $\mu_1 \oplus \mu_2 = \mu_2$.

C4. In general, $\mu_1 \oplus \mu_1 \neq \mu_1$. The bpa function $\mu_1 \oplus \mu_1$ believes in the same propositions as μ_1, but it will do so with twice the degree, as it were.

The bpa function $\mu_1 \oplus \mu_2$ represents aggregation of knowledge contained in bpa functions μ_1 and μ_2 only when the bpa functions μ_1 and μ_2 are independent; the bpa functions μ_1 and μ_2 do not contain some common knowledge. Property C4 tells us that double-counting of knowledge may lead to erroneous information. Thus it is important to ensure that the bpa functions being combined are independent.

We have already shown that axioms A1 and A2 are valid for bpa functions. Theorem 4 states that axiom A3 is also satisfied.

Theorem 4. Suppose μ_1 and μ_2 are bpa functions for h_1 and h_2, respectively. Suppose $X \notin h_1$, and suppose $X \in h_2$. Then $(\mu_1 \oplus \mu_2)^{\downarrow((h_1 \cup h_2) - \{X\})} = \mu_1 \oplus (\mu_2{}^{\downarrow(h_2 - \{X\})})$.

Since all three axioms required for local computation of marginals are satisfied, the fusion algorithm described in section 2.3 can be used for reasoning from knowledge expressed as bpa functions. The next section describes a small example to illustrate the use of the fusion algorithm to find marginals.

4. AN EXAMPLE

In this section, we describe an example in complete detail to illustrate the use of DS belief-function theory in managing uncertainty in expert systems.

Is Dick a Pacifist? Consider the following independent items of evidence. Most (at least 90 percent) Republicans are not pacifists. Most Quakers (at least 99 percent) are pacifists. Dick is a Republican (and we are more than 99.9 percent certain of this). Dick is a Quaker (and we are more than 99.9 percent certain of this). Is Dick a pacifist?

We will model the four items of evidence as bpa potentials as follows. Consider three variables R, Q, and P, each with two configurations in their respective frames. $R = r$ represents the proposition that Dick is a Republican, and $R = \sim r$ represents the proposition that Dick is not a Republican. Similarly for Q and P. The four items of evidence are represented by bpa potentials μ_1 for $\{R, P\}$, μ_2 for $\{Q, P\}$, μ_3 for $\{R\}$, and μ_4 for $\{Q\}$, respectively, as displayed in Table 18.2. Figure 18.3 shows the valuation network for this example.

Table 18.2: The bpa potentials μ_1, μ_2, μ_3 in the *Is Dick a Pacifist?* example.

$2^W \{R, P\}$	μ_1
$\{(r, \sim p), (\sim r, p), (\sim r, \sim p)\}$	.90
$\{(r, p), (r, \sim p), (\sim r, p), (\sim r, \sim p)\}$	.10

$2^W R$	μ_3
$\{r\}$	.999
$\{r, \sim r\}$	.001

$2^W \{Q, P\}$	μ_2
$\{(q, p), (\sim q, p), (\sim q, \sim p)\}$	.99
$\{(q, p), (q, \sim p), (\sim q, p), (\sim q, \sim p)\}$	.01

$2^W Q$	μ_4
$\{q\}$	.999
$\{q, \sim q\}$	.001

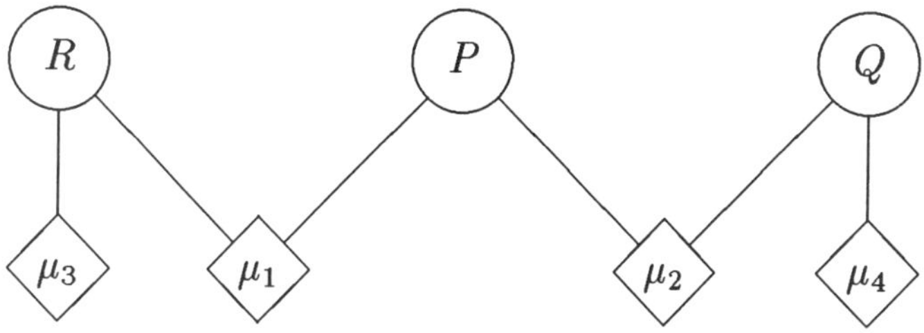

Figure 18.3: The valuation network for the *Is Dick a Pacifist?* example.

If we apply the fusion algorithm using deletion sequence RQ, we get $(\mu_1 \oplus \mu_2 \oplus \mu_3 \oplus \mu_4)^{\downarrow\{P\}} = (\mu_1 \oplus \mu_3)^{\downarrow\{P\}} \oplus (\mu_2 \oplus \mu_4)^{\downarrow\{P\}}$. The details of the computations are shown in Table 18.3. The degree of belief that Dick is a pacifist is 0.9008. Notice that we can avoid the normalization operation in Dempster's rule in the intermediate stages and do it just once at the very end (the last combination operation).

Table 18.3: The computation of $(\mu_1 \oplus \mu_3)^{\downarrow\{P\}} \oplus (\mu_2 \oplus \mu_4)^{\downarrow\{P\}}$.

$2^W \{R, P\}$	$\mu_1 \oplus \mu_3$
$\{(r, \sim p)\}$	.8991
$\{(r, p), (r, \sim p)\}$	.0999
$\{(r, \sim p), (\sim r, p), (\sim r, \sim p)$	.0009
$\{(r, p), (r, \sim p), (\sim r, p), (\sim r, \sim p)\}$	.0001

$2^W \{Q, P\}$	$\mu_2 \oplus \mu_4$
$\{(q, p)\}$	.98901
$\{(q, p), (q, \sim p)\}$	.00999
$\{(q, p), (\sim q, p), (\sim q, \sim p)$	.00099
$\{(q, p), (q, \sim p), (\sim q, p), (\sim q, \sim p)\}$	.00001

2^W P	$(\mu_1 \oplus \mu_3)^{\downarrow\{P\}}$	$(\mu_2 \oplus \mu_4)^{\downarrow\{P\}}$	$(\mu_1 \oplus \mu_3)^{\downarrow\{P\}} \oplus (\mu_2 \oplus \mu_4)^{\downarrow\{P\}}$
$\{p\}$	.0000	.98901	.9008
$\{\sim p\}$	.8991	.00000	.0892
$\{p, \sim p\}$	.1009	.01099	.0100

The use of local computation in computing marginals of the joint bpa function has been widely studied. Some of the influential works in this area are those by Shenoy and Shafer (1986, 1990), Kong (1986), Shafer et al. (1987), Mellouli (1987), and Dempster and Kong (1988). The fusion algorithm applied to the case of belief function theory is an abstraction of the methods described in these papers.

5. CONCLUSIONS

We described the framework of valuation-based systems (VBS), three axioms that permit the use of local computation in computing marginals of the joint valuation, and a fusion algorithm for computing marginals using local computation. Next, we described the essential features of DS theory of belief functions and how this theory fits in the framework of VBS. Elsewhere, we have described how VBs serve as a language for constructing expert systems (Shenoy, 1989). Thus, the correspondence between the theory of belief functions and the framework of VBS should facilitate the use of DS belief-function theory in expert systems.

6. PROOFS

In this section, we give proofs for all results in the paper. First we state and prove a lemma needed to prove Theorem 1.

Lemma 1. Suppose $\{\{\sigma_1,\ldots,\sigma_m\}, \oplus, \downarrow\}$ is a VBS where σ_i is a valuation for s_i, and suppose $\oplus$ and $\downarrow$ satisfy axioms A1-A3. Let **X** denote $s_1 \cup \ldots \cup s_m$. Suppose $X \in \mathbf{X}$. Then

$$(\sigma_1 \oplus \ldots \oplus \sigma_m)^{\downarrow(\bar{\mathrm{X}} - \{X\})} = \oplus \operatorname{Fus}_X\{\sigma_1,\ldots,\sigma_m\}$$

Proof of Lemma 1. Suppose σ_i is a valuation for s_i, $i = 1,\ldots,m$. Let $s = \cup\{s_i \mid X \in s_i\}$, and let $r = \cup\{s_i \mid X \notin s_i\}$. Let $\rho = \oplus\{\sigma_i \mid X \notin s_i\}$, and $\sigma = \oplus\{\sigma_i \mid X \in s_i\}$. Note that $X \in s$, and $X \notin g$. Then using axiom A3

$$\begin{aligned}(\sigma_1 \oplus \ldots \oplus \sigma_m)^{\downarrow(\mathfrak{X} - \{X\})} &= (\rho \oplus \sigma)^{\downarrow((r \cup s) - \{X\})} = \rho \oplus (\sigma^{\downarrow(s - \{X\})}) = \\ &= (\oplus\{\sigma_i \mid X \notin s_i\}) \oplus (\sigma^{\downarrow(s - \{X\})}) = \\ &= \oplus\ \mathrm{Fus}_X\{\sigma_1,\ldots,\sigma_m\}\end{aligned}$$

Proof of Theorem 1. By axiom A2, $(\delta_1 \oplus \ldots \oplus \sigma_m)^{\downarrow\{X\}}$ is obtained by sequentially marginalizing all variables but X from the joint valuation. A proof of this theorem is obtained by repeatedly applying the result of Lemma 1. At each step, we delete a variable and fuse the set of all valuations with respect to this variable. Using Lemma 1, after fusion with respect to X_1, the combination of all valuations in the resulting VBS is equal to $(\sigma_1 \oplus \ldots \oplus \sigma_m)^{\downarrow(\mathfrak{X} - \{X\})}$. Again, using Lemma 1, after fusion with respect to X_2, the combination of all valuations in the resulting VBS is equal to $(\sigma_1 \oplus \ldots \oplus \sigma_m)^{\downarrow(\mathfrak{X} - \{X, X_2\})}$. And so on. When all variables but X have been deleted, we have the result.

Proof of Theorem 2. Suppose μ is a bpa function for h, and suppose $X_1, X_2 \in h$. Then $(\mu^{\downarrow(h-\{X_1\})})^{\downarrow(h-\{X_1,X_2\})}(\mathbf{a}) = \Sigma\{\mu^{\downarrow(h-\{X_1\})}(\mathbf{b}) \mid \mathbf{b} \subseteq \mathbf{W}_{h-\{X_1\}}$ such that $\mathbf{b}^{\downarrow(h-\{X_1,X_2\})} = \mathbf{a}\}$

$= \sum\{\Sigma\{\mu(\mathbf{c}) \mid \mathbf{c} \subseteq \mathbf{W}_h$ such that $\mathbf{c}^{\downarrow(h-\{X_1\})} = \mathbf{b}\} \mid \mathbf{b} \subseteq \mathbf{W}_{h-\{X_1\}}$ such that $\mathbf{b}^{\downarrow(h-\{X_1,X_2\})} = \mathbf{a}\}$

$= \Sigma\{\mu(\mathbf{c}) \mid \mathbf{c} \subseteq \mathbf{W}_h$ such that $(\mathbf{c}^{\downarrow(h-\{X_1\})})^{\downarrow(h-\{X_1,X_2\})} = \mathbf{a}\}$

$= \Sigma\{\mu(\mathbf{c}) \mid \mathbf{c} \subseteq \mathbf{W}_h$ such that $\mathbf{c}^{\downarrow(h-\{X_1,X_2\})} = \mathbf{a}\}$

Similarly, we can show that

$(\mu^{\downarrow(h-\{X_1\})})^{\downarrow(h-\{X_1,X_2\})} = \Sigma\{\mu(\mathbf{c}) \mid \mathbf{c} \subseteq \mathbf{W}_h$ such that $\mathbf{c}^{\downarrow(h-\{X_1,X_2\})} = \mathbf{a}\}$

Proof of Theorem 3. All four properties follow trivially from the definition of Dempster's rule of combination.

Proof of Theorem 4. First, note that the normalization factor in the combination on the left-hand side, say K_1, is the same as the normalization factor in the combination on the right-hand side, say K_2, i.e., $K_1 = K_2$, as shown below:

$$K_2 = \Sigma\{\mu_1(\mathbf{a})\mu_2^{\downarrow(h_2-\{X\})}(\mathbf{e}) \mid (\mathbf{a}^{\uparrow(h_1\cup(h_2-\{X\}))}) \cap (\mathbf{e}^{\uparrow(h_1\cup(h_2-\{X\}))}) \neq \varnothing\}$$

$$= \Sigma\{\mu_1(\mathbf{a})\Sigma\{\mu_2(\mathbf{b}) \mid \mathbf{b}^{\downarrow(h_2-\{X\})} = \mathbf{e}\} \mid (\mathbf{a}^{\uparrow(h_1\cup(h_2-\{X\}))}) \cap (\mathbf{e}^{\uparrow(h_1\cup(h_2-\{X\}))}) \neq \varnothing\}$$

$$= \Sigma\{\mu_1(\mathbf{a})\,\mu_2(\mathbf{b})\,|\,(\mathbf{a}^{\downarrow(h_1\cup(h_2-\{X\}))})\cap(\mathbf{b}^{\downarrow(h_2-\{X\})})^{\uparrow(h_1\cup(h_2-\{X\}))}) \neq \emptyset\}$$
$$= \Sigma\{\mu_1(\mathbf{a})\,\mu_2(\mathbf{b})\,|\,(\mathbf{a}^{\uparrow(h_1\cup(h_2-\{X\}))})\cap(\mathbf{b}^{\uparrow(h_1\cup(h_2-\{X\}))}) \neq \emptyset\}$$
$$= \Sigma\{\mu_1(\mathbf{a})\,\mu_2(\mathbf{b})\,|\,(\mathbf{a}^{\uparrow(h_1\cup h_2)})\cap(\mathbf{b}^{\uparrow(h_1\cup h_2)}) \neq \emptyset\} = K_1 = K$$

Next,

$$(\mu_1 \oplus \mu_2)^{\downarrow(h_1\cup h_2)-\{X\})}(\mathbf{d}) = \Sigma\{\mu_1 \oplus \mu_2)(\mathbf{c})\,|\,\mathbf{c}^{\downarrow(h_1\cup h_2)-\{X\})} = \mathbf{d}\}$$
$$= \Sigma\{K^{-1}\Sigma\{\mu_1(\mathbf{a})\mu_2(\mathbf{b})\,|\,(\mathbf{a}^{\uparrow(h_1\cup h_2)})\cap(\mathbf{b}^{\uparrow(h_1\cup h_2)}) = \mathbf{c}\}\,|$$
$$\mathbf{c}^{\downarrow(h_1\cup h_2)-\{X\})} = \mathbf{d}\}$$
$$= K^{-1}\Sigma\{\mu_1(\mathbf{a})\,\mu_2(\mathbf{b})\,|\,((\mathbf{a}^{\uparrow(h_1\cup h_2)})\cap(\mathbf{b}^{\uparrow(h_1\cup h_2)}))^{\downarrow(h_1\cup h_2)-\{X\})} = \mathbf{d}\}$$
$$= K^{-1}\Sigma\{\mu_1(\mathbf{a})\,\mu_2(\mathbf{b})\,|\,(\mathbf{a}^{\uparrow(h_1\cup h_2)-\{X\}})\cap(\mathbf{b}^{\uparrow(h_1\cup h_2)-\{X\}}) = \mathbf{d}\}$$
$$= K^{-1}\Sigma\{\mu_1(\mathbf{a})\,\mu_2(\mathbf{b})\,|\,(\mathbf{a}^{\uparrow(h_1\cup(h_2-\{X\}))})\cap((\mathbf{b}^{\downarrow(h_2-\{X\})})^{\uparrow(h_1\cup(h_2-\{X\}))}) = \mathbf{d}\}$$
$$= K^{-1}\Sigma\{\mu_1(\mathbf{a})\,\Sigma\{\mu_2(\mathbf{b})|\mathbf{b}^{\downarrow(h_2-\{X\})} = \mathbf{e}\}\,|(\mathbf{a}^{\uparrow(h_1\cup(h_2-\{X\}))})\cap(\mathbf{e}^{\uparrow(h_1\cup(h_2-\{X\}))}) = \mathbf{d}\}$$
$$= K^{-1}\Sigma\{\mu_1(\mathbf{a})\,\mu_2{}^{\downarrow(h_2-\{X\})}(\mathbf{e})|(\mathbf{a}^{\uparrow(h_1\cup(h_2-\{X\}))})\cap(\mathbf{e}^{\uparrow(h_1\cup(h_2-\{X\}))}) = \mathbf{d}\}$$
$$= (\mu_1 \oplus (\mu_2{}^{\downarrow(h_2-\{X\})}))(\mathbf{d})$$

ACKNOWLEDGMENTS

This work was supported in part by the National Science Foundation under grant IRI-8902444. I am grateful to Leen-Kiat Soh for comments.

BIBLIOGRAPHY

Arnborg, S., Corneil, D. G., and Proskurowski, A. (1987). Complexity of finding embeddings in a k-tree. *SIAM Journal of Algebraic and Discrete Methods* 8: 277–84.

Dempster, A. P. (1967) Upper and lower probabilities induced by a multi-valued mapping. *Annals of Mathematical Statistics* 38: 325–39.

Dempster, A. P. and Kong. A. (1988). Uncertain evidence and artificial analysis. *Journal of Statistical Planning and Inference* 20: 355–68.

Kjaerulff, U. (1990). Triangulation of graphs – Algorithms giving small total state space. Technical Report R90-09, Institute for Electronic Systems, University of Aalborg, Denmark.

Kong, A. (1986). Multivariate belief functions and graphical models. Ph. D. dissertation, Department of Statistics, Harvard University, Cambridge, MA.

Mellouli K. (1987). On the propagation of beliefs in networks using the Dempster-Shafer's theory of evidence. Ph. D. thesis, School of Business, University of Kansas, Lawrence.

Saffiotti, A. and Umkehrer, E. (1991). Pulcinella: A general tool for propagating uncertainty in valuation networks. In D'Ambrosio, B., P. Smets, and P. P. Bonissone (eds.), *Uncertainty in Artificial Inteligence: Proceedings of the Seventh Conference*, pp. 323–31. San Mateo, CA: Morgan Kaufmann.

Shafer, G. (1976). *A mathematical theory of evidence*. Princeton NJ: Princeton University Press.

Shafer, G., Shenoy, P. P., and Mellouli, K. (1987). Propagating belief functions in qualitative Markov trees, *International Journal of Approximate Reasoning* 1 (4): 349–400.

Shenoy, P. P. (1989). A valuation-based language for expert systems, *International Journal of Approximate Reasoning*. 3 (5): 383–411.

Shenoy, P. P. (1990a). Valuation-based systems for propositional logic. In Ras, Z.W., M. Zemankova, and M. L. Emrich (eds.), *Methodologies for intelligent systems*, Vol. 5, pp. 305–12. Amsterdam: North-Holland.

Shenoy, P. P. (1990b). Consistency in valuation-based systems. Working Paper No. 216, School of Business, University of Kansas, Lawrence.

Shenoy, P. P. (1990c). Valuation-based systems for Bayesian decision analysis, Working Paper No. 220, School of Business, University of Kansas, Lawrence. To appear in 1992 in *Operations Research* **40** (3).

Shenoy, P. P. (1990d). A new method for representing and solving Bayesian decision problems. Working Paper No. 223, School of Business, University of Kansas, Lawrence. To appear in 1992 in Hand, D. J. (ed.), *Artificial intelligence and statistics III*. London: Chapman and Hall.

Shenoy, P. P. (1991a). On Spohn's rule for revision of beliefs. *International Journal of Approximate Reasoning* 5: 149–81.

Shenoy, P. P. (1991b). Valuation-based systems for discrete optimization. In Bonissone, P. P., M. Henrion, L. N. Kanal, and J. Lemmer (eds.), *Uncertainty in artificial intelligence*, Vol. 6, pp. 385–400. Amsterdam: North-Holland.

Shenoy, P. P. (1991c). Using possibility theory in expert system. Working Paper No. 233, School of Business, University of Kansas, Lawrence. To appear in 1992 in *Fuzzy Sets and Systems*.

Shenoy, P. P. (1991d). Independence in valuation-based systems. Working Paper No. 236, School of Business, University of Kansas, Lawrence.

Shenoy, P. P. (1992). Valuation-based systems: A framework for managing uncertainty in expert systems. In Zadeh, L. A. and J. Kacprzyk (eds.), *Fuzzy logic for the management of uncertainty*, pp. 83–104. New York: Wiley.

Shenoy, P. P. and Shafer, G. (1986). Propagating belief functions using local computations. *IEEE Expert* 1: 43–52.

Shenoy, P. P. and Shafer, G. (1988). Constraint propagation. Working Paper No. 208, School of Business, University of Kansas, Lawrence.

Shenoy, P. P. and Shafer, G. (1990). Axioms for probability and belief-function propagation. In Shachter, R. D., T. S. Levitt, J. F. Lemmer and L. N. Kanal (eds.), *Uncertainty in artificial intelligence*, Vol. 4, 169–98. Amsterdam: North-Holland. Reprinted in Shafer, G. and J. Pearl, eds. (1990), *Readings in uncertain reasoning*, pp. 575–610. San Mateo, CA: Morgan Kaufmann.

Spohn, W. (1988). Ordinal conditional functions: A dynamic theory of epistemic states. In Harper, W. L. and B. Skyrms (eds.), *Causation in decision, belief change, and statistics*, Vol. 2, pp. 105–34. Dordrecht: Reidel.

Zadeh, L. A. (1979). A theory of approximate reasoning. In Ayes, J. E., D. Mitchie, and L. I. Mikulich (eds.), *Machine intelligence*, Vol. 9, pp. 149–94. Chichester, UK: Ellis Horwood.

Zhang, L. (1988). Studies on finding hypertree covers of hypergraphs. Working Paper No. 198, School of Business, University of Kansas, Lawrence.

19 Issues of knowledge representation in Dempster-Shafer's theory

Alessandro SAFFIOTTI

Abstract: This contribution aims at matching Dempster-Shafer (DS) theory to the needs of knowledge representation (KR). We first survey the most common approaches to representing knowledge in DS theory, putting a stronger emphasis on recent work on graph-based approaches. We then pinpoint some limitations of these approaches. To overcome these limitations, we suggest marrying DS theory with KR by proposing a formal framework where DS theory is used for representing strength of belief about our knowledge, and the linguistic structures of an arbitrary KR language are used for representing the knowledge itself. We exemplify this framework by integrating (an extension of) the KRYPTON KR system with DS theory, and by showing how some nontrivial problems may be modeled in the integrated system (e.g., a problem involving multiple agents).

Keywords: Dempster-Shafer theory, knowledge representation, hybrid reasoning, network-based techniques for uncertainty.

1. INTRODUCTION

Already at an early stage of the research in knowledge representation (KR), the need to represent and to reason with uncertain knowledge has been recognized, and work in developing techniques for dealing with uncertainty has started. As a consequence, a distinguished field of "uncertain reasoning" has come into autonomous existence, with its own history, conferences, self-contained results, and schools of thought. We have witnessed a relative departure of the uncertain reasoning field from the issues and methodologies which had characterized the KR field together with an increasing lack of communication between these two fields. As a matter of fact workers in the field of uncertain reasoning have traditionally been rather unconcerned with the linguistic structures used to represent knowledge.

In this respect, the work in Dempster-Shafer (DS) theory is not an exception. Though the AI community has often acknowledged expressive power and epistemic adequacy to it, DS theory explicitly addresses only the problem of representing uncertainty. The other side of the problem of formalizing uncertain knowledge – namely, representing the knowledge itself, which uncertainty refers to – does not seem to have attracted the curiosity of workers in this field. The usual attitude consists in leaving to the user the burden of expressing the knowledge relevent to his or her problem in the mathematical framework provided by DS theory, that is, by means far away from the languages most commonly used in the KR field. Beside reducing the ease of applicability of DS theory to practical cases, this attitude weakens the expressiveness of the theory itself. For instance, though the two statements "Dogs are mammals" and "All of my friends like jazz" would be taken as expressing qualitatively different types of knowledge by most people in the KR community, they would be expressed by a single pattern in a DS framework (e.g., a mass function on the product space of two appropriate variables). Also, representing even simple patterns of generic knowledge (e.g., "Fathers are humans that have at least one child") may become highly problematic in a DS framework. On the other hand, this knowledge is normally easily represented by most KR systems.

In this way, we try to match DS theory to the needs of KR. By so doing, we hope to contribute to the task of defining the "operating instructions" of DS theory when considering its use in the AI practice. We first survey in Section 2 the ways knowledge is normally represented in DS theory, putting a particular emphasis on the recent works on belief networks. In Section 3, we pinpoint the limitations, from both the theorist's and the knowledge engineer's viewpoints, of these ways, and point at some of the solutions proposed in the literature. We then proceed to outline, in Section 4, our own way of rejoining DS theory to the KR field. A prerequisite of this rejoining is the understanding of the role that uncertainty should play in a KR system. In this respect, we shall insist on the epistemic interpretation of DS belief. Accepting this interpretation, we define a formal framework that uses DS theory for representing strength of belief about our knowledge, and the linguistic structures of an arbitrary KR language for representing the knowledge itself. Putting a KR system on top of DS theory may be seen as a means for extending its applicability to kinds of knowledge and problems whose formalization in a pure DS framework would otherwise be far from obvious. Formal results guarantee that both the properties of the given KR system and of DS theory are preserved. From a dual perspective, the proposed integration may be seen as a way of extending a KR system with the possibility of expressing DS degrees of belief. We give examples where first-order logic and (an extension of) KRYPTON are used as KR systems. Section 5 shows how some nontrivial problems are solved by the DS + KRYPTON integration (e.g., a problem involving multiple agents). Finally, Section 6 concludes with a discussion on related work.

2. REPRESENTING PROBLEMS IN THE DEMPSTER-SHAFER THEORY

We review here the most common AI approaches to representing problems in the DS theory.[1] The standard AI account of DS theory regards it as a convenient mathematical setting for expressing the strength of our belief over a set of possible hypotheses. In a nutshell, a unitary amount of belief (*belief mass*) is distributed among the subsets of a set Θ of (exhaustive and mutually exclusive) hypotheses (called the *frame of discernment*). Formally, a *basic probability assignment* (BPA) over Θ is a function $m: 2^{\Theta} \rightarrow [0,1]$ specifying how heavy a mass of belief is being allocated to each subset of Θ. A *belief function* bel_m is then defined on the subsets of Θ from m by $bel_m(A) = \Sigma_{B \subseteq A} m(B)$. Intuitively, $bel_m(A)$ measures the overall amount of belief committed to A according to m. Notice that it is not the case that $bel_m(A) + bel_m(-A) = 1$: when $bel_m(A) + bel_m(-A) < 1$ we say that we are *partially ignorant* about the status of A. (We can also be totally ignorant about A: $bel_m(A) = bel_m(-A) = 0$.) Two BPAs on the

[1] See, e.g., Dempster (1966), Shafer (1976), Smets (1988) for an introduction to the DS theory.

same space of hypotheses, corresponding to two distinct bodies of evidence, may be combined into a new BPA by means of *Dempster's rule of combination*: the resulting BPA is meant to represent the *agreement* (or consensus) of the two given BPAs regarding Θ. In order for Dempster's rule to be applicable, the sources of evidence must be independent. Notice that it is still unclear how independence of the sources of evidence can be guaranteed. This and other cautions that should be used when applying Ds theory, and Dempster's rule of combination in particular, are the subject of a number of studies (e.g., Smets, 1988; Halpern and Fagin, 1989; Ruspini et al., 1990). Acquisition of new evidence is typically performed by combining a preexisting BPA representing the evidence gathered until now with a new BPA representing the impact of the new evidence alone. The reasons that make DS an adequate tool for representing uncertainty have been listed many times, and we do not repeat them here. However, we do notice that, by offering the possibility to adequately represent partial (and total) ignorance, DS theory complies with the AI motto that the power of a representation language does not reside in what it allows you to say, but in what it allows you to leave unsaid.

2.1. The straightforward use

In a typical plain use of DS theory, the frame of discernment Θ contains all the possible (and mutually exclusive) answers to our problem, and an initial belief function is defined over Θ describing our prior information about the actual situation (the vacuous belief function will be used for total ignorance). Different sources of evidence (e.g., sensors, witnesses, experts,...) are then converted in corresponding belief functions over Θ, and all these belief functions are combined together through Dempster's rule, to give rise to a consensus answer to our problem. An example of this straightforward use can be found in Garvey et al. (1981).

2.2. The multivariate approach

The straightforward use of DS theory described above may be used (and has been used – e.g., Garvey et al., 1981) whenever our problem may be stated as: "given some independent sources of evidence, compute a consensus answer to a question for which a set of exhaustive and mutually exclusive possible answers is known." Many problems do not lend themselves to this simple formulation. Often, our problem is better thought of as composed of many simple elements that are connected together by a number of relations (e.g., the complex of valves and sensors that comprise the jets of the Space Shuttle). In these cases, we may apply what has been called the "multivariate approach" (Kong, 1986): the problem we want to deal with is represented through a number of variables, each associated with a relevant element of the problem. Each variable is allowed to take a number of alternative values, and the BPAs are defined over the sets of these values. For instance, one variable may be associated with each valve and sensor of the Space Shuttle jets. Values of the variables correspond to states of the associated object: knowledge about these states is expressed by BPAs over the values of the corresponding variables. A BPA on the product space of (the values of) a set of variables expresses a relationship among the states of the corresponding elements. Figure 19.1 summarizes the situation: variables

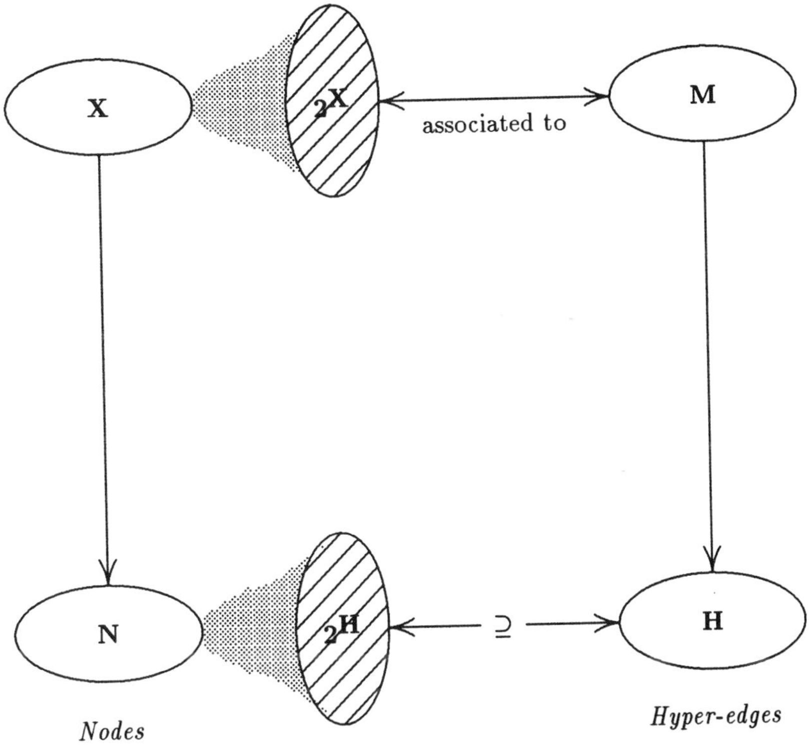

Figure 19.1

represent entities of the domain of discourse, and BPAs represent relational knowledge among the entities represented by these variables (or, as a particular case, prior knowledge about one single entity). For instance, let $Valve_1$ be a variable representing the status {open, closed} of a given valve, and $Probe_1$ a variable representing the reading {red, green} of the associated sensor. The possible values for the pair $\{Valve_1, Probe_1\}$ are $\Omega = \{\langle \text{open, red} \rangle, \langle \text{open, green} \rangle, \langle \text{closed, red} \rangle, \langle \text{closed, green} \rangle\}$. We may encode the relation between the state of the valve and the reading of the sensor as BPA m_{vp} over Ω: $m_{vp}(\{\langle \text{open, red} \rangle\ \langle \text{closed, green} \rangle\}) = 0.99$; $m_{vp}(\Omega) = 0.01$. Intuitively, this BPA encodes a strong belief (0.99) that whenever the reading is red the valve is open, and whenever it is green the valve is closed; and a small (0.01) belief that something goes wrong (i.e., that any other combination may show up).

Once we have modeled a problem this way, a DS solution is found by computing an overall BPA – the combination of all the available BPAs (i.e., those expressing prior belief, those expressing relationships, and those expressing acquired evidence) – on the overall space of values for all the variables. From this BPA, a BPA on each (set of) interesting variables can be computed by marginalization. Thus, Dempster's combination is used to model aggregation of different fragments of knowledge, and marginalization models a norrowing of the focus of interest by concentrating knowledge on a subset of variables. Notice that this implies that all the BPAs to be combined must be based on independent bodies of evidence. If new evidence is obtained concerning the value of some (sets of) variables, it is incorporated by creating a new BPA to represent it, and combining it with the previous overall BPA. We then marginalize the new overall BPA over the (sets of) variables of interest.

2.3. Graph-based approaches

The multivariate approach lends itself to a graphical representation of the problem. The basic elements of the approach, variables and subsets of variables over which a BPA is defined, may be represented as nodes and hyperedges[2] of a hypergraph, respectively (Figure 19.2).

[2] Hypergraphs generalize usual graphs in that they allow for n-ary (rather than binary) edges (called hyperedges) between nodes.

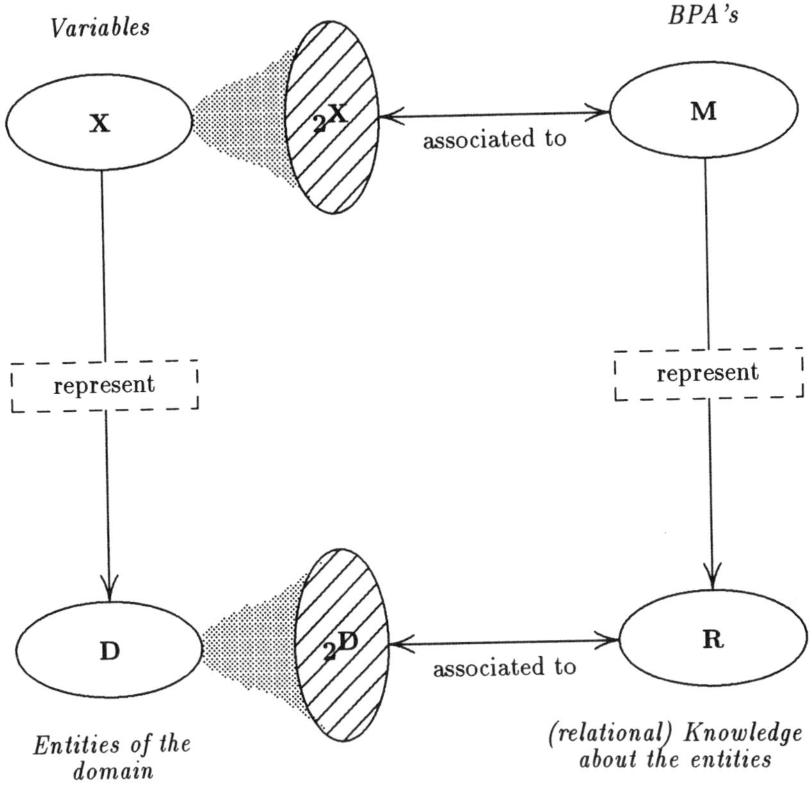

Figure 19.2

In the above example, the two variables, $Valve_1$ and $Probe_1$, and the relation between them, can be represented by the hypergraph in Figure 19.3, where rounds represent nodes, and rectangles hyperedges.

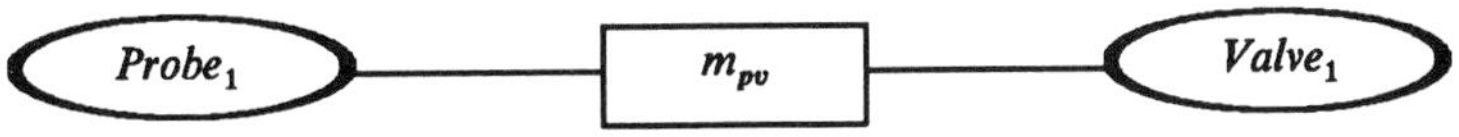

Figure 19.3

Besides providing an intuitive visual representation, hypergraphs form the basis of the local computation technique proposed by Shenoy and Shafer (1988). In their technique, the evaluation of a multivariate model (i.e., the aggregation of all the available evidence, and the marginalization over the variables of interest) is performed on a local basis: the overall BPA is never explicitly computed. Systems for creating and evaluating DS models based on the hypergraph representation and the local computation technique have been implemented (e.g., Hsia and Shenoy, 1989; Zarley et al., 1988; Saffiotti and Umkehrer, 1991; Xu, 1991). These systems offer both the representational appeal of the multivariate approach, and the computational efficiency of Shenoy and Shafer's local computation technique. Notice that this technique is not restricted to using BPAs for representing partial information: Shenoy (1989) generalizes the local computation technique into what he calls *valuation systems*.

3. WHY DO WE NEED MORE?

In the last section, we focused on the most popular ways of representing *problems* in DS theory. Why did we not say "of representing *knowledge*"? We will show here that, if we take the point of view of knowledge representation, we may arrive at the conclusion that DS theory is not an adequate tool for expressing the general *knowledge* that uncertainty refers to.

3.1. Odd representation tools

We have seen that, in typical uses of DS theory, *entities* of the object domain are represented by variables ranging over sets of possible values, and *relations* among them are expressed by mathematical functions defined over them. Unfortunately, these "representation tools" are not even part of the standard vocabulary in the KR field. Rather, researchers working in KR have developed, and used, formalisms for representing knowledge where the objects of discourse are represented as atoms of some logical language, concepts and attributes in a semantic network, frames, etc.; and relations among them are represented by logical formulae, production rules, taxonomies of concepts, "demons," etc. This lack of a common language has often caused well-grounded mathematical theories (viz. DS theory, but also probability theory, or possibility theory) developed by the uncertainty management community to be of scarce practical use in KR systems. It is interesting to contrast this fact with the different fortune of the Mycin-like certainty factors. Scant as they are from the viewpoint of formal soundness, epistemic adequacy, and cognitive plausibility, the fact that certainty factors are defined directly in the context and language of production rules has nonetheless made them a favorite choice in a number of existing KR tools (even disregarding their applicability conditions).

3.2. Missed distinctions

The mismatch between the language used by workers in the KR field and that used in DS theory is not only a matter of syntax. The concepts and tools developed in KR have been motivated by a constant need to adequately account for modes of organization of knowledge, and for distinctions among types of knowledge, that have been identified as relevant to the KR enterprise (see, e.g., Israel and Brachman, 1981, and Brachman and Levesque, 1985, for some flavors of this interesting debate). As an example, consider the statements:

(i) Elephants are mammals with four legs
(ii) Triangles are polygons with three edges
(iii) All of my friends like jazz music
(iv) Normally, birds fly
(v) Smoke suggests fire

Both (i) and (ii) express concept definitions, but while a "triangle" is completely defined by (ii), (i) refers to a concept that can never be fully characterized; (iii) expresses a universal that is contingently (but not "by definition") true; (iv) expresses a "default" statement; and (v) expresses a semiotic relation induced by a causal one. Most people in the KR community would argue for the need of representation formalisms capable of distinguishing between these (and other) different types of knowledge. For example, we want a concept definition like (i) to induce a universal belief like "all elephants are mammals"; however, we do not want a universal like (iii) to induce a concept definition like "(the concept) *my-friend* is a kind of (the concept) *jazz-connoisseur*." Unfortunately, these distinctions cannot be accounted for in DS theory: all the five statements above would typically be expressed by a single pattern in a DS framework, namely a BPA on the product space of two appropriate variables.

3.3. The unrepresentable

The last limitation we mention is probably the most annoying. When defining a DS model, all the knowledge we may talk about is instantiated knowledge. Thus, we can create a variable representing the state of a specific valve and a variable representing the reading of a specific sensor; and we can express a relation between that state and that reading. But we do not have any mechanism for expressing that *any* sensor reading is related to the state of the corresponding valve in a certain way. Said differently, we cannot represent a generic rule relating the reading of any instance of a sensor in our device to the state of the associated instance of a valve. To be sure, there are ways for circumventing this problem in small domains: we can still create separate variables and relations for each of our valves and sensors. However, the problem of representing patterns of generic knowledge becomes practically unsolvable for vast domains, or for patterns involving predicates of arity greater than one. For instance, consider the fact that parents are humans that have at least one child. This fact would be simply represented in first-order logic by

$$\text{for all } x, (\exists\, y, \text{child}(x, y) \rightarrow \text{parent}(x))$$

and in, say, the KRYPTON KR system (Brachman et al., 1985) by

DEFINE[Parent, (VRGeneric Human child Human)].

However, representing this fact in DS theory can become near to impossible. To fix ideas, suppose there are 100 individuals in our domain, and consider the multivariate approach: we would have to introduce 100 binary variables "parent(i)," each providing an answer to the question whether or not i is a parent; 10000 variables "child(i,j)," encoding the question whether or not i is a child of j; and 10000 relations, each encoding an implication relation between the state of a "child(i,j)" variable, and that of the corresponding "parent(j)" variable! (For example, "if 'child(Alex,Elisabeth)' is <u>true</u>, then 'parent(Elisabeth)' must be <u>true</u>," and so on.) One way to summarize this problem is by saying that the expressive power of DS theory is propositional, and does not allow quantification.

4. AN INTEGRATION PROPOSAL

In this section, we give an overview of our proposal for marrying DS theory with KR. The key idea is to embed belief functions into a logic whose language is better suited for representing knowledge. In other words, we propose to use DS theory for representing strength of belief about our knowledge, and the linguistic structures of an arbitrary KR language for representing the knowledge itself. The goal is to be able to represent items of uncertain knowledge as pairs of type:

$$\text{for all } x,(\exists\, y, \text{friend}(x,y) \wedge \text{smoker}(y) \rightarrow \text{smoker}(x)), \langle 0.7, 0\rangle \quad (1)$$

expressing our partial (0.7) belief in the fact that smoking is contagious (the second value measures our confidence in the negation of the statement: here, 0). Or of type:

$$\text{DEFINE[Piropirolus, (VRGeneric Insect habitat Moon)]}, \langle 0.95, 0\rangle \quad (2)$$

expressing our partial (0.95) belief that piropirolus is a kind of lunar insect. In the following, we assume that a KR language *L* is given, and show how to integrate *L* and DS theory into a hybrid language where uncertain knowledge is expressed by items like (1) and (2) above. Importantly, the proposed integration will preserve the formal properties of both DS theory and the given KR language.

The formal framework discussed here had been first presented, in a different from, in Saffiotti (1990a,b). A corresponding computational technique for integrating uncertainty calculi and KR languages is presented in Saffiotti (1991). Finally, Saffiotti (1992) presents a deeper analysis of the integration between DS and first-order logic.

4.1. DS belief as epistemic uncertainty

The first step we have to take is to clarify the nature of the uncertainty we want to talk about, and its relation with the knowledge it refers to. Given an item of knowledge, we call *epistemic uncertainty* on it a judgment as to the truth of that item. To exemplify, consider the following statements:

(i) I am pretty sure (90%) that piropirolus is a kind of insect
(ii) (I am sure that) 90% of birds fly

Statement (i) illustrates the epistemic notion of uncertainty: we can see (i) as a sharp implication ("for all x, piropirolus(x) $\rightarrow$ insect(x)") accompanied by information about its uncertainty; partial belief about the (complete) truth of a fact. On the contrary, we see statement (ii) as expressing just categorical knowledge, which refers to a statistical (but with a firm epistemic status) fact (complete belief about a statistical fact).[3]

We will take a stance here, and assert that DS theory should be thought of as addressing the epistemic notion of uncertainty. What is important for us is that epistemic uncertainty can be seen as just a type of knowledge: knowledge about our confidence in our knowledge. Thus, the problem of integrating knowledge and uncertainty about it becomes an instance of the problem of hybrid knowledge representation, namely integrating two different types of knowledge in a way that accounts for both the differences and the relationships between them. Sticking to this notion of uncertainty, we see uncertain knowledge as composed by just (categorical) knowledge plus (epistemic) uncertainty about it. Accordingly, we shall define DS theory to operate on (i.e., to measure our belief about the truth of) propositions expressed by the KR language L that we are using.

Formally, we identify items of knowledge with elements of a set P of "propositions."[4] As we express our knowledge through sentences of L, we need a mechanism for mapping sentences of L to the propositions they connote. To do this, we suppose that a set W of interpretations[5] (that we also call "worlds") for L is defined, together with a truth relation $\models$: if $w \in W$ and $\alpha \in L$, we read $w \models \alpha$ as "the formula α is *true* in the world w." For example, in first-order logic W is the set of standard first-order interpretation, and $\models$ is the standard truth relation. Following logical tradition, we identify here propositions with sets of possible worlds, namely those worlds in which the proposition holds: given a formula α of L, the proposition connoted by α in L, written $\|\alpha\|$, is given by:

---

[3] But notice that b will induce an epistemic uncertainty when we consider a particular instance of a bird.

[4] We remind the reader that, after Frege (1893), the *proposition* connoted by a sentence is its *sense*, its *meaning*; correspondingly, we say that a sentence *connotes* a proposition that corresponds to the knowledge it represents. The reader should never confuse propositions with sentences that express them; nor should he or she confuse them with propositional symbols, or variables, or any other syntactical element of any given language. Propositions are the *content* of the sentences.

[5] To avoid unnecessary complications, we pass over the issue of the cardinality of W. However, we do assume we have countable domains.

$$\|\alpha\| =_{df} \{w \in W \mid w \models \alpha\}$$

P is then given by the power-set of ***W***, equipped with the standard $\subseteq$ relation. ***P*** is the set on which we will asses our DS belief. In order to make the integration clean, however, we need one final formal machinery.

4.2. Belief bases

In a successful attempt at giving an abstract characterization of knowledge representation systems, Levesque (1984) suggested modeling knowledge by means of abstract data types (*knowledge bases*) characterized in terms of the operations that can be made on them. This approach allows us to describe the behavior of a knowledge representation system at the "knowledge level," that is, without having to care about the actual machineries and structures used to represent knowledge. Correspondingly, we will characterize our integration by defining *belief bases* (*BB*) on ***L*** as characterized by the following three primitive operations:

Ask: $L \times BB$ ([0,1] $\times$ [0,1]}
Tell: $L \times ([0,1] \times [0,1]) \times BB \rightarrow BB$
Empty: $\{\emptyset\} \rightarrow BB$

The intended semantics of these operations is the following. **Ask**[α, κ] inspects the *BB* κ to determine to what extent the sentence α of ***L*** is believed to be true: it returns a pair of numbers $\langle x_t, x_f \rangle$ that measure our degree of belief in the truth of α and of that of its negation – respectively – given all the knowledge in κ. **Tell**[$\alpha, \langle x_t, x_f \rangle, \kappa$] returns a new *BB* obtained by updating κ with a new evidence saying:

"I believe to a degree X_t that α is true,
and to a degree x_f that it is false." (3)

Empty[] simply returns the "empty belief base," i.e., the *BB* where nothing is believed (except the valid sentences of ***L***).

Different definitions of the above primitives can be given depending, among other things, on the calculus we want to use for representing uncertainty (cf. Saffiotti, 1990a, for other examples). In the present case, we model belief bases as BPAs over ***W***. Correspondingly, **Empty**[] returns the vacuous BPA, allocating all the mass to the whole set ***W***; the two values returned by **Ask**[α, κ] are interpreted as the values returned by bel_κ for the asked proposition[6] and its complement – respectively; and **Tell**$[\alpha,\langle x_t, x_f\rangle,\kappa]$ returns the new BPA obtained by combining, by Dempster's combination, the old BPA κ with a BPA representing the new evidence (3). For notational convenience, we represent here a BPA m on W as a set of pairs $\langle P, m_p\rangle$, where $P \subseteq W$ and $m_p = m(P)$ (hence, m_p is a number in $[0,1]$). We restate the basic definitions of DS theory in terms of sets of pairs:[7]

Defintion 1. Let κ be a set of pairs $\langle P, m_p\rangle$ as above, and $Q \subseteq W$. Then we let

$$Bel_\kappa(Q) =_{df} \sum\{m_p | \langle P, m_p\rangle \in \kappa \text{ and } P \subseteq Q\}$$

Definition 2. Let κ_1 and κ_2 be two sets of pairs as above. *Dempster's combination of* κ_1, and κ_2 is given by:

$$\kappa_1 \oplus \kappa_2 =_{df} \{\langle Q, m_Q\rangle | m_Q = \rho_{12}^{-1} \sum m_p m_{p'} \text{ for all } \langle P', m_{p'}\rangle \in \kappa_1, \langle P'', m_{p''}\rangle \in \kappa_2 \; s.t. \; Q = P' \cap P''\}$$

if $\rho_{12} \neq 0$, and it is undefined otherwise; ρ_{12} is given by:

$$\rho_{12} = 1 - \sum\{m_{p'} m_{p''} | \langle P', m_{p'}\rangle \in \kappa_1, \langle P'', m_{p''}\rangle \in \kappa_2, P' \cap P'' = \emptyset\}$$

We now have all the ingredients for giving the functional definition of belief bases.

Definition 3. Let L be a KR language, with corresponding W and $\|\cdot\|$ as above. *Belief bases on L* are functionally defined by the following operations:

$$\textbf{Empty}[\,] =_{df} \{\langle W, 1\rangle\}$$
$$\textbf{Ask}[\alpha, \kappa] =_{df} \langle Bel_\kappa(\|\alpha\|), Bel_\kappa({}^c\|\alpha\|)\rangle$$
$$\textbf{Tell}[\alpha, \langle x_t, x_f\rangle, \kappa] =_{df} \kappa \oplus \{\langle \|\alpha\|, x_t\rangle, \langle {}^c\|\alpha\|, x_f\rangle, \langle W, 1 - x_t - x_f\rangle\}$$

provided that, in Tell, the evidence represented by α is distinct from that represented by κ.

A belief base on Σ is built starting with **Empty**, and then by performing successive **Tell** operations on it. **Empty**[ ] allocates all the mass of belief to the whole set W. **Tell**$[\alpha,\langle x_t, x_f\rangle, \kappa]$ combines the old BPA κ with a BPA that allocates the desired amounts of belief to the Told proposition and to its complement and the remaining

[6] We will often use "the Asked (Told) proposition" to mean the proposition connoted by the sentence appearing in the Ask (Tell) operation.

[7] *The usual constraints* $Bel_\kappa(w_\Sigma) = 1$ and $Bel_\kappa(\emptyset) = 0$ will follow from the definition of belief bases given below.

amount to the tautology W. Very roughly, each set of worlds P in κ is split into three subsets: those worlds in P where α holds, those where α does not hold, and P itself. Mass of belief is redistributed over all the resulting sets of possible worlds according to Dempster's combination. **Ask**$[\alpha, \kappa]$ measures the total belief committed to the set of possible worlds $\|\alpha\|$(and to its complement) by the BPA κ. The condition "$P \subseteq Q$" *in the definition of* Bel_κ *corresponds to logical entailment between sentences of* L: given two sentences α and β of L, $\|\beta\| \subseteq \|\alpha\|$ is true whenever $\{w|w \models \beta\} \subseteq \{w|w \models \alpha\}$, that is, whenever $\beta \models \alpha$. Notice that, as all and only the valid sentences of L hold in all worlds, all and only the valid sentences of L will be believed (with unitary belief) in the empty belief base.

We interact with belief bases, via the **Ask** and **Tell** operations, by using *sentences* of L for expressing our knowledge, and numbers in [0,1] for expressing our belief in the truth (or falsity) of this knowledge. However, we emphasize once again that mass of belief is actually allocated to the *propositions* connoted by these sentences, and not to the *sentences* themselves.

Example 1. We can use belief bases to link together DS theory and first-order logic (FOL). Consider a FOL language L_{FOL}, and a standard truth relation $\models_{FOL}$. W_{FOL} is the set of standard FOL interpretations. Hence: $\|\alpha\|_{FOL} = \{w|w \models_{FOL} \alpha\}$; i.e., $\|\alpha\|_{FOL}$ is the set of all standard first-order models for α. Ask$_{FOL}$, Tell$_{FOL}$ and Empty$_{FOL}$ are plainly given in Definition 3. In the resulting belief bases, knowledge is represented in first-order logic, and belief about it obeys DS theory. Figure 19.4 illustrates the belief base κ obtained by

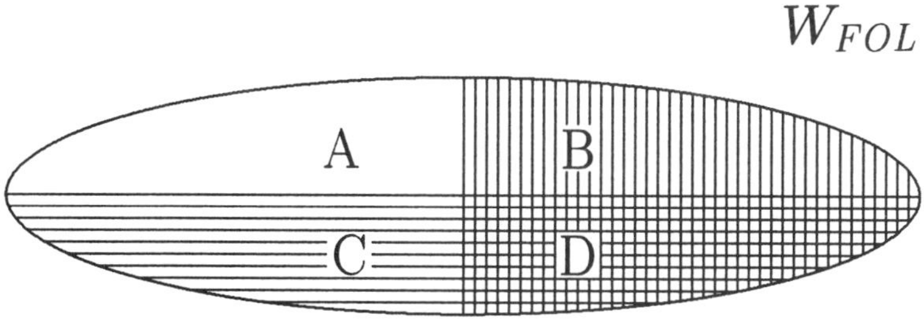

Figure 19.4

$\kappa \equiv$ **Tell**$_{FOL}$[dog(Alex), $\langle 0.7, 0.1\rangle$, **Tell**$_{FOL}$ [for all x, (dog(x) $\rightarrow$ animal(x)), $\langle 0.9, 0\rangle$, **Empty**$_{FOL}$[ ]]]

The vertically shaded part in the picture comprises worlds in which "for all x, (dog(x) $\rightarrow$ animal(x))" is true; the horizontally shaded one, worlds in which "dog(Alex)" is true; D corresponds to $\|$for all x, (dog(x) $\rightarrow$ animal(x)) $\wedge$ dog(Alex)$\|_{FOL}$. So, the first Tell allocates a mass of 0.9 to the subset $B \cup D$, and 0.1 to the whole space $A \cup B \cup C \cup D$. The second Tell combines this BPA with one in which a mass of 0.7 is allocated to $C \cup D$, 0.1 to $A \cup B$, and 0.2 to $A \cup B \cup C \cup D$. In the resulting belief base κ, a mass of 0.02 is being allocated to $A \cup B \cup C \cup D$, 0.01 to $A \cup B$, 0.07 to $C \cup D$, 0.18 to $B \cup D$, 0.09 to B, and 0.63 to D. By definition of FOL interpretation, the sentence "animal(Alex)" will uniformly hold in D (while it will in general hold in some of–but not all–the worlds in A, B and C); this means that the only proposition in κ which entails $\|$animal(Alex)$\|_{FOL}$ is D, while no proposition entails $\| \sim$animal(Alex)$\|_{FOL}$. Hence:

$$\mathbf{Ask}_{FOL}[\text{animal(Alex)}, \kappa] = \langle 0.63, 0 \rangle$$

Example 2. We continue Example 1 by illustrating how the celebrated Tweety problem may be formulated with belief bases on FOL:

$$\begin{aligned}
\kappa_1 &\equiv \mathbf{Tell}_{FOL}[(\text{for all } x, (\text{bird}(x) \wedge \sim\text{excp}(x)) \rightarrow \text{flier}(x)), \langle 1,0 \rangle,\\
&\qquad \mathbf{Empty}_{FOL}[\,]]\\
\kappa_2 &\equiv \mathbf{Tell}_{FOL}[(\text{for all } x, \sim\text{excp}(x)), 0.8, 0.2\rangle, \kappa_1]\\
\kappa_3 &\equiv \mathbf{Tell}_{FOL}[(\text{for all } x, \text{penguin}(x) \rightarrow (\text{bird}(x) \wedge \sim\text{flier}(x))),\\
&\qquad \langle 1,0 \rangle, \kappa_2]\\
\kappa_4 &\equiv \mathbf{Tell}_{FOL}[\text{bird(Tweety)}, \langle 1,0 \rangle, \kappa_3]\\
\kappa_5 &\equiv \mathbf{Tell}_{FOL}[\text{bird(Cippy)}, \langle 1,0 \rangle, \kappa_3]\\
\kappa_6 &\equiv \mathbf{Tell}_{FOL}[\text{penguin(Tweety)}, \langle 1,0 \rangle, \kappa_4]
\end{aligned}$$

Then we have, in κ_5:

$$\begin{aligned}
&\mathbf{Ask}_{FOL}[\text{flier(Tweety)}, \kappa_5] = \langle 0.8, 0 \rangle\\
&\mathbf{Ask}_{FOL}[\text{flier(Cippy)}, \kappa_5] = \langle 0.8, 0 \rangle
\end{aligned}$$

and, in κ_6:

$$\begin{aligned}
&\mathbf{Ask}_{FOL}[\text{flier(Tweety)}, \kappa_6] = \langle 0, 1 \rangle\\
&\mathbf{Ask}_{FOL}[\text{flier(Cippy)}, \kappa_6] = \langle 0.8, 0 \rangle\\
&\mathbf{Ask}_{FOL}[\text{excp(Tweety)}, \kappa_6] = \langle 1, 0 \rangle\\
&\mathbf{Ask}_{FOL}[\text{excp(Cippy)}, \kappa_6] = \langle 0, 0.8 \rangle
\end{aligned}$$

Belief bases as resulting from Definition 3 "behave well" as hybrid structures; that is, they preserve all the properties of both DS theory and the used KR system. For instance, we have:[8]

[8] Notice that a sentence holds in the empty belief base if and only if it holds in all belief bases.

Proposition 1.

(i) $\textbf{Ask}[\alpha, \textbf{Empty}[\,]] = \begin{cases} \langle 1, 0 \rangle \text{ if } \alpha \text{ is valid in } L; \\ \langle 0, 0 \rangle \text{ otherwise} \end{cases}$

(ii) $\textbf{Ask}[\alpha, \textbf{Tell}[\beta, \langle 1,0 \rangle, \textbf{Empty}[\,]]] = \begin{cases} \langle 1,0 \rangle \text{ if } \beta \text{ logically implies } \\ \alpha \text{ in } L; \\ \langle 0, 0 \rangle \text{ otherwise} \end{cases}$

So, belief bases on L obey the logic of L, and they reduce to it when belief measures are restricted to be 0 or 1. On the other hand, any DS model can be captured in our framework:

Proposition 2. **Let** $A = (\emptyset, m_1, m_2, \ldots, m_k)$ **be a DS model, where** $\emptyset = \{\theta_1, \ldots, \theta_n\}$ is a frame of discernment and the m_i's are BPAs on $\emptyset$; let $m = \oplus_i m_i$. Then there exists a belief base κ_m on propositional calculus such that, for all subsets A of Θ,

$$\textbf{Ask}[P_A, \kappa_m] = \langle x_t, x_f \rangle \text{ iff } x_t = bel_m(A) \text{ and } x_f = bel_m(\emptyset - A)$$

where P_A is the propositional calculus formula expressing "the answer to A is in A," and bel_m is the standard belief function associated to m.

5. AN EXAMPLE: MERGING M-KRYPTON WITH BELIEF FUNCTIONS

We illustrate the use of belief bases by giving an example of integration. The example is meaningful in that the chosen KR system incorporates some advanced KR features, which would not be available in DS theory. The resulting belief bases will therefore exhibit nontrivial KR capabilities, together with the power of the DS aproach in dealing with uncertainty. Our KR language is M−KRYPTON, an extension of the KRYPTON hybrid KR system (Brachman et al., 1985), developed to model the interaction between multiple agents.[9] Like KRYPTON, M-KRYPTON may accommodate both knowledge with an *assertional* content – facts which hold contingently in our world, like "(friend Alex Robert)"; and knowledge with a terminological content – definitions of our dictionary, like "(<u>IS</u> man (<u>A</u> human (<u>WITH</u> sex male)))." Unlike KRYPTON, M-KRYPTON can

[9] M-KRYPTON is fully described in Saffioti and Sebastiani (1988).

model belief[10] of multiple agents – like in "($\mathbf{B}_i\,\alpha$)," red "agent i believes that α," where α is any formula of M-KRYPTON. M-KRYPTON has been given semantics in a possible world framework, in terms of a truth relation $\models_{MK}$. Space limitation prevents us from even attempting a description of M-KRYPTON semantics. However, we need at least two clauses (in a simplified form) of the definition of $\models_{MK}$:

$$w \models_{MK} (P\,x) \quad \text{iff} \quad V(x, w) \in V(P, w)$$
$$w \models_{MK} (\mathbf{IS}\, g_1\, g_2) \quad \text{iff} \quad \text{for all } w' \in \underline{W} \text{ such that } w\underline{T}w',\ \mathbf{E}(g_1, w') \subseteq \mathbf{E}(g_2, w')$$

Very roughly, the first clause says that (P x) (e.g., (dog Scruffy)) holds in a world w iff the individual associated to x by V in w belongs to the extension of P (through V) in the same world (e.g., Scruffy happens to be a dog in w). The second clause says that a concept g_1 (e.g., "man") is subsumed by a concept g_2 (e.g., "(A human (WITH sex male))") iff the extention of g_1 (returned by the function E) is included in that of g_2 in all the worlds w' that are "terminologically possible" in w. The T relations decides which worlds are terminologically possible from any given world. Intuitively, fixing the terminology (i.e., the relations between the predicates we are using) means to fix a set of possible alternatives where the contingent facts may change, but the terminological definition must remain fixed.

Belief bases on M-KRYPTON are plainly given by Definition 3, by letting $\|\alpha\|_{MK} = \{\omega \in W_{MK} \mid w \models_{MK} \alpha\}$, where W_{MK} is the set of Kripke worlds on which $\models_{MK}$ is defined.

$$\mathbf{Empty}_{MK}[\,] =_{df} \{\langle W_{MK}, 1\rangle\}$$
$$\mathbf{Ask}_{MK}[\alpha, \kappa] =_{df} \langle \mathbf{Bel}_\kappa(\{w \models_{MK} \alpha\}), \mathbf{Bel}_\kappa(\{w \models_{MK} \sim\alpha\})\rangle$$
$$\mathbf{Tell}_{MK}[\alpha, \langle x_t, x_f\rangle, \kappa] =_{df} \kappa \oplus \{\langle\{w \models_{MK} \alpha\}, x_t\rangle, \langle\{w \models_{MK} \sim\alpha\}, x_f\rangle, \langle W_{MK}, 1 - x_t - x_f\rangle\}$$

We illustrate the behavior of the resulting belief bases through a couple of interesting problems.

Example 3. I have never been very learned in Paleontology: though I am almost sure that brontosaurs are animals, I am not quite sure about what the possible kinds of brontosaurus are; for instance, I am inclined to believe that researchers are one of these kinds. Given that I know for sure that Alex is a researcher, how strongly do I believe Alex is an animal?

---

[10] The traditional epistemic notion of (categorical) belief is meant here with no reference to Dempster-Shafer's belief.

The following is the set of M-KRYPTON sentences used to formulate our problem, and their associated belief values. A graphical representation of the situation is given in Figure 19.5.

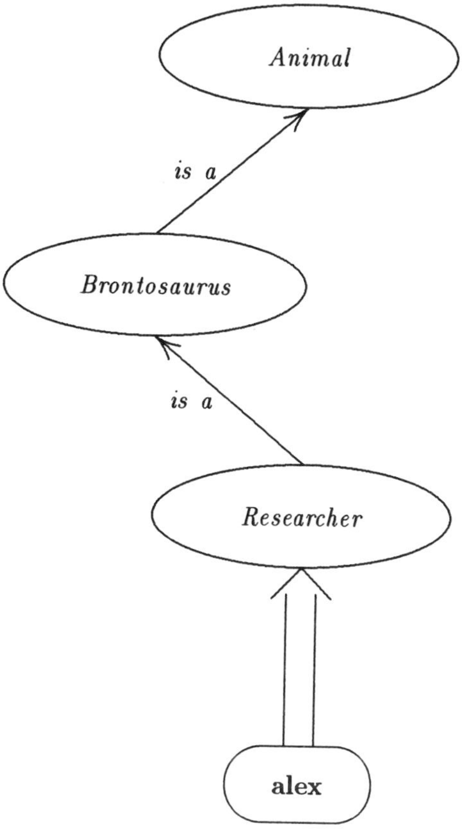

Figure 19.5

(IS Brontosaurus Animal)	$\langle 0.9, 0\rangle$	(brontosaurs are a kind of animal
(IS Researcher Brontosaurus)	$\langle 0.7, 0\rangle$	researchers are a kind of brontosaur)
(Researcher Alex)	$\langle 1, 0\rangle$	(Alex is an instance of a researcher)

We need some simplifications in order to be able to follow the evolution of Belief Sets; so, we limit ourselves to considering a small

W_{MK} composed of the only worlds $\{ø,r,b,a,rb,ra,ba,rba\}$, where the domain contains the only individual alex, and T relates each world only to itself; V is such that in the world "rb," alex is in the extension of Researcher and of Brontosaurus, but not in that of Animal; in "ra," he is in the extension of Researcher and of Animal, but not in that of Brontosaurus, etc. So, the proposition connoted by "(IS Animal Researcher)" consists of $\{ø,r,b,rb,ra,rba\}$, the set of worlds in which alex is in the extension of Researcher whenever he is in the extension of Animal. We then build the following Belief Bases:

$\kappa_1 \equiv$ **Tell**$_{MK}$ [(**IS** Researcher Brontosaurus), $\langle 0.7, 0\rangle$,
Empty$_{MK}$[ ]] = $\{\langle W, 0.3\rangle, \langle\{ø,b,a,rb,ba,rba\}, 0.7\rangle\}$
$\kappa_2 \equiv$ **Tell**$_{MK}$ [(**IS** Brontosaurus Animal), $\langle 0.9, 0\rangle$, κ_1] =
= $\{\langle W, 0.03\rangle, \langle\{ø,b,a,rb,ba,rba\}, 0.07\rangle, \langle\{ø,r,a,ra,ba,rba\}$,
$0.27\rangle, \langle\{ø,a,ba,rba\}, 0.63\rangle\}$
$\kappa_3 \equiv$ **Tell**$_{MK}$ [(**IS** Researcher alex), $\langle 1, 0\rangle$, κ_2] =
= $\{\langle\{r,rb,ra,rba\}, 0.03\rangle, \langle\{\text{rb,rba}\}\ 0.07\rangle$,
$\langle\{r,ra,rba\}, 0.27\rangle, \langle\{rba\}, 0.63\rangle\}$

From that we get, for instance:

Ask$_{MK}$[(Brontosaurus alex), κ_3] = $\langle 0.07+0.63, 0\rangle = \langle 0.7, 0\rangle$
Ask$_{MK}$[(Animal alex), κ_3] = $\langle 0.63, 0\rangle$

Our second problem makes use of the full representational power of the integrated system. Unfortunately, because of the relative complexity of the example, we will not be able to follow the evolution of the belief bases.

Example 4. After a long discussion, Robert and Alex come to a good agreement about which individuals are (or are not) human; also, most probably Alex knows that pets are animals owned by humans. Given that Alex knows that Tweety is a pet, and that Philippe owns it, will Robert believe Philippe to be a human?

$\kappa_1 \equiv$ **Tell**$_{MK}$[(FORALL x (**B**$_{alex}$ (human x))⟷(**B**$_{robert}$ (human x))),
$\langle 0.8, 0\rangle$, **Empty**$_{MK}$[ ]]
$\kappa_2 \equiv$ **Tell**$_{MK}$[(**B**$_{alex}$(**IS** Pet (AN Animal (WITH owner
(A human))))), $\langle 0.98, 0\rangle$, κ_1]
$\kappa_3 \equiv$ **Tell**$_{MK}$[(**B**$_{alex}$ (AND (pet Tweety) (owner Tweety Philippe))),
$\langle 1, 0\rangle$, κ_2]

Then: **Ask**$_{MK}$[(**B**$_{robert}$ (human Philippe)), κ_3] = $\langle 0.784, 0\rangle$

Notice that the kind of knowledge represented in this example is in no respect a trivial one: the first Tell expresses a contingent relation between the belief held by two different agents; the second one expresses the belief of an agent toward a terminological definition; and the third one expresses the belief of an agent toward some assertions. All these types of knowledge are adequately captured by the mechanisms of M-KRYPTON. By contrast, a formalization of this problem in a standard DS formalism appears far from being obvious. Moreover, the "good behavior" of belief bases, as resulting from Propositions 1 and 2, guarantees that the properties of M-KRYPTON are preserved in the integration. For instance, the essential distinction made between assertional and terminological knowledge still works as expected:

$$\mathbf{Ask}_{\mathrm{MK}}[(\underline{\text{FORALL}}\ x\ ((P\ x) \rightharpoonup (Q\ x))), \mathbf{Tell}_{\mathrm{MK}}[(\underline{\text{IS}}\ P\ Q), \langle 1,0\rangle, \mathbf{Empty}_{\mathrm{MK}}[\,]]] = \langle 1,0\rangle$$

$$\mathbf{Ask}_{\mathrm{MK}}[(\underline{\text{IS}}\ P\ Q), \mathbf{Tell}_{\mathrm{MK}}[(\underline{\text{FORALL}}\ x\ ((P\ x) \rightharpoonup (Q\ x))), \langle 1,0\rangle, \mathbf{Empty}_{\mathrm{MK}}[\,]]] = \langle 0,0\rangle$$

6. CONCLUSIONS

Building on the analysis of the current ways of using DS theory for modeling AI problems, and from the limitations of these ways from a KR viewpoint, we have proposed a framework for integrating DS theory with a KR system. This framework is "hybrid" in the sense that it accounts for both the differences and the relations between two essentially different types of knowledge. As such, it shares the practical advantages of hybrid systems, namely the ease of redefining one of the components without side-effects on the other, and the relative independence in the choice of data structures and algorithms to be used for each of the components. This framework is not limited to DS theory: in Saffiotti (1990b) we have extended it to other uncertainty calculi. Also, the proposed hybridization technique has a computational counterpart in the general technique for building integrated systems presented in Saffiotti (1991). This technique is based on the dynamic construction of a belief network that "mirrors" the inferences performed by the KR system.

The mismatch between the (usual formulation of) DS theory and the needs and traditions in the KR field seems to have scarcely attracted the attention of workers in the former field, who appear as being unconcerned with the linguistic structures used to represent knowledge. This seems to be a general attitude in the field of uncertain reasoning. In some cases, some attention has been devoted to this linguistic aspect, as in Zadeh (1989); however, Zadeh's proposal consists in advocating the use of fuzzy logic *as* a KR tool, while we suggest to combine DS theory *with* a KR tool. Other systems have recently been developed in which both the need of representing knowledge and that of representing uncertainty have been taken into consideration (e.g., Shastri, 1988; Yen and Bonissone, 1990; Heinsohn, 1991). Contrary to our proposal, these systems consider only a particular KR system: they do not address the general problem of integration. Moreover, they do not consider the issue of isolating formulae from propositions: by contrast, in our approach uncertainty is attached to the knowledge itself, rather than to the linguistic structures used to represent it. This move allows us to set our approach as a general integration paradigm.

Other researchers have proposed tightly coupled integrations between logical languages and some uncertainty formalisms. Two interesting examples are the work by Lang et al. (1991) on "Possibilistic Logic," and by the work of Baldwin (1986) on "Support Logic Programming." Possibilistic logic extends first-order logic by attaching degrees of possibility and necessity to formulae. So, possibilistic logic combines the advantages of a well-grounded uncertainty representation like possibility theory with the expressive power of first-order logic. Like our proposal, the uncertainty considered is epistemic uncertainty about the truth of formulae. Unlike our proposal, the uncertainty mechanism and the representation language are tightly (rather than loosely) integrated: this reflects the fact that possibilistic logic is meant to be a powerful logic for uncertain knowledge, rather than a general integration framework. Similarly, support logic programming tightly integrates Horn clauses and DS theory. However, Baldwin interprets the values attached to clauses in a very different way. Namely, Baldwin reads

$$P :- Q.\ \langle 0.7, 0.1 \rangle \tag{4}$$

as "when Q is the case, I believe to the extent 0.7 that P is true, and to the extent 0.1 that it is false." Contrast this with the reading of (4) under the epistemic uncertainty interpretation: "I believe to the extent 0.7 that whenever Q is true, so is P; and to the extent 0.1 that this is not the case." As a consequence of this peculiar reading of nonunit clauses, Baldwin's approach cannot be directly transported to other KR languages. If we wanted to use a different KR language (e.g., M-KKRYPTON), we would have to find some adequate special construct that, like (4), models uncertain inference. On the contrary, the only operation we have to do for applying our proposal to any given KR language is to integrate the corresponding definition of $\models$ in our Definition 3.

Finally, the possible world formalization given in this work is clearly related to other possible world accounts given in Dempster-Shafer's theory (e.g., Ruspini, 1986; Fagin and Halpern, 1989). However, our focus here is the linking of DS theory to an arbitrary KR system, by using propositions as a formal bridge: possible worlds are just one possible choice for modeling propositions. Moreover, the accounts referred to above are normally restricted to considering the propositional case, while the approach presented here allows us to extend DS theory to any suitable formal language.

ACKNOWLEDGMENTS

The warm human and intellectual environment of IRIDIA has been critical to the development of this research; in particular, discussions with Yen-Teh Hsia, Robert Kennes, Philippe Smets, Elisabeth Umkehrer, and Hong Xu have been a major source of inspiration, and their comments helped improve the quality of this paper. I also wish to thank all the partners of the DRUMS Basic Reasearch Action for many useful discussions.

BIBLIOGRAPHY

Baldwin, J.F. (1986). Support logic programming. *Int. J. of Intelligent Systems* 1: 73–104

Brachman, R.J. and Levesque, H.J. (eds.). *Readings in knowledge representation.* San Mateo, CA: Morgan Kaufmann.

Brachman, R.J., Pigman Gilbert, V., and Levesque, H.J. (1985). An essential hybrid reasoning system: Knowledge and symbol level accounts of Krypton. *Proc. of IJCAI-85,* pp. 532–39.

Dempster, A.P. (1966). Upper and lower probabilities induced by a multi-valued mapping. *Annals of Mathematical Statistics* 38: 325–39.

Fagin, R. and Halpern, J.Y. (1989). Uncertainty, belief and probability. *Proc. of IJCAI-89,* pp. 1161–67.

Frege, G. (1893). Über Sinn und Bedeutung. *Zeitschrift für Philosophie und philosophische Kritik* 100: 25–50. UK: Cambridge University Press.

Gervey, T.D., Lowrance, J.D., and Fisher, M.A. (1981). An inference technique for integrating knowledge from disparate sources. *Proc. of IJCAI-81.*

Halpern, J.Y. and Fagin, R. (1989). Two views of belief: Belief as generalized evidence and belief as evidence. IBM Technical Report RJ 7221. To appear in *Artificial Intelligence.*

Heinsohn, J. (1991). A probabilistic extension for term subsumption languages. *Proc. of the First European Conf. on Symbolic and Quantitative Approaches to Uncertainty.*

Hsia, Y. and Shenoy, P.P. (1989). MacEvidence: A visual environment for constructing and evaluating evidential systems. Working Paper No. 211, School of Business, University of Kansas, Lawrence.

Israel, D.J. and Brachman, R.J. (1981). Distinctions and confusions: A catalogue raisonné. *Proc. of IJCAI-81,* pp. 451-59.

Kong, A. (1986). Multivariate belief functions and graphical models. PhD thesis, Department of Statistics, Harvard University.

Lang, J., Dubois, D., and Prade, H. (199). A logic of graded possibility and certainty coping with partial inconsistency. *Proc. of the Seventh Conf. on Uncertainty in AI,* Los Angeles, CA, pp. 188–96.

Levesque, H.J. (1984). Foundations of a functional approach to knowledge representation. *Artificial Intelligence* 23: 155–212.

Ruspini, E.H. (1986). The logical foundations of evidential reasoning. Technical Note 408. Menlo Park, CA: SRI International.

Ruspini, E., Lowrance, J.D., and Strat, T.M. (1990). Understanding evidential reasoning. Technical Note 501. Menlo Park, CA: SRI International.

Saffiotti, A. (1990a). Using Dempster-Shafer theory in knowledge representation. In Bonissone, P., Henrion, M., Kanal, L.N. and Lemmer, J. (eds.) *Uncertainty in artificial intelligence, Vol. IV.* New York: North-Holland. Extended version as IRIDIA Technical Report TR/IRIDIA/90-5 (Université Libre de Bruxelles).

Saffiotti, A. (1990b). A hybrid framework for representing uncertain knowledge. *Proc. of AAAI-90,* Boston, MA, pp. 653–58.

Saffiotti, A. (1991). Inference-driven construction of valuation systems. IRIDIA Technical Report TR/IRIDIA/91-18 (Université Libre de Bruxelles, Bruxelles, Belgium).

Saffiotti, A. (1992). A belief-function logic. *Proc. of AAAI-92* (to appear). Extended version as IRIDIA Technical Report TR/IRIDIA/91-25 (Université Libre de Bruxelles).

Saffiotti, A. and Sebastiani, F. (1988). Dialogue modelling in M-KRYPTON, a hybrid language for multiple believers. *Proc. of the Fourth IEEE Conf. on AI Applications,* San Diego, CA, pp. 56–60.

Safiotti, A. and Umkehrer, E. (1991). PULCINELLA: A general tool for propagating uncertainty in valuation networks. *Proc. of the Seventh Conf. on Uncertainty in AI,* Los Angeles, CA, pp. 323–31.

Shafer, G. (1976). *A mathematical theory of evidence.* Princeton: Princeton University Press.

Shastri, L. (1988). *Semantic networks: An evidential formalization and its connectionist realization.* London: Pitman.

Shenoy, P.P. (1989). A valuation-based language for expert systems. *Int. J. of Approximate Reasoning* 3: 383–411.

Shenoy, P.P. and Shafer, G. (1988). An axiomatic framework for Bayesian and belief-function propagation. *Proc. of AAAI Workshop on Uncertainty in Al,* pp. 307–14.

Smets, P. (1988). Belief functions. In Smets, P., Mamdani, E.H., Dubois, D., and Prade, H. (eds.), *Non-standard logics for automated reasoning.* London: Academic Press.

Xu, H. (1991). An efficient implementation of belief function propagation. IRIDIA Technical Report TR/IRIDIA/91-4 (Université Libre de Bruxelles, Bruxelles, Belgium).

Yen, J. and Bonissone, P. (1990). Extending term subsumption systems for uncertainty management. In Bonissone, P., Henrion, M., Kanal, L.N. and Lemmer, J. (eds.), *Uncertainty in artificial intelligence, Vol. IV*. New York: North-Holland.

Zadeh, L.A. (1989). Knowledge representation in fuzzy logic. *IEEE Trans. on Knowledge and Data Engineering* 1: 89–100.

Zarley, D.K., Hsia, Y., and Shafer, G.R. (1988). Evidential reasoning using DELIEF. Working Paper No. 211, School of Business, University of Kansas, Lawrence.

20 Representing heuristic knowledge and propagating beliefs in the Dempster-Shafer theory of evidence

Weiru LIU, John G. HUGHES,
and Michael F. MCTEAR

Abstract: The Dempster-Shafer theory of evidence has been used intensively to deal with unertainty in knowledge-based systems. However, the representation of uncertain relationships between evidence and hypothesis groups (heuristic knowledge) is still a major research problem. This paper presents an approach to representing such heuristic knowledge by *evidential mappings* that are defined on the basis of mass functions. The relationships between evidential mappings and multivalued mappings, as well as between evidential mappings and Bayesian multivalued causal link models in Bayesian theory are discussed. Following this the detailed procedures for constructing evidential mappings for any set of heuristic rules are introduced. Several situations of belief propagation are discussed. Shafer's partition technique is used to get the mass function in a complex evidence space when the antecedent frame of a rule is made of several variables. Matrices and vectors are used to represent uncertain relaionships in heuristic knowledge and pieces of evidence respectively.

Keywords: evidential reasoning, representing heuristic knowledge, evidential mappings.

1. INTRODUCTION

In the design and implementation of expert systems and decision-making systems, the problem of uncertain knowledge and evidence has to be solved. Several approaches can be used to deal with this problem, such as Mycin's certainty factors, Prospector's inference nets, fuzzy sets, Bayesian nets, and Dempster-Shafer's belief functions.

Generaly speaking, there are two kinds of problems involving uncertainty: one is caused by uncertain evidence; another is caused by uncertain knowledge, that is, heuristic knowledge. The former is a result of ill-defined concepts in the observation, or due to inaccuracy and poor reliability of the instruments used to make the observations. The latter is a result of weak implication, which occurs when the expert or model builder is unable to establish a strong correlation between premise (or evidence) and conclusion (or hypotheses) (Bonissone and Tong, 1985).

The Dempster-Shafer (DS) theory of evidence provides a flexible approach to representing uncertain evidence. This theory, which is claimed as a generalization of Bayesian inference (Shafer, 1976, 1981), has the advantages of representing ignorance of evidence and narrowing the hypothesis space as a result of evidence accumulation. Several AI implementations have been undertaken (Laskey et al., 1989; Lowrance et al., 1986; Strat, 1987; Wesley, 1988; Yen, 1989; Zarley et al., 1988) based on the theory or extended versions of the theory (Laskey and Lehner, 1989; Yen, 1989). In this paper we argue that it is difficult to represent uncertain heuristic knowledge in this theory; however, in most complex domains heuristic knowledge plays an important role in solving problems.

Consider the following piece of heuristic knowledge: if X is X_1, then Y is Y_1 with a degree of belief r_1. If we get a piece of evidence which says that X is X_1 with a degree of a_1, by invoking this rule we should be able to obtain the corresponding degree y_1 for Y is Y_1. Certainly the value of y_1 must be a function F of a_1 and r_1 (i.e., $y_1 = F(a_1, r_1)$).

More generally, we suppose that a set of heuristic rules R includes:

R_1: if E_1 then H_1^1 with a degree of belief $r_{1,1}$;
H_1^2 with a degree of belief $r_{1,2}$;

...

$$
\begin{aligned}
&R_2\text{: if } E_2 \text{ then } H_2^1 \text{ with a degree of belief } r_{2,1};\\
&\qquad\qquad\quad H_2^2 \text{ with a degree of belief } r_{2,2};\\
&\qquad\qquad\quad \ldots\\
&\ldots \qquad\qquad\qquad\qquad\qquad\qquad\qquad\qquad\qquad (1)\\
&R_n\text{: if } E_n \text{ then } H_{n1} \text{ with a degree of belief } r_{n1};\\
&\qquad\qquad\quad H_{n2} \text{ with a degree of belief } r_{n2};\\
&\qquad\qquad\quad \ldots
\end{aligned}
$$

where $E_1, E_2, ..., E_n$ are values (or propostions) of the variable E, and E_i is called an antecedent of rule R_i. H_{ij} in rule R_i is a subset of the values (or propositions) of the variable H and it is called one of the conclusions of rule R_i. r_{ij} is called a rule strength.

Assume we have a piece of evidence which says that E_1 is confirmed with a_1; E_2 is confirmed with a_2, ..., E_n is confirmed with a_n; how can we solve the following problems:

1. What conditions should $\Sigma_i a_i$ satisfy?
2. What conditions should $\Sigma_j r_{ij}$ satisfy?
3. What is the function F to determine h_{ij} (the degree of belief on H_{ij}) from those a_i and r_{ij}?
4. If more than one set of rules is invoked and the same conclusion H_{ij} is obtained, what will be the final degree of belief on H_{ij} from those $h_{ij}, ..., h_{kl}$?

Generally, if the variable E is the Cartesian product of variables A, B, ..., C, that is, each E_i is in a form of (A_i and B_j and... and C_k), assuming we know the evidence for A, B, ..., C, then:

5. What is the function F' to determine the degree of belief on the premise (A_i and B_j and ... and C_k)?

These problems have been modeled in fuzzy theory using a fuzzy extension of modal logic, based on Zadeh's concepts of necessity and possibility (Prade, 1981). They were also solved in Mycin's certainty factor model (Shortliffe and Buchanan, 1976). Can these problems be solved in Dempster-Shafer's theory?

In this paper we analyze these problems and propose our approaches for solving them by extending the theory of evidence. The paper is organized as follows. In section 2 the basics of Dempster-Shafer's theory are introduced and the approach for representing heuristic knowledge by evidential mappings is described in which a matrix is used to represent the uncertain relationships between evidence and conclusion. In section 3 the relations between Bayesian inference and evidential mappings are examined in which it is proved that the multivalued causal links between hypothesis space H and evidence space E (Pearl, 1988) in Bayesian theory is consistent with the special case of evidential mappings. In section 4 the method of constructing a complete evidential mapping matrix for an evidential mapping of a heuristic rule is discussed. In section 5 belief propagation approaches are discussed for different situations. Finally a conclusion is given along with some consideration of related work.

2. REPRESENTING HEURISTIC KNOWLEDGE IN THE DEMPSTER-SHAFER THEORY

The Dempster-Shafer theory of evidence, which is also called the theory of belief functions (Smets, 1988; Shafer, 1990) provides an alternative approach to drawing plausible conclusions from uncertain and incomplete evidence. It is a generalization of the Bayesian theory of sujective probability, it is more flexible, and it allows us to derive degrees of belief for a question from probabilities of a related question (Shafer, 1990).

2.1. The basics of Dempster-Shafer's theory of evidence

Suppose Θ is a finite set that consists of mutually exclusive and exhaustive propositions of a problem or all values of a variable, 2^Θ is the set of all subsets of Θ. A function *Bel*: $2^\Theta \rightarrow [0,1]$ is called a belief function in Shafer (1976), if it satisfies the following conditions:

1. $Bel(\emptyset)=0$;
2. $Bel(\Theta)=1$;
3. For every positive integer n and every collection $A_1, ..., A_n$ of subsets of Θ,

$$Bel(A_1 \cup \ldots \cup A_n) \geqslant \Sigma_i Bel(A_i) - \Sigma_{i<j} Bel(A_i \cap A_j) +/- \ldots + (-1)^{n+1} Bel(A_1 \cap \ldots \cap A_n)$$

Such a set Θ is called a *frame of discernment*.

By knowing a belief function on a frame of discernment, another function m can be calculated as:

$$m(A) = \Sigma_{B \subseteq A}(-1)^{|A-B|}Bel(B) \text{ for all } A \subseteq \Theta$$

where $|A-B|$ denotes the number of elements in the set of $A-B$.

The function m is called a *basic probability assignment* (*bpa*) or a *mass function*. Obviously a mass function has the features that $m(\emptyset) = 0$ and $\Sigma m(A) = 1$ for all subsets A of Θ. A subset A is called a focal element of the belief function *Bel* if $m(A) > 0$. Recovering the belief function *Bel* from a mass function m is carried out by

$$Bel(B) = \Sigma_{A \subseteq B} m(A)$$

If all the focal elements of a belief function are singletons of Θ, then the corresponding mass function m is a Bayesian subjective probability distribution.

A belief function (or a mass function) on a frame Θ can either be directly obtained from a piece of evidence or calculated from a probability measure P on the related frame T by a multivalued mapping Γ between T and Θ. The term multivalued mapping was originally introduced by Dempster in his early article (Dempster, 1967) in which he defined that a multivalued mapping Γ assigns each element t of T to a subset A of Θ. Suppose we get a probability measure P on frame T; two other functions on frame Θ will be obtained by a multivalued mapping Γ as:

$$m(A) = \sum_{\Gamma(t) = A} P(t) \quad t \in T, A \subseteq \Theta$$

$$Bel(A) = \sum_{\Gamma(t) \subseteq A} P(t) \quad t \in T, A \subseteq \Theta$$

where $P(t)$ is the probability distributed on t by P and $\Sigma_i P(t_i) = 1$. Here we suppose that no element t of T maps to the empty set in Θ. It is easy to prove that m is a mass function and *Bel* is a belief function on Θ. Another name for multivalued mappings is compatibility relations, which is used in Shafer (1987), Lowrance et al. (1986), and Shafer and Srivastava (1990).

The impact of several belief functions (or mass functions) on the same frame of discernment is obtained by using Dempster's rule of combination, which treats Bayesian conditioning probabilities as a special case (Shafer, 1976). Dempster's rule of combining two belief functions Bel_1 and Bel_2 can be defined by a relatively simple rule in terms of the corresponding mass functions m_1 and m_2:

$$m(C) = \frac{\Sigma_{A \cap B = C} m_1(A) m_2(B)}{1 - \Sigma_{A \cap B = \varphi} m_1(A) m_2(B)}$$

This rule requires that the combined belief functions (or their mass functions) are independent. This condition has been further enhanced as *DS-independent* in Voorbraak (1991).

2.2. Representing heuristic knowledge in the Dempster-Shafer theory

It is obvious that a heuristic rule like {if X is X_1 then Y is Y_1, with a degree of belief r_1} cannot be directly represented in DS theory. Some work concerning this topic was carried out previously (Ginsberg, 1984; Yen, 1989; Liu, 1986; Hau and Kashyap, 1990). We propose that evidential mappings defined on the basis of mass functions can be used to represent the uncertain relationships between evidence and conclusions.

Definition 1. *An evidential mapping is the mapping from one frame of discernment to another, which represents causal links among elements of two frames of discernment in the form of mass functions. Formally an evidential mapping from frame* Θ_E *to frame* Θ_H *is a function* Γ^*: $\Theta_E \rightarrow 2^{2^{\Theta_H} \times [0,1]}$. *The image of each element in* Θ_E, *denoted by* $\Gamma^*(e_i)$, *is a collection of subset-mass pairs:*

$$\Gamma^*(e_i) = \{(H_{i1}, f(e_i \rightarrow H_{i1})), \ldots, (H_{im}, f(e_i \rightarrow H_{im}))\}$$

and let $\Theta_i = \cup_{j=1}^{m} H_{ij}$ $H_{ij} \subseteq \Theta_H$ *that satisfies the following conditions:*

$$(a)\ H_{ij} \neq \emptyset \qquad j = 1, \ldots, m$$
$$(b)\ f(e_i \rightarrow H_{ij}) > 0 \qquad j = 1, \ldots, m$$
$$(c) \Sigma_j (e_i \rightarrow H_{ij}) = 1$$

There is a set of heuristic rules, denoted as R, related to an evidential mapping, each of which is in the form of

$$R_i: e_i \rightarrow H_{i1(f(e_i \rightarrow H_{ij}))};$$
$$\ldots;$$
$$e_i \rightarrow H_{im(f(e_i \rightarrow H_{im}))}.$$

where $f(e_i \rightarrow H_{ij})$ represents our belief exactly on H_{ij} given condition e_i, and it is in the range of [0,1].

A rule states that if e_i is true then the truth of the problem carried by Θ_H is in H_{i1} with the degree of belief $f(e_i \rightarrow H_{i1})$ exactly committed to $H_{i1}, \ldots$, in H_{im} with the degree of belief $f(e_i \rightarrow H_{im})$ exactly committed to H_{im}. The e_i is called the antecedent of rule R_i and it is an element of Θ_E.

H_{ij} is called one of the conclusions of rule R_i, and it is a subset of Θ_H. We name Θ_E and Θ_H as antecedent frame and conclusion frame of R respectively.

$$\begin{array}{c} row/col \\ \{e_1\} \\ \{e_2\} \\ \\ \{e_n\} \end{array} \begin{array}{c} \begin{array}{cccc} H_1 & H_2 & \dots & \Theta \end{array} \\ \left[\begin{array}{cccc} m_{11} & m_{12} & \dots & m_{1l} \\ m_{21} & m_{22} & \dots & m_{2l} \\ & \dots & & \\ m_{n1} & m_{n2} & \dots & m_{nl} \end{array}\right] \end{array} = M$$

The size of matrix M is $n \times l$ where n is the number of elements in Θ_E and l equals $|2^{\Theta_H}|-1$ (except $\emptyset$). H_i is a subset of the elements of Θ_H. For any H_{ij} appearing in $(H_{ij}, f(e_i \rightarrow H_{ij}))$ there is H_k where $H_k = H_{ij}$. The (i, k)-th entry of M is defined as m_{ik} which equals $f(e_i \rightarrow H_{ij}))$ if the pair $(H_{ij}, f(e_i \rightarrow H_{ij}))$ is an element of $\Gamma^*(e_i)$ and $H_k = H_{ij}$; otherwise m_{ik} equals 0. Thus those $m_{i1}, m_{i2}, \dots, m_{il}$ of line i must satisfy the condition $\Sigma_j m_{ij} = 1$. More precisely based on $m_{i1}, m_{i2}, \dots, m_{il}$, we define a function m_i. In fact m_i is a mass function on $\Theta_E \times \Theta_H$, with its focal elements as $A_{i1} = \{(x,y) \mid x \in \neg \{e_i\}$ or $y \in H_{i1}\}, \dots, A_{im} = \{(x,y) \mid x \in \neg \{e_i\}$ or $y \in H_{im}\}$ and $m_i(A_{ij}) = m_{ij}$ for $j = 1, \dots, l$. So there are in total n mass functions on frame $\Theta_E \times \Theta_H$. But we define that the combination of any two of the above mass functions is meaningless.

In order to identify each row and column in m we call H_k the *title of column k*, $\{e_i\}$ the *title of row i*. We also call $[\{e_1\}, \{e_2\}, \dots, \{e_n\}]$ and $[H_1, H_2, \dots, \Theta]$ the *row title vector* and *column title vector* of M respectively. When we mention a matrix M of an evidential mapping, we assume the row title vector and the column title vector are known. Thus for any given evidential mapping the related heuristic rule set and the matrix are unique.

An evidential mapping from Θ_E to Θ_H states that for two related questions represented by Θ_E and Θ_H, if the truth for the question represented by Θ_E is e_i then the truth for the question represented by Θ_H is in a set Θ_i, but e_i has different interrelationships with different subsets of Θ_i. The $f(e_i \rightarrow H_{ij}))$ is used to reflect the sensitivity or strength of interrelation between e_i and H_{ij}. Certainly the total strength should be 1.

Example 1. If an evidential mapping Γ^* specifies a mapping from an evidence space Θ_E to a hypothesis space Θ_H as:

$$\Gamma^*(e_1) = \{(\{a_1, a_2\}, 0.7, (\{a_3, a_4\}, 0.3)\}$$
$$\Gamma^*(e_2) = \{(\{a_2, a_3\}, 0.8), (\Theta_H, 0.2)\}$$
$$\Gamma^*(e_3) = \{(\{a_4, a_5\}, 0.9, (\Theta_H, 0.1)\}$$

and a related set of heuristic rules is

$$\text{R: } e_1 \to \{a_1,a_2\}_{(0.7)}; \quad e_1 \to \{a_3,a_4\}_{(0.3)}.$$
$$e_2 \to \{a_2,a_3\}_{(0.8)}; \quad e_2 \to \Theta_{H(0.2)}.$$
$$e_3 \to \{a_4,a_5\}_{(0.9)}; \quad e_3 \to \Theta_{H(0.1)}.$$

where $\Theta_E=\{e_1,e_2,e_3\}$ and $\Theta_H=\{a_1,a_2,a_3,a_4,a_5\}$, then the matrix M has 2^5-1 columns, most of which have only zero m_{ij} such as columns $\{a_1\}$, $\{a_1,a_2,a_3\}$. Usually a matrix becomes too big when Θ_H contains several elements. So we delete all those columns that have only zero m_{ij} and form another matrix. We call such a simplified matrix the *basic matrix* and denote it as BM. Thus the title vector of a basic matrix of an evidential mapping only contains those H_{ij} which appear in $\Gamma^*(e_i)$. The BM of this evidential mapping in the above example is

$$\begin{array}{c} row/col \\ \{e_1\} \\ \{e_2\} \\ \{e_3\} \end{array} \begin{array}{c} \begin{array}{ccccc} \{a_1,a_2\} & \{a_2,a_3\} & \{a_3,a_4\} & \{a_4,a_5\} & \Theta_H \end{array} \\ \begin{bmatrix} 0.7 & 0.0 & 0.3 & 0.0 & 0.0 \\ 0.0 & 0.8 & 0.0 & 0.0 & 0.2 \\ 0.0 & 0.0 & 0.0 & 0.9 & 0.1 \end{bmatrix} \end{array} = BM$$

with row title vector $[\{e_1\},\{e_2\},\{e_3\}]$ and column title vector $[\{a_1, a_2\}, \{a_2, a_3\}, \{a_3, a_4\}, \{a_4, a_5\}, \Theta_H]$.

Obviously, multivalued mappings in section 2.1 and Bayesian multivalued causal link models (Pearl, 1988) can all be represented using such evidential mappings.

Corollary 1. *If all the m_{ij} in a basic matrix BM of an evidential mapping from Θ_E to Θ_H are either 1 or 0 then the evidential mapping is a multivalued mapping. For any e_i, the mass function m_i on $\Theta_E \times \Theta_H$ is a simple support function with a focal element $A_{ij}(A_{ij}=\{(x,y)\,|\,x\in\neg\{e_i\} \text{ or } y\in H_{ij}\})$, and $m_i(A_{ij})=1$.*

Corollary 2. *If a basic matrix BM has $|\Theta_H|$ columns, and the titles of all columns are singletons of Θ_H then the evidential mapping from Θ_E to Θ_H of this matrix is exactly a Bayesian multivalued causal link model. For any e_i, the mass function m_i on $\Theta_E \times \Theta_H$ is a Bayesian probability distribution. We refer to this kind of evidential mapping as a Bayesian evidential mapping.*

If a piece of evidence gives a probability distribution P on Θ_E, then a new function m on Θ_H can be calculated by the evidential mapping from Θ_E to Θ_H:

$$m(H_k)=\begin{cases}\Sigma_i P(e_i)\times m_{ik}=\Sigma_i P(e_i)\times f(e_i\rightarrow H_k)H_k & \text{is the title of a column}\\ 0 & \text{otherwise}\end{cases} \quad (2)$$

The function m is a basic probability assignment in the hypothesis space and has the following features:

1. $m(\emptyset)=0$
2. $\Sigma_k m(H_k)=1$ where $H_k \subseteq \Theta$

This can be proved by the following according to definition 1, probability distribution P and features of a mass function

$$\begin{aligned}\Sigma_k m(H_k) &= \Sigma_k\Sigma_i P(e_i)\times f(e_i\rightarrow H_k)\\ &= \Sigma_i\Sigma_k P(e_i)\times f(e_i\rightarrow H_k)\\ &= (\Sigma_i P(e_i))(\Sigma_k f(e_i\rightarrow H_k))\\ &= (\Sigma_i P(e_i))(\Sigma_j f(e_i\rightarrow H_k)) \quad \text{(because there exists an}\\ &= 1\times 1=1 \qquad H_{ij} \text{ such that } H_k=H_{ij})\end{aligned}$$

Corollary 3. *A function m is a mass function on frame Θ_H if it is given by formula 2 under the condition that P is a probability distribution on space Θ_E and Γ^* is an evidential mapping from Θ_E to Θ_H.*

The theoretical support of formula (2) is Bayes' formula

$$P(A)=\sum_i P(A\mid B_i)P(B_i)$$

where B_i is an element of an exhaustive and mutually exclusive event set (Pearl, 1988).

We suppose that any evidence e giving $P(B_i/e)$ has no effect on $P(A\mid B_i)$. This rule is also called Jeffrey's rule of conditioning (Jeffrey, 1965; Shafer, 1981).

2.3. Creating evidential mappings for incomplete heuristic rule sets

We have seen in the above section that an evidential mapping can be associated with a set of heuristic rules. The other way around, given a set of heuristic rules in the form of (1), if all the antecedents of rules can form a frame of discernment Θ_E, all the conclusions of rules can form another frame of discernment Θ_H, and for any heuristic rule R_i the sum of r_{ij}(for $j=1, ..., m$) is 1, then an evidential mapping can be established between Θ_E and Θ_H. Unfortunately, the antecedents (or conclusions) of a set of rules normally cannot form a frame of discernment that is mutually exclusive and exhaustive and usually the sum of r_{ij} for rule R_i is less than 1. For example, if there is only one rule in a set of heuristic rules: if X is X_1 then Y is Y_1 with a degree of belief r_1, then the antecedent (X is X_1) itself does not form a frame of discernment at all; nor does the conclusion (Y is Y_1).

Definition 2. *If at least one of the antecedent frame and conclusion frame of a heuristic rule set R is not a frame of discernment or there is a rule R_1 in rule set R where $\Sigma_j r_{ij} < 1$, then we define such a heuristic rule set as an incomplete heuristic rule set. Otherwise we call it a complete heuristic rule set.*

Corollary 4. *Given an incomplete heuristic rule set R, let $E=\{e_1, ..., e_n\}$ represent the antecedent set, and $H=\{h_1, ..., h_m\}$ represent the conclusion set of R:*

1. *If E is not a frame of discernment then define $e_{n+1} = \neg(e_1 \vee ... \vee e_n)$ and $\Theta_E = \{e_{n+1}\} \cup E$; otherwise define $\Theta_E = E$.*
2. *If H is not a frame of discernment then define $h_{m+1} = \neg(h_1 \vee ... \vee h_m)$ and $\Theta_H = \{h_{m+1}\} \cup H$; otherwise define $\Theta_H = H$.*
3. *If e_{n+1} exist then add the rule $R_{n+1}: (e_{n+1} \to \Theta_{H(1)})$ to rule set R.*

Then Θ_E and Θ_H are two frames of discernment representing the antecedent frame and the conclusion frame of R, respectively.

Corollary 5. *For each rule R_i in R, if $\Sigma_j r_{ij} < 1$ then we add an extra conclusion Θ_H with belief $r_{ik} = (1 - \Sigma_j r_{ij})$ to R_i. That is, if the original R_i is*

$$R_i: e_i \to H_{i1(r_{i1})}; ...; e_i \to H_{im(r_{im})} \quad \text{where } \Sigma_j r_{ij} < 1$$

then a new R_i' is

$$R'_i: e_i \to H_{i1(r_{i1})}; ...; e_i \to H_{im(r_{im})};\ e_i \to \Theta_{H(r_{ih})} \quad \text{where } r_{ih} = 1 - \Sigma_j r_{ij}.$$

Now the heuristic rule set R is complete and an evidential mapping from Θ_E to Θ_H can be created.

In fact, the added part of a rule represents our ignorance. In other words, based on the current knowledge of a specific domain, we have no knowledge to identify any more ad-hoc realionships among elements of reasons and results.

Example 2. Suppose we have a rule set R, which consists of a rule as follows:

Smoke alarm is ringing $\rightarrow$ There is a $\text{fire}_{(0.9)}$.

We construct $\Theta_E = \{$smoke alarm is ringing), not (smoke alarm is ringing)$\}$, $\Theta_H = \{$(there is a fire), not (there is a fire)$\}$ based on corollary 4, and a new rule set R' based on corollary 5,

R' has: R_1: Smoke alarm is ringing $\rightarrow$ There is a $\text{fire}_{(0.9)}$;
Smoke alarm is ringing $\rightarrow$ $\Theta_{H_{(0.1)}}$.
R_2: Not (Smoke alarm is ringing) $\rightarrow$ $\Theta_{H_{(1)}}$.

This rule set can be associated with an evidential mapping from Θ_E to Θ_H. In particular, if Θ_H is the same as Θ_E then the corresponding evidential mapping represents self-relations of Θ_E (it is also called delta-Θ_E compatibility relation by Lowrance et al., 1986).

Now we can represent any heuristic rule set (either complete or incomplete) in the Dempster-Shafer theory of evidence by the means of evidential mappings. In the following we simply use a triple (R, Θ_E, Θ_H) to represent an evidential mapping where R is a heuristic rule set, Θ_E is the antecedent frame of discernment of R, and Θ_H is the conclusion frame of discernment of R.

3. THE RELATION BETWEEN EVIDENTIAL MAPPINGS AND BAYESIAN CONDITIONAL PROBABILITIES

The Dempster-Shafer theory of evidence as a generalization of Bayesian inference includes two meanings: mass functions are the general form of Bayesian subjective probabilities in representing evidence; Bayesian conditional probabilities are a special case of Dempster's rule of combination (Shafer, 1976). Pearl (1988) gave a general formula to calculate posterior probabilities (on hypotheses) or predict future events in multivalued causal link models of Bayesian theory when a set of evidence (for evidence variable) is given. In fact, Pearl's work is the extension of traditional Bayesian inference theory to the situation when the relationships among elements of an evidence space and a hypothesis space are multivalued causal mappings. In this section we prove that Bayesian inference performed on multivalued causal link models can be carried out in the DS theory by using evidential mappings.

3.1. Predicting future events in DS theory

Example 3. Let S be a variable for "alarm sound" and D for "a person's call." If we use the same capital letter to represent both a variable name and the name of the frame that includes all the values of the variable, we have $S=\{alarm\ on, alarm\ off\}$ and $D=\{a\ person\ will\ call, a\ person\ will\ not\ call\}$, each of which represents an exhaustive and mutually exclusive set of propositions. Suppose the causal link between S and D is

S/D	*will call*	*will not call*
alarm on	0.7	0.3
alarm off	0.0	1.0

Bayesian inference produces

$$P(d_i)=\Sigma_j P(d_i \mid s_j)P(s_j) \tag{3}$$

which is a shorthand notation for the statement

$$P(d_i \mid e)=\sum_j P(d_i \mid s_j,e)P(s_j \mid e)$$

where d_i is an element of D and s_j is an element of S and we assume that a piece of evidence has no effect on the causal link between S and D. Given a probability distribution of a piece of evidence on S, the probabilities on D can be calculated from formula (3):

Suppose $P(s_1=on)=0.2686$, $P(s_2=off)=0.7314$, then

$$P(d_1=will\ call)=\sum_j P(d_1 \mid s_j)P(s_j)=[0.2686, 0.7314]\times \times \begin{bmatrix}0.7\\0.0\end{bmatrix}=0.188 \tag{4}$$

This is called *predicting future events* by Pearl in Bayesian inference.

Obviously the causal link above forms an evidential mapping from S to D in Dempster-Shafer theory. In the condition of prior probabilities $P(s_1=on)=0.2682$, $P(s_2=off)=0.7314$, applying formula (2) wet get a mass function on D which is the same as that shown in formula (4):

$$m(d_1)=\sum_i P(s_i)\times f(s_i\rightarrow\{d_i\})=0.2686\times 0.7+0.7314\times 0.0=0.188$$

$$m(d_2)=\sum_i P(s_i)\times f(s_i\rightarrow\{d_2\})=0.2686\times 0.3+0.7314\times 1.0=0.812$$

In Bayesian multivalued causal link models, the causal link between the hypothesis space H and the evidence space E is identified by an $n \times m$ matrix M, where n and m are the numbers of values of H and E respectively, and the (i,j)-th entry of M is $M_{ij} = P(e_j \mid h_i)$ (Pearl, 1988).

It is easy to see (corollary 3) that the causal link model above is consistent with the special case of evidential mappings. The mass function on D obtained from formula (2) is exactly the same as the probability distribution on D obtained in Bayesian inference.

3.2. Calculating posterior probabilities in DS theory

Furthermore, in Bayesian multivalued causal link models, given a prior probability distribution on hypothesis space H, causal link matrix M with $M_{ij} = P(e_j \mid h_i)$

$$\begin{array}{c} \\ \{h_1\} \\ \{h_2\} \\ \\ \{h_n\} \end{array} \begin{array}{c} \begin{array}{cccc} \{e_1\} & \{e_2\} & \cdots & \{e_m\} \end{array} \\ \begin{bmatrix} p(e_1 \mid h_1) & p(e_2 \mid h_1) & \cdots & p(e_m \mid h_1) \\ p(e_1 \mid h_2) & p(e_2 \mid h_2) & \cdots & p(e_m \mid h_2) \\ & \cdots & & \\ p(e_1 \mid h_n) & p(e_2 \mid h_n) & \cdots & p(e_m \mid h_n) \end{bmatrix} \end{array} = M$$

and a set of evidence $e^1, e^2, \ldots, e^N$ on evidence space E, then posterior-probability $P(h_i \mid e^1, e^2, \ldots, e^N)$ on h_i of H is:

$$P(h_i \mid e^1, e^2, \ldots, e^N) = \alpha P(e^1, e^2, \ldots, e^N \mid h_i) P(h_i) \tag{5}$$

where $\alpha = [P(e^1, e^2, \ldots, e^N)]^{-1}$ is a normalizing constant to be computed by requiring that (5) sum to unity. Assuming $e^1, e^2, \ldots, e^N$ are independent with each other and conditional independence of respect to each h_i, Pearl (1988) indicated that,

$$P(h_i \mid e^1, e^2, \ldots, e^N) = \alpha P(h_i) [\Pi_{k=1}^{N} P(e^k \mid h_i)] \tag{6}$$

Here we should make it clear that Pearl assumes that for each piece of evidence e^k there exists an element e_j in E where $p(e_j) = 1$ given by e^k so that $P(e^k \mid h_i) = P(e_j \mid h_i)$.

Can these posterior probabilities be calculated in DS theory using evidential mappings based on the above causal link matrix under these assumptions? The following theorem indicates that they can.

Theorem 1. *Let E and H be two frames of discernment, Γ^* be a Bayesian evidential mapping from H to E, BM be the basic matrix of* *the mapping* Γ^* *with (i,j)-th entry as* $p(e_j|h_i)$. *Assume the prior probability on* h_i *of H is* $p(h_i)$, *a set of evidence on E is* $e^1, e^2, \ldots, e^N$ *for each of which there exists an* e_l *where* $p(e_l)=1$. *Then the final belief function Bel on H using DS theory is*

$$Bel(h_i) = \alpha p(h_i)[\Pi_{k=1}^{N} p(e^k|h_i)]$$

where $\alpha = (\sum_{1}^{n}(p(h_i)[\Pi_{k=1}^{N} p(e^k|h_i)]))^{-1}$, and $p(e^k|h_i) = p(e_l|h_i)$ for each k when the evidence e^k makes $p(e_l)=1$.

The theorem can be proved by the following steps. (The mathematical proof is given in Appendix A.)

Step 1: Form an evidential mapping from a frame of discernment H to a frame of discernment E; the corresponding basic matrix BM is M in the Bayesian multivalued causal link model and m_{ij} in BM is $P(e_j|h_i)$. The titles of rows from 1 to n are $\{h_1\}, \ldots, \{h_n\}$, and the titles of columns from 1 to m are $\{e_1\}, \ldots, \{e_m\}$.

Step 2: A prior probability $p(h_i)$ is transformed into a basic probability assignment $m_0(h_i) = p(h_i)$ on H.

Step 3: Construct an evidential mapping from E to H through the evidential mapping from H to E; the corresponding basic matrix is BM′ with $(j, i)'$-th entry as

$$p'(h_i|e_j) = \frac{p(e_j|h_i)}{\Sigma_{i=1}^{N} p(e_j|h_i)} \tag{7}$$

and the titles of rows from 1 to m are $\{e_1\}, \ldots, \{e_m\}$, and the titles of columns from 1 to n are $\{h_1\}, \ldots, \{h_n\}$.

Step 4: For each probability distribution p_k on E provided by a piece of evidence e^k, calculate k-th mass function m_k on H using (2).

Step 5: Obtain the final belief function by using Dempster's combination rule to combine all those basic probability assignments because of independence of evidence.

Example 4 (from Pearl, 1988, p. 39).Let a hypothesis space have four propositions $H = \{h_1, h_2, h_3, h_4\}$ and an evidence space have three propositions $E = \{e_1, e_2, e_3\}$. The causal link matrix between H and E is

$$\begin{array}{c} \\ \{h_1\} \\ \{h_2\} \\ \{h_3\} \\ \{h_4\} \end{array} \begin{array}{c} \begin{array}{ccc} \{e_1\} & \{e_2\} & \{e_3\} \end{array} \\ \left[\begin{array}{ccc} 0.5 & 0.4 & 0.1 \\ 0.06 & 0.5 & 0.44 \\ 0.5 & 0.1 & 0.4 \\ 1{,}0 & 0.0 & 0.0 \end{array}\right] \end{array} = BM$$

Assume prior probabilities for the hypotheses in H are a vector $p(h_i)=[0.099\ 0.009\ 0.001\ 0.891]$, two pieces of evidence are e^1 providing $P(e_3)=1$, and e^2 providing $P(e_1)=1$.

* In Bayesian inference, applying formula (6), the posterior probabilities are

$$P(h_1|e^1,e^2)=0.919, \quad P(h_2|e^1,e^2)=0.0439,$$
$$P(h_3|e^1,e^2)=0.0375, \quad P(h_4|e^1,e^2)=0.0$$

* Now we use evidential mappings in DS theory to analyze the example again. Given the above causal link matrix we can form a set of heuristic rules with its evidential mapping as:

R:
$$h_1 \to e_1(0.5); h_1 \to e_2(0.4); h_1 \to e_3(0.1).$$
$$h_1 \to e_1(0.06); h_1 \to e_2(0.5); h_1 \to e_3(0.44).$$
$$h_1 \to e_1(0.5); h_1 \to e_2(0.1); h_1 \to e_3(0.4).$$
$$h_1 \to e_1(1.0); h_1 \to e_2(0.0); h_1 \to e_3(0.0).$$

Γ^*:
$$\Gamma^*(h_1)=\{(\{e_1\},0.5),(\{e_2\},0.4),(\{e_3\},0.1)\}$$
$$\Gamma^*(h_2)=\{(\{e_1\},0.06),(\{e_2\},0.5),(\{e_3\},0.44)\}$$
$$\Gamma^*(h_3)=\{(\{e_1\},0.5),(\{e_2\},0.1),(\{e_3\},0.4)\}$$
$$\Gamma^*(h_4)=\{(\{e_1\},1.0),(\{e_2\},0.0),(\{e_3\},0.0)\}$$

Based on this evidential mapping to construct another evidential mapping from E to H using formula (7), we get

$$\Gamma'^*(e_1)=\{(\{h_1\},50/206),(\{h_2\},6/206),(\{h_3\},50/206),(\{h_4\},100/206)\}$$
$$\Gamma'^*(e_2)=\{(\{h_1\},0.4),(\{h_2\},0.5),(\{h_3\},0.1),(\{h_4\},0.0)\}$$
$$\Gamma'^*(e_3)=\{(\{h_1\},10/94),(\{h_2\},44/94),(\{h_3\},40/94),(\{h_4\},0.0)\}$$

and

$$\begin{array}{c} \\ \{e_1\} \\ \{e_2\} \\ \{e_3\} \end{array} \begin{array}{c} \begin{array}{cccc} \{h_1\} & \{h_2\} & \{h_3\} & \{h_4\} \end{array} \\ \begin{bmatrix} 50/206 & 6/206 & 50/206 & 100/206 \\ 0.4 & 0.5 & 0.1 & 0.0 \\ 10/94 & 44/94 & 40/94 & 0.0 \end{bmatrix} \end{array} = BM'$$

Based on the prior probability distributions on H, the first mass function on H is obtained as:

$$m_0(h_1)=0.099;\ m_0(h_2)=0.009;\ m_0(h_3)=0.001;\ m_0(h_4)=0.891$$

According to two pieces of evidence on E, the evidential mapping from E to H, and corollary 1, w get another two mass functions:

$$m_1(h_1)=P(e_3)\times f(e_3\rightarrow\{h_1\})=1\times 10/94=10/94$$
$$m_1(h_2)=P(e_3)\times f(e_3\rightarrow\{h_2\})=1\times 44/94=44/94$$
$$m_1(h_3)=P(e_3)\times f(e_3\rightarrow\{h_3\})=1\times 40/94=40/94$$
$$m_1(h_4)=P(e_3)\times f(e_3\rightarrow\{h_4\})=1\times 0.0=0.0$$

and

$$m_2(h_1)=P(e_1)\times f(e_1\rightarrow\{h_1\})=1\times 50/206=50/206$$
$$m_2(h_2)=P(e_1)\times f(e_1\rightarrow\{h_2\})=1\times 6/206=6/206$$
$$m_2(h_3)=P(e_1)\times f(e_1\rightarrow\{h_3\})=1\times 50/206=50/206$$
$$m_2(h_4)=P(e_1)\times f(e_1\rightarrow\{h_4\})=1\times 100/206=100/206$$

Combining these three mass functions using Dempster's rule of combination we eventually get $m(h_i)=m_0\oplus m_1\oplus m_2(h_i)$, that is,

$$m(h_1)=0.099\times 0.1\times 0.5\alpha=\alpha P(h_1)[\Pi_{k=1,2}P(e^k\,|\,h_1)]$$
$$m(h_2)=0.009\times 0.44\times 0.06\alpha=\alpha P(h_2)[\Pi_{k=1,2}P(e^k\,|\,h_2)]$$
$$m(h_3)=0.001\times 0.4\times 0.5\alpha=\alpha P(h_3)[\Pi_{k=1,2}P(e^k\,|\,h_3)]$$
$$m(h_4)=0.891\times 0.0\times 1.0\alpha=\alpha P(h_4)[\Pi_{k=1,2}P(e^k\,|\,h_4)]$$

where α is $(0.099\times 0.1\times 0.5+0.009\times 0.44\times 0.06+0.001\times 0.4\times 0.5+0)^{-1}$. The result of DS theory is exactly the same as what we get in Bayesian inference.

4. CONSTRUCTING COMPLETE EVIDENTIAL MAPPING MATRICES TO PROPAGATE MASS FUNCTIONS FROM AN EVIDENCE SPACE Θ_E TO A HYPOTHESIS SPACE Θ_H

In Dempster-Shafer theory a multivalued mapping is used to calculate a mass function on a frame based on either a probability distribution or a mass function on another frame (Lowrance et al., 1986; Zarley, 1988; Laskey et al., 1989). What we have assumed in the previous two sections is that a piece of evidence on an evidence space (a frame of discernment Θ_E) is represented in the form of Bayesian subjective probabilities. A mass function on Θ_H will be obtained based on the probability distribution on Θ_E through an evidential mapping from Θ_E to Θ_H.

In section 2, we gave the definition of evidential mappings. Let Θ_E and Θ_H be two frames of discernment, Γ^* be an evidential mapping from Θ_E to Θ_H. Assuming a piece of evidence indicates that $m(E)=p$, $m(\Theta_E)=1-p$, E is a subset of Θ_E, what is the impact of the evidence on Θ_H? Obviously the impact of the evidence on Θ_H is easily obtained if Γ^* is a multivalued mapping. But it is not so easy when Γ^* is an evidential mapping.

In this section, we introduce the approach to constructing complete evidential mapping matrices between two frames. A complete evidential mapping matrix between two frames allows the propagation of a mass function from one frame to another.

Definition 3. *If Γ^* is an evidential mapping from Θ_E to Θ_H BM is the basic matrix of Γ^* with m_{ij} as its (i,j)-th entry, the titles of rows of BM are $\{e_1\}$, ..., $\{e_n\} \subseteq \Theta_E$, the titles of columns of BM are A_1, ..., $A_m \subseteq \Theta_H$, then a matrix is called a complete evidential mapping matrix of BM, denoted as CEM, if it is defined as:*

1. *All the subsets of Θ_E except Ø are titles of rows of CEM and $\{e_1\}$, ..., $\{e_n\}$ are first n row titles; A_1, ..., A_m are the titles of the first m columns of CEM.*
2. *The m_{ij} of BM is the value of (i,j)-th entry of CEM and denoted as m'_{ij}.*
3. *For a row l with the title E, and $l>n$, suppose $E=\{e_{l_1}, e_{l_2}...,$ $e_{l_k}\}$, then (l,j)-th entry of CEM is*

$$m_{l_j} = \begin{cases} (m_{l_{1j}}+m_{l_{2j}}+...+m_{l_{kj}})/k & \text{if } m_{l_{ij}} \neq 0 \text{ for } i=1, ...k \\ 0 & \text{otherwise} \end{cases}$$

4. *For $m_{l_j}=0$, create a column r with the title A_r; let $A_r=\cup_i\Theta_i$ for $i=l_1$, ..., l_k. (for Θ_i see definition 1 in 2.2). If A_r is not an element of column title vector, then add A_r as an column title and the value of (l,r)-th entry is $m_{l_r}=(m_{l_{1j}}+m_{l_{2j}}+...$ $+m_{l_{kj}})/k$. Otherwise there is a column r' satisfying $A_{r'}=A_r$ and we update $m_{l_{r'}}$ as $m_{l_{r'}}+(m_{l_{1j}}+m_{l_{2j}}+...+m_{l_{kj}})/k$.*
5. *For any other entry (x,y), define $m_{xy}=0$.*

Obviously we have the inequality

$$\begin{aligned} max(m_{l_{1j}}, m_{l_{2j}}...m_{l_{kj}}) &\geq (m_{l_{1j}}+m_{l_{2j}}+...+m_{l_{kj}})/k \\ &\geq min(m_{l_{1j}}, m_{l_{2j}},...,m_{l_{kj}}) \end{aligned} \tag{8}$$

The basic idea of constructing a complete evidential mapping matrix is that if the causal links from e_{l1}, e_{l2} ..., e_{lk} to A' are $m_{l_{1j}}, m_{l_{2j}}...,m_{l_{kj}}$ respectively, then the causal link from $\{e_{l1}, e_{l2}, ...,$ $e_{lk}\}$ to A' is something between max $(m_{l_1}, m_{l_2},... m_{l_{kj}})$ and min $(m_{l_{1j}},$

$m_{l_2 j},\ldots,m_{l_k j}$). Here we use the average value of $m_{l_1 j},\ldots,m_{l_2 j},\ldots,m_{l_k j}$ to represent approximate causal link from $\{e_{l1}, e_{l2}, \ldots, e_{lk}\}$ to A'.

Example 5. Assume a BM of an evidential mapping from $\Theta_E=\{e_1,e_2,e_3\}$ to $\Theta_H=\{h_1,h_2,h_3,h_4\}$ is

$$\begin{array}{c} \\ \{e_1\} \\ \{e_2\} \\ \{e_3\} \end{array} \begin{array}{c} \begin{array}{ccc} \{h_1,h_2\} & \{h_3\} & \{h_4\} \end{array} \\ \begin{bmatrix} 0.5 & 0{,}5 & 0.0 \\ 0.7 & 0.0 & 0.3 \\ 0.0 & 0.0 & 1.0 \end{bmatrix} \end{array} = BM$$

with row title vector $[\{e_1\},\{e_2\},\{e_3\}]$, and column title vector $[\{h_1,h_2\},\{h_3\},\{h_4\}]$. Then the corresponding CEM is

$$\begin{array}{c|ccccc} & \{h_1,h_2\} & \{h_3\} & \{h_4\} & \Theta_E & \{h_1,h_2,h_4\} \\ \hline \{e_1\} & 0.5 & 0.5 & 0 & 0 & 0 \\ \{e_2\} & 0.7 & 0 & 0.3 & 0 & 0 \\ \{e_3\} & 0 & 0 & 1 & 0 & 0 \\ \{e_1,e_2\} & (0.5+0.7)/2 & 0 & 0 & 0.5/2+0.3/2 & 0 \\ \{e_1,e_3\} & 0 & 0 & 0 & 0.5/2+0.5/2+1/2 & 0 \\ \{e_2,e_3\} & 0 & 0 & (0.3+1)/2 & 0 & 0.7/2 \\ \Theta_E & 0 & 0 & 0 & (0.5+0.7)/3+0.5/3+(0.3+1)/3 & 0 \end{array}$$

with row title vector $[\{e_1\}, \{e_2\}, \{e_3\}, \{e_1, e_2\}, \{e_1, e_3\}, \{e_2, e_3\}, \Theta_E]$ and column title vector $[\{h_1,h_2\}, \{h_3\}, \{h_4\}, \Theta_E, \{h_1,h_2,h_4\}]$.

Example 6. Assume a BM of an evidential mapping from $\Theta_E=\{e_1,e_2,e_3\}$ to $\Theta_H=\{h_1,h_2,h_3,h_4\}$ is multivalued mapping as:

$$\begin{array}{c|cc} & \{h_1,h_2\} & \{h_2,h_3,h_4\} \\ \hline \{e_1\} & 1 & 0 \\ \{e_2\} & 1 & 0 \\ \{e_3\} & 0 & 1 \end{array}$$

Then the corresponding CEM is

$$\begin{array}{c|ccc} & \{h_1,h_2\} & \{h_2,h_3,h_4\} & \Theta_H \\ \hline \{e_1\} & 1 & 0 & 0 \\ \{e_2\} & 1 & 0 & 0 \\ \{e_3\} & 0 & 1 & 0 \\ \{e_1,e_2\} & 1 & 0 & 0 \\ \{e_1,e_3\} & 0 & 0 & 1 \\ \{e_2,e_3\} & 0 & 0 & 1 \\ \Theta_E & 0 & 0 & 1 \end{array}$$

It is easy to prove that a CEM is a basic matrix of an evidential mapping from 2^{Θ_E} to Θ_H. So any piece of evidence which is in the form of *bpa* on Θ_E can be propagated to Θ_H through the CEM. If a BM is the matrix of a multivalued mapping then its related CEM is also associated with the same multivalued mapping.

Certainly if a rule in a rule set specifies the causal link between a subset E of Θ_E and $A_1, \ldots, A_n$ of Θ_H, then the values of row i, with the row title as E, are $(f(E \rightarrow A_1), \ldots, f(E \rightarrow A_n))$ in CEM. But these $f(E \rightarrow A_i)$ must satisfy the condition of (8).

5. PROPAGATING BELIEFS USING HEURISTIC KNOWLEDGE

Belief propagation in a rule-based system such as that described above indicates that, given belief functions on an antecedent frame and a set of rules with rule strengths in the form of mass functions, the belief functions on the conclusion frame can be deduced. If (R, Θ_E, Θ_H), $(R', \Theta_H, \Theta_H')$, $(R'', \Theta_E', \Theta_H)$, $(R_1, \Theta_E, \Theta_H)$ and $(R_2, \Theta_E, \Theta_H)$ are five triples associated with five evidential mappings, generally we need to solve the following belief propagation problems:

(i) given a piece of evidence on Θ_E, (R, Θ_E, Θ_H) is known, to deduce belief on Θ_H.
(ii) given a piece of evidence on Θ_E, (R, Θ_E, Θ_H), and $(R', \Theta_H, \Theta_H')$ are known, to deduce belief on Θ_H'.
(iii) given two pieces of evidence on Θ_E and Θ_E' respectively, (R, Θ_E, Θ_H) and $(R'', \Theta_E', \Theta_H)$ are known, to deduce belief on Θ_H.
(iv) given a piece of evidence on Θ_E, $(R_1, \Theta_E, \Theta_H)$ and $(R_2, \Theta_E, \Theta_H)$ are given independently, to deduce belief on Θ_H.
(v) given several pieces of evidence each of which is on $A, B, \ldots, C$ respectively, (R, Θ_E, Θ_H) is known where $\Theta_E = A \times B \times \ldots \times C$, to deduce belief on Θ_H.

These problems can be solved by the following three theorems.

Theorem 2. *Let (R, Θ_E, Θ_H) be a triple associated with an evidential mapping Γ^*, BM and CEM are the basic matrix and the complete evidential mapping matrix of Γ^*, if a mass function m on Θ_E is known, then a mass function m_1 on Θ_H is calculated by the formula*

$$[m_1(H_1)...m_1(H_m)]=[m(E_1)...m(E_n)]\times\begin{bmatrix}m_{11} & ... & m_{1m}\\ & ... & \\ m_{n1} & ... & m_{nm}\end{bmatrix}(=CEM)(9)$$

where $[E_1,...,E_n]$ *is the row title vector of CEM, and* $[H_1,...,H_m]$ *is the column title vector of CEM.*

Specifically, if m is a Bayesian subjective probability assignment then m_1 on Θ_H is calculated by

$$[m_1(H_1)...m_1(H_m)]=[m(e_1)...m(e_n)]\times\begin{bmatrix}m_{11} & ... & m_{1m}\\ & ... & \\ m_{n1} & ... & m_{nm}\end{bmatrix}(=BM)$$

Example 7. Assume there are two rules in a rule set R:

R_1: $p\rightarrow\{q\}_{(c)}$; $p\rightarrow\neg\{q\}_{(1-d)}$; $p\rightarrow\Theta_{H(d-c)}$
R_2: $\neg p\rightarrow\Theta_{H(1)}$.

and a piece of evidence says that $[m(p)m(\neg p)m(\Theta_E)]=[a 1-b\ b-a]$, where a, b, c, and d are all real numbers between [0,1] with conditions $b>a$, and $d>c$, what is the belief distribution on q?

Obviously the CEM of this evidential mapping is

$$\begin{array}{c} \\ \{p\}\\ \{\neg p\}\\ \Theta_E\end{array}\begin{array}{c}\begin{array}{ccc}\{q\} & \{\neg q\} & \Theta_H\end{array}\\ \begin{bmatrix}c & 1-d & d-c\\ 0 & 0 & 1\\ 0 & 0 & 1\end{bmatrix}\end{array}=CEM$$

with row title vector $[\{p\},\{\neg p\},\Theta_E]$ and column title vector $[\{q\},\{\neg q\},\Theta_H]$.

Applying formula (9) to (R, Θ_E, Θ_H), we get

$$[m_1(q)\ m_1(\neg q)\ m_1(\Theta_H)]=$$
$$=[m(p)\ m(\neg p)\ m(\Theta_E)]\times\begin{bmatrix}c & 1-d & d-c\\ 0 & 0 & 1\\ 0 & 0 & 1\end{bmatrix}=$$
$$=[ac\ a(1-d)\ 1-ac-a+ad]$$

This result is the same as formula (12) by Hau and Kashyap (1990).

Theorem 3. *Let* (R, Θ_E, Θ_H) *and* $(R', \Theta_H, \Theta_H')$ *be two triples associated with two evidential mappings* Γ^* *and* Γ'^*, CEM_1 *and* CEM_2 *are two complete evidential mapping matrices of* Γ^* *and* Γ'^*, *if a mass function m on* Θ_E *is known, then a mass function* m_1 *on* Θ_H' *is calculated by the formula*

$$[m_1(H'_1)...m_1(H'_m)] = [m(\mathrm{E}_1)...\mathrm{m}(E_n)] \times \begin{bmatrix} m_{11} & \dots & m_{1m} \\ & \dots & \\ m_{n1} & \dots & m_{nm} \end{bmatrix}$$

where $CEM = CEM_1 \times CEM_2$.

Theorem 3 indicates that if we know a series of evidential mappings from Θ_{E_1} to Θ_{E_2}, ..., from $\Theta_{E_{n-1}}$ to Θ_{E_n} and those CEM$_i$ of evidential mappings from Θ_{Ei} to Θ_{Ei+1} for $i = 1, \dots, n-1$, then we wil get an evidential mapping from Θ_{E1} to Θ_{En} with its CEM as CEM$_1$ $\times \dots \times$ CEM$_{n-1}$.

Example 8. Assume two rule sets R and R' are as follows:

R: $A \to B_{(a)}$; $A \to \neg B_{(1-b)}$; $A \to \Theta_{B(b-a)}$.
$\neg A \to \Theta_{B(1)}$.
R': $B \to C_{(c)}$; $B \to \neg C_{(1-d)}$; $B \to \Theta_{C(d-c)}$.
$\neg B \to \Theta_{C(1)}$.

CEM$_1$ and CEM$_2$ are:

$$\begin{array}{c} \\ A \\ \neg A \\ \Theta_A \end{array} \begin{array}{c} \begin{array}{ccc} B & \neg B & \Theta_B \end{array} \\ \begin{bmatrix} a & 1-b & b-a \\ 0 & 0 & 1 \\ 0 & 0 & 1 \end{bmatrix} \end{array} = CEM_1$$

and

$$\begin{array}{c} \\ B \\ \neg B \\ \Theta_B \end{array} \begin{array}{c} \begin{array}{ccc} C & \neg C & \Theta_C \end{array} \\ \begin{bmatrix} c & 1-d & d-c \\ 0 & 0 & 1 \\ 0 & 0 & 1 \end{bmatrix} \end{array} = CEM_2$$

Given a mass function m on Θ_A, the mass function on Θ_C is

$$[m_1(C)\ m_1(\neg C)\ m_1(\Theta_C)] =$$
$$= [m(A)\ m(\neg A)\ m(\Theta_A)] \times$$
$$\begin{bmatrix} ac & a(1-d) & a(d-c)+1-a \\ 0 & 0 & 1 \\ 0 & 0 & 1 \end{bmatrix} \ (= CEM)$$

This formula is identical to (14) in Hau and Kashayap (1990) and formula (4) in Ginsberg (1984).

Theorems 2 and 3 can be used to solve problems (i) and (ii). Dempster's combination rule is used to deal with the problem in (iii) where we suppose that any two pieces of evidence bearing on the same frame are DS-independent (Voorbraak, 1991). DS-independence will guarantee that if we use Dempster's rule to combine two probability distributions we should obtain the same result as what we get from Bayesian theory.

Theorem 4. *Let $(R_1, \Theta_E, \Theta_H)$ and $(R_2, \Theta_E, \Theta_H)$ be two triples associated with two evidential mappings Γ^* and Γ'^*, m_i and m_i' are two mass functions indicating causal links from e_i to Θ_H in Γ^* and Γ'^* respectively (for $i=1, \ldots, n$), that is,*

$$\Gamma^*(e_i)=\{(H_{i1}, f(e_i \rightarrow H_{i1})), \ldots, (H_{in'}, f(e_i \rightarrow H_{in'}))\}$$
$$m_i(A_{il})=\mathrm{F}(e_i \rightarrow H_{il}) \text{ where } \mathrm{A}_{il}=\{(x,y) \mid x \in \neg\{e_i\} \text{ or } y \in H_i^l\} \text{ for } l=1, \ldots, n'$$

and

$$\Gamma'^*(e_i)=\{(H'_{i1}, f(e_i \rightarrow H'_{i1})), \ldots, (H'_{in''}, f(e_i \rightarrow H'_{in''}))\}$$
$$m'_i(A'_{ir}=f(e_i \rightarrow H'_{ir}) \text{ where } A'_{ir} = \{x,y) \mid x \in \neg\{e_i\} \text{ or } y \in H'_{ir}\} \text{ for } r = 1, \ldots, n''$$

then the joint impact of two evidential mappings is the third evidential mapping Γ''^* from Θ_E to Θ_H in which:

$$\Gamma''^*(e_i)=\{(H''_{i1}, f(e_i \rightarrow H''_{i1})), \ldots, (H''_{ik}, f(e_i \rightarrow H''_{ik}))\} \tag{10}$$
$$m_i(A''_{ij})=f(e_i \rightarrow H''_{ij} = m_i \oplus m'_i(A''_{ij}) \text{ for } j=1, \ldots, k$$
$$\text{where } A''_{ij}=A_i^l \cap A'_{ir}, \text{ and } H''_{ij} = H_{il} \cap H'_{ir}.$$

Here $\oplus$ indicates that Dempster's rule is used to combine m_i and m'_i.

Proof. Because $m_i \oplus m'_i$ is still a mass function in the Dempster-Shafer theory, we need only prove that any focal element A''_{ij} in $m_i \oplus m'_i$ is in the form of $\{(x,y) \mid x \in \neg\{e_i\} \text{ or } y \in H''_{ij}\}$.

Given that $A''_{ij} = A_{il} \cap A'_{ir}$, $A_{il}=\{(x,y) \mid x \in \neg\{e_i\}$ or $y \in H_{il}\}$ and $A'_{ir}\{(x,y) \mid x \in \neg\{e_i\}$ or $y \in H'_{ir}\}$, we have

$$\begin{aligned}
A''_{ij} &= A_{il} \cap A'_{ir} \\
&= \{(x,y) \mid x \in \neg\{e_i\} \text{ or } y \in H_{il}\} \cap \{(x,y) \mid x \in \neg\{e_i\} \text{ or } y \in H'_{ir}\} \\
&= (\neg\{e_i\} \times \Theta_H \cup \Theta_E \times H_{il}) \cap (\neg\{e_i\} \times \Theta_H \cup \Theta_E \times H'_{ir}) \\
&= (\neg\{e_i\} \times \Theta_H \cup \{e_i\} \times H_{il}) \cap (\neg\{e_i\} \times \Theta_H \cup \{e_i\} \times H'_{ir}) \\
&= ((\neg\{e_i\} \times \Theta_H) \cup (\{e_i\} \times H_{il} \cap \{e_i\} \times H'_{ir}) \\
&= (\neg\{e_i\} \times \Theta_H) \cup (\{e_i\} \times (H_{il} \cap H'_{ir}) \\
&= \{(x,y) \mid x \in \neg\{e_i\} \text{ or } y \in H_{il} \cap H'_{ir}\} \\
&= \{(x,y) \mid x \in \neg\{e_i\} \text{ or } y \in H''_{ij} = H_{il} \cap H'_{ir}\}
\end{aligned}$$

The meaning of this theorem is that if there are two independent heuristic rule sets (as in Figure 20.1) given by different domain experts respectively, each of those specifies one kind of causal link from frame Θ_E to frame Θ_H; then the joint impact of the two causal links can be substituted by the third heuristic rule set that is produced from them.

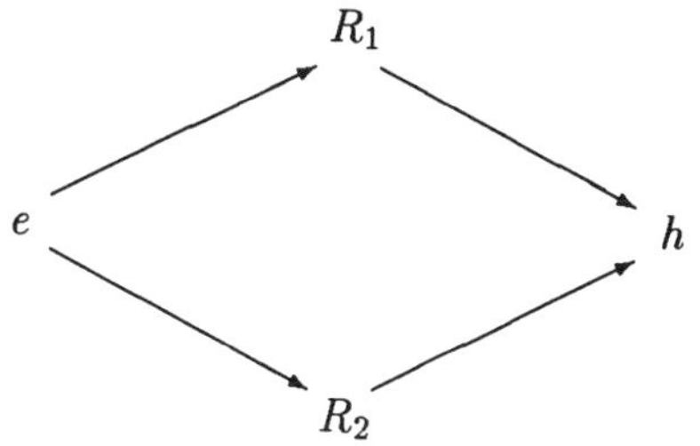

Figure 20.1: Two evidential mappings from e to h.

Here we need to address the issue that the meaning of this theorem is different from using theorem 2 twice through two evidential mappings. Using theorem 2 in that way gives a wrong result because of the dependency of the two mass functions on Θ_H.

Formula (6) given by Ginsberg (1984) is achieved from formula (10) in a special case when $(R_1, \Theta_E, \Theta_H)$ and $(R_2, \Theta_E, \Theta_H)$ are as follows:

$$R_1\text{:}\ e \to H_{(a)};\ e \to \neg H_{(b)};\ e \to \Theta_{H(1-b-a)}$$
$$\neg e \to \Theta_{H(1)}.$$

and

$$R\text{:}\ e \to H_{(c)};\ e \to H_{(d)};\ e \to \Theta_{H(1-c-d)}$$
$$\neg e \to \Theta_{H(1)}.$$

Then the joint evidential mapping produces a new rule set as:

$$R\text{:}\ e \to H \quad (1 - \frac{(1-a)(1-c)}{1-(ad+bc)}) = x;$$
$$e \to \neg H \quad (1 - \frac{(1-b)(1-d)}{1-(ad+bc)}) = y;$$
$$e \to \Theta_H \quad (1-x-y).$$
$$\neg e \to \Theta_H \quad (1).$$

Here if $b=0$ and $d=0$, then it is identical with the result of parallel reduction given by Pearl (1990).

For problem (v), given a triple of an evidential mapping $(R, \Theta_E,$

Θ_H), $\Theta_E = a \times b \times .... \times C$, and a series of evidence in the form of mass functions on $A, B, ..., C$ respectively, we must first get the joint mass function on Θ_E in order to obtain the impact of those pieces of evidence on Θ_H. Shafer's partition theory and technique (Shafer, 1976; Shafer et al., 1987; Shafer and Logan, 1987) provide a sound background for propagating mass functions (or belief functions) from $A, B, ..., C$ to their Cartesian product frame of discernment Θ_E. Thus applying theorem 2 the mass function on Θ_H will be calculated. Certainly computational complexity is a major problem that has been widely researched (Barnett, 1981; Shafer and Logan, 1987).

Generally speaking, when $\Theta_E = A \times B \times ... \times C$, we can solve problem (v) by the following steps:

1. Establish evidential mappings Γ_A, Γ_B, ..., Γ_C (in fact they are multivalued mappings) from A, B, ..., C to Θ_E, respectively.

   $\Gamma_A(a_i) = \{(\{a_i\} \times B \times ... \times C, 1)\}$ for each a_i in A
   $\Gamma_B(b_i) = \{(A \times \{b_i\} \times ... \times C, 1)\}$ for each b_i in B
   ...
   $\Gamma_C(c_i) = \{(A \times B \times ... \times \{c_i\}, 1)\}$ for each c_i in C (11)

2. Given a series of pieces of evidence on $A, B, .., C$, based on those evidential mappings, get a number of mass functions on the joint frame from each simple frame.

3. Suppose $A,B,...,C$ are different from each other and the pieces of evidence are independent; using Dempster's combination rule, get the final mass function on Θ_E.

4. Based on this final mass function on Θ_E and an evidential mapping associated with (R, Θ_E, Θ_H), apply theorem 2 eventually to deduce a mass function on Θ_H.

Example 9. Assume we have four heuristic rules as follows. Given that p, q, v are certain, what is the degree of belief on c?

$r_1 : p \wedge q \rightarrow s(m_1)$;
$r_2 : s \wedge t \rightarrow c(m_2)$;
$r_3 : v \rightarrow u(m_3)$;
$r_4 : u \rightarrow c(m_4)$.

Intuitively, the relations of the rules can be described as in Figure 20.2. The degree of belief on c will be contained through the following steps.

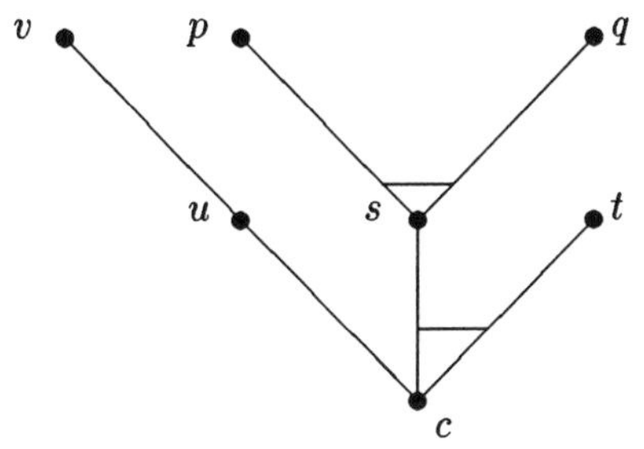

Figure 20.2: An AND/OR graph representing four heuristic rules

Step 1: Construct a rule set for each rule above:

R_1: $p \wedge q \rightarrow s_{(m_1)}$; $p \wedge q \rightarrow \Theta_{S(1-m_1)}$.
$\neg p \wedge q \rightarrow \Theta_{S(1)}$.
$p \wedge \neg q \rightarrow \Theta_{S(1)}$.
$\neg p \wedge \neg q \rightarrow \Theta_{S(1)}$.
R_2: $s \wedge t \rightarrow c_{(m_2)}$; $s \wedge t \rightarrow \Theta_{C(1-m_2)}$.
$\neg s \wedge t \rightarrow \Theta_{C(1)}$.
$s \wedge \neg t \rightarrow \Theta_{C(1)}$.
$\neg s \wedge \neg t \rightarrow \Theta_{C(1)}$.
R_3: $v \rightarrow u_{(m_3)}$; $v \rightarrow \Theta_{U(1-m_3)}$.
$\neg v \rightarrow \Theta_{U(1)}$.
R_4: $u \rightarrow c_{(m_4)}$; $u \rightarrow \Theta_{C(1-m_4)}$.
$\neg u \rightarrow \Theta_{C(1)}$.

Step 2: Construct the corresponding basic matrices and complete evidential mapping matrices of those rule sets.

Step 3: According to formula (11) for rule set R_1, because p and q are certain, the joint mass function m_{pq} on Θ_{pq} is calculated by:

$m_{pq}(\{(p,q)\}) = 1$
(because of $m'_{pq}(\{p\} \times \Theta_q) = 1$ and $m''_{pq}(\Theta\Theta_p \times \{q\}) = 1$)

Then, based on theorem 2, calculate a mass function on Θ_s:

$m_s(s) = m_1$; $m_s(\Theta_s) = 1 - m_1$

Step 4: According to formula (11), for rule set R_2, because t is certain and the mass function on Θ_s is known in step 3, then the joint mass function on Θ_{st} is:

$$m_{st}(\{(s,t)\})=m_1;\ m_{st}(\Theta_s\times\{t\})=1-m_1$$

Then, based on theorem 2, a mass function on Θ_c is

$$m_c(c)=m_1m_2;\ m_c(\Theta_c)=m_1(1-m_2)+1-m_1=1-m_1m_2$$

Step 5: Using theorem 3 to rule sets R_3 and r_4, we obtain another mass function on Θ_c as

$$m_c'(c)=m_3m_4;\ m_c'(\Theta_C)=1-m_3m_4$$

Step 6: Because m_c and m_c' are independent, we get a mass function on Θ_C by combining them:

$$m_c''(c)=1-(1-m_1m_2)(1-m_3m_4);$$
$$m_c''(\Theta_C)=(1-m_1m_2)(1-m_3m_4)$$

Eventually we have $Bel(c)=1-(1-m_1m_2)(1-m_3m_4)$.

In fact, this example is a variation of Pearl's example (1990, p. 561). In r_3, we use the logical formula $v\rightarrow u$ with m_1 instead of $p\rightarrow u$ with m_1 in order to avoid the dependency problem. We achieve the same result as Pearl did using his own explanation (random-switch metaphor).

6. CONCLUSIONS

6.1. Related work

Several approaches to dealing with heuristic knowledge in the Dempster-Shafer theory of evidence have been proposed (Ginsberg, 1984; Liu, 1986; Yen, 1989; Hau and Kashyap, 1990). Pearl (1990) also mentions this problem. The approach proposed in this paper is different from those approaches among which Liu's approach and Yen's approach are two proper subsets of our evidential mappings. In Ginsberg's as well as in Hau and Kashyap's representation formalisms of heuristic rules, a rule is associated with a pair of real numbers between [0,1] in the form of

if E then H with uncertainty $[c,d]$

The meaning of c and d defined by Ginsberg is: c is the extent to which we believe a given proposition to be confirmed by the available evidence, and d is the extent to which it is disconfirmed. That is:

$E \rightarrow H$ with c and $E \rightarrow \neg H$ with d

Hau and Kashyap gave two explanations:

1. c is the credibility to which E supports h, d is the plausibility to which E supports H, so $1-d$ is the degree to which E supports $\neg H$. That is:

   $E \rightarrow H$ with c and $E \rightarrow H$ with $1-d$

2. Let $\Theta = \Theta_E \oplus \Theta_H$ where Θ_E and Θ_H are frames of discernment of E and H, then c and d form a mass function on Θ:

   $m(A)=c,\ m(\neg A)=1-d$, and $m(\Theta)=d-c$

   where $A=\{(x,y) \mid x \in \neg E \text{ or } y \in H\}$.

Obviously, Ginsberg's representation can be incorporated into an evidential mapping from Θ_E to Θ_H by the rule set R:

$$R:\ E \rightarrow H_{(c)};\ E \rightarrow \neg H_{(d)};\ E \rightarrow \Theta_{H_{(1-d-c)}}$$
$$\neg E \rightarrow \Theta_{H_{(1)}}$$

Hau and Kashyap's first explanation can also be incorporated into an evidential mapping from Θ_E to Θ_H by the rule set R'

$$R':\ E \rightarrow H_{(c)};\ E \rightarrow \neg H_{(1-d)};\ E \rightarrow \Theta_{H_{(d-c)}}$$
$$\neg E \rightarrow \Theta_{H_{(1)}}$$

In fact, the second explanation given by Hau and Kashyap is to construct a mass function (furthermore a belief function) on a joint frame of discernment. Similar explanations of a rule are adopted by Laskey and Lehner (1989), by Lowrance et al. (1986), and by Zarley et al. (1988). This is also consistent with our explanation in section 2.2.

In section 5 we discuss only one situation involving the dependency problem. Hau and Kashyap (1990) discussed several situations based on their representation of heuristic rules.

6.2. Summary

Evidential mappings are the main concept proposed in this paper. The extended Dempster-Shafer theory is more powerful for propagating beliefs while at the same time keeping all the features of the original theory. The following are main features in our approach: (1) representing uncertain relations between evidence spaces and hypothesis spaces by evidential mappings; (2) by creating evidential mappings for incomplete heuristic rule sets, more heuristic knowledge can be represented in DS theory; (3) by constructing complete evidential mapping matrices any piece of evidence bearing on an evidence space can be propagated to the corresponding hypothesis space; (4) when a set of heuristic rules is detailed enough to form a Bayesian multivalued causal link model, any result produced by Bayesian inference can also be carried out by DS theory under evidential mappings; (5) evidential mappings are consistent with other previous research work in this respect; (6) a series of belief propagation procedures are easily deduced based on evidential mappings.

Heuristic knowledge is important in knowledge-based systems. Representing this kind of knowledge and propagating beliefs are the main and most difficult tasks for designers of knowledge-based systems. This paper makes some progress in this area. Future work concerning evidential mappings in the Dempster-Shafer theory should focus on exploring more features of evidential mappings and more approaches to dealing with dependency relations.

APPENDIX A:

Let E and H be two frames of discernment, Γ^* be a Bayesian evidential mapping from H to E, BM be the basic matrix of the mapping Γ^* with (i,j)-th entry as $p(e_j|h_i)$. Assume the prior probability on h_i of H is $p(h_i)$, a set of evidence on E is $e^1, e^2, \ldots, e^N$, for each of which there is an e_l where $p(e_l)=1$. Then the final belief function Bel on H using DS theory is

$$Bel(h_i)=\alpha p(h_i)\Pi_{k=1}^{N} p(e^k\,|\,h_i)$$

where $\alpha=\sum_{1}^{n} p(h_i)\Pi_{k=1}^{N} p(e^k\,|\,h_i)))^{-1}$, and $p(e^k\,|\,h_i)=p(e_l\,|\,h_i)$ for each k when the evidence e^k makes $p(e_l)=1$.

PROOF:

Step 1: According to the conditions in the theorem, the given BM of the evidential mapping from H to E is:

$$\begin{array}{l} \\ \{h_1\} \\ \{h_2\} \\ \\ \{h_n\} \\ \Sigma_i p(e_j\,|\,h_i) \end{array} \begin{array}{ccccc} \{e_1\} & \{e_2\} & \cdots & \{e_m\} & \Sigma_j p(e_j|h_i) \end{array} \atop \left[\begin{array}{ccccc} p(e_1\,|\,h_1) & p(e_2\,|\,h_1) & \cdots & p(e_m|h_1) & (=1) \\ p(e_1\,|\,h_2) & p(e_2\,|\,h_2) & \cdots & p(e_m|h_2) & (=1) \\ & & \cdots & & \\ p(e_1\,|\,h_n) & p(e_2\,|\,h_n) & \cdots & p(e_m|h_n) & (=1) \\ (\beta_1^{-1}) & (\beta_2^{-1}) & \cdots & (\beta_m^{-1}) & \end{array}\right]$$

where we suppose H contains n elements and E contains m elements. Then another matrix from E to H will be obtained as follows and it is also a Bayesian evidential mapping from E to H.

$$\begin{array}{c} \\ \{e_1\} \\ \{e_2\} \\ \\ \{e_m\} \end{array} \quad \begin{array}{cccc} \{h_1\} & \{h_2\} & \cdots & \{h_n\} \\ \left[\begin{array}{c} p(e_1\,|\,h_1)\beta_1 \\ p(e_2\,|\,h_1)\beta_2 \\ \\ p(e_m\,|\,h_1)\beta_m \end{array}\right. & \begin{array}{c} p(e_1\,|\,h_2)\beta_1 \\ p(e_2\,|\,h_2)\beta_2 \\ \\ p(e_m\,|\,h_2)\beta_m \end{array} & \begin{array}{c} \cdots \\ \cdots \\ \cdots \\ \cdots \end{array} & \left.\begin{array}{c} p(e_1\,|\,h_n)\beta_1 \\ p(e_2\,|\,h_n)\beta_2 \\ \\ p(e_m\,|\,h_n)\beta_m \end{array}\right] \end{array}$$

where β_j is $(\Sigma_{i=1}^{n} p(e_j\,|\,h_i))^{-1}$ for $j=1, .., m$.

Step 2: Assume we only get one piece of evidence e^1, and there exists an e_j that e^1 makes $p(e_j)=1$. Applying theorem 2 to $p(e_j)=1$ and the Bayesian evidential mapping from E to H, a mass function m_1 on H is calculated as

$$m_i(h_i)=p(e_j\,|\,h_i)\beta_j \text{ for } i=1, .., n$$

The prior probability gives another mass function on H

$$m_0(h_i)=p(h_i)$$

Applying Dempster's combination rule to m_0 and m_1, there will be

$$m_0 \oplus m_1(h_i)=\frac{(m_1(h_i)p(e_j\,|\,h_i)\beta_j)}{(\Sigma_{i=1}^{n} m_0(h_i)p(e_j\,|\,h_i)\beta_j)}$$

let $\alpha_1=(\sum_{i=1}^{n} m_0(h_i p(e_j\,|\,h_i))^{-1}$. Then

$$\begin{aligned} m'_1(h_i) &= m_0 \oplus m(h_i) \\ &= \alpha_1 m_0(h_i)p(e_j\,|\,h_i) \\ &= \alpha_1 p(h_i)p(e_j\,|\,h_i) \text{ (because of } p(h_i)=m_0(h_i)) \\ &= \alpha_1 p(h_i)p(e^1\,|\,h_i) \text{ (we use } e^1 \text{ instead of } e_j \text{ because of } e^1 \text{ making } p(e_j)=1) \\ &= \alpha_1 p(h_i)\Pi_{k=1}^{1} p(e^k\,|\,h_i) \end{aligned}$$

So $Bel'_1(h_i)=\alpha_1 p(h_i)\Pi_{k=1}^{1} p(e^k\,|\,h_i)$; the theorem is true when $N=1$.

Step 3: Assume for $N-1$ pieces of evidence we have proved the theorem, that is,

$$\begin{aligned} m'_{N-1}(h_j) &= m_0 \oplus m_1 \oplus \ldots \oplus m_{N-1}(h_i) \\ &= Bel'_{N-1}(h_i) \\ &= \alpha_{N-1} = p(h_i)\Pi_{k=1}^{N-1} p(e^k\,|\,h_i) \end{aligned}$$

Step 4: Given n-th evidence e^N, e^N makes $p(e_r)=1$ for a particular e_r, then m_N is a corresponding mas function produced from $p(e_r)=1$ and the Bayesian evidential mapping. That is,

$$m_N(h_i)=p(e_r \mid h_i)\beta_r \text{ for } i = 1, \ldots, n$$

So

$$\begin{aligned} m'_N(h_i) &= m_N \oplus m'_{N-1}(h_i) \\ &= \frac{m_N(h_i)m'_{N-1}(h_i)}{(\Sigma_{i=1}^{n} m_N(h_i)m'_{N-1}(h_i))} \\ &= \frac{\alpha_{N-1}p(h_i)\Pi_{k=1}^{N-1}p(e^k \mid h_i)p(e_r \mid h_i)\beta_r}{(\Sigma_{i=1}^{n}(\alpha_{N-1}p(h_i)\Pi_{k=1}^{N-1}p(e^k \mid h_i)p(e_r \mid h_i)\beta_r))} \\ &= \alpha_N p(h_i)\Pi_{k=1}^{N}p(e^k \mid h_i) \text{ (by using } e^N \text{ instead of } e_r) \end{aligned}$$

where $\alpha_N=(\Sigma_{i=1}^{n}p(h_i)\Pi_{k=1}^{N}p(e^k \mid h_i)))^{-1}$ because $Bel(h_i)=m'_N(h_i)$. The theorem is true for N pieces of evidence.

ACKNOWLEDGMENTS

The research work was supported by "Information Systems Committee (of UFC)" when the first author was working in the Department of Information Systems, University of Ulster. The authors are grateful for useful comments from Prof. Smets and Dr. Hong.

BIBLIOGRAPHY

Barnett, J.A. (1981). Computational methods for a mathematical theory of evidence. *Proc. IJCAI-81*, pp. 868–75.

Bonissone, P.P. and Tong, R.M. (1985). Editorial: Reasoning with uncertainty in expert systems. *Int. J. Man-Machine Studies*: 241–50.

Dempster, A.P. (1967). Upper and lower probabilities induced by a multivalued mapping. *Annals Mathematical Statistics* 38: 325–39.

Ginsberg, M.L. (1984). Non-monotonic reasoning using Dempster's rule. *Proc. AAAI-84*, pp. 126–29.

Hau, H.Y. and Kashyap, R.L. (1990). Belief combination and propagation in a lattice-structured inference network. *IEEE Transactions on Systems, Man and Cybernetics* 20 (1): 45–57.

Jeffrey, R. (1965). *The logic of decisions*. New York: McGraw-Hill.

Laskey, K.B., Cohen, M.S., and Marin, A.W. (1989). Representing and elicting knowledge about uncertain evidence and its implications. *IEEE Transactions on Systems, Man and Cybernetics* 19 (3): 536–45.

Laskey, M.B. and Lehner, P.E. (1989). Assumptions, beliefs and probabilities. *Artificial Intelligence 41*: 65–67.

Liu, G.S.H. (1986). Causal and plausible reasoning in expert systems. *Proc. AAAI-86*, pp. 220–25.
Lowrance, J.D., Garvey, T.D. and Strat, T.M. (1986). A framework for evidential-reasoning systems. *Proc. AAAI-86*, pp. 896–903.
Prade, H. (1981). Modal semantics and fuzzy set theory. In Yager, R.R. (ed.), *Fuzzy set and possibility theory: Recent developments*, pp. 232–46. New York: Pergamon Press.
Pearl, J. (1988). *Probabilistic reasoning in intelligence systems: Networks of plausible inference*. San Mateo, CA: Morgan Kaufmann.
Pearl, J. (1990). Bayesian and belief-functions formalisms for evidential reasoning: A conceptual analysis. In Shafer, G. and Pearl, J. (eds.), *Readings in uncertain reasoning*, pp. 540–74. San Mateo, CA: Morgan Kaufmann.
Shafer, G. (1976). *A mathematical theory of evidence*. Princeton: Princeton University Press.
Shafer, G. (1981). Jeffrey's rule of conditioning. *Philosophy of Science* 48: 337–62.
Shafer, G. (1987). Probability judgment in artificial intelligence and expert systems. *Statistical Science* 2 (1): 3–44.
Shafer, G. (1990). Perpectives on the theory and practice of belief functions. Working Paper No. 218, University of Kansas, Lawrence.
Shafer, G., Shenoy, P.P., and Mellouli, K. (1987). Propagating belief functions in qualitative Markov trees. *International Journal of Approximate Reasoning* 1: 349–400.
Shafer, G. and Logan, R. (1987). Implementing Dempster's rule for hierarchical evidence. *Artificial Intelligence* 33: 271–98.
Shafer, G. and Srivastava R. (1990). The Bayesian and belief-function formalisms: A general perspective for auditing. In Shafer, G. and Pearl, J. (eds.), *Readings in uncertain reasoning*, pp. 482–521. San Mateo, CA: Morgan Kaufmann.
Shortliffe, E.H. and Buchanan, B.G. (1976). A model of inexact reasoning in medicine. In Buchanan and E.H. Shortiffe (eds.), *Rule-based expert systems*. Reading, MA: Addison-Wesley.
Smets, P. (1988). Belief functions. In Smets, P., Mamdani, E.H., Dubois, D. and Prade, H. (eds.), *Non-standard logics for automated reasoning*, pp. 213–52. London: Academic Press.
Strat, T.L. (1987). Evidential-based control in knowledge-based systems. Ph.D. thesis, University of Massachusetts.
Voorbraak, F. (1991). On the justification of Dempster's rule of combination. *Artificial Intelligence* 48: 171–97.
Wesley, L.P. (1988). Evidential-based control in knowledge-based systems. Ph.D. thesis, University of Massachusetts.
Yen, J. (1989). Gertis: A Dempster-Shafer approach to diagnosing hierarchical hypotheses. *Communications of the ACM* 32: 573–85.
Zarley, D., Hsia, Y.T., and Shafer, G. (1988). Evidential reasoning using DELIEF. *Proc. AAAI-88*, pp. 205–209.

21 Representation of evidence by hints

Jürg KOHLAS and Paul-André MONNEY

Abstract: This paper introduces a mathematical model of a hint as a body of imprecise and uncertain information. Hints are used to judge hypotheses: the degree to which a hint supports a hypothesis and the degree to which a hypothesis appears plausible in the light of a hint are defined. This leads in turn to support- and plausibility functions. Those functions are characterized as set functions which are normalized and monotone or alternating of order ∞. This relates the present work to Shafer's mathematical theory of evidence. However, whereas Shafer starts out with an axiomatic definition of belief functions, the notion of a hint is considered here as the basic element of the theory. It is shown that a hint contains more information than is conveyed by its support function alone. Also hints allow for a straightforward and logical derivation of Dempster's rule for combining independent and dependent bodies of information. This paper presents the mathematical theory of evidence for general, infinite frames of discernment from the point of view of a theory of hints.

Keywords: hints, evidence, support functions, plausibility functions, Dempster's rule.

1. HINTS: AN INTUITIVE INTRODUCTION

Intuitively, a hint is a body of information relative to some question that is in general *imprecise* in that it does not point to a precise answer but rather to a range of possible answers. It is also often *uncertain* in the sense that the information allows for several possible interpretations and it is not entirely sure which is the correct one. There may be internal conflict within a hint because different interpretations may lead to contradictory answers. Also there can be external contradictions between distinct and different hints relative to the same question. The goal of this paper is to develop a mathematical model of this intuitive notion of a hint and to study some of its basic properties. It takes as its starting point Dempster's (1967) multivalued mapping and develops along similar lines to Shafer's (1976) mathematical theory of evidence. The theory will, however, be developed for the most general case and not be limited to the case of finite frames as in Shafer's book.

For an introduction, and as a motivation, the simpler case of finite hints will first be discussed. Let Θ be an arbitrary finite set whose elements θ represent the possible answers to a given question that has to be considered. One of the elements of Θ represents the true, but unknown answer. Θ is called the *frame of discernment*. The subsets of Θ represent possible propositions about the answer to the question considered. Let Ω denote the finite *set of possible interpretations* of the information contained in the hint to be represented. One of the elements $\omega \in \Omega$ must be the *correct* interpretation, but it is unknown which one. However, not all possible interpretations are equally likely. Thus, a probability $p(\omega)$ for the interpretations $\omega \in \Omega$ is introduced.

Each possible interpretation ω restricts the possible answers within Θ somehow. If ω is the correct interpretation, then the correct answer θ is known to be within some nonempty subset $\Gamma(\omega)$ of Θ, the *focal set* of the interpretation. Alternatively, for any possible interpretation ω, the family S of the propositions (subsets of Θ) *implied* by the interpretation ω can be considered. S is simply the family of supersets of the focal set $\Gamma(\omega)$. It thus has trivially the following properties:

(1) $H \in S$ and $H \subseteq H'$ imply $H' \in$ S.
(2) $H_1 \in S$, $H_2 \in S$ imply $H_1 \cap H_2 \in$ S.
(3) Θ belongs to S, $\emptyset$ does not belong to S.

In addition, the intersection of all implied sets of an interpretation equals $\Gamma(\omega)$. Furthermore, for any possible interpretation, one can also look at the family **P** of propositions which are *possible* under the interpretation. A subset $H \subseteq \Theta$ is possible, when H intersects the focal set $\Gamma(\omega)$ of the interpretation. Equivalently, H is possible, iff its complement is not implied, $H^c \notin$ S. **P** has the following properties:

(1′) $H \in \mathbf{P}$ and $H \subseteq H'$ imply $H' \in \mathbf{P}$.
(2′) $H_1 \in \mathbf{P}$, $H_2 \in \mathbf{P}$ imply $H_1 \cup H_2 \in \mathbf{P}$.
(3′) Θ belongs to $\mathbf{P}$, $\emptyset$ does not belong to $\mathbf{P}$.

Furthermore, if $H \in \mathrm{S}$, then $H^c \notin \mathrm{S}$ and thus $\mathrm{S} \subseteq \mathbf{P}$.

A *hint* is thus defined by a frame of discernment Θ to which it refers, a set of possible interpretations Ω together with a probability $p(\omega)$ and finally a multivalued mapping Γ from the set of interpretations into the frame Θ. If the interpretation ω happens to be the correct one, then the answer to the question considered is restricted to the set $\Gamma(\omega)$. So far, any hint $\mathbf{H}$ is a quadruple $(\Omega, p, \Gamma, \Theta)$.

If a proposition $H \subseteq \Theta$ is fixed as a hypothesis about the correct answer, then it will be interesting to judge this hypothesis in the light of a hint $\mathbf{H}$. Let $\mathbf{S}(\omega)$ and $\mathbf{P}(\omega)$ denote the families of implied and possible propositions of an interpretation ω. Then one can look at the subsets of interpretations under which H is *implied*, $u(H)$, or *possible*, $v(H)$,

$$\begin{aligned} u(H) &= \{\omega \in \Omega : H \in \mathbf{S}(\omega)\} \\ v(H) &= \{\omega \in \Omega : H \in \mathbf{P}(\omega)\} \end{aligned} \tag{1}$$

A hypothesis H, which is implied or supported by many possible interpretations, or more important, by very probable interpretations, is very *credible* in light of the hint. Also, if the hypothesis is possible under many interpretations, or under very probable interpretations, then the hypothesis is very *plausible* in light of the hint. Thus, in order to measure the *degree of credibility* or *support* $sp(H)$ and the *degree of plausibility* $pl(H)$, the probabilities of $u(H)$ and $v(H)$ can be considered:

$$\begin{aligned} sp(H) &= P(u(H)) \\ pl(H) &= P(v(H)) \end{aligned} \tag{2}$$

The values $sp(H)$ and $pl(H)$ are defined for all subsets of Θ. sp is called a *support* (or belief) *function* and pl a *plausibility function* (or upper probability). These concepts were introduced by Dempster (1967) and extensively studied by Shafer (1976) for finite frames of discernment.

The goal of this contribution is to study hints with respect to arbitrary, especially infinite frames. To the best of our knowledge, only very few papers study evidence theory in this general case (Goodman and Nguyen, 1985; Nguyen, 1978; Shafer, 1979; Strat, 1984). The case of belief functions on infinite frames of discernment was in particular studied by Shafer (1979). In this paper belief functions are axiomatically defined as Choquet capacities, monotone of order ∞. Using an integral representation theorem of Choquet (1953, 1969) an *allocation of probability* for belief functions is derived. This concept provides for an interpretation of the meaning of belief. However, with this interpretation, the definition of Dempster's rule for the combination of belief functions is less straightforward. In an unpublished paper Shafer (1978) defines first product belief functions on a product space $\Theta \times \Theta$ and then Dempster's rule as a conditioning of the product belief function to the diagonal of $\Theta \times \Theta$. This seems somehow to be a detour. Hints, on the other hand, allow for a straightforward and logical derivation of Dempster's rule for combining independent and also dependent bodies of information.

Furthermore and more importantly, it will be seen that in the general case a hint contains more information than is conveyed by its support function alone. Therefore, hints cannot be combined on the basis of their support functions alone as proposed in Shafer's (1978) paper! This would result in a loss of information. This will be one of the main results of this paper. Another main result is that support- and plausibility functions as defined by (2) can be characterized as Choquet capacities, monotone of order ∞. The proof of this result rejoins Shafer's (1979) development and will only be sketched here. Finally, a new inclusion relation between hints will be introduced in this paper that generalizes a similar relation between support functions introduced by Yager (1985; see also Dubois and Prade, 1986).

In section 2 the general mathematical concept of a hint will be defined. In section 3 support- and plausibility functions will be introduced. A process of refining hints is presented in section 4. It leads to a relation of inclusion between hints. Section 5 studies inclusion relations between hints that are equivalent in the sense that they define partially the same support- and plausibility functions. Finally, in section 6, the combination of hints will be discussed and Dempster's rule derived. In particular, it will be shown that inclusion of hints is maintained under Dempster's rule. The results of this section show that Dempster's rule cannot be defined in terms of support functions only.

2. THE MATHEMATICAL MODEL OF HINTS

The frame of discernment Θ is now an arbitrary set and in particular it can be infinite. The set of possible interpretations Ω can then also be arbitrary. However, Ω will be a probability space (Ω, **A**, **P**) with a σ-algebra **A** and a probability measure **P** on it. As before (section 1) any possible interpretation $\omega \in \Omega$ restricts the possible answers in Θ somehow. It will be assumed here that to any $\omega \in \Omega$ a family $\mathbf{S}(\omega)$ of implied propositions $H \subseteq \Theta$, satisfying conditions (1) to (3) of section 1, is assigned. A family of subsets satisfying conditions (1) to (3) of section 1 is called a *filter*. The family $\mathbf{P}(\omega) = \{H \subseteq \Theta : H^c \notin \mathbf{S}(\omega)\}$ of possible propositions satisfies conditions (1′) to (3′) of section 1 above. A pair of such dual families $\mathbf{R} = (\mathbf{S}, \mathbf{P})$ will be called a *restriction.*

A restriction **R** is called *vacuous,* if **S** contains only Θ (and **P** all subsets of Θ except the empty set). A vacuous restriction does not restrict at all the possible answers. It is used to represent the situation that, under some interpretations, a hint contains possibly no information at all concerning the question considered.

The set $R = \cap \{H : H \in \mathbf{S}\}$ is called the *base* of the restriction **R**. One might wonder whether **S** should not be closed under arbitrary intersections and thus $R \in \mathbf{S}$. This will not be assumed here – for reasons that will become clear later. However, a restriction **R** with $R \in \mathbf{S}$ will be called *set-based,* because in this case $\mathbf{S} = \{H \subseteq \Theta : R \subseteq H\}$ and $\mathbf{P} = \{H \subseteq \Theta : R \cap H \neq \emptyset\}$. For a set-based restriction we write $\mathbf{R} = R$. Similarly, if (2) and (2′) of secton 1 hold for countable families, the restriction will be called a *σ-restriction.*

To go back to the model of a hint, it will thus be assumed that every possible interpretation $\omega \in \Omega$ has assigned a *nonempty* restriction $\Gamma(\omega) = (\mathbf{S}(\omega), \mathbf{P}(\omega))$ describing its implied and possible propositions. Γ is a mapping from Ω into the set $\mathbf{R}(\Theta)$ of restrictions on Θ. This is a generalization of the multivalued mappings considered by Dempster (1967). A *hint* **H** is thus finally a quintuple $\mathbf{H} = (\Omega, \mathbf{A}, P, \Gamma, \Theta)$ of elements as described above.

A hint $\mathbf{H} = (\Omega, \mathbf{A}, P, \Gamma, \Theta)$ is called *set-focused,* iff its restrictions $\Gamma(\omega)$ are set-based for all $\omega \in \Omega$. The bases of $\Gamma(\omega)$ are then called *focal sets.* If Θ is a finite set, then all restrictions and thus all hints are set-based. But even in the general case many important classes of hints are set-focused. For all $\omega \in \Omega$, if $\Gamma(\omega)$ is either a fixed set-based restriction R or the vacuous restriction, then the hint is called *simple.* If $\Gamma(\omega)$ equals the vacuous restriction for all $\omega \in \Omega$, then the hint is called *vacuous;* it represents full ignorance about the question at hand. If **H** is a set-focused hint whose focal sets $\Gamma(\omega)$ all contain only one single point $\theta(\omega)$ of Θ, then the hint is called *precise.* A precise hint corresponds essentially to a random variable (under reserve of the appropriate measurability condition).

Restrictions are fundamental to the theory. In many respects they behave like ordinary subsets of Θ. Especially the operation of *intersection* or *conjunction* can be defined: If $\mathbf{R}_1$ and $\mathbf{R}_2$ are two restrictions known to hold on Θ, then their conjunction forms a new restriction $\mathbf{R} = \mathbf{R}_1 \cap \mathbf{R}_2$ defined by $\mathbf{S} = \{H_1 \cap H_2 : H_1 \in \mathbf{S}_1, H_2 \in \mathbf{S}_2\}$. It is easily verified, that $\mathbf{S}$ is a filter if $\emptyset$ does not belong to $\mathbf{S}$. If $\emptyset \in \mathbf{S}$, then $\mathbf{R}_1$ and $\mathbf{R}_2$ are called *contradictory*. If $\mathbf{R}_1 = R_1$ and $\mathbf{R}_2 = R_2$, then $\mathbf{R}_1 \cap \mathbf{R}_2 = R_1 \cap R_2$. In the same way, the intersection is defined for arbitrary families of restrictions, not only for finite ones.

In order to judge hypotheses $H \subseteq \Theta$ in light of a hint $\mathbf{H}$, the subset $u(H)$ of interpretations that imply H and the subset $v(H)$ of interpretations under which H is possible are defined as in (1). u and v are mappings from the power set $\mathbf{P}(\Theta)$ to the power set $\mathbf{P}(\Omega)$. The following theorem lists some of their elementary properties:

Theorem 1.

(1) $u(\emptyset) = v(\emptyset) = \emptyset$

(2) $u(\Theta) = v(\Theta) = \Omega$

(3) $u(H) = v(H^c)^c$

(4) $v(H) = u(H^c)^c$

(5) $u(\cap\{H_i : i \in \mathbf{C}\}) = \cap\{u(H_i) : i \in \mathbf{C}\}$, *where* $\mathbf{C}$ *is finite in general, countable for hints with σ-restrictions* $\Gamma(\omega)$, $\omega \in \Omega$, *and arbitrary for set-focused hints.*

(6) $u(\cup\{H_i : i \in \mathbf{C}\}) \supseteq \cup\{u(H_i) : i \in \mathbf{C}\}$ *for an arbitrary* $\mathbf{C}$.

(7) $v(\cup\{H_i : i \in \mathbf{C}\}) = \cup\{v(H_i) : i \in \mathbf{C}\}$, *where* $\mathbf{C}$ *is finite in general, countable for hints with σ-restrictions* $\Gamma(\omega)$, $\omega \in \Omega$, *and arbitrary for set-focused hints.*

(8) $v(\cap\{H_i : i \in \mathbf{C}\}) \subseteq \cap\{v(H_i) : i \in \mathbf{C}\}$ *for an arbitrary* $\mathbf{C}$.

(9) $u(H') \subseteq u(H'')$ *if* $H' \subseteq H''$.

(10) $v(H') \subseteq v(H'')$ *if* $H' \subseteq H''$.

Proof. (1) and (2) are trivial. By definition, $v(H)^c = \{\omega \in \Omega : H^c \in \mathbf{S}(\omega)\} = u(H^c)$ and (4) is proved. (3) follows by applying (4) to H^c. (5): If $\omega \in u(H_i)$ for all $i \in \mathbf{C}$, then $H_i \in \mathbf{S}(\omega)$, thus $\cap\{H_i : i \in \mathbf{C}\} \in \mathbf{S}(\omega)$ and therefore $\omega \in u(\cap\{H_i : i \in \mathbf{C}\})$. Inversely, $\omega \in u(\cap\{H_i : i \in \mathbf{C}\})$ implies $\cap\{H_i : i \in \mathbf{C}\} \in \mathbf{S}(\omega)$, hence $H_i \in \mathbf{S}(\omega)$ and $\omega \in u(H_i)$ for all $i \in \mathbf{C}$. (6): If $\omega \in u(H_i)$ for some $i \in \mathbf{C}$, then $H_i \in \mathbf{S}(\omega)$, thus $\cup\{H_i : i \in \mathbf{C}\} \in \mathbf{S}(\omega)$ and $\omega \in u(\cup\{H_1 : i \in \mathbf{C}\})$. (7) and (8) are proved using (3), (4), (5) and (6) together with de Morgan laws. (9) and (10) follow immediately from the definitions of u and v.

In view of (5) u is called a $\cap$-homomorphism, and in view of (7) v is called a $\cup$-homomorphism.

3. SUPPORT AND PLAUSIBILITY FUNCTIONS

For a hint $\mathbf{H} = (\Omega, \mathbf{A}, P, \Gamma, \Theta)$ the degree of support $sp(H)$ and the degree of plausibility $pl(H)$ are defined by (2) for any subset H of Θ for which $u(H) \in \mathbf{A}$ and $v(H) \in \mathbf{A}$, respectively. Let $\mathbf{E}_s$ be the class of all subsets H of Θ for which $u(H) \in \mathbf{A}$, i.e., for which the degree of support is defined. The sets of $\mathbf{E}_s$ are called *s*-measurable and $\mathbf{E}_s$ is the domain of the set-function *sp*. Similarly let $\mathbf{E}_p$ be the class of all subsets $H \subseteq \Theta$ for which $v(H) \in \mathbf{A}$, i.e., for which the degree of plausibility is defined. The sets of $\mathbf{E}_p$ are called *p*-measurable and $\mathbf{E}_p$ is the domain of the set-function *pl*.

Note that there is a strong link between the support- and the plausibility function. In fact, according to theorem 1 (4) and (3)

$$\begin{aligned} pl(H) &= P(v(H)) = P(u(H^c)^c) = 1 - sp(H^c) \\ sp(H) &= P(u(H)) = P(v(H^c)^c) = 1 - pl(H^c) \end{aligned} \tag{3}$$

whenever the corresponding probabilities are defined.

Theorem 2.

(1) $\mathbf{E}_s$ *is a multiplicative class (i.e., closed under finite intersections) or a σ-multiplicative class (closed under countable intersections) depending on whether* $\Gamma(\omega)$, $\omega \in \Omega$ *are general restrictions or σ-restrictions.*

(2) $\mathbf{E}_p$ *is an additive class (i.e., closed under finite unions) or a σ-additive class (closed under countable unions) depending on whether* $\Gamma(\omega)$, $\omega \in \Omega$ *are general restrictions or σ-restrictions.*

(3) $\mathbf{E}_p = \{H \subseteq \Theta : H^c \in \mathbf{E}_s\}$, $\mathbf{E}_s = \{H \subseteq \Theta : H^c \in \mathbf{E}_p\}$ *and* $\emptyset$, Θ *belong to both* $\mathbf{E}_s$ *and* $\mathbf{E}_p$.

Proof. (1) and (2) are direct consequences of theorem 1 (5) and (7) and the fact that $\mathbf{A}$ is a σ-algebra. (3): $H \in \mathbf{E}_s$ is equivalent to $u(H) \in \mathbf{A}$, which is equivalent to $v(H^c) \in \mathbf{A}$ (theorem 1 (3) and (4)) which finally is equivalent to $H^c \in \mathbf{E}_p$. $\emptyset$, Θ belong to $\mathbf{E}_s$ and $\mathbf{E}_p$ because of theorem 1 (1) and (2).

$\mathbf{E}_s$ and $\mathbf{E}_p$ are called *dual classes* of s- and p-measurable sets. If Ω is a finite set, then all subsets of Θ are *s*- and *p*-measurable. However, in general $\mathbf{E}_s$ and $\mathbf{E}_p$ are strict subclasses of the power set of Θ. Let's illustrate theorem 2 by a simple, albeit somewhat pathological example: If $(\Omega, \mathbf{A}, P)$ is a probability space and $B \subseteq \Omega$ a subset that does not belong to $\mathbf{A}$, $\Gamma(\omega) = F \subseteq \Theta$ for all $\omega \in B$, $\Gamma(\omega) = \Theta$ otherwise, then $\mathbf{E}_s$ contains all subsets of Θ that do not contain F plus the set Θ. We have $u(H) = \emptyset$ for all $H \in \mathbf{E}_s$, $H \neq \Theta$ and thus $sp(H) = 0$, unless $H = \Theta$. $\mathbf{E}_p$ contains all subsets of Θ that are not contained in F^c plus $\emptyset$.

Theorem 3. *The support and plausibility functions of a hint* $\mathbf{H} = (\Omega, \mathbf{A}, P, \Gamma, \Theta)$, $sp: \mathbf{E}_s \to [0,1]$ *and* $pl: \mathbf{E}_p \to [0,1]$, *respectively, satisfy the following conditions:*

(1) $sp(\emptyset) = pl(\emptyset) = 0$ *and* $sp(\Theta) = pl(\Theta) = 1$.
(2) sp *is monotone of order* ∞, *i.e.,*

$$sp(E) \geqslant \sum\{(-1)^{|I|+1} sp(\cap_{i \in I} E_i) : \emptyset \neq I \subseteq \{1, \ldots, n\}\} \tag{4}$$

for all $n \geqslant 1$ *and sets* $E, E_i \in \mathbf{E}_s$, *such that* $E \supseteq E_i$; *and* pl *is alternating of order* ∞, *i.e.,*

$$pl(E) \leqslant \sum\{(-1)^{|I|+1} pl(\cup_{i \in I} E_i) : \emptyset \neq I \subseteq \{1, \ldots, n\}\} \tag{5}$$

for all $n \geqslant 1$ *and sets* $E, E_i \in \mathbf{E}_p$, *such that* $E \subseteq E_i$.

Furthermore, if all $\Gamma(\omega)$, $\omega \in \Omega$ *are* σ*-restrictions, then the following conditions hold:*

(3) sp *and* pl *are continuous, i.e., if* $E_1 \supseteq E_2 \supseteq \ldots$ *is a monotone decreasing sequence of sets of* $\mathbf{E}_s$, *then*

$$sp(\cap_{i=1}^{\infty} E_i) = \lim_{i \to \infty} sp(E_i) \tag{6}$$

and if $E_1 \subseteq E_2 \subseteq \ldots$ *is a monotone increasing sequence of sets of* $\mathbf{E}_p$, *then*

$$pl(\cup_{i=1}^{\infty} E_i) = \lim_{i \to \infty} pl(E_i) \tag{7}$$

Proof. (1) follows from theorem 1 (1) and (2). In order to prove (2) for the support function, the well-known inclusion-exclusion formula of probability theory, together with theorem 1 (5), (6) and (9) is used:

$$\begin{aligned} sp(E) &= P(u(E)) \geqslant P(u(\cup\{E_i : i = 1, 2, \ldots, n\})) \\ &\geqslant P(\cup\{u(E_i) : i 1, 2, \ldots, n\}) \\ &= \sum\{(-1)^{|I|+1} P(\cap_{i \in I} u(E_i)) : \emptyset \neq I \subseteq \{1, \ldots, n\}\} \\ &= \sum\{(-1)^{|I|+1} P(u(\cap_{i \in I} E_i)) : \emptyset \neq I \subseteq \{1, \ldots, n\}\} \\ &= \sum\{(-1)^{|I|+1} sp(\cap_{i \in I} E_i) : \emptyset \neq I \subseteq \{1, \ldots, n\}\} \end{aligned}$$

Condition (2) for the plausibility function is proved in the same way or by using (4) together with (3).

$E_1 \supseteq E_2 \supseteq \ldots$ implies $u(E_1) \supseteq u(E_2) \supseteq \ldots$ (theorem 1 (9)) and $\cap_{i=1}^{\infty} E_i \in \mathbf{E}_s$ (theorem 2 (1)). By the continuity of probabilities and theorem 1 (5)

$$\begin{aligned} sp(\cap_{i=1}^{\infty} E_i) &= P(u(\cap_{i=1}^{\infty} E_i)) \\ &= P(\cap_{i=1}^{\infty} u(E_i)) \\ &= \lim_{i=\infty} P(u(E_i)) = \lim_{i=\infty} sp(E_i) \end{aligned}$$

and condition (3) is proved.

Note that in particular set-focused hints have continuous support- and plausibility functions.

Does it make sense to define the degree of support for a hypothesis $H \subseteq \Theta$ outside the class $\mathbf{E}_s$ of s-measurable subsets? If $u(H) \subseteq \Omega$ is not measurable, the model of the hint $\mathbf{H}$ does not contain the necessary information to determine the probability of the set of interpretations supporting H. But any measurable set of interpretations $A \subseteq \Omega$ that is contained in $u(H)$ is a support for H. Hence, one may say that the unknown support for H must be at least $P(A)$, for any $A \subseteq u(H)$ and $A \in \mathbf{A}$. Thus, in the absence of further information the support of H could be defined as

$$sp_e(H) = sup\{P(A) : A \subseteq u(H), A \in \mathbf{A}\} = P_*(u(H)) \tag{8}$$

where P_* is the inner probability to P. This is an extension of the support function sp onto the whole power set $P(\Theta)$ because the restriction of sp_e to $\mathbf{E}_s$ equals sp. We call sp_e the *vacuous extension* of sp to underline that no information not contained in the hint $(\Omega, \mathbf{A}, P, \Gamma, \Theta)$ has been added.

By duality, we may also extend the plausibility functions pl from $\mathbf{E}_p$ to $P(\Theta)$:

$$pl_e(H) = 1 - sp_e(H^c) \tag{9}$$

This is similarly called the vacuous extension of pl. This name is justified by the following proposition:

Theorem 4. *The equality*

$$pl_e(H) = inf\{P(A) : A \supseteq v(H), A \in \mathbf{A}\} = P^*(v(H)) \tag{10}$$

holds. P^* *is the outer probability to* P.

Proof. From definitions (8) and (9) and theorem 1 (4) it follows that

$$\begin{aligned} pl_e(H) &= 1 - sp_e(H^c) = 1 - sup\{P(A): A \in \mathbf{A}, A \subseteq u(H^c)\} \\ &= 1 - sup\{P(A): A \in \mathbf{A}, u(H^c)^c \subseteq A^c\} = \inf\{P(A^c): \\ &\quad A \in \mathbf{A}, v(H) \subseteq A^c\} = inf\{P(A): A \in \mathbf{A}, v(H) \subseteq A\} \end{aligned}$$

Furthermore, it turns out that sp_e and pl_e satisfy also the conditions of theorem 3.

Theorem 5. *Let sp_e and pl_e be the extended support and plausibility functions of a hint $\mathbf{H} = (\Omega, \mathbf{A}, P, \Gamma, \Theta)$. Then*

(1) sp_e and pl_e are monotone and alternating of order ∞, respectively on $\mathbf{P}(\Theta)$.
(2) If $\Gamma(\omega)$ is a σ-restriction for all ω, then sp_e and pl_e are also continuous.

The proof of this theorem will not be given here. It seems to be surprisingly difficult and relies on the notion of an allocation of probability (Shafer, 1979). See Kohlas (1990) for a proof of this theorem. The connection between inner probability measures and support or belief functions have also been noted by Ruspini (1987) and Fagin and Halpern (1989), see also Shafer (1990).

4. REFINING HINTS

A hint $\mathbf{H} = (\Omega, \mathbf{A}, P, \Gamma, \Theta)$ can be refined in several respects by adding supplementary information to it:

(1) The restrictions $\Gamma(\omega)$ associated with the interpretations ω may become more precise: A restriction $(\mathbf{S}', \mathbf{P}')$ is said to be more precise than (or included in) a restriction $(\mathbf{S}, \mathbf{P})$ iff $\mathbf{S}' \supseteq \mathbf{S}$ (or equivalently $\mathbf{P}' \subseteq \mathbf{P}$), i.e., if it implies more propositions and if less propositions are possible. We write then $(\mathbf{S}', \mathbf{P}') \subseteq (\mathbf{S}, \mathbf{P})$.

(2) Some interpretations that originally are considered as possible may become known as impossible: The new set of possible interpretations Ω' becomes a subset of Ω. This implies also that the original probability P must be conditioned on Ω'. This leads to a new probability space $(\Omega', \mathbf{A}', P')$ of possible interpretations, where $\mathbf{A}' = \mathbf{A} \cap \Omega'$ and $P'(A) = P^*(A \cap \Omega')/P^*(\Omega')$, provided that $P^*(\Omega')$

> 0. Note that Ω' is not necessarily measurable; P' is still a probability measure on $\mathbf{A}'$ (Neveu, 1964).

(3) The probability measure P′ on the set of possible interpretations Ω' may be extended from the σ-algebra $\mathbf{A}'$ to a probability measure P'' on a larger σ-algebra $\mathbf{A}''$ containing $\mathbf{A}'$. Let's note that in this case

$$P'_*(A) \leqslant P''(A \leqslant P'^*(A) \tag{11}$$

for all $A \in \mathbf{A}''$.

Thus, combining all three refining steps in the above sequence, a new, refined hint $\mathbf{H}'' = (\Omega'', \mathbf{A}'', P'', \Gamma'', \Theta)$ may be obtained, such that $\Omega'' \subseteq \Omega$, $\mathbf{A}'' \supseteq \mathbf{A} \cap \Omega''$, P'' is an extension to $\mathbf{A}''$ of the probability measure $P'(A) = P^*(A \cap \Omega'')/P^*(\Omega'')$ on $\mathbf{A} \cap \Omega''$ and $\Gamma''(\omega) \subseteq \Gamma(\omega)$ for all $\omega \in \Omega''$. In this case we write $\mathbf{H}'' \subseteq \mathbf{H}$ and say that $\mathbf{H}''$ is *included* in or is *finer* than $\mathbf{H}$ (and $\mathbf{H}$ is *coarser* than $\mathbf{H}''$). Of course, many times not all three refining steps are present; often only step (1) or steps (1) and (3) are considered. These particular cases correspond to Yager's (1985) definition of inclusion.

This notion of inclusion of hints leads to the following comparison of the corresponding support- and plausibility functions:

Theorem 6. *Let* $\mathbf{H}'' = (\Omega'', \mathbf{A}'', P'', \Gamma'', \Theta)$ *and* $\mathbf{H} = (\Omega, \mathbf{A}, P, \Gamma, \Theta)$ *be two hints such that* $\mathbf{H}'' \subseteq \mathbf{H}$ *and with* sp''_e, pl''_e *and* sp_e, pl_e *as their respective extended support- and plausibility functions. If* $k = P^*(\Omega'')$, *then:*

(1) $sp_e(H) \leqslant k \cdot sp''_e(H) + (1-k)$ *for all* $H \subseteq \Theta$
(2) $pl_e(H) \geqslant k \cdot pl''_e(H)$ *for all* $H \subseteq \Theta$.

Proof. Let $v''(H)$ and $v(H)$ be the subsets of interpretations of Ω'' and Ω, respectively, under which H is possible. Then clearly $v''(H) \subseteq v(H) \cap \Omega''$ by the refining step (1).

Now, for any $H \subseteq \Theta$,

$$pl_e(H) = P^*(v(H)) \geqslant P^*(v(H) \cap \Omega'') \geqslant P^*(v''(H)) = P^*(v''(H) \cap \Omega'')$$

Let $P'(A) = P^*(A \cap \Omega'')/P^*(\Omega'')$ for $A \in \mathbf{A} \cap \Omega''$ and $P'^*(A)$ denote the outer probability measure with respect to P'. Then it follows easily that $P'^*(v''(H) \cap \Omega'') = P^*(v''(H) \cap \Omega'')/P^*(\Omega'')$ and hence

$$pl_e(H) \geqslant P'^*(v''(H) \cap \Omega'')\, P^*(\Omega'')$$

If $P''^*(A)$ is the outer measure with respect to the probability measure P'' on $\mathbf{A}''$, then clearly $P'^*(A) \geqslant P''^*(A)$ for any $A \subseteq \Omega''$. Thus

$$pl_e(H) \geqslant P''^*(v''(H) \cap \Omega'')\, P^*(\Omega'') = P''^*(v''(H))\, P^*(\Omega'') = \\ = pl''_e(H)\, P^*(\Omega'') = k \cdot pl''_e(H)$$

and this proves (2).

By (9) we have

$$sp_e(H) = 1 - pl_e(H^c) \leqslant 1 - k \cdot pl''_e(H^c) \\ = 1 - k \cdot (1 - sp''_e(H)) = k \cdot sp''_e(H) + (1 - k)$$

and this proves (1).

If only refining steps (1) and possibly (3) are present, then $k = 1$ and

$$[sp''_e(H), pl''_e(H)] \subseteq [sp_e(H), pl_e(H)]$$

To any hint $\mathbf{H} = (\Omega, \mathbf{A}, P, \Gamma, \Theta)$ a vacuous hint $\mathbf{V} = (\Omega, \mathbf{A}, P, \Gamma_{vac}, \Theta)$ can be associated, where $\Gamma_{vac}(\omega)$ is the vacuous restriction for all ω. Clearly $\Gamma(\omega) \subseteq \Gamma_{vac}(\omega)$ for all ω and therefore we have always $\mathbf{H} \subseteq \mathbf{V}$.

5. FAMILIES OF HINTS RELATED TO A SUPPORT FUNCTION

A hint generates a support function sp on some multiplicative class $\mathbf{E}_e$. This function has the properties (1) and (2), possibly (3) as stated in theorem 3. If now sp is a function on a multiplicative class $\mathbf{E}_e$, satisfying conditions (1) and (2) of theorem 3, is there always a hint which generates this support function? The answer is affirmative. This is a consequence of an integral theorem of Choquet (1953) as was noted by Shafer (1979). But it can easily be seen that different hints may generate the *same* support function sp on $\mathbf{E}_s$, but with *different* extensions sp_e to $\mathbf{P}(\Theta)$. In fact, let $(\Omega, \mathbf{A}, P)$ be a probability space and let B_1, B_2 be two different nonmeasurable subsets of Ω which have different inner probabilities. Furthermore, let Θ be a frame of discernment and F a strict subset of Θ. This allows us to define two distinct hints $\mathbf{H}_i = (\Omega, \mathbf{A}, P, \Gamma_i, \Theta)$, $i = 1,2$, where

$$\Gamma_i(\omega) = \begin{cases} F & \text{if } \omega \in B_i \\ \Theta & \text{otherwise} \end{cases}$$

For both hints, the class $\mathbf{E}_s$ equals all subsets of Θ that do not contain F plus the set Θ and the support functions of $\mathbf{H}_1$ and $\mathbf{H}_2$ coincide. But if sp_{1e} and sp_{2e} denote their respective extended support functions, then

$$sp_{1e}(F) = P_*(B_1) \neq P_*(B_2) = sp_{2e}(F)$$

Thus there exists a whole family of hints related to a support function sp on $\mathbf{E}_s$. The goal of this section is to study this family of hints. In a similar vein, Shafer (1979) studied various extensions of support (or belief) functions. This section puts some of his results into the perspective of hints.

In the context of the theory of hints Choquet's theorem can be stated as follows:

Theorem 7. *Let* $\mathbf{E}_s$ *be a multiplicative class and* $sp:\mathbf{E}_s \to [0,1]$ *a function satisfying conditions (1) and (2) of theorem 3. Then there exists a hint whose support function is sp. If furthermore* $\mathbf{E}_s$ *is a* σ*-multiplicative class and sp satisfies condition (3) of theorem 3 (continuity), then there exists a hint whose restrictions are all* σ*-restrictions and whose support function is sp.*

For a formal proof we refer to Choquet (1953) (see also Shafer, 1978 and Kohlas, 1990). Let's only describe the hint constructed in this proof: As a set of possible interpretations the set $\mathbf{R}(\mathbf{E}_s)$ of all filters on the multiplicative class $\mathbf{E}_s$ is selected. Note that to any restriction $\mathbf{R} = (\mathbf{S}, \mathbf{P})$ in $\mathbf{R}(\Theta)$ can be associated a filter $\varphi(\mathbf{R}) = \mathbf{S} \cap \mathbf{E}_s$ on $\mathbf{E}_s$. The mapping φ from $\mathbf{R}(\Theta)$ to $\mathbf{R}(\mathbf{E}_s)$ is onto because for any filter $\mathbf{F} \in \mathbf{R}(\mathbf{E}_s)$ the restriction $\mathbf{R}_c(\mathbf{F}) \in \mathbf{R}(\Theta)$ defined by its class of implied propositions $\mathbf{S} = \{H \subseteq \Theta: \textit{there is an } E \in \mathbf{F} \textit{ such that } E \subseteq H\}$ is in $\varphi^{-1}(\mathbf{F})$. This shows that $\{\varphi^{-1}(\mathbf{F}): \mathbf{F} \in \mathbf{R}(\mathbf{E}_s)\}$ is a partition of $\mathbf{R}(\Theta)$. Moreover, $\mathbf{R}_c(\mathbf{F})$ is the coarsest restriction in $\varphi^{-1}(\mathbf{F})$: if $\mathbf{R}' \in \varphi^{-1}(\mathbf{F})$, then $\mathbf{R}' \subseteq \mathbf{R}_c(\mathbf{F})$. Define $\Gamma''(\mathbf{F}) = \mathbf{R}_c(\mathbf{F})$ for any $\mathbf{F} \in \mathbf{R}(\mathbf{E}_s)$. Then there is according to Choquet (1953) a σ-algebra $\mathbf{A}''$ in $\mathbf{R}(\mathbf{E}_s)$ and a probability measure P'' defined on it such that the hint $(\mathbf{R}(\mathbf{E}_s), \mathbf{A}'', \mathbf{P}'', \Gamma'', \Theta)$ has sp as support function.

Note that using φ the probability space $(\mathbf{R}(\mathbf{E}_s), \mathbf{A}'', P'')$ induces a probability space $(\mathbf{R}(\Theta), \mathbf{A}', P')$. If we define $\Gamma_c(\mathbf{R}) = \mathbf{R}_c(\varphi(\mathbf{R}))$, then the hint $(\mathbf{R}(\Theta), \mathbf{A}', P', \Gamma_c, \Theta)$ generates clearly also the support function sp on $\mathbf{E}_s$. Let $u_c(H)$, $v_c(H)$ be the functions (1) defined with respect to Γ_c and let $u_c(\mathbf{E}_s)$, $v_c(\mathbf{E}_p)$ (where $\mathbf{E}_p$ is the dual class to $\mathbf{E}_s$) be the images of $\mathbf{E}_s$ and $\mathbf{E}_p$ with respect to u_c and v_c, respectively. By theorem 1 (5) and (7), $u_c(\mathbf{E}_s)$ is a multiplicative class and $v_c(\mathbf{E}_p)$ an additive class. Both $u_c(\mathbf{E}_s)$ and $v_c(\mathbf{E}_p)$ are contained in $\mathbf{A}'$. Now, let $\mathbf{A}_c$ be the smallest σ-algebra containing $u_c(\mathbf{E}_s)$ and $v_c(\mathbf{E}_p)$; $\mathbf{A}_c$ is subalgebra of $\mathbf{A}'$. Let finally P_c be the restriction of P' to $\mathbf{A}_c$. Then the hint $\mathbf{H}_c = (\mathbf{R}(\Theta), \mathbf{A}_c, P_c, \Gamma_c, \Theta)$ still has sp on $\mathbf{E}_s$ as support function. This hint is called the *canonical hint* of the support function sp on $\mathbf{E}_s$. We shall see that $\mathbf{H}_c$ is in some sense the coarsest hint that generates sp on $\mathbf{E}_s$: among all hints generating sp, it contains the least information. This will be formulated more precisely using the inclusion relation between hints introduced in the previous section.

Thus, let $\mathbf{H} = (\Omega, \mathbf{A}, P, \Gamma, \Theta)$ be any hint that defines the support function sp on $\mathbf{E}_s$. More precisely, suppose that the class of s-measurable sets of $\mathbf{H}$ contains $\mathbf{E}_s$ and that on $\mathbf{E}_s$ its support function equals sp. Hints that define in this sense identical support functions on $\mathbf{E}_s$ are called *equivalent*. In order to compare equivalent hints among themselves and in particular with the canonical hint, they must be represented with respect to an identical set of possible interpretations. By the mapping Γ, the σ-algebra $\mathbf{A}$ and the probability measure P can be transported to the set $\mathbf{R}(\Theta)$ in the usual way: Consider the σ-algebra $\mathbf{A}'$ of all subsets $B \subseteq \mathbf{R}(\Theta)$ for which $\Gamma^{-1}(B) \in \mathbf{A}$ and define a probability P' on $\mathbf{A}'$ by $P'(B) = P(\Gamma^{-1}(B))$. This leads to an equivalent hint $(\mathbf{R}(\Theta), \mathbf{A}', P', id, \Theta)$ where id stands for the identical mapping $id(\mathbf{R}) = \mathbf{R}$. This is called the *canonical representation* of $\mathbf{H}$. In particular, note that this new hint defines the same extended support function sp'_e as $\mathbf{H}$. In this sense $\mathbf{H}$ and its canonical representation $\mathbf{H}_{cr}$ contain exactly the same information.

The following theorem states now that the canonical hint is the coarsest hint among all equivalent hints with respect to a support function sp on $\mathbf{E}_s$.

Theorem 8. *Let* $\mathbf{H}_c$ *be the canonical hint with respect to a support function sp on a multiplicative class* $\mathbf{E}_s$. *If* $\mathbf{H}$ *is any equivalent hint with respect to this support function and* $\mathbf{H}_{cr}$ *its canonical representation, then* $\mathbf{H}_{cr} \subseteq \mathbf{H}_c$.

Proof. Both $\mathbf{H}_{cr}$ and $\mathbf{H}_c$ have the same set of possible interpretations $\mathbf{R}(\Theta)$. Moreover, clearly $id(\mathbf{R}) \subseteq \mathbf{R}_c(\varphi(\mathbf{R}))$, $\mathbf{A}' \supseteq \mathbf{A}_c$ and the restriction of P' to $\mathbf{A}_c$ equals P_c.

As a consequence of this theorem, it follows that $[sp_e(H), pl_e(H)] \subseteq [sp_{ce}(H), pl_{ce}(H)]$ for all $H \subseteq \Theta$, if sp_{ce}, pl_{ce} denote the extended support and plausibility functions of the canonical hint and sp_e, pl_e the extended support and plausibility functions of the hint $\mathbf{H}$. Shafer

(1979) studied extensions of support functions and identified among others the minimal extension of a support function sp on $\mathbf{E}_s$. It turns out that this minimal extension is in fact, as one may expect, the extension of the canonical hint with respect to sp on $\mathbf{E}_s$.

Theorem 9. *If sp_{ce}, pl_{ce} are the extended support and plausibility functions of the canonical hint $\mathbf{H}_c$ with respect to a support and plausibility function sp and pl on a multiplicative class $\mathbf{E}_s$ and its dual additive class $\mathbf{E}_p$, then*

$$sp_{ce}(H) = \sup\{\textstyle\sum\{(-1)^{|I|+1} sp(\cap_{i\in I} E_i) : \emptyset \neq I \subseteq \{1,\dots,n\}\} : E_i \subseteq H, E_i \in \mathbf{E}_s, i = 1,\dots,n;\ n = 1,2,\dots\} \tag{12}$$

$$pl_{ce}(H) = \inf\{\textstyle\sum\{(-1)^{|I|+1} pl(\cup_{i\in I} E_i) : \emptyset \neq I \subseteq \{1,\dots,n\}\} : E_i \supseteq H, E_i \in \mathbf{E}_p, i = 1,\dots,n;\ n = 1,2,\dots\} \tag{13}$$

Proof. Note that by theorem 1 (6) $\cup_{i=1}^{n} u_c(E_i) \subseteq u_c(\cup_{i=1}^{n} E_i)$. Furthermore

$$\begin{aligned} sp_{ce}(H) &= P_{c*}(u_c(H)) \\ &\geqslant \sup\{P_c(\cup_{i=1}^{n} u_c(E_i)) : E_i \subseteq H, E_i \in \mathbf{E}_s, i = 1,\dots,n; n = 1,2,\dots\} \\ &= \sup\{\textstyle\sum\{(-1)^{|I|+1} P_c(\cap_{i\in I} u_c(E_i)) : \emptyset \neq I \subseteq \{1,\dots,n\}\} : E_1 \subseteq H, E_i \in \mathbf{E}_s, i = 1,\dots,n; n = 1,2,\dots\} \\ &= \sup\{\textstyle\sum\{(-1)^{|I|+1} sp(\cap_{i\in I} u_c \mathrm{E}_i) : \emptyset \neq I \subseteq \{1,\dots,n\}\} : E_1 \subseteq H, E_i \in \mathbf{E}_s, i = 1,\dots,n; n = 1,2,\dots\} \end{aligned}$$

On the other hand, Shafer (1979) proves that the right-hand side of (12) defines indeed a support function sp_m on the power set $\mathbf{P}(\Theta)$ satisfying the conditions of theorem 7. There exists, therefore, a hint $\mathbf{H}'$ that generates this support function, and let $\mathbf{H}'_{cr}$ be its canonical representation. But theorem 8 implies that $\mathbf{H}'_{cr} \subseteq \mathbf{H}_c$ and by theorem 6 $sp_{ce}(H) \leqslant sp_{cre}(H) = sp_m(H)$ since $k = 1$. Thus we obtain finally $sp_{ce}(H) = sp_m(H)$ which proves (12).

(13) is deduced from (12) using (3) and theorem 1 (3) and (4) together with the de Morgan laws.

Theorem 9 together with theorems 6 and 8 show that sp_m is the smallest support function that extends sp from $\mathbf{E}_s$ to all of $\mathbf{P}(\Theta)$.

If the support function sp on a σ-multiplicative class $\mathbf{E}_s$ is *continuous* (satisfies condition (3) of theorem 3), then a canonical hint associated to this support function can be constructed in a similar way with respect to the set of σ-restrictions $\mathbf{R}_\sigma(\Theta)$ on Θ. For any hint for which all restrictions are σ-restrictions, a canonical representation with respect to $\mathbf{R}_\sigma(\Theta)$ can be defined along similar lines as above.

Then two further results corresponding to theorems 8 and 9 can be proved:

Theorem 10. *Let* $\mathbf{H}_c$ *be the canonical hint with respect to a continuous support function sp on a* σ*-multiplicative class* $\mathbf{E}_s$. *If* $\mathbf{H}$ *is any equivalent hint with respect to this support function and* $\mathbf{H}_{cr}$ *its canonical representation, then* $\mathbf{H}_{cr} \subseteq \mathbf{H}_c$.

Theorem 11. *If* sp_{ce}, pl_{ce} *are the extended support and plausibility functions of the canonical hint* $\mathbf{H}_c$ *with respect to continuous support and plausibility functions sp and pl on a* σ*-algebra* $\mathbf{E}_s = \mathbf{E}_p$, *then*

$$sp_{ce}(H) = \sup\{ \lim_{i\to\infty} sp(E_i): E_1 \supseteq E_2 \supseteq \dots, E_i \in \mathbf{E}_s, \cap E_i \subseteq H\} \quad (14)$$

$$pl_{ce}(H) = \inf\{ \lim_{i\to\infty} pl(E_i): E_1 \subseteq E_2 \subseteq \dots, E_i \in \mathbf{E}_p, \cup E_i \supseteq H\} \quad (15)$$

These theorems will not be proved here. The proofs develop along similar lines as those of theorems 8 and 9. Note that for theorem 11 Shafer (1979) showed that the right-hand side of (14) is indeed a continuous support function. This theorem shows that it is the smallest continuous support function that extends the continuous support function *sp* from $\mathbf{E}_s$ to $\mathbf{P}(\Theta)$.

6. COMBINING HINTS

Let $\mathbf{H}_1$ and $\mathbf{H}_2$ be two hints relative to the same frame Θ and defined by $(\Omega_1, \mathbf{A}_1, P_1, \Gamma_1, \Theta)$ and $(\Omega_2, \mathbf{A}_2, P_2, \Gamma_2, \Theta)$. The basic idea for the combination of these hints into a combined body of information is that in each hint there must be exactly one correct interpretation ω_i, $i = 1, 2$ such that – looking at both hints together – ω_1 and ω_2 must be simultaneously correct interpretations. Hence (ω_1, ω_2) must be the correct combined interpretation. Therefore, in order to combine the two hints $\mathbf{H}_1$ and $\mathbf{H}_2$ into one new combined hint, we form first the product space of the combined interpretations from the two hints $(\Omega_1 \times \Omega_2, \mathbf{A}_1 \oplus \mathbf{A}_2, P')$ where P' is any probability measure on $\mathbf{A}_1 \oplus \mathbf{A}_2$ reflecting the common likelihood of combined interpretations. The two hints are called *independent* if the interpretations of the two hints are stochastically independent. Then P is the product measure of P_1 and P_2. This is the case that will be pursued here, although other cases would be equally possible.

If the combined interpretation (ω_1, ω_2) is the correct one, then the restriction

$$\Gamma(\omega_1, \omega_2) = \Gamma_1(\omega_1) \cap \Gamma_2(\omega_2) \tag{16}$$

must necessarily hold. Note that it is possible that $\Gamma_1(\omega_1)$ and $\Gamma_2(\omega_2)$ are contradictory. Then ω_1 and ω_2 are called contradictory interpretations.

Define now

$$\begin{aligned} u'(H) &= \{(\omega_1, \omega_2) \in \Omega_1 \times \Omega_2 : H \textit{ is implied by } \Gamma(\omega_1, \omega_2)\} \\ v'(H) &= \{(\omega_1, \omega_2) \in \Omega_1 \times \Omega_2 : H \textit{ is implied under } \Gamma(\omega_1, \omega_2)\} \end{aligned} \tag{17}$$

Theorem 1 – except (1) and (2) – clearly applies to u' and v'; (1) is replaced by $v'(\emptyset) = \emptyset$ and (2) by $u'(\Theta) = \Omega_1 \times \Omega_2$. $u'(\emptyset)$ represents the set of contradictory interpretation pairs. Such a pair can never be the correct one because contradictions are not possible. Therefore, contradictory interpretations must be eliminated and the probability must be conditioned on the event that there is no contradiction. Provided that $u'(\emptyset)$ is measurable, i.e., $u'(\emptyset) \in \mathbf{A}_1 \oplus \mathbf{A}_2$ and $P'(u'(\emptyset) < 1$, the new combined hint $\mathbf{H}_1 \oplus \mathbf{H}_2 = (\Omega, \mathbf{A}, P, \Gamma, \Theta)$ can be formed, where

$$\begin{aligned} \Omega &= u'(\emptyset)^c = v'(\Theta), \\ \mathbf{A} &= u'(\emptyset)^c \cap \mathbf{A}_1 \oplus \mathbf{A}_2, \\ P(A) &= P'(A) / P'(u'(\emptyset)^c) \end{aligned}$$

and Γ is defined by (16) (and restricted to Ω). This method of combining hints is called *Dempster's rule* (Dempster, 1967).

Let u and v be defined by (1) relative to the hint $\mathbf{H}_1 \oplus \mathbf{H}_2$. Then $u(H) = u'(H) \cap \Omega = u'(H) - u'(\emptyset)$ and $v(H) = v'(H)$.

Dempster's rule may be extended even to the case where $u'(\emptyset)$ is not measurable. In this case the conditional probability space $(\Omega, \mathbf{A}, P)$ can be considered, where $(\Omega, \mathbf{A})$ is defined as above and $P(A) = P'^*(A \cap u'(\emptyset)^c) / P'^*(u'(\emptyset)^c)$, provided that $P'^*(u'(\emptyset)^c) > 0$. This leads to the combined hint $\mathbf{H}_1 \oplus \mathbf{H}_3 = (\Omega, \mathbf{A}, P, \Gamma, \Theta)$.

As before, we have $u(H) = u'(H) \cap \Omega = u'(H) - u'(\emptyset)$ and $v(H) = v'(H)$. Let $\mathbf{E}_s$ and $\mathbf{E}_p$ be the classes of s- and p-measurable sets relative to the hint $\mathbf{H}_1 \oplus \mathbf{H}_2$. Denote by $\mathbf{E}'_s$ and $\mathbf{E}'_p$ the classes of sets H such that $u'(H)$ and $v'(H)$ are measurable with respect to $\mathbf{A}_1 \oplus \mathbf{A}_2$. From $u'(H) \in \mathbf{A}_1 \oplus \mathbf{A}_2$ it follows that $u(H) \in \Omega \cap \mathbf{A}_1 \oplus \mathbf{A}_2$ and thus $\mathbf{E}'_s \subseteq \mathbf{E}_s$. Similarly, because $v'(H) \subseteq \Omega$, $v'(H) \in \mathbf{A}_1 \oplus \mathbf{A}_2$ implies $v(H) \in \Omega \cap \mathbf{A}_1 \oplus \mathbf{A}_2$ or $\mathbf{E}'_p \subseteq \mathbf{E}_p$. If $u'(\emptyset)$ is measurable, then $\mathbf{E}'_s = \mathbf{E}_s$ and $\mathbf{E}'_s = \mathbf{E}_p$.

The next theorem states that inclusion of hints is maintained under Dempster's rule.

Theorem 12. *Let* $\mathbf{H}_1, \mathbf{H}_2, \mathbf{H}''_1, \mathbf{H}''_2$ *be four hints such that* $\mathbf{H}''_1 \subseteq \mathbf{H}_1$ *and* $\mathbf{H}''_2$ $\mathbf{H}_2$. *Then* $\mathbf{H}''_1 \oplus \mathbf{H}''_2 \subseteq \mathbf{H}_1 \oplus \mathbf{H}_2$.

Proof. $\Gamma''_1(\omega_1) \subseteq \Gamma_1(\omega_1)$ and $\Gamma''_2(\omega_2) \subseteq \Gamma_2(\omega_2)$ imply $\Gamma''_1(\omega_1) \cap \Gamma''_2(\omega_2) \subseteq \Gamma_1(\omega_1) \cap \Gamma_2(\omega_2)$. This, together with $\Omega''_1 \subseteq \Omega_1$ and $\Omega''_2 \subseteq \Omega_2$ implies $\Omega'' \subseteq \Omega$. Also $\mathbf{A}''_1 \supseteq \mathbf{A}_1 \cap \Omega''_1$ and $\mathbf{A}''_2 \supseteq \mathbf{A}_2 \cap \Omega''_2$ imply that

$$\begin{aligned}\mathbf{A}'' &= \mathbf{A}''_1 \oplus \mathbf{A}''_2 \cap \Omega'' \supseteq (\mathbf{A}_1 \cap \Omega''_1) \oplus (\mathbf{A}_2 \cap \Omega''_2) \cap \Omega'' \\ &= (\mathbf{A}_1 \oplus \mathbf{A}_2) \cap (\Omega''_1 \times \Omega''_2) \cap \Omega'' \\ &= \mathbf{A}_1 \oplus \mathbf{A}_2 \cap \Omega'' = (\mathbf{A}_1 \oplus \mathbf{A}_2 \cap \Omega) \cap \Omega'' = \mathbf{A} \cap \Omega''\end{aligned}$$

It remains to show that

$$P''(A) = P^*(A)/P^*(\Omega'')$$

for any $A \in \mathbf{A} \cap \Omega''$. Let Q'' and Q denote the product measures of P''_1 and P''_2, and P_1 and P_2 on the product spaces $(\Omega''_1 \times \Omega''_2, \mathbf{A}''_1 \oplus \mathbf{A}''_2)$ and $(\Omega_1 \times \Omega_2, \mathbf{A}_1 \oplus \mathbf{A}_2)$ respectively. Then by definition $P''(A) = Q''^*(A)/Q''^*(\Omega'')$ for any $A \in \mathbf{A} \cap \Omega''$. It is thus sufficient to show that $Q''^*(A) = k \cdot P^*(A)$ for some constant k independent of A.

To begin with, let's suppose that the sets Ω''_1, Ω''_2, Ω'' and Ω are measurable with respect to $\mathbf{A}_1$, $\mathbf{A}_2$, $\mathbf{A}$ and $\mathbf{A}_1 \oplus \mathbf{A}_2$ respectively. Then $P''(A) = Q''(A)/Q''(\Omega'')$ and $P^*(A)/P^*(\Omega'') = P(A)/P(\Omega'')$ for $A \in \Omega''$ and we must prove that $Q^*(A) = k \cdot P(A)$. Let X_2 denote the indicator function of A. Then

$$Q''(A) = \int P''_1(d\omega_1)\, P''_2(d\omega_2) X_A$$

Because X_A is a measurable function with respect to $\mathbf{A}$, it is sufficient to take the restrictions of the probability measures P''_1 and P''_2 to $\mathbf{A}_1$ and $\mathbf{A}_2$. But there these probabilities are conditional probabilities such that

$$\begin{aligned}Q''(A) &= \int P_1(d\omega_1)\, P_2(d\omega_2) X_A / P_1(\Omega''_1) P_2(\Omega''_2) \\ &= Q(A)/P_1(\Omega''_1) P_2(\Omega''_2) = P(A)(Q(\Omega)/P_1(\Omega''_1) P_2(\Omega''_2))\end{aligned}$$

This proves the theorem in the case of measurable sets Ω''_1, Ω''_2, Ω'' and Ω. If Ω is not measurable, then there exists a measurable set $\bar{\Omega}$, containing Ω, such that $Q^*(\Omega) = Q(\bar{\Omega})$. If $A \in \mathbf{A} \cap \Omega$, then $\bar{A} = A \cap \bar{\Omega}$ is measurable, contains A, and $Q^*(A) = Q(\bar{A})$.

Thus $P(\bar{A}) = P(A)$ for all $A \in \mathbf{A} \cap \Omega$ and Ω may be replaced by $\bar{\Omega}$ and $\mathbf{A} \cap \Omega$ by $\mathbf{A} \cap \bar{\Omega}$ without changing the relevant probability values. In this way the case where some or all sets Ω_1'', Ω_2'', Ω'' and Ω are not measurable can be reduced to the former case. This proves the theorem.

In the case of theorem 12, the constant k appearing in theorem 6 equals $P^*(\Omega'')$, where Ω'' contains all combined interpretations (ω_1, ω_2) that are not contradictory under $\mathbf{H}_1'' \oplus \mathbf{H}_2''$. Some combined interpretations, which are not contradictory under $\mathbf{H}_1 \oplus \mathbf{H}_2$, may, however, be contradictory under $\mathbf{H}_1'' \oplus \mathbf{H}_2''$. This accounts for the possible difference between Ω and Ω''. If the situation is such that $\Omega'' = \Omega$, then $k = 1$ and $[sp_e''(H), pl_e''(H)] \subseteq [sp_e(H). pl_e(H)]$.

Let $\mathbf{V}$ be the vacuous hint associated with $\mathbf{H}_2$. Then theorem 12 implies that $\mathbf{H}_1 \oplus \mathbf{H}_2 \subseteq \mathbf{H}_1 \oplus \mathbf{V}$. Similarily $\mathbf{H}_1 \oplus \mathbf{H}_2 \subseteq \mathbf{V} \oplus \mathbf{H}_2$. As the combination of a hint with a vacuous hint does not add new information to the hint, this result shows that a combined hint $\mathbf{H}_1 \oplus \mathbf{H}_2$ is always finer than each of the two hints $\mathbf{H}_1$ and $\mathbf{H}_2$ alone. And in particular, if sp is the support function of $\mathbf{H}_1 \oplus \mathbf{H}_2$, then we have $[sp_e(H), pl_e(H)] \subseteq [sp_{1e}(H), pl_{1e}(H)]$ and $[sp_e(H), pl_e(H)] \subseteq [sp_{2e}(H), pl_{2e}(H)]$, if $\mathbf{H}_1$ and $\mathbf{H}_2$ have no contradictory interpretations.

BIBLIOGRAPHY

Choquet, G. (1953). Theory of capacities. *Ann. Inst. Fourier (Grenoble)* 5: 131–295.

Choquet, G. (1969). *Lectures on analysis*. New York: Benjamin Cummings.

Dempster, A. P. (1967). Upper and lower probabilities induced by a multivalued mapping. *Annals of Mathematical Statistics* 38: 325–39.

Dubois, D. and Prade, H. (1986). A set-theoretic view of belief functions. Logical operations and approximations by fuzzy sets. *Int. J. General Systems* 12: 193–226.

Fagin, R. and Halpern, J. Y. (1989). Uncertainty, belief, and probability. *Proc. of IJCAI-89*, pp. 1161–67.

Goodman, I. R. and Nguyen, H. T. (1985). *Uncertainty models for knowledge-based systems*. New York: North-Holland.

Kohlas, J. (1990). A mathematical theory of hints. Working Paper No. 173, Institute for Automation and Operations Research, University of Fribourg, Switzerland.

Neveu, J. (1964). *Bases mathématiques du calcul des probabilités*. Paris: Masson.

Nguyen, H. T. (1978). On random sets and belief functions. *J. Math. Anal. Appl.* 65: 531–42.

Ruspini, E. H. (1987). Epistemic logics, probability, and the calculus of evidence. *Proc. of IJCAI-87*, pp. 924–931.

Shafer, G. (1976). *A mathematical theory of evidence.* Princeton: Princeton University Press.

Shafer, G. (1978). Dempster's rule of combination. Unpublished manuscript. University of Kansas, School of Business, Lawrence.

Shafer, G. (1979). Allocations of probability. *Annals of Probability* 7: 827–39.

Shafer, G. (1990). Perspectives on the theory and practice of belief functions. *Int. J. Approx. Reas.* 4: 323–62.

Strat, T. M. (1984). Continuous belief functions for evidential reasoning. *Proc. of AAAI-84*, pp. 308–13.

Yager, R. R. (1985). The entailment principle for Dempster-Shafer granule. Tech. Report MII-512, Iona College, New Rochelle, NY.

22 Evidential reasoning with conditional events

Marcus SPIES

Abstract: A new approach to the treatment of conditioning in the Dempster-Shafer theory of evidence is described. The approach is based on a purely algebraical definition of conditioning via conditional objects. Based on this theory conditional belief functions are defined and combination of evidence on such functions is introduced. Then, the generalization of stochastic matrices to conditional belief functions is given. It is shown that there are straightforward generalizations of computations known from Bayesian networks to networks of multivariate conditional belief functions.

Keywords: Dempster-Shafer theory, combination of evidence, conditional objects.

1. INTRODUCTION

Recently, the problem of defining conditional belief functions has attracted the attention of several researchers. Jaffray (1990) and Hestir et al. (1991) provide the most encompassing summaries of the situation. It has been proved that there is no conditionalization function for belief functions that does not violate the interpretation of belief functions in terms of lower and upper probabilities. In this respect I will consider an alternative approach that uses conditional objects as defined by Goodman and Nguyen (1988). Basically, conditional objects provide a set-theoretical representation of conditionals. Therefore it is a simple idea to define conditional belief functions as belief functions whose focal elements are (sets of) conditional objects. In a previous paper (Spies, 1991 a), I proved that this view leads to an elegant use of the qualitative Markov property that is needed to define local reasoning schemes for belief functions. In that paper, I restricted the valuation of conditional objects to focal elements that are Boolean functions of antecedent and consequent. Such valuations lead to a representation of conditional probabilities. In the present paper, I introduce the definition of a conditional belief function.

An important consequence of this method is that Bayesian conditioning can always be recovered from a conditional object representation of conditional probabilities. Thus, my method is rather orthogonal to the negative results found by Jaffray (1990). While, in the conventional view, conditioning is a restriction operation on a probability space, in the view presented here it applies to a newly partitioned but otherwise unrestricted universe. In this way, the problem of "redistributing" evidence mass on a subalgebra of the original σ-algebra can be circumvented. It is this problem that genuinely leads to the difficulties encountered in a conventional definition of conditional belief functions.

2. BASIC DEFINITIONS

The basic purpose of introducing conditional events is to have a way to refer to the rule

"If X is A, then Y is B"

as an event in some event algebra. It has been proved (Goodman and Nguyen, 1988) that ordinary probability theory offers no support in this respect. Namely the probability that

"Y is B, given X is A"

is usually not the probability of an event in the σ–algebra of the underlying probability space $(\Omega, \mathbf{A}, P)$. In general, there is no Boolean function f, such that, for $A, B, Z \in \mathbf{A}$ with

$$Z = f(A, B)$$

we have

$$p(Z) = \frac{p(A \cap B)}{p(A)}$$

This is a remarkable fact. Basically it is due to the difference between conditioning and material implication that has also been noted. It makes a difference whether I ask for those rainy days on which a rainbow appears or whether I ask for how many days the condition

"If the day is rainy, then a rainbow appears"

holds true. In the former case, the universe (all days) is restricted to the subset of rain days, whereas in the second case, all days are taken into account. Moreover, in this case, all nonrainy (cloudy to sunny) days fulfill trivially the implication

$$p(A \cap B)/p(A) \leqslant p(\bar{A} \cup B)$$

Therefore, the material implication gives us just an upper bound on conditionalization. This leads to thinking of conditionals as something set-valued. Acually, a conditional can range from all cases in which antecedent and consequent are true to all cases in which the antecedent is false but the consequent is true. Probabilistically, this can be expressed by

$$p(A \cap B) \leqslant p(B|A) \leqslant p(\bar{A} \cup B)$$

We shall see that conditional events generalize this inequality to a mere set-theoretic framework prior to any valuations.

These considerations led Goodman and Nguyen (1988) to the following definitions. For an extanded introduction to the formalism of conditional events, the reader is referred to an edited volume by Goodman et al. (1991).

We shift from a set-oriented perspective to an algebra-oriented perspective. This facilitates notations. Let $\mathbf{R}(+,\bigstar)$ denote a Boolean ring of sets over a universe U with the unit element 1 (or $\top$) and the zero element 0 (or $\bot$). Usually, the elements of a Boolean ring are denoted by lowercase letters $a, b, \ldots$ in order to stress the algebraic aspect. In a Boolean ring we have $a \bigstar a = a$, for all $a \in \mathbf{R}$. This is the set-theoretic idempotency property. Moreover, $\mathbf{R}$ is commutative. As for the ring addition, it corresponds to the symmetric difference in set theory; therefore, we have $a + a = 0$, for all $a \in \mathbf{R}$. In the sequel $x \bigstar y$ will usually be abbreviated by xy. Similarly, in some formulae, the complement of x, $1 - x$ will be referred to by x'.

A *conditional object* is defined by Goodman and Nguyen (1988) as a set of subsets whose elements all fulfill a given implication.

Therefore, the conditional object $[b|a]$ is a set of elements x of $\mathbf{R}$ such that the intersection of x with a is the same as the intersection of b with a:

$$[b|a] := \{x \in \mathbf{R} | x \bigstar a = b \bigstar a\}$$

It is easily seen that *a conditional object, or event, precisely spans the intervals of those subsets in* $\mathbf{R}$ *for which the material implication*

"if x is in a, then x is in b"

holds. We can therefore write equivalently:

$$[b|a] = [ab, 1 + a + ab]$$

This notation is the easiest for intuitively understanding conditional events. $\mathbf{R}(+, \bigstar)$ is a lattice. We denote the infimum and supremum of $[b|a]$ by $\sqcap[b|a]$ and $\sqcup[b|a]$, respectively.

In a recent paper, Nguyen and Rogers (1990) have provided a more general view of conditional objects in terms of partitions of a Boolean ring modulo an ideal. The basic point is that the definition of conditional objects can be equivalently written as

$$[a|b] = b + \mathbf{R}a'$$

Since the term $\mathbf{R}a'$ denotes a (principal) ideal of a Boolean ring, there is a partition of this ring modulo this ideal, written as $\mathbf{R}_{/\mathbf{R}a'}$. Thus, the conditional objects of a given antecedent are cosets (or equivalence classes) of this partition. The conditional object of a particular consequent is the coset containing this consequent. These results will be used in the section on combination of evidence.

Let us now introduce valuations into the merely set-theoretic notion of conditionals we have defined. Let us assume a probability measure to be given on our universe of discourse U. Then the valuations (probabilities) of then lower and upper bounds of a conditional have a nice logical interpretation (Spies, 1991a): we may call $p(\sqcap[b|a])$ the *degree of verification* since, in a frequentistic interpretation of probability, it measures the proportion of cases verifying the implication "if x is in a, then x is in b." On the other hand, $p(\sqcup[b|a])$ measures the proportion of cases that do not violate the material implication. Thus $1 - p(\sqcup[b|a])$ measures how many cases actually violate the implication. This number can therefore, in a logical interpretation of probability, be called a *degree of falsification*.

If a probability measure is given on U, the conditional probability $p(b|a)$ can be recovered from $p(\sqcap[b|a])$ and $p(\sqcup[b|a])$ by

$$p(b|a) := = \frac{p(\sqcap[b|a])}{1 - (p(\sqcup[b|a]) - p(\sqcap[b|a]))}$$

This is equivalent to the results on the Bayesian conditioning investigated in Jaffray (1990). In this perspective, a valuation of a conditional object is a *distributed representation* of a conditional probability.

3. HOW IMPORTANT IS CONDITIONAL INFORMATION?

In probability theory, there is a prominent way to operate on conditional probabilities. This method is based on a "locality" assumption: if I know all relevant antecedents of a certain consequent I can discard from my computations all probabilities of irrelevant antecedents. On the basis of such locality assumptions the powerful theories of Markov chains (Freedman, 1983) and Markov random fields (Lauritzen and Spiegelhalter, 1988) have been built. As for applications to knowledge-based systems, it was the research of Pearl that made a widely accepted point in introducing locality assumptions into reasoning systems including uncertainty management (Pearl, 1988). Lauritzen and Spiegelhalter, in parallel to Pearl, have developed a different algorithm that achieves the same goal as Pearl's work: establishing a probabilistic reasoning system based on graphical multivariate models. In the sequel, I will assume some familiarity with this work. Again in parallel to research on probabilistic reasoning systems, Shafer and his colleagues worked out reasoning systems using multivariate belief functions (see Kong, 1986; Mellouli, 1987; Shafer et al., 1987; Kohlas and Monney, 1990; Shenoy, 1989). While the underlying independence concepts in both lines of research are different (Spies, 1991b), the principal ideas are highly correlated. Again, this work will be assumed familiar in the sequel of the present paper.

It is typical of the work on multivariate belief functions quoted before that conditionalization plays a marginal role only. On the one hand, this is motivated by a more philosophical point: conditional probabilities seem somehow "derived" from unconditional ones (Shafer, 1986). On the other hand, there are severe technical difficulties to consistently formulate conditional beliefs. In all approaches that have been made in this realm, conditionalization appears as a derived concept; there is some multivariate belief function, and a conditional belief is derived by restricting values of some of the variables. As mentioned in the introduction, it is by now well known that this approach to conditional beliefs always leads into trouble. However, despite this, the importance of being able to use conditional beliefs is undoubted. In practice, expert judgments are nearly always conditional. Thus, a method that allows for conditional beliefs only "after" knowing unconditional ones, is of low practical value.

The method of propagating evidence through qualitative Markov trees (Shafer et al., 1987) clearly shows the footprints of this absence of genuine conditional beliefs. In conventional probabilistic reasoning, one usually concludes from a given marginal probability of a disjoint and exhaustive set of quasi causal events B_i; $i \in \{1,...,n\}$, say, and the conditional probabilities of an event showing the effects of this cause, A, say, to an updated or posterior probability of this event.

$$p(A) = \sum_{i=1}^{n} p(A|B_i)\,p(B_i)$$

This equation is generally referred to as Jeffrey's rule. The underlying reasoning scheme can be expressed as: mariginal probability (A) $\Leftarrow$ f (conditional probability (A given B) marginal probability (B)).

What is important is that you never need to know the multivariate unconditional probabilities of the various combinations of variable states $A_i \cap B_j$. Now, in propagating belief functions, things work differently. Since there is no genuine formulation of conditional beliefs, we must know the multivariate unconditional beliefs of the various $A \cap B_i$ to obtain conditional beliefs. Thus, we have the reasoning scheme conditional belief (A given B) $\Leftarrow$ g (marginal belief (B), multivariate unconditional belief (A, B)).

Here, g corresponds to a composition of

1. vacuously extending *Bel* on frame B to the product frame $A \times B$,
2. applying Dempster's rule of combination on the product frame, and
3. projecting the resulting belief function to the frame corresponding to variable A.

The main point of this paper is that using conditional events as defined in the previous section we can

- consistently define genuine conditional belief functions,
- compute prior bounds for unconditional beliefs given conditional belief functions, and

- formulate an analogon of Jeffrey's rule for conclusions on the basis of such conditional belief functions.

As a consequence, conditional belief functions will enable us to freely move between conditional and marginal representations without the pervasive need to know multivariate unconditional belief functions.

4. CONDITIONAL BELIEF FUNCTIONS

Using the definitions and observations on conditional events, it is plausible to say that conditional belief refers to an uncertainty with respect not to a single set but to a whole interval of sets, namely those in the conditional object. This motivates the following simple definition.

Definition 1 (CBF). *A conditional belief function w.r.t. (with respect to) an element a of a Boolean ring* $\mathbf{R}$ *is a belief function whose focal elements are elements of* $\mathbf{R}_{/\mathbf{R}a'}$.

Three points should be noticed:

1. According to this definition, the focal elements of a CBF are sets of ring elements. Thus they are sets of subsets of the underlying frame of discernment. As a consequence, an ordinary belief function is a CBF on the atoms of the underlying frame of discernment.
2. The definition does not allow focal elements of CBFs to be themselves sets of conditional events. The reason for this lies in random set theory: a probability measure on an interval algebra defines a random set on the underlying event algebra (see Hestir et al., 1991, the first canonical construction of a random set). However, in practice, this is no restriction, since the focal element to be used when assessing a conditional belief of, say, $(B \cup C)|A$, is just the single conditional event $[b \sqcup c | a]$, where $\sqcup$ denotes the usual supremum operation in lattices.
3. As it is usual in evidence theory, no mass will be commited to an empty conditional $[\perp | a]$. Thus, we assume $m([\perp | a]) = 0$, for all $a \in \mathbf{R}$.

The important consequence of this definition is that a conditional belief function is *not* a belief function on a subalgebra $\mathbf{R}a$. Therefore, the difficulties in moving probability masses from the full algebra to the subalgebra vanish. It was these difficulties that caused the incompatibility of a conventional definition of conditioning in the Dempster-Shafer framework (see Jaffray, 1990). The usefulness of the present definition will become clear by discussing the following simple, albeit challenging example.

4.1. Ruspini's problem

At the Workshop on Uncertainty Modeling held at the FAW in Ulm (see Kämpke et al., 1990), Ruspini posed the following problem to me (see also Ruspini, 1987):

Let two frames be given. The one (Θ_1) distinguishes nationalities German (G) and Italian (I), the other one (Θ_2) drinking preferences for beer (B) versus not-beer, say wine ($\bar{B}$). Now assume the following conditional information comes in:

- $m(B|G) = 0.7$, $m(\bar{B}|G) = 0.2$, $m(\Theta_1|\text{G}) = 0.1$
- $m(B|I) = 0.4$, $m(\bar{B}|I) = 0.6$

Moreover, we are told that

$$m(G \cup I) = 1$$

that is, we may restrict our attention to $\Theta_1 = \{G, I\}$.

Now the question being posed is what can be said about, say, $p(B)$ or other marginal probabilities on frame Θ_2.

This question cannot be answered with traditional Dempster-Shafer methods, since it involves marginalizing conditional probabilities – a thing not being defined in this theory up to now. In order to give an answer to this problem, the first task evidently is to *define* what the conditional information really means, because, as explained in the previous section, such quantities do not exist *per se* in the belief function formalism. Here, I will use the definition given previously of conditional belief functions (CBFs). To get started, we have to build up a frame $\Theta_1 \times \Theta_2$. The Boolean ring of sets corresponding to this frame has the atoms

$$gb, gb', g'b, g'b'$$

which correspond, respectively, to the sets

$$G \cap B, G \cap \bar{B}, I \cap B, I \cap \bar{B}$$

This Boolean ring will be denoted **R** in all developments of the present example. It is depicted in Figure 22.1.

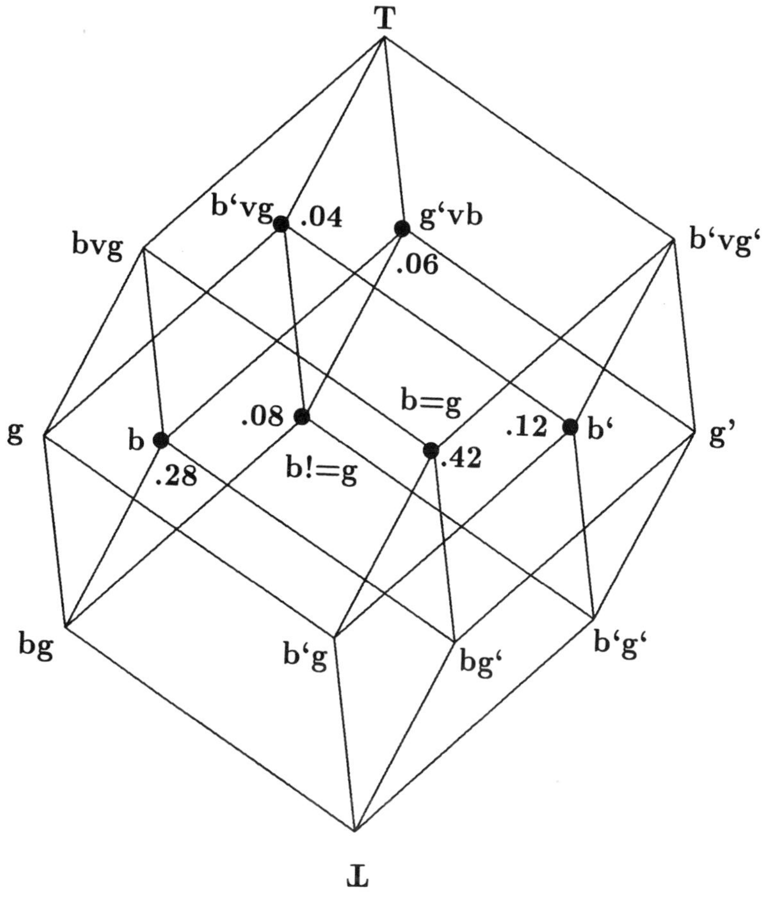

Figure 22.1: The Boolean ring corresponding to Ruspini's problem. As in text, ′ denotes complements; for brevity, notations $b! = g$ for $bg' \sqcup b'g$ and $b = g$ for $bg \sqcup b'g'$ are used.

With this definition in mind, we can model conditional information as *basic probability assignments* on the conditional objects of a single antecedent. Thus, the first piece of conditional information would be focused on elements of $\mathbf{R}_{/\mathbf{R}_{g'}}$. (Remember that the ring partition used for a specific antecedent is made up from a principal ideal corresponding to the complement of this antecedent). Similarly, the second piece of conditional information would be focused on elements of $\mathbf{R}_{/\mathbf{R}g'}$. The two conditional belief functions corresponding to our pieces of eidence can then be formulated as depicted in Figure 22.2.

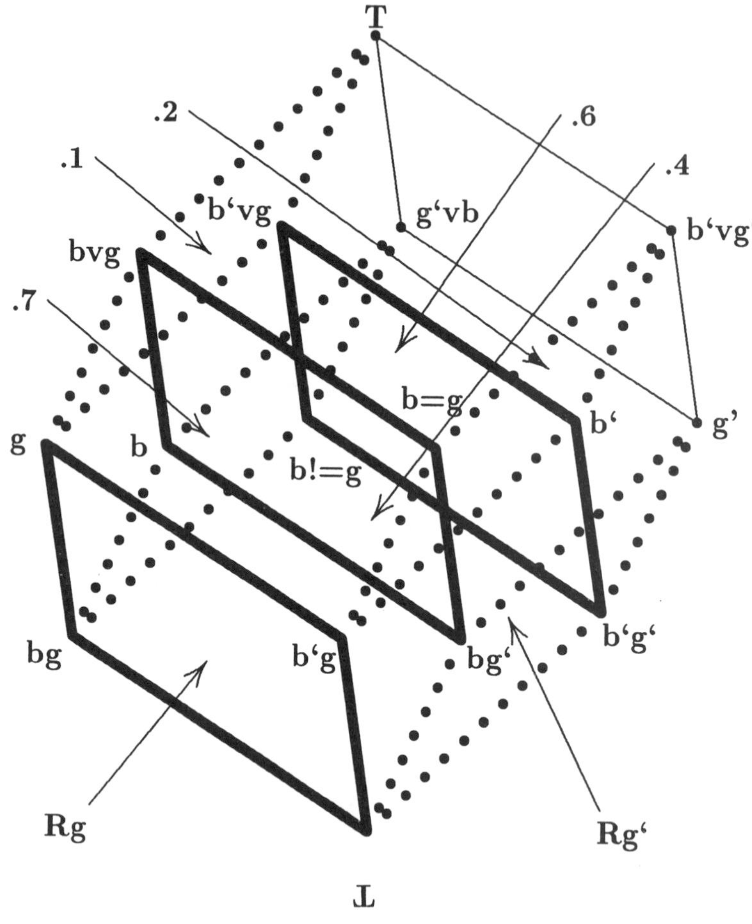

Figure 22.2: On the Boolean ring corresponding to Ruspini's problem two conditional belief functions are visualized. The dotted rectangles show conditional events w.r.t. antecedent g, starting with the principal ideal $\mathbf{R}g'$; the solid rectangles show conditional events w.r.t. antecedent g', starting with principal ideal $\mathbf{R}g$.

This picture implies that we use the following CBFs to model Ruspini's problem:

- $m([b|g]) = 0.7$
  $m([b'|g]) = 0.2$
  $m([\top|g]) = 0.1$
- $m([b|g']) = 0.4$
  $m([b'|g']) = 0.6$

Now let us suppose the two CBFs are independent. Then we may combine them like ordinary belief functions using Dempster's rule. The resulting numbers and focal elements are depicted in Figure 22.3.

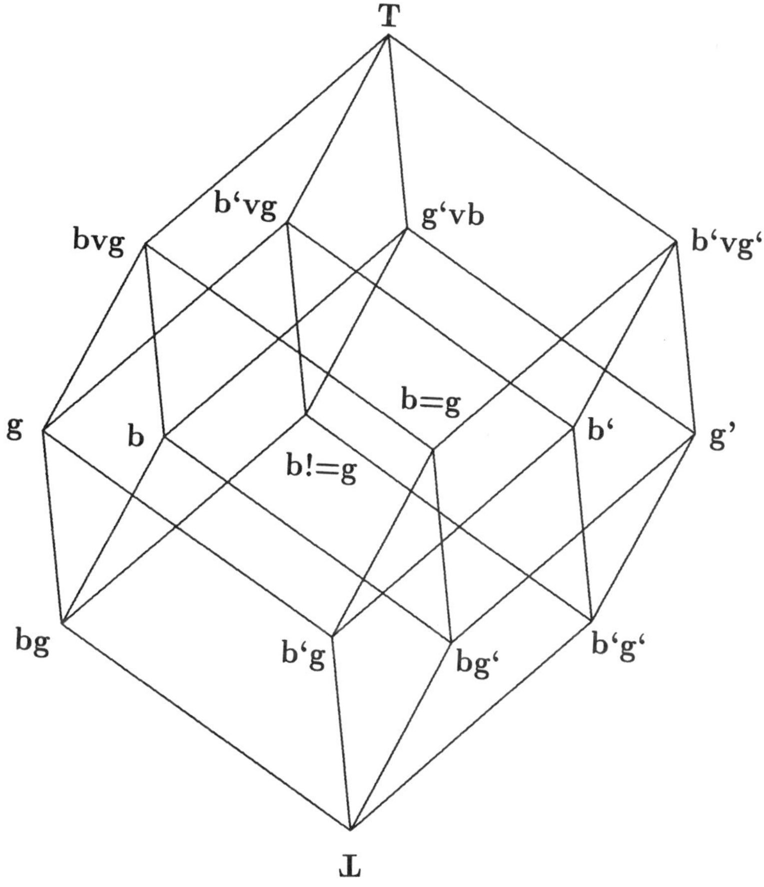

Figure 22.3: On the Boolean ring corresponding to Ruspini's problem the combination of two conditional belief functions is visualized. As shown in a theorem, this combination yields a belief function on singletons in **R** if the two antecedents are complements of each other. Moreover, the numbers in the figure are shown to be in accordance with usual probability estimates if all CBFs are probabilities.

Rewriting results for subsets instead of algebra elements, we find for instance, that $m(B) = 0.28$, $m(\bar{B}) = 0.12$, implying that

$$0.28 \leqslant p(B) \leqslant 0.88$$

or

$$0.12 \leqslant p(\bar{B}) \leqslant 0.72$$

Here, we tacitly mapped $\{b\}$ to b. The procedure is of striking simplicity: We established two CBFs on complementary antecedents, combined them, and found a marginal belief function that we can easily project down to Θ_2. Thus, we are able to accomplish the marginalization of conditional beliefs. The next theorem shows that the resulting belief function will always look like a marginal belief function if we have antecedents that exhaust the frame Θ_1. It will be tacitly assumed that we may shift from a belief function on singletons in $\mathbf{R}$ to a belief function on $\mathbf{R}$ itself, as we have done already in evaluating Dempster's rule.

Theorem 1. *Let A on frame Θ_1 and B on frame Θ_2 be discrete variables with mutually exclusive and exhaustive states $A = \{a_1,...,a_m\}$, $B = \{b_1,...,b_n\}$. Let $F_A = \{A_{I1},...,A_{IK}\}, k \leqslant 2^m$ be a set of state subsets of A $({}^I{}_i \subseteq \{1,...,m\}$ for all $i \in \{1,...,k\})$ such that*

$$\bigcup_{i=1}^{i} A_{Ii} = A$$

Let $m_{A_{Ii}} = m([x|A_{I_i}])$ be CBFs *on $\mathbf{R}_{\mathbf{R}A_{I_i'}}$. Then*

$$m_{F_A} := \bigoplus_{i=1}^{k} m_{A_{I_i}}$$

is a basic probability assignment on singletons in $\mathbf{R}$.

Proof. In a Boolean ring, there is an isomorphism between congruence relations and ring ideals (see Spies, 1991a – Lemmas 3 to 5, Theorem 1). Since each CBF has focal elements in the elements of precisely one congruence relation (as shown in Section 2), the focal elements of the combination of the $m_{A_{I_i}}$ will be the system of intersections of the elements of the congruence relations $\mathbf{R}_{/\mathbf{R}A_{I_i'}}$. Because of the isomorphism this will be the congruence relation based on the ideal that is the intersection of all $\mathbf{R}A_{I_i'}$. Now since

$$\sqcup_{i=1}^{k} A_{I_i} = \top$$

we have

$$\sqcup_{i=1}^{k} A_{I_i} = \perp$$

and therefore

$$\sqcap_{i=1}^{k} \mathbf{R}_{\mathbf{R}A_{Ii}} \mathbf{R}_{\mathbf{R}\sqcap_{i=1}^{k} A_{Ii}} = \mathbf{R}_{\mathbf{R}\perp}$$

Now $\mathbf{R}_{/\mathbf{R}\perp}$ is the congruence relation corresponding to conditional objects $[x|\top]$, which can be identified with the ring elements themselves.

The next theorem establishes that m_{F_A} is indeed a generalization of ordinary probability relationships.

Theorem 2. *If, in the preceding theorem, F_A is a set of mutually disjoint subsets or singletons in A, then m_{F_A} is a lower bound of posterior probabilities $p(b)$.*

Proof. If F_A partitions the set of states A, we have

$$p(b) = m \sum_{i=1}^{k} m([b|A_{I_i}]) * m(A_{I_i}) \geqslant \min_{i=1\ldots k} m([b|A_{I_i}])$$
$$\geqslant \prod_{i=1}^{k} m([b|A_{I_i}])$$

The first inequality holds since $\Sigma_{i=1}^{k} m(A_{I_i}) = 1$ (convex combination of conditional m numbers). The second inequality then follows from the fact that all factors in the product are positive and bounded from above by 1.0.

Since the belief function on the Boolean ring thus obtained is derived from marginalizing prior conditional belief functions, we are entitled to call it a *prior marginal belief evaluation*. It should be noted that m_{F_A} is a very conservative estimate of marginal probabilities. However, it is a very useful information if we do have nothing but conditional belief functions. Actually, it shows which probabilities can be compatible with the conditional belief given in a particular situation. The bounds obtained are necessary but not sufficient conditions for probabilities to be compatible with the conditional knowledge expressed in the CBFs. In order to infer marginal probabilities from conditional ones and marginal ones as in ordinary probability calculus we must go one step further.

4.2. Jeffrey's rule

In the present framework, we are able to generalize Jeffrey's rule. The basis for that is the simple observation that

$$[b|a] \cap \{a\} = \{x|xa = ab \wedge x \leqslant a\} = \{ab\}$$

which is a set-theoretic version of the famous equation

$$p(B|A)p(A) = p(AB)$$

With the notation of the two preceding theorems, we have:

Lemma 1 (Jeffrey's Rule for Belief Functions). *Let for* $i = 1,\ldots,k$ m_{A_i} *be a set of* CBFs *on exhaustive states* A_{I_i} *of a variable* A. *Let* m_A *be a marginal belief function on variable* A *with focal elements* $A_{I_1},\ldots,A_{I_k}$ *in* F_A. *Then the set of m-numbers defined by*

$$\hat{m}(A_{I_{iy}}) = m_{A_i}(y) * m_A(A_{I_i})$$

is a basic probability assignment on singletons in **R**. Its projection on the frame Θ_2 is called *prior belief function w.r.t. variable B.*

Proof. $\hat{m}$ is defined if the antecedent of a conditional event equals a given subset A_i of variable states. Therefore,

$$\sum_{i=1,\ldots,k;\, y\in\mathbf{R}} \hat{m}(A_i y) = \sum_{i=1,\ldots,k} m_A(\mathrm{A}_{I_i}) \sum_{y\in\mathbf{R}} m_{A_i}(y) = 1$$

It is easily seen that this reduces to Jeffrey's rule in the case of ordinary probabilities. Let us demonstrate in a modification of Ruspini's example how this rule works. Let us assume evidence (E) concerning the belief that someone is Italian g' or not (g) comes in.

$$\bullet m_E: \quad \begin{aligned} m(g) &= 0.3 \\ m(g') &= 0.5 \\ m(\Theta) &= 0.2 \end{aligned}$$

In order to be able to combine this with the conditional belief functions m_g and $m_{g'}$ we have to introduce a vacuous conditional belief function m_Θ with

$$m(x|\Theta) = \begin{cases} 0 & \text{if } x \neq \Theta \\ 1 & \text{if } x = \Theta \end{cases}$$

This is necessary because Θ is not among the antecedents of the CBFs m_g and $m_{g'}$. Now we are ready to calculate Jeffrey's rule for belief functions. For instance, we obtain

$$m([b|g]) * m_E(g) = 0.3 * 0.7 = 0.21$$
$$m([b|g']) * m_E(g') = 0.5 * 0.4 = 0.2$$

Projecting the result to frame Θ_2 corresponding to variable B, we find

$\hat{m}(b) = 0.41$

Similar calculations give

$\hat{m}(b') = 0.36$
$\hat{m}(\Theta) = 0.23$

4.3. Multivariate antecedents

In propagating beliefs through variable networks, an important case arises when severe variables are immediate predecessors of a given variable. This case is generally managed by graph triangulation (see Lauritzen and Spiegelhalter, 1988; Pearl, 1988; Kohlas and Monney 1990; Shenoy, 1989). In each triangle we need joint conditional information of two antecedent variables to one consequent variable. For instance if we know that drinking preferences are affected by climate besides nationality, we have to make up conditional belief functions for each combination of climate states with nationalities in order to get our inference process started.

I will now briefly show what these CBFs look like in the corresponding Boolean ring. One might expect the various conditional information to operate on ever finer partitions of this ring. However, it turns out that the opposite happens: The more complex the antecedent, the simpler the congruence relation of the corresponding conditional events.

As was noted in the definitory section on conditional objects, conditional obiects are cosets (or equivalence classes) in a ring being partitioned modulo the ideal generated by the negated antecedent. For antecedent b we have

$$\text{for all } a \in \mathbf{R} : [a \mid b] \in \mathbf{R}_{/\mathbf{R}b'}$$

The problem of multiple antecedents can be stated in the most general form as follows:

Given $[a \mid b]$ *and* $[a \mid c]$, *what is* $[a \mid b \star c]$?

The main result of Spies (1991a) is that in this situation a striking qualitative independence property holds. (For detailed explanation of qualitative and qualitative conditional independence, see Shafer et al., 1987; Shenoy and Shafer, 1988; Shenoy, 1989; Nguyen and Rogers, 1990; Spies, 1991b.) Denoting, as before, the partition generated by the complement of antecedent x, relative to the ring universe $\mathbf{R}$, as $\mathbf{R}_{/\mathbf{R}x'}$, and conditional Q-independence by the operator $\perp_Q$ between conditional independent partitions, and by separating the conditioning partition from these by a |, we have:

Theorem 3. *The set of conditional objects corresponding to a conjunction of two antecedents forms a partition that is qualitative conditional independent from the partitions corresponding to the set of conditional objects of each antecedent:*

$$\mathbf{R}_{/\mathbf{R}x'} \perp_Q \mathbf{R}_{/\mathbf{R}y'} | \mathbf{R}_{/\mathbf{R}(xy)'}$$

Moreover, this partition is coarser than the partitions corresponding to conditional event generated by each single antecedent.

The proof for this is in Spies (1991a).

Combining different antecedents in conditional events thus *always* satisfies the QC-independence for *pairs of antecedents*. This is in itself a remarkable fact. It leads to easier computations of multivariate antecedent CBFs than one might have expected.

4.4. Conditional beliefs in transition matrices

In propagation of evidence in multivariate models we use finite-valued variables to express the different "sites" of the underlying Markov random field (Pearl, 1988). Variables will be denoted henceforth by capital letters A, B,...

If we are able to express conditional beliefs we should be able to arrange them in stochastic matrices or transition matrices. Each row in such a matrix corresponds to a single antecedent while each column corresponds to one consequent of a conditional.

Now, take a transition matrix with row variable A with state subsets (!) A_i and for column variable B with state subsets B_j. In the cells of this matrix, we write the conditional *bpa*-numbers $m([B_j|A_i])$. Note again that these numbers sum up to unity in each row.

$$\sum_j m([B_j|A_i]) = 1$$

Thus, each row in a transition matrix corresponds to a single conditional belief function.

Two rows in the transition matrix deserve a comment: The first row conditions the consequents B_j under the empty set of antecedent states. In this row, the entry $m11$ must equal one, since the fact that no states of the antecedent variable are true amounts to a contradiction;

as a consequence, no states of the consequent variable can be true. In the last row the state-subsets of the consequent variable are conditioned under the antecedent

$$\bigcup_i A_i$$

that is, the universe of discourse. This row should contain the marginal beliefs in sets of states of variable B. Since we assume not to know these beliefs we write down a vacuous belief function with all probability mass attributed to the union

$$\bigcup_j B_j$$

of states of B. With these definitions and stipulations, we may write down a stochastic matrix for an arbitrary numerical example.

5. CONCLUSION

This paper introduces conditional belief functions. Their definition is made possible by the theory of set-theoretic conditioning, or conditional events. If one combines this theory with a simple view of belief functions as discrete random sets, the way to a straightforward generalization of probability propagation rules in Bayesian networks to networks representing multivariate belief functions is possible. It should be noted that the underlying view of belief functions is not shared by all researchers working on the Dempster-Shafer theory and that some of them also firmly assert that there is no need for a genuine concept of conditional belief functions. However, the ability to express conditional beliefs (or to assess conditional relative frequencies of random sets) is of practical importance. Therefore, I hope that the suggestions made in this paper will enhance the applicability of the Dempster-Shafer theory to practical problems.

BIBLIOGRAPHY

Dubois, D. and Prade, H. (1989). Measure-free conditioning, probability, and non-monotonic reasoning. *Proc. 11th IJCAI,* Detroit, pp. 1110–14.

Freedman, D. (1983). *Markov chains.* New York–Heidelberg: Springer-Verlag.

Goodman, I. and Nguyen, H. (1988): Conditional objects and the modelling of uncertainties. In M.M. Gupta and T. Yamakawa (eds.), *Fuzzy computing*, pp. 119–38, New York: Elsevier.

Goodman, I., M.M. Gupta, H.T. Nguyen, and G. Rogers, eds. (1991). *Conditional logic in expert systems*. Amsterdam: North-Holland

Heckerman, D. (1986). Probabilistic interpretations for MYCIN's certainty factors. In L.N Kanal and J.F. Lemmer (eds.), *Uncertainty in artificial intelligence* (1), pp. 167-96. New York: North-Holland.

Hestir, K., H.T. Nguyen, and G. Rogers (1991). A random set formalism for evidential reasoning. In I. Goodman, M.M. Gupta, H. Nguyen, and G. Rogers (eds.), *Conditional logic in expert systems*, pp. 309–44. Amsterdam: North-Holland.

Jaffray, J.-Y. (1990). Bayesian conditioning and belief functions. Working Paper. Université Paris VI.

Kämpke, Th., Kohlas, J., Radermacher, F.J., and Rieder, U., eds. (1990). *Uncertainty in knowledge-based systems*. Workshop, FAW Ulm, July 8–13, 1990. FAW-B-90025.

Kohlas, J. and Monney, P.A. (1990). Modeling and reasoning with hints. University of Fribourg, Institute for Automation and OR, Working Paper 174.

Kong, A. (1986). Multivariate belief functions and graphical models. Ph.D. thesis. Department of Statistic. Harvard University.

Lauritzen, S., and Spiegelhalter, D. (1988). Local computations with probabilties on graphical structures and their application to expert systems. *J. R. Statistical Society* 50 (2): 157–224.

Mellouli, K. (1987). On the propagation of beliefs in networks using Dempster-Shafer's theory of evidence. Ph.D. thesis. School of Buslness, University of Kansas, Lawrence.

Nguyen, H.T. and Rogers, G. (1990). Conditioning operators in a logic of conditionals. In I. Gooodman, M.M. Gupta, H.T. Nguyen and G. Rogers (eds.), *Conditional logic in expert systems*, pp. 159–80. Amsterdam: North-Holland.

Pearl, J. (1988). *Probabilistic reasoning in intelligent systems. Networks of plausible inference*. San Mateo, CA: Morgan Kaufmann.

Ruspini, E. (1987). The logical foundations of evidential reasoning. Technical Note 408 SRI International, Menlo Park, CA.

Shafer, G. (1986). Conditional probability. Memo.

Shafer, G., Shenoy, P., and Mellouli, K. (1987). Propagating belief functions in qualitative Markov trees. *Int. J. Approximate Reasoning* 1: 349-400

Shenoy, P. (1989). A valuation-based language for expert systems. *Int. J. Approximate Reasoning* 3: 383–411.

Shenoy, P. and Shafer, G. (1988). An axiomatic framework for Bayesian and belief function propagation. *Proc. 4th Workshop on Uncertainty in AI*, Minneapolis, MN, pp. 307–14.

Spies, M. (1991a). Combination of evidence with conditional objects and its application to cognitive modeling. In I.R. Goodman, M.M. Gupta, H.T. Nguyen, and G. Rogers (eds.), *Conditional logic in expert systems*, pp. 181–210. Amsterdam: North-Holland.

Spies, M. (1991b). Application aspects of qualitative conditional independence. In B. Bouchon-Meunier, R.R. Yager, and L.A. Zadeh (eds.), *Uncer-*

tainty in knowledge bases (*Proceedings Third IPMU Conference*, Paris, 1990). Lecture Notes in Computer Science 521, pp. 31-40. New York – Heidelberg: Springer-Verlag.

Zadeh, L.A. (1985). Syllogistic reasoning in fuzzy logic and its application to usuality and reasoning with dispositions, University of California at Berkeley. Institute of Cognitive Studies, Report 34.

23 A calculus for mass assignments in evidential reasoning

James F. BALDWIN

Abstract: This paper develops a theory of the mass assignment suitable for representing uncertain evidence in knowledge engineering. A pseudo-Boolean algebra for FMAs (family of mass assignments) is given in terms of meet and join operators representing the intersection and aggregated union of mass assignments. The SPLIT algorithm is described for computing the meet and join of mass assignments. An iterative assignment algorithm is also given for "filling in" the mass assignment with respect to prior information. This represents a conditioning process that can be considered as an extension of Bayesian updating to the case of updating mass assignments with uncertain evidence expressed as a mass assignment. This theory solves the non-monotonic logic problem and can be used for modeling uncertainty and incompleteness in many applications in the fields of artificial intelligence and evidential reasoning.[1]

Keywords: probability logic, Bayesian conditioning, evidential reasoning, logic programming, expert systems, fuzzy logic.

1. INTRODUCTION

In this paper we present an algebra for mass assignments, or to be more correct, an algebra for families of mass assignments. A mass

[1] Professor Baldwin is a SERC Senior Research Fellow.

assignment represents a family of probability distributions defined over a set F.

This theory is applicable to situations in which the probability distributions or point probabilities cannot be precisely specified. It can therefore handle cases in which a probability can only be specified as being contained in a certain interval. If this interval is chosen as [0,1], then nothing is known about the probability. The theory is also applicable to the analysis of fuzzy sets. Fuzzy sets are interpreted as mass assignments and the mass assignment theory brings together the fuzzy set and probability theories for handling uncertainty. More generally, the theory is applicable to combining inconsistent evidences and amalgamating evidences from examples.

Examples are given to illustrate the various definitions and theorems presented. Applications of such a theory combined with the iterative assignment method for updating prior mass assignments with a set of mass assignments are given in the literature (Baldwin 1989, 1990a, b, c, d, e, 1991, 1992a, b). The theory of mass assignments has relevance for knowledge engineering systems that have inherent uncertainties, both probabilistic and fuzzy. It has been shown to solve the nonmonotonic logic problem. More specifically, it can form the basis of handling uncertainty in expert systems and relational databases involving uncertain data. It is also applicable for learning systems, control theory, combining subjective expert opinions, and decision support systems.

2. MASS ASSIGNMENTS

2.1. Definition of mass assignments

A complete mass assignment over a finite frame of discernment F is a function $m: P(F) \rightarrow [0,1]$ where $P(F)$ is the powerset of F, such that

$$\sum_{A \in P(F)} m(A) = 1$$

and $m(A)$ for any $A \subseteq F$ represents a probability mass allocated to exactly the subset A of F and to no subset of A.

This is similar to the basic probability assignment function of the Dempster-Shafer theory of evidence (Shafer, 1976; Smets, 1988, 1990; Shenoy, 1989; Shenoy and Shafer, 1990), but the constraint that $m(\emptyset) = 0$ is not imposed. The theory also differs from that of the

Dempster-Shafer theory of evidence since the method of combining mass assignments is different. The theory presented here is consistent with probability theory.

If $m(\emptyset) \neq 0$ for some mass assignment, the mass assignment is said to be incomplete. This incompleteness arises because of some form of inconsistency.

A family of mass assignments can be denoted by $m(.|z1,\ldots,zn)$ where zi are parameters defining the family and satisfy constraints $\alpha_i \leqslant C_i(z1,\ldots,zn) \leqslant \beta_i$; $0 \leqslant \alpha_i, \beta_i \leqslant 1$, $\alpha_i \leqslant \beta_i$ where C_i are linear.

We will see below that, in general, a family of mass assignments results from combining mass assignments.

2.2. Support measures

A *necessary support measure* is a function

$$Sn: P(F) \to [0,1]$$

satisfying the following axioms

$$Sn(\emptyset) = 0 \text{ and } Sn(F) = 1$$

$$Sn(\cup_i A_i) \geqslant \sum_i Sn(A_i) - \sum_{i<j} Sn(A_i \cap A_j) + \ldots + (-1)^{n+1} Sn(\cap_i A_i)$$

where $A_k \subseteq F$, for all k; thus

$$Sn(A) = \sum_{B \subseteq A} m(B); \text{ for any } A \subseteq F$$

is such a measure that we call the necessary support measure for the mass assignment m.

A possible support measure Sp is dual to the necessary support measure. It satisfies $Sp(A) = 1 - Sn(\bar{A})$; for any $A \subseteq F$, where $\bar{A}$ is the complement of A with respect to F,

$$Sp(A) = \sum_{A \cap B \neq \emptyset} m(B); \quad \text{for any } A \subseteq F$$

is such a measure, which we call the possible support measure for the mass assignment m. It should be noted that

$$Sn(A) = 1 - Sp(\bar{A}); \text{ for any } A \subseteq F$$

A *support pair* for any $A \subseteq F$ resulting from the family of mass assignments $m(. \mid \alpha_1, \ldots, \alpha_n)$ is given by

$$[\min_{\alpha_i} Sn(A), \max_{\alpha_i} Sp(A)]$$

which defines an interval containing $\Pr(A)$.

2.3. Focal elements

Every subset, A, of F for which $m(A) > 0$ is called a focal element. If M is the set of focal elements of $P(F)$ for m, then the mass assignment can be represented by $\{L_i : m_i)$ where $L_i \in M$ and $m(L_i) = m_i$. This can also be written as $m = \{L_i : m_i\}$.

We can also denote this mass assignment by (m, F), which we will often write simply as m. Total ignorance is then represented by the mass assignment $F : 1$. In this case the only focal element is F so that $m(F) = 1$ and $m(A) = 0$ for all subsets, A, of F other than F.

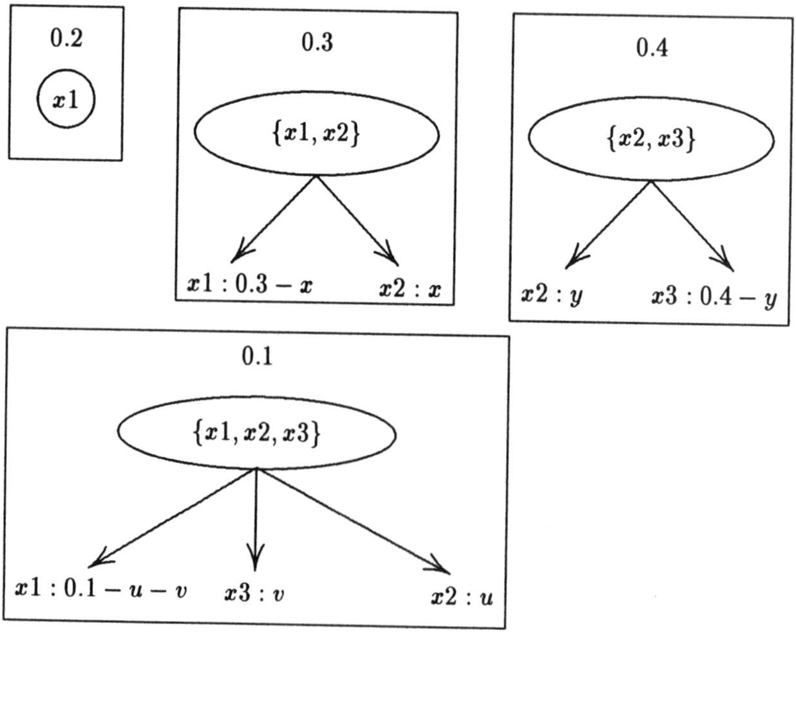

Figure 23.1

Example 1. Let $X = \{x_1, x_2, x_3\}$ be a frame of discernment, $P(X) = \{\{\}, \{x_1\}, \{x_2\}, \{x_3\}, \{x_1, x_2\}, \{x_1, x_3\}, \{x_2, x_3\}, \{x_1, x_2, x_3\}$ and $m = \{x_1\}:0.2, \{x_1, x_2\}:0.3, \{x_2, x_3\}:0.4, \{x_1, x_2, x_3\}:0.1$. Therefore

> mass associated with *exactly* $\{x_1\}$ is 0.2; mass associated with *exactly* $\{x_1, x_2\}$ is 0.3; mass associated with *exactly* $\{x_2, x_3\}$ is 0.4; mass associated with *exactly* $\{x_1, x_2\ x_3\}$ is 0.1

This mass assignment defines a family of probability distribution (Figure 23.1),

> $\Pr(x_1) = 0.6 - x - u - v$; $\Pr(x_2) = x + y + u$; $\Pr(x_3) = 0.4 - y + v$

where: $0 \leqslant x \leqslant 0.3$; $0 \leqslant y \leqslant 0.4$; $0 \leqslant u + v \leqslant 0.1$; $u, v \geqslant 0$.

2.4. Restrictions

If $m = \{L_i : m_i\}$ and, for some k, L_1' and L_2' are chosen such that $L_1' \cup L_2' = Lk$ and $m(L_1')$, $m(L_2')$ are chosen such that $0 < m(L_1') + m(L_2') \leqslant mk$, then

$$m' = \begin{cases} \{L_i : m_i \mid i \neq k\} \cup \{L_1' : m(L_1')\} \cup \{L_2' : m(L_2')\} \\ \quad \text{if } m(L_1') + m(L_2') = m_k \\ \{L_i : m_i \mid i \neq k\} \cup \{L_1' : m(L_1')\} \cup \{L_2' : m(L_2')\} \cup \{L_k : m_k - \\ \quad m(L_1') - m(L_2')\} \text{ if } m(L_1') + m(L_2') < mk \end{cases}$$

is a *restriction of m* and is denoted by $m' < m$.

Example 2. If $m = \{a, b\}:0.6, \{a, b, c\}:0.4$ then $m' = a:0.2, b:0.2, c:0.2, \{a, b\}:0.2, \{a, b, c\}:0.2$ is a restriction of m.

2.5. Labels and projector operator

If F is a set of elements where each $f \in F$ is a possible instantiation of the variables $X_1, \ldots, X_m$ in the conjunction $X_1 \wedge \ldots \wedge X_m$ where X_i can take values from the set F_i, for $i = 1, \ldots, n_i$ then F represents a set of labels defined on the space $X_1, \ldots, X_m$. The powerset of F, $P(F)$, represents all possible subsets of labels.

Let m be a mass assignment defined over F; $m = \{E_i : a_i\}$ where E_i is a subset of F. We can project this mass assignment m over a subset of

$\{X_1, \ldots, X_m\}$, say $\{X_1, \ldots, X_s\}$, where $s < m$, to obtain the mass assignment m' where $m' = \{E'_j : a'_j\}$ and a'_j is the sum of a_i over labels E_i that contain the label E'_j.

3. COMBINING MASS ASSIGNMENTS

3.1. Concepts of meet and join

If we are given two mass assignments (m_1, M_1) and (m_2, M_2), how can we combine them to give a mass assignment (mM)? Two questions can be asked. What do we mean by the concept "combining" and for any definition of such a concept is the result a unique mass assignment or a family of mass assignments?

We will define two concepts of combining. One corresponds to the intersection of the mass assignments, that is, finding the mass assignment corresponding to taking the conjunction of statements S_1 and S_2 where S_1, S_2 are statements corresponding to the mass assignments m_1, m_2, respectively. When no inconsistency arises the intersection of the mass assignments corresponds to taking the intersection of the families of probability distributions represented by the mass assignments.

The other corresponds to the aggregation of the mass asignments. This requires careful attention since it is not the operation of union in the sense of taking the union of the families of probability distributions corresponding to the mass assignments. If, for example, two mass assignments are given by $m_1 = a{:}0.2, b{:}0.8$; $m_2 = b{:}0.3, c{:}0.7$, the aggregation of m_1 and m_2, that is,

$$\alpha[a{:}0.2, b{:}0.8] + (1-\alpha)[b{:}0.3, c{:}0.7] = a{:}0.2\alpha, b{:}0.3 + 0.5\alpha, c{:}0.7(1-\alpha)$$

where $0 \leqslant \alpha \leqslant 1$. We can interpret this as follows. Subjects 1 and 2 observe a process to determine the value of a variable X that can take values from $\{a, b, c\}$. These observations are not made at the same time. Subject 1 observes that for 20% of the time X has the value a and for 80% of the time it has the value b. Subject 2 observes that for 30% of the time X has the value b and for 70% of the time it has the value c. The above result gives the most general result for the aggregation of these results. The parameter α reflects the typicality of the particular set of results for subject 1 relative to subject 2. We can also think of the judgments of subject 1 and subject 2 as expert judgments on the value of X. The parameter α then represents the relative expertise of subject 1 relative to subject 2.

The combination of these two mass assignments with respect to intersection is given by $b:0.3$, $\emptyset:0.7$, illustrating that both mass assignments indicated that the probability of b is at least 0.3, but otherwise they are inconsistent. It can be noted that the Dempster-Shafer theory of combining evidences would give $b:1$ for this example. Smets has suggested that an open world model for interpreting a mass to $\emptyset$ can be used to avoid the normalization process of the Dempster-Shafer theory.

The basic algorithm for performing the combining operations and the complete definitions is given by the general assignment method. This will give the most general family of solutions for the combinations. The split algorithm is a variation of the general assignment method, which allows the family of mass assignments resulting from combining two mass assignments to be expressed as a linear sum of base mass assignments. A set of base mass assignments for a given family of mass assignments, M_f, is a set of orthogonal mass assignments $\{s_i\}$ such that any member of M_f is given by the linear sum

$$\sum_i \alpha_i s_i; \ \sum_i \alpha_i = 1$$

Two mass assignments s_i and s_j are orthogonal if s_i cannot be obtained from s_j by restriction or vice versa, i.e., $\neg(s_i < s_j) \vee \neg(s_j < s_i)$.

The split algorithm will give the most general assignment for the combination with respect to intersection and the aggregation combination when combining with respect to the union. For this latter case the general assignment method can give more general solutions. The split algorithm picks out a least upper bound for the aggregation of the mass assignments and a greatest lower bound for the intersection case.

3.2. General assignment method

Consider the two mass assignments (m_1, M_1) and (m_2, M_2) where $M_1 = \{L_{1_k}\}$ for $k = 1,2,\ldots,n_1$ and $M_2 = \{L_{2_k}\}$ for $k = 1,2,\ldots,n_2$ where each L_{ij} are subsets of F for which $m_1(L_{1_k}) \neq 0$; $k = 1,\ldots,n_1$, $m_2(L_{2_k}) \neq 0$; $k = 1,\ldots,n_2$.

Let* be a binary set theoretic operation, intersection or union. Let (m, M) be the result of combining (m_1, M_1) and (m_2, M_2) with respect to * and we will denote this by

$$(m(.\mid\alpha), M) = (m_1, M_1) + *(m_2, M_2)$$

where m represents a unique assignment or family of mass assignments. If a unique assignment results then $m = m(.\mid\{\})$.

The combination operation * is defined by the general assignment algorithm now stated. Let $M = \{L_{m_{ij}}\}$ for which $L_{m_{ij}} = L_{1_i} * L_{2_j}$ for all i,j such that $L_{1_i} * L_{2_j} \neq \emptyset$ and

$$m(Y) = \sum_{i,j: L_{1_i} * L_{2_j} = Y} m'(L_{1_i} * L_{2_j}); \text{ for any } Y \subseteq M$$

where $m'(L_{1_i} * L_{2_j})$, for $i = 1, \ldots, n_1$ and $j = 1, \ldots, n_2$ satisfies

$$\sum_j m'(L_{1_i} * L_{2_j}) = m_1(L_{1_i}) \text{ for } i = 1, \ldots, n_1$$

$$\sum_i m'(L_{1_i} * L_{2_j}) = m_2(L_{2_j}) \text{ for } j = 1, \ldots, n_2$$

and

$$m'(L_{1_i} * L_{2_j}) = 0 \text{ if } L_{1_i} * L_{2_j} = \emptyset, \text{ for } i = 1, \ldots, n_1 \text{ and } j = 1, \ldots, n_2$$

Consider a matrix of cells C_{ij} where $i = 1, \ldots, n_1$ and $j = 1, \ldots, n_2$. Let cell C_{ij} contain label $L_{1_i} * L_{2_j}$ with associated mass $m'_{ij} = m'(L_{1_i} * L_{2_j})$. Then the ith row masses of the cell tableau must add up to $m_1(L_{1_i})$ for all ith and the jth columm masses must add up to $m_2(L_{2_j})$ for all j. Cells with null set entries are allocated the mass 0. This will not in general give a unique solution. For the nonunique case, any allocation can be modified by alternatively adding and subtracting a quanitity at vertices around a loop made up of alternative horizontal and vertical jumps. The quantity must be such that no cell mass entries go negative. This is simply the assignment algorithm from the field of operations research. If, in the case for intersection, the constraints cannot be satisfied, then the mass assignments are incompatible. An incomplete mass assignment for the combination can then be obtained by allowing masses to be associated with cells with null set entries.

If a unique solution is not obtained, the family of solutions can be parametrized. We will use the split algorithm defined below for obtaining the family of mass assignments rather than the loop method since the latter is difficult to handle computationally except for the more simple cases.

3.3. The split algorithm for the combination of two mass assignments

Step 1. Label cells of cell tableau as for general assignment method, i.e., label in each cell is the intersection (union) of associated column and row labels of the given mass assignments.

Step 2. Allocate a mass of zero to any Ø label and complete any necessary allocations arising from this.

Step 3. IF a label L, corresponding to a subset S of F, exists such that all labels in the same row and the same column correspond to subsets of S,
THEN allocate maximum possible mass to L and complete assignment to any other cells that have a unique allocation arising from this,
ELSE choose a column (row) and make a copy of the cell allocation tableau for each member of this column (row). Allocate the maximum possible mass to the member cell for each of these tableaus and complete assignment to any other cells which have a unique allocation.

Step 4. REPEAT step 3 until all tableaus have complete mass assignments.

Step 5. IF a complete allocation cannot be completed using steps 1, 2, 3 and 4
THEN complete steps 2, 3 and 4 as far as possible and allocate the remaining mass to Ø's.

The tableau splitting can be represented as a tree. Let the leaves of this tree, corresponding to final tableaus, be represented by the mass assignments $s_1, \ldots, s_m$. Let $\{s_1, \ldots, s_n\}$ be an independent set from $\{s_1, \ldots, s_m\}$. Then the result of combining the original mass assignments is given by

$$\sum_{i=1}^{n} \alpha_i s_i; \quad \sum_{i=1}^{n} \alpha_i = 1$$

This defines a family of mass assignments, P. The vector $\{s_1, \ldots, s_n\}$ is called a mass assignment basis for P.

This algorithm gives a family of mass assignments satisfying the row and column constraints of the general assignment algorithm and assumes a least commitment model for allocating the masses (step 3). If the mass assignments correspond to fuzzy sets then this model is equivalent to using MIN rule for fuzzy set intersection. For more general mass assignments it does not necessarily give the most general solution. A split algorithm without least commitment model assumption gives the most general solution.

This algorithm for combining mass assignments with respect to intersection gives the meet of the mass assignments, that is, $m_1 + m_2 = m_1 \wedge m_2$.

3.4. The split algorithm for the join of two mass assignments

Step 1. IF a label L, corresponding to a subset S of F, exists such that S is a subset of each set corresponding to all labels in the same row and column as L,

THEN allocate maximum possible mass to L and complete assignment to any other cells which then have a unique allocation,

ELSE choose a column (row) and make a copy of the cell allocation tableau for each member of this column (row). Allocate the maximum possible mass to the member cell for each of these tableaus and complete assignment to any other cells that have a unique allocation.

Step 2. REPEAT step 1 until all tableaus have complete mass assignments.

The tableau splitting can be represented as a tree. Let the leaves of this tree, corresponding to final tableaus, be represented by the mass assignments $s_1, \ldots, s_m$. Let $\{s_1, \ldots, s_n\}$ be an orthogonal set from $\{s_1, \ldots, s_m\}$. Then the result of combining the original mass assignments is given by

$$\sum_{i=1}^{n} \alpha_i s_i; \quad \sum_{i=1}^{n} \alpha_i = 1$$

This defines a family of mass assignments, P. The vector $\{s_1, \ldots, s_n\}$ is called a mass assignment basis for P.

This algorithm gives the join, $m_1 \vee m_2$, of the mass assignments. The join satisfies the row and column constraints of the general assignment algorithm since each final tableau satisfies the row and column constraints. Step 1 assumes the least committment model and is consistent with the use of the max rule for fuzzy set union when the mass assignments correspond to fuzzy sets. The split algorithm can be used without assuming this model.

4. ALGEBRA OF MASS ASSIGNMENTS

4.1. FMAs and basic operations

Let the frame of discernment be F and $\{s_1, \ldots, s_n\}$ be orthogonal mass assignments defined over F. The linear form

$$\mathbf{m} = \sum_{i=1}^{n} \alpha_i s_i; \quad \sum_{i=1}^{n} \alpha_i = 1$$

represents a family of mass assignments formed from the orthogonal mass assignments $\{s_i\}$. We will call this an FMA. The algebra of mass assignments given here is strictly an algebra of FMAs.

Let $\mathbf{m}_1, \mathbf{m}_2$ be two FMAs defined over F as

$$\mathbf{m}_1 = \sum_{i=1}^{n} \alpha_i u_i; \quad \sum_{i=1}^{n} \alpha_i = 1; \quad \mathbf{m}_2 = \sum_{i=1}^{m} \beta_i v_i; \quad \sum_{i=1}^{m} \beta_i = 1$$

then $\mathbf{m}_1 \leqslant \mathbf{m}_2$ iff $u_i \leqslant v_j$ for all $i = 1, \ldots, n, j = 1, \ldots, m$ where $\leqslant$ is the restriction ordering relation defined above.

Then:

$$\mathbf{m}_1 \wedge \mathbf{m}_2 = \sum_{i=1}^{n} \varphi_{ij}(u_i \wedge v_j); \quad \sum_{i=1}^{n} \varphi_{ij} = 1;$$

where, for any $i, j, \varphi_{ij} = 0$ if $u_i \wedge v_j \leqslant u_r \wedge v_s$ for any r, s, and

$$\mathbf{m}_1 \vee \mathbf{m}_2 = \sum_{i=1}^{n} \varphi_{ij}(u_i \vee v_j); \quad \sum_{i=1}^{n} \varphi_{ij} = 1;$$

where, for any $i, j, \varphi_{ij} = 0$ if $u_r \wedge v_s \leqslant u_i \wedge v_j$ for any r, s.

The following indempotence, commutativity, associativity, and absorption properties hold:

(1) $\mathbf{m} \vee \mathbf{m} = \mathbf{m}; \quad \mathbf{m} \wedge \mathbf{m} = \mathbf{m}$

(2) $\mathbf{m}_1 \vee \mathbf{m}_2 = \mathbf{m}_2 \vee \mathbf{m}_1; \; \mathbf{m}_1 \wedge \mathbf{m}_2 = \mathbf{m}_2 \wedge \mathbf{m}_1$

(3) $\mathbf{m}_1 \vee (\mathbf{m}_2 \vee \mathbf{m}_3) = (\mathbf{m}_1 \vee \mathbf{m}_2 \vee \mathbf{m}_3); \; \mathbf{m}_1 \wedge (\mathbf{m}_2 \wedge \mathbf{m}_3) = \mathbf{m}_1 \wedge \mathbf{m}_2) \wedge \mathbf{m}_3$

(4) $\mathbf{m}_1 \vee (\mathbf{m}_1 \wedge \mathbf{m}_2) = \mathbf{m}_1 \wedge (\mathbf{m}_1 \vee \mathbf{m}_2) = \mathbf{m}_1$

Also $\mathbf{m}_1 \leqslant \mathbf{m}_2$ is equivalent to

$\mathbf{m}_1 \vee \mathbf{m}_2 = \mathbf{m}_2$ and $\mathbf{m}_1 \wedge \mathbf{m}_2 = \mathbf{m}_1$

Furthermore, the following distributive properties hold:

$$\mathbf{m}_1 \vee (\mathbf{m}_2 \wedge \mathbf{m}_3) = (\mathbf{m}_1 \vee \mathbf{m}_2) \wedge (\mathbf{m}_1 \vee \mathbf{m}_3)$$

$$\mathbf{m}_1 \wedge (\mathbf{m}_2 \vee \mathbf{m}_3) = (\mathbf{m}_1 \wedge \mathbf{m}_2) \vee (\mathbf{m}_1 \wedge \mathbf{m}_3)$$

4.2. Complementation

The complement of a mass assignment (m, M), denoted by $\overline{(m, M)}$, is (m', F') where the set of focal elements $\mathbf{F}' = \{L'_i\}$ where L'_i is the complement of L_i with respect to F and the mass associated with L'_1 is $m(L'_i) = m(L_i)$. If for m a mass is associated with F, then this mass will be associated with $\emptyset$ for $\overline{m}$ and the complement is an incomplete mass assignment. If m is an incomplete mass assignment, then the mass associated with $\emptyset$ is associated with F for $\overline{m}$.

Let

$$\mathbf{m} = \sum_{i=1}^{n} \alpha_i s_i; \quad \sum_{i=1}^{n} \alpha_i = 1$$

be an FMA defined over F, then the complement FMA $\overline{\mathbf{m}}$ is defined as

$$\overline{\mathbf{m}} = \sum_{i=1}^{n} \alpha_i \overline{s_i}; \quad \sum_{i=1}^{n} \alpha_i = 1$$

De Morgan's laws hold. For FMAs $\mathbf{m}, \mathbf{m}_1, \mathbf{m}_2$ defined over F, we have

$$\overline{\mathbf{m}_1 \wedge \mathbf{m}_2} = \overline{\mathbf{m}_1} \vee \overline{\mathbf{m}_2}; \qquad \overline{\mathbf{m}_1 \vee \mathbf{m}_2} = \overline{\mathbf{m}_1} \wedge \overline{\mathbf{m}_2}$$

and the involution law holds

$$\overline{\overline{\mathbf{m}}} = \mathbf{m}$$

4.3. Lattice

Let **M** represent all FAMs over F. $\langle \mathbf{M}, \vee, \wedge \rangle$ is an algebra with indempotence, commutativity, associativity, absorption, distributivity, and complementation properites given above. Full complementation properties are not satisfied. The algebra is a pseudo-Boolean algebra.

We can also view the structure in lattice terms. $\langle \mathbf{M}, \leqslant \rangle$ is a poset and further is a lattice since the join and meet are defined everywhere. $\emptyset : 1$ and $F : 1$ are the universal bounds of the lattice **M**. The lattice is distributive but not completely complemented. $\langle \mathbf{M}, \leqslant \rangle$ is a pseudo-complemented distributed lattice.

5. EXAMPLES

5.1. Probability logic example

Suppose variables P, Q, R, S can take values $\{p, \neg p\}$, $\{q, \neg q\}$, $\{r, \neg r\}$, $\{s, \neg s\}$, respectively, and we are given the statements (axioms):

(1) $\Pr\{p \supset q\} = 0.9$; (2) $\Pr\{\neg r \supset \neg q\} = 0.8$;
(3) $\Pr\{r \supset \neg s\} = 0.7$

What can we conclude about $\Pr\{p \supset \neg s\}$?

The mass assignments corresponding to the given axioms are:

$$m_1 = \{pq, \neg p\_\} : 0.9,\ p \neg q : 0.1$$
$$m_2 = \{\neg r \neg q, r\_\} : 0.8,\ \neg rq : 0.2$$
$$m_3 = \{r \neg s \neg r\_\} : 0.7,\ rs : 0.3$$

where an underscore represents any appropriate value. In m_1 $\neg p\_$ represents $\{\neg pq, \neg p \neg q\}$.

Combining these mass assignments (cf. Table 23.1) gives $m_1 \wedge m_2 = \{pqr, \neg p \neg q \neg r, \neg p\_r\} : 0.7,\ \{\_q \neg r\} : 0.2,\ \{p \neg q\_\} : 0.1$.

Table 23.1

	0.8 $\{\_\neg q \neg r, \_\_r\}$	0.2 $\{\_q \neg r\}$
0.9 $\{pq\_, \neg p\_\_\}$	$\{pqr, \neg p \neg q \neg r, \neg p\_r\}$ 0.7	$\{\_q \neg r\}$ 0.2
0.1 $\{p \neg q\_\}$	$\{p \neg q\_\}$ 0.1	$\emptyset$ 0

Also $m_1 \wedge m_2 \wedge m_3 = (m_1 \wedge m_2) \wedge m_3 = \text{Proj}_{PR}(m_1 \wedge m_2) \wedge m$ and $\text{Proj}_{PR}(m_1 \wedge m_2) = \{pr, \neg p\_\}:0.7, \ \{\_\neg r\}:\{p\_\}:0.1$ so that $\text{Proj}_{PS}(m_1 \wedge m_2 \wedge m_3) = \alpha \text{Proj}_{PS}\, s_1 + (1-\alpha)\, \text{Proj}_{PS}\, s_2$; $\quad 0 \leqslant \alpha \leqslant 1$, where $s_1 = \{\_r \neg s, \neg p \neg r\_\}:0.4, \ \{\_rs\}:0.3, \ \{\_\neg r\_\}:0.2$, $\{\text{pr} \neg s, p \neg r\_\}:0.1$, and $s_2 = \{\_r \neg s, \neg p \neg r\_\}:0.5, \{\_rs\}:0.2$, $\{\_\neg r\_\}:0.2$, prs$:0.1$ (cf. Table 23.2) so that $m_1 \wedge m_2 \wedge m_3 = \{\_\neg s$, $\neg p\_\}:0.5\text{-}0.1\alpha, \ \{\_s\}:0.2 + 0.1\alpha, \ \{\_\ \_\}:0.2, \ \{p\_\}:0.1\alpha, \ ps:0.1$ $(1-\alpha)$, so that $\Pr(p \supset \neg s) \in [0.5\text{-}0.1\alpha, 09. + 0.1\alpha]$; $0 \leqslant \alpha \leqslant 1$, $\text{Sn}((p \supset \neg s) = 0.4$ and $\text{Sp}(p \supset \neg s) = 1$, and the support pair for $(p \supset \neg s)$ is $(p \supset \neg s):[0.4, 1]$.

Table 23.2

	0.7 $\{r\neg s, \neg r\_\}$	0.3 rs
0.7 $\{pr, \neg p\_\}$	$\{\_r\neg s, \neg p\neg r\_\}$	$\{\_rs\}$
0.2 $\{\_\neg r\}$	$\{\_\neg r\_\}$ 0.2	Ø 0
0.1 $\{p\_\}$	$\{p\neg r\neg s, p\neg r\_\}$	prs

0.5 max	0.2
0.2	0
0	0.1

0.4	0.3 max
0.2	0
0.1	0

5.2. Algebraic Example

Let $F = \{a, b, c\}$, $\mathbf{m} = a:0.4, \{b, c\}:0.3, \{a, b, c\}:0.3$, $\overline{\mathbf{m}} = \{b, c\}:$ $0.4, a:0.3, \varnothing:0.3$ so that $\mathbf{m} \vee \overline{\mathbf{m}} = a:0.4, \{b, c\}:0.3, \{a, b, c\}:0.3$, (cf. Table 23.3).

Table 23.3

	0.4 $\{b, c\}$	0.3 a	0.3 Ø
0.4 a	$\{\_\}$	a 0.3 max	a
0.3 $\{b, c\}$	$\{b, c\}$	$\{\_\}$ 0	$\{b, c\}$
0.3 $\{\_\}$	$\{\_\}$	$\{\_\}$ 0	$\{\_\}$

0	0.3	0.1 max
0.1	0	0.2
0.3	0	0

$s_1 =$
$a:0.4$
$\{b, c\}:0.3$
$\{\_\}:0.3$

$s_1 < s_2$

0.1	0.3	0
0	0	0.3 max
0.3	0	0

$s_2 =$
$a:0.3$
$\{b, c\}:0.3$
$\{\_\}:0.4$

This illustrates the need to test for independence in the split algorithm. Moreover (cf. Table 23.4), $\mathbf{m}\wedge\overline{\mathbf{m}} = a:0.3,\ \{b, c\}:0{,}4,\ Ø:0.3$ so that $\overline{\mathbf{m}\wedge\overline{\mathbf{m}}} = a:0.4,\ \{b, c\}:0.3,\ \{a, b, c\}:0.3$ showing that $\overline{\mathbf{m}\wedge\overline{\mathbf{m}}} = \mathbf{m}\vee\overline{\mathbf{m}}$.

Table 23.4

	0.4 $\{b, c\}$	0.3 a	0.3 Ø
0.4 a	Ø 0	a 0.3 $\max_2$	Ø
0.3 $\{b, c\}$	$\{b, c\}$ 0.3 $\max_1$	Ø 0	Ø 0
0.3 $\{\_\}$	$\{b, c\}$ 0.1 $\max_3$	a 0	Ø 0.2

Result is
$a:0.3$
$\{b, c\}:0.4$
$Ø:0.3$
where $\max_i$ indicates that the maximization was the ith case of this operation

6. ITERATIVE ASSIGNMENT METHOD

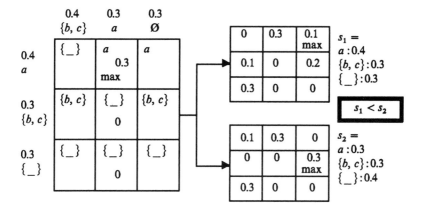

The interative assignment method for updating an a priori mass assignment with a sequence of evidences, each expressed as a mass assignment, is discussed in Baldwin (1990b, c, d). We summarize the method. The update is a generalization of Bayesian updating to the case when the evidence is uncertain. If the prior mass assignment is a probability distribution over F and the specific evidence is a probability distribution over a partition of F then the update algorithm given below is equivalent to minimizing the relative entropy of the update with respect to the prior subject to the specific evidence probability constraints. It is in special cases equivalent to using Jeffrey's rule. It can also be viewed as a "filling in" process for the incompleteness expressed by the mass assignment.

Suppose an a priori mass assignment m_a is given over the focal set A whose elements are subsets of the powerset $P(F)$.

Suppose we also have a specific evidence E where E is (m, M) where M is the set of focal elements of $P(F)$ for E and m is the mass assignment for these focal elements.

We wish to update the a priori assignment m_a with E to give the updated mass assignment m. This iterative assignment method updates m_a with E to give m'. The a priori is a replaced with m' and the update process repeated to give a new m'. This is repeated until the process converges.

The one-step algorithm is as follows:

Let prior mass be $m = (t,\ T)$ where $t = \{t_1, \dots, t_m\}$, $T = \{T_1, \dots, T_m\}$, T_i is a subset of $P(X)$, and

$$m = T_1 : t_1, \dots, T_m : t_m$$

and let $E = (t^E,\ T^E)$ be a specific evidence, where $t = \{t_1^E, \dots, t_s^E\}$, $T^E = \{T_1^E, \dots, T_s^E\}$, T_i^E is a subset of $P(X)$.

$$E = T_1^E : t_1^E, \dots, T_s^E : t_s^E$$

Let m' be the update mass assignment, i.e., $m' = (t',\ T')$ where $t' = \{t'_1, \dots, t'_r\}$ and $T' = \{T'_1, \dots, T'_r\}$.

From

$$T' = \{T_i \cap T_j^E \mid T_i \cap T_j^E \neq \emptyset\} \text{ and } t'_k = \sum_{i,j : T_i \cap T_j^E = T'_k} K_j t_i t'_j$$

for $k = 1, \dots, r$, where $K_j = \dfrac{1}{1 - \sum_{q : T_q \cap T_j^E = \emptyset} t_q}$, for $j = 1, \dots, s$. It should be noted that the label set, T′, can change from stage to stage of the complete iteration process.

This algorithm can be thought of as combining the prior mass and the specific evidence mass using a modified Dempster rule. The prior mass represents the rows of the Dempster matrix and the specific evidence mass represents its columns. The cell intersections are found and the cell masses found using the multiplication rule as in the Dempster case. If there are no null sets in the matrix then this represents the update. More generally, when null sets occur in the matrix, each column containing one or more null sets is renormalized so that the sum of the column masses associated with nonnull sets adds up to the corresponding column mass of the specific evidence and the masses of the null sets put to 0.

Modifications of this algorithm to account more generally for partial matches of prior and specific evidence masses has been discussed by Baldwin (1992a, b, c) but we will not consider this here.

Example 3. We use the probability logic example given above to illustrate the "filling in" process of the iterative assignment algorithm. The meet of the mass assignments

$$m_1 = \{pq, \neg p\_\}:.09, p\neg q:0.1$$
$$m_2 = \{\neg r\neg q, r\_\}:0.8, \neg rq:0.2$$
$$m_3 = \{r\neg s, \neg r\_\}:0.7, rs:0.3$$

is given by

$$\mathbf{m} = m_1 \wedge m_2 \wedge m_3 = \alpha s_1 + (1-\alpha)s_2$$

where $s_1 = \{pqr\neg s, \neg p\neg q\neg r\_, \neg p\_r\neg s\}:0.5$, $\{pqrs, \neg p\_ rs\}:0.2$, $p\neg qrs:0.1$, $\{\_q\neg r\_\}:0.2$, $s_2 = \{pqr\neg s, \neg p\neg q\neg r\_, \neg p\_r\neg s\}:0.4$, $\{pgrs, \neg p\_rs\}:0.3$, $\{p\neg qr\neg s, p\neg qr\_\}:0.1$, $\{\_q\neg r\_\}:0.2$. This is abtained as above but without using any projections.

The "filling in" is achieved by updating an equally likely a priori probability distribution over the set of labels that all possible instantiations of *PQRS* for a given α, i.e., 0.0625 to *pqrs*, etc. Suppose this update gives the set $\{\text{yi}(\alpha)\}$ over $\{\text{PQRS}\}$ then α is chosen such that

$$\min_\alpha \mathrm{I}(\alpha) = \sum y_i(\alpha).L_n(y_i/0.0625)$$

The mass assignment over labels $\{PQRS\}$ can then be projected over $\{PS\}$ giving the results ps: 0.1921, $p\neg s$:0.1844, $\neg ps$:0.3177, $\neg p\neg s$:0.3058 which gives $p \supset \neg s$:0.8079 where the optimal value of α is 0.2263.

This result can also be obtained by first updating the equally likely prior over $\{PQRS\}$ with m_1, and updating this with m_2 and updating this result with m_3 and iterating as shown diagrammatically in Figure 23.2.

Figure 23.2

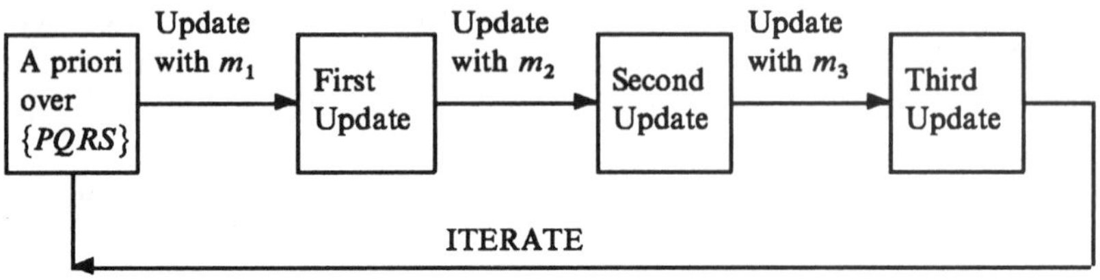

The iteration converges and the final solution can be projected onto $\{PS\}$ to give $ps:0.1921$, $p\neg s:0.1844$, $\neg ps:0.3177$, $\neg p\neg s$: 0.3058 which gives $p \supset \neg s:0.8079$ which is the same result as obtained previously.

It should be noted that if projections are formed prior to updating with the update with respect to an equally likely distribution over the resulting label set, the final update will not be the same as that obtined above. Possible interactions are lost when projecting.

7. CONCLUSION

An algebra for families of mass assignments has been given and a updating process for prior mass assignments with respect to uncertain evidence expressed as mass assignments analogous to Bayesian updating for probability distribution. This conditioning process can act as a "fill in" method for incompleteness associated with mass assignments.

BIBLIOGRAPHY

Baldwin, J. F. (1989). A new approach to combining evidences for evidential reasoning. ITRC 151. Report, University of Bristol.

Baldwin, J. F. (1990a). Computational models of uncertainty reasoning in expert systems. *Computers Math. Applic.* 19: 105–19.

Baldwin, J. F. (1990b). Combining evidences for evidential reasoning. *Int. J. of Intelligent Systems* 6: 569–617.

Baldwin, J. F. (1990c). Towards a general theory of intelligent reasoning. *Proc. Third Int. Conf. IPMU*, Paris, July 1990.

Baldwin, J. F. (1990d). Inference under uncertainty for expert system rules. ITRC 152 Report, University of Bristol. To appear.

Baldwin, J. F. (1991). Fuzzy and probabilistic databases with automatic reasoning. ITRC 160 Report, University of Bristol. To appear.

Baldwin, J. F. (1992a). Inference for information systems containing probabilistic and fuzzy uncertainties. In L. A. Zadeh and J. Kacprzyk (eds.), *Fuzzy logic for the management of uncertainty*. New York: Wiley.

Baldwin, J. F. (1992b). Fuzzy and probabilistic uncertainties. In S. C. Shapiro (ed.), *Encyclopedia of artificial intelligence, second ed.* New York: Wiley.

Baldwin, J. F. (1992c). Evidential reasoning under probabilistic and fuzzy uncertainties. In R. R. Yager and L. A. Zadeh, (eds.), *An introduction to fuzzy logic applications in intelligent systems*. Dordrecht: Kluwer.

Shafer, G. (1976). *A mathematical theory of evidence*. Princeton: Princeton University Press.

Shenoy, P. P. (1989). A valuation-based language for expert systems. *Int. J. of Approx. Reasoning* 3: (5).

Shenoy, P.P. and Shafer, G. (1990). Axioms for probability and belief-function propagation. In Shachter et al., *Uncertainty in artificial intelligence* 4. Amsterdam: North-Holland.

Smets, P. (1988). Belief function. In Smets et al. (eds.), *Non-standard logics for automated reasoning*, pp. 253–86. New York: Academic Press.

Smets, P. (1988). The combination of evidences in the transferable belief model, *IEEE Trans. PAMI* 12. 442–258

Zadeh, L. A. (1965). Fuzzy sets. *Information and Control* 8: 338–53.

Zadeh, L. A. (1975). Fuzzy logic and approximate reasoning. *Synthese* 30: 407–28.

Zadeh, L. A. (1978). Fuzzy sets as a basis for a theory of possibility. *Fuzzy Sets and Systems* 1: 3–28.

Zadeh, L. A. (1983). The role of fuzzy logic in the management of uncertainty in expert systems. *Fuzzy Sets and Systems* 11: 199–227.

Zadeh, L. A. (1986). A simple view of the Dempster-Shafer theory of evidence and its implications for the role of combination. *AI Magazine* 7: 85–90.

24 Nonmonotonic reasoning with belief structures

Ronald R. YAGER

Abstract: We discuss the Dempster-Shafer theory of evidence. We introduce a concept of monotonicity that is related to the diminution of the range between belief and plausibility. We show that the accumulation of knowledge in this framework exhibits a nonmonotonic property. We show how the belief structure can be used to represent typical or commonsense knowledge.

Keywords: nonmonotonic reasoning, belief structure, default values, aggregation, uncertainty.

1. INTRODUCTION

A considerable debate exists in regard to the most appropriate manner in which to represent commonsense or default knowledge. A number of researchers have suggested extensions of the classic logic. These include Reiter's (1980) default logic, McCarthy's (1986) circumscription, and Doyle and McDermott's (1980) nonmonotonic logic. Moore (1985) introduced an approach based on modal logic. Yager (1987a) suggested a version of possibilistic logic based on fuzzy set theory. In another direction, a number of approaches based on the use of probabilistic concepts have been introduced. Zadeh (1984) has suggested an approach based on the concept of usuality and dispositions. Yager (1986a; 1989b) has suggested an approach involving the use of possibility-probability granules. Pearl (1988) has suggested another approach based on his causal network.

What appears to be a central characteristic of commonsense knowledge is the possibility of nonmonotonicity. By this we mean that the addition of knowledge may cause us to withdraw some previously made inference.

In this paper, we look at the theory of evidence (Dempster, 1967; Shafer, 1976) and particularly at the process of normalization. We show that this process introduces an inherent nonmonotonicity into the Dempster-Shafer framework. This inherent nonmonotonicity, we feel, makes this representation scheme a suitable one for the representation of default knowledge. We then show how the belief structure provides a formalism for representing commonsense knowledge. The work here can be seen as an extension of the work in Yager (1989a).

2. THE DEMPSTER-SHAFER FRAMEWORK

In this section we briefly review the mathematical theory of evidence. More comprehensive and detailed information can be found in the literature (Dempster, 1967; Shafer, 1976; Yager, 1987b).

Assume V is a variable taking its value in the set X. A belief structure (or Dempster-Shafer's evidence) consists of a collection of nonnull subsets $A_1,...A_n$ of X, called focal elements, and a set of weights $m(A_i)$ such that

(1) $m(A_i) > 0$
(2) $\sum_i m(A_i) = 1$

An alternative view of this structure that is more in the spirit of Dempster 1967) can also be described. In this alternative view we have in addition to the set X a set $Y = \{Y_1,...Y_n\}$ and a relation R on $Y \times X$. In this view, we have associated with the set Y a probability distribution, P, where $p_i = \text{Prob}\{y_i\}$ and it is assumed that $p_i = m(A_i)$. In this view we perform an experiment on the space Y. As result of the outcome of this experiment we are concerned with the occurrence of the element in X. This occurrence is effected through the relationship R. In particular, if y_i occurs, then the possible values for V lie in the set $A_i = \{x|(y_i, x) \in R\}$. Thus a focal set is a subset of elements in X that are possible values when a particular Y occurs.

In order to provide a unified view of this theory we introduce two important concepts. Assume A and B are two subsets of X. We define

$$\text{Poss}\,[B/A] = \max\,[A(x) \wedge B(x)]$$

where $A(x)$ and $B(x)$ are the characteristic functions of A and B. We also note $\wedge$ is the min operator. It can be easily seen that

$$\text{Poss}[B/A] = 1 \text{ if } A \cap B \neq \emptyset$$
$$\text{Poss}[B/A] = 0 \text{ if } A \cap B = \emptyset$$

Thus Poss$[B/A]$ is a measure of the degree of intersection of A and B. We shall denote Poss$[A]$ = Poss$[A/X]$, thus Poss$[A] = 0$ if and only if $A = \emptyset$.

A second concept we shall find useful is Cert$[B/A]$, which we define as

$$\text{Cert}[B/A] = 1 - \text{Poss}[\bar{B}/A]$$

It can easily be shown that Cert$[B/A] = 1$ if $A \subset B$ and Cert[B/A] $= 0$ if $A \not\subset B$.

Two important concepts used in the theory of evidence are the concepts of plausibility and belief. Assume m is a belief structure on X and A is any subset of X, then

$$\text{Pl}(A) = \textstyle\sum_j \text{Poss}[A/A_j] * m(A_j)$$

and

$$\text{Bel}(A) = \textstyle\sum_j \text{Cert}\,[A/A_j] * m(A_j)$$

Assume A is any subset of X. Given some belief structure m we are interested in determining the probability of A, denoted Prob(A). It can be shown (Dempster, 1967) that

$$\text{Bel}(A) \leqslant \text{Prob}(A) \leqslant \text{Pl}(A)$$

Based on this observation Bel(A) and Pl(A) can be seen as the lower and upper probability bounds of the probability of A.

A fundamental concern in the theory of evidence is the aggregation of multiple belief strucutres. The standard procedure for accomplishing this task is the use of Dempster's rule.

Assume m_1 and m_2 are two belief structures with focal elements $A_1,\ldots A_q$ and $B_1,\ldots B_m$ respectively. The conjunction of these belief structures, m, denoted

$$m = m_1 \cap m_2$$

is defined so that the focal elements of m are all the nonnull sets D such that there exists a pair A_i and B_j, where

$$D = A_i \cap B_j$$

The weights associated with a focal element D in m is expressed as

$$m(D) = 1/(1-k) \sum_{i,\,j;\,A_i \cap B_j = D} m_1(A_i) * m_2(B_j)$$

where

$$k = \sum_{i,\,j;\,A_i \cap B_j = \varnothing} m_1(A_i) * m_2(B_j)$$

The term k is called the degree of conflict and the process of dividing by 1-k is called normalization. Dubois and Prade (1988) have a comprehensive discussion of this process.

The degree of conflict can be seen as closely related to the plausibility of one belief function given a second belief function. Assuming m_1 is a belief structure, then for any B

$$\mathrm{Pl}_1(B) = \textstyle\sum_j \mathrm{Poss}[B/A_j] * m_1(A_j)$$

Furthermore, if m_2 is a belief structure with focal elements B_i, then the plausibility of a focal element of m_2 with m_1 is

$$\mathrm{Pl}_1(B_i) = \textstyle\sum_j \mathrm{Poss}[B_i/A_j] * m_1(A_j)$$

In addition we can define the expected plausibility of m_2 given m_1 as

$$\begin{aligned}\mathrm{Pl}_1(m_2) &= \textstyle\sum_i \mathrm{Pl}_1(B_i) * m_2(B_i)\\ &= \textstyle\sum_i \sum_j \mathrm{Poss}[B_i|A_j] * m_1(A_j) * m_2(B_i)\end{aligned}$$

From the properties of Poss it follows that

$$\mathrm{Pl}_1(m_2) = \sum_{A_i \cap B_j = \varnothing} m_1(A_j) * m_2(B_i)$$

From the above we note that

$$k = 1 - \mathrm{Pl}_1(m_2)$$

Therefore

$$m(D) = \frac{1}{\mathrm{Pl}_1(m_2)} \sum_{i,\,j:\,A_i \cap B_j = D} m_1(A_i) * m_2(B_j)$$

It should be noted that $\mathrm{Pl}_1(m_2) = \mathrm{Pl}_2(m_1)$.

3. INFORMATION AND MONOTONICITY IN THE THEORY OF EVIDENCE

In this section, we discuss a number of issues related to the information contained in a belief structure and provide a concept of monotonicity for the belief structures.

Assume m is a belief structure on the set X. Basically the information contained in a belief structure consists of knowledge about the probabilities of events (subsets) of X. This view is very much in the spirit of Dempster's original work. We note that the essential feature of the belief structure is that the information it contains about the probabilities is generally imprecise (lacks specificity).

As we previously noted given the belief structure m for any subset A of X, the probability of A is known to satisfy the following inequality

$$\text{Bel}(A) \leqslant \text{Prob}(A) \leqslant \text{Pl}(A)$$

Thus our knowledge about Prob(A) based on m is that it lies in the interval [Bel(A), Pl(A)]. For a given event A, we can use the term

$$r_A = \text{Pl}(A) - \text{Bel}(A)$$

to measure the uncertainty associated with our knowledge of the probability of A. If $r_A = 0$, then we know exactly the probability of A. Shafer calls a belief structure in which $r_A = 0$, for all A, a Bayesian belief structure. This type of structure requires that the focal elements be all singletons. It is essentially the classical probability structure.

In order to motivate and justify the work that follows, we make the following simple observation. Assume

$$a_1 \leqslant \text{Prob}(A) \leqslant b_1$$

then it naturally follows that

$$a_2 \leqslant \text{Prob}(A) \leqslant b_2$$

for any $a_2 \leqslant a_1$ *and* $b_2 \geqslant b_1$.

Putting it another way, given that Prob(A) $\in [a_1, b_1]$, we can infer that Prob(A) $\in [a_2, b_2]$. We note that the second interval is wider, less specific, but still valid. In the above we note that $[a_1, b_1] \subset [a_2, b_2]$.

This observation provides the basis for the introduction of an inference among belief structures that was introduced by Yager (1986b).

Assume m_1 and m_2 are two belief structures on X such that for every subset A of X the following condition is satisfied

$$[\mathrm{Bel}_1(A), \mathrm{Pl}_1(A)] \subset [\mathrm{Bel}_2(A), \mathrm{Pl}_2(A)]$$

If the above condition holds then it follows that knowledge that m_1 is true allows us to infer that m_2 is true. A more general formulation of this observation is possible.

Definition: Assume m_1 is a belief structure in which $A_1,\ldots,A_p$ are the focal elements with weights $m_1(A_i) = a_i$. Let m_2 be another belief structure in which the focal elements can be represented as

$$B_{11}, B_{12},\ldots,B_{1n_1}, B_{21}, B_{22},\ldots,B_{2n_2},\ldots,B_{p1}, B_{p2},\ldots,B_{pn_p}$$

where $m_2(B_{ij}) = b_{ij}$. In addition, assume that for each $i = 1,\ldots,p$ the following two conditions are satisfied

(1) $A_i \subset B_{ij}$ for all $j = 1,\ldots,n_i$

(2) $\sum_{j=1}^{n_i} m_2(B_{ij}) = a_i$

In this situation we say that m_1 entails m_2 and denote this as $m_1 \subset m_2$.

Yager (1986b) proves the following result.

Theorem: If $m_1 \subset m_2$, then for every subset A

$$[\mathrm{Bel}_1(A), \mathrm{Pl}_1(A)] \subset [\mathrm{Bel}_2(A), \mathrm{Pl}_2(A)]$$

As a result of this theorem we see that if $m_1 \subset m_2$, then the knowledge that m_1 is a valid description of the world allows us to infer that m_2 is also true. We can see that if $m_1 \subset m_2$, then $m_1 \vdash m_2$. We can sy that if $m_1 \subset m_2$, then m_1 is a more specific representation.

We should note that the process of gaining knowledge in the Dempster-Shafer framework can be seen as obtaining more specific belief functions as the representation of our knowledge.

In logic the concept of monotonicity plays a fundamental role. It essentially is a manifestation of the fact that the gaining of knowledge allows us to know more about the world.

Assume $P_1, P_2,\ldots,P_n$ are a collection of propositions from which we can deduce the proposition H; we denote this as

$$(P_1, P_2,\ldots,P_n) \vdash H$$

The environment is considered to be monotonic if the addition of any proposition, p_{n+1}, still allows us to infer H, that is,

$$(P_1, P_2,\ldots,P_n, P_{n+1}) \vdash H$$

The environment is called nonmonotonic if the addition of some proposition may require us to withdraw the validity of H.

We are now in a position to introduce an analogous concept of monotonicity in the Dempster-Shafer framework. In this framework the role of propositions is played by belief structures. Assume m_1, $m_2,\ldots,m_q$ are a collection of belief structures. The process of reasoning in this framework consists of the aggregation (conjunction) of pieces of evidence. In particular if

$$m^* = m_1 \cap m_2 \cap \ldots \cap m_q$$

then

$$(m_1, m_2,\ldots,m_q) \vdash m$$

where m is any belief structure such that $m^* \subset m$.

Thus in the Dempster-Shafer framework we can infer any belief structure that contains (is entailed by) the intersection of the constituent belief structures. We shall say that the situation is monotonic if for any additional m_{q+1}, the conjunction

$$m_1 \cap m_2 \cap \ldots \cap m_q \cap m_{q+1} = m^+$$

satisfies

$$m^+ \subset m^* \, (m^* \cap m_{q+1} \subset m^*)$$

This concept of monotonicity is based on the fact that, if m^+ then from m^+ we can use the entailment principle to infer any belief structure inferred by m^*.

We should note that the view taken in this Dempster-Shafer approach is essentially a generalization of the model theoretic approach in logic. In that view, we associate with any proposition P_i a set S_i of possible worlds that are true under P_i. Then

$$S^* = S_1 \cap \ldots \cap S_q$$

are the worlds acceptable to all the propositions. A proposition H is inferable if the set of possible worlds, S_H, that make H true satisfies

$$S^* \subset S_H$$

We should note that there is one important characteristic of logic not available in the Dempster-Shafer framework. This characteristic is that of stepwise deduction. In particular if

$$(P_1, \mathrm{P}_2) \vdash H$$
$$(P_1, \mathrm{P}_3) \vdash G$$

and if

$$(G,H) \vdash Q$$

then

$$(P_1, P_2, P_3) \vdash Q$$

This stepwise deduction process doesn't work in the Dempster-Shafer environment. That is, if

$$(m_1, m_2) \vdash m_a$$
$$(m_1, m_3) \vdash m_b$$

and

$$(m_a, m_b) \vdash m_c$$

then it is *not* the case that

$$(m_1, m_2, m_3) \vdash m_c$$

The reason for this is that m_a and m_b are no longer independent and the use of Dempster's rule becomes invalid. One implication of this is that one must aggregate all the evidence together. Shenoy and Shafer (1990) introduced the use of hypergraphs to help deal with this property.

4. NORMALIZATION AND NONMONOTONICITY

In this section we shall investigate the reasoning process in the Dempster-Shafer theory, the conjunction of pieces of evidence, in regard to its satisfying the previously described monotonicity condition. We shall show that in general monotonicity is not always guaranteed in the Dempster-Shafer framework. More specifically, when the aggregation of evidence has conflicts, focal elements that have null intersection, then a nonmonotonicity is introduced. On the other hand, if there is no conflict among the evidence, then monotonicity is guaranteed. The most fundamental manifestation of this potential nonmonotonicity appears when starting with a piece of evidence m_1 we add a new piece of evidence m_2; it is generally *not* the case that

$$m_1 \cap m_2 \subset m_1$$

This only holds when there are no conflicts.

The following example will help illustrate the issues. Assume that m_1 and m_2 are two belief structures such that

$$m_1(A) = \alpha \qquad m_2(B) = \beta$$
$$m_1(X) = 1 - \alpha = \bar{\alpha} \; m_2(X) = 1 - \beta = \bar{\beta}$$

Using Dempster's rule, if $A \cap B \neq \emptyset$ the aggregation of these two pieces of evidence results in the belief structure m where

Focal element	Weight
$A \cap B$	$\alpha\beta$
A	$\alpha\bar{\beta}$
B	$\bar{\alpha}\beta$
X	$\bar{\alpha}\bar{\beta}$

We note in this case that $m_1 \cap m_2 \subset m_1$ as well as $m_1 \cap m_2 \subset m_2$. The fact that $m_1 \cap m_2 \subset m_1$ follows from the fact that $A \cap B$ and A are both contained in A and have a sum of weights equal α. In addition, both B and X are contained in X and sum to $\bar{\alpha}$.

More generally, we can prove the following theorem (Yager, 1986b):

Theorem: Assume m_1 and m_2 are two belief structures with focal elements $A_1, \ldots, A_p$ and $B_1, \ldots, B_q$. If for all A_i and B_j, $A_i \cap B_j \neq \emptyset$, then

$$m_1 \cap m_2 \subset m_1, \text{ and } m_1 \cap m_2 \subset m_2$$

Thus we see that if no conflicts arise, the reasoning process is monotonic. An implication of this observation is that, as we obtain more information, in terms of additional belief structures, which don't conflict with what we already have, then our overall knowledge increases. This follows since our ranges, the r_A's, get smaller, and are contained in previous ones.

In the case in which conflicts arise between focal elements the situation becomes different. If we consider the previous example but with the case in which $A \cap B = \emptyset$, then we get

Focal element	Weight
A	$\dfrac{\alpha\bar{\beta}}{1-\alpha\beta}$
B	$\dfrac{\bar{\alpha}\beta}{1-\alpha\beta}$
X	$\dfrac{\bar{\alpha}\bar{\beta}}{1-\alpha\beta}$

In this case it is not necessarily true that $m_1 \cap m_2 \subset m_1$. This can be seen from the following. We first note that $\mathrm{Pl}_1(A) = 1$ and $\mathrm{Bel}_1(A) = \alpha$ thus $\mathrm{Prob}_1(A) \in [\alpha, 1]$. If $m = m_1 \cap m_2$, since $A \cap B = \emptyset$, then $\mathrm{Pl}(A) = (1 - \bar{\alpha}\beta)|(1 - \alpha\beta) = \mathrm{a}$ and $\mathrm{Bel}(A) = \alpha\bar{\beta}/1 - \alpha\beta = b$ thus $\mathrm{Prob}(A) \in [b, a]$. However since

$$b = \alpha\bar{\beta}/1 - \alpha\beta = \alpha(1 - \beta)/1 - \alpha\beta < \alpha$$

then

$$\mathrm{Bel}(A) < \alpha$$

thus

$$[\mathrm{Bel}(A), \mathrm{Pl}(A)] \not\subset [\mathrm{Bel}_1(A), \mathrm{Pl}_1(A)]$$

The process exhibits a nonmonotonicity. Thus it appears the introduction of conflict and the requirement for normalization introduces a nonmonotonicity into the process.

As a first step in reducing this nonmonotonicity we may try to use a different process for normalization than that used in Dempster's rule. We note that Dempster's rule essentially allocates the weights in the conflict set proportionately among the nonconflicting focal elements.

Dubois and Prade (1988) provide a comprehensive discussion of the issue of normalization in the aggregation of belief structures. In this paper they discuss a number of alternative procedures for aggregation. We shall look at a number of these and see their effect on the monotonicity issue.

One alternative approach to normalization was suggested by Yager (1987b). In that approach, instead of proportionately distributing the conflict among all the focal elements we give it all to the base set X. Thus, using this approach we get when $A \cap B = \emptyset$,

$$m_1 \cap m_2 = m^*$$

where in this case

$$m^*(A) = \alpha\bar{\beta}$$
$$m^*(B) = \bar{\alpha}\beta$$
$$m^*(X) = \bar{\alpha}\bar{\beta} + \alpha\beta$$

Hence in this case

$$\mathrm{Pl}^*(A) = \alpha\bar{\beta} + \bar{\alpha}\bar{\beta} + \alpha\beta = 1 - \bar{\alpha}\beta = a^*$$
$$\mathrm{Bel}^*(A) = \alpha\bar{\beta} = b^*$$

Again we note that

$$b^* = \alpha\bar{\beta} < \alpha$$

and hence

$$[\mathrm{Bel}^*(A), \mathrm{Pl}^*(A)] \not\subset [\mathrm{Bel}_1(A), \mathrm{Pl}_1(B)]$$

Thus the nonmonotonicity has not been eliminated. A second approach, suggested by Dubois and Prade (1988), is to replace conflict sets with the union of the two sets. Thus, if $A \cap B = \emptyset$, then use $A \cup B$. In this case we get

$$m_1 \cap m_2 = m^+$$

where

$$\begin{aligned} m^+(A \cup B) &= \alpha\beta \\ m^+(A) &= \alpha\bar{\beta} \\ m^+(B) &= \bar{\alpha}\beta \\ m^+(X) &= \bar{\alpha}\bar{\beta} \end{aligned}$$

Thus we see that

$$\begin{aligned} \mathrm{Pl}^+(A) &= 1 - \bar{\alpha}\beta = a^+ \\ \mathrm{Bel}^+(A) &= \alpha\bar{\beta} = b^+ \end{aligned}$$

Since $b^+ = b^*$ and $a^+ = a^*$, the situation is the same as in the previous method and the nonmonotonicity still exists.

A third approach consists of applying a type of weighted averaging, which essentially corresponds to a discounting. In this approach we calculate, for $c \in [0, 1]$,

$$m^\circ = cm_1 + (1 - c)m_2$$

It can be shown that this approach still does not reduce the nonmonotonicity.

Is there any procedure we can use that will reduce the nonmonotonicity? Essentially we see that we must assign the conflict weight $\alpha\beta$ in a manner that brings up the Bel(A) to α. Thus we must assign $\alpha\beta$ to some set D such that $D \subset A$, because in that case Bel $(A) = \alpha\bar{\beta} + \alpha\beta = \alpha$. But we must also do it in a way that $D \subset B$, so that we keep the monotonicity with respect to m_2; this requires that $D \subset B$. Since $B \cap A = \emptyset$, the only possible value for D is the null set. Thus one possibility is to forgo the proces of normalization. In this case we get

$$m^\nabla = m_1 \cap m_2$$

where

$$m^{\nabla}(\varnothing) = \alpha\beta$$
$$m^{\nabla}(A) = \alpha\bar{\beta}$$
$$m^{\nabla}(B) = \bar{\alpha}\beta$$
$$m^{\nabla}(X) = \bar{\alpha}\bar{\beta}$$

Thus we get that

$$m^{\nabla} \subset m_1$$

and hence the situation is monotonic. However, in this case it happens when conflict exists that

$$\text{Bel}(X) = \text{Pl}(X) \neq 1$$

The intuitive appeal of this result is that the appearance of conflict in our knowledge base raises the possibility that the underlying base set may be greater than X. That is, there is some value x^+ not in X that could be the real value.

We can consider a more general rule for the intersection of focal elements in the Dempster rule. Assume A and B are two focal elements from m_1 and m_2; then we define their conjunction as

$$D(x) = (A(x) \wedge B(x)) \vee (1 - \text{Poss}(B/A)) * F(A, B)(x))$$

In the above the function $F(A, B)$ results in some subset of X. In all cases when $\text{Poss}(B/A) = 1$ we always get $A \cap B$. When $\text{Poss}(B/A) = 0$, the value depends on the choice of F.

In particular if we set

$$F(A, B) = A \cup B$$

then when $\text{Poss}(B/A) = 0$ we get that

$$D = A \cup B$$

which is the suggestion of Dubois and Prade (1988).

If we let

$$F(A, B) = \bar{A} \cup \bar{B}$$

then when $A \cap B = \varnothing$ we get

$$F(A, B) = X$$

which is the suggestion of Yager (1987b).

If we let

$$F(A, B) = A$$

then when $A \cap B = \emptyset$ we get

$$D = A$$

The use of this last rule guarantees, even if conflicts arise, that

$$m_1 \cap m_2 \subset m_1$$

but not

$$m_1 \cap m_2 \subset m_2$$

This last approach introduces an idea of priority. It can be seen as a form of discounting, where m_2 is discounted if it conflicts with m_1; otherwise we don't discount it.

It should be noted that a close parallel exists between the conflict case in the Dempster-Shafer theory and that of classical logical reasoning. In the classical logic conflict results in $S^* = \emptyset$ and hence for any proposition H, $S^* \subset S_H$; thus everything is inferable. In the Dempster-Shafer theory, if we take the option of not normalizing, then for any subset A the difference between Pl(A) and Bel(A) starts getting smaller and thus allows the inference of more belief structures. the shrinkage of r_A is directly related to the amount of mass assigned to the null set. When all the mass is assigned to the null then any belief structure is inferable.

5. DEFAULT KNOWLEDGE IN BELIEF STRUCTURES

In this section we show that the appearance of the nonmonotonicity rather than being a problem provides a natural facility for introducing default knowledge in the framework of belief structures.

Assume V is a variable that takes its value in the set X. Assume we have two pieces of knowledge with respect to V, the first a categorical and the second a typical piece of knowledge:

P_1: V is A
P_2: typically V is B

As discussed by Yager (1987a), essentially what we desire to happen in this case is that, if $A \cap B \neq \emptyset$, we obtain $A \cap B$ as our inference. If they don't intersect, we want to discount the default knowledge and be left with A. We shall see that the reasoning mechanism in the theory of evidence essentially provides this capability.

Yager (1986a, 1989b) has suggested that one can represent a statement like

typically V is B

by a belief structure

V is m_2

where

$$m_2(B) = \alpha$$
$$m_2(X) = 1 - \alpha$$

where α is close to one, the idea being that by typical knowledge we are saying that there is a high probability that V lies in the set B but some small chance it can be anywhere.

Thus the above knowledge base can be represented in the Dempster-Shafer framework as two belief structures m_1 and m_2, where

$$m_1(A) = 1 \qquad m_2(B) = \alpha \qquad m_2(X) = 1 - \alpha$$

Taking the conjunction of these two pieces of information we get

$$m = m_1 \cap m_2$$

If $A \cap B \neq \emptyset$, then we get

$$m(A \cap B) = \alpha$$
$$m(A) = 1 - \alpha$$

In this case

$$\mathrm{Pl}(A) = \mathrm{Bel}(A) = \mathrm{Prob}(A) = 1$$

thus we are certain that V lies in A. In addition

$$\mathrm{Pl}(A \cap B) = 1$$
$$\mathrm{Bel}(A \cap B) = \alpha$$

thus

$$\alpha \leqslant \mathrm{Prob}(A \cap B) \leqslant 1$$

So, as desired, there is a high probability that V lies in $A \cap B$. We note that if $A \subset B$, then $A \cap B = A$ and we get $m(A) = 1$. Thus, when the categorical knowledge is more specific than the default knowledge, no use is made of the default knowledge. In the other case, where $B \subset A$, then $m(B) = \alpha$ and $m(A) = 1 - \alpha$.

On the other hand, if $A \cap B = \emptyset$ and we use Dempster's normalization process, we get

$$m(A) = 1$$

Thus we see that we get the desired result that the typical knowledge is completely discounted when a conflict with absolute knowledge arises.

If we use another normalization procedure this nice result doesn't necessarily follow. For example, if we put all the conflict weight into $A \cup B$ we get

$$m(A) = 1 - \alpha$$
$$m(A \cup B) = \alpha$$

In this case we get

$$\text{Bel}(A) = 1 - \alpha$$

while still retaining

$$\text{Pl}(A) = 1$$

Dubois and Prade (1988) suggest the choice of normalization may be a function of the characteristics of the base knowledge. So it appears that when typicality arises, Dempster's aggregation is an appropriate one.

6. PRIORITIES AND STRENGTHS OF DEFAULTS

We next consider the case in which we have two pieces of default knowledge:

P_1: typically V is A
P_2: typically V is B

In addressing this problem by one of the logical extension-type methods we are faced with the issue of priority among the default rules. In particular, if one of the default rules has a higher priority, it is introduced first in the deduction process. If $A \cap B \neq \emptyset$ no problems arise and we infer $A \cap B$. If $A \cap B = \emptyset$ and if P_1 is considered to have a higher priority, then we should infer A. If P_2 is considered to have a higher priority we should infer B. If P_1 and P_2 are considered to have some priority, we should get a different result, which is essentially the union of the two. Subsequently, we shall see that the role of priority in the Dempster-Shafer framework is played by the probability assigned to the default set in each case.

We can represent the above knowledge base by two belief structures m_1 and m_2 where

$$m_1(A) = \alpha \qquad m_2(B) = \beta$$
$$m_1(X) = 1 - \alpha \qquad m_2(X) = 1 - \beta$$

In this representation we can see that α essentially describes the strength of the first default rule since $\text{Bel}(A) = \alpha$. That is, α measures how certain we are that A holds.

In the above example, our inferred belief structure is

$$m = m_1 \cap m_2$$

If $A \cap \text{B} \neq \emptyset$, then we get

$$m(A \cap B) = \alpha\beta$$
$$m(A) = \alpha\bar{\beta}$$
$$m(B) = \bar{\alpha}\beta$$
$$m(X) = \bar{\alpha}\bar{\beta}$$

In this case

$$\text{Pl}(A \cap B) = 1$$
$$\text{Bel}(A \cap B) = \alpha\beta$$

thus

$$\text{Prob}(A \cap B) \geqslant \alpha\beta$$

Since both α and β are very close to one, this result essentially says that the inferred value for V is $A \cap B$. Since both A and B have small probabilities, we can use the entailment principle to replace the above by

$$m(A \cap B) = \alpha\beta$$
$$m(X) = 1 - \alpha\beta$$

This essentially says that we get typically $A \cap B$ with a little less strength than the typicality of either A or B.

If $A \cap B, = \emptyset$, then we get

$$m(A) = \alpha\bar{\beta}/(1 - \alpha\beta)$$
$$m(B) = \bar{\alpha}\beta/(1 - \alpha\beta)$$
$$m(X) = \bar{\alpha}\bar{\beta}/(1 - \alpha\beta)$$

Let us consider the case in which P_1 is a stronger default rule than P_2, $\alpha > \beta$. This essentially corresponds to P_1 having a priority over P_2. In the above since

$$\mathrm{Bel}(A) = \alpha\bar{\beta}/(1 - \alpha\beta)$$
$$\mathrm{Bel}(B) = \bar{\alpha}\beta/(1 - \alpha\beta)$$

and with $\alpha > \beta$, it follows thag $\alpha\bar{\beta} > \bar{\alpha}\beta$, and we see that Bel($A$) > Bel($B$). The actual distinction depends on the values for α and β, the strengths of the defaults.

Example: If $\alpha = 0.99$ and $\beta = 0.9$, then $m(A) = 0.9$, $m(B) = 0.08$, and $m(X) = 0.02$. In this case $0.9 \leqslant \mathrm{Prob}(A) \leqslant 0.92$ and $0.08 \leqslant \mathrm{Prob}(B) \leqslant 0.1$. Thus there is a high probability that V lies in A and a small chance that V lies in B. In addition, $\mathrm{Prob}(A \cup B) \geqslant 0.98$.

In the case when P_1 and P_2 have the same strength (priority), then $\alpha = \beta$. In this case $m(A) = \alpha\bar{\alpha}/(1 - \alpha^2)$, $m(B) = \alpha\bar{\alpha}/(1 - \alpha^2)$, and $m(X) = \alpha\bar{\alpha}/(1 - \alpha^2)$. Thus the belief and plausibility of A and B are equal.

Example: If $\alpha = 0.95$ then $m(A) = 0.49$, $m(B) = 0.49$, and $m(X) = 0.02$. In this case Prob(A) and Prob(B) are contained in [0.49, 0.51]. This essentially says that we are about 50 percent certain of each. From a pragmatic point of view, if two rules are conflicting and are of equal priority, it would appear that we should not assign too high a strength to each. Thus if we let $\alpha = 0.5$ we get $m(A) = 1/3$, $m(B) = 1/3$, and $m(X) = 1/3$. In this case $1/3 \leqslant \mathrm{Prob}(A) \leqslant 2/3$ and $2/3 \leqslant \mathrm{Prob}(A \cup B) \leqslant 1$.

Assume we have a proposition

typically V is A

to which we assign a strength α. Therefore

$$m(A) = \alpha$$
$$m(X) = 1 - \alpha$$

From the entailment principle we can infer

$$m^*(A) = \alpha_1$$
$$m^*(X) = 1 - \alpha_1$$

where

$$\alpha_1 < \alpha$$

Essentially what this implies is that we can always hedge, make less the degree of typicality, and still be correct.

7. REPRESENTATION OF DEFAULT RULES

In this section we consider the representation and manipulation of default rules within the framework of the Dempster-Shafer theory of evidence. Further details in regard to this case can be found in Yager (1986a, 1989b).

Consider first a categorical rule such as

"if V is A then U is B" $(A \rightarrow B)$

where V and U are variables taking their values in the sets X and Y. A and B are subsets of X and Y, respectively. We can represent this rule as a relationship on V and U such that

(V, U) is $\bar{A} \cup B$

where $\cup$ is a co-product. That is,

$$A \cup B = \{(x, y) \mid x \in \bar{A} \text{ or } y \in B\}$$

Next we consider a default rule such as

typically [if V is A then U is B]

As suggested by Yager (1986a, 1989b) we can represent this in the Dempster-Shafer framework as a belief structure by indicating that there is a high probability α, the strength of the rule, that it holds and a $(1 - \alpha)$ probability that the rule does not hold. In this case we get a belief structure m on $X \times Y$ such that

$$m(A \rightarrow B) = \alpha$$
$$m(A \rightarrow Y) = 1 - \alpha$$

Consider a knowledge base in which we have

P_1: typically [if V is A then U is B]
P_2: V is Q

We can represent this by two belief structures m_1 and m_2, where

$$m_1(A \rightarrow B) = \alpha \qquad m_2(Q) = 1$$
$$m_1(A \rightarrow Y) = 1 - \alpha$$

The reasoning process consists of the conjunction of these pieces of information to get

$$m = m_1 \cap m_2$$

where

$$m([A \to B) \cap Q]) = \alpha$$
$$m([A \to Y) \cap Q]) = 1 - \alpha$$

Two cases are of interest. The first case is when $Q \subset A$, then we get that

$$m(U \text{ is } B) = \alpha$$
$$m(U \text{ is } Y) = 1 - \alpha$$

hence we infer that

typically V is B

We note that the stronger the rule, the larger α, the higher the certainty of B. In particular

$$\text{Prob}(B) \geqslant \alpha$$

If $Q \not\subset$ A, then the rule does not fire and we obtain

$$m(V \text{ is } Y) = 1$$

that is,

V is Y

We next consider a classic example from the nonmonotonic literature. In this case we have two default rules:

P_1: typically if Quaker then Pacifist ($Q \to P$)
P_2: typically if Republican then not Pacifist ($R \to \bar{P}$)

These two pieces of knowledge can be represented as belief structures as

$$m_1(Q \to P) = \alpha_1 \qquad m_2(Q \to \bar{P}) = \alpha_2$$
$$m_1(Q \to Y) = 1 - \alpha_1 \quad m_2(Q \to Y) = 1 - \alpha_2$$

Where $Y = P \cup \bar{P}$.

We shall assume in addition that we have

P_3: Q
P_4: R.

In this case we get

$$m_1(P) = \alpha_1 \qquad m_2(\bar{P}) = \alpha_2$$
$$m_1(Y) = 1 - \alpha_1 \quad m_2(Y) = 1 - \alpha_2$$

Taking the conjunction of these two pieces of information, we get $m = m_1 \cap m_2$.

$$m(P) = \frac{\bar{\alpha}_2 \alpha_1}{1 - \alpha_1 \alpha_2}$$
$$m(\bar{P}) = \frac{\bar{\alpha}_1 \alpha_2}{1 - \alpha_1 \alpha_2}$$
$$m(P) = \frac{\bar{\alpha}_1 \bar{\alpha}_2}{1 - \alpha_1 \alpha_2}$$

Since both P_1 and P_2 have the same priority, then $\alpha_1 = \alpha_2 = \alpha$ hence

$$m(P) = m(\bar{P}) = \frac{\bar{\alpha}\alpha}{1 - \alpha\alpha} = \frac{(1 - \alpha)\,\alpha}{1 - \alpha^2} = \frac{\alpha}{1 + \alpha}$$
$$m(Y) = \frac{1 - \alpha}{1 + \alpha}$$

In this situation we get

$$\frac{\alpha}{1 + \alpha} \leqslant \text{Prob}(P) \leqslant 1 - \frac{\alpha}{1 + \alpha}$$

and the same holds for $\text{Prob}(\bar{P})$.

8. PROBABILISTIC AND DEFAULT KNOWLEDGE

Probabilistic knowledge is representable in the Dempster-Shafer structure by a Bayesian belief structure (Shafer, 1976). Let X be our base set and assume we have a probability distribution on X where[1]: $p(x_1) = b_1$, $p(x_2) = b_2$, $p(x_3) = b_3$ and $p(x_4) = b_4$. We can represent this as a belief structure m_1 with focal elements $B_i = \{x_i\}$ and $m_1(B_i) = b_i$, for $i = 1, 2, 3, 4$. This type of belief structure is called a Bayesian belief structure and is characterized by the property that all its focal elements are singletons. In addition to the above knowledge assume we have a piece of default knowledge:

$$m_2(A) = \alpha$$
$$m_2(X) = 1 - \alpha$$

Let $m = m_1 \cap m_2$ be the conjunction of these two pieces of knowledge. Let us look at this for various special situations:

---

[1] It is assumed that $\{x_1, x_2, x_3, x_4\} \subset X$.

(i) $x_i \in A$ for all i. In this case $m = m_1$.
(ii) $x_i \notin A$ for all i. In this case $m = m_1$.
(iii) $x_i \in A$ for some i. With loss of generality assume x_1 and x_2 are contained in A. In this case we get m to have the following weights:

$$m(B_1) = \frac{b_1}{1 - \alpha(b_3 + b_4)}$$

$$m(B_2) = \frac{b_2}{1 - \alpha(b_3 + b_4)}$$

$$m(B_3) = \frac{(1 - \alpha) b_3}{1 - \alpha(b_3 + b_4)}$$

$$m(B_4) = \frac{(1 - \alpha) b_4}{1 - \alpha(b_3 + b_4)}$$

Thus we see that in this case those x_i's lying in A are enhanced while those lying in $\bar{A}$ are discounted.

9. CONCLUSION

We have investigated the representation of default knowledge in the framework of the Dempster-Shafer theory of evidence.

BIBLIOGRAPHY

Dempster, A.P. (1967). Upper and lower probabilities induced by a multi-valued mapping. *Ann. Math. Statistics* 38: 325–39.

Dubois, D. and Prade, H. (1988). Representation and combination of uncertainty with belief functions and possibility measures. *Computational Intelligence* 4; 244–64.

McCarthy, J. (1986). Applications of circumscription to formalizing common sense knowledge. *Artificial Intelligence* 28: 89–116.

McDermott, D. and Doyle, J. (1980). Non-monotonic logic I. *Artificial Intelligence* 13: 41–72.

Moore, R.C. (1985). Semantical considerations on nonmonotonic logic. *Artificial Intelligence* 25: 75–94.

Pearl, J. (1988). *Probabilistic reasoning in intelligent systems*. Palo Alto, CA: Morgan Kaufmann.

Reiter, R. (1980). A logic for default reasoning. *Artificial Intelligence* 13: 81–132.

Shafer, G. (1976). *A mathematical theory of evidence*. Princeton: Princeton University Press.

Shenoy, P.P. and Shafer, G. (1990). Axioms for probability and belief-function propagation. In Shafer, G. and Pearl, J. (eds.), *Readings in uncertain reasoning*, pp. 576–610. San Mateo, CA: Morgan Kaufmann.

Yager, R.R. (1986a). On implementing usual values. *Proc. Second Workshop on Uncertainty in Artificial Intelligence*, Philadelphia, pp. 339–46.

Yager, R.R. (1986b). The entailment principle for Dempster-Shafer granules. *Int. J. of Intelligent Systems* 1: 247–62.

Yager, R.R. (1987a). Using approximate reasoning to represent default knowledge. *Artificial Intelligence* 31: 99–112.

Yager, R.R. (1987b). On the Dempster-Shafer framework and new combination rules. *Information Sciences* 41: 93–137.

Yager, R.R. (1989a). Normalization and representation of nonmonotonic knowledge in the theory of evidence. *Proceedings of Fifth Workshop on Uncertainty in Artificial Intelligence*, Windsor, Ont., pp. 395–403.

Yager, R.R. (1989b). On usual values in commonsense reasoning. *Fuzzy Sets and Systems* 30: 239–55.

Zadeh, L.A. (1984). A theory of commonsense knowledge. In Skala, H., Termini, S. and Trillas, E. (eds.), *Aspects of vagueness*, pp. 257–96. Dordrecht: Reidel.

25 How far are we from the complete knowledge? Complexity of knowledge acquisition in the Dempster-Shafer approach

Bassam A. CHOKR and
Vladik Ya. KREINOVICH

Abstract: When a knowledge base represents experts' uncertainty, then it is reasonable to ask how far we are from the complete knowledge, that is, how many more questions we have to ask these experts or ask nature by means of experimenting, etc. in order to attain the complete knowledge. Of course, since we do not know what the real world is, we cannot get the precise number of questions from the very beginning: it is quite possible, for example, that we could ask the right question first and thus guess the real state of the world after the first question. So we have to estimate this number and use this estimate as a natural measure of completeness for a given knowledge base. We give such estimates for Dempster-Shafer's formalism. Namely, we show that this average number of questions can be obtained by solving a simple mathematical optimization problem. In principle, this characteristic is not always sufficient to express the fact that sometimes we have more knowledge. For example, it has the same value if we have an event with two possible outcomes and nothing else is known, and if there is an additional knowledge that the probability of every outcome is 0.5. We'll show that from the practical viewpoint this is not a problem, because the difference between the necessary number of questions in both cases is practically negligible.

Keywords: complexity of knowledge acquisition, Dempster-Shafer formalism.

1. BRIEF INTRODUCTION TO THE PROBLEM

Knowledge is usually not complete. The vast majority of modern knowledge bases include uncertain knowledge, that is, statements the truth about which the experts themselves are not 100% sure. This uncertainty leads to uncertainty in the answers to the queries: instead of yes-no answers, we get answers like "probably" and "with probability 0.8." Sometimes the uncertainty is too high, and we cannot get anything definite from the resulting expert system. We can get only *estimates* for the number of necessary questions. These estimates are a natural measure of completeness for a given knowledge base.

Estimates of incompleteness are useful. Such estimates can be useful in several cases. For example, suppose that we feel our knowledge base needs updating and we want to estimate the cost of the update. The main part of updating is the acquisition of the new knowledge from the experts. Since it is desirable to take the best (and therefore highly paid) specialists as experts, the knowledge acquisition cost is an essential part of the total update cost. From our previous experience, we can get the expected per-question cost c by dividing the previous update cost by the number of questions asked. To estimate the total acquistion cost, we multiply c by the number of necessary questions.

Another situation where these estimates are applicable is when we choose between the existing knowledge bases (for example, when we decide which of them to buy). When choosing we must take into consideration cost, performance time and so on. But the main characteristic of the knowledge base is how much information it contains. It is difficult to estimate this amount of information directly, but we can use the estimates of the number of questions if they are available: evidently the fewer questions we need to ask in order to obtain the complete knowledge, the more information was there initially. So the knowledge base for which we have to ask the fewest questions is the one with the greatest amount of information.

What we are planning to do. There exist several different formalisms for representing uncertainty (see, e.g., Smets, et al., 1988). In the present paper we estimate the necessary number of questions for the case of Dempster-Shafer's formalism. Namely, we show that this average number of questions can be obtained by solving a simple mathematical optimization problem.

It turns out that the same techniques can be applied to estimate the complexity of knowledge acquistion for the probabilistic approach to uncertainty (Nilsson, 1986).

It seems desirable to have a characteristic of uncertainty such that if we add additional information (i.e., diminish uncertainty), we decrease the value of this characteristic. Strictly speaking, our characteristic (average number of binary question) does not satisfy this property. For example, it has the same value if we have an event with two possible outcomes and nothing else is known, and if there is an additional knowledge that the probability of every outcome is 0.5. We'll show that from the practical viewpoint this is not a problem, because the difference between the necessary number of questions in both cases is practically negligible. The main results of this paper appeared first in Chokr and Kreinovich (1991).

The structure of the paper is as follows: There exists a well-known case where a formula for the average number of questions is known: the case of probabilistic knowledge, which was considered in the pioneer Shannon papers on information theory. We are planning to use the same methods that were used in its derivation. Since the derivation is not as well known as Shannon's formula itself, we'll briefly describe it in Section 2. In Section 3, we'll formulate a corresponding problem for Dempster-Shafer formalism in mathematical terms and present our results. In Section 4, we'll show that this characteristic is sometimes not sufficient, but from a practical viewpoint there is no need to worry. In Section 5 we apply the same techniques to the case of a probabilistic knowledge. Proofs are in Section 6.

2. SHANNON'S FORMULA REVISITED

First let's analyze the simplest possible case: formulation. Before we actually analyze Shannon's formula, let us recall how to compute the complexity of knowledge acquisition in the simplest case; namely, we consider one event, and we know beforehand that it can result in one of finitely many incompatible outcomes. Let's denote these outcomes by $A_1, A_2, \ldots$, and their total number by n. For example, in the coin-tossing case n equals two, and A_1 and A_2 are "heads" and "tails." If we are describing weather, then it is natural to take "raining" as A_1, "snowing" as A_2, and so on. How many binary questions do we have to ask in order to find out which of the outcomes occurred?

The simplest case: result. The answer is well known: we must ask Q questions, where Q is the smallest integer that is greater than or equal to $\log_2 n$. This number is sometimes called the *ceiling* of $\log_2 n$ and is denoted by $\lceil \log_2 n \rceil$. And if we ask less than Q questions, we will be unable to always find the outcome.

Although the proof of this fact is well known (Horowitz and Sahni, 1984), we repeat it here, because this result will be used as a basis for all other estimates.

The simplest case: proof. First we have to prove that Q questions are sufficient. Indeed, let's enumerate all the outcomes (in arbitrary order) by numbers from 0 to $n-1$, and write these numbers in the binary form. Using binary numbers with q digits, one gets numbers from 0 to $2^q - 1$, that is, a total of 2^q numbers. So one digit is sufficient for $n = 1,2$; two digits for $n = 1,2,\ldots,4$, q digits for $n = 1,2,\ldots,2^q$, and in order to represent n numbers we need to take the minimal q such that $2^q \geqslant n$. Since this inequality is equivalent to $q \geqslant \log_2 n$, we need Q digits to represent all these numbers. So we can ask the following Q questions: "is the first binary digit 0?," "is the second binary digit 0?," etc., up to "is the q-th digit 0?"

The fact that we cannot use less than Q questions is also easy to prove. Indeed, suppose we use $q < Q$ questions. After we ask q binary questions, we get a sequence of q 0's and 1's (q bits). If there is one bit, we have 2 possibilities: 0 or 1. We have q bits, so we have $2 \cdot 2 \cdot 2 \ldots \cdot 2$ (q *times*) $= 2^q$ possible sequences. This sequence is the only thing that we use to distinguish outcomes, so if we need to distinguish between n outcomes, we need at least n sequences. So the number of sequences 2^q must be greater than or equal to n: $2^q \geqslant n$. Since logarithm is a monotonic function, this inequality is equivalent to $q \geqslant \log_2 n$. But Q is by definition the smallest integer, that is, greater than or equal to this logarithm, and q is smaller than Q. Therefore q cannot be $\geqslant \log_2 n$, and hence $q < Q$ questions are not sufficient.

Situations that are covered by Shannon's formula. The above formula works fine for the case when we have a single event and we need to find what its outcome is. But in many real-life cases the same types of events happen again and again: for example, we can toss the coin again and again; we must predict weather every day. In such cases there is a potentially infinite sequence of repeating independent events. By the moment when we are asking about the otucome of the current event, we normally already know what outcomes happened before, which of them were more frequent, which were more seldom.

In some cases these frequencies change essentially in course of time: for example, in case of the global warming the frequencies of cold weather days will become smaller and smaller. But in many cases we can safely assume that these frequencies are more or less the same. This means that the outcomes that were more frequent in the past will still be more frequent, and vice versa.

Of course, the frequencies with which some outcome occurs in two long sequences of n events, are not precisely equal. But it is usually assumed that the larger N is, the smaller is the difference between them. In other words, when N tends to ∞, the frequencies converge to a number that is called a *limit frequency*, or a *probability* p_i of an outcome i. We can also express the same supposition by saying that the frequencies are estimates for these probabilities: the bigger the sample we take, the better are these estimates. These frequencies are the additional information that Shannon (1948) used to diminish the number of necessary questions.

Why probabilities help to diminish the number of questions: explanation in commonsense terms. If we have just one event, then probabilities or no probabilities, we still have to ask all $Q=[\log_2 n]$ questions. However, if we have N similar events, and we are interested in knowing the outcomes of all of them, we do not have to ask Q questions all N times: we can sometimes get away with less than QN questions and still know all the outcomes.

Let's give a simple example why it is possible. Suppose we have 2 outcomes ($n=2$), and their probabilities are $p_1=0.99$ and $p_2=0.01$. If there is just one event, we have to ask $Q=1$ question. Let's now consider the case of 10 events. If we knew no probabilities, there would be $2^{10}=1024$ possible combinations of outcomes, and so we need to ask at least $10 = \log_2 1024$ questions in order to find all the outcomes.

But we do know the probabilities. And due to the fact that the probability of the second event is very small, it is hardly unprobable that there will be 2 or more cases out of 10 with the second outcome. If we neglect these unprobable cases, we conclude that there are not 1024, but only 11 possible combinations: second outcome in first event, first in all the others; second outcome in the second event, first in all the others, ... (10 such combinations), and the eleventh that corresponds to first outcome in all these events. To find a combination out of 11 possible we need only $\lceil \log_2 11 \rceil = 4$ questions. On average we have 4/10 questions per event.

So, if we neglect low probability combinations of outcomes then we can drastically reduce the average number of questions. What if we do not neglect them? Let us show that the average number of binary questions can still be kept small. Indeed, in the above example, we can consider 12 mutually exclusive classes: 11 defined as above (classes that consist of a single sequence of outcomes), and a twelfth class that contains all rare outcome sequences (in this example, outcome sequences with 2 or more second outcomes). We still need 4 questions to figure out to which of these 12 mutually exclusive classes the sequence of 10 actual outcomes belongs. If it belongs to one of the first 11 classes (that consist of one sequence each), then we know the outcomes of all 10 events. In case we are in the twelfth class, we still have to ask 10 additional questions to find out the actual outcomes of all 10 events. In this case we need 10 additional questions, but this case is very rare (probability $\leqslant 0.01$). Therefore, it adds $\leqslant 0.01 \cdot 10 = 0.1$ to the average number of questions. So, we can handle rare cases with a small effect on the average number of questions.

The above-given example may look purely mathematical, but it has lots of real-world applications. As an example, let us take diagnosis: a system doesn't work, and we must find out which of n components failed. Here we have two outcomes: good and failed. In case the reliability of these components is sufficiently high so that $p_2 \ll 1$, we can neglect the possibility of multiple failures, and thus simplify the problem.

Some statistics. When talking about Shannon's (1948) theory one cannot avoid using statistics. However, we will not copy Shannon; instead we reformulate so that it would be easy to obtain a Dempster-shafer modification.

Suppose we know the probabilities p_i, and we are interested in the outcome of N events, where N is given. Let's fix i and estimate the number of events N_i, in which the outcome is i.

This number N_i is obtained by adding all the events in which the outcome was i, so $N_i = n_1 + n_2 + \dots + n_N$, where n_k equals to 1 if in k-th event the outcome is *id* and 0 otherwise. The average $E(n_k)$ of n_k equals to $p_i \cdot 1 + (1 - p_i) \cdot 0 = p_i$. The mean square deviation $\sigma[n_k]$ is determined by the formula $\sigma^2[n_k] = p_i(1 - E(n_k))^2 + (1 - p_i)(0 - E(n_k))^2$. If we substitute here $E(n_k) = p_i$, we get $\sigma^2[n_k] = p_i(1 - p_i)$. The outcomes of all these events are considered independent; therefore n_k are independent random variables. Hence the average value of N_i equals to the sum of the averages of

n_k: $E[N_i]=E[n_1]+E[n_2]+...+E[n_N]=Np_i$. The mean square deviation $\sigma[N_i]$ satisfies a corresponding equation $\sigma^2[N_i]=\sigma^2[n_1]+\sigma^2[n_2]+...=Np_i(1-p_i)$, so $\sigma[N_i]=\sqrt{p_i(1-p_i)N}$.

For big N the sum of equally distributed independent random variables tends to a Gaussian distribution (the well-known *central limit theorem*), therefore for big N we can assume that N_i is a random variable with a Gaussian distribution. Theoretically, a random Gaussian variable with the average a and a standard deviation σ can take any value. However, in practice, if for example one buys a measuring instrument with guaranteed 0.1 V standard deviation and it gives an error 1 V, it means that something is wrong with this instrument. Therefore it is assumed that only some values are practically possible. Usually a "k-sigma" rule is accepted that the real value can only take values from $a-k\sigma$ to $a+k\sigma$, where k is 2, 3 or 4. So in our case we can conclude that N_i lies between $Np_i-k\sqrt{p_i(1-p_i)N}$ and $Np_i+k\sqrt{p_i(1-p_i)N}$. Now we are ready for the formulation of Shannon's result.

Comment. In this quality control example the choice of k matters, but, as we'll see, in our case the results do not depend on k at all.

2.1. Formulation of Shannon's results

Definitions. Suppose a real number $k>0$ and a positive integer n are given. n is called the *number of outcomes*. By a *probabilistic knowledge* we mean a set $\{p_i\}$ of n real numbers, $p_i \geqslant 0$, $\Sigma p_i=1$. p_i is called a *probability* of i-th event.

Suppose that an integer N is given; it is called *the number of events*. By a *result of n events* we mean a sequence r_k, $1 \leqslant k \leqslant N$ of integers from 1 to n. r_k is called the *result of k*-th event. The number of events that resulted in i-th outcome will be denoted by N_i^i. We say that the result of N events is consistent with the probabilistic knowledge $\{p_i\}$ if for every i the following inequality is true: $Np_i-k\sqrt{p_i(1-p_i)N} \leqslant N_i \leqslant N_{p_i}+k\sqrt{p_i(1-p_i)N}$.

Let's denote the number of all consistent results by $N_{cons}(N)$. The number $[\log_2(N_{cons}(N))]$ will be called the *number of questions necessary to determine the results of N events* and denoted by $Q(N)$. The fraction $Q(N)/N$ will be called the *average number of questions*. The limit of the average number of questions will be called the *complexity of knowledge acquisition*.

Theorem (Shannon). *When the number of events N tends to infinity, the average number of questions tends to* $\Sigma - p_i log_2(p_i)$.

Comments:

1. This sum is known as an *entropy* of a probabilistic distribution $\{p_i\}$ and denoted by S or $S(\{p_i\})$. So Shannon's theorem says that if we know the probabilities of all the outcomes, then the average number of questions that we have to ask in order to get a complete knowledge equals to the entropy of this probabilistic distribution. In other words: in case we know all the probabilities, the complexity of knowledge acquisition equals the entropy of this probabilistic distribution.
2. As promised, the result does not depend on k.
3. Since we modified Shannon's definitions, we cannot use the original proof. Our proof is given in Section 6.

3. DEMPSTER-SHAFER'S CASE

Dempster-Shafer's (DS) formalism in brief (Smets et al., 1988). The basic element of knowledge in this formalism is as follows: an expert gives several hypotheses $E_1, \ldots, E_p$ about the real world (these hypotheses are not necessarily incompatible), and describes his degrees of belief $m(E_1)$, $m(E_2), \ldots, m(E_p)$ in each of these hypotheses. These values are called *masses*, and their sum is supposed to be equal to 1. There are also combination rules that allow us to combine the knowledge of several experts; as a result we again get a set of hypotheses (that combine the hypotheses of several experts), and their masses (degrees of belief).

So in general the knowledge consists of a finite set of statements E_1, E_2, ..., E_p about the real world, and a set of real numbers $m(E_i)$ such that $\Sigma m(E_i)=1$.

What "complete knowledge" means in DS. This knowledge is incomplete: first of all, we do not know which of the hypotheses E_i is true. But even if we manage to figure that out, the uncertainty can still remain because this hypothesis E_i does not necessarily determine uniquely the state of our system. Therefore, if we want to estimate how far we are from the complete knowledge, we must know what is meant by a complete knowledge. In other words, we need to know the set W of possible states of the analyzed system (these states are sometimes called *possible worlds*). Of course, there are infinitely many states of any real objects, but usually we are interested only in finitely many properties $P_1, P_2, \ldots, P_m$. It means that if for some pair of states s_1, s_2 each of these properties is true in s_1 if and only if it is true in s_2, then we consider them as one state. In this sense a state is uniquely determined by the m-dimensional Boolean vector that consists of truth values $P_i(s)$. So the set of all possible worlds consists of all such vectors for which a state s with these properties is possible at all.

Where do we take the masses from? In order to use this formalism to describe actual knowledge we must somehow assign the masses to the experts' beliefs. The fact that the sum of these masses equals 1 prompts the interpretation of masses as probabilities. And, indeed, the very formalism stemmed from probabilities; therefore a probabilistic way is one of the possible ways to estimate masses.

For example, we can ask several experts what statement better describes their knowledge, take all these statements for E_i and for $m(E_i)$ take the fraction $N(E_i)/N$, where N is the total number of experts, and $N(E_i)$ is the number of experts whose knowledge is described by the statement E_i. Or, alternatively, we can ask one expert, and by analyzing the similar situations he can say that in the part $m(E_i)$ of all these cases a hypothesis E_i was true. It is also possible that the expert does not know so many cases, but he tries to make a guess, based on his experience of similiar cases.

There exist other methods to determine masses that are not of probabilistic origin, but we'll consider only probabilistic ones for three reasons (more detailed explanations of the pro-probabilistic viewpoint can be found in Pearl, 1989; Dubois and Prade, 1989; Halpern and Fagin, 1990; Shafer and Pearl, 1990):

Why do we consider only probabilistic methods to determine masses?

1. There are arguments (beginning with Savage, 1954, 1962) that if an expert assigns the degrees of belief to several mutually exclusive events and assigns them in a rational manner, then they automaticaly satisfy all the properties of probabilities (they are called *subjective probabilities*). In Dempster-Shafer's case, the mass $m(E)$ represents an expert's degree of belief in the statement "the set of all possible alternatives coincides with E." Such statements for different E are mutually exclusive, and therefore, we can apply the abovementioned arguments.
2. Several nonprobabilistic methods of assigning degrees of belief that we successfully applied turned out to have probabilistic origin; for example, for the rules of MYCIN, the famous

successful expert systems (Shortliffe, 1976; Buchanan ad Shortlife, 1984), it was proved in Heckerman (1986).

3. Finally, in case we interpret masses as probabilities, we know precisely what we mean by saying that we believe in E_i with the degree of belief $m(E_i)$: namely, as we'll show right now, this knowledge can be easily reformulated in terms of the future behavior of the system. Therefore, we can understand in precise terms what is meant by this knowledge, and what knowledge we need in addition so that we would be able to narrow our predictions to one actual outcome and thus get a complete knowledge. In case we do not use a probabilistic interpretation, what restrictions this knowledge imposes on future outcomes is difficult to figure out.

What does a DS knowledge mean? In case we accept a probabilistic interpretation, then the knowledge that the hypothesis E_i is true with mass $m(E_i)$ can be interpreted as follows: if we have N similar events, then among these N cases there are approximately $Nm(E_1)$ in which the outcomes satisfy the statement E_1; among the remaining ones there are approximately $Nm(E_2)$ cases in which E_2 is true, and so forth.

Warning. This does not mean that E_1 is true only in $Nm(\mathrm{E}_1)$ cases. According to the original interpretation of Dempster and Shafer, the relation between masses and probabilities is more complicated. In this interpretation, when our knowledge is given in a DS form, it means that we do not know all the probabilities p. Instead, we know a class $\mathbf{P}$ of probability distributions that contains the actual distribution p. For each event E, different distributions p from this class lead to different values of $p(E)$. These values form an interval $[p^-, p^+]$. The smallest possible value (it is also called a *lower probability*) is equal to our belief $bel(E)$ in E, and the biggest possible value p^+ coincides with the plausibility $pl(E)$ of the event E.

To illustrate this point, let us give an example when masses are different from probabilities.

Example. Suppose that the whole knowledge of an expert is that to some extent he believes in some statement E. If we denote the corresponding degree of belief by m, we can express this knowledge in DS terms as follows: he believes in $E_1 = E$ with degree of belief $m(E_1) = m$, and with the remaining degree of belief $m(E_2) = 1 - m$

he knows nothing, i.e., E_2 is a statement that is always true. In our terms this knowledge means that out of N events there are $\approx Nm$ in which E is true, and $\approx N(1-m)$ in which E_2 is true. But E_2 is always true, so the only conclusion is that in at least $\approx Nm$ events E is true. It is possible that E is always true (if it is also true for the remaining $N(1-m)$ events), and it is also possible that E is true only in Nm cases (if E is false for the outcomes of the remaining events).

We are almost ready to formalize this idea; the only problem is how to formalize "approximately." But since we interpret masses as probabilities, we can apply the same statistical estimates as in the previous section. So we arrive at the following definitions.

3.1. Definitions and the main result

Denotation. For any finite set X, we'll denote by $|X|$ the number of its elements.

Definitions. Suppose that a real number $k > 0$ is given. Suppose also that a finite set W is given. Its elements will be called *outcomes*, or *possible worlds*.

Comment. In the following text we'll suppose that the possible worlds are ordered, so that instead of talking about a world we can talk about its number $i = 1,...,n = |W|$. In these terms W is equal to the set $\{1,2,...,n\}$.

By a *Dempster-Shafer (DS) knowledge* we mean a finite set of pairs $< E_i, m_i >, 1 \leqslant i \leqslant p$, where E_i are subsets of W (called *statements*) and m_i are real numbers (called *masses* or *degrees of belief*) such that $m_i \geqslant 0$ and $\Sigma m_i = 1$.

If an outcome r belongs to the set E_i, we'll say that r *satisfies* E_i. Suppose that an integer N is given; it is called *the number of events*. By a *result of N events* we mean a sequence r_k, $1 \leqslant k \leqslant N$ of integers from 1 to n. r_k is called the *outcome of k-th event*. We say that the result of N events is *consistent* with the DS knowledge $< E_i, m_i >$, if the set $\{1,2,...,N\}$ can be divided into p subsets H_1, H_2,...,H_p with no common elements in such a way that:

1. if k belongs to H_j, then the outcome r_k of k-th event satisfies E_i;
2. the number $|H_i|$ of elements in H_i satisfies the inequality $Nm_i - k\sqrt{m_i(1-m_i)N} \leqslant |H_i| \leqslant Nm_i + k\sqrt{m_i(1-m_i)N}$.

Let's denote the number of all results that are consistent with a given DS-knowledge by $N_{cons}(N)$. The number $\lceil log_2(N_{cons}(N)) \rceil$ will be called *the number of questions necessary to determine the results of N events,* and denoted by $Q(N)$. The fraction $Q(N)/N$ will be called the *average number of questions*. The limit of average number of questions, when $N \to \infty$, will be called the *complexity of knowledge acquisition*.

To formulate our estimate we need some additional definitions.

Definitions. By a *probabilistic distribution* we mean an array of n nonnegative numbers $p_1,...,p_n$ such that $\Sigma p_j = 1$. We say that a probabilistic distribution is *consistent* with the DS knowledge $\langle E_i, m_i \rangle$, $i = 1,..., p$, if and only if there exist nonnegative numbers z_{ij} such that $\Sigma_i z_{ij} = P_j$, $\Sigma_j z_{ij} = m_i$ and $z_{ij} = 0$ if j does not belong to E_i.

Comments.

1. Informally, we want to divide the whole fraction m_i of events, about which the expert predicted that E_i is true, into the groups with fractions z_{ij} for all $j \in E_i$, so that the outcome in a group z_{ij} is j.
2. This definition is not explicitly constructive, but if we fix a probabilistic distribution and a DS knowledge, the question whether they are consistent or not is a linear programming problem so we can use the known algorithms to solve it (the simplex method or the algorithm of Karmarkar, 1984).

By an *entropy* of a DS knowledge we mean a maximum entropy of all probabilistic distributions that are consistent with it.

In other words, this entropy is a solution to the following mathematical problem: $-\Sigma p_j \log_2 p_j \to \max$ under the conditions that $\Sigma_i z_{ij} = p_j$, $\Sigma_j z_{ij} = m_i$, $z_{ij} \geqslant 0$ and $z_{ij} = 0$ for j not in E_i, where i runs from 1 to p, and j from 1 to n.

If we substitute $p_j = \Sigma_i z_{ij}$, we can reformulate it without using p_j: Entropy is a solution of the following mathematical optimization problem:

$$-\sum\left(\sum_i z_{ij}\right)\log_2\left(\sum_i z_{ij}\right) \to \max$$

under the conditions that $\Sigma_j z_{ij} = m_i$, $z_{ij} \geqslant 0$ and $z_{ij} = 0$ for j not in E_i.

Comments.

1. Entropy is a smooth convex function; all the restrictions are linear in z_{ij}, so in order to compute the entropy of a given DS knowledge we must maximize a smooth convex function on a convex domain. In numerical mathematics there exist sufficiently efficient methods for doing that.
2. For the degenerate case, when a DS knowledge is a probabilistic one, i.e., when $n = p$ and $E_i = \{i\}$, there is precisley one probabilistic distrubution that is consistent with this DS knowledge: this very p_j; therefore the entropy of a DS knowledge in this case coincides with Shannon's entropy.

Main theorem. *The complexity of knowledge acquisition for a DS knowledge $\langle E_i, m_i \rangle$ is equal to the entropy of this knowledge.*

Comments.

1. Our definition of entropy is thus a natural generalization of Shannon's entropy to a DS case. This does not mean, of course, that this is *the* generalization. The notion of entropy is used not only to compute the average number of questions, but in several other applications: in communication theory, in pattern recognition, etc. Several different generalizations of entropy to DS formalism have been proposed and turned out to be efficient in these other problems (Yager, 1983; Pal and Dutta Majumer, 1986; Dubois and Prade, 1987; Nguyen, 1987; Klir and Folger, 1988; Dubois and Prade, 1989; Pal, 1991; Kosko, 1992).
2. That the complexity of knowledge acquisition must be greater than or equal to the entropy of a DS knowledge is rather easy to prove. Indeed, if a probabilistic distribution p_j is consistent with a DS knowledge, and a result of N events is consistent with this distribution, then it is consistent with a DS-knowledge as well. Therefore, there are at least as many results consistent with DS knowledge as there are results consistent with p_j. Therefore, the average number of questions in a DS case must be not smaller than the average number of questions (entropy) for every probabilistic distribution that is consistent with this knowledge. So it must be greater than or equal to the maximum of all such probabilistic entropies; we have called this maximum an entropy of a DS knowledge. The fact that it is precisely equal, and not greater, is more difficult to prove, and demands combinatorics (see Section 6).

4. THE ABOVE COMPLEXITY CHARACTERISTIC IS NOT SUFFICIENT, BUT WE NEED NOT WORRY ABOUT THAT

Example. The above characteristic describes the average number of questions that we need to ask in order to attain the complete knowledge. However, we'll now show that it is sometimes possible that although we add the new information, this characteristic remains the same. The simplest of such situations is as follows: suppose that there are only two possible outcomes. If we know nothing about them, this can be expressed in DS terms as follows: there is only one statement ($p = 1$), and this statement E_1 is identically true (i.e., $E_1 = W = \{1, 2\}$). In this case the above mathematical optimization problem is easy to solve, and yields 1. This result is intuitively very reasonable: if we know nothing, and there are two alternatives, we have to ask one binary question in order to figure out which of the outcomes actually occurred.

Suppose now that we analyzed the previous cases and came to a conclusion that on average in half of these cases the first outcome occurred, in half of them the second one. In other words, we add the new information that the probability of both outcomes is equal to 1/2. This is really new information, because it diminishes the number of possibilities: For example, if we observed 100 events, in case we knew nothing it was quite possible that in all the cases we would observe the first outcome. In case we know that the probability is 1/2, then the possible number N_1 of cases, in which the first outcome occurs, is restricted by the inequalities $1/2 \cdot 100 - k\sqrt{1/2(1-1/2)100} \leqslant N_1 \leqslant 1/2 \cdot 100 + k\sqrt{1/2(1-1/2)100}$, or $50 - 5k \leqslant N_1 \leqslant 50 + 5k$. Even for $k = 4$ the value $N_1 = 100$ does not satisfy this inequality and is therefore negligibly rare (therefore for $k < 4$ it also cannot be equal to 100).

In other words, we added a new information. But if we compute the uncertainty (entropy) of the resulting probabilistic distribution, we get $-1/2\log_2(1/2) - 1/2\log_2(1/2) = -1 \cdot \log_2(1/2) = 1$, i.e., again 1! We added the new information, but the uncertainty did not diminish. We still have to ask an average of one question in order to get a complete knowledge.

Isn't it a paradox? No, because we were estimating the *average* amount of questions $\lim Q(N)/N$. We have two cases, in which the necessary number of questions $Q_1(N)$ in the first case is evidently bigger than in the second one ($Q_1(N) > Q_2(N)$), but this difference disappears in the limit. In order to show that it is really so, let us compute $Q(N)$ in both cases.

If we know nothing, then all sequences of 1 and 2 are possible as the results, that is, in this case N_{cons} is equal to 2^N. Therefore $\log_2 N_{cons} = N$, and $Q_1(N) = \lceil \log_2 N_{cons} \rceil = N$.

In the second case computations are more complicated (so we moved them to Section 6), and the result for big N is $Q_2(N) = N - c$, where c is a constant depending on k. Since $c/N \to 0$, in the limit this difference disappears and so it looks like in these two cases the uncertainty is the same.

Do we need to worry about that? To answer this question let's give a numeric estimate of the difference between $Q_1(N)$ and $Q_2(N)$; this difference occurs only when the inequality $N/2 - kN/2 \leqslant N_1 \leqslant N/2 + kN/2$ really restricts the possible values of N. If $k = 2$, then for $N \leqslant 4$ all possible values of N_1 from 0 to N satisfy it, so $Q_1 = Q_2$. Therefore, the difference starts only with $N = 5$. The bigger k, the bigger is the N, from which the difference appears. The value of this difference $c = Q_1(N) - Q_2(N)$ depends on k (see the proof in Section 6). The smaller the k, the bigger is c. The smallest value of k that is used in statistics is $k = 2$. For $k = 2$, we have $c \approx 0.1$. In comparison with 5 it is 2%. For bigger N or bigger k it is even smaller.

So this difference makes practical sense, if we can somehow estimate $Q(N)$ with a similar (or better) precision. But $Q(N)$ is computed from the initial degrees of belief (masses) m_i. There is already a tiny difference between, say, 70% and 80% degree of belief, and hardly anyone can claim that in some cases he is 72% sure, and in some other cases 73%, and that he feels the difference. There are certainly not so many subjective degrees of belief. In view of that the degrees of belief are defined initially with at best 5–10% precision. Therefore the values of $Q(N)$ are known with that precision only, and in comparison to that adding $\leqslant$ 2% of c is, so to say, under the noise level.

So the answer to the question is: no, we don't need to worry.

5. PROBABILISTIC KNOWLEDGE

Let's analyze the case of a probabilistic knowledge as described in Nilsson (1986), when we know the probabilities of several statements. In this case, we can repeat the definitions given above almost verbatim.

Definitions. Suppose that a real number $k > 0$ is given. Suppose also that a finite set $W = \{1, 2,...,n\}$ is given. Its elements will be called *outcomes*, or *possible worlds*. By a probabilistic knowledge we mean a finite set of pairs $\langle E_i, p(E_i)\rangle$, $1 \leqslant i \leqslant p$, where E_i are subsets of W and $0 \leqslant p(E_i) \leqslant 1$. Subsets E_i are called *statements*, and the number $p(E_i)$ is called a *probability* of i-th statement.

If an outcome r belongs to the set E_i, we'll say that r *satisfies* E_i.

Suppose that an integer N is given; it is called *the number of events*. By a *result of N events* we mean a sequence r_k, $\leqslant k \leqslant N$ of integers from 1 to n. r_k is called the *outcome of k-th event*. We say that the result of N events is *consistent* with the probabilistic knowledge $< E_i, p(E_i) >$, if for all i from 1 to p the number N_i of all r_k that belong to E_i satisfies the inequality $Np(E_i) - k\sqrt{p(E_i)(1 - p(E_i))N} \leqslant N_i \leqslant Np(E_i) + k\sqrt{p(E_i)(1 - p(E_i))N}$.

Let's denote the number of all results that are consistent with a given probabilistic knowledge, by $N_{cons}(N)$. The number $\lceil \log_2(N_{cons}(N))\rceil$ will be called *the number of questions necessary to determine the results of N events*, and denoted by $Q(N)$. The fraction $Q(N)/N$ will be called the *average number of questions*. The limit of average number of questions, when $N \to \infty$, will be called the *complexity of knowledge acquisition*.

By a *probabilistic distribution* we mean an array of n nonnegative numbers $p,...,p_n$ such that $\Sigma p_j = 1$. We say that a probabilistic distribution is *consistent* with a probabilistic knowledge $< E_i, p(E_i) >, i = 1,...,p$, if and only if for every i: $\Sigma_{j\in E_i} = p_i$. By an *entropy* of a probabilistic knowledge we mean a maximum entropy of all probabilistic distributions that are consistent with it, that is, the solution to the following mathematical optimization problem: $-\Sigma_{pj}\log_2 p_j \to \max$ under the conditions $\Sigma_{j\in E_i} p_j = p(E_i), p_j \geqslant 0$ and $\Sigma_{j=1}^{n} p_j = 1$.

Comment. This is also a convex optimization problem.

Theorem. *The complexity of knowledge acquisition for a probabilistic knowledge is equal to the entropy of this knowledge.*

Comments.

1. Main Theorem and this result can be combined as follows: if our knowledge is not sufficient to determine all the probabilities uniquely, so that several different probabilistic distributions are compatible with it, then the uncertainty of this knowledge is

equal to the uncertainty of the distribution with the maximal entropy. It is worth mentioning that the distribution with maximal entropy has many other good properties, and is therefore often used as a most "reasonable" one when processing incomplete data in science (for a survey see Jaynes, 1979, and references therein; see also Kosheleva and Kreinovich, 1979, and Cheeseman, 1985).

2. Similar maximum entropy result can be proved for the case when part of the knowledge is given in a DS form, and part in a probabilistic form. In this case we can also formulate what we mean by saying that probabilities are consistent with a given knowledge, and prove that the complexity of knowledge acquisition is equal to the maximum entropy of all probabilistic distributions that are consistent with a given knowledge.

6. PROOFS

Proof of Shannon's Theorem. As we have mentioned in the main text, the Theorem that we prove is not Shannon's original, but a modification: Shannon was interested in data communication, and not in asking questions, so we must modify the proof. The proof we are using first appeared in Kreinovich (1989). Let's first fix some values N_i that are consistent with the given probabilistic distribution. Due to the inequalities that express the consistency demand, the ratio $f_i = N_i/N$ tends to p_i as $N \to \infty$. Let's count the total number C of results for which for every i the number of events with outcome i is equal to this N_i. If we know C, we will be able to compute N_{cons} by adding these C's.

Actually we are interested not in N_{cons} itself, but in $Q(N) \approx \log_2 N_{cons}$, and moreover, in $\lim Q(N)/N$. So we'll try to estimate not only C, but also $\log_2 C$ and $\lim ((\log_2 C)/N)$.

To estimate C means to count the total number of sequences of length N in which there are N_1 elements, equal to 1, N_2 elements, equal to 2, etc. The total number C_1 of ways to choose N_1 elements out of N is well known in combinatorics, and is equal to $\binom{N_1}{N} = N!/((N_1)!(N - N_1)!)$. When we choose these N_1 elements, we have a problem in choosing N_2 out of the remaining $N - N_1$ elements, where the outcome is 2; so for every choice of 1's we have $C_2 = \binom{N_2}{N-N_1}$ possibilities to choose 2's. Therefore in order to get the total number of possibilities to choose 1's and 2's, we must multiply

C_2 by C_1. Adding 3's, 4's,...,n's, we get finally the following formula for C:

$$C = C_1 C_2 \ldots C_{n-1} = \frac{N!}{N_1!(N-N_1)!}\frac{(N-N_1)!}{(N_2!(N-N_1-N_2)!}\cdots$$
$$= \frac{N!}{N_1!N_2!\ldots N_n!}$$

To simplify computations let's use the well-known Stirling formula, according to which $k!$ is asymptotically equivalent to $(k/e)^k\sqrt{2\pi k}$. If we substitute these expressions into the above formula for C, we conclude that

$$C \approx \frac{(N/e)^N\sqrt{2\pi N}}{(N_1/e)^{N_1}\sqrt{2\pi N_1}(N_2/e)^{N_2}\sqrt{2\pi N_2}\ldots(N_n/e)^{N_n}\sqrt{2\pi N_n}}$$

Since $\Sigma N_i = N$, terms e^N and e^{N_i} annihilate each other.

To get further simplification, we substitute $n_i = Nf_i$, and correspondingly $N_i^{N_i}$ as $(Nf_i)^{Nf_i} = N^{Nf_i}f_i^{Nf_i}$. Terms N^N in the numerator and $N^{Nf_1} N^{Nf_2} \ldots N^{Nf_n} = N^{Nf_1+Nf_2+\ldots+Nf_n} = N^N$ in the denominator cancel each other. Terms with $\sqrt{N}$ lead to a term that depends on N as $cN^{-(n-1)/2}$. Now we are ready to estimate $\log_2 C$. Since logarithm of the product is equal to the sum of logarithms, and $\log a^b = b \log a$, we conclude that $\log_2 C \approx -Nf_1 \log_2 f_1 - Nf_2 \log_2 f_2 - \ldots - Nf_n \log_2 f_n - 1/2(n-1)\log_2 N - const$. When $N \to \infty$, we have $1/N \to 0$, $\log_2 N/N \to 0$ and $f_i \to p_i$, therefore $\log_2 C/N \to -p_1 \log_2 p_1 - p_2 \log_2 p_2 - \ldots - p_n \log_2 p_n$, i.e., $\log_2 C/N$ tends to the entropy of the probabilistic distribution.

Comment. We used the denotation $A \approx B$ for some expressions A and B meaning that the difference between A and B is negligible in the limit $N \to \infty$ (i.e., the resulting difference in $(\log_2 C)/N$ tends to 0).

Now that we have found an asymptotic expression for C, let's compute N_{cons} and $Q(N)/N$. For a given probabilistic distribution $\{p_i\}$ and every i possible values of n_i form an interval of length $L_i = 2k\sqrt{p_i(1-p_i)}\sqrt{N}$. So there are no more than L_i possible values of N_i. The maximum value for $p_i(1-p_i)$ is attained when $p_i = 1/2$, therefore $p_i(1-p_i) \leqslant 1/4$, and hence $L_i \leqslant 2k\sqrt{N/4} = k\sqrt{N/2}$. For every i from 1 to n there are at most $(k/2)\sqrt{N}$ possible values of N_i, so the total number N_{co} of possible combinations of N_i is smaller than $((k/2)\sqrt{N})^n$.

The total number N_{cons} of consistent results is the sum of N_{co} different values of C (that correspond to different combinations $N_1, N_2, \ldots N_n$). Let's denote the biggest of these C by C_{max}. Since N_{cons} is the sum of N_{co} terms, and each of them is not greater than the biggest of them C_{max}, we conclude that $N_{cons} \leqslant N_{co}C_{max}$. On the other hand the sum N_{cons} is bigger than each of its terms, i.e., $C_{max} \leqslant N_{cons}$. Combining these two inequalities, we conclude that $C_{max} \leqslant N_{cons} \leqslant N_{co}C_{max}$. Since $N_{co} \leqslant ((k/2)\sqrt{N})^n$, we conclude that $C_{max} \leqslant N_{cons} \leqslant ((k/2)\sqrt{N})^n C_{max}$. Turning to logarithms, we find that $\log_2(C_{max}) \leqslant \log_2(N_{cons}) \leqslant \log_2(C_{max}) + (n/2)\log_2 N + const$. Dividing by N, tending to the limit $N \to \infty$ and using the fact that $\lim_{N\to\infty}(\log_2 N)/N = 0$ and the already proved fact that $\log_2(C_{max})/N$ tends to the entropy S, we conclude that $\lim Q(N)/N = S$.

Proof of the Main Theorem. Let's denote by h_i some integer numbers that satisfy the inequalities $Nm_i - k\sqrt{m_i(1-m_i)N} \leqslant h_i \leqslant Nm_i + k\sqrt{m_i(1-m_i)N}$ from Section 3. Let's denote the ratios h_i/N by g_i. Due to these inequalities, when $N \to \infty$, $g_i \to m_i$.

Unlike the previous theorem, even if we know g_i, that is, know how many outcomes belong to E_i for every i, we still cannot uniquely determine the frequencies f_j of different outcomes. If there exists a result of N events with given frequencies g_i and f_j, then we can further subdivide each set H_i into subsets Z_{ij} that correspond to different outcomes $j \in E_i$. In this case $\Sigma_j Z_{ij} = h_i$ and $\Sigma_i Z_{ij} = Nf_j$; therefore the frequencies $t_{ij} = Z_{ij}/N$ satisfy the equalities $\Sigma_j t_{ij} = g_i$ and $\Sigma_i t_{ij} = f_i$. Vice versa, if there exist values t_{ij} such that these two equalities are satisfied, and $N t_{ij}$ is an integer for all i,j, then we can divide W into sets of size h_i, each of them into sets with $N t_{ij}$ elements and thus find a result with given g_i and f_j. If such t_{ij} exist, we'll say that the frequencies d_i and f_j are *consistent* (note an evident analogy between this concept and the definition of consistency between a DS knowledge and a probabilistic distribution).

Let's now prove that if the set of frequencies $\{f_j\}$ is consistent with the set $\{g_i\}$, and we have a result in which there are Nf_1 outcomes that are equal to 1, Nf_2 outcomes that are equal to 2, etc., then this result is consistent with the original DS knowledge. Indeed, we can subdivide the set of all the outcomes that are equal to j into subsets with Nt_{ij} elements for all i such that $j \in E_i$. We'll say that the elements that are among these Nt_{ij} ones are *labeled by i*. In total there are $\Sigma_j Nt_{ij} = N\Sigma_j t_{ij} = Ng_i = h_i$ elements that are labeled by i, and for all of them E_i is true. Since h_i was chosen so as to satisfy the inequalities that are necessary for consistency, we conclude that this result is really consistent with a DS knowledge.

The number C of results with given frequencies $\{f_j\}$ has already been computed in the proof of Shanon's theorem: lim $((\log_2 C)/N) = -\Sigma f_j \log_2 f_j$.

The total number of the results N_{cons} that are consistent with a given DS knowledge is the sum of N_{co} different values of C that correspond to different f_j. For a given N there are at most $N + 1$ different values of $N_1 = Nf_1$ $(0,1,...,N)$, at most $N + 1$ different values of N_2, etc., in total at most $(N + 1)^n$ different sets of $\{f_j\}$. So, as in the proof of Shannon's theorem, we get an inequality $C_{max} \leqslant N_{cons} \leqslant (N + 1)^n C_{max}$, from which we conclude that lim $Q(N)/N =$ lim $(log_2 C_{max})/N$.

When $N \to \infty$, the values g_i tend to m_i, and therefore these frequencies f_j tend to the probabilities p_j that are consistent with a DS knowledge. Therefore $(\log_2 C)/N$ tends to the entropy of the limit probabilistic distribution and $(\log_2 C_{max})/N$ tends to the maximum of such entropies. But this maximum is precisely the entropy of a DS knowledge as we defined it. So lim$(Q(N)/N)$ equals the entropy of a DS knowledge.

The estimates for a probabilistic case are proved likewise.

Proof of the statement from Section 4. We have to consider the case when $n = 2$ (there are two possible outcomes). In this case the result of N events is a sequence of 1's and 2's. A result is consistent with our knowledge if and only if the number N_1 of 1's satisfies the inequality $N/2 - k\sqrt{N}/2 \leqslant N_1 \leqslant N/2 + k\sqrt{N}$ (actually we must demand that the similar inequality is true for $N_2 = N - N_1$, but one can easily see that this second inequality is equivalent to the first one). Let's estimate the number N_{cons} of such results.

In order to get this estimate let's use the following trick. Suppose we have N independent equally distributed random variables r_k, each of which attains two possble values 1 and 2 with equal probability 1/2. Then the probability of each of 2^N possible sequences of 1's and 2's is the same: 2^{-N}. The probability P that a random sequence satisfies the above inequalities is equal to the sum of the probabilities of all the sequences that satisfy it, that is, equal to the sum of N_{cons} terms that are equal to 2^{-N}. So $P = N_{cons} 2^{-N}$. Therefore, if we manage to estimate P, we'll be able to reconstruct N_{cons} by using a formula $N_{cons} = 2^N P$.

So let us estimate P. Let's recall the arguments that lead to the inequalities that we are using. The total number N_1 of 1's in a sequence $\{r_k\}$ is equal to the sum of terms that are equal to 1 if r_k

$= 1$ and to 0 if $r_k = 2$. In other words, it is the sum of $2 - r_k$. So N_1 is the sum of several equally distributed variables, and therefore for big N its distribution is close to Gaussian, with the average $N/2$ and the standard deviation $\sigma = \sqrt{N}/2$. Therefore, for big N the probability that N_1 satisfies the above inequalities is equal to the probability that the value of a Gaussian random variable with the average a and standard deviation σ lies between $a - k\sigma$ and $a + k\sigma$. This probability P depends only on k and does not depend on N at all. For example, for $k = 2$ $P \approx 0.95$, and for bigger k P is bigger. Since $N_{cons} = P2^N$, we conclude that $Q(N) \approx \log_2(P2^N) = N - c$, where $c = -\log_2 P$. For $k = 2$ we get $c = -log_2 P \approx 0.1$, and for bigger k it is even smaller.

ACKNOWLEDGMENTS

This work was supported by NSF Grant No. CDA-9015006, NASA Research Grant No. 0-482 and the Institute for Manufacturing and Materials Management grant. One of the authors (V.K.) is greatly thankful to Professors Joe Halpern, Vladimir Lifshitz, and Patrick Suppes (Stanford), Peter Cheeseman (Palo Alto), Michael Gelfond (El Paso), Yuri Gurevich (Ann Arbor), and Sankar Pal (NASA Johnson Space Center) for valuable discussions, to Didier Dubois and Henry Prade (France), and Judea Pearl (UCLA) for stimulating preprints, and to anonymous referees for their important suggestions.

BIBLIOGRAPHY

Buchanan, B.G. and Shortliffe, E.H. (1984). *Rule-based expert systems.* Reading, MA: Addison-Wesley.

Cheeseman, P. (1983). In defense of probability. *Proceedings of the Eighth International Joint Conference on AI,* Los Angeles, pp. 1002–1009.

Chokr, B.A. and Kreinovich, V. (1991). How far are we from the complete knowledge: Complexity of knowledge acquisition in Dempster-Shafer approach. *Proceedings of the Fourth University of New Brunswick Artificial Intelligence Workshop,* Fredericton, N.B., Canada, pp. 551–61.

Dubois, D. and Prade, H. (1987). Properties of measures of information in possibility and evidence theory. *Fuzzy Sets and Systems* 24: 279–300.

Dubois, D. and Prade, H. (1989). Fuzzy sets, probability and measurements. *European Journal of Operational Research* 40: 135–54.

Halpern, Y.H. and Fagin, R. (1990). Two views of belief: Belief as generalized probability and belief as evidence. *Proceedings of the Eighth National*

Conference on Artificial Intelligence AAAI-90, AAAI Press/MIT Press, Menlo Park, Cambridge, London, Vol. 1, pp. 112–29.

Hackerman, D. (1986). Probabilistic interpetations for MYCIN's certainty factors. In L. N. Kanal and J.F. Lemmer (eds.), *Uncertainty in artificial intelligence,* pp. 167–96. Amsterdam: North Holland.

Horowitz E., and Sahni, S. (1984). *Fundamentals of computer algorithms.* Rockville, MD: Computer Science Press.

Jaynes, E.T. (1979). Where do we stand on maximum entropy? In R. D. Levine and M. Tribus (eds.), *The maximum entropy formalism.* Cambridge, MA: MIT Press.

Karmarkar, N. (1984). A new polynomial-time algorithm for linear programming. *Combinatorica* 4: 373–95.

Klir G. and Folger, T. (1988). *Fuzzy sets, uncertainty and information.* Englewood Cliffs, NJ: Prentice-Hall.

Kosheleva, O.M. and Kreinovich, V. (1979). A letter on maximum entropy method. *Nature* 281: 708–709.

Kosko, B. (1992). *Neural networks and fuzzy systems.* Englewood Cliffs, NJ: Prentice-Hall.

Kreinovich, V. (1989). *Entropy approach for the description of uncertainty in knowledge bases.* Technical Report, Center for the New Informational Technology "Informatika," Leningrad (in Russian).

Nguyen, H.T. (1987). On entropy of random sets and possibility distributions. In J.C. Bezdek (ed.), *Analysis of fuzzy information,* Vol. 1. *Mathematics and logic,* pp. 145–56. Boca Raton, FL: CRC Press.

Nilsson, N.J. (1986). Probabilistic logic. *Artificial Intelligence* 18: 71–87.

Pal, S. (1991). Fuzziness, image information and scene analysis. In R.R. Yager and L.A. Zadeh (eds.), *An introduction to fuzzy logic applications to intelligent systems.* Dordrecht: Kluwer.

Pal, S. and Dutta Majumer, D.K. (1986). *Fuzzy mathematical approach to pattern recognition.* New York, Delhi: Wiley.

Pearl, J. (1989). *Probabilistic reasoning in intelligent systems: Networks of plausible inference.* San Mateo, CA: Morgan Kaufmann.

Savage, L.J. (1954). *The foundations of statistics.* New York: Wiley.

Savage, L.J. (ed.) (1962). *The foundations of statistical inference.* New York: Wiley.

Shannon, C.E. (1948). A mathematical theory of communication. *Bell Systems Technical Journal* 27: 379–423, 623–56.

Shafer, G. and Pearl, J. (eds.). (1990). *Readings in uncertain reasoning.* San Mateo, CA: Morgan Kaufmann.

Shortliffe, E.H. (1976). *Computer-based medical consultation: MYCIN.* New York: Elsevier.

Smets, P. et al. (eds.) (1988). *Nonstandard logics for automated reasoning.* London: Academic Press.

Yager, R.R. (1983). Entropy and specificity in a mathematical theory of evidence. *International Journal of General Systems* 9: 249–60.

26 Mass assignments and fuzzy sets for fuzzy databases

James F. BALDWIN

Abstract: In this paper we use methods associated with the theory of mass assignments and fuzzy set theory to provide a method of automatic reasoning with relational type databases that can contain fuzzy relations, mass assignments, apriori mass assignments, and virtual relations defined by means of rewrite rules. Attribute values of the base fuzzy relations can be precise values or fuzzy sets. Both continuous and discrete fuzzy sets can be used. Fuzzy sets can also represent interval values and also lists of values taken from the domain.[1]

Keywords: evidential reasoning, fuzzy logic, relational databases, logic programming, fuzzy control, expert systems.

1. INTRODUCTION

A row of a database table, corresponding to a fuzzy relation, will have a membership value in its final column corresponding to the degree to which the row tuple satisfies the relation. This extends the usual notion of a relational database to the fuzzy case.

---

[1] Professor Baldwin is a Senior SERC Research Fellow.

Base relations correspond to tables of the fuzzy relational database. Virtual relations can be defined in terms of rewrite rules involving base relations and other virtual relations but avoiding recursive structures.

When a query is asked, the problem generator uses the base relations, virtual relation definitions, and mass assignments to determine a sequence of fuzzy relational and mass assignment operations to answer the query. This sequence of operations is then performed to obtain the solution in the form of a fuzzy relation expressed as a table or a mass assignment.

When the solution is given as a mass assignment a certain filling-in process can then occur to obtain a probability distribution. For this, relevant apriori information must be available. This prior information can be part of the database or supplied on request by the user asking the query. The filling-in process is performed by the iterative assignment algorithm.

The general approach of inference under both probabilistic and fuzzy uncertainties given in this paper can be applied to knowledge bases of a relational type with rewrite rules excluding recursive structures. It can be used in fields such as expert systems, control and robotics, diagnostics, and decision support systems. It brings together methods of handling more specialized forms of uncertainty. Fuzzy relational databases concentrate on handling fuzzy uncertainties. The theory of mass assignments is generally applicable to both probabilistic and fuzzy uncertainty inference. This paper shows how this can be applied to knowledge bases of the form given above. It generalizes on the usual relational database theory to include uncertainties, fuzzy relations, and virtual relations. In this sense, from a modeling point of view, it is more like a logic programming language although it does not use resolution methods of inference. Since recursive structures are not allowed it does not have the full power of an extended version of a logic programming language that can handle uncertainties. Nevertheless for many applications containing uncertainties of different forms it is a powerful tool that can be computationally efficient. Many of the relational operations can be handled by parallel processing, but this will not be discussed in this paper.

2. KNOWLEDGE BASE

2.1. Relations

A knowledge base can contain:

- Fuzzy base relations
- Mass assignments
- Rewrite rules (optional)
- A priori relations (optional)

A fuzzy base relation $R(A_1, \ldots, A_n)$, where A_i are attributes, is defined by the mapping

$$X_R : D_1 \times \ldots \times D_n \rightarrow [0, 1]$$

where D_i is the domain of attribute A_i; $i = 1, \ldots, n$ and can be depicted as in Table 26.1 where $t = (a_1, \ldots, a_n)$ is a row tuple satisfying the relation R to degree $X(t)$. We can say that the tuple t is compatible with R to the degree $X(t)$.

Table 26.1

R	A_1	■ ■ ■	A_n	X
	a_1	■ ■ ■	a_n	$X(t)$

Each a_i in the tuple t is one of the following: (1) a value from D_i or (2) a fuzzy set defined on D_i.

If D_i is a finite set then the fuzzy set defined on D_i will be a discrete fuzzy set. This notation is for convenience and the tuple $t = (\ldots, g, \ldots)$ where g is a fuzzy set on D_i can be expanded to give the set of tuples $\{t_k\} = \{(\ldots, e, \ldots \mid X_g(e))\}$. If on expansion a repeated tuple results, duplicates are removed and only the one with the largest membership value is included. The X value for an expanded tuple is the smallest of the membership values associated with the tuple containing the fuzzy set and the X value of the element in the fuzzy set.

Several fuzzy set entries in the relation can be handled by expanding the relation by considering one fuzzy set at a time. For example, if we have the situation as in Table 26.2, where $g = b_1/1 + b_2/0.8$, then expanding gives tuples $(a_1\, b_1 \,|\, 0.9)$, $(a_1\, b_2 \,|\, 0.8)$, $(a_2\, b_2 \,|\, 1)$, $(a_1\, b_1 \,|\, 0.7)$ giving the relation $\{(a_1\, b_1 \,|\, 0.9), (a_1\, b_2 \,|\, 0.8), (a_2\, b_2 \,|\, 1)\}$. If D_i is an interval, then the fuzzy set defined on D_i will be a continuous fuzzy set.

A discrete fuzzy set can represent a list of domain elements. We allow the more usual notation of writing the value directly as a list of values from D_i. A continuous fuzzy set can represent a domain interval. The base relation is a fuzzy set defined on the Cartesian product $D_1 \times \ldots \times D_n$.

Table 26.2

R	A	B	X
	a_1	g	0.9
	a_2	b_2	1
	a_1	b_1	0.7

3. FUZZY SETS AND MASS ASSIGNMENTS

The theory of FMAs (Baldwin, 1991) also includes fuzzy set theory as a given in, e.g., Zadeh (1965).

Let f be a normalized fuzzy set, $\mathrm{f} \subseteq_f X$, such that

$$\mathrm{f} = \sum_{x_i \in X} x_i / X_\mathrm{f}(x_i); \quad X_\mathrm{f}(x_1) = 1, X_\mathrm{f}(x_k) \leqslant X_\mathrm{f}(x_j), \text{ for } k > j$$

where $X_\mathrm{f}(x)$ is the membership level, $x \in X$, of x in f.

The mass assignment associated with f is

$$x_1 : 1 - X_\mathrm{f}(x_2),\ \{x_1, \ldots, x_i\} : X_\mathrm{f}(x_i) - X_\mathrm{f}(x_{i+1}) \text{ for } i = 2, \ldots; \\ \text{with } X_\mathrm{f}(x_k) = 0 \text{ for } x_k \notin X$$

This defines a family of probability distributions over F for the instantiation of variable X, given the statement X is f.

This definition is consistent with the voting model with the constant threshold model (Baldwin, 1991). In this voting model $X_\mathrm{f}(x)$ is the percentage of a representative population P who accept x as satisfying f with the constraint imposed on the voting behavior of

P that any member of P who accepts $y \in X$ with membership value $X_{\mathbf{f}}(y)$ in $\mathbf{f}$ as satisfying $\mathbf{f}$, will also accept any $z \in X$ such that $X_{\mathbf{f}}(z) \geqslant X_{\mathbf{f}}(y)$.

Let $\mathbf{f}$ be an unnormalized fuzzy set, $\mathbf{f} \subseteq X$, such that $\max_i\{X_{\mathbf{f}}(x_i)\} = \beta < 1$ where

$$\mathbf{f} = \sum_{x_i \in X} x_i / X_{\mathbf{f}}(x_i); \quad X_{\mathbf{f}}(x_1) = \beta, \; X_{\mathbf{f}}(x_k) \leqslant X_{\mathbf{f}}(x_j) \text{ for } k > j$$

Then the mass assignment associated with $\mathbf{f}$ is

$x_1 : \beta - X_{\mathbf{f}}(x_2)$, $\{x_1, \ldots, x_i\} : X_{\mathbf{f}}(x_i) - X_{\mathbf{f}}(x_{i+1})$, $\emptyset : 1 - \beta$ for $i = 2, \ldots$; with $X_{\mathbf{f}}(x_k) = 0$ for $x_k \notin X$

Example 1. Let $F = \{a, b, c, d, e\}$. If $\mathbf{f} = a/1 + b/0.7 + c/0.4 + d/0.3$, then the associated mass assignment is

$$m_{\mathbf{f}} = a:0.3, \{a, b\}:0.3, \{a, b, c\}:0.1, \{a, b, c, d\}:0.3$$

If $\mathbf{f} = a/0.8 + b/0.7 + c/0.4 + d/0.3$, then the associated mass assignment is

$$m_{\mathbf{f}} = a:0.1, \{a, b\}:0.3, \{a, b, c\}:0.1, \{a, b, c, d\}:0.3, \emptyset:0.2$$

3.1. Intersection, union, meet and join

Fuzzy set intersection and fuzzy set union, using the min and max rules respectively, are equivalent to mass assignment meet and join respectively.

Example 2. Let

$$\mathbf{f}_1 = a/1 + b/0.7 + c/0.4 + d/0.3$$
$$\mathbf{m}_{\mathbf{f}_1} = a:0.3, \{a, b\}:0.3, \{a, b, c\}:0.1, \{a, b, c, d\}:0.3$$
$$\mathbf{f}_2 = a/0.7 + b/1 + c/0.3 + d/0.4$$
$$\mathbf{m}_{\mathbf{f}_2} = b:0.3, \{a, b\}:0.3, \{a, b, d\}:0.1, \{a, b, c, d\}:0.3$$

Then, as given in Table 26.3: $\mathbf{m}_{\mathbf{f}_1} \wedge \mathbf{m}_{\mathbf{f}_2} = \{a, b\}:0.4, \{a, b, c\}:0.3, \emptyset:0.3$

This mass assignment is in the form of nested sets, and therefore it is the mass assignment associated with the fuzzy set $\mathbf{f} = a/0.7 + b/0.7 + c/0.3 + d/0.3$. Therefore, $\mathbf{f}_1 \cap \mathbf{f}_2 = \mathbf{f}$ illustrating the equivalence

Table 26.3

	0.3 b	0.3 $\{a, b\}$	0.1 $\{a, b, d\}$	0.3 $\{a, b, c, d\}$
0.3 a	$\emptyset$ 0.3	a 0	a 0	a 0
0.3 $\{a, b\}$	b 0	$\{a, b\}$ 0.3 max 3	$\{a, b\}$ 0	$\{a, b\}$ 0
0.1 $\{a, b, c\}$	b 0	$\{a, b\}$ 0	$\{a, b\}$ 0.1 max 2	$\{a, b, c\}$ 0
0.3 $\{a, b, c, d\}$	b 0	$\{a, b\}$ 0	$\{a, b, d\}$ 0	$\{\_\}$ 0.3 max 1

between mass assignments and fuzzy set theory with respect to intersection of fuzzy sets and the meet of mass assignments (cf. Table 26.4).

$$\mathbf{m}_{\mathbf{f}_1} \vee \mathbf{m}_{\mathbf{f}_2} = \{a, b\}:0.6, \{a, b, c, d\}:0.4$$

Table 26.4

	0.3 b	0.3 $\{a, b\}$	0.1 $\{a, b, d\}$	0.3 $\{a, b, c, d\}$
0.3 a	$\{a, b\}$ 0.3 max	$\{a, b\}$ 0	$\{a, b, d\}$ 0	$\{\_\}$ 0
0.3 $\{a, b\}$	$\{a, b\}$ 0	$\{a, b\}$ 0.3 max	$\{a, b, \mathrm{d}\}$ 0	$\{\_\}$ 0
0.1 $\{a, b, c\}$	$\{a, b, c\}$ 0	$\{a, b, c\}$ 0	$\{\_\}$ 0.1	$\{\_\}$ 0
0.3 $\{a, b, c, d\}$	$\{\_\}$ 0	$\{\_\}$ 0	$\{\_\}$ 0	$\{\_\}$ 0.3

This mass assignment is in the form of nested sets, and therefore it is the mass assignment associated with the fuzzy set $\mathbf{f} = a/1 + b/1 + c/0.4 + d/0.4$. Therefore, $\mathbf{f}_1 \cup \mathbf{f}_2 = \mathbf{f}$ illustrating the equivalence between mass assignments and fuzzy set theory with respect to union of fuzzy sets and the join of mass assignments.

Let $F = \{a, b, c\}$ and

$$\mathbf{f}_1 = a/1 + b/0.7 + c/0.3$$
$$\mathbf{m}_{\mathbf{f}_1} = a{:}0.3,\ \{a, b\}{:}0.4,\ \{a, b, c\}{:}0.3$$
$$\mathbf{f}_2 = a/0.9 + b/0.5 + c/0.4$$
$$\mathbf{m}_{\mathbf{f}_2} = a{:}0.4,\ \{a, b\}{:}0.1,\ \{a, b, c\}{:}0.4,\ \varnothing{:}0.1$$

Then (Table 26.5): $\mathbf{m}_{\mathbf{f}_1} \wedge \mathbf{m}_{\mathbf{f}_2} = a{:}0.4,\ \{a, b\}{:}0.2,\ \{a, b, c\}{:}0.3,\ \varnothing{:}0.1$ corresponding to the fuzzy set $a/0.9 + b/0.5 + c/0.3$. Also $\mathbf{f}_1 \cap \mathbf{f}_2 = a/0.9 + b/0.5 + c/0.3$.

Table 26.5

	0.4 a	0.1 $\{a, b\}$	0.4 $\{a, b, c\}$	0.1 $\varnothing$
0.3 a	a 0.3	a 0	a 0	$\varnothing$ 0
0.4 $\{a, b\}$	a 0.1	$\{a, b\}$ 0.1 max 3	$\{a, b\}$ 0.1 max 2	$\varnothing$ 0.1
0.3 $\{a, b, c\}$	a 0	$\{a, b\}$ 0	$\{a, b, c\}$ 0.3 max 1	$\varnothing$ 0

3.2. Complementation

Complementation to the fuzzy set is equivalent to the complementation of mass assignments.

Example 3. Let

(a) $F = \{a, b, c, d\}$

If $\mathbf{f} = a/1 + b/0.7 + c/0.3$ with associated mass assignment $\mathbf{m}_\mathbf{f} = a{:}0.3,\ \{a, b\}{:}0.4,\ \{a, b, c\}{:}0.3$, then from fuzzy set theory the complement of $\mathbf{f}$ is $\bar{\mathbf{f}} = b/0.3 + c/0.7 + d/1$ and the complement of $m_\mathbf{f}$ is

$$\bar{\mathbf{m}}_\mathbf{f} = \{b, c, d\}{:}0.3,\ \{c, d\}{:}0.4,\ d{:}0.3$$

This is equivalent to the fuzzy set $b/0.3 + c/0.7 + d/1$ showing the equivalence of complementation between the two theories.

(b) $F = \{a, b, c\}$

If $\mathbf{f} = a/1 + b/0.7 + c/0.3$ with associated mass assignment $\mathbf{m}_f = a{:}0.3, \{a, b\}{:}0.4, \{a, b, c\}{:}0.3$, then from fuzzy set theory the complement of $\mathbf{f}$ is $\bar{\mathbf{f}} = b/0.3 + c/0.7$ and the complement of m_f is

$$\bar{\mathbf{m}}_f = \{b, c\}{:}0.3, \{c\}{:}0.4, \emptyset{:}0.3$$

This is equivalent to the fuzzy set $b/0.3 + c/0.7$ showing the equivalence of complementation between the two theories.

A mass assignment can be expressed in relational form as exemplified in Table 26.6. This notation is useful to reexpress a mass assignment over a different space through reference with a database relation. This is illustrated in an example later in the paper.

Table 26.6

Mass Assignment	X	Mass
	x_1	0.2
	$\{x_1, x_2\}$	0.3
	$\{x_2, x_3\}$	0.4
	$\{x_1, x_2, x_3\}$	0.1

corresponding to the mass assignment
$x_1{:}0.2$
$\{x, x_2\}{:}0.3$
$\{x_2, x_3\}{:}0.4$
$\{x_1, x_2, x_3\}{:}0.1$

4. VIRTUAL RELATIONS AND SUBRELATIONS

A virtual relation can be defined as a rewrite rule containing base relations and other virtual relations. Fuzzy logic connectives such as AND(τ), OR(τ) can be used to connect relations in the right-hand side of the rewrite rule and these can be nested using brackets. This is explained more fully in Baldwin (1979, 1981), and Baldwin and Zhou (1984). For example:

$$R(X, Y) \leftarrow R_1(X, \_, \_) \text{ AND } (R_2(Y, \_) \text{ OR } R_3(Y, \_)) \text{ AND } R_4(X, Y)$$

where R_1, R_2, R_3 and R_4 are defined base relations. There are no common attributes corresponding to the underscore positions in R_2, R_3 and R_4. The connectives AND and OR are equivalent to AND(true) and OR(true), respectively (Baldwin, 1979, 1981).

Variables are used to represent attribute values, common attributes in various relations, and to define which attributes are to be in the relation being defined and the position in which they are to be placed.

Thus, for the last example, the tuple (x_1, y_1) is in R if the tuple $(x_1,\_,\_)$ is in R_1 and, either the tuple $(y_1,\_)$ is in R_2 or the tuple $(y_1,\_)$ is in R_3, and the tuple (x_1, y_1) is in R_4. In terms of relational algebra involving union, intersection, and join operations the tuples of the relation R are given by

$$R(X, Y) = \mathrm{Proj}_X R_1(X,\_)\,\&\,((\mathrm{Proj}_Y R_2(Y,\_) \cup \mathrm{Proj}_Y R_3(Y,\_))\,\&\, R_4(X, Y))$$

where $\mathrm{Proj}_X R$ represents the projection of the relation R onto the attribute represented by X, and $R_1 \,\&\, R_2$ is a join of R_1 and R_2 over common attributes of R_1 and R_2.

The membership value of the tuple (x_1, y_1) in R is given by

$$X_R(x_1,y_1) = \bigvee_W X_{R_1}(x_1, W) \wedge \left(\bigvee_W X_{R_2}(y_1, W) \vee \bigvee_W X_{R_3}(y_1, W)\right) \wedge X_{R_4}(x_1,y_1)$$

where $\bigvee_W X_{R_1}(x_1, W)$ represents the maximum value of $X_{R_1}(x_1, w)$ over all possible values of w. This will be further explained in the section dealing with fuzzy relational algebra.

A nonfuzzy relation R, as defined above, can be denoted by $R(\_,\ldots,\_)$ where the underscores denote the possible values from the table defining R, $R(X_1,\ldots,X_n)$ where the X_i are variables that can take any value from the domain D_i.

A capital letter by itself or followed by numerals is a variable and can take any value from the appropriate domain.

A *subrelation* of R can be denoted by giving one or more variables in $R(X_1,\ldots,X_n)$ appropriate values. For example $R(a_1, X_2,\ldots,X_n)$ is a subrelation of R with all the first elements of its tuples having the value a_1 assuming a_1 is an element of D_1. If a_1 is not in D_1 then the resulting subrelation is empty.

A fuzzy relation is similarly denoted by $R(X_1,\ldots,X_n \mid X)$, although this can be abbreviated to $R(X_1,\ldots,X_n)$, and we can form the subrelation $R(X_1,\ldots,X_n \mid \geqslant 0.7)$, which contains all those tuples of R whose membership value is greater than or equal to 0.7. In place of $\geqslant$ we can use $=$ or $<$, $\leqslant$, $>$ with obvious meaning.

We can select a subrelation by specifying the value of an attribute A_i using a fuzzy set g_1 defined over D_i. The resulting selection is given by

$$R(\ldots, \mathbf{a}_i^* \cap \mathbf{g}_1, \ldots \mid X(t))$$

where

$$\mathbf{a}_i^* = \begin{cases} a_i/1 & \text{if } a_i \text{ is an element of } D_i \\ \mathbf{g} & \text{if } a_i \text{ is the fuzzy set } \mathbf{g} \text{ over } D_i \end{cases}$$

The resulting relation can be expanded as described above.

Example 4. If R is as shown in Table 26.7

Table 26.7

R	A	B	X
	a_1	b_2	0.9
	a_2	b_2	1
	a_1	b_1	0.7

and $\mathbf{g}_1 = b_1/0.6 + b_2/1$, then $R(\_, \mathbf{g}_1)$ is as shown in Table 26.8 which can be expanded to give $R(\_, \mathbf{g}_1)$ as in Table 26.9.

Table 26.8

$R(\_, \mathbf{g}_1)$	A	B	X
	a_1	$b_2/1$	0.9
	a_2	$b_2/1$	1
	a_1	$b_1/0.6$	0.7

Table 26.9

$R(\_, \mathbf{g}_1)$	A	B	X
	a_1	b_2	0.9
	a_2	b_2	1
	a_1	b_1	0.6

If R is as shown in Table 26.10, where $\mathbf{g} = b_1/1 + b_2/0.8$ and $\mathbf{g}_1 = b_1/0.6 + b_2/1$, then $R(\_, \mathbf{g}_1)$ is as in Table 26.11 which expands to give $R(\_, \mathbf{g}_1)$ as in Table 26.12.

Table 26.10

R	A	B	X
	a_1	g	0.9
	a_2	b_2	1
	a_1	b_1	0.7

Table 26.11

$R(\_, g_1)$	A	B	X
	a_1	$b_1/0.6 + b_2/0.8$	0.9
	a_2	$b_2/1$	1
	a_1	$b_1/0.6$	0.7

Table 26.12

$R(\_, g_1)$	A	B	X
	a_1	b_1	0.6
	a_1	b_2	0.8
	a_2	b_2	1

5. FUZZY RELATIONAL ALGEBRA

Fuzzy relational algebra is a collection of operations on fuzzy relations. Each operation takes one or more fuzzy relations as its operand(s) and produces a new fuzzy relation as its result. Basic operations are union, difference, intersection, cross product, join, projection, and truth functional modification. These take definitions as follows.

Union, difference, and intersection. The union, difference, and intersection of two compatible fuzzy relations A and B, denoted by $A \cup B$, $A - B$, and $A \cap B$, respectively, is a set of tuples t with the following degree of compatibility $X(t)$, respectively, to which the tuple t satisfies the resulting relation:

$$X_{A \cup B}(t) = X_A(t) \vee X_B(t)$$
$$X_{A - B}(t) = X_A(t) \vee (1 - X_B(t))$$
$$X_{A \cap B}(t) = X_A(t) \wedge X_B(t)$$

Two relations A and B are compatible if they have the same arity, n say, and the ith attribute of them (i in the range 1 to n) must be drawn from the same domain, that is, relation A and B are two subsets of the product space of domains $D_1 \times \ldots \times D_n$.

Cross product. The cross product of two fuzzy relations A and B, denoted by $A \times B$, is the set of all tuples t with the membership value $X(t)$ defined by

$$X_{A \times B}(t) = X_A(a) \wedge X_B(b),\ A \subseteq_f M,\ B \subseteq_f N, \text{ for all } a \in M, \text{ for all } b \in N,\ t = (a, b)$$

where $X \subseteq_f Y$ signifies that X is a fuzzy subset of Y.

Join. The join of two fuzzy relations A and B with common attributes drawn from domains $C_1, \ldots, C_k$, denoted by $A \,\&\, B$, is a set of tuples t with the membership value $X(t)$ defined by $X_{A\&B}(t) = X_A(a) \wedge X_B(b)$ where

$$A \subseteq_f C_1 \times \ldots \times C_k \times AD_1 \times \ldots \times AD_m,$$
$$B \subseteq_f C_1 \times \ldots \times C_k \times BD_1 \times \ldots \times BD_n$$

$a = (c, bd)$, for all $a \in A$, for all $c \in C_1 \times \ldots \times C_k$, for all $ad \in AD_1 \times \ldots \times AD_m$, $b = (c, bd)$, for all $b \in B$, for all $bd \in BD_1 \times \ldots \times BD_n$, $t = (c, ad, bd)$.

If the relations have fuzzy sets as attribute values then the methods of selection associated with forming subrelations are used in the join process.

We can also join a fuzzy relation with mass assignment expressed in relational form. The join is obtained ignoring the mass column associated with the mass assignment. This column is simply included in the resulting table and renormalized if necessary.

Projection. The projection of a fuzzy relation $R(A_1, A_2) \subseteq_f D_1 \times D_2$ onto D_2, denoted by $\mathrm{Proj}_{A_2} R$ is a set of tuples a_2 with the membership value $X(a_2)$ defined by

$$X \mathrm{Proj}_{A_2} R(a_2) = \bigvee_{a_1 \in D_1} X_R(a_1, a_2)$$

This definition can easily be generalized to projections of n-ary relations onto compound spaces.

5.1. Truth functional modification

Let A be a fuzzy relation and τ a fuzzy set, acting as a truth modifier, defined on the interval [0,1]. The result of truth functional modification of A using τ, denoted by R_τ, is a relation such that each tuple t has the membership value given by $X_{B_\tau}(X_A(t))$. For example, if $A = \{(a, \alpha \mid 1), (b, \beta \mid 0.8), (c, \chi \mid 0.4), (d, \delta \mid 0.2)\}$ and $\tau = \{(0.5, 0), (1,1)\}$ an i type fuzzy set, then $A_\tau = \{(a, \alpha \mid 1), (b, \beta \mid 0.6)\}$.

Fuzzy sets can themselves be truth-functionally modified, so that, for example, if $\mathbf{g} = a/1 + b/0.8 + c/0.4 + d/0.2$, then $\mathbf{g}_\tau = a/1 + b/0.6$.

6. QUERIES AND SOLUTION GENERATION

A query can be written as WHICH((X, Y,...) $\Psi(X, Y, Z, ...)$) where the first argument is a list of variables representing the attributes to be included in the solution relation and the second argument is a logic pattern, Ψ, containing variables corresponding to attributes. The logic pattern can be a relation, NOT relation, relation*logic pattern where*can be AND or OR.

We can also ask DOES(R), which simply returns the $\max \chi_R()$ associated with R. Since WHICH() is a relation we can ask DOES (WHICH()).

The query can be answered by selecting a sequence of fuzzy relational algebraic and mass assignment algebraic statements which, taken together, answers the query. This selection is done using the database problem generator, which has rules and heuristics to guide it in its choice of sequence to answer the query. For a given query, in general the sequence to provide the answer will not be unique. The rules of the generator are used to select a sequence and the heuristics are used to optimize the computation for performing this sequence of operations. We do not discuss the problem generator further in this paper but examples are given below to illustrate its behavior.

Example 5. Let the relations be as in Tables 26.13, 26.14, 26.15 and 26.16 where the fuzzy sets $\mathbf{f}_1$, $\mathbf{f}_2$, $\mathbf{f}_3$, and $\mathbf{f}_4$ are defined as

$\mathbf{f}_1 = \text{fair}/1 + \text{dark}/0.4$; $\mathbf{f}_1 \subset_f$ Hair Color
$\mathbf{f}_2 = \text{medium}/1 + \text{tall}/0.4 + \text{short}/0.2$; $\mathbf{f}_2 \subset_f$ Height
$\mathbf{f}_3 = \text{right}/1 + \text{left}/0.3$; $\mathbf{f}_3 \subset_f$ Dexterity

Let the rules be

hair_satisfactory(N) ← Witness Evidence(X,_,_) AND
    Properties(N, X,_,_)
height_satisfactory(N) ← Witness Evidence(_,X,_) AND
    Properties(N,_,X,_,_)
dexterity_satisfactory(N) ← Witness Evidence(_,_, X) AND
    Properties(N,_,_, X,_)
build_probable(N) ← Witness MA(X) AND
    Properties(N,_,_,_, X)
criminal(N) ← Suspect(N) AND hair_satisfactory(N) AND
    height_satisfactory(N) AND dexterity_satisfactory(N)
    AND Build_probable(N)

Table 26.13

Suspect	Name	χ
	Joe	0.6
	Mary	0.4
	Harry	0.7
	June	0.9

Table 26.14

Properties	Name	Hair Color	Height	Dexterity	Build
	Joe	fair	tall	left	big
	Mary	dark	short	right	small
	Harry	dark	medium	left	average
	June	fair	medium	right	small

Table 26.15

Witness Evidence	Hair Color	Height	Dexterity
	f1	f2	f3

Table 26.16

Witness MA	Build	Mass
	small	0.8
	{big, medium}	0.2

This database represents suspects for a given crime. A χ value in the suspects relation represents the degree to which the given crime is compatible with the types of crimes the suspect has committed in the past. The properties relation gives the hair color, height, dexterity, and build for each of the suspects. The three fuzzy sets represent evidence of witnesses and this is indicated in the witness relation. For example, all witnesses thought it possible that the criminal was fair while 40% of witnesses thought it possible that the criminal had dark hair. A similar interpretation can be given to the other evidences concerning height and dexterity. The evidence for the build of the criminal, expressed as a mass assignment, was estimated by the police on technical considerations.

In response to the query

WHICH((N), criminal(N))

the problem generator gives the following sequence of computations:

1. Proj_N(Witness Evidence(X,_,_) & Properties(N, X,_,_,_)) = $R_1(N)$
2. Proj_N(Witness Evidence(_, X,_) & Properties(N,_, X,_,_)) = $R_2(N)$
3. Proj_N(Witness Evidence(_,_, X) & Properties(N,_,_,X,_)) = $R_3(N)$
4. $R_1(N) \cap R_2(N) \cap R_3(N) = R_4(N)$
5. $R_4(N) \cap \text{Suspects}(N) = R_5(N)$
6. $\text{MA}(R_5(N)) = M_1(N)$
7. Proj_N(Witness MA(X) & Properties(N,_,_,_, X)) = $M_2(N)$
8. $M_1(N) \wedge M_2(N) = M(N)$.
9. $\text{Relation}(M(N)) = \text{criminal}(N)$

which gives the results shown in Table 26.17.

Table 26.17

Criminals	Name	Mass
	June	0.7
	{Joe, Harry}	0.2
	{Mary, June}	0.1

7. FILLING-IN SOLUTIONS USING APRIORI INFORMATION

The solution of a WHICH query can be further processed if relevant apriori information is available or can be supplied by the user. An apriori mass assignment must be given over the space of the solution fuzzy relation, understood as a fuzzy set.

The iterative assignment method for updating an apriori mass assignment with a sequence of evidences, each expressed as a mass assignment, is discussed in Baldwin (1989, 1990a, b, c, d, 1991, 1992a, b). We summarize those aspects of the method that are relevant to the filling-in process associated with solutions of database queries expressed as mass assignments. The update is a generalization of Bayesian updating to the case when the evidence is uncertain. It is in special cases equivalent to using Jeffrey's rule (Jeffrey, 1965).

Suppose an apriori mass assignment m_a is given over the focal set A whose elements are subsets of the powerset $P(X)$. This represents the apriori mass assignment of the query solution.

Suppose we also have a specific evidence E where E is (m, F), where F is the set of focal elements of $P(X)$ for E, and m is the mass assignment for these focal elements. This represents the mass assignment corresponding to the query solution obtained using the methods given in the previous section.

We wish to update the apriori assignment m_a with E to give the updated mass assignment m. The iterative assignment method updates m_a with E to give m'. The apriori is replaced with m' and the update process repeated to give a new m'. This is repeated until the process converges.

Example 6. Consider the example above. We are given the apriori mass assignment over the set of criminals. This is updated with the mass assignment found as the solution of the query, i.e., June: 0.7, {Joe, Harry}: 0.2, {Mary, June}: 0.1. The apriori mass is shown in Table 26.18 and the first update is given in Table 26.19.

Table 26.18

Criminal	Name	Apriori Mass
	Joe	0.7
	Mary	0.1
	Harry	0.1
	June	0.1

Table 26.19

EVIDENCE

Apriori	0.7 June	0.2 {Joe, Harry}	0.1 {Mary, June}	Update
0.7 Joe	Ø:0	Joe:0.175	Ø:0	0.175
0.1 Mary	Ø:0	Ø:0	Mary:0.05	0.05
0.1 Harry	Ø:0	Harry:0.025	Ø:0	0.025
0.1 June	June:0.7	Ø:0	June:0.05	0.75
	$K_1 = 1/0.1$	$K_2 = 1/0.8$	$K_3 = 1/0.2$	

This updating process will converge to Joe: 0.175, Harry: 0.025, June: 0.8. We call it a "filling-in" process since, as can be seen in this example, the 0.2 in the evidence for {Joe, Harry} is split between Joe and Harry in the proportions proportional to the apriori values for Joe and Harry, i.e., 0.175 for Joe and 0.025 for Harry. The 0.1 associated with {Mary, June} is similarly split equally between June and Mary. This provides the update. This process is then repeated with the same evidence and the updated apriori to produce the next update.

8. CONCLUSIONS

A form of knowledge representation allows for both fuzzy and probabilistic uncertainties to be used for databases with automatic answering of queries. The automatic inference is in terms of a problem generator that provides a sequence of fuzzy relational and mass assignment computations. These computations are carried out to determine the solution to a given query. This solution can be used to update a given apriori solution if required and this process acts as a "filling-in" mechanism for the incomplete solution obtained from the database query. The approach provides the means to represent many applications with uncertain data and fuzzy concepts in a database form with rewrite rules.

BIBLIOGRAPHY

Baldwin, J. F. (1979). A new approach to approximate reasoning using a fuzzy logic. *Fuzzy Sets and Systems* 2: 309–25.

Baldwin, J. F. (1981). A theory of fuzzy logic. In E. Mamdani and B. Gaines (eds.), *Fuzzy reasoning and its applications*, pp. 133–48. New York: Academic Press.

Baldwin J. F. (1989). A new approach to combining evidences for evidential reasoning. ITRC University of Bristol Report.

Baldwin, J. F. (1990a). Combining evidences for evidential reasoning. *Int. J. of Intelligent Systems* 6.

Baldwin, J. F. (1990b). Towards a general theory of intelligent reasoning. *Third Int. Conf IPMU*, Paris.

Baldwin, J. F. (1990c). Evidential reasoning under probabilistic and fuzzy uncertainties. In R. R. Yager and L. A. Zadeh (eds.), *An introduction to fuzzy logic applications in intelligent systems*. Dordrecht: Kluwer.

Baldwin, J. F. (1990d). Inference under uncertainty for expert system rules. ITRC 152 University of Bristol Report. To appear.

Baldwin, J. F. (1991). A calculus for mass assignments in evidential reasoning. In this volume.

Baldwin, J. F. (1992a). Inference for information systems containing probabilistic and fuzzy uncertainties. In L. A. Zadeh and J. Kacprzyk (eds.), *Fuzzy logic for the management of uncertainty*. New York: Wiley.

Baldwin, J. F. (1992b). Fuzzy and probabilistic uncertainties. In S. C. Shapiro (ed.), *Encyclopedia of artificial intelligence*, 2nd ed. New York: Wiley.

Baldwin, J. F. and Zhou, S. Q. (1984). A fuzzy relational inference language. *Fuzzy Sets and Systems* 14: 155–74.

Jeffrey, R. (1965). *The logic of decision*. New York: McGraw-Hill.

Shafer, G. (1976). *A mathematical theory of evidence*. Princeton: Princeton University Press.

Zadeh, L. (1965). Fuzzy sets. *Information and Control* 8: 338–53.

INDEX